Quick Reference Editing Shortcut Keystrokes

To:	Press:
Cut	Ctrl+X
Copy	Ctrl+C
Paste	Ctrl+V
Start a new document	Ctrl+N
Save	Ctrl+S
Print	Ctrl+P
Undo	Ctrl+Z
Select All	Ctrl+A
Select a paragraph	Double-click in the left border
Check thesaurus for a selected word	Shift+F7
Cancel a selection	Esc

Quick Reference Formatting

To:	Do This:
Start a new line within a paragraph	Shift+Enter
Keep words together	Press Ctrl+Shift+Space between the words you want to keep together
Repeat formatting with Format Painter	Highlight the text whose formatting you want to repeat. Double-click Format Painter and highlight the new text to be formatted. When you are finished, press Esc.
Reveal formatting information	Shift+F1, then click the text
Start a new page	Ctrl+Enter
Create an unnumbered or unbulleted item within a bulleted or numbered list	Shift+Enter

Quick Reference Navigation

To Move To:	Press:
The location of your last edit	Shift+F5
A page within a document	F5 (GoTo key and type page number)
A word or phrase	Ctrl+F

Using Microsoft Word 97, Third Edition

Quick Reference Table Edits

To:	Do This:
Append a row at the end of a table	Click the last cell of the last row and press Tab.
Insert a row	Right-click in the row below where you want to insert the new row(s). Choose **Insert Rows.**
Append a column to the right of	Click outside of the last column of a table column and open the **Table** menu, choose **Select Column**. Then choose **Table** from the submenu, and select **Insert Columns.**
Insert a column	Select the column to the left of where you want to insert the new column(s). Right-click and choose **Insert Columns.**
Insert blank line or text above a table	Click in the first row. Open the **Table** menu and choose **Split Table.**
Turn a table into an AutoText entry	Select the table and then open the **Insert** menu, choose **AutoText**, then choose **New**. Assign a name to the table. Insert the table by choosing **Insert**, and hold down the Shift key as you select **AutoText**. Click the table name in the AutoText list.

Quick Reference Customization

To:	Do This:
Turn ScreenTips on/off	Open the **Tools** menu and choose **Options**, click the **View** tab, select/deselect **ScreenTips**.
Show/don't show field codes	Open the **Tools** menu and choose **Options**, click the **View** tab, select/deselect **Field codes**.
Change default folder	Open the **Tools** menu and choose **Options**, click the **File Locations** tab, then select what you want to change and click **Modify**.
Add or remove an AutoCorrect item	Open the **Tools** menu and choose **AutoCorrect**, select an entry, and click **Delete** or type a new entry and click **Add**.
Edit custom dictionary	Click **Start** on the Windows Taskbar, choose **Find**, then choose **Files or Folders**. Search for custom.dic. Double-click the file to open it. Edit the document and save your changes.
Change default font	Open the **Format** menu and choose **Font**, select the font to use as the default, and click **Default**. Click **OK**.

Using Microsoft Word 97

Third Edition

Jane Calabria

Rob Kirkland

Dorothy Burke

QUE®

A Division of Macmillan Computer Publishing, USA
201 W. 103rd Street
Indianapolis, Indiana 46290

Contents at a Glance

Using Microsoft® Word 97, Third Edzition

Library of Congress Catalog No.: `CIP data available upon request.`

ISBN: 0-7897-1568-6

00 99 98 6 5 4 3 2 1

Interpretation of the printing code: the rightmost double-digit number is the year of the book's printing; the rightmost single-digit number, the number of the book's printing. For example, a printing code of 98-1 shows that the first printing of the book occurred in 1998.

Credits

Executive Editor
Jim Minatel

Acquisitions Editor
Jill Byus

Development Editor
Rick Kughen

Technical Editor
Doug Klippert

Managing Editor
Thomas F. Hayes

Project Editor
Gina Brown

Copy Editor
Linda Seifert

Indexer
Tim Tate

Production
Betsy Deeter
Rebekah Stutzman

Book Designers
Nathan Clement
Ruth Harvey

Contents

V Add Objects to Documents

VII Automate and Customize

About the Authors

Jane Calabria has authored 11 Que books. As a consultant, Jane works on a national level with large corporations and training organizations, developing user training programs and modeling help desk support structures. As a trainer, Jane teaches Microsoft desktop applications, operating systems, and Lotus Notes. She is a **Certified Lotus Notes Professional (Principal level)** and a **Certified Microsoft User Specialist**. Jane is heard weekly in the Philadelphia area on KYW News Radio 1060 AM, giving reports on computing and computer news as "JC on PCs." Her weekly radio reports are also found on AOL. Jane can be reached at: `jc_on_pcs@compuserve.com`

Rob Kirkland is a **Certified Lotus Notes Instructor (CLI)**, a **Certified NetWare Engineer (CNE)**, and a **Microsoft Certified Product Specialist (MCPS)** for Windows NT. He is a contributing author of several Que books including, *Using Windows NT Workstation*, *Intranet Publishing*, *Running a Perfect Intranet*, and *Intranet HTML*. Rob began his computer teaching career as a word processing and desktop publishing guru. Today, Rob also teaches Lotus Notes, Novell NetWare, Windows NT, numerous application programs, and hardware management. As a consultant, he sets up networks, designs applications, and subdues unruly hardware and software. In his spare time, Rob picked up a law degree. Rob can be reached at: `74754.3360@compuserve.com`

Rob and Jane are husband and wife and coauthored the *Professional Developers Guide to Domino 4.5*. They live in beautiful Chester County, PA.

Dorothy Burke started life as a technical magazine editor and went on to sales and then office management. She has been an independent consultant and trainer since 1988. Dorothy contributed to several Que books, including *Special Edition, Using PowerPoint 97*. As a trainer, she teaches word processing, desktop publishing, operating systems, spreadsheets, and graphics programs, as well as Lotus Notes and Domino. As a consultant, Dorothy works with Lotus Notes and Domino, developing applications. Dorothy is a **Certified Lotus Instructor (CLI)**. Dorothy can be reached at: `dburke@compuserve.com`

Jane and Dorothy have teamed up successfully on several Que books, including the *Certified Microsoft Office User Exam Guides for Microsoft Word 97*, *Microsoft Excel 97* and *Microsoft Power Point 97*. They also coauthored *Microsoft Works 6-in-1*, *Microsoft Windows 95 6 in 1* and several Lotus Notes books.

About the Technical Editor

Doug Klippert is an independent contract trainer living in Tacoma, Washington. He is an **MCSE** and an **Expert Microsoft Office User Specialist (MOUS)** in Word 97, Excel 97, and PowerPoint 97.

Doug has been working with Word/WinWord since 1991. He's the Credit Manager for a Public utility and has a BA in Accounting and an MBA.

Dedication

To Zanna and Spence for growing into strong, independent, and beautiful people.

Acknowledgments

Thanks to John Pierce and Jill Byus for presenting this new series opportunity to my team. It is a privilege to work on such an important project for MCP.

A special thanks to Jim Minatel, Executive Editor, for his endless attention to detail and long hours of hard work. His multifaceted publishing and writing experiences enabled us to meet a tremendous challenge in an otherwise impossible time frame.

Thanks too, to Doug Klippert, Gina Brown, and Linda Seifert for their invaluable editorial work.

Finally, (but hardly least) thanks for the "Que East" team: Janet Crawford and Carol Manieri for their late hours, research, keystroking, food breaks, and exercise demands.

We'd Like to Hear from You!

Que Corporation has a long-standing reputation for high-quality books and products. To ensure your continued satisfaction, we also understand the importance of customer service and support.

Tech Support

If you need assistance with the information in this book or you have feedback for us about the book, please contact Macmillan Technical Support by phone at 317-581-3833 or via email at: `support@mcp.com`.

Orders, Catalogs, and Customer Service

To order other Que or Macmillan Computer Publishing books, catalogs, or products, please contact our Customer Service Department:

Phone: 1-800-428-5331

Fax: 1-800-835-3202

International Fax: 1-317-228-4400

Or visit our online bookstore: `http://www.mcp.com/`

Introduction

We first started using Microsoft Word when it was still in version 1.1. It was a DOS-based program in those days—graphical user interfaces like the Macintosh and Windows didn't exist yet. At that time Word was a pioneering program, unique among word processors in its treatment of characters, paragraphs, and pages as discreet objects—each having its own properties. Word's object orientation made it uniquely easy to use for the creation of great-looking, highly formatted documents. Clearly Microsoft was on to something when it came up with this word processor because now virtually all programs designed for laying out pages or editing and formatting text have adopted the same paradigm that we first encountered in Word 1.1.

Over the years we have learned, used, taught, and written about many other software programs. For awhile, when WordPerfect dominated the world of computerized word processing, we hardly thought about Word. But Word had impressed us because of its power and ease of use and we found ourselves returning to it again and again. With each revision, it became more powerful, more relevant and easier to use. Now it has become our preferred word-processing program. It is our great pleasure to present the latest version of Word to you.

Microsoft has long developed Word with an eye to three things:

- *Power*. They want you to be able to use Word to do anything that can be done with words.
- *Ease of use*. They want it to be so easy that you don't hesitate to do it just because it is too much effort. They want it to be so easy that the process doesn't distract you from your ultimate goal of communication with words.
- *Ease of learning*. They want it to be easy to master so that you don't hesitate to try tasks simply because you have never done so.

One of a programmer's most difficult challenges is to add power while retaining ease of use and ease of learning in a program. Microsoft has never lost sight of these goals. As a result, not only has Word gained new features with each new release, but its existing features have become easier to use. Also, some of the new features—for example, wizards and the

Office Assistant—have had the soul purpose of making it easy for you to discover and begin using Word's power.

That is our goal too. We want you to get your word processing done quickly, efficiently, and painlessly. We'll help you to quickly discover the power of Word. We'll help you to quickly learn the tools that Word provides. We'll show you the easiest and most efficient ways of using those tools. In the end, we hope you will feel the same excitement we feel about Word and the same pleasure that we feel in having mastered a powerful set of tools.

Why This Book?

Have you ever purchased a *Using* book from Que?. The *Using* books have proven invaluable to readers as both learning guides and as references for many years. The *Using* series is an industry leader, and has practically become an industry standard. We encourage and receive feedback from readers all the time and we consider and implement their suggestions whenever possible.

Using Microsoft Word 97, Third Edition incorporates fresh new ideas and approaches to the *Using* series. This book is not a compiled authority on all the features of Word. Instead, it is a streamlined, conversational approach for using Word productively and efficiently. New features include

- *Improved Index. To help you find information the first time you look!* What do you call tasks and features? As we wrote, we anticipated every possible name or description of a task that we've heard people call it. For example, if you wanted to know how to include artwork in your letterhead, where do you look? Should you check the index for artwork, clip art, scanned images, graphics, letterhead, or pictures? The answer is ***yes***—check the index for any of those terms and you will find your answer on the first pass.
- *Real-life answers.* Throughout the book you will find *our* real life examples and experiences. We recommend when to use tables versus tabs versus columns. We tell you why you don't want to create a database with a field containing first names and last names. We even suggest when wizards save you time and when you might be more productive creating your own documents from scratch. After all,

we've been there and done that! We understand that *how* to perform a task is only one question you may have, and perhaps the bigger questions are *why* and *what for*?

- *Relevant information written just for you!* We have carefully scrutinized which features and tasks to include in this book and have included those that apply to your everyday use of Word.

  We realize that very few people use as much as 50% of Word's capabilities. Our experience tells us that there are two reasons for this:

  - *Time.* You can't spare the time from work to attend classes on Word 97. You don't have the time at work to explore every nook and cranny of the software. And, when you do need to perform a task that is new to you, you need to get it done quickly.
  - *Need.* Why invest in material that teaches you how to perform tasks you will never need to perform? Word is a powerful (and potentially complex) software program. But your work does not involve powerful, complex word processing tasks? Will it ever? Why spend time on features you don't need?

- *Reference or Tutorial.* You can learn to quickly perform a task using step-by-step instructions, or you can investigate the why and wherefore of a task with our discussions preceding each task.
- *Wise Investment.* Pay the right price for the right book. We won't waste your valuable bookshelf real estate with redundant or irrelevant material, nor do we assume you "know it all" or need to "know it all." Here is what you need, when you need it, how you need it, with an appropriate price tag.
- *Easy to find procedures.* Every numbered step-by-step procedure in the book has a short title explaining exactly what it does. This saves you time by making it easier to find the exact steps you need to accomplish a task.
- *Cross referencing, to give to additional, related information.* We've looked for all the tasks and topics that are related to a topic at hand and referenced those for you. So, if you need to look for coverage that leads up to what you are working on, or if you want to build on the new skill you just mastered, you have the references to easily find the right coverage in the book.

- *Sidebar elements with quick-read headlines save you time.* Often times, we'll want to give you a little tip or note about how to make something work best. Or we'll need to give you a caution or warning about a problem you may encounter. By giving these SideNotes precise titles that explain their topic and by placing them in the margins, we make each one easy to skip while still preserving the flow of the text around it.

Who Should Use this Book

Anyone who uses Word and needs to accomplish a specific task, solve a problem, or wants to learn a technique that applies to something they need to get done. Basically, anyone who:

- Has basic Windows skills but is new to Word.
- Uses Word, but wants to become more proficient in Word.
- Uses Word at work.
- Uses Word at home.
- Needs to create special documents, such as newsletters or letterhead.
- Wants to manage small databases and mailing lists such as club memberships or client lists.

This book is not for you if you have never used a Windows-based computer program. In that case, we recommend you read *Sams' Teach Yourself Word 97 in 24 Hours*. This book is also not for you if your goal is to learn everything there is to know about Word 97. In that case, we recommend you read *Special Edition Using Word 97 Best Seller Edition*.

How this Book is Organized

Using Microsoft Word 97, Third Edition has task-oriented, easy-to-navigate tutorials and reference information presented in a logical progression from simple to complex tasks. It covers features of the program you use in your daily work. Features are explained thoroughly. Examples are real life. You can work through the book lesson by lesson or you can find specific information when you need to perform a job quickly.

Using Word 97 is divided into seven parts:

Part I: Use Everyday Word-Processing Techniques
This is fundamental information for those who are new (or fairly new) to Word. You learn the basics of word processing. You learn to navigate documents, select and format text, run spell check and grammar check, and manage files. Even if you think you know all these basics, you will find shortcuts, hints, and trainer information to help you use Word more productively. And, you'll have this basic information handy if you need a quick refresher.

Part II: Work with Paragraphs
The paragraph is a key component in a word-processing program. Learn to create numbered and bulleted lists, apply styles, indent paragraphs, set tabs, and control line breaks.

Part III: Create Professional-Looking Documents
Formatted pages using headers, footers, columns, custom templates, and proper margin settings are what differentiate between amateur and professional-looking documents. Here, you learn to produce great-looking documents quickly and efficiently.

Part IV: Print with Ease
Learn to select printers, share printers, change print options, print envelopes and labels, and even send a fax or mail a document.

Part V: Add Objects to Documents
Discover how to use tables to organize information, add graphics and drawings, use Object Linking and Embedding, and create or embed a chart in your document.

Part VI: Create Special Purpose and Custom Documents
Show off your skills with custom letterhead and Web documents. Or incorporate a customer list with a custom letter by using Mail Merge. Also, learn how to track document changes and revisions within a workgroup.

Part VII: Automate and Customize
Write macros to automate your word-processing tasks and learn to use wizards to create elaborate documents. Learn how to customize Word features.

Be sure to make use of the tearout card inside the book's cover. Tear this out and take it with you wherever you use Word. It contains some of the most common information you'll need that isn't easy to remember. So keep it next to your computer when you are using Word.

Conventions Used in this Book

Commands, directions, and explanations in this book are presented in the clearest format possible. The following items are some of the features that will make this book easier for you to use:

- *Menu and dialog box commands and options.* You can easily find the onscreen menu and dialog box commands by looking for bold text like you see in this direction: Open the **File** menu and click **Save**.
- *Hotkeys for commands.* The underlined keys onscreen that activate commands and options are also underlined in the book as shown in the previous example.
- *Combination and shortcut keystrokes.* Text that directs you to hold down several keys simultaneously is connected with a plus sign (+), such as Ctrl+P.
- *Graphical icons with the commands they execute.* Look for icons like this in text and steps. These indicate buttons onscreen that you can click to accomplish the procedure.
- *Cross references.* If there's a related topic that is prerequisite to the section or steps you are reading, or a topic that builds further on what you are reading, you'll find the cross reference to it after the steps or at the end of the section like this:

SEE ALSO

➤ *To see how to create newspaper columns, see page 222*

- *Glossary terms.* For all the terms that appear in the glossary, you'll find the first appearance of that term in the text in *italic* along with its definition.
- *Sidebars.* Information related to the task at hand or "inside" information from the author is offset in sidebars as not to interfere with the task at hand and to make it easy to find this valuable information. Each of these sidebars has a short title to help you quickly identify the information you'll find there. You'll find the same kind of information in these that you might find in notes, tips, or warnings in other books but here, the titles should be more informative.

Your screen may look slightly different from some of the examples in this book. This is due to various options during installation and because of hardware setup.

PART

I

Use Everyday Word-Processing Techniques

CHAPTER

1

Get Acquainted with Word

Start and close Word and Word documents

Create a basic document

Use menus, keyboard commands, and toolbar icons to work efficiently

Get help with Word from built-in help or Microsoft's Web site

Understand Word

Microsoft Word 97 is a word-processing program designed for Windows 95 and Windows NT 4.0. Word can integrate information with other Microsoft Office products such as Excel and PowerPoint. You, for example, can create a document in Word, and send the document's outline to PowerPoint.

Word is a powerful program and it is the most popular word-processing program today. Word includes capabilities to create charts, drawings, and databases within documents (such as those used in mail merges). Word also has the capability to link to charts, drawings, and databases that were created in other programs.

Files you create in Word can be mailed, saved, converted to other file formats—so that you can open them in other programs—and saved as HTML documents for the Internet.

Microsoft Word files are called *documents* and by default, filenames are given the extension .doc. When you save a report you want to name "First Quarter Budget", Word assigns the file extension .doc so that the full filename of your report becomes First Quarter Budget.doc.

This chapter reviews the basics of Word. The following sections are filled with reminders of and refreshers on the fundamental elements of Word.

SEE ALSO

- *Learn more about charts, see page 381*
- *Creating drawings, see page 358*
- *For information on databases and mail merge, see page 403*
- *Linking Word information to other programs, see page 335*
- *Creating HTML and Internet documents, see page 458*

Start Word 97

Word 97 can be started in several different ways. The method that you use depends on your personal preference and your system configuration. One way to start Word is by locating the Word program on the Windows **Start** button and clicking the program icon.

If you have Office 97 installed, you can start Word from the Office toolbar (if you elected to display the Office toolbar when you start Windows). You also can start Word by choosing the **Start** menu and then selecting either **New Office Document** or **Open Office Document.** The New Document dialog box appears. Click the **General** tab and choose **Blank Document**. You are now ready to begin working in your new document.

If you have a Word shortcut on your desktop, you can start Word by clicking the shortcut icon. 

Set up a Word shortcut

1. Locate the Word Program file by clicking the **Start** button and then choosing **Find**. Then select the **Files or Folders** option.
2. The Find: All Files dialog box appears. In the **Named** field, type `Winword.exe`. If you know that the program files for Word are located on a drive other than c:, choose the other drive in the **Look in** field.
3. Click the **Find Now** button. When Windows is finished searching, the Word file appears in the dialog box as shown in Figure 1.1. If the file did not appear, try searching another drive by selecting a different drive in the **Look in** field.
4. To add a shortcut to your desktop, click and drag the Winword.exe file to your desktop.
5. As you release your mouse, the icon changes from a file icon to a shortcut icon.

Turning off the Office toolbar

To turn off the Microsoft Office toolbar, right-click the toolbar and click **Exit**. Choose **Yes** or **No** to display the toolbar the next time you start your computer. To view the toolbar again, select the Microsoft Office Shortcut bar from your **Start** menu's list of programs.

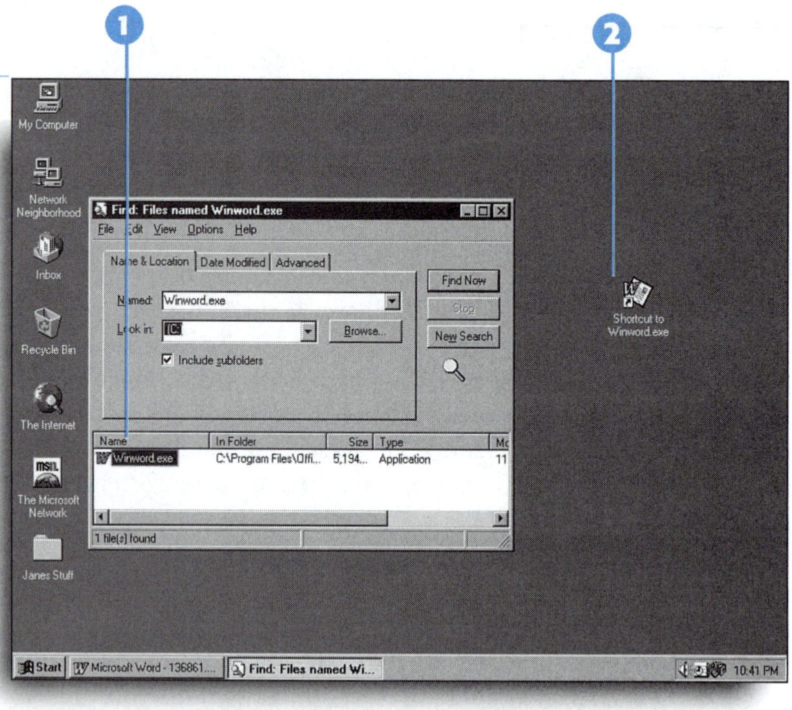

FIGURE 1.1
Add a Word shortcut to your desktop by dragging the Winword.exe file onto the desktop.

1. Drag from here…
2. …to here.

Don't see the Formatting toolbar?

To display the Formatting toolbar, go to the **View** menu and select **Toolbars**. From the **Toolbars** submenu select **Formatting**. Also, your screen may have other toolbars showing or they may be arranged in a different order. Alternately, you can right-click the menu and select **Formatting** from the pop-up menu.

Understand the Word Workspace

Word contains elements that are common to other Windows programs—title bar, menu bar, status bar, scrollbars, Minimize button, Restore/Maximize button, Close button, and Control button. Depending on your default setup, you also might see a Formatting toolbar.

You should have a basic understanding of Windows and of these elements to use Word 97 effectively. Figure 1.2 shows the major elements of the Word window.

FIGURE 1.2
Basic elements of the Word window.

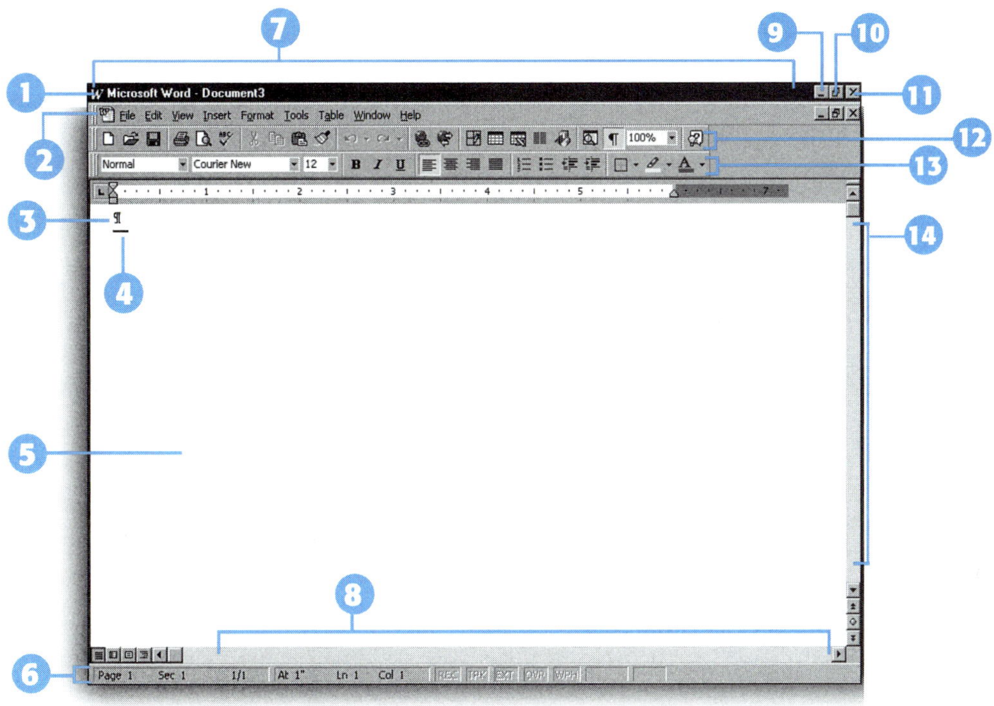

1. Control menu
2. Menu bar
3. Cursor
4. End-of-document marker
5. Work area
6. Status bar
7. Title bar
8. Horizontal scrollbar
9. Minimize button
10. Restore/Maximize button
11. Close button
12. Formatting toolbar
13. Standard toolbar
14. Vertical scrollbar

Use Menus, Toolbars, and Keyboard Shortcuts

To do almost anything in Word 97 (except the actual writing), you must use a command. In Word, as in most Windows applications, commands can be invoked in three ways:

- *Menu*. Select a command from a menu.
- *Toolbar*. Click an icon in a toolbar or on a scrollbar.
- *Keyboard shortcuts*. Use a key combination.

You can navigate a menu with a mouse or the keyboard. You can click icons only with the mouse. You can use key combinations only with the keyboard.

To access a command in the menu by mouse, click the menu name (such as **File**). To access a menu using the keyboard, hold down the Alt key, then press the underlined letter in the menu (such as Alt+F to access the **File** menu).

To activate a toolbar item, click its icon on the toolbar. You should take some time to become familiar with toolbars and menus. Knowing *where* to find features in the menu system helps you work efficiently.

Work more efficiently with keyboard shortcuts

We encourage you to use the keyboard techniques as much as possible. Push yourself to do it. The mouse is a crutch. Use the Alt key to open the menus and the arrow keys or hotkeys to navigate them. Use keyboard shortcuts whenever they are available.

Keyboard shortcuts are keystrokes that activate a command directly. Keyboard shortcuts are not Alt plus a key to open the menu; they are keystrokes that bypass the menu.

Word can help you become familiar with keyboard shortcuts by displaying the shortcut keys in the ScreenTips boxes that appear when you point at an icon on a toolbar. To activate the ScreenTips feature, go to the **Tools** menu and select **Customize**. In the Customize dialog box click the **Options** tab. In this tab select the **Show shortcut keys in ScreenTips** check box.

The basic tasks you need to create letters are used in many types of documents. The following section walks you through how to create letters so that you may review the basics of working with Word documents.

SEE ALSO

➤ *Learn more about keyboard shortcuts, see page 24*

➤ *Learn more about customizing Word defaults, see page 537*

Create and Save a Basic Letter

The fastest way to start creating letters is by using the Letter Wizard. To open the Letter Wizard, select the **File** menu and choose **New**. The New dialog box appears. Click the **Letters & Faxes** tab and then open the **Letter Wizard** file. Here's a quick refresher and a list of reminders regarding how to enter text, dates, and time. The basics of editing, saving, and closing documents are also covered in the following pages.

- The blinking vertical line represents your cursor position (insertion point). Whatever you type appears at the insertion point. The horizontal line is the end-of-document marker.
- The word wrap function fits text within the margins. You need only use the Enter key when you want to start a new line or a new paragraph.
- You can insert a date (instead of typing a date) by choosing the **Insert** menu and then selecting **Date and Time**. The Date and Time dialog box appears as shown in Figure 1.3. Select the date format you want and click **OK**. By inserting a date in this way, the date becomes part of your document text. If you click the **Update automatically** option in the Date and Time dialog box, the date is inserted as a field and is automatically updated each time you print or open your letter.

Caution: Automatic update

If the date of your letter is important, do *not* choose to automatically update. The date will change with future printings and the letter will appear to have been composed on a date other than its original date.

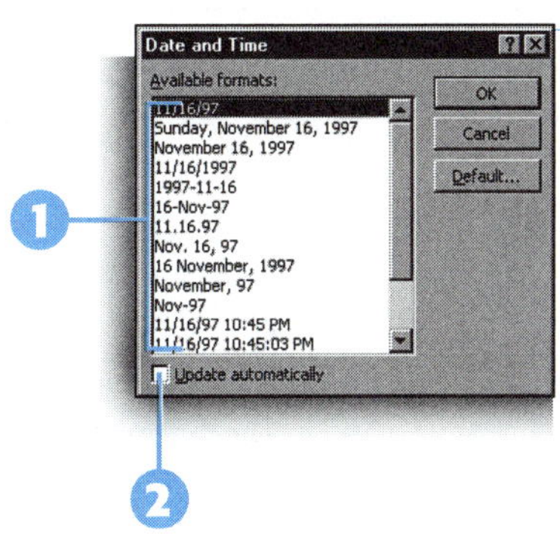

FIGURE 1.3

Automatically inserting a formatted date can save you time.

1. Choose a date format here.
2. Click here to insert a field.

- Consider turning on Word's **Show/Hide** option, which displays non-printing characters such as paragraph marks. Using this option, you can easily see where you have placed unnecessary spaces, where tabs were used instead of spaces, and where line and paragraph breaks are. Throughout this book you will find that non-printing characters display whenever you work in Word. To display these characters, click the Show All icon on the Standard toolbar. ¶
- If you make a mistake while typing, use the Backspace key to erase characters one at a time. You also can delete text by pressing the Delete key. This deletes characters one at a time to the right of your cursor position. Another way to delete text is by selecting a word and pressing the Delete key.
- To save your letter, click the Save icon on the Standard toolbar. The Save As dialog box appears as shown in Figure 1.4. Name your document by typing a name in the **File name** field. It is likely that your default settings will save this document in a file folder called My Documents. (If you are familiar with Windows and want to save to a different folder, select where you want to save the file and click the **Save** button.)

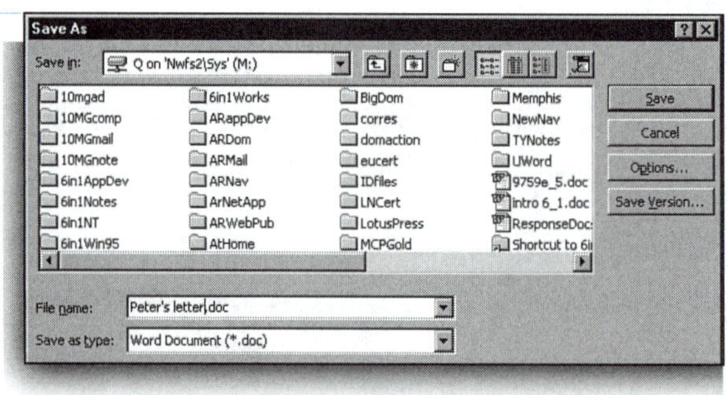

FIGURE 1.4
Choose a filename and location to save your letter.

- To print your letter, you can view your document in Print Preview mode or you can print without previewing. To view the document before printing, click the Print Preview button on the Standard toolbar. Figure 1.5 shows a letter as viewed in Preview mode. To print directly from Print Preview, click the Print button on the toolbar. To return to your document, click the Close button. To print without previewing, click the Print icon on the Standard toolbar.

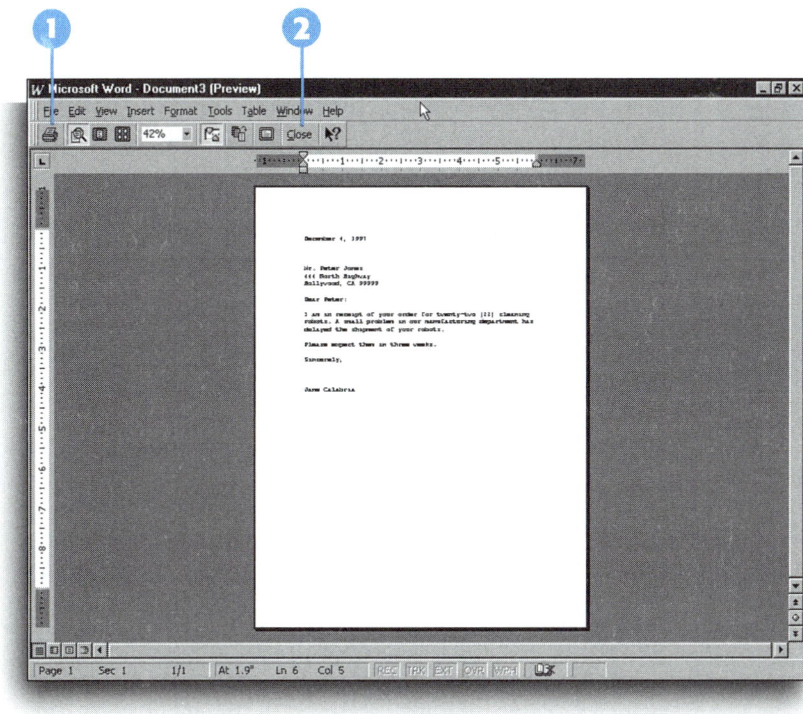

FIGURE 1.5

Save paper by seeing in Print Preview what your printed page will look like. This letter would probably overprint the letterhead.

1. Click here to print from this view.
2. Click here to close Print Preview.

- To close your letter, click the Close button on the menu bar. You also can close a letter by selecting the **File** menu, and then choosing **Close**.

SEE ALSO

➤ *Learn more about using fields in document merging, see page 467*
➤ *Learn more about saving documents and folders and file management, see page 86*
➤ *Learn more about printing and Print Preview mode, see page 258 and 260*

Find Help

Word has onscreen help and, like all *Microsoft* products, additional help can be found by searching Microsoft Web sites. Help can be accessed in five ways, as described in the following list:

- Get onscreen help by accessing the Help Topics window. (Open the **Help** menu and select **Contents and Index**.)
- Get interactive help by asking the Office Assistant. (Choose the **Help** menu and select **Microsoft Word Help** or press F1.)
- Find the definition of a screen element by using the What's This? feature. (Choose the **Help** menu and select **What's This?** or press Shift+F1.)
- Reveal a ScreenTip by pointing at an onscreen object.
- This method requires an Internet connection. Access online support and view frequently asked questions by visiting a Microsoft Web site. (Choose the **Help** menu and select **Microsoft on the Web**.)

The purpose of each help method differs slightly. If you know where to go in the help databases to find something, or you want to find every help topic on a given topic, you can browse the **Contents** tab in Help Topics. If you know the name of a feature, you can search the **Index** tab for it in Help Topics. If you don't know the name of a feature or its location in the help databases, you can do a full-text search. You can do this in two different places—in the **Find** tab in Help Topics or in the Office Assistant. If you want to know what some item on the screen is supposed to do, point at it with the mouse pointer. For some items a Help Tip pops up and tells you about the object. If that doesn't happen, click the object using What's This? help. A more comprehensive explanation pops up. If all else fails, you can go to Microsoft's Web site where you can look up information in the Microsoft Office Frequently Asked Questions (FAQ) page. You also can seek help directly from a Microsoft support personnel.

We usually access help with the Office Assistant because it is the most accessible. If the Office Assistant isn't on the screen, pressing F1 displays it. If we need more help, we go to help topics. If we still need help, we then go to the Microsoft Web site. Each of these methods is outlined in the following sections.

Browsing the Help Contents Screen

If you know exactly where to go in Help to find the information you need, or you want to research a topic thoroughly, then Help Contents is for you. Access Help Contents by choosing the **Help** menu and selecting **Contents and Index**. The Help Topics dialog box appears.

The **Contents** tab displays categories of information. When you double-click a category (symbolized by), it expands to display an indented list of either related subcategories or help topics (symbolized by), as shown in Figure 1.6.

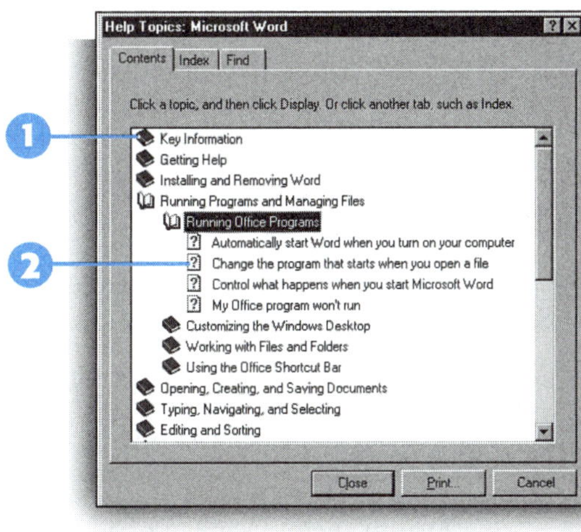

FIGURE 1.6

Book icons represent expandable categories of topics. Document icons represent help topics.

1. Double-click a book icon to expand it.
2. Double-click a document icon to view help information.

When you double-click a help topic , the Help Topics window closes and the help topic opens in a new window. This window floats on top of all the other screen windows so that you can (if you want to) keep the help topic information open for reference while you work. Help articles may contain a labeled screen, a series of step-by-step instructions, or an explanation of a concept (see Figure 1.7).

A help topic that instructs you to carry out some task typically opens as narrow windows on the right side of your screen so that you can leave them open while you work. Some help topics include a **Show me** button, which when clicked, indicates the menu or dialog box you need to access to perform the action you are querying. One or more **For more information** buttons also may appear. These buttons open more detailed help topic windows. Finally, clicking text highlighted by underlining and colored green displays a definition of the highlighted term.

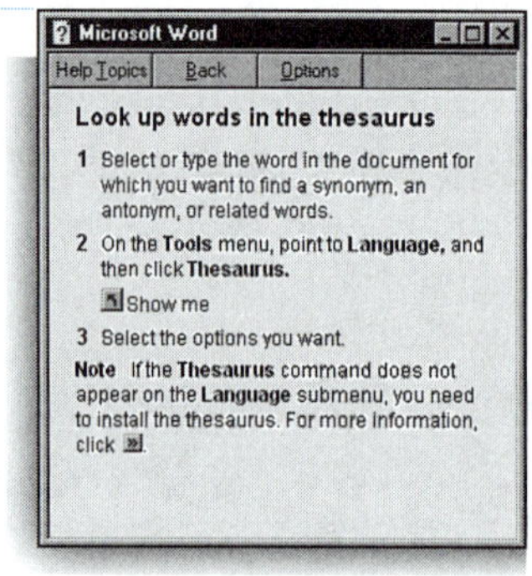

FIGURE 1.7
Click to have Word demonstrate the action. Click for more detailed help.

Useful Help Options

Each help topic window also has the following elements:

- **Help Topics** button. Used to return to the **Contents** tab of the Help Topics window so that you can select another topic
- **Back** button. Used to display the previously viewed Help Topics window (if applicable)
- **Options** menu. A menu of additional help features

On the **Options** menu, the **Print Topic** option (see Figure 1.8) is very useful because it allows you to print out the help topic. You can also use the **Copy** option to copy the help topic to the Clipboard so that you can paste the information in to another window or application. You can use the **Annotate** option to add your own insights to the help topic so that someone coming along after you can benefit from your experience—especially helpful for a company help desk. You also can use the **Bookmark** feature to mark a help topic so that you can return to it quickly in the future.

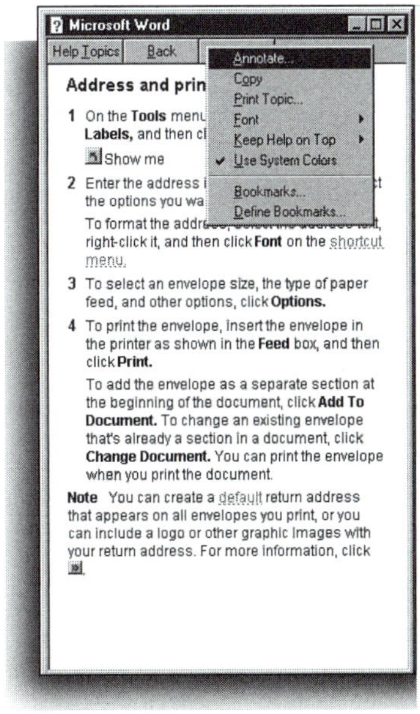

FIGURE 1.8

Use the **Options** menu to print a help screen or copy it to the Clipboard.

Browsing the Help Index

If you know the name of a Word feature, you can locate all references to that feature in the Help Index. The index, available on the **Index** tab of the Help Topics window, is an alphabetical list of terms that appears in the titles of the help topics (see Figure 1.9). Either scroll through the index list or enter the first characters of a word into the text field. As you type each character, the index scrolls closer and closer to the item you are typing. If you type a word that does not appear in the index, the index list scrolls past the point where your word should have appeared. If that happens, just backspace and type another word.

If, for example, you type the word `print`, the index scrolls to the first word beginning with "p" when you type the letter `p`, then scrolls to the first word beginning with "pr" when you type the `r`, and so on. In general, the most efficient way to use the index is to type enough of the word you are looking for to get to that vicinity of the index, then scroll through that part of the index looking for promising entries.

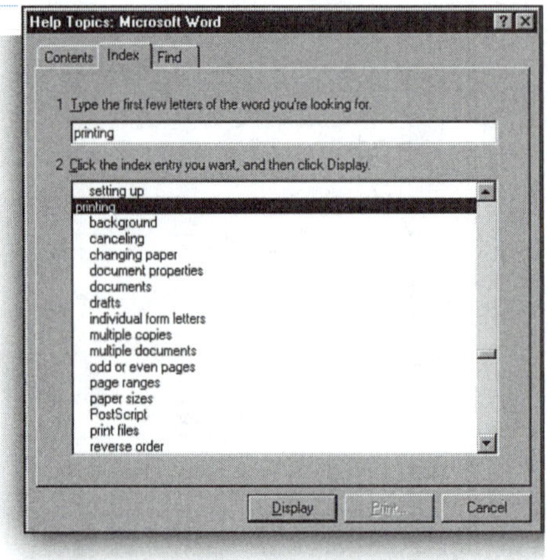

FIGURE 1.9
Use the **Index** tab to find specific words and phrases in Help.

Using Full-Text Search

Word Help has two search features—the **Find** tab, located in the Help Topics dialog box, and the Office Assistant. Find uses a full-text index to enable you to search for any word that appears in the help database. This differs from the Help Index (described in the previous section of this chapter), which lists only words that appear in help topic titles. The advantage of using the **Find** tab over the **Index** is that you might find relevant topics because you searched on a term that was significant but did not appear in the title of the help topic. That's why we say use the **Index** if you know the name by which Word refers to a topic, and use the **Find** feature (or Office Assistant, described in the next section), when you aren't sure how Word refers to a topic.

The first time you open the **Find** tab in the Help Topics dialog box, a wizard appears and informs you that you must build a word list for Word to search on when you initiate a search. You can choose one of three options for building the word list:

- **Minimize database size (recommended).** The wizard indexes just the main help database.
- **Maximize search capabilities.** The wizard indexes all the help databases.
- **Customize search capabilities.** The wizard indexes the help databases you choose.

Word includes several help databases. The main help database is by far the biggest and most relevant to almost all searches. The **Minimize database size (recommended)** option indexes just that database, which keeps the index relatively small (about two megabytes smaller than the **Maximize** option) and keeps search results more relevant.

When Word finishes creating the word list, the **Find** tab appears, containing a text box, a word list, and a topic list, as shown in Figure 1.10. To search, enter a word or phrase into the text box (field 1 in Figure 1.10). If the word or phrase is in the word list, it appears in the first list (field 2), and the topics it appears in appear in the second list (field 3). You can select a word in the first list to narrow the list of topics in the second list. You also can browse the second list and double-click a topic to open it.

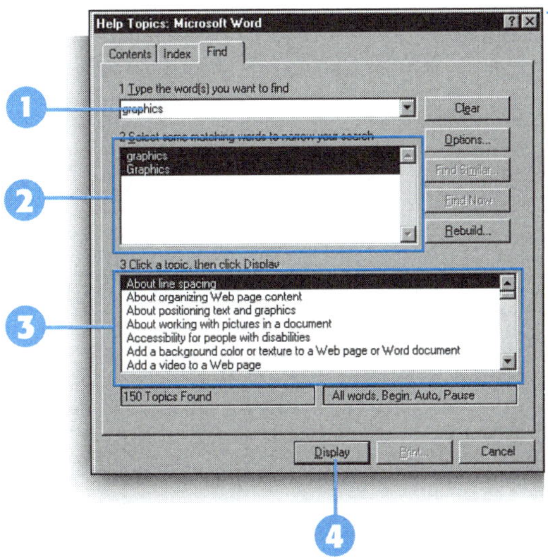

FIGURE 1.10

As you type a search term in field 1, matching indexed terms appear in field 2, and the corresponding help topics appear in field 3.

1. Type a word or phrase here (box 1).
2. (Optional)Select words here to narrow your search (box 2).
3. Select a topic from here (box 3).
4. Choose **Display** to view the selected topic.

Searching with Office Assistant

The Office Assistant is the animated cartoon character that initially appears in a window in the bottom-right corner of your screen. This fellow can be amusing, helpful, and annoying. It uses what Microsoft calls *IntelliSense natural-language technology*, which means that it can interpret questions you pose to it, and it can anticipate what kinds of help you may need and offer that help unbidden—based on what you are doing in your document. One of Office Assistant's more helpful features is its search feature, which you access by popping up the balloon that asks **"What would you like to do?"**

If the Office Assistant is currently visible on your screen, click it to reveal the **"What would you like to do?"** balloon. If the Office Assistant isn't visible on your screen, press F1 (or choose **Microsoft Word Help** from the **Help** menu) to pop it up. The **"What would you like to do?"** balloon also pops up (see Figure 1.11).

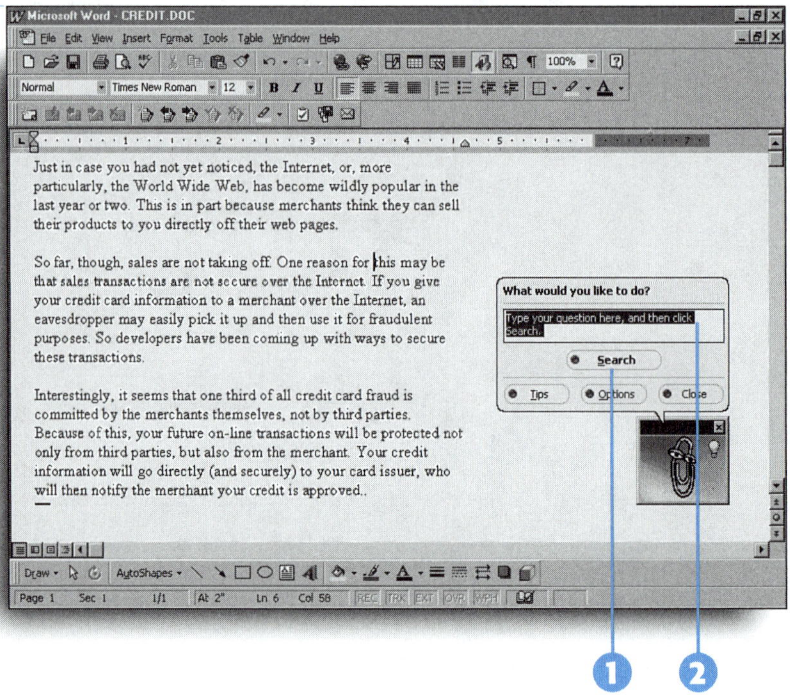

FIGURE 1.11

Type a word, phrase, or question in the Office Assistant bubble text box to get advice or help.

1. Click **Search**.
2. Type keywords here.

Enter any word, phrase, sentence, or question in the text field of the balloon, then press Enter. The IntelliSense search engine tries to figure what help topics you might be looking for. The search engine pops up a list of help topics. You can select a help topic that you want by clicking it. A Help Topics window opens for the topic that you choose.

As a demonstration of how the Office Assistant search engine works, enter the word `keystroke` into the balloon, then press Enter. The list of topics that pops up should include the item "Shortcut Keys". Click that item and the Shortcut Keys Help Topic window pops up. Browse through it; this window contains an exhaustive list of all the keyboard shortcuts you can use in Word.

No Office Assistant?

Run **Setup for Microsoft Office or Microsoft Word** and select the Office Assistant as an installation option. Close Word and access the Control Panel by choosing the **Start** menu, and selecting **Settings**. Then select **Control Panel** from the submenu. Double-click the Add/Remove Programs icon. Choose Microsoft Office or Microsoft Word and follow the instructions as the wizard guides you through setup.

Optimizing the Office Assistant

The Office Assistant can be very helpful. If you are finding that you don't agree—that it's either not helpful or is way too intrusive—you should try to optimize it to your liking before you give up on it. The Office Assistant can do a lot of other things besides search for help topics. It also can display the following things:

- *Suggested Help.* The Office Assistant can guess what help you might look for based on what you are doing. So, when you click the Office Assistant, the help topics appear even though you haven't entered a query.
- *Tips.* If the Office Assistant thinks you could be doing something more efficiently, it offers to tell you so by displaying a lightbulb icon. If the Office Assistant is currently visible on your screen, the lightbulb appears in its window. If it is not currently visible, the lightbulb appears in the toolbar as part of the Office Assistant icon. Click the lightbulb to pop up the tip.
- *Messages.* If something happens that the Office Assistant thinks you would like to know about, it pops up a message onscreen, either in a balloon or in a message box. If, for example, Word cannot AutoSave your document (say, because you are low on disk space), Office Assistant pops up a message that AutoSave was postponed.

If Office Assistant is not doing these things for you, or if it is and you find them unbearably annoying, you can change the Office Assistant options. Click the Office Assistant to pop up its balloon, then choose **Options** in the balloon to open the Office Assistant dialog box with the **Options** tab displayed (see Figure

1.12). Set the options as desired—don't be afraid to experiment with them, and remember to use What's This? help to get an explanation of any unclear item in the dialog box—then close the dialog box and see if the Office Assistant behaves more to your liking.

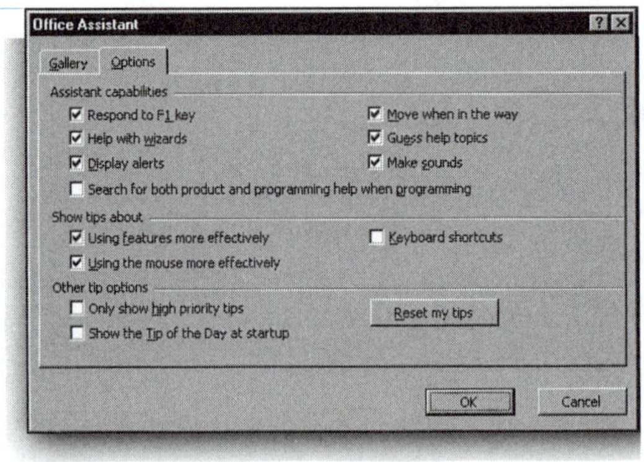

FIGURE 1.12
Change the behavior of the Office Assistant here.

Finding Out About Screen Objects

If you want to know what a particular icon, label, or other object is in the Microsoft Word window or a dialog box, you can find out in two different ways. First, in the Word window, point at any object on the screen. After a second or so, the name of the object might pop up. This alone may be enough to tell you what the object is for. If not, or if no name pops up at all, try using What's This? help. Either press Shift+F1 or choose the **Help** menu and select **What's This?** Your mouse pointer will change to an arrow and a question mark.  With this pointer, click any object on the screen. A balloon usually pops up with a description of the object (see Figure 1.13).

Depending on what you point at, the question mark pointer may disappear after you click an object. If it disappears, then you are back in normal pointer mode and you can continue working, or, if you want help on another screen object, you have to press Shift+F1 again. Alternately, if the pointer remains in What's This? mode (question mark in mouse pointer), and you want to turn off that mode, you can press Esc, and the mouse pointer returns to normal.

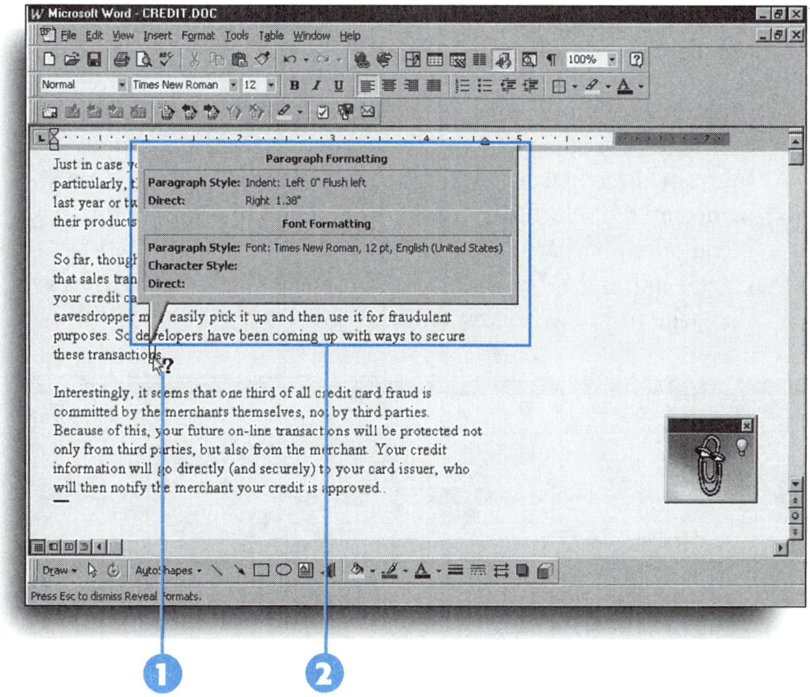

FIGURE 1.13

Using What's This? to click text in the document opens a window that displays the formatting of the selected text.

1 Click here.

2 What's This? help describes the formatting of the text you clicked.

In a dialog box, you can right-click an object to pop up a menu that has the entry **What's This?** in it, then click **What's This?** to display the pop-up Help window. Alternately, click the **?** icon in the upper-right corner of the dialog box, then click an object in the dialog box (see Figure 1.14).

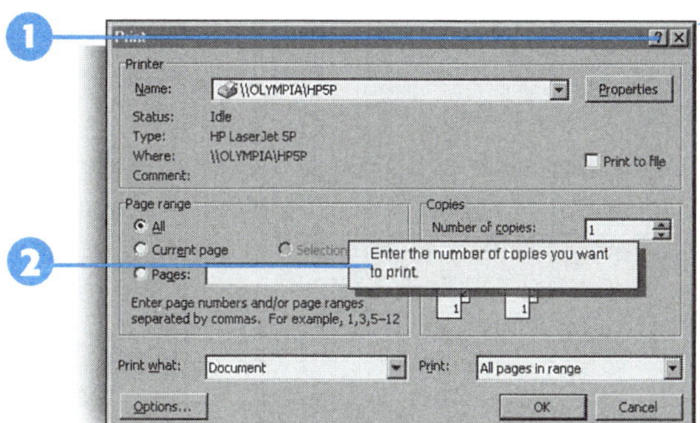

FIGURE 1.14

Using What's This? in this dialog box opened a window offering more detailed instructions about the **Number of copies** field.

1 Click here.

2 Then click an element of the dialog box.

Getting Help from the Microsoft Web Site

If you have a connection to the World Wide Web and you feel a need to seek help directly from Microsoft (or if you just want to take a short break to surf the Web), you can reach the Microsoft Web site directly from within the **Help** menu. Open the **Help** menu and the select **Microsoft on the Web** to display a submenu of relevant Microsoft Web page links (see Figure 1.15). Click a link and Word opens your browser, which then retrieves that page from the Microsoft Web site.

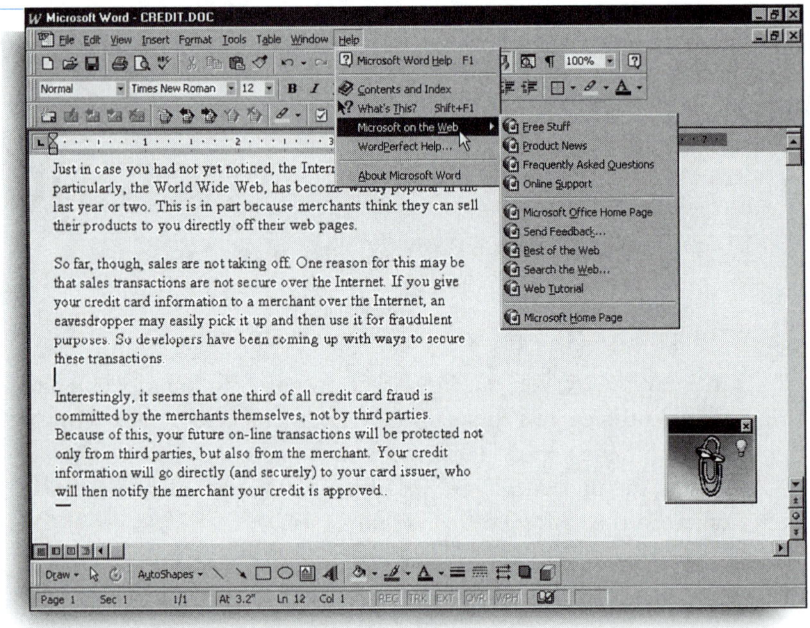

FIGURE 1.15
If you have access to the World Wide Web, you can go to Microsoft's Web site directly from the **Help** menu.

At the Microsoft Web site, you can search a library of technical notes for topics relevant to your problem, or you can submit a query directly to Microsoft support. You can see what updates are available for Word (and other Microsoft programs) and download them if they look helpful.

Like many other companies, Microsoft is making greater and greater use of the World Wide Web to provide support to users of its products. If you don't have access to the World Wide Web yet, this may be just the excuse you need to finally obtain Web access—of necessity.

CHAPTER

2

Navigate, Select, and Edit Text

Move quickly from place to place in your documents

Cut, copy, and paste text efficiently

Correct mistakes with undo and redo

Navigation and Selection Techniques

Word is designed to make writing easy. You can compose, navigate, edit, and format your text effortlessly thanks to Word's sophisticated navigation and selection tools. By becoming aware of the full range of tools available to you, you can learn to get the most out of your time writing in Word.

A glance at the tables in the following pages might suggest that you will never be able to remember them all and, in fact, most people start out using only the basic techniques.

As you become more experienced using Word, you'll appreciate eliminating the need to reach for the mouse, thus increasing your productivity.

Although expedient navigation is a time-saving technique, text selection is a *required* technique for efficient word processing. Many features of Word require that you select text before employing the feature. You *must*, for example, select text to cut, copy, delete, or move it. To add a word to your custom dictionary or to use the thesaurus, you must first select the word (see Figure 2.1). Table 2.1 lists the most frequently used keystroke combinations for navigating and selecting text. As shown in Figure 2.2, many keystroke combinations are shown on menus.

FIGURE 2.1
Selected text appears highlighted in black on your screen.

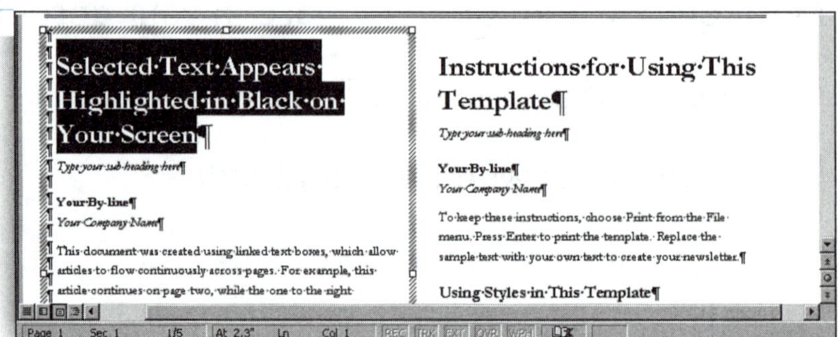

TABLE 2.1 **Keystroke combinations for navigating a document and selecting text**

To Move by a:	Direction:	Keystrokes to Move:	Keystrokes to Select (Note: Selection works from insertion point.)
Word	Right	Ctrl+Right arrow	Shift+Ctrl+Right arrow
To select entire words, place the insertion point at the beginning of the word.			
	Left	Right, or end	Shift+Ctrl+Left arrow
To select entire words, place the insertion point at the end of the word.			
Line of Text	Down	Down arrow	Shift+End
To select an entire line, place the insertion point at the beginning of the line.			
	Up	Up arrow	Shift+Home
To select an entire line, place the insertion point at the end of the line.			
Paragraph	Down	Ctrl+Down arrow	Shift+Ctrl+Down arrow
To select an entire paragraph, place the insertion point at the beginning of the paragraph.			
	Up	Ctrl+Up arrow	Shift+Ctrl+Up arrow
To select an entire paragraph, place the insertion point at the end of the paragraph.			
Screen	Down	Page Down	Shift+Page Down
To select an entire screen, place the insertion point at the beginning of the screen.			
	Up	Page Up	Shift+Page Up
To select an entire screen, place the insertion point at the end of the screen.			
Page	Down	Ctrl+Page Down	Shift+Ctrl+Page Down
To select an entire page, place the insertion point at the beginning of the screen.			
	Up	Ctrl+Page Up	Shift+Ctrl+Page Up
To select an entire page, place the insertion point at the end of the page.			
Document	Down	Ctrl+End	Shift+Ctrl+End
To select an entire document, place the insertion point at the beginning of the document.			
	Up	Ctrl+Home	Shift+Ctrl+Home
To select an entire document, place the insertion point at the end of the document.			
To select an entire document, press Ctrl+A.			

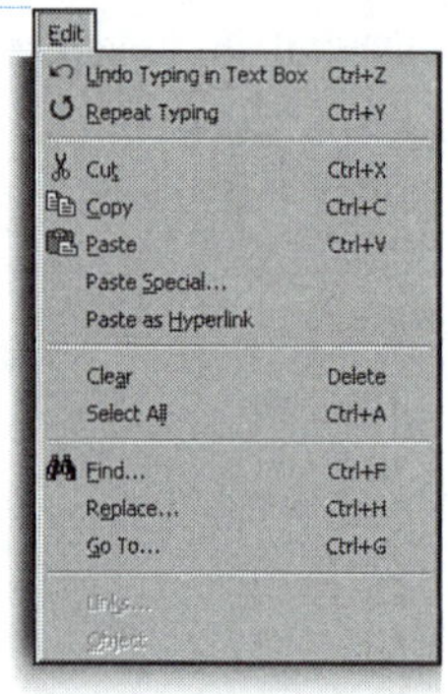

FIGURE 2.2
The **Edit** menu displays keystrokes that can be used in lieu of using the menu.

As you can see from Table 2.1, selecting text is just an extension of moving the insertion point. You use the same techniques as you do when navigating text, but you add the Shift key to your keystroke combination.

If keyboard combinations don't do it for you, or you can't break the habit of reaching for the mouse, consult Table 2.2 for mouse techniques. Clicking the mouse is faster and more accurate than dragging the mouse. The following are several techniques for using mouse clicks to select text.

For example, did you know that double-clicking inside of a word selects the word? Also, place your mouse in the left margin of a document and when the pointer changes to an arrow, click:

- Once to select a line
- Twice to select a paragraph
- Three times to select the entire document—triple-clicking within a paragraph selects an entire paragraph

Click again anywhere in the document to deselect lines, paragraphs, or text.

TABLE 2.2 **Mouse text-selection techniques**

To Select:	Position Your Mouse:	Do This:
Any amount of text	At the beginning of the text	Drag to the end of the text.

To Select:	Position Your Mouse:	Do This:
A word	Anywhere in the word	Double-click the word.
Multiple words	In the first word	Double-click the word, hold down the mouse key, and drag.
A line	In the left margin of the line	Click.
A sentence	Anywhere in the sentence	Hold down Ctrl and then click.
Multiple sentences	Anywhere in the sentence	Ctrl+click, then drag.
A paragraph	In the left margin of the paragraph	When the pointer changes to an arrow, double-click.
	Anywhere in the paragraph	Triple-click.
Multiple paragraphs	Anywhere in the first paragraph	Triple-click, hold down the mouse key, and drag.
	In a left margin of the first or last paragraph	When the pointer changes to an arrow, drag the mouse up or down.
An entire document	In the left margin of the document	When the point changes to an arrow, triple-click.

Check your default settings for word selection

When you use the drag method to select words, Word automatically selects whole words as you drag. If you prefer to disable this feature, choose the **Tools** menu and select **Options**, and click the **Edit** tab. Deselect **When selecting, automatically select entire word**.

SEE ALSO

- *Selecting text within a table, see page 285*
- *Selecting text while in Outline view, see page 207*
- *Learn how to select graphics with the mouse, see page 314*

Edit Text

When you edit text, you begin to see the importance of efficient text-selection techniques. Many editing functions are performed on selected text, such as cut, copy, move, and delete. Table 2.3 describes Word's editing tools, the shortcut keys for each, and the toolbar icons for each. The following are a few of the many tools provided by Word to help you edit text.

The Cut and Copy commands replace the Clipboard contents

Each time you cut or copy, the new selection replaces the contents of the Clipboard. If you are pasting information, be certain to complete your paste before you cut or copy again.

- *Cut*, *copy*, and *paste*, are actions that involve the Windows Clipboard. Cutting and copying items places the items on the Clipboard and pasting items places the contents of the Clipboard in to your document. *Items* can be text, graphics, tables, and any object that can be selected in a Word document. Cut, copy, and paste can be performed with the mouse or with keystroke combinations. Use cut, copy, and paste when you need to move or reuse text.
- Move is an action associated with the mouse—no keystroke combinations are dedicated for moving text. However, if you cut and paste items using keystroke combinations, you have effectively moved text with keystroke combinations.
- Insert mode describes the program mode that adjusts spacing when you add new text to a document.
- Overtype mode replaces existing text with your new text. Insert mode is the default mode.
- *Delete* is an action you should reserve for text you want to permanently remove. Deleted text is not placed in the Windows Clipboard. You can delete text with either mouse techniques or keystroke combinations.
- **Undo** and **Redo** are internal to Word and do not involve the Windows Clipboard. With the **Undo** and **Redo** commands, you can reverse tasks that you have performed.

TABLE 2.3 **Text-editing techniques**

	Cut	Copy	Paste	Move	Delete	Undo	Redo
Keyboard Shortcuts	Ctrl+X	Ctrl+C	Ctrl+V	Ctrl+X then Ctrl+V	Backspace or Delete	Ctrl+Z	Ctrl+Y
Menu Commands	**Edit, Cut**	**Edit, Copy**	**Edit, Paste**	**Edit, Copy** then **Edit, Paste**	**Edit, Clear**	**Edit, Undo**	**Edit, Redo**

	Cut	Copy	Paste	Move	Delete	Undo	Redo
Toolbar Icon				 then 			
Right Mouse Click	Select **Cut**.	Select **Copy**.	Select **Paste**.	Select **Cut**, then **Paste**.	Select **Cut**.		
Mouse Technique		Select text, then drag.		Select text, hold down the mouse button+ Ctrl and drag.			

Cut, Copy, and Paste Text

The **Cut** command removes text and places the text in the Windows Clipboard. Text must be selected before you can use the **Cut** command. After selecting the text, press Ctrl+X or right-click and choose **Cut** from the pop-up menu (see Figure 2.3).

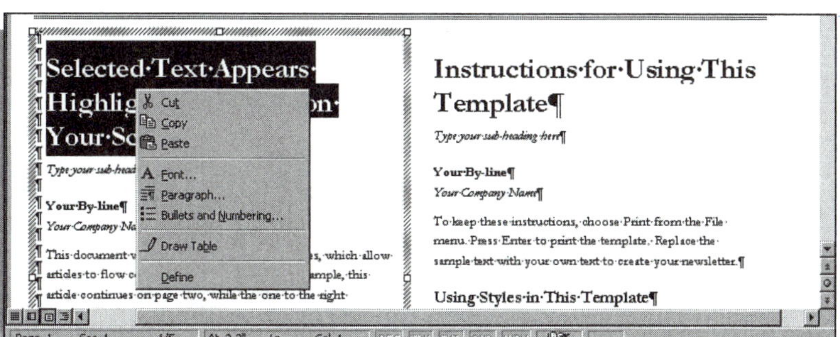

FIGURE 2.3
Right-click for the convenient pop-up menu. The **Cut** option is active only after you have selected text.

The **Copy** command copies the selected text and places the text in the Windows Clipboard. The same methods used to cut text are used when copying text. Select the text and press Ctrl+C, or right-click and choose **Copy** from the pop-up menu.

Three basic editing keystrokes

If you aren't a fan of shortcut keys, so be it. But, if you memorize just these five, you'll find your productivity increases: Ctrl+X to cut, Ctrl+V to paste, Ctrl+C to copy, Ctrl+S to save, and Ctrl+P to print.

The **Paste** command inserts the contents of the Windows Clipboard in to your document at your insertion point. Check your insertion point before pasting and press Ctrl+V or right-click and choose **Paste**.

If the contents of the Clipboard are empty, **Paste** is not an available option. To copy and paste in the same mouse movement, select text and hold down the Ctrl key as you drag it to a new location. Word copies the highlighted text and inserts it in the new location. When you copy and paste using this method, the cursor appears with a + sign while dragging.

Warning: Check for selected text before pasting

Selected text will be replaced with the contents of the Windows Clipboard when you choose **Paste**, meaning that you could inadvertently overwrite important text in your document. You can always use **Undo** if you inadvertently paste text. The replacement of text in this way is the default setting in Word. Should you want to disable this setting, choose the **Tools** menu and select **Options**. Then in the Options dialog box click the **Edit** tab. Deselect the **Typing replaces selection** option.

Cut, **Copy**, and **Paste** commands are also found in the **Edit** menu and on the standard toolbar:

- **Cut**
- **Copy**
- **Paste**

Move Text

Moving text is a function of the mouse—unless you use the keystrokes for **Cut** (Ctrl+X) and **Paste** (Ctrl+V). To move text with the mouse:

Moving text to a new screen or page

We find the drag-and-drop method of moving text inconvenient if we are moving text far from its original location. In that case, we prefer to use the **Cut** and **Paste** commands.

Move text using the mouse

1. Select the text you want to move.
2. Point to the middle of the selected text.
3. Hold down your mouse button and drag the text. As you drag, the mouse pointer displays a small box around its tail.
4. A vertical line appears above your pointer (see Figure 2.4). This line acts as the insertion point. Move the insertion point to your desired position on the document and release the mouse button.

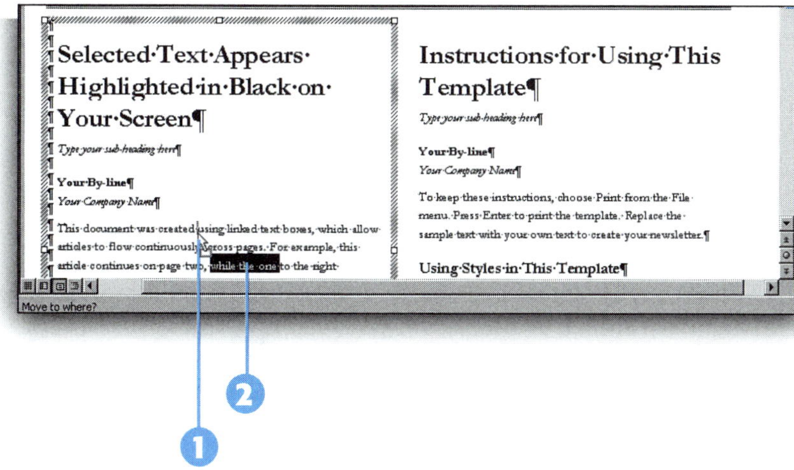

FIGURE 2.4

The drag-and-drop method enables you to see the *from* and *to* positions of selected text if you are moving within a screen.

1. Move text to this position.
2. Copy the highlighted text.

Move Multiple Text Entries with Spike

If you need to move text from one place to another, most of the time you will use the Windows **Cut** and **Paste** commands or Word's drag-and-drop method. But Word does provide another, specialized method for moving text—the AutoText Spike entry.

The *Spike* is like the Windows Clipboard, in that it stores text for you temporarily while you move it. But it is different from the Clipboard in that it can store multiple text entries. You append each item to the Spike, in the order you want them to appear. Then you paste them as a group in to a new location. You can paste the same group again and again. They remain in the Spike until you empty it, and you must empty the Spike to add a different set of items to it.

- *Adding text to the Spike*. To move selected text to the Spike, press Ctrl+F3. Do the same for each subsequent item you want to add to the Spike, being careful to do it in the order you want the text to appear when you paste out the group.
- *Inserting the Spike's contents without emptying it*. Position your insertion point where you want to put the contents. Open the **Insert** menu and select **AutoText**. Then select **AutoText** from the submenu. From the list below **Enter**

AutoText entries here, select **Spike**, and then choose **Insert**. Alternately, you may enter the word `Spike` where you want its contents to appear, then press F3.

- *Inserting the Spike's contents and emptying the Spike.* With your insertion point in the position where you want the Spike's contents to appear, press Ctrl+Shift+F3. This inserts the Spike's contents at the insertion point and empties the Spike.

An example of a use for the Spike would be the assembly of a contract from a library of boilerplate paragraphs. You could scroll through the library and collect the paragraphs you want onto the Spike, then change to a new document and empty the Spike. All the spiked paragraphs would appear there in the order that they were spiked. Another example would be the assembly of a list of items from a larger list. Say you have a directory of names and you want to address a memo to a subset of them. You could scroll through the directory, adding names of addressees to the Spike, then empty the Spike into the addressee field of the memo.

Insert Text

No menu command or special instructions are needed to add new text to a document. The generic term for adding new text is insert; however, this term should not be confused with the menu choice **Insert**, which is used when you need to insert AutoText and other objects.

To add new text to your document, place your cursor at the insertion point and type. Text to the right of your insertion point moves as you type, allowing the required space you need for your new text. This is the default mode of all word-processing programs and it's called Insert mode.

Insert mode is the preferred mode for most people. However, there may be times when you want to replace large blocks of text. In these instances you can switch to Overtype mode.

To switch to Overtype mode double-click the grayed-out OVR button located on the status bar.

When the OVR button is displayed in black text, Overtype mode is active. To turn off Overtype mode, double-click the OVR icon again. When the button is gray, Overtype mode is disabled.

SEE ALSO

- *Creating a list of frequently used words, text, and formatting using the AutoText feature, see page 81*
- *Inserting page numbers, see page 193*
- *Inserting tables, see page 280*

Undo and Redo

What happens when you paste or move text to the wrong place in your document? Or if you delete text that you didn't mean to delete? Word provides a few ways to undo what you have done. Choose the **Edit** menu and select **Undo**, or press Ctrl+Z, to reverse your last command.

You also can view a list of the most recent changes you have made to your document, allowing you to undo several steps by clicking the arrow key located next to the Undo icon. To reverse an undo action, click the Redo button on the toolbar. Figure 2.5 shows a list of recent actions.

Warning: Undo undoes all actions above it

Undo is a cumulative list. Actions you select from the Undo list also undoes all actions above it in the list.

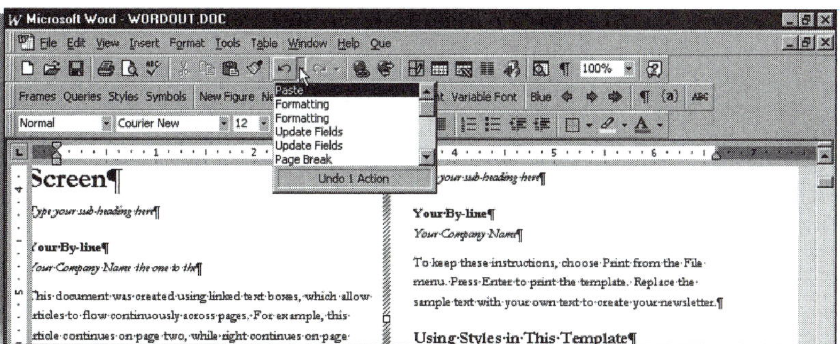

FIGURE 2.5

Select an action you want to undo from the list of the most recent actions.

CHAPTER

3

Format Text

Format text with different fonts and sizes as well as bold, italic, and underline

Copy text formatting quickly and efficiently

Bring text to life onscreen with animation

Format Text

Watch out for "font du jour" syndrome

Be prudent in your formatting options. It is a generally accepted rule of desktop publishing that no more than three fonts should be used within a document.

Writing consists of two main activities—composing/editing text and formatting text. When you compose text or edit it, you create and refine content. When you format text, you make the content presentable. You make it readable. You may argue that the most important task is the creation of the content, and we might agree. But formatting is also of vital importance because, if people won't or cannot read what you wrote, then you might as well not have wasted your time writing it.

Chapter 2, "Navigate, Select, and Edit Text," discussed the features of Word that help you to create and refine content. Here and later chapters discuss formatting.

Word has always divided formatting into four categories:

- *Character formatting*. How individual characters look.
- *Paragraph formatting*. How individual paragraphs look.
- *Page formatting*. How pages look.
- *Section formatting*. How major divisions of a document look.

This chapter discusses character formatting. Other kinds of formatting are discussed in later chapters. Character formatting includes the following characteristics of text:

- Font (or typeface)
- Type size
- Type style

When you format characters, you choose a font (typeface), a size, and one or more character styles.

SEE ALSO

➤ *Learn how to format paragraphs, see page 159*
➤ *See how to format pages and sections, see page 178*

Choose a Font

Fonts are identified by their names and are typically classed according to certain general characteristics shared by all fonts. These include whether the font has serifs and whether it is proportional or monospaced. The default Windows fonts (and therefore the most commonly appearing fonts in Windows programs) are Arial, Times New Roman, and Courier New.

Serifs are the short lines that appear at the ends of the main strokes of individual characters (see Figure 3.1). A font whose characters have serifs is a serif font. A font without serifs is a sans serif font. Courier and Times New Roman are serif fonts. Arial is a sans serif font.

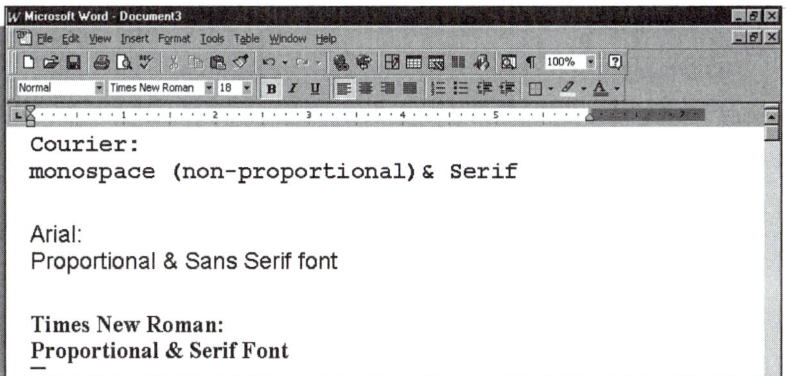

FIGURE 3.1
Fonts in this example are all 18 point. Note the difference in the space requirements for proportional versus nonproportional fonts.

Serif fonts are considered to be easier to read than sans serif fonts and therefore are favored for body text. Sans serif fonts are generally cleaner looking than serif fonts, and are favored for headlines. Sans serif fonts are also easier to read on some computer screens than serif fonts, and so may be the default font for body text in some programs.

A *monospace font* or *nonproportional font* is one in which all characters are the same width onscreen or on the printed page. A proportional font is one in which each character is only as wide as it needs to be. Arial and Times New Roman are proportional fonts. Courier (Courier New and all forms of Courier) is a monospace font.

Some fonts are designed for your computer screen (screen fonts), others for your printer (printer fonts), and still others for both screen and printer (TrueType and PostScript fonts). Printers typically use 300 dots or more per inch, whereas computer monitors display the width of your page in 800 or more dots (which amounts to only about 72 dots per inch for most monitors). Although your final printed version of your document may look slightly different (a different resolution) than the document onscreen, line lengths onscreen and on the printed paper will be the same.

Choose a font using the Formatting toolbar or menus.

To choose a font before you type, position your cursor at the insertion point from which you want to affect the font change. To change an existing text's font, select the text and right-click your mouse. From the pop-up menu, choose **Font**. The Font dialog box appears (see Figure 3.3). Click the **Font** tab. Scroll through the Font box and click the name of the font you want.

Alternately, select a font by clicking the Font Name drop-down list on the Formatting toolbar (see Figure 3.2), or by clicking the **Format** menu and selecting **Font**.

If you choose a font *before* you type your text, the font change is in effect for the rest of the document until, and unless, you change the font. If you select text before you choose a font, the font change applies to that selected text only, unless what you select includes the last paragraph in the document, in which case anything you add to the end of the document appears in that font.

Displaying the Formatting toolbar

If your Formatting toolbar does not show up (see Figure 3.2), click the **View** menu, and select **Toolbars**. Then select **Formatting** from the submenu.

Choose a default font

To make a font the default font for Word, click the **Default** button located in the Font dialog box (see Figure 3.3). The default font is associated with your current template and will affect all future documents created with that template.

Choose a Size

Word measures fonts by their height, not by characters per inch. Word measures height by points, with 72 points per inch.

To choose a font size for text not yet typed, position your cursor at the point from which you want to affect the font size. To choose a font size for existing text, select the text. The quickest way to change size is to click the Size drop-down list on the Formatting toolbar. Click the size of the font you desire. Alternately, you can right-click your mouse and choose **Font**, or select the **Format** menu and choose **Font**. Some fonts are

FIGURE 3.2

The Formatting toolbar displays under the Standard toolbar. To move or float the toolbar, drag it.

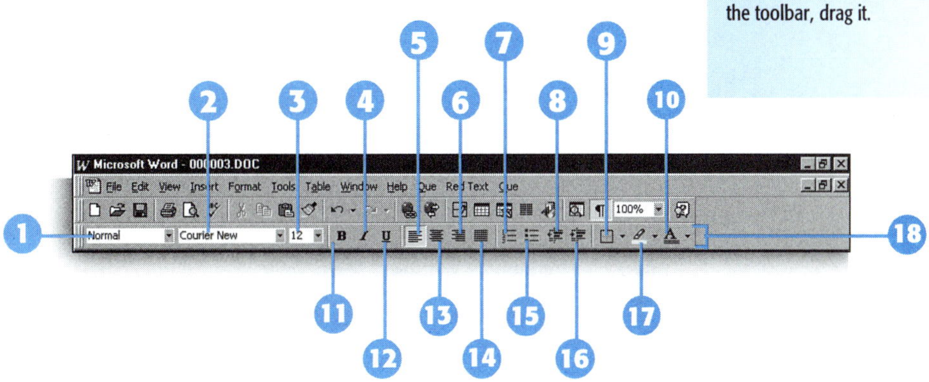

1. Style
2. Font name
3. Font size
4. Italic
5. Left align
6. Right align
7. Numbered list
8. Decrease Indent
9. Outside border
10. Font color
11. Bold
12. Underline
13. Center align
14. Justify
15. Bulleted list
16. Increase Indent
17. Highlight
18. Formatting toolbar

scalable. That means they will print or display at any size that you choose within some size ranges. For example, if you need to squeeze a certain amount of text onto a single page, you might find that 11.5 points is the largest possible size that lets you do that. A scalable font would let you use that size. Nonscalable fonts are available only in discrete sizes, for example, 8 points, 10 points, 12 points, 14 points, 18 points, and 24 points. In this example, you would have to choose 10-point text to fit all the text on the page.

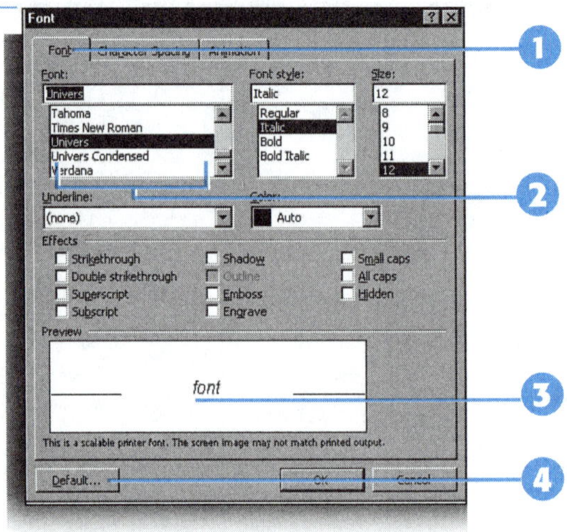

FIGURE 3.3

As you choose a font in the Font dialog box, Word displays a sample of the font in the Preview pane.

1. Font tab
2. List of available fonts
3. Font Preview
4. Use as default font

When you select a scalable font, if you want a size other than those listed, you can type the font size you want in the font **Size** box.

To determine whether a font is scalable, consult the Font dialog box. Right-click some text and choose **Font**. The Font dialog box appears. A description of the font appears under the **Preview** pane as shown in Figure 3.4. Select a different font in the dialog box, and the information regarding the font will change accordingly. If it says it is a *TrueType* font, it is a scalable font. Other scalable fonts include PostScript fonts and some printer fonts.

Scalable fonts include scalable printer fonts and TrueType fonts. TrueType fonts are scalable to any font size. Several TrueType fonts are automatically installed when Windows is installed on your system. Depending on your printer, you might see scalable printer fonts as an option.

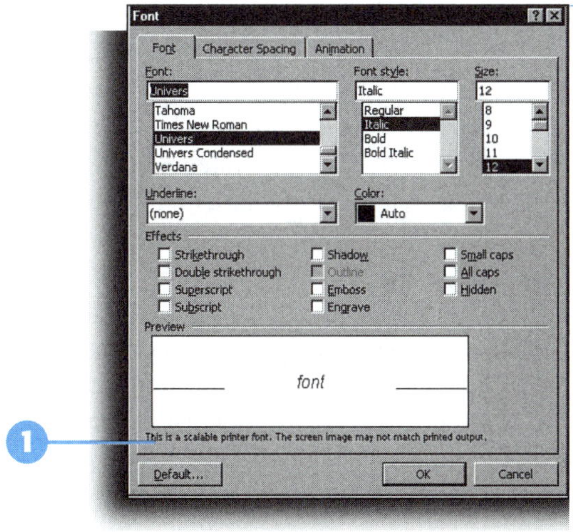

FIGURE 3.4

Font information tells you the relationship between the screen font and the printed font.

1. Find additional font information here.

Choose a Style

Font style options in Word include Regular (also known as Roman, as in Times Roman), *Italic*, **Bold** and ***Bold Italic***. Style selection can be made before or after typing text. Although Word 97 does not classify underlining as a style per se, most people think of underlining as an alternative to boldfacing and italicizing; so we mention underlining here as well.

Bold, italic, and underlining are used to emphasize text. It is generally accepted that italicizing a word is the preferred method for emphasizing text within paragraphs and bold is reserved for titles or headings. Using underlining for emphasis is passé; don't do it.

To apply a font style for text that has not yet been typed, position your cursor where you want the style to begin. Use shortcut keystrokes or toolbar buttons to apply a style.

- *Bold.* Press Ctrl+B or click the Bold icon. 
- *Italic.* Press Ctrl+I or click the Italic icon. 
- *Underline.* Press Ctrl+U or click the Underline icon. 

Using styles for emphasis

Professional typesetters always used italic for emphasis. Because most of us can easily print and display italic with modern printers and computers, we too should use italic. Use underlining, boldface, or all CAPS only if your printer can't produce italic.

You can use these font styles in any combination. To apply a font style for existing text, select the text and click the toolbar icons

You can also select font styles in the **Style** box of the Font Properties box. Styles are displayed in the **Preview** section of the dialog box as you select them.

Like fonts and font sizes, styles are toggle keys; that is, the style will stay in effect for all text until you turn off the style. To disable a style, click the indented button on the Formatting toolbar.

Underline Text

In other word-processing programs, underline is categorized as a font *style*. Microsoft assigns underline to its own category, perhaps because Word provides so many underlining options.

You can underline a word, a string of text, a paragraph, or an entire document. Like bold and italic, you can turn on underlining before you type or apply underlining to existing text. Use the Underline icon [U] on the Formatting toolbar for a single underline. To turn off underlining, click the icon again.

When and how to apply formatting

We prefer to write first, format later. That way we can stay focused on one thing at a time. We also prefer to use keystrokes rather than the mouse to apply formatting, because it's faster.

To underline existing text, select the text and click the Underline icon on the Formatting toolbar.

The Underline icon underlines empty spaces if you select a block of text before clicking it. You can change the options to underline words only by accessing the Font dialog box.

On the **Font** tab of the Font dialog box, use the drop-down menu in the **Underlining** box to choose an underlining option. As you select underlining options they are displayed in the **Preview** pane (see Figure 3.5).

Figure 3.6 displays underlining options.

Choose a Color

Don't choose black as a text color

Choosing black as a text color disables the built-in formatting features of Automatic.

Like all other text formatting features, you can choose a different text color for a single word, a string of text, a paragraph, or an entire document. The default font color is set at Automatic, also referred to as Auto. The Auto or Automatic color setting sets black as the color of text. However, if you shade a paragraph, with formatting of 80 percent or greater, Auto changes the text color to white for readability purposes.

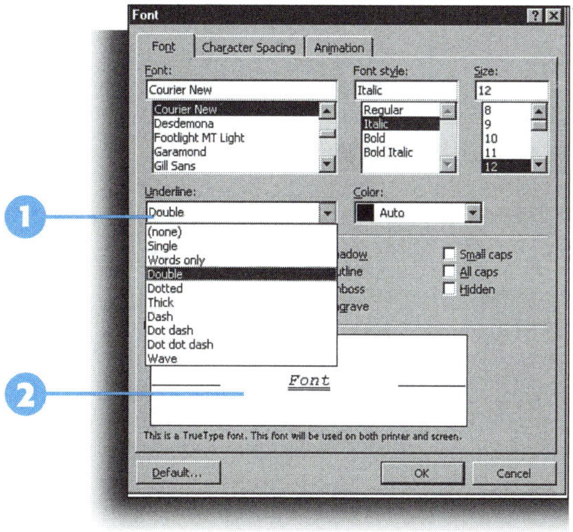

FIGURE 3.5

As you select underlining options, they are displayed in the **Preview** pane of the Font dialog box.

1. Click here to select underlining options.
2. Preview options here.

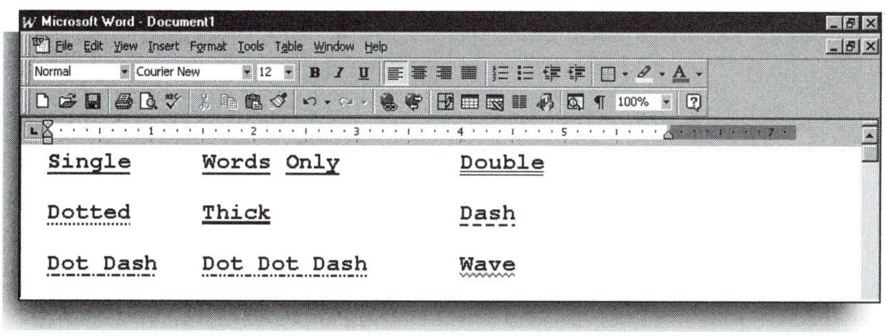

FIGURE 3.6

These examples show Word's available underlining options.

Use the Font Color icon on the Formatting toolbar for quick color selection. To apply color to text you have not yet typed, click the Font Color icon on the Formatting toolbar and then type your text. To apply color to existing text, select the text, then click the Font Color icon.

If you need more colors than the choices provided from the Formatting toolbar, use the Font dialog box. Right-click your mouse and choose **Font** from the menu. Click the drop-down list in the **Color** section to select a color. Colors are displayed in the Preview section of the dialog box as you select them. When you have selected a color, click **OK**.

Like other font features, color selection stays in effect until and unless you select another color or reset to Auto.

SEE ALSO

➤ *To shade a paragraph, see page 48*

Choose Font Effects

Font effects can be selected in the Font dialog box. If you find that you frequently use font effects, you may want to customize your toolbar by adding an icon for font effects.

To apply effects, select the text and choose your options in the Font dialog box. Alternately, choose your options in the Font dialog box, type the text, and then disable the options in the Font dialog box when you are finished.

To view the Font dialog box, right-click and select **Font** from the pop-up menu or click the **Format** menu, and select **Font**. Table 3.1 describes the font effects available in the **Effects** section of the Font dialog box. Figure 3.7 demonstrates those effects.

SEE ALSO

➤ *Customizing toolbars, see page 527*

TABLE 3.1 **Font effects**

Effect:	Description:
Strikethrough	Draws a line through the text.
Double Strikethrough	Draws a double line through the text.
Superscript	Changes the font to a smaller font size (if available) and raises the font above the baseline.
Subscript	Changes the font to a smaller font size (if available) and lowers the font below the baseline.
Shadow	Places a shadow beneath and to the right of characters.
Outline	Displays the inner and outer lines of each character. Not available for all fonts.

Effect:	Description:
Emboss	Makes characters appear raised off the page.
Engrave	Makes characters appear depressed into the page.
Small caps	Changes all letters to capital letters and reduces their size.
All caps	Changes all lowercase letters to capitals.
Hidden	Hides text.

Some effects look better than others

The shadow, outline, emboss, and engrave effects do not display well onscreen or at small point sizes. These are best used for printed documents in titles, headings, or on large fonts.

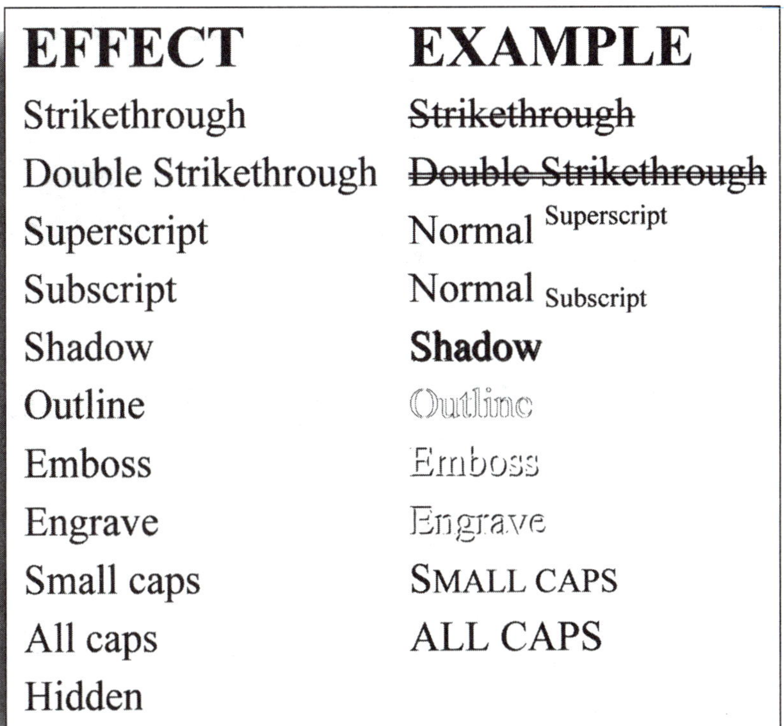

EFFECT	EXAMPLE
Strikethrough	Strikethrough
Double Strikethrough	Double Strikethrough
Superscript	Normal Superscript
Subscript	Normal Subscript
Shadow	Shadow
Outline	Outline
Emboss	Emboss
Engrave	Engrave
Small caps	SMALL CAPS
All caps	ALL CAPS
Hidden	

FIGURE 3.7

Font effects can dramatically change a document's appearance.

Repeat Formatting

Applying formatting options may take several steps. Word provides methods to shortcut your efforts to repeat formatting.

They include

- Using **Find** to locate text and **Replace** to replace text with formatted text.
- AutoCorrect and AutoText to apply formatting options.
- Creating styles that include the formatting options you want to apply.
- Using the **Edit** menu to repeat formatting selections.
- Using Format Painter to repeat formatting selections.

You should use the **Edit** menu and the Format Painter if you occasionally need to repeat formatting options or on a small document. If your work frequently involves special formatting, you should consider creating styles, using AutoText, or using AutoCorrect.

SEE ALSO

➤ *Learn how to create styles and apply automatic formatting, see page 165*

➤ *Create formatted AutoCorrect and AutoText entries, and replace text with formatted text, see page 76*

Repeat Formatting with Menu Commands

When you apply a formatting option, Word keeps track of those options and the **Edit** menu displays the last formatting option that you applied. For example, as soon as you apply color to a word, view the **Edit** menu and you find **Undo font color** and **Redo font color** as a menu selection. This is useful for repeating formatting options that do not otherwise have shortcut keystrokes. Keep in mind, however, that the **Edit** menu tracks only your last action. If you bold and underline a word, only the underline action appears in the **Edit** menu. Additionally, as soon as you type new text, formatting options are replaced by typing options. Using the Format Painter is a more accurate way of repeating formatting options and saves you time.

Use Format Painter

The Format Painter  enables you to copy formatting from a selected object or text and apply it to other objects or text within your document. For example, you may have words within your document that you want to appear in subscript and small caps; SUCH AS THIS. To apply subscript and small caps, you must select the text and access the Font dialog box, click **Subscript** and click **Small Caps**. This can be labor intensive. Alternately, you can apply the formatting to one word or phrase then use the Format Painter to apply the same formatting to other words or phrases. This saves time and keystrokes. Additionally, you can use the Format Painter to quickly apply formatting to one word or phrase, or you can toggle it on to use it for many words or phrases, then turn it off when you are done.

Apply formatting to text with Format Painter

1. Click once inside the text whose formatting you want to copy.
2. Click the Format Painter icon on the Standard toolbar. Your mouse pointer turns to a paintbrush.
3. Select the text to which you want to apply the formatting. To apply the formatting to only one word or object, click once inside of the word or click the object. You don't need to drag over the word or object. To apply the formatting to an entire paragraph, select the paragraph by clicking in the margin. If, however you are applying the formatting to several words or objects, you must drag the mouse over the words or objects to select them. When you release the mouse button, the formatting is applied to the new text and your pointer returns to normal appearance.

Keep Format Painter on

To keep the Format Painter on and repeat formatting throughout your document, double-click the Format Painter icon. The Format Painter stays active so that you can continue to format nonadjacent text. When you are finished, press the Esc key or click the Format Painter icon again to deactivate it.

Animate Text

Animated text can bring a document to life on the screen. However, you should know that animated text features will not convert to HTML if you are creating a document for the Web. Of course, animated text can't translate to the printer, so text animation features should be reserved for documents that will be read online and in Word.

Apply animation effects to text

1. Select the text you want to animate.
2. Right-click the text and choose **Font** from the pop-up menu.
3. The Font dialog box appears. Click the **Animation** tab (see Figure 3.8).

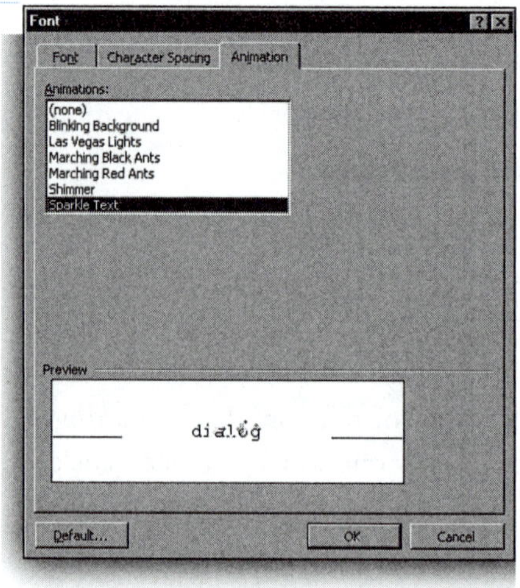

FIGURE 3.8
As you select animation effects, they appear in the **Preview** window.

4. Choose an effect from the **Animations** list. Click **OK** to close the dialog box and to apply the animation effect to your text.

Other character formatting techniques in Word 97 include character spacing, scaling, kerning, and character styles. Character spacing, scaling, and kerning are covered in *Special Edition Using Microsoft Word 97 Best Seller Edition* published by Que.

SEE ALSO

➤ *Learn how to apply character styles, see page 160*

➤ *Learn more about creating HTML pages, see page 458*

Apply Shading and Borders

A great way to emphasize headlines, captions, and other important text is to apply a border or shading to that text. Borders and shading can also separate a piece of text from the rest of the text on a page, such as a sidebar story in a newsletter.

Apply borders and shading

1. Carefully select the text to which you want to apply borders or shading. What you select determines what gets shaded/bordered. The rules are as follows:
   - If you don't select any text, the results affect the entire paragraph in which the insertion point appears.
   - If you select text within a single paragraph, but the paragraph mark itself is not included in the selection, the results affect only the selected text.
   - If you select text included in more than one paragraph (so that at least one paragraph mark is included in the selection), the results affect all the paragraphs in which any of the selected text resides.

   You can override these rules in the Borders and Shading dialog box, however.
2. Open the **Format** menu, and select **Borders and Shading** to display the Borders and Shading dialog box.
3. Click the **Borders** tab to work with border options (see Figure 3.9).

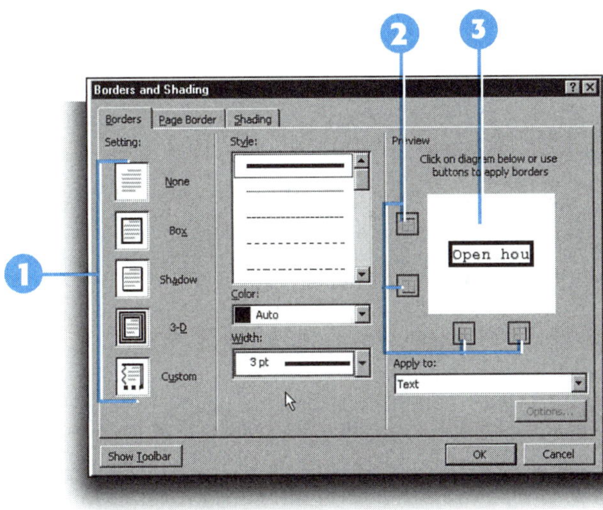

FIGURE 3.9
Select the style of the border line, the color, and the width.

1. Predefined borders
2. Border buttons (to select each line)
3. Preview

- Under Setting, click one of the preset border options: **None** to remove all borders from the selected paragraph(s), **Box** to insert a box border around the selected paragraph(s), **Shadow** to insert a box border around the selected paragraph(s) and apply preset shadow formatting to the border, **3-D** to insert a box border around the selection and apply preset 3-D border formatting, or **Custom** to create a border using the options you click in the Preview window. When you choose any of these settings, the current selections in **Style**, **Color**, and **Width** apply to the borders.
- From the **Style** list, select the type of line you want to use for the border, including dotted, dashed, and wavy lines.
- Click the **Color** drop-down list to select a color to apply to the border.
- From the **Width** drop-down list, choose the thickness of the border line from 1/4-point to 6 points.
- In the **Preview** box, click the individual border lines or use the border line buttons to apply or remove borders or change the attributes for a particular border (select the attributes first and then add the border).
- From the **Apply to** drop-down list, select whether to apply the border to just the selected text or to the whole paragraph(s).

4. Select the **Shading** tab to choose shading options (see Figure 3.10).
   - Under **Fill**, select the color or shade of gray with which you want to fill the selection.
   - From the **Patterns Style** drop-down list, choose a shading percentage for the color you selected under **Fill** or a pattern of lines such as Lt Horizontal or Dk Trellis.
   - If you selected a pattern of lines, select the **Color** of the lines from the drop-down list. The Fill color then becomes the background color for the pattern.

Effective use of patterns with text

When using patterns behind text, make the pattern small, the color light, and the text big and bold.

- From the **Apply to** drop-down list select whether to apply the shading options to just the selected text or to whole paragraph(s).

5. Click **OK**.

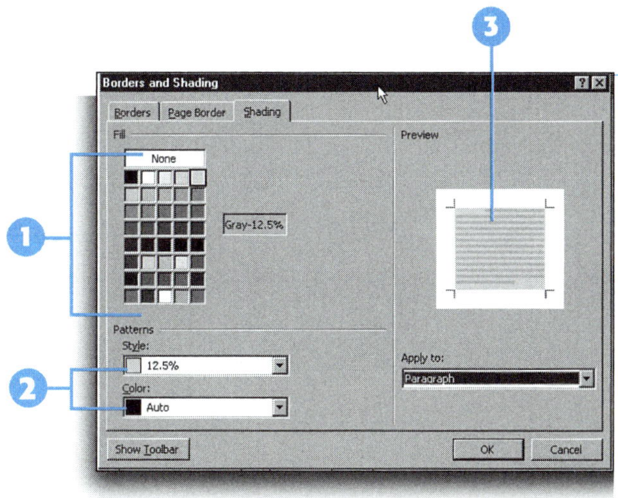

FIGURE 3.10
On the **Shading** tab, select the background fill color for your text or paragraph.

1. Fill colors
2. Patterns
3. Preview

To quickly choose shading colors, border line styles, border line colors, and border line widths, use the Tables and Borders toolbar. Click the **View** menu, and select **Toolbars**. From the submenu select **Tables and Borders** to display the toolbar, or choose Tables and Borders on the Standard toolbar.

Select the text to which you want to add borders and shading, and then click the appropriate button on the toolbar. Table 3.2 lists the buttons on the toolbar that apply to borders and shading. Figure 3.11 shows the full toolbar.

TABLE 3.2 **The Tables and Borders toolbar buttons**

Button:	Description:
Line Style	Sets the style of the border lines (dotted, dashed, wavy, double, and so on)
Line Weight	Sets the thickness of the border lines

continues...

TABLE 3.2 Continued

Button:	Description:
Border Color	Sets the color of the border lines
Border Options	Specifies where the border appears (top, bottom, left, right, box)
Shading Color	Sets the color of the **background** shading for the paragraph (you cannot specify the percentage)

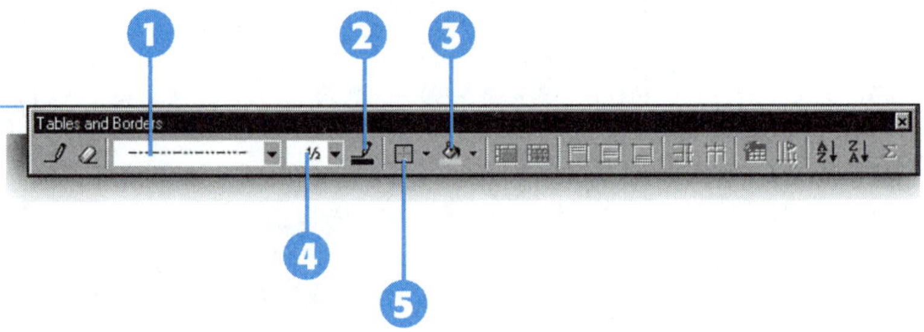

FIGURE 3.11

Shading options appear on the Tables and Borders toolbar.

1. Line Style
2. Border Color
3. Shading Color
4. Line Weight
5. Border Options

CHAPTER 4

Use Proofing Tools

- Correct spelling errors for individual words or an entire document
- Check for correct grammatical usage and correct errors
- Replace words with synonyms or antonyms from the thesaurus
- Find and replace text and formatting
- Automate common word-and-phrase entries and corrections with AutoText and AutoCorrect

Run Spell Check

Spell check is useful because everyone makes typos, even if you consider yourself to be a good speller. Word's spell check is especially easy to use because it operates while you type and flags errors the moment you make them.

As you type, Word continuously checks your spelling and flags any suspect words with a wavy red underline. You might notice as you type, toward the right end of the status bar, a little book icon with turning pages. That's the spell checker at work. When you stop typing, the pages stop turning and the book has either a red "x" or a red check mark on it. The "x" means that, somewhere in your document, a spelling (or grammar) flag is unresolved. The check mark means that all flags are resolved.

Spell check doesn't work?

If Word doesn't seem to be catching your spelling errors, it may be that **(no proofing)** is set as your language option. Open the **Tools** menu and select **Language**. In the Language dialog box that appears, select the **Set Language** option. If **(no proofing)** is selected, choose a language instead, such as **English (United States)**. Word then checks your writing against the spelling dictionary.

Even though Word may flag a word for spelling, that doesn't necessarily mean the word is misspelled. Word flags a word for spelling if the word doesn't appear in Word's spelling dictionary, or in the personal dictionary to which Word adds entries that you flag as correct spellings, or in any custom dictionary you might be using. If a correctly spelled word doesn't appear in any of those dictionaries, Word assumes it is incorrect and flags it.

Other times, Word fails to flag a word even though, in the context in which it is used, the word is misspelled. Word, for example, would not flag the word "merry" as a misspelling in the following sentence: "He wants to merry her." You still need to proofread your work.

Spell Checking a Flagged Word

You can either stop and correct errors flagged by Word immediately, or you can wait and correct them later. To correct a word flagged by the automatic spell checker, right-click the word. A menu pops up. Suggested replacement words (if there are any) appear in the pop-up menu, as well as commands for dealing with the misspelling (see Figure 4.1).

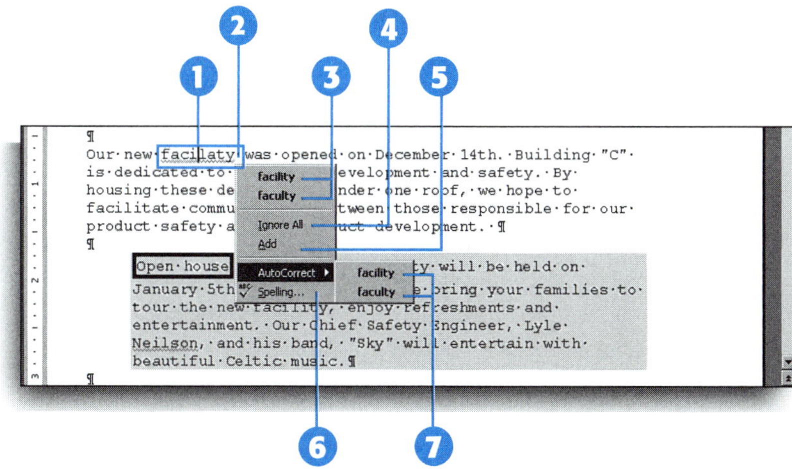

FIGURE 4.1

A pop-up menu appears when you right-click a word marked with a wavy red underline.

1. The wavy red underline indicates a misspelling.
2. Right-click here.
3. Choose replacement word.
4. Ignore all occurrences.
5. Add to custom dictionary.
6. Start spell check.
7. Add replacement word to AutoCorrect.

The choices in the pop-up menu and their uses are as follows:

- Click the appropriate replacement word to replace the word with one of the suggestions.
- Click **Ignore All** to ignore all occurrences of that spelling of the word in the document.
- Click **Add** to add the word to your custom dictionary.
- Click **AutoCorrect** to add the misspelling to the AutoCorrect list, and then select the proper replacement spelling from the submenu that appears.
- Click **Spelling** to start a regular spell check as discussed in the next section.

SEE ALSO

➤ *Learn how to create a custom dictionary, see page 59*
➤ *Learn more about AutoCorrect, see page 76*

Spell Checking an Entire Document or a Selected Block of Text

Instead of correcting spelling as you type, you can correct the whole document at once. You may prefer to wait until after you finish composing the document to take care of such chores as spell checking. Maybe you don't want to be distracted from writing, so you disable automatic spell checking. Or, you might conclude that it's more efficient to spell check the whole document in a single pass (so that, for example, you can have Word correct every instance of a misspelled word with one command, rather than having to correct each instance individually).

When you do a manual spell check, Word checks the document beginning at the location of your insertion point. After the spell checker reaches the end of the document, a dialog box appears asking if you want to continue from the beginning. When you choose to have the spell checker continue, it checks the remainder of the document and finishes when it reaches the original position of your insertion point.

To check only a portion of a document, select the text you want to check before starting the spell checker. Word checks the selected text from beginning to end.

You can start the spell checker in one of three ways:

- Select the **Tools** menu and choose **Spelling and Grammar**.
- Press F7.
- Choose the Spelling and Grammar button on the Standard toolbar. 

When the Spelling and Grammar dialog box appears (see Figure 4.2), make sure the **Check Grammar** check box is clear if you only want to check spelling. If this option is selected, the checker also checks for grammar errors (covered later in the "Grammar Check " section of this chapter).

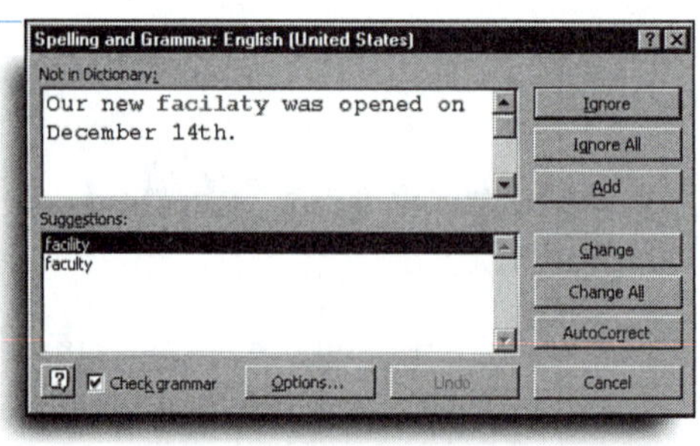

FIGURE 4.2
The sentence containing the possibly misspelled word appears in the **Not in Dictionary** box, with the suspect word in red.

When spell checker finds a word in the document that has no match in the spelling or custom dictionaries, it displays the word and its surrounding text in the **Not in Dictionary** box. The suspect word appears in red. (The word is also selected and highlighted in the body of the document.) In the **Suggestions** box is a list of possible correct spellings for the highlighted word. You can then do one of the following:

- Select the appropriate replacement word in the **Suggestions** box and choose **Change** to use one of the suggested replacements.
- If none of the suggested replacements is appropriate, correct the word manually by editing it in the **Not in Dictionary** box. Then choose **Change**.
- Choose **Change All** to replace this and all other instances of the word in the document with either the manual correction you made or one of the suggested replacement words. Note: This corrects all instances of a particular misspelling of a word, but does not correct other misspellings of the same word.
- Choose **Ignore** to leave the word unchanged in the document.
- Choose **Ignore All** to ignore this and all other instances of the word in the document.
- Choose **Add** to add the word to the custom dictionary.
- Choose **AutoCorrect** to add the misspelling and its correction to the AutoCorrect list. Then, if this misspelling appears in later documents, Word automatically corrects your spelling as you type. To learn more about AutoCorrect, refer to the section, "Define and Modify AutoCorrect Entries," later in this chapter.
- Choose **Cancel** to terminate the spell check process without finishing the entire document or selection.

Spell check stops at each suspect word in the document or selection, and you have the same alternatives for each misspelling. When the entire document or selection has been checked, Word

Interrupt the spell check whenever you want

Sometimes spell check highlights a word and you notice that you need to edit other words around it. If so, just click in the document and make your changes. Spell check suspends its operation when you click in the document. When you finish editing, choose the **Resume** button in the Spelling/Grammar dialog box to resume the spell check.

displays a message stating that spell check is complete. Choose **OK** to return to your document.

Setting Spell Check Options

If you don't want to deal with spelling while you're entering text, you can either hide the spell check marks while you work, or turn off automatic spell checking entirely. You also can control how spell check works by setting options.

To see what spell check options are available, to hide the spell check marks, or to turn off automatic spell checking, you must display the Spelling and Grammar Options dialog box. You can do this in two ways: Either choose the **Options** button when the Spelling dialog box is open, or from the **Tools** menu choose **Options**, then select the **Spelling & Grammar** tab (see Figure 4.3).

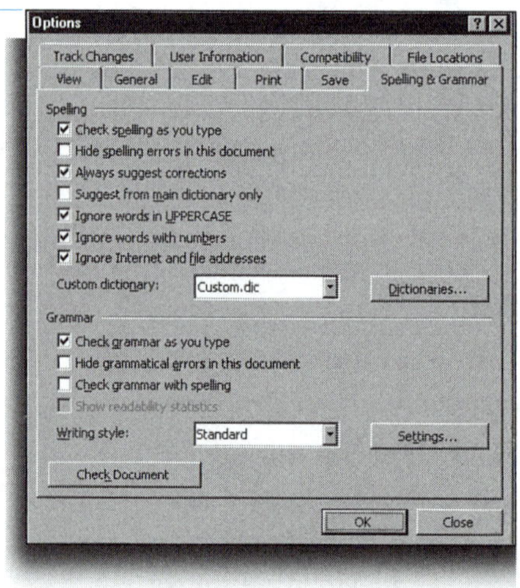

FIGURE 4.3
The **Spelling & Grammar** tab of the Options dialog box displays the name of your custom dictionary.

To hide the spell check marks while you work, click **Hide spelling errors in this document**. To turn automatic spell checking off, deselect **Check spelling as you type**. Other options you can set include the following:

- **Always suggest corrections.** Turn this off if you have a slow computer.

- **Suggest from main dictionary only.** When checked, only the main dictionary is checked and Word does not search other dictionaries.
- **Ignore words in UPPERCASE.** When this option is selected, Word ignores acronyms.
- **Ignore words with numbers.** When this option is selected, Word ignores words with numbers.
- **Ignore Internet and file addresses.** When this option is selected, Word ignores URLs and filenames.

Create and Edit a Custom Dictionary

When you spell check your document, you have the option to add new words to the Custom.dic dictionary file provided by Word. You can add proper names and terminology you use frequently that are not contained in Word's standard spelling dictionary. When you are performing a spell check of your document and Word finds one of these terms for the first time, choose **Add** in the Spelling and Grammar dialog box to add that word to the custom dictionary. If such a word is marked by the automatic spell check, right-click the word and click **Add** in the pop-up menu that appears.

If you add a misspelled word to the custom dictionary by mistake, you can edit the word or delete it from the custom dictionary. Also, when you have a list of names or words you need to add to the dictionary, you can add them all at once, instead of waiting for the words to appear in a document.

Misspelled words in the custom dictionary

Before you add a word to the custom dictionary, make sure that it is spelled correctly. If you add a misspelled word to the custom dictionary, Word will never detect the misspelled word in the future. To correct the situation, you have to edit the word in the custom dictionary.

Add, edit, and delete words in a custom dictionary

1. From the **Tools** menu, select **Options**.
2. When the Options dialog box appears, click the **Spelling & Grammar** tab (refer to Figure 4.3).
3. Choose **Dictionaries**.
4. From the list of custom dictionaries (see Figure 4.4), select the one you want to edit. Be careful not to clear its check mark.

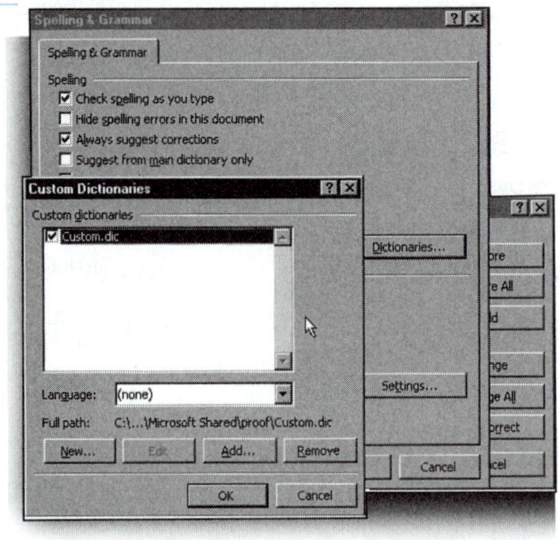

FIGURE 4.4
In the Custom Dictionaries dialog box, select the dictionary in which you want to add, delete, or edit entries.

5. Choose **Edit**. A warning appears saying that Word will turn off the automatic spelling and grammar checking. Choose **OK** to continue.
6. The dictionary document opens (see Figure 4.5). Make your additions, deletions, and corrections to the listed entries. Press Enter after each added word so that every word is on a separate line. If you need to search for a word on the **Edit** menu, use the **Find** command, or sort the list alphabetically if you like by opening the **Table** menu and selecting **Sort**.

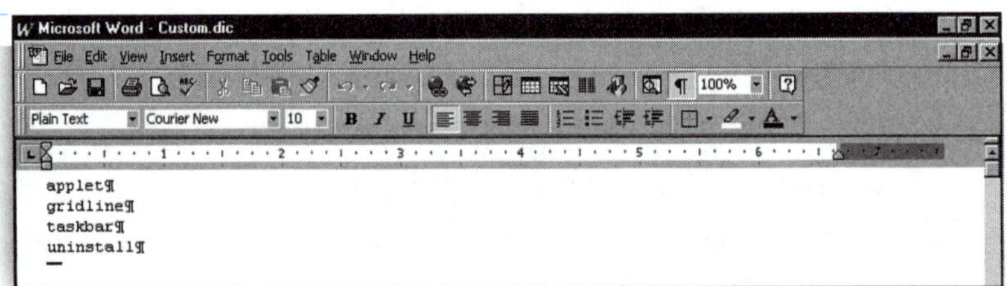

FIGURE 4.5
The dictionary file is a Word document with a list of words, each on a separate line.

7. After making your changes and additions, save the document and close it.
8. To reactivate the automatic spell check, from the **Tools** menu select **Options**. Select the **Spelling & Grammar** tab

from the Options dialog box (refer to Figure 4.3). Click **Check spelling as you type** to place a check mark in the box. Click **OK**.

Quick access to spelling and grammar options

Right-click the Spelling and Grammar icon on the status bar and choose **Options**.

Microsoft Word stores the Custom.dic dictionary in the C:\Program Files\Common Files\Microsoft Shared\Proof folder or the C:\Windows\Msapps\Proof folder on your PC, or in a similar location on a network drive (ask your system administrator). Word allows you to use other custom dictionaries, such as legal or medical dictionaries, that contain words often used in your business or profession. You must specify the location of these dictionaries and then activate them for use.

Selecting additional custom dictionaries

1. From the **Tools** menu, select **Options**.
2. Select the **Spelling & Grammar** tab in the Options dialog box (refer to Figure 4.3).
3. Choose **Dictionaries**.
4. In the Custom Dictionaries dialog box (refer to Figure 4.4), choose **Add**.
5. Enter the name of the dictionary file in the **File name** box of the Add Custom Dictionary dialog box (see Figure 4.6) or click the name of the file in the list of files.

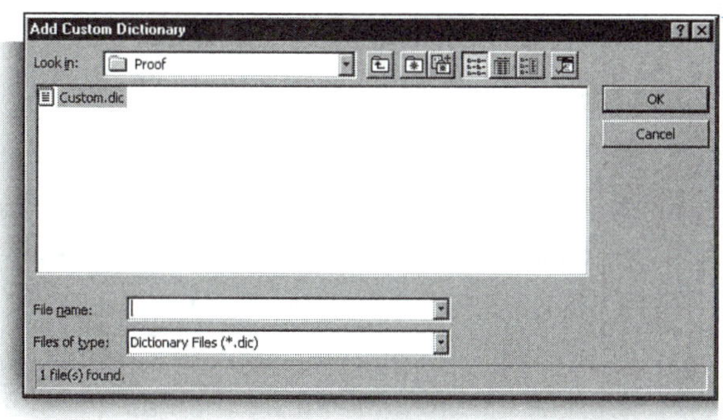

FIGURE 4.6
Select the location and name of the custom dictionary or enter the name of the dictionary in the **File name** box.

6. Choose **OK**.
7. From the **Tools** menu, select **Options** and then select the **Spelling & Grammar** tab in the Options dialog box.

8. Choose **Dictionaries**.
9. The name of the new dictionary is listed in the **Custom Dictionaries** box. Click the check box in front of the filename to place a check mark there.
10. Choose **OK**. Then choose **OK** in the Options dialog box. The next time you spell check your document, Word will also check the new custom dictionary.

SEE ALSO

➤ *Learn more about sorting lists, see page 154*

Share Custom Dictionaries

In certain industries, particularly medical and engineering, it is useful to share custom dictionary entries by distributing the dictionaries to others via email or network access. One person in the office, for example, can invest the time to create a dictionary of terms or acronyms, even names of clients. He or she can then save the custom dictionary as described in the preceding steps. The dictionary file can then be mailed to others, or access to it can be provided via a network. Individual users who receive the dictionary through email or from a network should save it to their Word dictionaries folder. The default directory for Word dictionaries is C:\Program Files\Common Files\Microsoft Shared\Proof. Users can then activate the custom dictionary by including it in the **Custom Dictionaries** list.

Adding a new custom dictionary

1. Open the **Tools** menu and select **Spelling and Grammar**.
2. Click the **Options** button in the Spelling and Grammar dialog box, then click the **Dictionaries** button.
3. In the Custom Dictionaries dialog box, click the **Add** button.
4. Select the new dictionary from the Proof folder and click **OK**.

Word now uses this new dictionary in conjunction with the user's own custom dictionary. If preferred, users can open the new dictionary file and copy all entries into their own custom dictionary. The advantage of keeping a separate dictionary is that the custom dictionaries can be disabled or enabled at any time by removing or adding their check marks in the **Custom Dictionaries** list. Another advantage of keeping the dictionary separate is that the separation enables the dictionary to be replaced (if the dictionary administrator has additions or corrections) without affecting any entries they may have saved in their own custom dictionary.

Grammar Check

Word's grammar check reviews your grammar as you write, just as spell check reviews spelling as you write. Whereas spell check flags suspect spelling with a wavy red underline, grammar check flags suspected grammatical problems with a wavy green underline. You can either check grammar flags on the spot, or wait until you have finished writing and then check all flags in one pass—just as you can with spell check.

Grammar check is a more complex tool than spell check. Spell check just compares words against its spelling dictionary and flags them if they are not in the dictionary. Grammar check reviews your writing using a mass of rules to flag a wide variety of problems, including not only grammar problems, but punctuation, capitalization, and style problems.

The importance of this fact is that grammar check is even less accurate than the spell check. It does not catch every problem. It flags text that is grammatically accurate. It flags ungrammatical text but then identifies the wrong grammar problem. You should carefully scrutinize grammar flags before accepting Word's opinion. If you find that Word repeatedly misidentifies a particular kind of problem, don't hesitate to turn off that type of grammar checking. To turn off grammar check settings, go to the **Tools** menu and select **Options**. In the Options dialog box, select the **Spelling & Grammar** tab, and then select **Settings**.

Grammar check isn't perfect

Word's grammar check is a useful tool, but it's not intelligent. It just follows rules. Don't assume that grammar check catches every error and don't assume every solution it offers is any better than your own or, even correct. Grammar check certainly cannot check to see if you actually wrote what you meant to write. It is no substitute for careful writing, editing, and proofreading.

Correcting a Single Grammar Error

You can correct a single flagged grammar error by right-clicking the green-underlined text. A pop-up menu appears, as shown in Figure 4.7. The pop-up menu offers the following choices:

- Click the flagged word(s) to get an explanation of why the grammar check thinks something is incorrect.
- Click **Ignore Sentence** to ignore the possible error and to make the wavy line disappear.
- Click **Grammar** to start a regular grammar check.

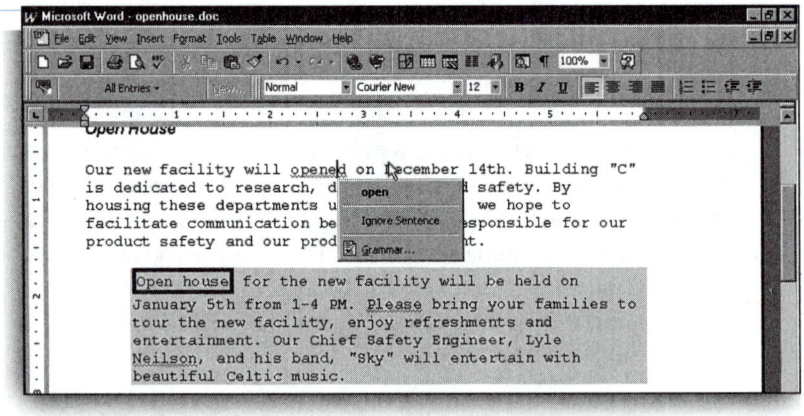

FIGURE 4.7
To quickly correct grammatical errors, right-click the flagged word(s) and choose a correction from the pop-up menu.

Grammar Checking an Entire Document or a Selected Block of Text

You may prefer to write first and check all grammar and spelling later. That way, if grammar check repeatedly flags things that you consider to be acceptable, you can choose **Ignore All** once and grammar check will not flag it again—and you save time. In that case, you can run a grammar check when you are ready by starting grammar check. If you have selected a block of text, grammar check checks only grammar within the selection. Otherwise, it checks the whole document. You can start grammar check in one of three ways:

- From the **Tools** menu, select **Spelling and Grammar**.
- Press F7.
- Choose the Spelling and Grammar button on the Standard toolbar. 

The Spelling and Grammar dialog box appears and Word now works its way through either the whole document or the selected text, searching for errors. Note that it checks for both grammar and spelling errors. Each time Word locates a phrase with a suspected grammatical error, it highlights the phrase in the body of the document and displays the phrase and its surrounding text in the Spelling and Grammar dialog box (see Figure 4.8), with the suspect phrase appearing in green text in the dialog box. A description of the problem appears at the top of the dialog box and sometimes the Office Assistant displays a more detailed description of the problem. The **Suggestions** box lists any suggested fixes.

Grammar check isn't working

Make sure the **Check grammar** option is checked in the Spelling and Grammar dialog box.

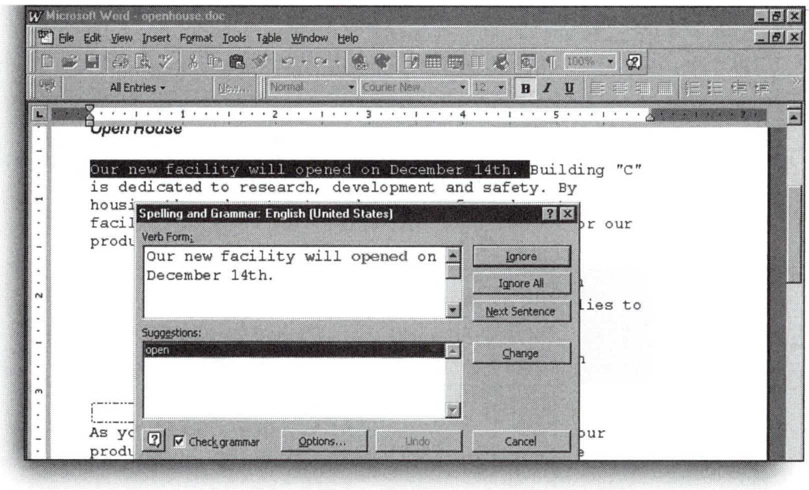

FIGURE 4.8

The suspected grammar error is marked in green with a description of the error appearing in the pop-up.

Make one of the following choices with respect to each suspected grammar error:

- Select one of the suggested fixes in the **Suggestions** list box and then choose **Change**.
- Edit the text to correct the error and then choose **Change**.
- Choose **Ignore** to ignore this instance of the problem.
- Choose **Ignore All** to ignore this instance and all other instances of the problem in the document.
- Choose **Next Sentence** to go on to the next sentence and ignore the current problem.

- Choose **Close** (X) or **Cancel** to stop grammar check and close the dialog box.
- Choose **Options** to set options for how grammar check works.

Unless you close the dialog box, Word continues to check each possible spelling and grammar error throughout the document. Each time, you have the same set of choices. A message box appears when the spelling and grammar checking are complete. Choose **OK** to return to your document.

Setting Grammar Checking Options

If you don't want to deal with grammar issues while you are entering text, you can either hide the grammar check marks while you work or turn off automatic grammar checking entirely. You also can control how grammar check works by setting options.

To see what grammar check options are available, to hide the grammar check marks, or to turn off automatic grammar checking, display the Spelling and Grammar Options dialog box. You can do this in one of two ways: Either choose the **Options** button when the Grammar dialog box is open, or from **Tools**, choose **Options**, and then choose the **Spelling & Grammar** tab in the Options dialog box.

To hide the grammar check marks while you work, click **Hide grammatical errors in this document**. To turn automatic grammar checking off, deselect **Check grammar as you type**. Other options you can set include whether you want Word to check your grammar as it checks your spelling, whether you want to see readability statistics at the end of the grammar check, and writing style.

Readability statistics tell you the grade-level in school that a theoretical reader must have attained to read what you have written. In general, if you use big words and long sentences, you are writing to a more educated audience.

The **Writing** style option (standard, formal, casual, or technical) determines what set of grammatical rules grammar check uses.

How many spaces between sentences?

The general rule is: Use one space between sentences if you are writing with a proportional font, such as Arial or Times; use two spaces between sentences if you are writing with a non-proportional font, such as Courier. Word's grammar check can check the number of spaces between sentences for you. To set up grammar check to check spacing, go to Grammar Settings. (From the **Tools** menu select **Options**. In the Options dialog box select the **Spelling & Grammar** tab and then **Settings**. Then select the **Spaces between sentences** option.)

You may also select a custom writing style, in which case you may select which grammar and style options you want checked. To turn a particular kind of grammar checking on or off, choose the **Tools** menu and select **Options**. In the Options dialog box, select the **Spelling & Grammar** tab and then choose **Settings**.

Consult the Thesaurus

Word 97 includes a thesaurus to help you find *synonyms* (words with similar meanings) and *antonyms* (words with opposite meanings) for words in your document. Using the thesaurus not only helps your vocabulary, but gives you alternatives to using the same word over and over again throughout your text.

Finding alternate words with thesaurus

1. Place the insertion point in the word that you want to look up in the thesaurus. (If the insertion point appears between words, the thesaurus automatically selects the word preceding the insertion point.)
2. From the **Tools** menu, choose **Language**. Then select **Thesaurus** on the menu or press Shift+F7. The Thesaurus dialog box opens (see Figure 4.9).
3. Choose the options you want.

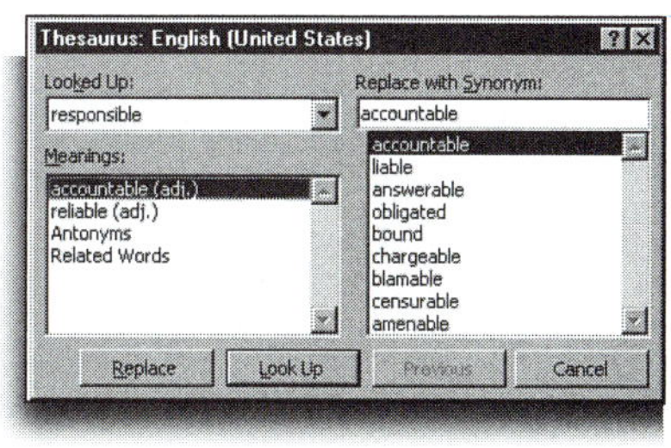

FIGURE 4.9
Click the **Look Up** button if you want to find a synonym for another word.

The following options are available in the thesaurus:

- If Word provides synonyms for the looked-up word, you can choose the meaning of the word as you are using it. After you choose a synonym, you can either replace your word with the chosen synonym or look up synonyms for the synonym.

- If Word provides antonyms for the looked-up word, you can choose one. After you choose an antonym, you can either replace your word with the chosen antonym or look up synonyms for the antonym.
- Sometimes Word provides a list of words similar to the looked-up word. You can choose a similar word, then choose a meaning and a synonym for the similar word.
- Sometimes Word is unable to provide synonyms, antonyms, or related words for a looked-up word. When this happens, Word displays an alphabetical list of words spelled similar to the looked-up word. You can choose a word from the alphabetical list, then choose a synonym, antonym, or related word for the chosen word.
- You can enter another word in the **Looked up** field or pick a word in the list of synonyms, then choose **Look up** to find synonyms for your new word.
- If you have looked up synonyms for synonyms, you can go back to a previous synonym by choosing **Previous**.

Find and Replace Text

Someday, you might need to find every instance of a particular word or phrase in a document. Or, you might need to replace every instance of underlining with italics. You could do it manually, but you don't have to because Word 97 has a versatile tool—Find and Replace—that can find or replace text, formatting, and special characters (such as tab markers). Specifically, Find and Replace can find and/or replace the following things:

- *Text strings*. Either strings of text embedded in words, or discrete words or whole phrases.
- *Text strings with formatting*. Strings of text that are formatted a particular way, such as underlining.
- *Formatting*. Font formatting options, such as underlining and bold, that are not necessarily associated with words or text.

- *Styles*. Find all instances of a named style or replace one named style with another.
- *Special characters*. Tab markers, forced line breaks, nonbreaking spaces, nonbreaking hyphens, whitespace, and so on.

SEE ALSO

➤ *For information about styles, see page 157*

Find Text

When you activate the Find feature, Word normally searches the entire document to find each occurrence of the text. To limit the scope of the search, select the text you want to search through before starting Find, and Find only searches through the selected text.

To activate Find, do one of the following:

- Open the **Edit** menu and select **Find**.
- Press Ctrl+F.
- Click the Select Browse Object icon in the vertical scrollbar (see Figure 4.10), then, in the pop-up menu, click the Find icon.

The Find and Replace dialog box appears (see Figure 4.11), and the **Find** tab should already be selected.

Search for text

1. Type the text that you are seeking in the **Find what** text box. This word or phrase is also referred to as the *search string*.
2. Choose the **More** button (if necessary) to specify search options, as explained in the section "Use Search Options," later in this chapter.
3. Choose **Find Next**. Find looks through the document for text that matches your search string. When it finds matching text, Word highlights the text in the document and stops. The Find and Replace dialog box remains on the screen.

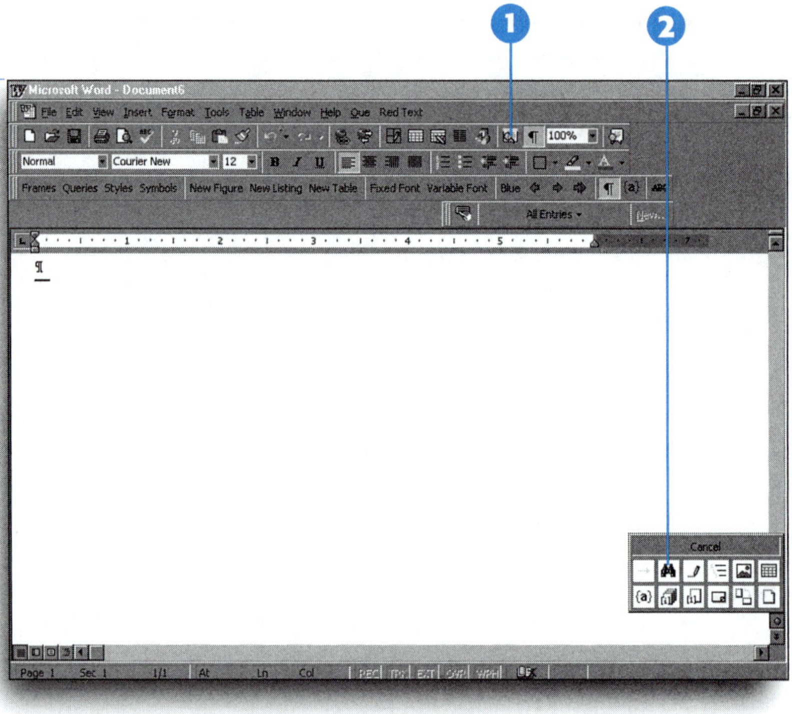

FIGURE 4.10

Click the Select Browse Object icon located on the scrollbar to view the Find and Replace dialog box.

1 Select Browse Object icon

2 Find icon

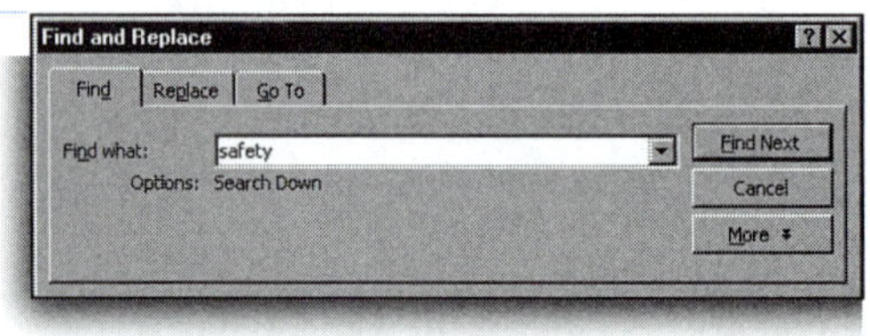

FIGURE 4.11

Enter the word or phrase you are seeking in the **Find what** box.

Using the Select Browse Object icon

The Find/Go To and Previous Find/Go To buttons display the next or previous item currently selected in the **Select Browse Object** menu. This could be footnotes, endnotes, comments, sections, and so forth. The default selection is page, in which case these buttons work

continues

4. Choose **Find Next** if you want to continue the search for another instance of the search string. Click **Cancel** or press Esc to close the dialog box and return to the document. The text in the document is still highlighted.

When Word finishes searching the entire document, or if it couldn't find the search string in the document, a dialog box displays a message to that effect. Choose **OK** to continue working in the document.

When you open the Find and Replace dialog box a second time during the same session of Word, the previous search string (if any) still displays in the **Find what** text box. This makes it easy to repeat the previous search.

If you exit the Find and Replace dialog box, you can quickly jump to the next or previous occurrence of the search string text in your document by clicking on the Next Find/Go To or Previous Find/Go To buttons in the vertical scrollbar (as shown in Figure 4.12).

like a page up or page down button. When page is the current selection, the buttons appear in black. When any other item is selected, the buttons appear in blue. To reset the buttons so that they work as page up or page down, click the Browse By Object button and choose the **Browse By Page** option in the pop-up menu.

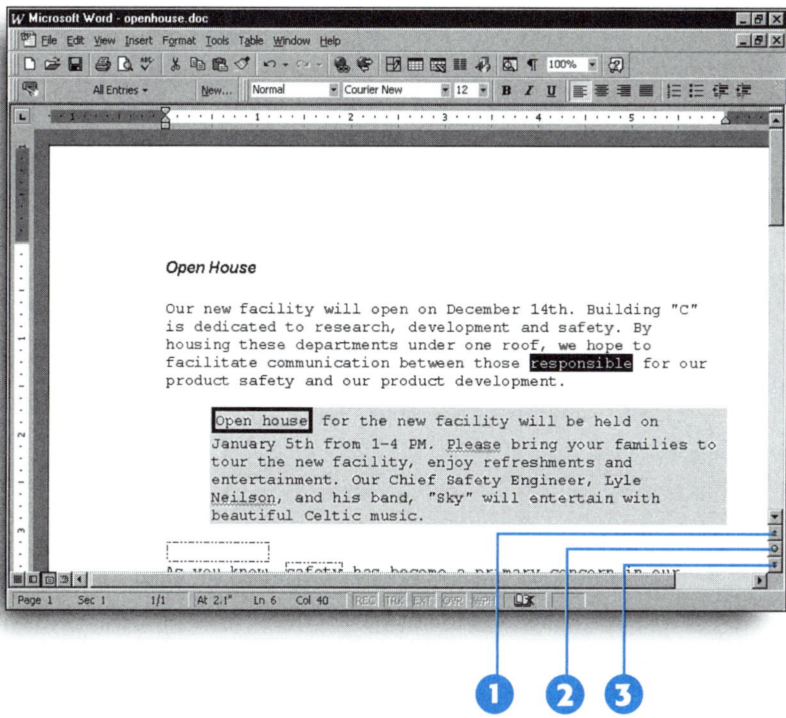

FIGURE 4.12

Use the Find/Go To buttons to find text without opening the Find and Replace dialog box.

1. Previous/Find Go To
2. Select Browse Object
3. Next/Find Go To

Replace Text

In addition to finding text in your document, Word's Replace feature can replace your search string with new text. To replace text, do one of the following:

- From the **Edit** menu, select **Replace**.

- Press Ctrl+H.
- Click the Select Browse Object icon in the vertical scrollbar, then, in the pop-up menu, click the Find icon.

When the Find and Replace dialog box appears, select the **Replace** tab if it is not already selected (see Figure 4.13).

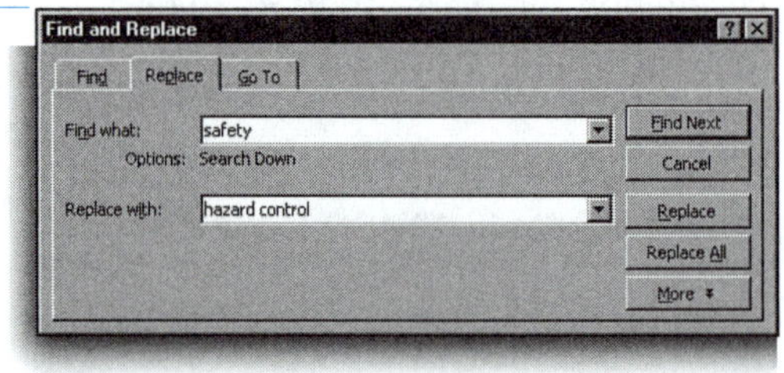

FIGURE 4.13
Type the text you want to find in the **Find what** box and the replacement text in the **Replace with** box.

Replace text

1. Type the text you want to replace in the **Find what** text box. You can leave this field blank only if you want to search for formatting only. However, you have to search for something.
2. Type the replacement text in the **Replace with** text box. If you search for text and leave this field blank, you are in effect telling Word to delete all instances of the search string.
3. Choose the **More** button (if necessary) to specify search options as explained in the next section of this chapter.
4. Choose **Find Next** to locate and highlight the first occurrence of text that matches your search string.
5. Then do one of the following:
   - Choose **Replace** to replace the text matching the search string with the replacement text and then locate the next occurrence of the search string in your document.
   - Choose **Find Next** to leave the text matching the search string unchanged and to locate the next occurrence of the search string.

- Choose **Replace All** to replace all text in the entire document that matches the search string with the replacement text.

6. Choose **Cancel** or press Esc to close the Find and Replace dialog box and return to your document.

When Word has finished searching through the document and has replaced all occurrences of the search text or can't find any further occurrences, a message box appears. Click **OK** to return to your document.

Use Search Options

Unless you change the options, Find locates the search string even if it's in a different case or is part of another word. The search string "ten", for example, finds "ten", "TEN", "often", and so on. You can narrow your search with Word's search options by choosing **More** in the Find and Replace dialog box (it doesn't matter if you have the **Find** tab or the **Replace** tab selected). When you do, the dialog box expands to offer additional options (see Figure 4.14); choose **Less** to shrink the dialog box.

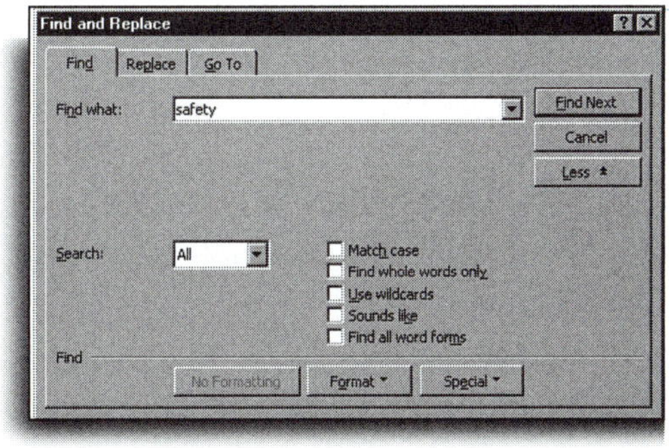

FIGURE 4.14
Choose **More** to expand the Find and Replace dialog box and to display options to narrow your search.

The following options are available in the Find and Replace dialog box:

- Click **Match case** to require an exact match for uppercase and lowercase letters. When selected, "Ten" matches only "Ten" and not "ten" or "TEN".

- Click **Find whole words only** to avoid finding text that is part of another word. Then, "ten" matches only "ten" and not "often", "attention", and so on.
- Click **Use wildcards** to use * and ? wildcards in the search string. You use the * wildcard to match any sequence of 0 or more characters and the ? wildcard to match a single character. The search string "ca?" would match "car", "can", but not "came" or "catch". The search string "ca*" would match "came", "catch", "canter", and so on.
- Click **Sounds like** to find words that sound similar to the search string. For example, "fare" would match "fair."
- Click **Find all word forms** to find alternate forms of the search string, such as "came" or "coming" to match "come." You can't use this option if you selected the **Use wildcards** option.

To determine what part of the document you want to search, click the **Search** drop-down arrow and select one of the following:

- Select **All** to search the entire document. Word searches from the insertion point to the end of the document, then from the beginning of the document back to the insertion point.
- Select **Down** to search from the insertion point to the end of the document. Word searches from the insertion point to the end of the document, then asks you if it should continue searching from the top of the document back to the insertion point.
- Select **Up** to search from the insertion point to the beginning of the document. Word searches from the insertion point to the beginning of the document, then asks you if it should continue searching from the end of the document back to the insertion point.

Finding and Replacing Formatting and Special Characters

To use a character in the **Find what** or **Replace with** box that is a punctuation mark or a break, choose **Special** to select from a pop-up list of unusual characters, such as paragraph marks, column breaks, graphics, nonbreaking spaces, tabs, and so on. (To search for regular spaces, press the Spacebar in the **Find what** text box.)

You also can use the Find and Replace dialog box to find and replace text with specified formatting, such as replacing underlining with italics. Suppose, for example, that you want to replace a bolded word with bold and italics. Instead of searching for every instance of the word and manually applying italics, you can search for the bolded occurrences of the word and replace them with bold and italics.

Find and replace text with specified formatting

1. Open the **Edit** menu and choose **Replace**.
2. In the **Find what** text box, type the word you want to replace. If you want to find only those bolded occurrences of the word, click the **Format** button, choose **Font** and in the **Font style** box select **Bold**. Otherwise, skip to step 3.
3. Click once in the **Replace with** text box to activate it. If you want to change only the formatting of text, you don't have to retype the text here; you can skip to step 4. If you are replacing the text with new text, type the new text in the **Replace with** box.
4. Click the **Format** button to select formatting options. Choose **Font** and select the formatting options you want. Note that the effects options all have gray check marks as shown in Figure 4.15. By default, these options are all selected even though they appear to be grayed out. To find or replace text that is only bold and italic, you must deselect the effect options that do not apply and reselect those that do. Reselecting changes the check mark to black.

Be very careful with formatting options

Word remembers the last search that you performed, including formatting options. Formatting can be applied to text you want to find and text you want to replace. Be certain to select the **Find what or Replace with** text boxes *before* you click the **Format** button. To clear formatting options, click the **No Formatting** button as shown in Figure 4.14. It's a good idea to clear the formatting before beginning each new search.

5. Click **Find Next** to find each occurrence of your search, and **Replace** to replace each occurrence of your search. Alternately, click **Replace All** to replace all occurrences of the word in your document.

To find formatting of text, but not the text itself, leave the **Find what** and **Replace with** text boxes empty, but choose the formatting options for each. In this way, you can replace formatting on any word, not just specific words.

FIGURE 4.15

When you select **Font** as the formatting type, the Find Font dialog box appears.

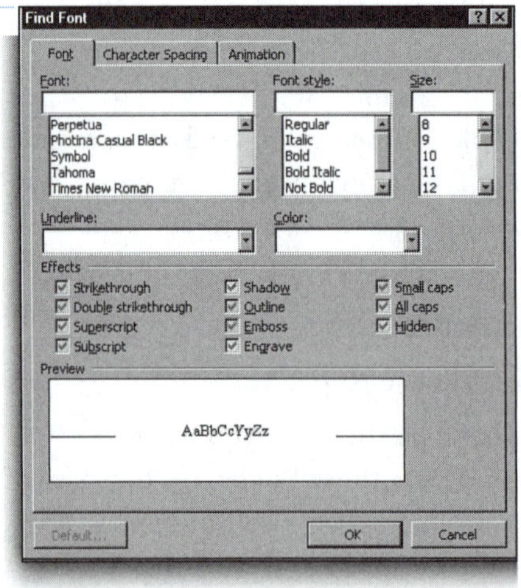

Define and Modify AutoCorrect Entries

AutoCorrect is a handy feature of Microsoft Word that automatically corrects common typing, capitalization, and spelling errors for you as you type. It also enables you to type shortcuts that AutoCorrect replaces with the full text, such as typing `MS` and having AutoCorrect replace it with `Microsoft`. Although Word has a number of default AutoCorrect entries, you can add your own common misspellings and shortcuts.

AutoCorrect checks only whole words, so if you type `adn` Word won't replace it with `and` until you press Spacebar, period, or some other key that indicates the word is complete.

AutoCorrect is also a useful tool for applying formatting options. In a business letter, for example, you might want your company name to always appear in a certain font and size, regardless of the font you are using for the letter. By creating an AutoCorrect entry of your company name with formatting options, you eliminate the need to format while you type, or to run search and replace when you have finished the letter.

Replacing Text as You Type

You can add new entries to AutoText during a spell check (see the "Run Spell Check" section at the beginning of this chapter), or in the AutoCorrect dialog box. After an entry has been added to the AutoCorrect list, corrections (or formatting options) are applied to the word at the time you type it and press the Spacebar after the word.

To see how AutoCorrect works with its default entries, type the characters `adn`. When you press the Spacebar, Word corrects your typo to `and`. With some special characters, Word does not wait until you press the Spacebar. For example, to create a registered trademark, ®, type (r). When you press the right parenthesis, the registered trademark replaces your text. If you don't want the trademark, but really want (r), press the Backspace key immediately after you type the right parenthesis and before you press the Spacebar.

Add AutoCorrect With entries without formatting

1. From the **Tools** menu, select **AutoCorrect** to open the AutoCorrect dialog box (see Figure 4.16). Click the **AutoCorrect** tab if it's not already selected.
2. Click **Replace text as you type** to place a check mark there, if it isn't already checked.
3. In the **Replace** box, enter the text you want AutoCorrect to automatically replace for you, such as your initials or a word you commonly misspell.
4. If it is not selected, click **Plain Text** to insert text without formatting options.

5. Choose **Add**. If the text in the **Replace** box is already listed, choose **Replace** to replace the existing replacement text with the text you entered in the **With** box.
6. Choose **With** and then choose **OK**.

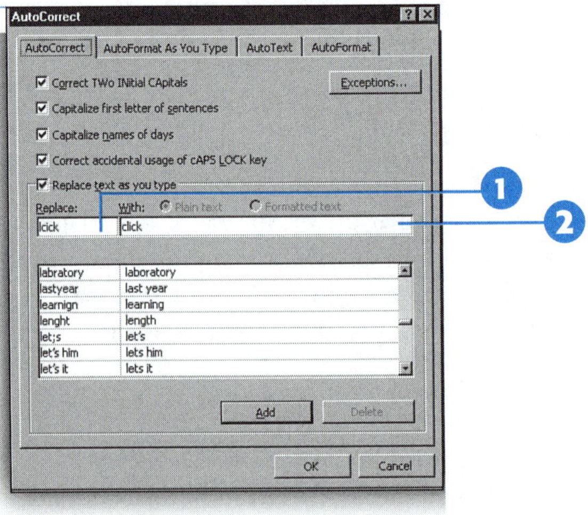

FIGURE 4.16

Define or modify AutoCorrect entries by typing the misspelling or shortcut text in the **Replace** box and the text to replace it in the **With** box.

1. Type text you want to replace here.
2. Type replacement text here.

Test your new AutoCorrect entry by typing the word in a document and pressing the Spacebar.

Add new AutoCorrect entries with formatting

1. Type the text in your document and format it.
2. Select the text. To store paragraph formatting with your entry, include the paragraph mark at the end of the text in your selection.
3. From the **Tools** menu, select **AutoCorrect**. The AutoCorrect dialog box appears (see Figure 4.17).
4. In the **Replace** text box, type a name for the AutoCorrect entry (an abbreviation, or the entire word or phrase).
5. Click **Formatted Text**.
6. To save the entry and close the dialog box, click **Add**.

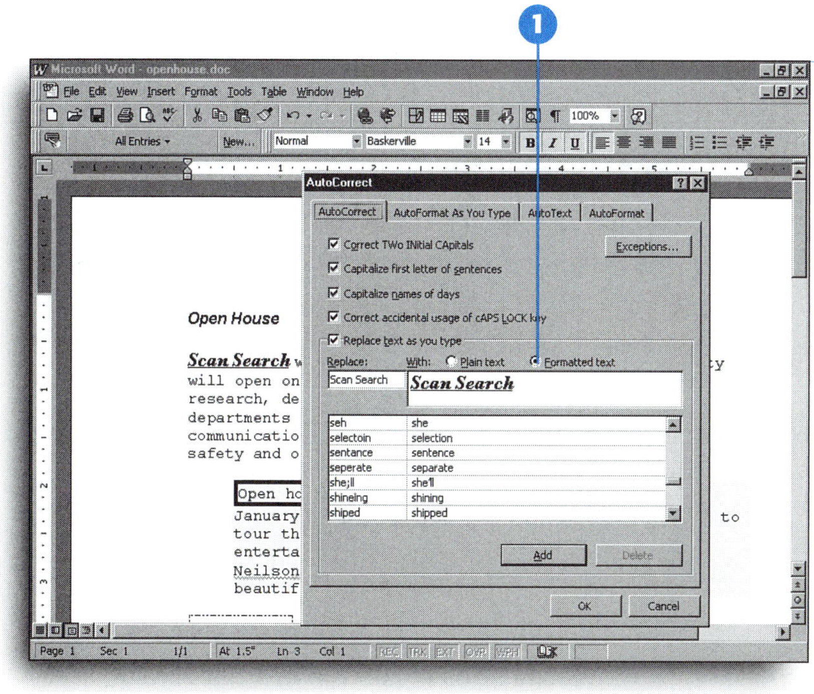

FIGURE 4.17

Formatted AutoCorrect entries display their formatting in the AutoCorrect dialog box.

1 Click here for **Formatted text**.

Changing How Word Handles Capitalization

By default, AutoCorrect handles common capitalization problems. It, for example, capitalizes the first letter of the first word in a sentence. Word also corrects or changes the following:

- *Two initial capitals.* If you do not release the Shift key quickly enough and your word contains two initial capital letters, Word changes the second letter to lowercase.
- *Days of the week.* Word capitalizes days of the week.
- *Accidental use of Caps Lock key.* If you accidentally leave the Caps Lock key on, Word switches uppercase letters to lowercase and vice versa.

In most cases, the Word default settings for handling capitalization work well. However, there are exceptions. Two areas in which you may find exceptions are the use of abbreviations that contain periods and the use of two initial capitals. For example, you can abbreviate included, including, or inclusive using "incl". But if this abbreviated word appears in the middle of a sentence, whatever immediately follows it will be capitalized by Word. Word views the period as the end of a sentence. What if your company name is "IBeam"? Word's default settings change the company name to "Ibeam". When you encounter these situations, you have two choices: Disable the first letter of sentence or two initial caps options, or create exceptions to those rules.

To disable any of the capitalization settings, open the **Tools** menu and select **AutoCorrect**. Deselect the capitalization option.

Removing or deleting AutoCorrect entries

To remove or delete an AutoCorrect entry, open the **Tools** menu, and choose **AutoCorrect**. Scroll through the entries and select the entry you want to delete. Click the **Delete** button. To remove exceptions, click the **Exceptions** button in the AutoCorrect dialog box, select the exception, and click the **Delete** button.

Create exceptions to word capitalization settings

1. Open the **Tools** menu and choose **AutoCorrect**.
2. Click the **Exceptions** button (see Figure 4.18).
3. The AutoCorrect Exceptions dialog box appears as shown in Figure 4.18.
   - To add an initial caps exception (such as IBeam), click the **INitial CAps** tab and type your exception in the **Don't correct** text box.
   - To add an abbreviated word that includes a period (such as incl.) click the **First Letter** tab and type the word with its period in the **Don't capitalize after** text box (see Figure 4.18).
4. Click **OK** to return to the AutoCorrect dialog box.
5. Click **OK** to return to your document.

To modify the AutoCorrect entries, do one of the following:

- Select an AutoCorrect entry and choose **Delete** to delete it from the list.
- Select an entry that you want to modify, edit the text in the **With** text box, and choose **Replace**.

Choose **OK** to accept your changes and to close the AutoCorrect dialog box. Choose **Cancel** to close the dialog box without saving your changes.

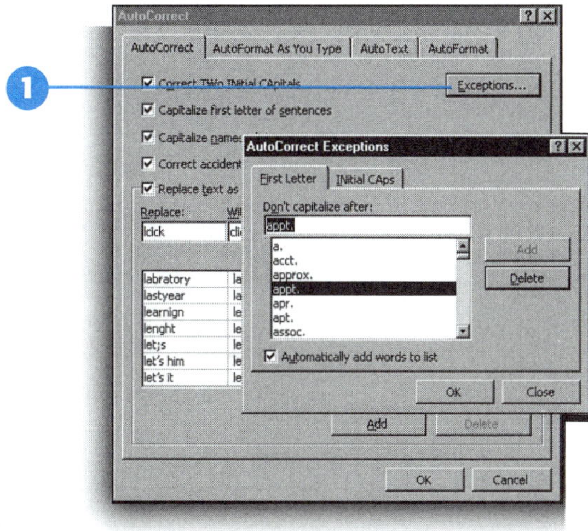

FIGURE 4.18

In the AutoCorrect Exceptions dialog box, you can specify which words you don't want automatically followed by a capital letter or which words are exceptions to the two-initial caps rule.

1 **Exceptions** button

Create and Insert AutoText

AutoCorrect stores frequently used text or graphics that automatically replace designated text entries. AutoText (called the Glossary in older versions of Word) also keeps frequently used text and graphics for you but inserts them in the document only when you call for them—not automatically. For example, you could store your company logo as an AutoText entry and insert it in your document when you press the appropriate keys. AutoText is also useful for abbreviating entries of larger bodies of text, such as addresses or frequently used boilerplate paragraphs.

Using the AutoText toolbar

If you use AutoText frequently, you may find it convenient to have the AutoText toolbar displayed. From the **View** menu select **Toolbars**. Then select **AutoText**.

Creating an AutoText entry

1. Select whatever text and/or graphics you want to include in the AutoText entry. Be sure to include the paragraph marker in the selection if you want the text's paragraph formatting to be part of the entry.
2. From the **Insert** menu, select **AutoText**. Then select the option **New**. You also can press Alt+F3, or choose **New** on the AutoText toolbar. The Create AutoText dialog box appears (see Figure 4.19).

FIGURE 4.19

Enter a short name for your AutoText entry in the Create AutoText dialog box.

1. AutoText
2. AutoText toolbar
3. All Entries
4. New
5. Type the name of the entry here.

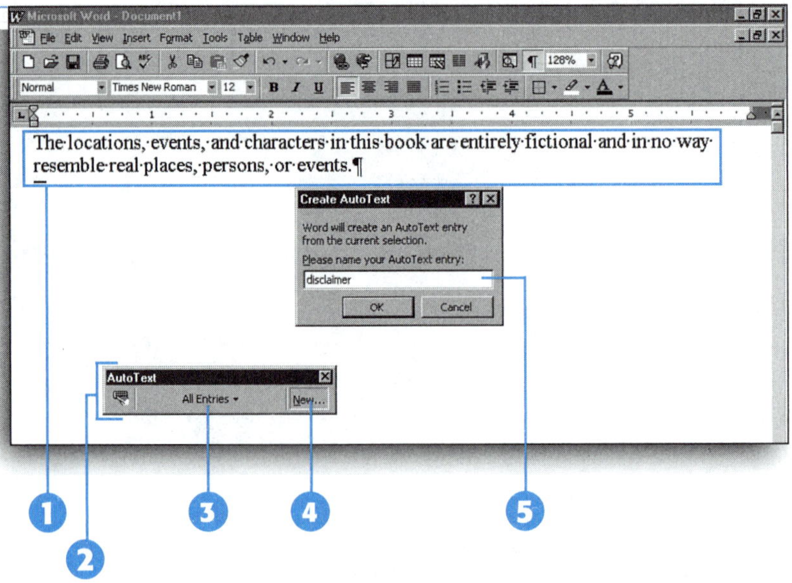

3. Accept the entry name that automatically appears or enter your own in the **Please name your AutoText entry** text box.
4. Choose **OK**.

AutoText entries can be inserted into your documents in several different ways:

- Type the name of the AutoText entry and then press F3.
- From the **Insert** menu, select **AutoText.** Then select the desired entry from the submenu.
- Choose the middle button on the AutoText toolbar to see a list of available AutoText entries. If the current text style is Normal, this button is labeled **All Entries**. Otherwise, the button has the name of the current paragraph style (see Figure 4.20). Then select the entry you want from the list that appears.
- When AutoComplete is enabled (as explained later in this section), Word displays a matching AutoText entry in a small pop-up menu next to the insertion point when you have typed enough of the AutoText entry name to identify the

entry, as shown in Figure 4.21. Press F3 or Enter to insert the entire entry. To ignore it, keep typing.

SEE ALSO

➤ *To learn more information about paragraph styles, see page 159*

As mentioned previously, the AutoText list displays only those entries that match the current paragraph style, unless the current style is Normal. To display all entries, regardless of style, hold down the Shift key while clicking the AutoText toolbar or from the **Insert** menu, choose **AutoText**.

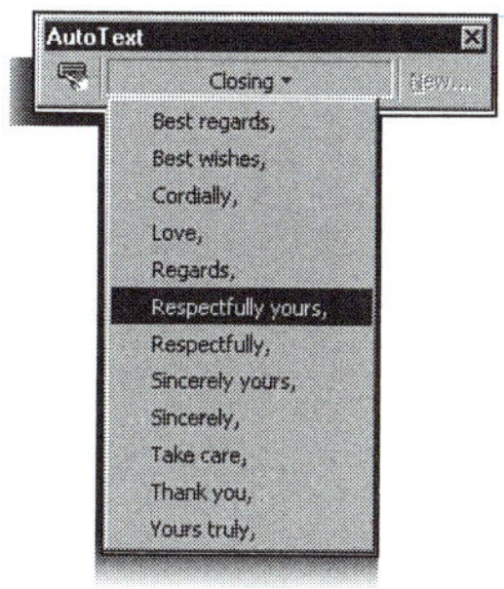

FIGURE 4.20
When you choose the middle button on the AutoText toolbar, you see a list of AutoText entries for the same paragraph style as the current paragraph.

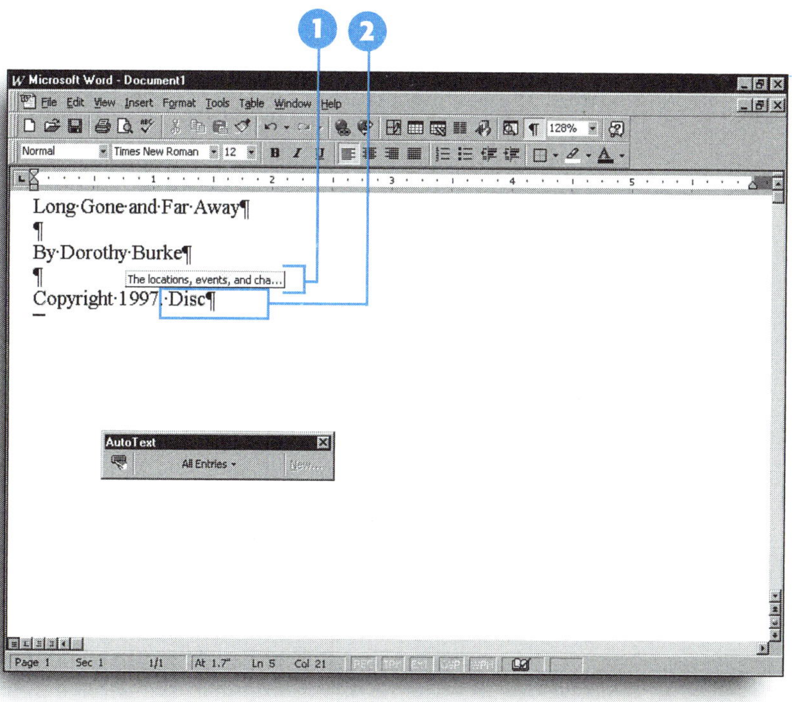

FIGURE 4.21
A small pop-up menu appears when you begin typing the name of the AutoText entry.

1. AutoText entry pop-up
2. Beginning of AutoText entry

Activate the AutoComplete option

1. On the **Insert** menu, select **AutoText** and then select **AutoText...** from the submenu, or choose AutoText on the AutoText toolbar to open the AutoText dialog box. You also can select the **Tools** menu and then choose **AutoCorrect.** Then click the **AutoText** tab to open the dialog box (see Figure 4.22).

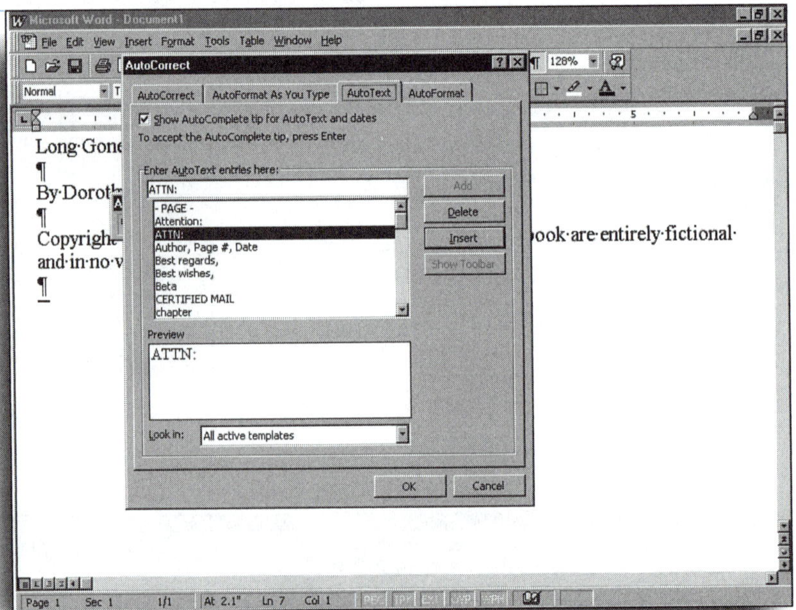

FIGURE 4.22
Enable the AutoComplete feature of AutoText by clicking the **Show AutoComplete** option.

2. Click **Show AutoComplete tip for AutoText and dates** to place a check mark there.
3. Choose **OK**.

When you want to remove an AutoText entry from the AutoText list, open the AutoText dialog box using AutoText (as described in step 1).

Select the entry you want to remove from the list, and then choose **Delete**. Choose **OK**.

CHAPTER 5

Manage Files

- Find and open an existing file
- Create folders to organize and store your documents
- Rename your documents
- Save your documents in formats acceptable to other applications or other versions of Word
- Use the summary data Word stores with your file

Use the Open and Save As Dialog Boxes to Your Best Advantage

The Open and Save As dialog boxes are designed to help you locate and manipulate files. In that way, they are like the Windows Explorer and they incorporate many features of the Windows Explorer. You can frequently save yourself the trouble of opening the Windows Explorer by just going to the Open dialog box or Save As dialog box.

Some of the features available in the Open and/or Save As dialog boxes include the following:

- Standard file management tools, such as delete, rename, cut, copy, paste files or folders, create new folders, print files, use **Send To** to send files to various destinations (floppy disk, mail recipient, My Briefcase), create shortcuts, and map network drives.
- Add files to Zip files (if you have WinZip installed).
- Select multiple files with the Shift and Ctrl keys, then perform file management (such as **Open**, **Print**, **Cut**, **Copy**, **Delete**, or **Create Shortcut**) on them all at once.
- Open files in a variety of ways, including **Open Read-Only** and **Open as Copy**.
- Open files located on FTP servers on the Internet or an intranet, and save files to FTP servers.
- View files in several different ways with the List, Details, Properties, and Preview buttons.
- Sort files by name, file type, size, or date modified.
- View the contents of multiple folders in one view, either sorted by name, file type, size, or data modified, or grouped by folder.
- View the properties or preview the contents of files.

You can reach the various functions available in the Open and Save As dialog boxes in three ways (see Figure 5.1):

- Right-click a file or folder to pop up a menu of commands. Some of the commands vary, depending whether you are in the Open or Save As dialog box and on whether you right-click a file or folder.
- Click the buttons across the top of the Open and Save As dialog boxes. Some of the buttons only appear in one dialog box or the other, not both.
- Click the **Commands and Settings** button to drop down a menu of commands. The commands vary depending on whether you are in the Open or Save As dialog box.

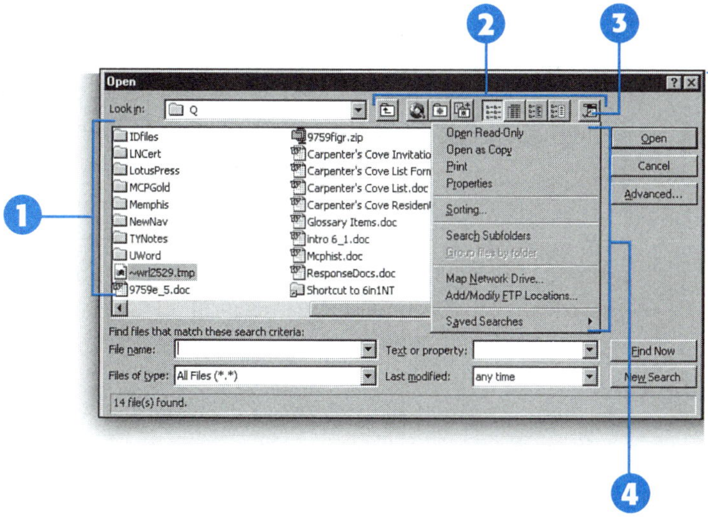

FIGURE 5.1

Use the buttons and menus to reach the advanced features of the Open and Save As dialog boxes.

1. Right-click a file or folder.
2. Click a button.
3. Commands and Settings button.
4. Commands and Settings menu.

Locate and Open Existing Files

There are several ways to find and open a Word document. You can use the Most Recently Used list in the **File** menu, use the Open dialog box and name the file you want to open, search the document summary information as described in this chapter, or use Windows 95 methods such as the **Start** menu or Explorer.

The best method for finding and opening an existing Word document depends on your circumstances. If you have worked on the document recently, you can probably pick the filename from a Most Recently Used list of files. When you know the name and location of a file, you can use a method that allows you to enter that information. In cases where you can't find the file in a list and can't remember the filename or location, you can use a search tool to locate the file.

The advantage of opening a file by using the Open dialog box is that you can do many file management tasks from Word, instead of opening the Windows Explorer, My Computer, or the **Start** menu.

Opening Recently Used Files

The easiest method for finding and opening a file is usually to use one of the **Most Recently Used** (MRU) lists, found either in the **Documents** submenu of the **Start** menu or in the Word 97 **File** menu (see Figure 5.2). These lists contain the names of the last few files you have saved (the number of files in each list varies). To access a file from this list, click the filename (alternately, press the number of the document). Provided you have not moved the file from its original location (disk and folder) or renamed it, Word automatically opens the file.

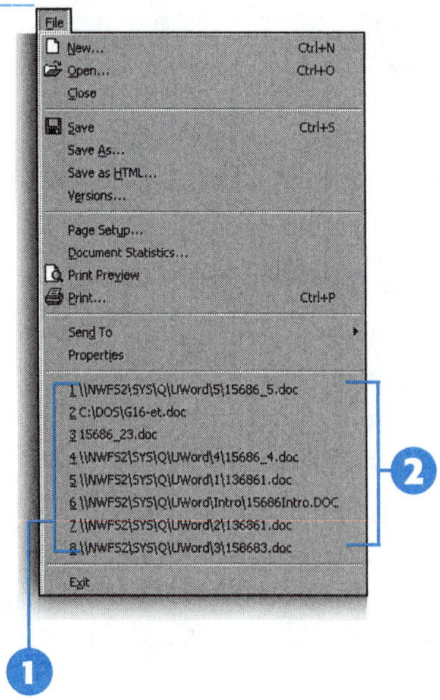

FIGURE 5.2

By default, Word lists only four files on the MRU list but you can change this as you can see from this figure. To change the number of files that appear in the MRU, open the **Tools** menu and select **Options**

1. Press file number on the keyboard.
2. Click file here.

To change the number of files that appear in Word 97's MRU, access the Options dialog box. You can display as many as nine filenames or disable the MRU by removing the check mark next to the Most Recently Used file list.

Change how many files are listed in the Most Recently Used files list

1. Choose **Tools**, then select **Options** from the menu.
2. Click the **General** tab of the Options dialog box (see Figure 5.3).
3. Use the arrow keys in the **entries** box to indicate the number of files you would like to see listed in the MRU list.

   To disable the MRU, remove the check mark next to **Recently used** file list.
4. Click **OK**.

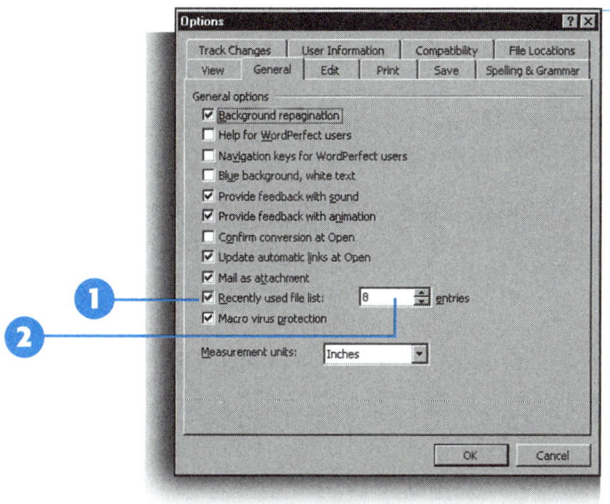

FIGURE 5.3

Display up to nine filenames in the Most Recently Used list of the **File** menu.

1. Disable/Enable here.
2. Use arrow keys to increase/decrease number of files here.

Opening Files Not Found in the Most Recently Used List

It's very possible that you need to open a file that does not appear in the Most Recently Used list. This could be a file that you haven't accessed recently, or one that was created with another program, such as WordPerfect.

Where are the file extensions?

If the file extensions aren't displayed, open the Windows Explorer. Select the **View** menu and then choose **Options**. Deselect **Hide file extensions for known file types**. Click **OK**.

To open a file, choose **File**, then select **Open** from the menu or click the Open icon on the Standard toolbar. The Open dialog box appears as shown in Figure 5.4. The file list displays all Word documents found in the current folder (documents with the file extension .doc). The current folder is identified in the **Look in:** box. Folders are represented by Folder icons. Documents have Page icons.

The following list describes options and actions you take in the Open dialog box:

- To open a file, click the filename and click **Open**. Alternately, double-click a filename or click the filename and press Enter. If you know the exact name of a file, type the filename in the **File name** box.
- To open a file in Read-only mode, right-click it, then choose **Open Read-Only** from the menu that appears.
- To open a copy of a file, right-click the file or select the file and click the **Commands and Settings** button, then choose **Open as Copy** from the menu that appears. The file appears in a window titled **Copy of [*filename*]**.
- To preview a file, click the filename then click the **Preview** button. The file appears in the preview pane.
- To navigate through folders, click the **Up One Level** button, or double-click a folder to open it. To locate a folder not found in the file list, click the drop-down arrow in the **Look in** box, and select another folder.
- To see a list of files other than Word documents, click the drop-down arrow in the **Files of type** box and select the types of files you want to view. Select **All Files** if you are unsure of a file type.
- If you want frequent quick access to a file or folder, select it then click Add to Favorites. That adds a shortcut for the file or folder to the Favorites folder. Later you can quickly locate the shortcut by clicking Look in Favorites.

FIGURE 5.4
From the Open dialog box you can preview, search for, and open files.

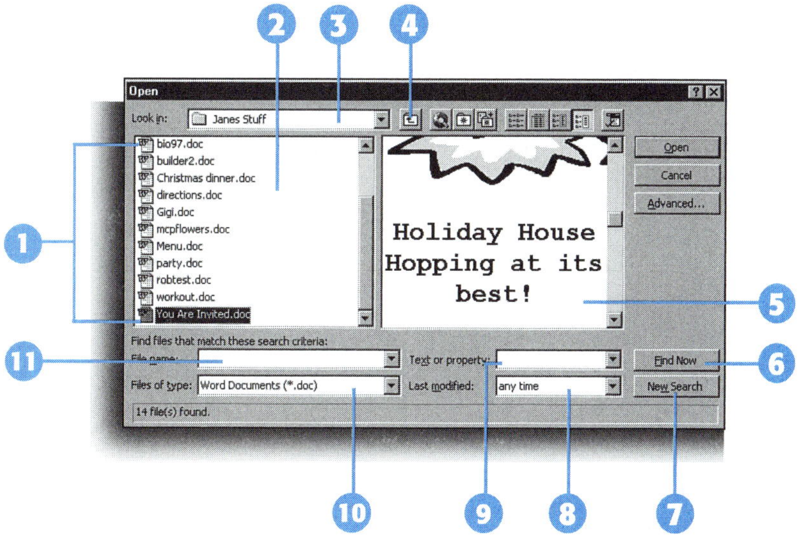

1. File list
2. Filenames
3. **Look in** list box
4. Up One Level button
5. Preview pane
6. Click here to search for text.
7. Click here to begin a new search.
8. Select a time period for last modification.
9. Type search criteria here.
10. **Files of type** list box
11. **File name** list box

You can also open Word files from My Computer or Windows Explorer by double-clicking the file. This starts the Word program and opens the file.

Search for Files by Document Text

If you know certain text that is in a document or have a rough idea when you created the document, you can still find it even if you don't know where it's located or what the correct name of the file is.

Finding a file by its contents

1. From the **File** menu, select **Open** or click the Open button on the Standard toolbar.
2. When the Open dialog box appears, type a word or phrase in the **Text or property** box. If you type a phrase or group of words, surround the phrase by quotation marks. For example, to search for toys, type `toys`, to search for toys for kids, type `toys for kids`. The **Text or property** box is also used to search summary information, as described later in this chapter.
3. From the **Look in** drop-down list, select the folder or drive that you want to search. When you're not sure of the location, select the drive so that Word searches all the folders. Whatever you choose, Word can search all subfolders beneath it as well.
4. Click **Find Now**. Word returns a list of all files that meet your criteria. Select the file you wanted. If Word returned more than one file, select a file and then click the Preview button to scan the file and see if it is the correct one.
5. Click the filename and then choose **Open**.

Search for Files by Date Modified

What if you don't know the name or location of the file, but you're sure it was created within the last month? The Open dialog box enables you to search for files by the modification date (the date the file was last saved). In the Open dialog box, click the drop-down arrow in the **Last modified** field and select a period when the file was last changed (today, last week, this week, all month, this month, anytime). Word begins the search immediately and displays documents fitting your criteria in the file list. Select the file you need and click **Open**.

Advanced File Searches

If you need to search for files based on their properties or if you need to search for files using the same search criteria repeatedly, you can use Word's Advanced Find feature to define complex searches and to save searches for reuse later. Open the Advanced Find dialog box (see Figure 5.5) by choosing the **Advanced** button in the Open dialog box.

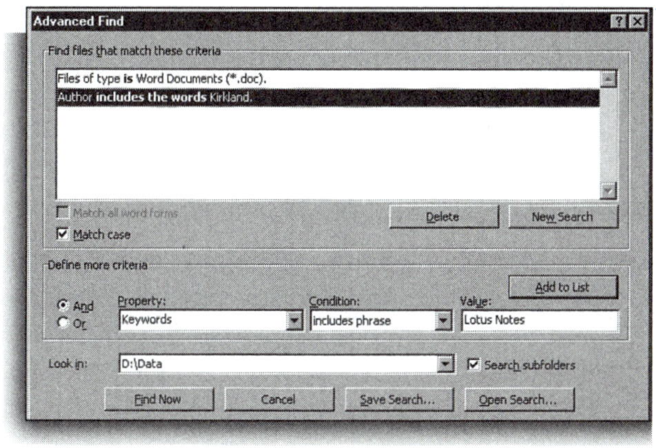

FIGURE 5.5
Use Advanced Find to combine multiple search criteria to locate files.

In the Advanced Find dialog box, you can define searches based on multiple search criteria. If you made entries in any of the search fields (**File name**, **Files of type**, **Text or property**, **Last modified**) in the Open dialog box before you chose **Advanced**, those entries appear in the Advanced Find dialog box's list of search criteria.

You can delete those search criteria by selecting them and choosing **Delete**. You can clear all the search criteria by choosing **New Search.** You can retrieve a previously saved set of search criteria by choosing **Open Search.** You can add search criteria by filling in the fields in the **Define more criteria** section.

Choose **And** or **Or**, choose a **Property**, choose a **Condition**, and (depending on the property and condition you chose) optionally enter a **Value**. Then choose **Add to List**.

Enter the pathname of the folder through which Word should search in the **Look in** field. Check **Search subfolders** if you want Word to look in subfolders. Check **Match all word forms** and **Match case** to further refine your search.

If you think you will want to reuse the search, choose **Save Search** and give the search a name. Otherwise choose **Find Now** to return to the Open dialog box and have Word conduct the search. Word returns the search results in the Open dialog box.

Ways to View Files

Normally, Word searches for files only one folder at a time; that is, Word displays files only from the currently selected folder. However, if you want, you can have Word search a selected folder and all its subfolders, and display the files in all the searched folders in a single window.

You can activate this in the Open dialog box or in the Advanced Find dialog box. In the Open dialog box, click the **Commands and Settings** button, then choose **Search subfolders** in the drop-down menu. In the Advanced Find dialog box, choose **Search subfolders**.

You can view the files sorted by filename, file type, size, or modification date, or you can see them grouped by folder. To sort the files, click the **Commands and Settings** button, then select **Sorting**. To see the files grouped by folder (as in Figure 5.6), turn on **Search subfolders** and **Group files by folder** in the **Commands and Settings** menu.

Watch Out for Macro Viruses when Opening Files

Word documents can harbor macro viruses. A *macro virus* is a macro that "infects" Word documents, that is, the virus inserts itself in the document without your knowledge or permission, and usually runs automatically when you open the document.

When you open an infected document, the macro virus executes and, among other things, infects your normal.dot template. Thereafter, every document you open becomes infected by the macro virus.

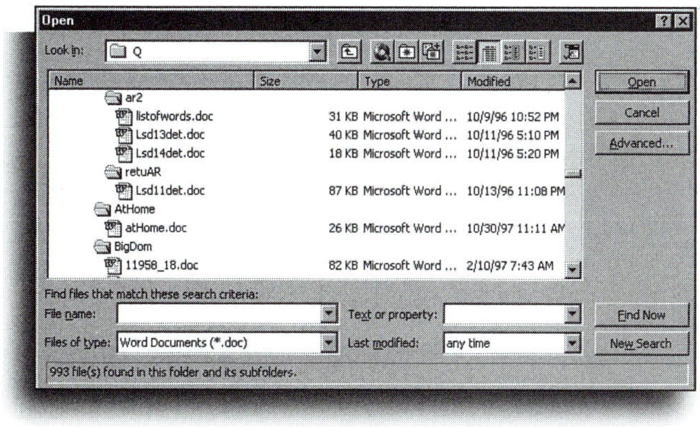

FIGURE 5.6
You can list files in multiple folders, grouped by folder.

Macro viruses typically find their way into your computer by way of an infected document that you receive from someone else. They usually act by running at the time that you open the document.

Word 97 warns you when a document or template you are about to open has macros in it. You can then decide to open the document with or without its macros. If you know that the document or template is supposed to have macros, and you know and trust the origin of the document or macro, you can open the document normally. If you don't think a document should contain macros or you don't trust its source, you can open it with the macros disabled.

To protect yourself from macro viruses, you need antivirus software that can detect and remove viruses. To find out more about macro viruses and antivirus software, you can download virus protection information from the Microsoft Web site, `www.microsoft.com`.

SEE ALSO

➤ *For information on Word 97 macros, see page 494*

Create Folders

The default working folder (the folder that is active when the Save As dialog box appears) for Office 97 is the My Documents folder. You might not want to keep all your Office documents in one folder. You might want to create new folders—for example, one for each client or project to help you locate and organize your files.

Although you can create new folders using My Computer or the Windows Explorer, you would have to switch programs to do so. It's more convenient to stay in Microsoft Word and create the folders. In addition to creating new folders, you can change the working folder for Word.

Create a new folder when you save a document

1. From the **File** menu, select **Save As**. The Save As dialog box appears (see Figure 5.7).

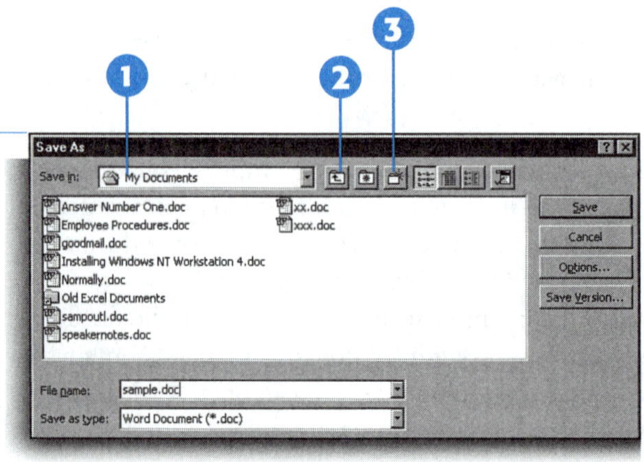

FIGURE 5.7

Choose Create New Folder on the Save As toolbar to add a new folder.

1 **Save in**

2 Up One Level

3 Create New Folder

2. Open the folder in which you want to place your new folder (choose **Up One Level** to move up in the folder hierarchy or tree; click the arrow next to the **Save in** box to see the folder tree and select a folder or drive).

3. Choose the **Create New Folder** icon in the Save As dialog box. The New Folder dialog box appears (see Figure 5.8).

FIGURE 5.8
Enter the name of the new folder and choose **OK**.

4. Type a **Name** for your new folder and then choose **OK** to return to the Save As dialog box.
5. Your new folder now appears in the Save As dialog box. Double-click the new folder to open it, enter a name for your document in the **File name** box, and then choose **Save**.

Changing the default working folder for Word 97

1. Choose **Tools**, and then select **Options** from the menu. The Options dialog box appears (see Figure 5.9). Click the **File Locations** tab.

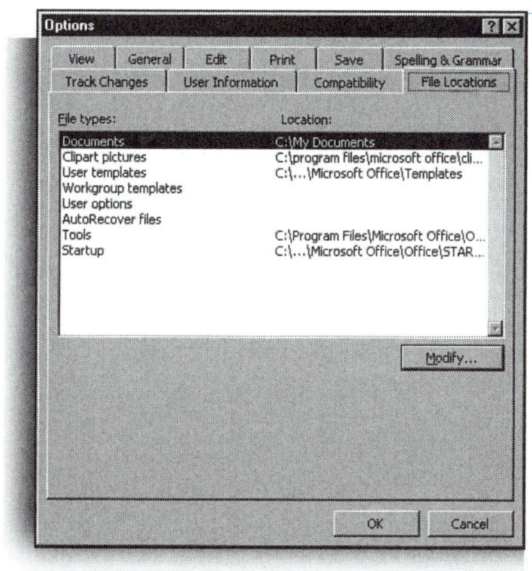

FIGURE 5.9
Select **Documents** and then click **Modify** to change the default folder for your Word documents.

2. In the **File types** list, click **Documents**.
3. Choose **Modify**. Locate and click the folder you want to use as your default working folder from the drives and folders in the **Look in** drop-down list.

4. Choose **OK** in the Modify Location dialog box. Choose **OK** in the Options dialog box to close the dialog boxes and save your changes.

SEE ALSO

➤ *Learn how to change other Word program defaults, see page 537*

Protect Your Files with AutoRecover and Backup Copies

Word provides features—AutoRecover and automatic creation of backup copies when you save your file—to protect yourself against loss of your hard work. The two features protect you from slightly different risks. AutoRecover protects you against loss of unsaved work caused by a system crash or power failure. Creation of backup copies protects you if a problem arises with the saved copy of your file.

Recover Unsaved Work with AutoRecover

AutoRecover protects you from losing unsaved edits by periodically (every 10 minutes by default) saving your document for you. It saves the document in the Windows temporary directory and names it **AutoRecovery save of [*filename*]** (where [*filename*] is the name of your file). When you close the file or exit Word, Word deletes the AutoRecovery version of your file. But if Word terminates abnormally—it crashes, your system crashes, or the power fails—Word does not delete the AutoRecovery version of your file.

When you terminate abnormally and restart Word, it automatically opens the AutoRecovery version of your file. You can then compare it with the last saved version of your file. If it contains edits that you never had a chance to save, you can use **Save As** to save the AutoRecovery version in place of your last saved version. Alternately, you can close the AutoRecovery version without saving it, and it will cease to exist.

AutoRecover is active by default, but you can turn it off if you want. You might want to turn it off if you have limited memory or free disk space or a slow processor, because it taxes all these resources. You can also change the default 10-minute save interval and you can tell Word where to save AutoRecovery files.

You do all these things in the Options dialog box (from the **Tools** menu, choose **Options**). Activate or deactivate AutoRecover on the **Save** tab, in the **Save AutoRecover info every** field. Change the time interval in the **minutes** field (see Figure 5.10). Define a location for AutoRecover files in the **File Locations** tab.

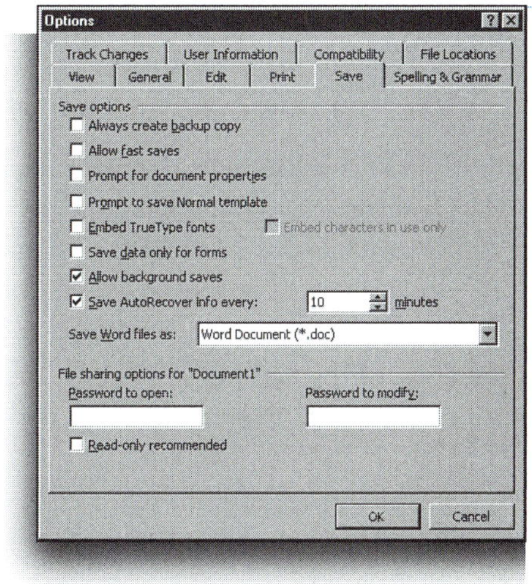

FIGURE 5.10

Set up AutoRecover, automatic creation of backups, fast saves, and background saves in this panel of the Options dialog box.

Protect Yourself from Deleted or Corrupted Files with Automatic Backups

Normally, when you save a file, Word just overwrites the currently saved copy of the file. You end up with only one copy of the file, which puts you at high risk of losing it. Word can help you reduce this risk by keeping the previously saved copy of your file as a backup copy whenever you save your file.

The first time you save a document, Word saves it as [*filename*].doc (where [*filename*] is the name of your file). The second time you save, Word renames the currently saved version of your file to [*filename*].bak. Then it saves the copy in memory, giving it the name [*filename*].doc. The third time you save, Word deletes the copy named [*filename*].bak (which was your first saved copy), renames the copy named [*filename*].doc to [*filename*].bak, and saves the copy in memory to [*filename*].doc. From the second save on, you end up with your two most recent revisions of the file saved on disk.

This is not a fully secure backup scheme by any definition, but it does give you some level of comfort. It also lets you retrieve edits that you may have deleted in your most recent version of your file. The drawback is that it doubles the amount of disk space occupied by your Word data files. If you are short of disk space, don't turn on this feature. You also can't activate Fast Saves (read more on Fast Saves in the next section).

To activate automatic backups, open the **Tools** menu, choose **Options**, choose the **Save** tab on the Options dialog box, and select **Always create Backup copy.**

Speed Up Saves with Fast Saves and Background Saves

If your file is large, saving it can take several seconds, even more on a slow computer. This can be a real distraction to a writer on a roll, trying to get her thoughts into words. Word lets you alleviate the distraction with two features that speed up saves—fast saves and background saves.

The alternative to a full save is a *fast save*. When Word does a fast save, it saves changes you have made only since the last save; it appends the changes to the end of the previously saved copy of the file. When Word does a full save, it resaves the whole document, replacing the disk copy entirely with the copy in memory.

As you can imagine, a fast save is potentially much faster than a full save. The downside is that the file keeps getting bigger as successive edits keep getting appended to the end of the file. If you activate fast saves, Microsoft recommends that you turn off fast saves at the end of each session, then do one last save. This is a full save and it shrinks the file back to its minimum size. We recommend that you stay away from fast saves. We recommend that you accomplish the same thing by doing a **Save As** to the same filename; that way you don't have to turn fast saves off then on again.

Activate fast saves by opening the Options dialog box (choose the **Tools** menu and then select **Options**) to the **Save** tab, and choose **Allow fast saves**.

We recommend that you do not allow fast saves

Experience has shown us that the upside of using fast saves is much smaller than the potential for disaster. There are times when deleted text is never really deleted, causing havoc with virus detection software, among other problems. It's best to stick with **Save As** as your alternative.

You can also activate background saves—choose **Allow background saves** on the **Save** tab of the Options dialog box. If background saving is active, when you tell Word to save a document, it does so in the background. This allows you to continue working on the document while Word is saving it (Word saves the changes you made only before commanding it to save). The problem with background saving is that Word needs processor time and memory to accomplish it. If your computer has a slow processor or is low on RAM, background saves will tax it so heavily that you may not be able to work anyway until after Word finishes saving the document.

Change Document Names

When you're working with a saved document or file, you might need to rename and save it with a different name. Typically, you do this when you want to create a document that is similar to an existing one. You open the original document and save it to a different name. Then your modifications are made in the new file and the original file remains intact.

Saving a file with a different filename

1. Click **File**, and then select **Save As** on the menu. The Save As dialog box appears (see Figure 5.11).
2. The current document name appears in the **File Name** text box. The name is highlighted, so typing the new filename automatically replaces the current filename.
3. (Optional) To save the document in a different folder or on a different drive, select the folder and/or drive from the **Save in** list box.

4. Choose **Save**. The document is saved with the new name (it appears on the Word title bar) but the original file still exists under its original name.

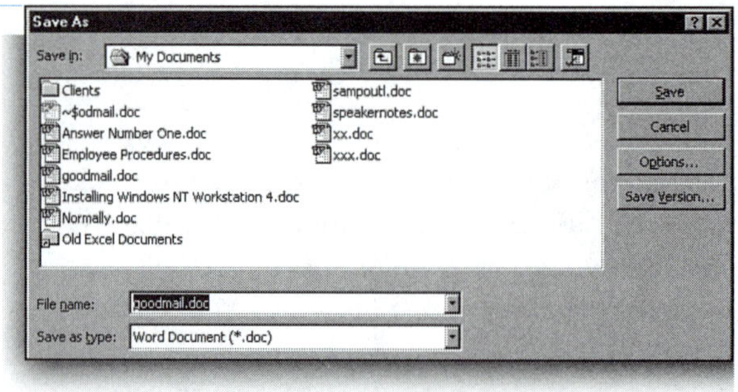

FIGURE 5.11

Replace the name of the file with the new name and then choose **Save**.

Word 6.0/Word 95 file sizes

When you save a file in the Word 6.0/Word 95 format, the file you save can be significantly larger than the original Word 97 file. Also, if you work with huge documents or many graphics in Word 97, you will have to break documents over 32MB into smaller pieces to save them in Word 6.0/Word 95.

SEE ALSO

➤ *Save successive versions of the same document, see page 434*

Save Files in Different File Formats

When you're sharing files with others, on your office network or through email or Internet mail, you may need to save the document in a format the recipient can use with their version of Word or with another word processing program.

Saving a file in a different format

1. With your document open, click **File**, and then select **Save As** on the menu.
2. When the Save As dialog box opens (see Figure 5.12), enter the name you want to give the file in the **File name** box. If you're converting the file to another version of Word (that uses the same .doc file extension as Word 97), you may want to give the file a different name than your current document so that you don't overwrite your original Word 97 document.
3. From the **Save in** box, select the drive and folder where you want to store the file.

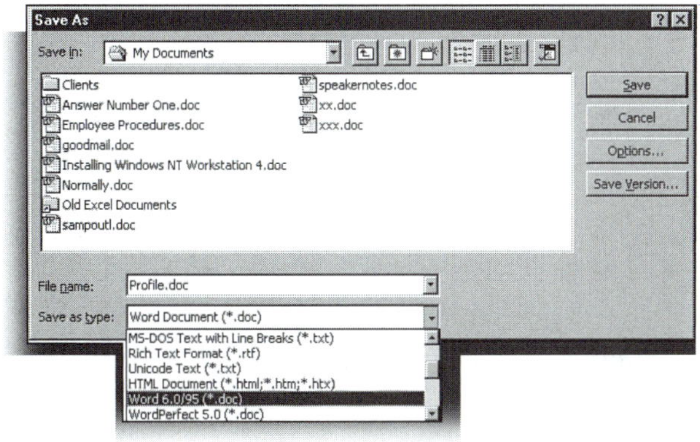

FIGURE 5.12

Select the file format you want to use from the **Save as type** drop-down list.

4. Select the file format in which you want to save the file from the **Save as type** drop-down list. Use **Word 6.0/95** to exchange files with users of Microsoft Word 6.0 or 7.0 for Windows 95. Select **HTML Document** to save the document as a Web-ready page for your Internet or intranet Web site. If the word processor file format you need isn't listed, ask the person who will be opening the file to tell you what formats his word processor can accept, such as Text Only or Rich Text Format.
5. Choose **Save** to convert your document to the format you have chosen.

If you are creating pages for your Internet or intranet Web site, the formatting instructions in the document must be in Hypertext Markup Language (HTML). Word converts documents to HTML for you when you follow the preceding steps. However, if you need to save your file only in HTML format and don't need to convert a file you already saved as a Word document, you should use the following steps.

Saving a document in HTML format

1. With the document open, click the **File** menu, and then select **Save as HTML** on the menu to open the Save As HTML dialog box (see Figure 5.13).

The Word 6.0/Word 95 file format problem

Word 97 saves Word 6.0/Word 95 files with a .doc extension but it doesn't save them in true Word 6.0/95 format. Word 6.0 and Word 95 can both open these files but Microsoft has a new converter (Wrd6ex32.exe) that you can install to save from Word 97 into real Word 6.0/Word 95 format. Download this from their web site (`www.microsoft.com/officefreestuff/word/` or by opening the **Help** menu then selecting **Microsoft on the Web** and choosing **Free Stuff**.

Users of Word 6.0 and Word 95 can install a converter (Wrd97cnv.exe) to read Word 97 files directly. Also, check your version of Word (press **Help**, **About**) If you have SR1 installed, it is fully backward compatible with Word 95. You can upgrade to SR1 by downloading the upgrade from the Microsoft Web site. It will take you a minimum of 40 minutes to download and install the file.

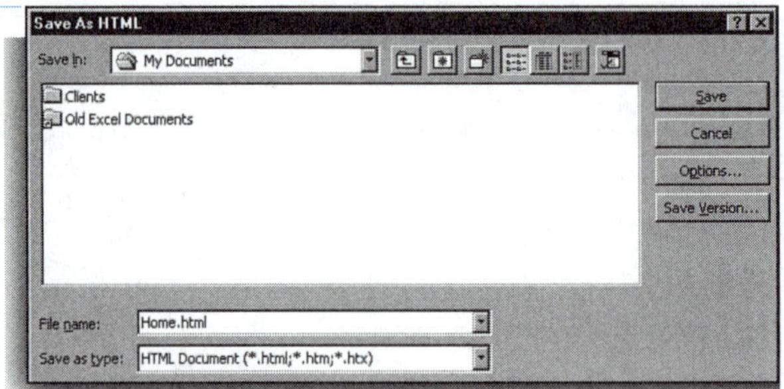

FIGURE 5.13
In the Save As HTML dialog box, the **HTML Document** file format is automatically selected.

2. Enter a name for the document in the **File name** box. The HTML or HTM (or, HTM if you have Word version SR1 installed) file extension is automatically added to the filename. The **Save as type** automatically displays **HTML Document** as the file format.
3. From the **Save in** drop-down list, select the drive and folder where you want to store the file.
4. Choose **Save**.

View Document Properties

Word keeps a set of information, called *properties*, about each document you create. Document properties contain information such as filename, location and size of the file, and summary and statistical information. Word gathers and maintains much of the information automatically. Some of it you add yourself, either because Word makes you (for example, the filename) or optionally (for example, the summary information). In fact, you can record just about any information about a document that you think might be useful to you later. Document properties are useful for a variety of reasons:

- You can keep a library of Word documents organized.
- You can locate lost documents.
- You can analyze the contents of a document using document properties.

- You can track the history of a document through document properties.

Viewing a document's properties

1. With the document open, click the **File** menu, and then select **Properties** to open the Properties dialog box (see Figure 5.14).

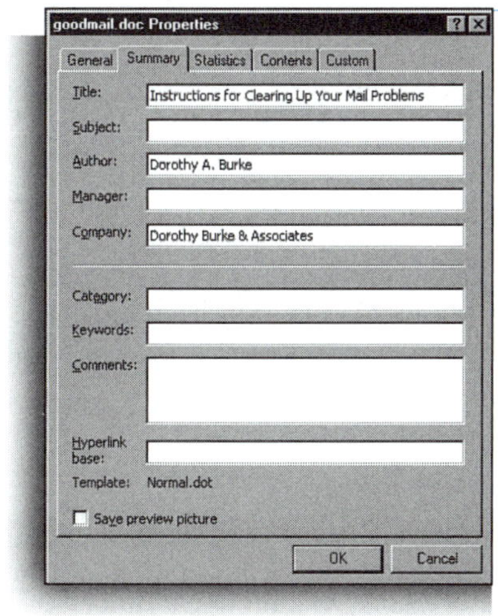

FIGURE 5.14
Word stores information about your document in the Properties dialog box.

2. Click the tab that contains the information you want to see:
   - **General**. Information on this tab includes the filename and location, the type of file, the size (in bytes), and the created, modified, and last accessed dates.
   - **Summary**. Although you can modify the data on this tab, Word supplies a title, the author's name, and the author's company. You can add a subject, a manager, a document category, keywords to help find the document when you're searching for it, a hyperlink base (the generalized location that all your hyperlinks in the document have in common), and the name of the template on which the document is based. If **Save preview picture** is checked, an image of the first page of the document appears in the Open dialog box when you select the document.

- **Statistics**. From the **Statistics** tab, you can learn who saved the document last, what revision this version of the document is, how much time was involved when the document was last edited, and how many pages, paragraphs, lines, words, and characters there are in the document.
- **Contents**. This tab lists the headings in the document, but only if you selected **Save preview picture** on the **Summary** tab.
- **Custom**. Use this tab to create your own properties that you want to track. You must give each custom property a name, assign a type, and enter a value for the property.

3. When you have finished viewing the properties, choose **OK** to accept any changes you made or choose **Close** to close the dialog box without saving changes.

About Document Summary

The Document Summary collects important information about each document such as the document author and title. You can search for a document on the basis of Document Summary information or incorporate the Document Summary information into the document. To incorporate Document Summary information into the document, you add to the document fields whose content is derived from the Document Summary. For example, add fields that automatically place the author's name and the document filename in the footer.

Inserting document summary field codes in a document

1. Position your insertion point where you want the field to appear in the document.
2. Click the **Insert** menu, and then select **Field** on the menu. The Field dialog box appears (see Figure 5.15).
3. From the **Categories** list box, click **Document Information**.

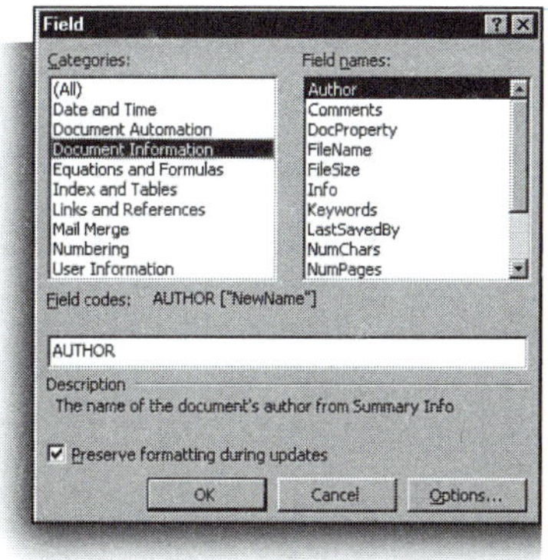

FIGURE 5.15
Choose a field name that matches one of the fields in the Document Summary.

4. A list of fields appears in the **Field names** box. These names reference fields in the Document Properties dialog box, many of which are from the Document Summary. Click a field name and then refer to the **Description** at the bottom of the dialog box for an explanation of that field.
5. Click the field name you want to use and choose **OK**. The data appears in your document. Refer to Figure 5.16 to see the field codes in a header. (To see field codes in your document, from the **Tools** menu, select **Options**, then click the **View** tab, and click **Field Codes** under **Show**. Choose **OK**.)

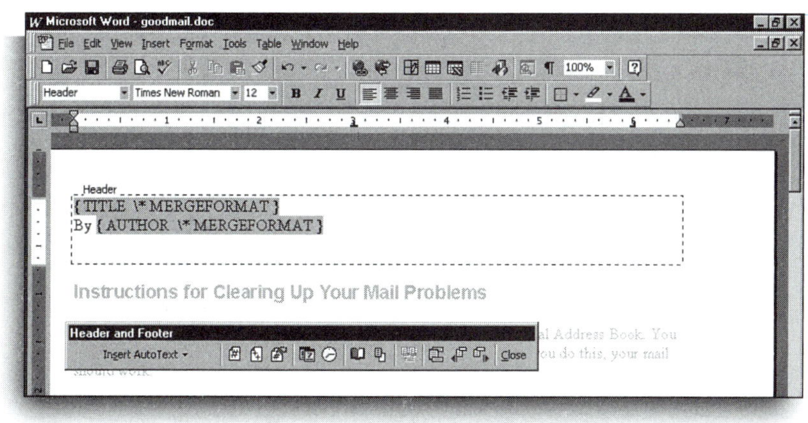

FIGURE 5.16
The field codes in this header pull information from the Document Summary.

SEE ALSO

➤ *Learn more about creating headers and footers, see page 187*

Find a Document Using Summary Information

Finding files can be simplified if you use the field information on the **Summary** tab of the **Document** properties.

Use document summary information to find documents

1. Click the **File** menu, then select **Open** or choose the Open button on the Standard toolbar. The Open dialog box appears.
2. In the **Look in** box, display the drive or folder that you want to search for the file.
3. Make sure that Word Documents shows in the **Files of type** box.
4. Choose **Advanced**. The Advanced Find dialog box opens (see Figure 5.17).

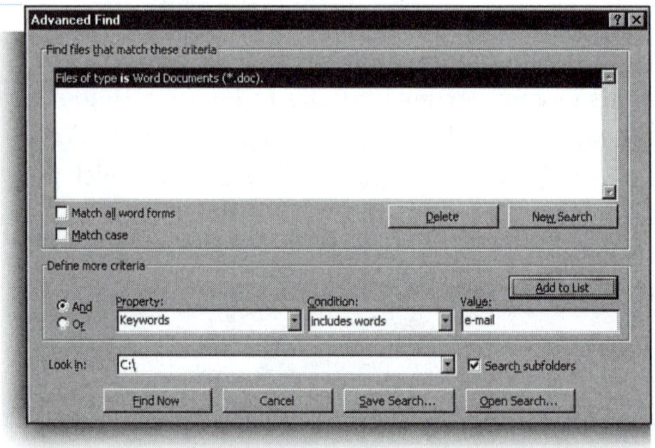

FIGURE 5.17
In the Advanced Find dialog box, you specify which **Summary** field you want to use in your search and for what value you're looking.

5. Under **Define more criteria**, click **And** or **Or**. When you choose **And**, the file found must meet all the criteria; when you use **Or**, the file found must meet one criterion or the other but not all.
6. From the **Property** box, select the **Summary** field that contains the information on which you want to base your search, such as **Author**, **Category**, **Keywords**, and so on.
7. From the **Condition** box, select a condition such as **includes** or **begins with**. For example, if you choose

Keywords as the **Property**, **Includes Words** as the **Condition**, and **e-mail** as the **Value**, Word finds all the files in the Document Summary where the Keywords property contains the text "e-mail."

8. In the **Value** box, enter the text for which you're searching.
9. The **Look in** box should contain the drive and file path you selected in the Open dialog box. To also search the subdirectories under that, click **Search Subfolders**.
10. Choose **Add to List**.
11. Choose **Find Now**. Click **Yes** if you are prompted to add the Advanced Options to the search.
12. The Open dialog box reappears (see Figure 5.18), displaying only the files that met the search criteria. Select the file you want and choose **Open**.

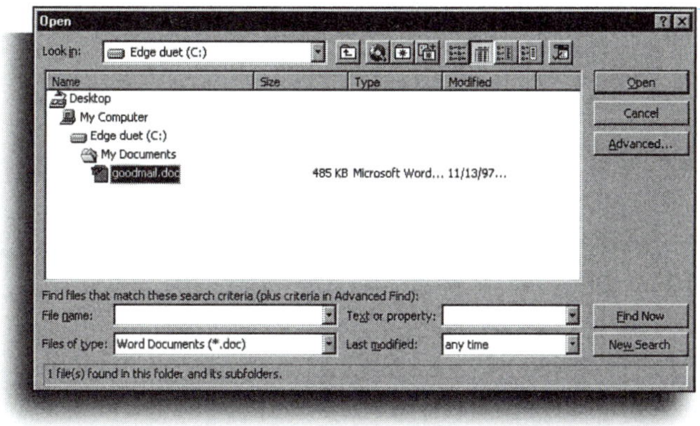

FIGURE 5.18
The result of the search appears in the Open dialog box.

Password Protect Your Document

Documents that you intend for use by others can have restricted access. You can require the user to enter a password to either open or edit a document, or you can recommend to the user that they open the file in read-only mode to view it (which means they have to save it to a different name to modify the document).

Assign a password

1. With the document open, click the **File** menu, and select **Save As**. The Save As dialog box appears.
2. Choose **Options**. The Save dialog box appears (see Figure 5.19).

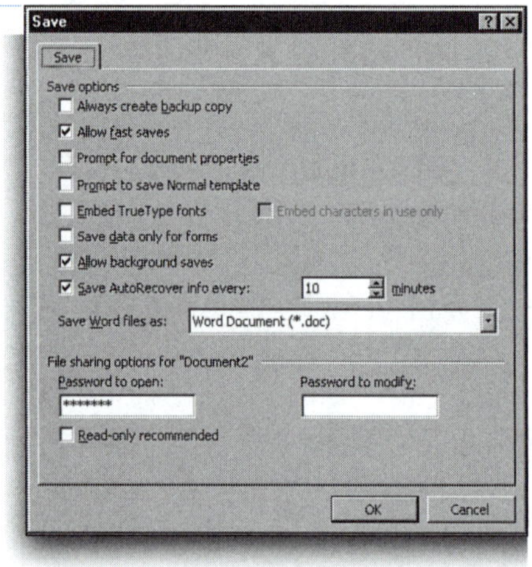

FIGURE 5.19

You enter passwords in the File sharing options section of the Save dialog box.

3. To restrict who may open the document, enter the password you want to assign the document in the **Password to open** box under File sharing options. Passwords can be as many as 15 characters long and can include letters, numbers, symbols, and spaces. As you enter a password, only asterisks appear in the box. This keeps anyone from reading the password over your shoulder, but it means you have to be careful as you type to not make any mistakes.
4. To restrict who may edit the document, enter the password in the **Password to modify** box (you may enter both passwords for any document).
5. If you don't want to set a password, you can practice a little preventative medicine by clicking the **Read-only recommended** option, so that you can recommend to others that the file be opened in a read-only mode when they open the document. Keep in mind, this will not protect your file;

users can still open it without restrictions, but it suggests that you want no changes to be made to your file.

6. If you entered a password to open the file, the Reenter Password to Open dialog box appears (see Figure 5.20). Confirm the password by entering it again exactly as before (passwords are case-sensitive, so be sure to capitalize the password the same way as the original). It appears as asterisks in the text box. Then choose **OK**.

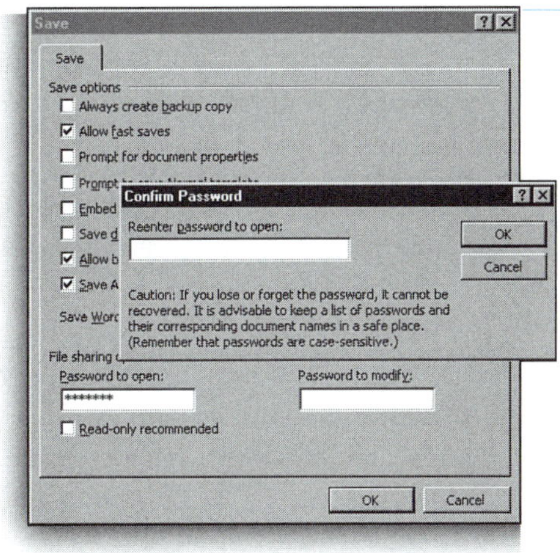

FIGURE 5.20
You must confirm the password you entered.

7. The Reenter Password to Modify dialog box appears if you entered a password to modify the document. Confirm the password by entering it again exactly as before and then choose **OK**.

8. Choose **Save** to save the file with its password.

SEE ALSO

➤ *To protect parts of a form from unauthorized users, see page 448*

When someone attempts to open the document, a dialog box appears requesting the password (see Figure 5.21). The user must enter the password exactly as you did when you created it. After a user enters the password and chooses **OK**, the document opens in a read-only mode. Users can't change the original document when it is read-only; they must save the document with a new name to save any modifications they make.

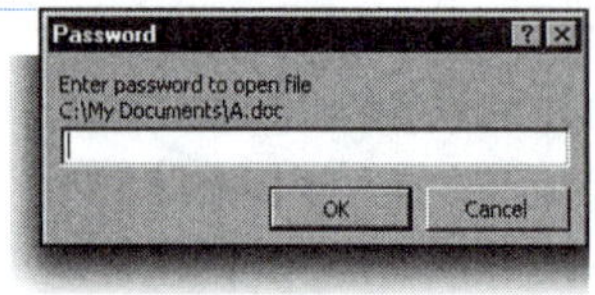

FIGURE 5.21
You must enter the correct password to open the document.

A dialog box appears that requests the modify password when a user tries to open the document if you entered a password to modify the document.

If the user doesn't know the password and chooses OK, the document opens in read-only mode. Users who enter the correct password can make changes and save the modifications in the original file.

If you selected the read-only recommendation option when you saved the file, a dialog box appears (see Figure 5.22) when a user opens the document, recommending that the document be opened as read-only. The user clicks **Yes** to open the file as read-only. This does not apply the Windows read-only attribute to the file, because it's only in a read-only mode for that particular user. Another user having the modify password can edit that same file.

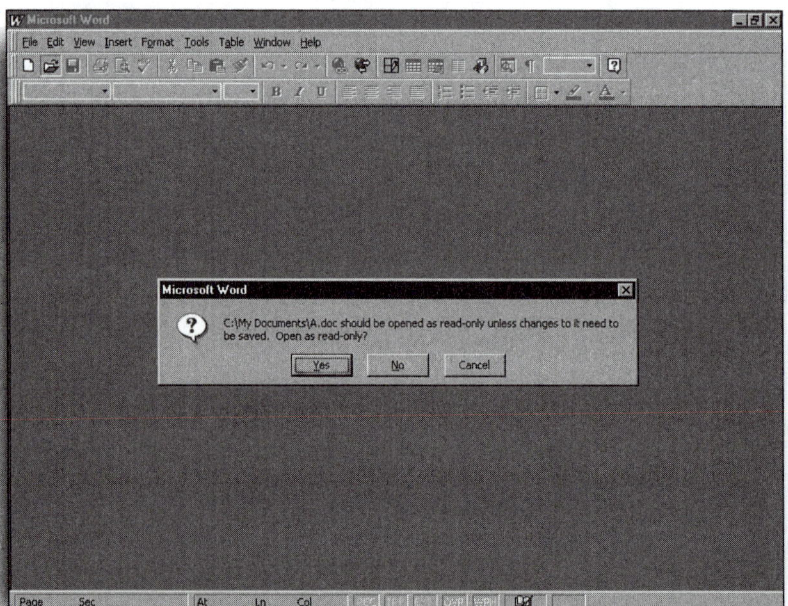

FIGURE 5.22
Click **Yes** to accept the recommendation that the file be opened as read-only.

Remember that, if you want others to be able to read or edit a document, you have to store it somewhere that others will be able to access it. Normally, your home directory on a local area network is completely private—closed to all users except you. Any shared documents must be stored in publicly accessible directories, normally on *file servers*.

SEE ALSO

➤ *For more information on using Word in groups or in collaborative settings, see page 422*

PART

II

Work with Paragraphs

CHAPTER

6

Control Paragraph Alignment and Text Flow

Align text horizontally and vertically

Control where words, sentences, paragraphs, lines, and pages break

Use hyphenation and nonbreaking spaces

Set and change tab settings

About Alignment and Text Flow

After character-level formatting (covered in Chapter 5, "Manage Files"), the next formatting unit in Word is the paragraph. Word treats the paragraph as a single unit for formatting purposes. The kinds of paragraph formatting you can apply that affect alignment and text flow include

- *Horizontal alignment.* The way the paragraph appears within the right and left margins. You can left align, right align, center align, and justify paragraph text.
- *Vertical alignment.* Distribution of paragraphs on a page, inserting only as much space as necessary to evenly distribute the paragraphs on the page. You can align text with the top or bottom of a page, center text, or distribute text equally between the top and bottom margins.
- *Indentation.* The amount of space between the paragraph and the page margin. You can set paragraph indents from the left margin or the right margin or both.
- *Line and paragraph spacing.* Line spacing is the vertical space between lines. Paragraph spacing is the vertical space before and after paragraphs. By controlling these two types of spacing separately, you can create single-line spacing within paragraphs (line spacing) and double-line spacing between paragraphs (paragraph spacing) without pressing the Enter key twice between paragraphs.
- *Line and page breaks.* Determines where a new page starts or where a new line starts on a page.

Align Text Horizontally

Horizontal text alignment describes how lines of text align with the left and right margins on the page. The purpose of alignment is to make documents attractive and readable, and you should strive for balance between each of these attributes. The four alignment options in Word are (see Figure 6.1):

- *Left-aligned.* In a left-aligned paragraph, the left ends of lines are even and the right ends are uneven. Standard text paragraphs are generally either left aligned or justified. The default setting for Word paragraphs is left-aligned. Left-aligned—*ragged right*—paragraphs are considered to be easier to read, than other alignment types, because the uneven line lengths help you to maintain your place vertically when reading long blocks of text. Left-aligned paragraphing is popular among publishers of material that is not inherently easy to read—reports, technical manuals, and so on.
- *Right-aligned.* In a right-aligned paragraph, the right ends of lines are even and the left ends are uneven. Right-alignment is useful only in rare circumstances, such as when you want to right align page numbers.
- *Centered.* In a centered paragraph, the lines of the paragraph are centered between the left and right margins. Both ends of lines are uneven. Centered alignment is commonly used for headings and title pages, invitations, or text that you need to emphasize by placing it alone on a line within a paragraph.
- *Justified.* In a justified paragraph, the lines are even on both the right and left, except for the last line. The amount of space between words varies, however. Justified paragraphs appear mostly in printed matter—books, magazines, and newspapers. Justified text can look very attractive on the printed page. Word adjusts the amount of space between words to achieve even line lengths. This variation in word spacing from line to line can become a problem with justified paragraphs. If the spacing variation from line to line is too radical, it can make your work both harder to read (because the spacing problem distracts the reader) and unattractive to look at (with "rivers" of whitespace running down your paragraphs).

  Should you decide to use justified paragraphs, you should do a few things to minimize word spacing problems:

  - *Hyphenate words at line endings.* Hyphenation enables Word to minimize the amount of word spacing variation between lines. Word can help you with hyphenation; see the section "Use Hyphenation to Control Line Breaks" later in this chapter. But watch out for excessive hyphenation that can detract from the readability of your writing.

- *Keep text lines relatively long.* More words per line translate into less variation in word spacing. If you will be using two or more text columns, consider abandoning justified paragraphs.
- *Use a proportional font such as Times or Arial.* Nothing you can do will make monospaced fonts and paragraph justification work well together.

Alignment versus justification

Some software programs refer to horizontal paragraph alignment as *justification*. In these programs, text will be *left justified*, *center justified*, *right justified*, and *fully justified*.

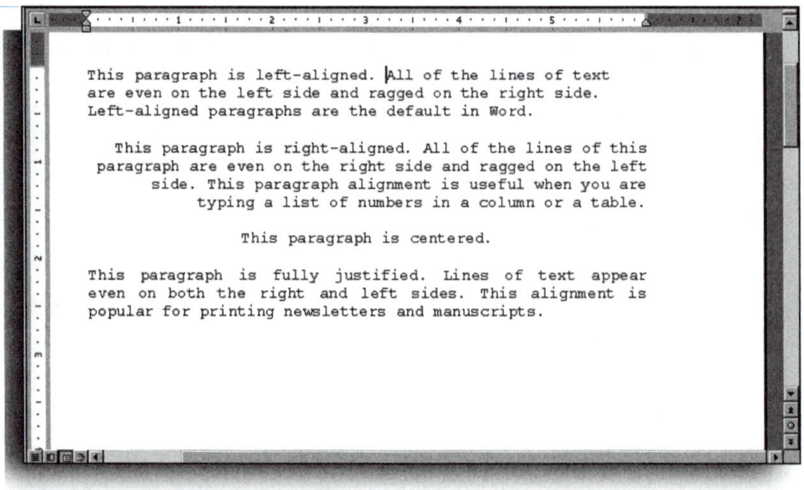

FIGURE 6.1

Four types of paragraph alignment are available in Word.

Aligning Text Horizontally

1. Position your insertion point in the paragraph. Alternately, select several paragraphs.
2. Click the appropriate paragraph alignment button as shown in Table 6.1.

When your cursor is in a paragraph you can identify the paragraph's alignment by looking at the alignment buttons; the button for the current alignment setting is depressed.

TABLE 6.1 **Horizontal alignment shortcuts**

To:	Click:	Press:
Left align a paragraph		Ctrl+L
Center a paragraph		Ctrl+E
Right align a paragraph		Ctrl+R
Justify a paragraph		Ctrl+J

You can also set paragraph alignment from within the Paragraph dialog box.

Align paragraphs using the Paragraph dialog box

1. Open the **Format** menu, and select **Paragraph** to open the Paragraph dialog box, as shown in Figure 6.2. Click the **Indents and Spacing** tab, if it's not already selected.

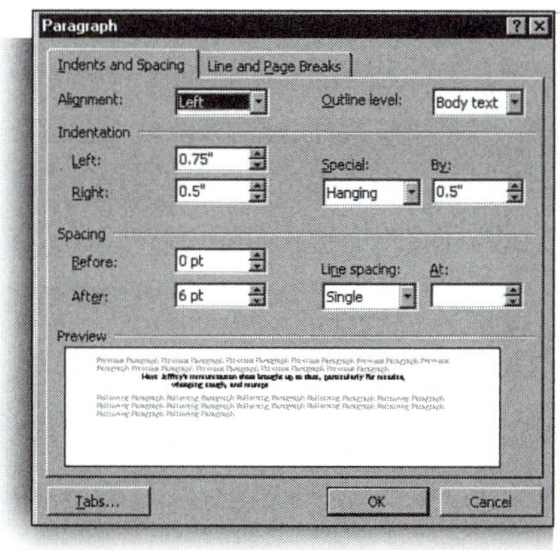

FIGURE 6.2
The sample box in the Paragraph dialog box shows how the current indentation settings appear.

2. From the **Alignment** drop-down list, select **Left**, **Centered**, **Right**, or **Justified**.
3. Click **OK**.

Right mouse click to format paragraphs

Access the Paragraph dialog box by placing your cursor in a paragraph, right-clicking your mouse, and choosing **Paragraph** from the pop-up menu.

When you need varying alignment on the same line of text

You can separate text into tabbed columns and align each column separately. For example, you may need one column decimal aligned and another left aligned. The easiest way to do this is through the use of tables. See Chapter 14, "Use Tables to Organize Information," to learn how to create tables.

Align Text Vertically

Most of the time you won't care about vertical alignment of text. You want text to print from the top of the page down, and that's what Word does. But occasionally you might want to center text on a page vertically. For example, you might want to create a title page in which text is centered both horizontally and vertically. Perhaps you might want to print a short letter, and by centering it vertically, it fills the printed page in a more balanced look.

Also, you can justify an entire page vertically. This means that Word distributes the paragraphs on the page evenly, inserting as much space as necessary.

Center or justify text vertically on a page

1. Open the **File** menu, and select **Page Setup** to open the Page Setup dialog box.
2. Click the **Layout** tab (see Figure 6.3).

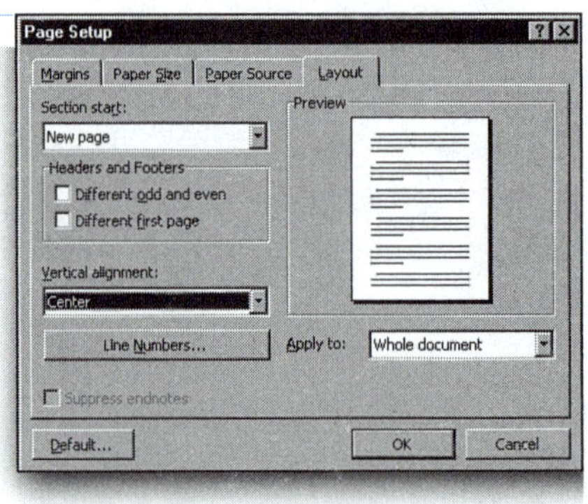

FIGURE 6.3
Select how you want your text to align between the top and bottom margins.

3. From the **Vertical Alignment** drop-down list, select **Top** (aligns with top margin), **Center** (centers the text between the top and bottom margins), or **Justified** (distributes paragraphs evenly from top to bottom margin).
4. From the **Apply to** drop-down list, select the portion of the document to which you want to apply this setting—**This Section, This Point Forward**, or **Whole document**. If you

have not divided your document into sections, This section does not appear in the list.

5. Click **OK**.

Generally, you would want to apply vertical centering or justification to a single-page document or, if applying it to a page in a multipage document, you would want to define that page as a separate section of the document. For example, if you want to vertically center or justify the title page of a document, you would first insert a section break between that page and the rest of the document. Then you would apply the vertical alignment to the section consisting of the title page.

SEE ALSO

➤ *Learn more about section breaks, see page 178*

Set Indents

In a paragraph that is *not* indented, the lines of text begin at the left margin and end at the right margin. An *indent* is additional whitespace inserted between the margin and the paragraph text. Use paragraph indentation to set paragraphs apart from one another.

You can set paragraph indents from the left margin, the right margin, or both. Word permits you to indent either entire paragraphs, just the first line of a paragraph, or to create a *hanging indent*. The three methods of setting indentation in Word are by using the ruler, menu commands, or keyboard shortcuts.

Indent Using the Ruler

Because indentation is a paragraph attribute, you need to select the paragraphs you want to indent prior to choosing indentation preferences. However, if you're only setting the indentation for one paragraph, you can position the insertion point anywhere in the paragraph. After the indentation for a paragraph has been set, that setting carries down to any new paragraphs you create by pressing Enter while in the current paragraph.

Tabs are useful for indenting first lines

You can always indent the first line of a paragraph by inserting a tab at the beginning of the paragraph. However, if you use the techniques outlined here, you can automate the indentation of your paragraphs, thus avoiding the necessity of inserting whitespace at the beginning of each paragraph.

Don't use spaces to indent paragraphs

Never use the Spacebar to indent paragraphs. This wastes time and keystrokes and makes your document look sloppy. Use the Tab key or, better yet, use Word's indentation tools described here.

To use the ruler to set paragraph indentation, you must be able to view it. Display the ruler by clicking the **View** menu, and selecting **Ruler** (to turn off the ruler display choose the **View** menu, and then select **Ruler** again). Or, to quickly display the ruler without leaving it permanently on, move your mouse pointer to the top edge of the work area; keep the mouse there for a second or two, and the ruler slides down onto your work area and disappears when you move the mouse pointer away.

The *ruler* has triangles that mark the paragraph indents (see Figure 6.4). By dragging these markers, you change the indent settings for the selected paragraphs. A dotted vertical line shows the new position of the indent as you drag the indent markers. With ScreenTips enabled, you can more easily identify the ruler markers.

SEE ALSO

➤ *Learn how to enable ScreenTips, see page 531*

To change indentation using the ruler markers:

- Drag the First Line Indent marker to change the left indent of the first line of a paragraph.
- Drag the Hanging Indent marker to change the left indent of all lines of a paragraph except the first one (that is, to create a hanging indent).
- Drag the Left Indent marker to change the left indent of the whole paragraph, including the first line.
- Drag the Right Indent marker to change the right indent of the whole paragraph, including the first line.

Indent Using Menu Commands

Paragraph indentation also can be set in the Paragraph dialog box.

Setting paragraph indentation

1. Position your cursor in the paragraph or select the paragraphs you want to indent.

FIGURE 6.4

Drag the appropriate indent marker to set the indentation for the selected paragraphs.

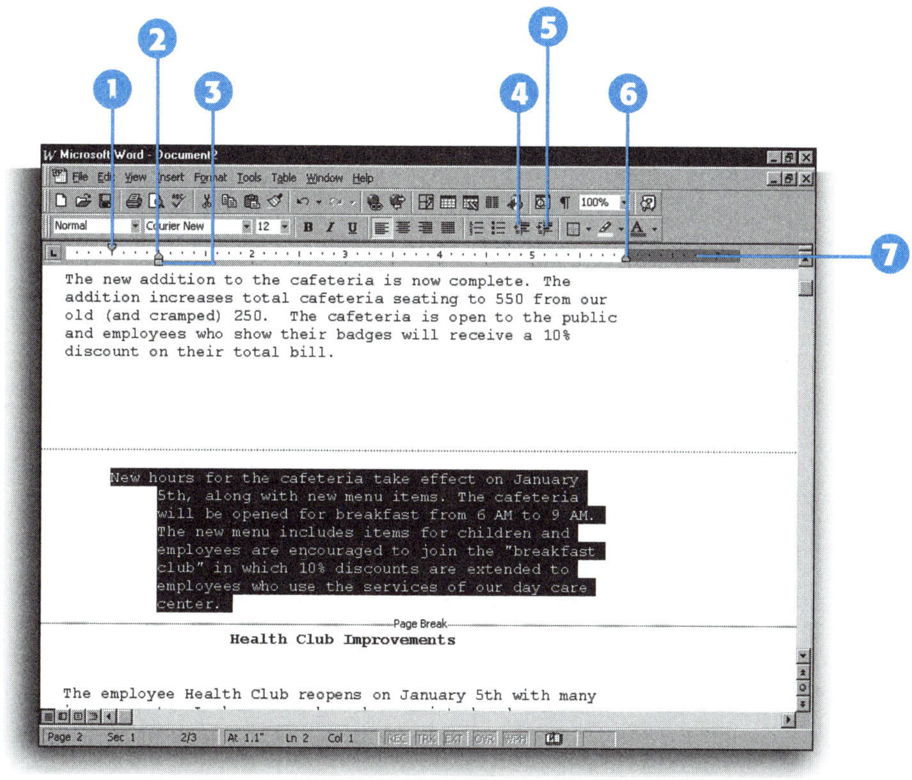

1. First Line Indent marker
2. Hanging Indent marker
3. Left Indent marker
4. Decrease Indent button
5. Increase Indent button
6. Right Indent marker
7. Ruler

2. Open the **Format** menu, and select **Paragraph** to open the Paragraph dialog box. Alternately, right-click and select **Paragraph**. Click the **Indents and Spacing** tab if it isn't already selected.
3. In the **Indentation** area of the dialog box, enter the number of inches you want to indent the paragraph in the **Left** or **Right** boxes, or click the up and down arrows on the boxes to increase or decrease the indentation settings.

   To indent the first line of the paragraph, select **First Line** from the **Special** drop-down list. Then enter the number of inches you want to indent the first line in the **By** box, or use the up and down arrows to select the measurement.

   To indent all the lines of the paragraph on the left except the first line of the paragraph, select **Hanging** from the **Special** drop-down list. Then in the **By** box enter the number of inches you want to indent all but the first line, or use the up and down arrows to select the measurement. Unless you specify a left indent for the entire paragraph, the first line of the paragraph remains flush with the left margin.
4. Click **OK** to apply the settings.

Indent Using Keyboard Shortcuts

To quickly indent paragraphs using only the keyboard, use the shortcuts listed in Table 6.2.

TABLE 6.2 **Indenting shortcuts**

To:	Do This:
Indent whole paragraph 1/2 inch from the left margin.	Choose Increase Indent or press Ctrl+M.
Decrease the left indent of a paragraph by 1/2 inch.	Choose Decrease Indent or press Ctrl+Shift+M.
Indent the first line of a paragraph.	Press Tab.
Create a hanging indent	Press Ctrl+T.
Remove a hanging indent.	Press Ctrl+Shift+T.
Remove all paragraph formatting.	Press Ctrl+Q.

The easiest way to indent the first line of a paragraph is to use the Tab key. However, this does not create an "inheritable" indent, as the other methods do. That is, if you indent a paragraph using the Tab key, then press **Enter** to create a new paragraph, the new paragraph inherits the indentation of the original paragraph, all except the first line indent created by inserting a tab character. If you want to create an inheritable first line indent, create it by using a style.

SEE ALSO

➤ *Learn how to create and apply paragraph styles, see page 159*

Work with Tabs

Tab stops help you align text at a horizontal position on your page, such as two inches from the left margin. When you press the Tab key, Word moves the insertion point (and any paragraph text to the right of it) to the next tab stop. By default, Word sets tab stops at half-inch intervals across the width of the page. You may find that half-inch tabs do not suit your text layout and you can change the position of the tab stops. You can also define how the text aligns at each tab stop.

We find that the default tab settings, or the use of tables serves us well in everyday use of Word and we rarely have occasion to change tab settings. We do, however, change the default tab settings when we use tabs in headers and footers, tables of contents and indexes, or inside table cells.

Consider tables instead of tabs

We frequently use tables instead of changing tab stops. Even if you are creating a list that contains as few as two columns, it's faster to insert a two-column table (with no borders) than setting tab stops and using the Tab key. Most importantly, tables wrap text within a cell, tab settings do not wrap text.

SEE ALSO

➤ *Learn how to create a table of contents and an index, see page 477*
➤ *Creating tables, see page 279*
➤ *Using tab settings within table cells, see page 290*
➤ *Creating headers and footers, see page 187*

The five types of tab stops are as follows (see Figure 6.5):

- *Left*. The left edge of text lines up at the tab stop (this is the default and standard type of tab stop).
- *Center*. The text centers on the tab stop.
- *Right*. The right edge of the text lines up at the tab stop.

- *Decimal.* The decimal point lines up at the tab stop. This is occasionally useful for aligning columns of numbers.
- *Bar.* A straight vertical line appears at the tab stop. The text does not realign on this type of tab. Also, you can only set a bar from the Tabs dialog box. The bar is a relic of versions of Word in which you had to set up tables with tabs. You used the bar to set vertical borders between columns in tabbed tables.

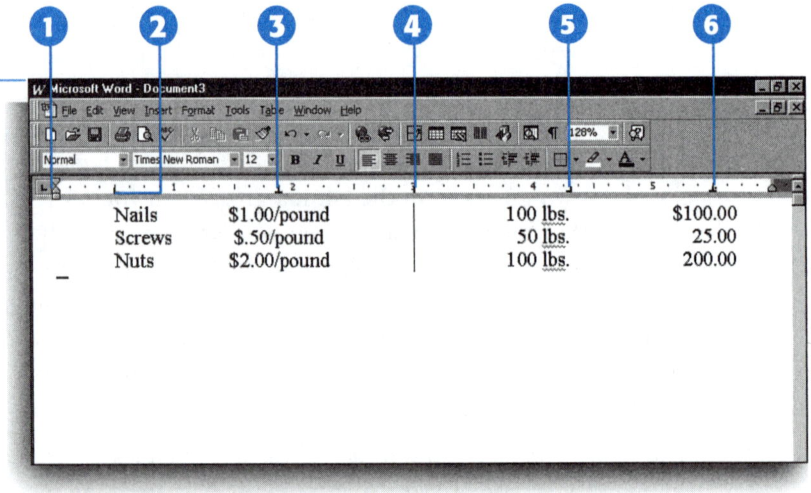

FIGURE 6.5

Five types of tabs are available.

1. Click here to select the type of tab you want to set.
2. Left tab
3. Center tab
4. Bar tab
5. Right tab
6. Decimal tab

Create Custom Tab Stops

Although Word provides tab stops at every ½ inch from the left to right margins on your page, you can move, remove, or add tab stops. You can use the ruler to set tab stops or you can specify them in the Tabs dialog box.

Set custom tab stops with the ruler

1. Make sure the insertion point is in the paragraph in which you want to set tab stops. If you want to set tab stops for more than one paragraph, select the paragraphs that you want to affect.
2. Click the tab symbol on the ruler (refer to Figure 6.5) until you see the symbol for the type of tab you want to set.

3. Point at the location on the ruler where you want to place the tab stop (keep your mouse pointer near the bottom gray border of the ruler).
4. Hold down the left mouse button. A tab symbol of the type you selected in step 3 appears in the ruler, along with a dashed vertical line on your page, showing where the tab stop falls in relation to your text.
5. Drag the mouse left or right until the tab stop is at the correct position and then release the mouse button. If you release the mouse button before you have moved the tab symbol where you want it, point at the tab symbol again and drag it left or right until it appears where you want it.
6. Repeat steps 2 through 5 as necessary until you have set all desired tab stops.

All the default tab stops to the left of manually set tab stops disappear. Default tab stops to the right of your rightmost manually set tab stop remain in effect.

The ruler method of setting tabs is the most intuitive. However, some people prefer to use the Tabs dialog box to set tabs. Using the dialog box, you can set the exact position of a tab by indicating its position on the ruler using measurements instead of eyeballing the tab setting.

Position tab stops precisely with the Tabs dialog box

1. Make sure the insertion point is in the paragraph in which you want to set tab stops. If you want to set tab stops for more than one paragraph, select the paragraphs that you want to affect.
2. Open the **Format** menu, and select **Tabs**, or double right-click the ruler.
3. The Tabs dialog box appears (see Figure 6.6).
4. In the **Tab stop position** text box, enter the tab position as number of inches from the left margin.
5. Under **Alignment**, click the type of tab stop you want to set—**Left**, **Center**, **Right**, **Decimal**, or **Bar**.
6. Click **Set**.

Removing a tab stop

If you set a tab stop by mistake and you want to remove it entirely, drag its tab symbol below the ruler. The tab symbol disappears.

About tab settings and inheritance

When you press Enter at the end of a paragraph, the new paragraph will inherit the tab settings of the original paragraph. You therefore have to clear the tab settings if you want the new paragraph to return to the default tabs at every 1/2 inch.

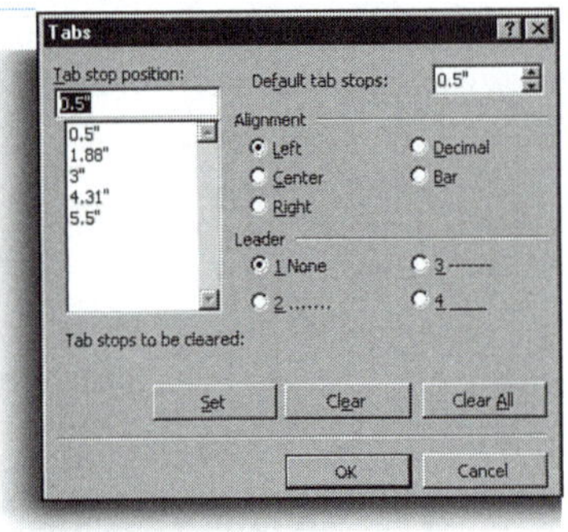

FIGURE 6.6
In the Tabs dialog box you can set and clear tabs.

Setting even spaced tab stops

By changing the default tab stop setting to something other than 0.5," you can create a set of evenly spaced tab stops automatically. To do this, enter the spacing you want to use in the **Default tab stops** box in the Tabs dialog box.

7. Repeat steps 4 through 6 for each tab stop you want to set. When finished, click **OK**.

Set Tabs with Leaders

Leaders are repeated characters that appear to the left of a tab stop. They "lead up" to the tab stop. The most commonly used characters for leaders are periods, but Word also offers dash and underline leaders (see Figure 6.7). The most common use for leaders is in tables of contents and indexes to make it easier for the reader to line up a table entry with its page number on the right side of the page. You can also use leaders in paper-based forms to create underlined spaces for people to complete.

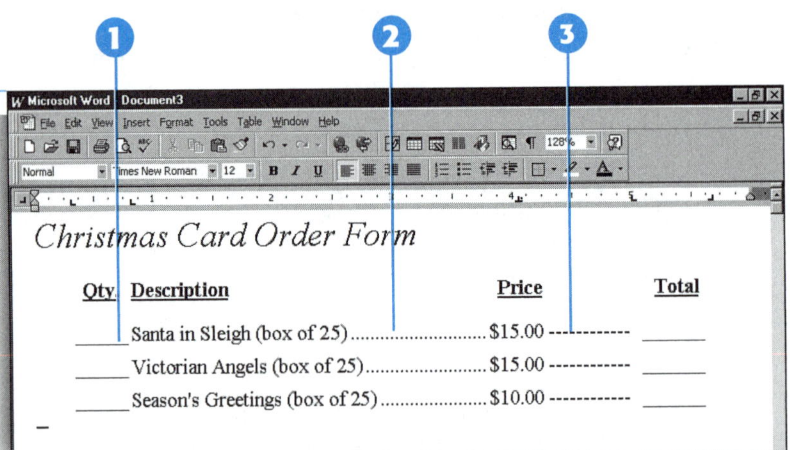

FIGURE 6.7
Dot leaders and dash leaders often separate items and numbers; underline leaders are useful for forms.

1. Underline leaders
2. Dot leaders
3. Dash leaders

Add tab leaders

1. Make sure the insertion point is in the paragraph where you want to set tab stops. If you want to set tab stops for more than one paragraph, select the paragraphs that you want to affect.
2. Open the **Format** menu, and select **Tabs** or double right-click the ruler.
3. The Tabs dialog box appears (refer to Figure 6.6).
4. Enter a new tab stop position in the **Tab stop position** text box, or select one of the existing tab stops listed beneath it.
5. Under **Leader**, select **1 None** to remove leaders, 2 for dot leaders, 3 for dash leaders, or 4 for underline leaders.
6. Click **Set**, then click **OK**.

Move and Delete Custom Tab Stops

You can move or delete tab stops with either the ruler and mouse or the Tabs dialog box.

Moving a tab stop with the mouse

1. Point at the tab symbol on the ruler.
2. Hold down the left mouse button and drag the tab symbol to its new position.
3. Release the mouse button.

To quickly delete a tab stop, point at the tab symbol, hold down the left mouse button, and drag the tab symbol down and off the ruler. The symbol disappears.

You also can use the Tabs dialog box to clear a tab (open the **Format** menu and select **Tabs**). Select the tab from the list beneath **Tab stop position** and then click **Clear**. Click **Clear All** to remove all the tab stops and restore the default tabs. Then click **OK** to close the dialog box.

Tips on modifying tab settings

When you want to modify the tab settings for a paragraph or group of paragraphs, you must click in the paragraph you want to change or select all the paragraphs you want to change. Don't assume that by changing one paragraph with the tab settings you are affecting the other paragraphs with the same settings.

Set Line Spacing and Paragraph Spacing

The amount of vertical space between lines in a paragraph is the *line spacing*. The amount of space between paragraphs is *paragraph spacing*. By default, Word uses single-spacing for both line and paragraph spacing. This means that the amount of space between lines depends on the design of the font you are using; and, in general, that means there is just enough space to keep the *descenders* of letters above from touching the *ascenders* of letters below.

Most people use single-spacing for their finished documents, but you may want to print a draft with double- or triple-spacing to leave room for an editor to insert comments. If you really want to refine the look of a document, you may want to make fine adjustments to vertical spacing by specifying the point size of the spacing between the lines.

Most people also add one line of space between paragraphs to set the paragraphs apart by pressing the Enter key twice. But you can automatically set spacing between paragraphs so that you need to press the Enter key only once. You can set the amount of space above a paragraph, the amount below, or both. Most experienced users only set the space above paragraphs. It seems to work more cleanly than setting the space below, and is easier than trying to set space both above and below.

Setting paragraph spacing automatically may only save you one keystroke per paragraph, but it can have much impact on your editing time. For example, a letter whose second page contains only a few lines of text is unattractive and not economical. In this case, you could play with changing the top and bottom margins of page one, or you can reset paragraph spacing from two lines to 1.5 lines. If you space paragraphs by hitting Enter twice, this is a lot of work. But if you have Word insert the space automatically, it is easy to have Word reset the amount of space.

Change line or paragraph spacing

1. Make sure the insertion point is in the paragraph where you want to set spacing. If you want to set spacing for more than one paragraph, select the paragraphs that you want to affect.

2. Open the **Format** menu and select **Paragraph**. The Paragraph dialog box opens (see Figure 6.8). Click the **Indents and Spacing** tab if it isn't already selected.

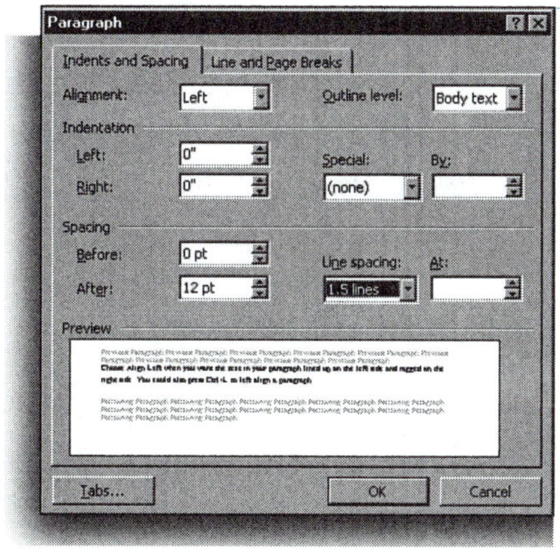

FIGURE 6.8
Select the desired vertical spacing between lines of text from the **Line spacing** drop-down list.

3. To change line spacing, select the desired spacing from the **Line spacing** drop-down list.
   - **Exactly**. Space between lines is exactly the value, in points, that you enter in the **At** text box. (There are 72 points in an inch.)
   - **At Least**. Space between lines is at least the value, in points, you enter in the **At** text box; Word increases the spacing if the line has characters with larger font sizes or graphics that need more vertical space.
   - **Multiple**. Changes spacing by the factor you enter in the **At** text box. For example, enter **3** to triple the line spacing.
4. To add additional spacing before or after the paragraph, enter the desired amount of space (in points) in the **Before** or **After** text boxes, or click the up and down arrows to increase or decrease paragraph space in half-line increments.
5. Click **OK**.

To change line and paragraph spacing, you also can right-click and choose **Paragraph** to open the Paragraph dialog box.

Control Where Words, Sentences, Paragraphs, Lines, and Pages Break

When you create a document, Word helps you control the flow of text on the printed page. You control where words, sentences, and paragraphs break. Word controls where lines and pages break. In a document organized in columns, Word controls where the columns break. In a long or complex document, you might want to control organization by breaking the document into sections. Usually you insert section breaks manually, but Word occasionally inserts section breaks for you. For example, when Word creates a table of contents, it separates the table of contents from the rest of the document by inserting a section break.

SEE ALSO

➤ *Inserting sections, see page 178*

➤ *Ceating columns, see page 223*

Although Word controls line and page breaks, you can force line and page breaks whenever you need to. You can also use hyphenation and nonbreaking spaces to influence where Word breaks lines. You can use Word's pagination tools to influence where page and column breaks occur.

Insert Line Breaks

Normally, if you want to force text to appear on the next line, you press Enter, which forces a paragraph break. Occasionally, however, you may want to force text to appear on the next line without starting a new paragraph. You want to continue typing in the same paragraph. You want to force a line break. You can do this by pressing Shift+Enter.

One example of a line break application is to center a title that is more than one line long. You want to balance the lengths of the lines by choosing where the lines break. If you have defined the paragraph so that it has whitespace below it, pressing Enter to force a paragraph break inserts extra, unwanted space between the lines. But pressing Shift+Enter to force a line break does not introduce extra whitespace.

Use Hyphenation to Control Line Breaks

Normally during word wrap, Word breaks lines at spaces or hyphens. If you don't want a hyphenated word (say, for example, a hyphenated last name) to be separated by a line break, you can use a *nonbreaking hyphen* instead. Press Ctrl+Shift+Hyphen where you would normally type the hyphen, or click the **Insert** menu, and select **Symbol**, select the **Special Characters** tab, click **Nonbreaking Hyphen** in the **Character** box to select it, and choose **Insert**.

On the other hand, you may want to define where a long word should break, to prevent Word from moving the entire word down to the next line and creating a gap in the line above. You could insert a hyphen, which would cause the word to break at the hyphen. The problem with this is, if you ever edit the paragraph, the word might no longer fall at the end of the line. But the hyphen still appears. The solution is either to insert an *optional hyphen* or to turn on automatic hyphenation.

You only see an optional hyphen if the word it is in falls at the end of a line where it extends past the right margin. In that circumstance, the line breaks at the hyphen and the hyphen appears, separating the word between lines. But if the word does not appear at the end of a line, the hyphen is invisible.

To insert an optional hyphen, position your insertion point in the word where you want to put the hyphen and then press Ctrl+Hyphen.

Using optional hyphens and nonbreaking hyphens enables you to manually control the hyphenation of your text. The other alternative is to have Word hyphenate line endings automatically or have Word prompt you for hyphens where it thinks they are appropriate.

Turn on automatic or prompted hyphenation

1. Open the **Tools** menu, and select **Language**. Then choose **Hyphenation** from the submenu. The Hyphenation dialog box appears (see Figure 6.9).
2. Click **Automatically hyphenate document** to place a check mark there.

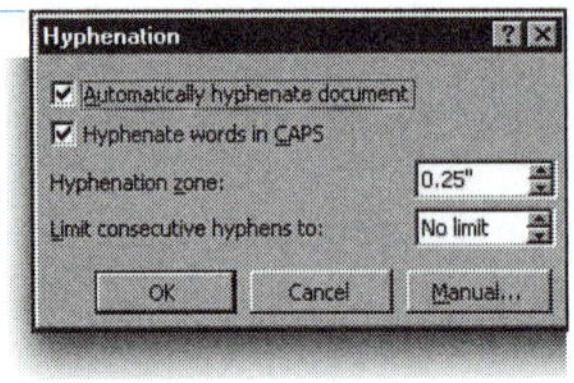

FIGURE 6.9
Set the hyphenation zone and the number of consecutive hyphens you want.

3. (Optional) If you want to hyphenate words that appear in all uppercase letters, click **Hyphenate words in CAPS** to place a check mark there.
4. Specify the amount of space to leave between the end of the last word in the line and the right margin in the **Hyphenation zone** box. To reduce the number of hyphens, make the hyphenation zone wider. Make the hyphenation zone narrower to reduce the raggedness of the right margin. In justified paragraphs, a narrower zone causes Word to permit less variation in the amount of space it allows between words on each line.
5. Enter the maximum number of consecutive lines that you want Word to hyphenate in the **Limit consecutive hyphens to** box. By default, Word allows unlimited consecutive hyphenated lines. But hyphenated line endings make a document harder to read (and uglier), so you may want to use this feature to limit the number of consecutive hyphenated lines.
6. Click **OK** to apply your settings to the document. Choose **Manual** to have Word immediately begin the hyphenation process but stop at each possible hyphen to allow you to accept, reject, or change the hyphen position (see Figure 6.10).

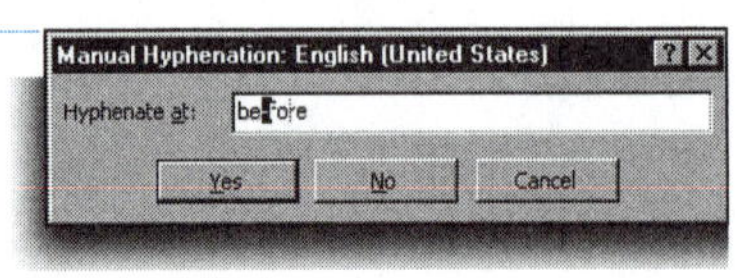

FIGURE 6.10
During manual hyphenation, Word requests a hyphenation decision from you each time a word needs to be hyphenated.

When you choose **OK** or **Manual** in the Hyphenation dialog box, Word immediately begins hyphenating your document. If you choose **Manual** in the Hyphenation dialog box, Word prompts you with a dialog box whenever it thinks a word needs to be hyphenated. Choose **Yes** to accept the hyphen position or **No** to reject hyphenation of the word. If you prefer to hyphenate the word at a position other than that offered by Word (this often happens with technical jargon that doesn't appear in the spelling dictionary), use the arrow keys to move the insertion point to that location, and then choose **Yes**. When the manual hyphenation process is complete, a dialog box appears stating that hyphenation is complete. Click **OK** to return to your document.

If you selected **Automatically hyphenate document** in the Hyphenation dialog box, and then you continue entering new text, Word automatically hyphenates line endings each time it wraps text to the next line. It does so even if you closed the Hyphenation dialog box by choosing **Manual**.

On the other hand, if you did not select **Automatically hyphenate document**, but closed the dialog box by choosing **Manual**, then Word only does the prompted hyphenation. When it is finished with that, if you enter new text into the document, Word does not automatically hyphenate line endings as you type.

Use Nonbreaking Spaces to Control Line Breaks

Because Word breaks lines at spaces or hyphens, it may separate words that you want to be kept on the same line, such as a person's first and last name.

To prevent two words from being separated onto different lines, use a *nonbreaking space*. A nonbreaking space has the same appearance as any other space in your text, but Word won't treat it as a space when it determines where to wrap a line of text to the next line. The two words on either side of the nonbreaking space stay together on the same line.

To use a nonbreaking space in your text, position your insertion point where you want to put the nonbreaking space and then do one of the following:

- Open the **Insert** menu and select **Symbol**. Select the **Special Characters** tab (see Figure 6.11) and then click **Nonbreaking Space** to select it. Click **Insert** and then click **Close** to exit the dialog box.
- Press Ctrl+Shift+Space.

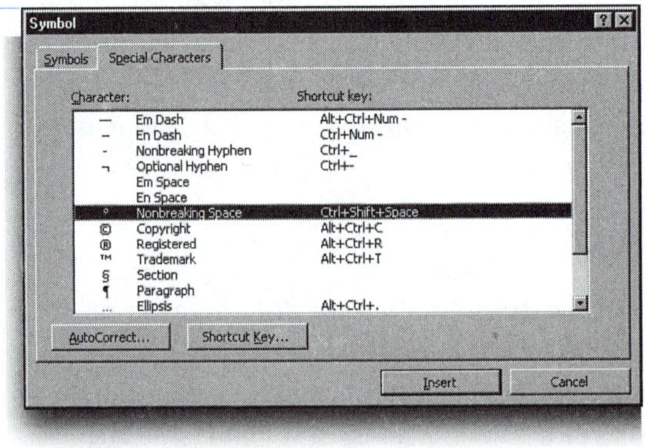

FIGURE 6.11
Use **Special Characters** to insert typesetting characters, such as the nonbreaking space.

Insert Page Breaks

Word automatically creates a new page when the text you are entering reaches the bottom margin of the current page. However, you can also create page breaks in your document.

To insert a *page break*, place your insertion point where you want to start the new page and then do one of the following:

- Open the **Insert** menu, and select **Break**. Click **Page break** in the Break dialog box (see Figure 6.12) and click **OK**.
- Press Ctrl+Enter.

FIGURE 6.12
To start a new page, click **Page break** and then click **OK**.

In Page Layout view, you can clearly see the end of one page and the beginning of another. In Normal view, automatic page breaks appear as dotted lines that stretch across the page while manual page breaks display as a dotted line with the notation "Page Break" in the middle (see Figure 6.13).

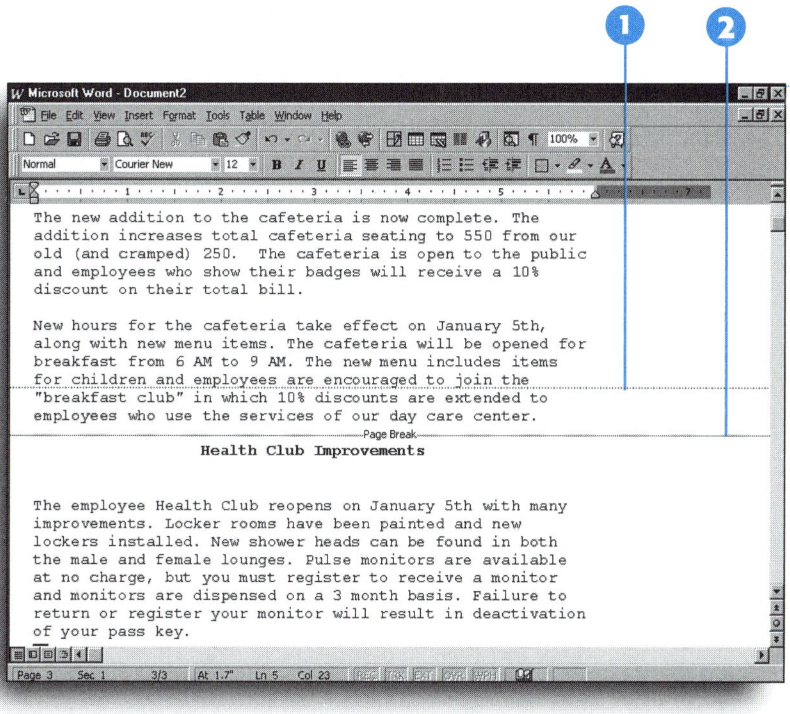

FIGURE 6.13
The page break you insert looks like a dotted line with "Page Break" in the middle when seen in Normal view.

1. Automatic page break
2. Manual page break

To remove a manual page break, click to place your insertion point on the break line and then press the Delete key. Or, place your insertion point immediately after the page break and press Backspace. Inserting a manual page break, of course, affects the automatic page breaks that follow it, causing them to be repositioned.

Use Pagination Tools to Control Page and Column Breaks

Word normally inserts page breaks automatically, based on the paper and margin sizes you select, so that text fills each page from margin to margin. You can prevent Word from inserting page breaks in or between certain paragraphs. For example, you might not want page breaks to appear between headings and the body text that follows them. Or you might not want a page break to appear within a list. Finally, you can cause a page break to occur whenever a certain kind of paragraph appears.

Keeping the First and Last Lines with a Paragraph

A document of more than one page or column may contain a paragraph that begins its first line or column on page one and continues the rest of the paragraph on page two. This single line of text at the bottom of the first page or column is called an *orphan*.

When all the lines of the paragraph except the last one are on one page or column, and the last line is on the next page or column, the single line on the next page or column is a called a *widow*.

Leaving widows and orphans is considered to be poor page layout. By default, Word prevents widows and orphans from occurring in your text. In the case of an orphan, Word moves the first line of the paragraph to the next page or column. Where a widow occurs, Word moves the previous line in the paragraph to the next page or column to join the widow line, so that two lines of the paragraph appear at the top of the next page or column. Either way leaves a blank line at the bottom of the page or column, so that the bottom margin won't be even with the bottom margin of the other pages or columns in your document.

Turn off automatic widow and orphan control

1. Select the paragraph to control then click the **Format** menu, and select **Paragraph**, or right-click and then click **Paragraph**, to open the Paragraph dialog box.
2. Select the **Line and Page Breaks** tab (see Figure 6.14).
3. Click **Widow/Orphan control** under **Pagination** to deselect the option.
4. Click **OK**.

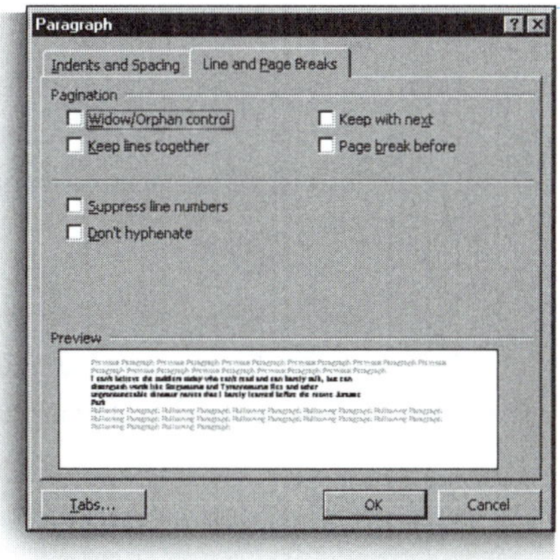

FIGURE 6.14
You can control the flow of text in your document by selecting one of the Pagination options.

Widow and orphan control is an alternative to using the tried and true system of editing the text to eliminate the problem, which is more precise but far more time-consuming.

Prevent a Page Break Within a Paragraph

You can specify that a paragraph not be split by a column or page break.

Prevent page breaks or column breaks within a paragraph

1. Select the paragraph or paragraphs you want to keep from breaking.
2. Click the **Format** menu and select **Paragraph**, or right-click and then click **Paragraph** to open the Paragraph dialog box.
3. Click the **Line and Page Breaks** tab (refer to Figure 6.14).
4. Under **Pagination**, click **Keep lines together**.
5. Click **OK**.

If you set this for multiple consecutive paragraphs, Word does not insert a page or column break within any of the paragraphs. But it might insert a page or column break between the paragraphs.

Keeping Multiple Paragraphs Together

You may not want a page or column break to separate two paragraphs from each other. For example, you never want a heading to appear at the bottom of a page, without any text following it.

Keep two paragraphs together

1. Make sure the insertion point is in the heading paragraph.
2. Open the **Format** menu and select **Paragraph**, or right-click and then click **Paragraph** to open the Paragraph dialog box.
3. Click the **Line and Page Breaks** tab (refer to Figure 6.14).
4. Under **Pagination**, click **Keep with next**.
5. Click **OK**.

Forcing Page Breaks At Headings

In a long document with multiple main headings, you might want each main heading to appear at the top of a new page.

Start a new page for a new heading

1. Make sure the insertion point is in the heading paragraph.
2. Open the **Format** menu and select **Paragraph**, or right-click and then click **Paragraph** to open the Paragraph dialog box.
3. Click the **Line and Page Breaks** tab (refer to Figure 6.14).
4. Under **Pagination**, click **Page break before**.
5. Click **OK**.

Typically, you would use this feature as part of the definition of a paragraph style.

SEE ALSO

➤ *Learn more about paragraph styles, see page 159*

CHAPTER

7

Work with Lists

Create numbered or bulleted lists

Sort lists

Create a Numbered or Bulleted List

Lists help to organize and clarify your writing. Bulleted lists clearly set forth the points you want to make. Numbered lists set forth the order of action or importance. Multilevel lists organize more complex ideas. Word makes it easy by automatically applying the proper paragraph formatting to your bulleted and numbered paragraphs. Word indents the paragraphs for you, applies the number or bullet style to each new paragraph as you type, and adjusts the number sequence automatically when you add or subtract items.

Start a numbered or bulleted list as you are entering text

1. Position your insertion point where you want the first bulleted or numbered item to appear.
2. Choose Bullets or Numbering from the Formatting toolbar.

Word automatically inserts the first bullet or number, properly punctuated and tabbed (see Figure 7.1), and sets up the paragraph formatting with a hanging indent (a paragraph where all the lines are indented except the first line). When you press Enter at the end of the paragraph, a new bullet or the next number appears at the beginning of the next paragraph. This happens each time you press Enter.

You can discontinue the bullets or numbering two ways:

- Press Enter twice at the end of the last paragraph in the list. The first time you press Enter, a new, bulleted/numbered paragraph appears. The second time you press enter, a new, standard paragraph appears and the bullet/number formatting disappears from the blank paragraph above.
- Press Enter, then Backspace. Pressing Enter creates a new bulleted or numbered paragraph. Pressing Backspace removes the bullet or number and causes the paragraph to revert to normal paragraph formatting, but does not remove the paragraph entirely. Pressing Backspace a second time would remove the paragraph and move the insertion point to the end of the preceding paragraph.

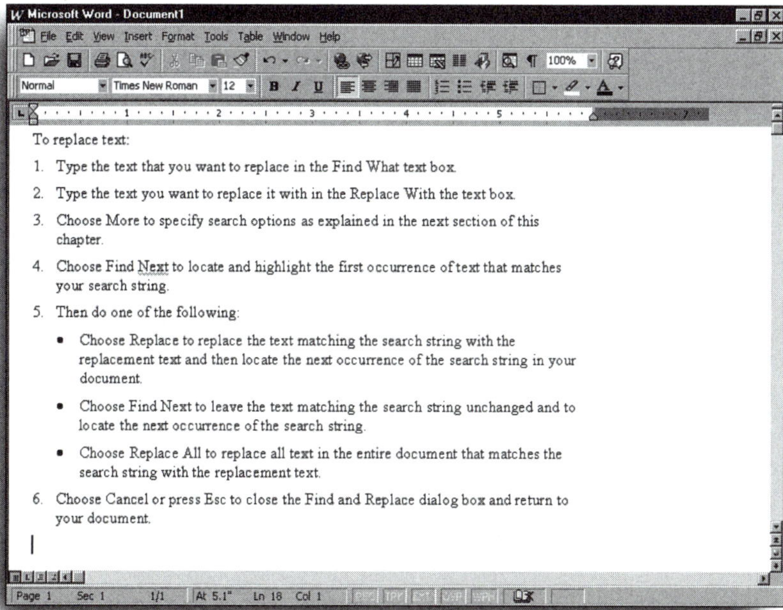

FIGURE 7.1

Bulleted lists are generally used for lists of items, while numbered lists work well for steps that must be done in order or paragraphs that must be assigned a value (such as priority).

If you are still in the habit of pressing Enter twice to insert whitespace between paragraphs, then the action described in the first bullet point initially thwarts your effort to create a bulleted or numbered list, because your bulleting/numbering disappears as you press Enter the second time. However, if Word is *AutoFormatting* a numbered list for you, you can make Word add the extra carriage return. Start the numbering and press Enter twice at the end of the first item paragraph. Then, for the second item in your list, restart the numbering. Thereafter, when you press Enter once, Word automatically inserts two hard returns for you after each numbered paragraph.

Word AutoFormats lists by default. If Word does not behave as described previously, perhaps list AutoFormatting has been turned off. Turn it on again by opening the **Format** menu, then selecting **AutoFormat**, and then **Options** from the submenu. You also can select the **Tools** menu, and then choose **AutoCorrect.** In the AutoCorrect dialog box that opens, select the **AutoFormat** tab. Make sure a check mark appears in the **Lists** check box in the **Apply** section of the dialog box. You

AutoFormat starts numbered lists for you

Word automatically starts a numbered list if you type a number followed by a period, hyphen, closing parenthesis, or greater than sign and then type a space or tab and more text.

AutoFormat starts bulleted lists for you

When you type an asterisk, one or two hyphens, a greater than sign, or an arrow created by a greater than sign and a hyphen or equal sign, Word starts a bulleted list. Word also turns a symbol or an inline graphic (a picture that's treated like a character) followed by two or more spaces into the start of a bulleted list.

should also click the **AutoFormat as You Type** tab and check both **Automatic bulleted lists** and **Automatic numbered lists** under **Apply as you type**.

When you need to apply bullets or numbers to existing text, select the paragraphs that will constitute the bulleted or numbered paragraphs, then click the Bullets or Numbering icon on the Formatting toolbar. Word automatically reformats the selected paragraphs and bullets them or numbers them in order. If you have two hard returns between paragraphs, you'll discover that Word is clever enough not to bullet or number the blank paragraphs between each of your bulleted/numbered paragraphs.

SEE ALSO

- *Adding spacing between paragraphs without adding extra carriage returns, see page 132*
- *Learn more about AutoFormat and controlling AutoFormat options, see page 169*

Edit a Numbered or Bulleted List

Add new items to an existing bulleted or numbered list

1. Position the insertion point at the end of the paragraph after which you want to add the new item.
2. Press Enter. A new paragraph appears with a new bullet or number. Word automatically renumbers any subsequent numbered paragraphs.
3. Type the new text. If you press Enter at the end of the paragraph, a new bulleted or numbered paragraph starts.
4. Repeat steps 1 through 3 as many times as needed.

To delete a bulleted or numbered paragraph from a list, select the paragraph and press Delete. Any subsequent numbered paragraphs are automatically renumbered. Word also renumbers the list if you move paragraphs within a numbered list.

If you interrupt the list with paragraphs that don't have bullets or numbering, and then you want to continue the list from where you left off, do one of the following:

- For bulleted lists, click where you want the new paragraph to begin and choose Bullets from the Formatting toolbar.
- For numbered lists, click where you want the new paragraph to begin. Open the **Format** menu, and select **Bullets and Numbering** or right-click and select **Bullets and Numbering** to open the Bullets and Numbering dialog box. Select the **Numbered** tab, and then select the numbering style you are using in the list. Select **Continue previous list** and then click **OK**.

To restart the numbering in a list at 1, click **Restart numbering** in the Bullets and Numbering dialog box.

Use Multilevel Lists

You use a *multilevel list* when you need two or more levels of bullets or numbering in the same list. Examples of multilevel lists include numbered outlines and a bulleted list within a bulleted list.

In a multilevel list, such as the one shown in Figure 7.2, the numbers or bullets are assigned to paragraphs based on how far they're indented from the left margin. A Level 1 paragraph is on the left margin, a Level 2 paragraph is indented 1/4 inch from the left margin, a Level 3 paragraph is indented 1/2 inch from the left margin, and so on. All the Level 1 paragraphs share the same style bullet or number, all the Level 2 paragraphs share the same style (although different from what is used at Level 1), and so on. For example, in the traditional outline style, the Level 1 paragraphs have Roman numerals (I, II, III), the Level 2 paragraphs have capital letters (A, B, C), and the Level 3 paragraphs have Arabic numerals (1, 2, 3).

Create a multilevel list as you type the list

1. Open the **Format** menu, and select **Bullets and Numbering** to open the Bullets and Numbering dialog box.
2. Click the **Outline Numbered** tab (see Figure 7.3).

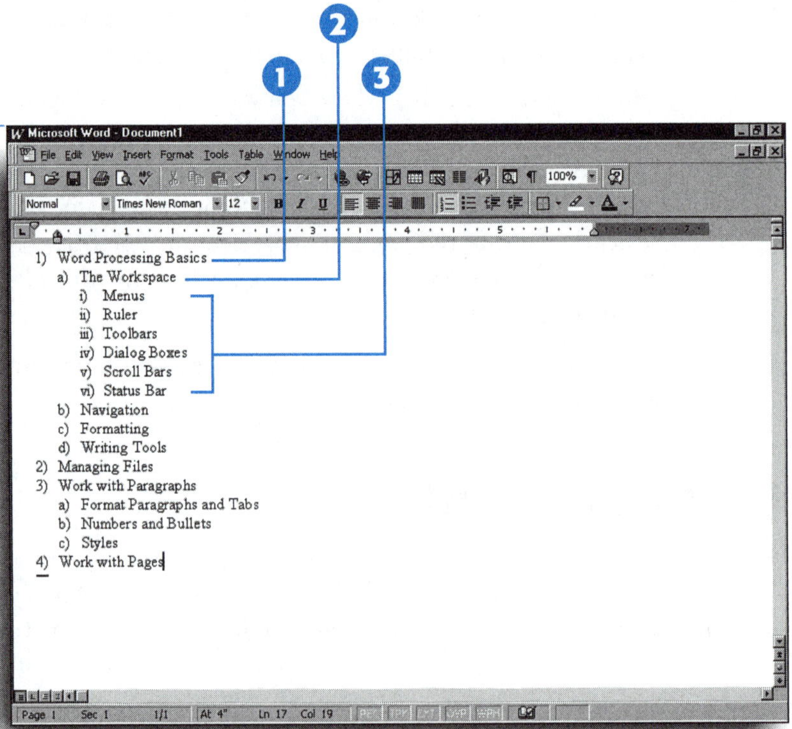

FIGURE 7.2

This multilevel list has different numbers and letters for each item based on how far the paragraph is indented from the left margin.

1. Level 1
2. Level 2
3. Level 3

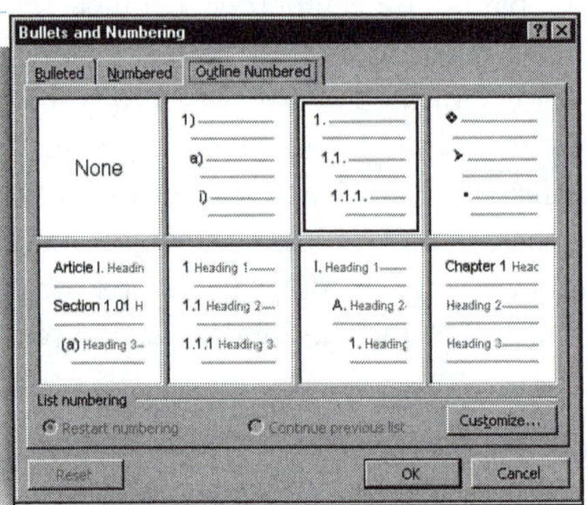

FIGURE 7.3

Select the style of multilevel list you want and then choose **OK**.

3. Select the style of numbering/lettering or bullets you want.
4. Click **OK**.

When you type the list, press Enter at the end of each paragraph. The next paragraph will have the same number, letter, or bullet style as the one above it. To demote a paragraph to a lower level number/bullet style (for example, to change a Level 1 paragraph to a Level 2 paragraph), or promote it to a higher level (for example, to change a Level 2 paragraph to a Level 1 paragraph), do the following:

- *Demote*. Press Tab or choose Increase Indent from the Formatting toolbar.
- *Promote*. Press Shift+Tab or choose Decrease Indent from the Formatting toolbar.

After you type the last paragraph in the list, press Enter, and then choose Numbering from the Formatting toolbar to end the list or press Enter twice; or, press Enter, then Backspace. Any of these actions terminate the list.

SEE ALSO

➤ *To learn more about styles, see page 157*

Tabs don't work

Not all the outline numbering styles work when you use the Tab key to set the levels. When that happens, try the Increase Indent or Decrease Indent buttons on the Formatting toolbar. The traditional outline style (I, A, 1, a) automatically assigns heading styles to the paragraphs. Change the style of all the paragraphs to Normal and the numbering should work.

Convert existing text into a multilevel list and modify list styles

1. Select all the paragraphs that you want to include in the list.
2. Open the **Format** menu, and select **Bullets and Numbering** on the menu.
3. When the Bullets and Numbering dialog box appears, select the **Outline Numbered** tab.
4. Select a multilevel style and then click **OK**.
5. Move the insertion point to the beginning of an item in the list whose level you want to change.
6. Press Tab or click Increase Indent on the Formatting toolbar to demote the item. Press Shift+Tab or click Decrease Indent on the Formatting toolbar to promote the item.
7. Repeat steps 5 and 6 as needed to set the different levels for each paragraph in the list.

Remove Numbers and Bullets

When you no longer need the numberings or bullets but want to retain text, select the paragraphs from which you want to remove the bullets or numbering and click Bullets or Numbering on the Formatting toolbar.

Change Number or Bullet Formatting

When you apply bullets or numbers to your paragraphs, Word applies its *default* formatting. For a bulleted paragraph, this means that Word places a round bullet on the left margin and indents the rest of the paragraph 1/4 inch. For a numbered paragraph, it means that Word places an Arabic number and a period on the left margin and indents the rest of the paragraph 1/4 inch.

Change the bullet or number style of existing lists

1. Select the paragraphs to which you want to apply the bullets or numbering; or, if creating new paragraphs, place the insertion point where you begin typing.
2. Click the **Format** menu, and select **Bullets and Numbering** or right-click and select **Bullets and Numbering** to open the Bullets and Numbering dialog box (see Figure 7.4).

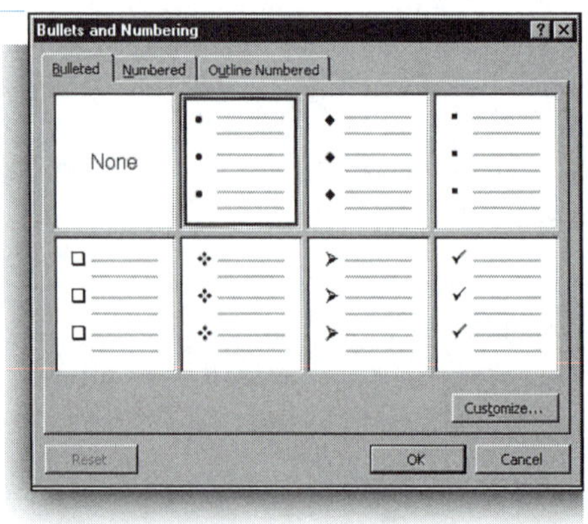

FIGURE 7.4
Select the style of bullets you want to use by clicking in the appropriate preview box.

3. Click the **Bulleted** tab and click the desired style to change the style of bullets. Select **None** to remove bullets.

   Click the **Numbered** tab and select the desired numbering style (see Figure 7.5), or click **None** to remove the numbering from the list.

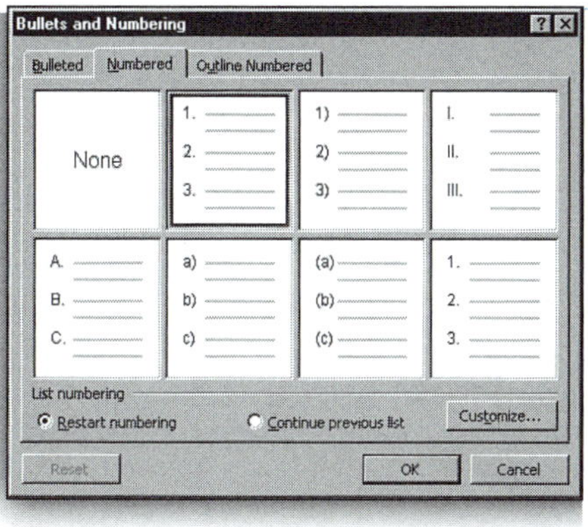

FIGURE 7.5
Select the style of numbering that you want to use by clicking in the appropriate preview box.

4. Click **OK**.

If none of the number or bullet styles offered by Word meets your needs, you can create your own number styles or select different symbols for your bulleted lists.

Create custom numbering styles

1. Position your insertion point where you want the numbered list to start or select the existing paragraphs to which you want to apply the numbering.
2. Open the **Format** menu, and select **Bullets and Numbering** on the menu to open the Bullets and Numbering dialog box.
3. Click the **Numbered** tab or the **Outline Numbered** tab.
4. Click **Customize**.
5. The Customize Numbered List dialog box (see Figure 7.6) or Customize Outline Numbered List dialog box appears (see Figure 7.7).

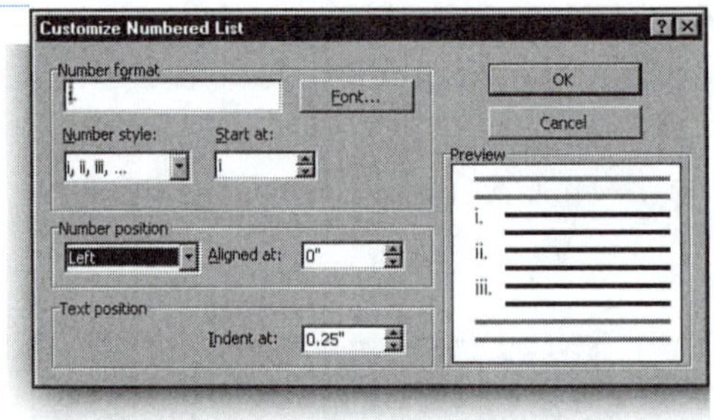

FIGURE 7.6

Set the options to create your own numbering style for your list.

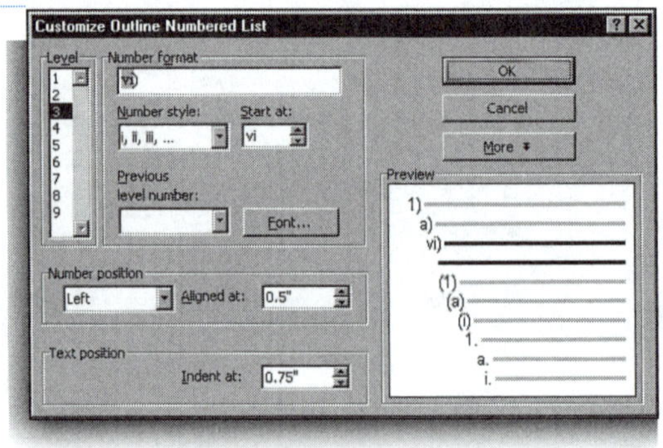

FIGURE 7.7

Set the style options for each level of numbering your multi-level list uses.

6. Set the options to customize your list:

   For numbered lists, choose **Font** to set the font options for the numbers. Select a **Number style** from the drop-down list and specify what number or letter to **Start at**. Select the alignment of the paragraph under **Number position** and set the **Aligned at** position, and specify the number of inches the paragraph text is indented in the **Indent at** box.

   For outline numbered lists, you must specify options for each level. Select the **Level** (you can have as many as nine) and then set the options as you would for numbered lists.

7. Click **OK**.

Select a different symbol for your bulleted list

1. Position your insertion point where you want the bulleted list to start or select the existing paragraphs to which you want to apply the bullets.

2. Open the **Format** menu, and select **Bullets and Numbering** to open the Bullets and Numbering dialog box.
3. Click the **Bulleted** tab.
4. Choose **Customize**.
5. The Customize Bulleted List dialog box appears (see Figure 7.8).

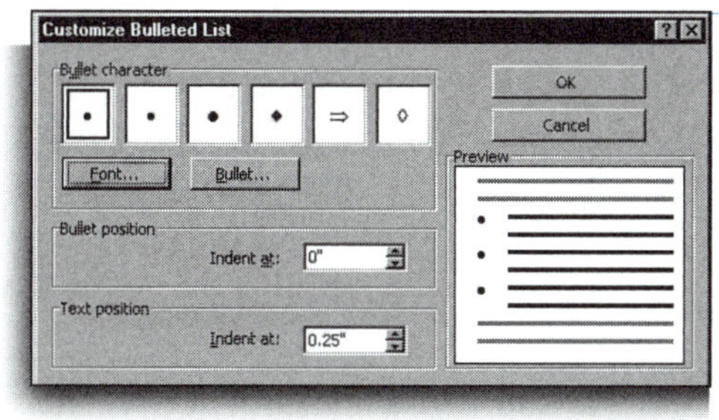

FIGURE 7.8
Select a bullet style and set font and position options in the Customize Bulleted List dialog box.

6. Set the options to customize your list:
   - Select a **Bullet character** from the bullet styles shown.
   - Click **Font** to change the font options (such as size or bold) for the bullet symbol.
   - Click **Bullet** to open the Symbol dialog box (see Figure 7.9). Select an appropriate symbol font from the **Font** box, click the symbol you want to use (hold down your mouse button on a symbol to magnify it), and click **OK**. The symbol replaces whichever **Bullet character** is currently selected.

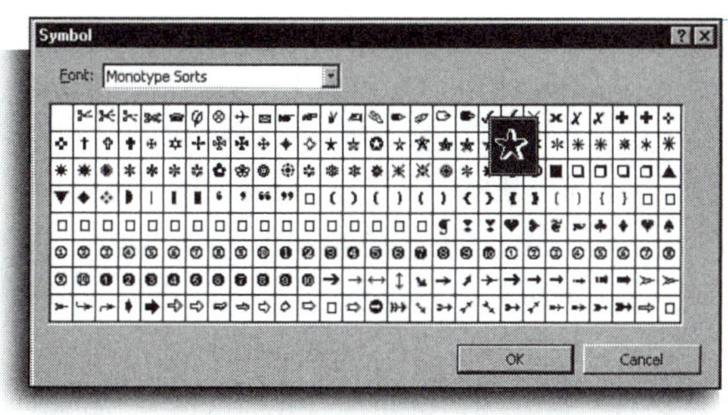

FIGURE 7.9
Select a font that has the symbol you need and then click the symbol you want to use.

- Set the position of the bullet relative to the left margin by specifying the number of inches in the **Indent at** box under **Bullet position**.
- Specify the left indentation of the following lines of text in the **Indent at** box under **Text position**.

7. Click **OK**.

Sort Lists

When Microsoft Word sorts text, rules govern the sort order. It helps to understand how Word sorts text:

- You choose whether you want to sort alphabetically, numerically, or by date.
- You have a choice of sorting in ascending order (A to Z or zero to nine) or in descending order (Z to A or nine to zero).
- Paragraph marks (¶) separate items to be sorted. Tabs separate fields within each item.
- Items beginning with punctuation marks or symbols (such as !, #, $, %, or &) are sorted first, followed by items beginning with numbers and then by items beginning with letters. Dates are treated as three-digit numbers.
- If the sort is by numbers, all other characters are ignored. The numbers can be anywhere in a paragraph.
- If the sort is by date, only the following are accepted as date separators: a hyphen (-), a forward slash (/), comma (,), and period (.). Only the colon (:) is recognized as a time separator. If the item isn't recognized as a date or time, Word puts the item at the beginning or end of the list (depending on whether the list is sorted in ascending or descending order).
- When more than one item begins with the same character, Word looks to subsequent characters to determine the sort order.

Paragraph marks make a list

You don't necessarily have to set out text in a "list" format to use Word's sorting feature. Because Word defines list items as text followed by paragraph marks (hard returns), any set of paragraphs can be sorted as a list.

We find sorting lists convenient because we enter text in whatever order is easiest, and then sort the list. Word sorts lists by the first word in the list, unless you have tabs separating columns of items. In that case Word considers the tabs as field markers (a *field* is a single piece of information, usually associated with databases, which in this case refers to the text in a particular tabbed column). The text in the first column is considered Field 1, the text in the second column is Field 2, and so on. That way it's possible to sort based on the second or subsequent column items instead of the first word of the line.

SEE ALSO

➤ *Learn more about fields and sorting, see page 408*

Sort a list

1. Select the text you want to sort. Each item in the list should be on a separate line. Related items on the same line should be separated by tabs.
2. Click the **Table** menu, and select **Sort**. The Sort Text dialog box appears (see Figure 7.10).

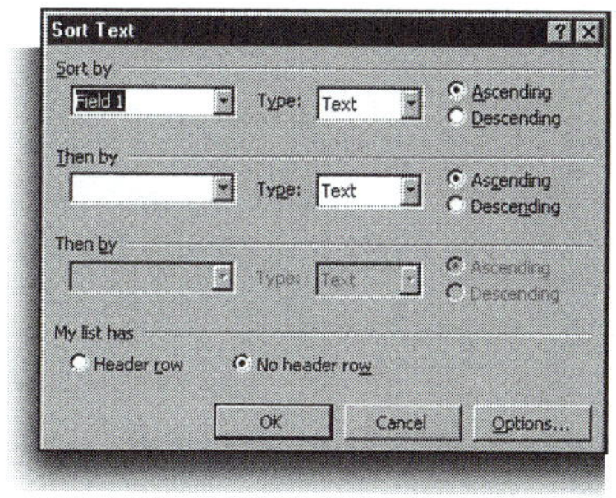

FIGURE 7.10
For a tabbed list, select the field by which you want to sort.

3. From the **Sort by** drop-down list, select **Field 1** if you want to sort the lines based on the first word on each line, select **Field 2** if you want to sort the lines based on the text in the second tabbed column, and so on. If the items in the list don't have tabbed columns or you don't want to use the tabs as field separators, select **Paragraphs** (especially if the items have more than one line in the paragraph).
4. From the **Type** drop-down list, select **Text** to sort the list alphabetically, **Number** to sort numerically, or **Date** to sort by date or time.

Sorting tabbed columns

It can get a little difficult to keep track of which text is in Field 1 and which is in Field 2 when you have a list with tabbed columns. An easier way to handle this is to convert the text to a table and then sort the table text. You can convert the text back to tabbed columns after sorting.

5. Click **Ascending** to sort the list in A to Z, 0 to 99 order. Click **Descending** to sort the list in Z to A, 99 to 0 order.
6. When you choose a field for the first (primary) sort, the **Then by** drop-down list is available. This lets you set a secondary sort criteria so if two items in the first sort are the same, the secondary sort sets the order. For example, if you have a list with last name, first name, and phone number for a set of people, you would sort alphabetically by last name. However, if you have two Smiths, you would want Ellen Smith to come before John Smith, so you want the secondary sort to be by first name. Select the options for the **Then by** sort the same way you did for the primary sort.
7. If your list has a line of column titles, select **Header row** under **My list has** in order to avoid including that line in the sorting.
8. Click **OK**.

SEE ALSO

➤ *Learn how to convert tabbed text to tables and how to sort tables, see page 291*

CHAPTER 8

Format Using Styles

Create and assign paragraph and character styles

Modify styles

Use automatic formatting

Use Styles for Consistency and Efficiency

Styles make formatting documents easier. Styles eliminate the tedium of repeating the same formatting tasks over and over. A *style* is a set of formatting commands saved under a single name, and each time you want to apply those same commands to another text selection you only have to call up that name.

For instance, when you format a heading so that it is 24-point Times New Roman bold, centered, and colored blue, each time you create a new heading that you want formatted in the same way, you must reformat. Alternately, you can save the formatting as a style, and select the style name from the Style list on the Formatting toolbar to apply that same formatting to the text.

Using styles is not only faster but also ensures a consistent look throughout your document. You are assured that all paragraphs with a given style assigned to them are formatted identically.

Plus, if you need to change the formatting of all your headings, you can change the style definition and the new formatting is applied to all the text assigned that style. You don't have to work through the document changing one paragraph at a time with the attendant risk that you will miss a paragraph or make a mistake.

Also, because Word lets you base one style on another you can create families of styles. For example, you may have three different heading styles for different types of headings. Main Head is the main heading style. Subhead 1 is for lower-level headings and is based on the Main Head style. Subhead 2 is for the lowest-level headings and is based on the Subhead 1 style. After the document is written, you may decide to change the font of headings from Times New Roman to Arial. You make that change to Main Head. Because Subhead 1 is based on Main Head, and Subhead 2 is based on Subhead 1, the new font affects them as well. So you have changed the font of every paragraph heading in the document with a single change.

The two types of styles in Word are

- *Paragraph styles.* These affect entire paragraphs. Every paragraph has a style; the default style is called Normal.
- *Character styles.* These affect portions of text that are not necessarily paragraphs and affect only the character formatting of the selected text. Word doesn't have a default character style.

Assign Paragraph Styles

Paragraph styles can include both character and paragraph formatting definitions—font, size, color, font styles (bold, italic, underline), font effects (subscript, superscript, small caps, strikethrough, and so on), as well as shaded backgrounds and borders, indents, alignment, line and paragraph spacing, and so on.

Apply paragraph styles

1. To apply a style to existing text, select the paragraph or paragraphs to which you want to assign the style (or place your insertion point in the paragraph to affect only that paragraph). If you want to apply a style when entering new text, place your insertion point where you want the newly styled text to appear.
2. Choose a style from the Style list on the Formatting toolbar. When you click the down arrow next to the Style box, you see each style name displayed in the style's font. The symbols to the right of the style name indicate whether the style is a paragraph or a character style and show the font size and paragraph alignment of the style (see Figure 8.1).
3. Click the name of the style you want to apply to the selected paragraph(s).

Faster navigation

If you apply heading styles in your document, you can navigate quickly through your document using the *Document Map*. This is an outline listing of the document's headings, in a separate pane to the left of your document window. To turn it on, click the **View** menu, and select **Document Map**. Move your insertion point to a part of the document by clicking the heading for it in the Document Map.

Styles are applied to entire paragraphs

You don't have to select the entire paragraph to apply a paragraph style. Select a part of a paragraph, or place your cursor in the paragraph before you select the style, and the style will be applied to the entire paragraph. This is true for paragraph styles only, not character styles.

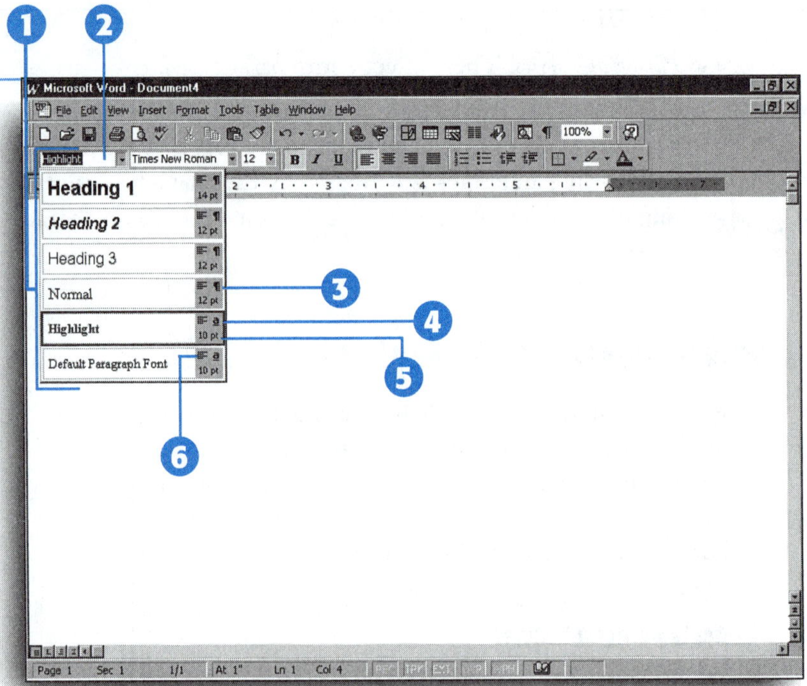

FIGURE 8.1

Paragraph styles display a paragraph mark next to them; character styles show an underlined letter "a" next to them.

1. Style list
2. Style name
3. Paragraph style symbol
4. Character style symbol
5. Font size
6. Alignment symbol

Assign Character Styles

Character styles add to the current formatting of text. For example, if the text is 12-point Arial italic and your character style applies bold and strikethrough, the text to which you apply the character style will be 12-point Arial bold, italic, and strikethrough.

Assign a character style

1. To apply a style to existing text, select the text to which you want to assign the style. If you want to apply a style as you are entering new text, place your insertion point where you want the newly styled text to appear.
2. Choose a style from the Style list on the Formatting toolbar. When you click the down arrow next to the Style box, you see each style name displayed in the style's font. An underlined "a" indicates a character style (refer to Figure 8.1).
3. Click the name of the style you want to use to apply the style to the selected text.

When you want to remove the character style from selected text, apply the character style Default Paragraph Font. The text reverts to the formatting defined in the paragraph style assigned to the paragraph in which the selected text is located.

View Style Names

Word displays the name of the paragraph style of selected text (or text where your insertion point is located) in the Style list on the Formatting toolbar. When the selected text has a character style applied to it, the Style box on the Formatting toolbar displays the character style name.

View formatting applied to text

1. From the **Help** menu, select **What's This?**, or press Shift+F1 to activate What's This Help. The mouse pointer looks like a question mark.
2. Click in the text. A balloon appears with information about character and paragraph formatting (see Figure 8.2).

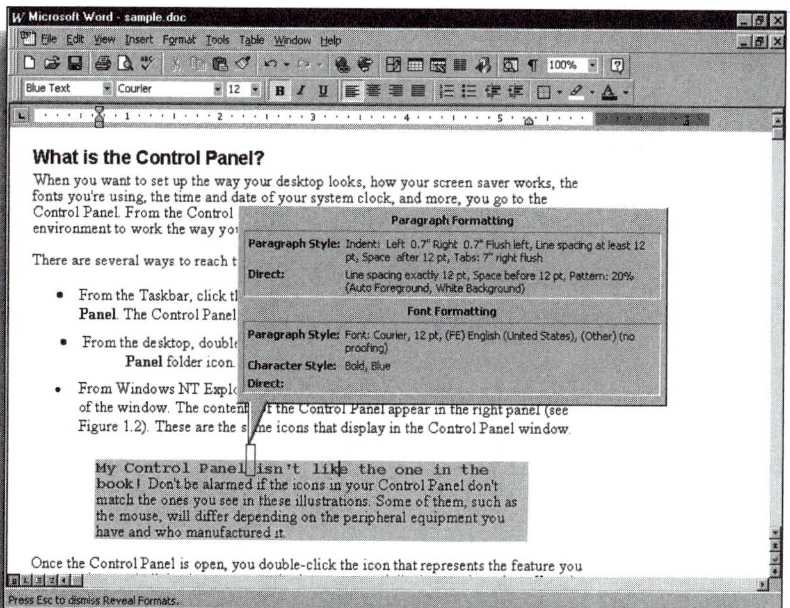

FIGURE 8.2
Click in the text with the What's This? mouse pointer to see the applied character and paragraph formatting.

3. Repeat step 2 as needed for other text.
4. Press Esc to turn off the What's This? pointer.

View the names of paragraph styles next to the document window

1. Switch to Normal view (click the **View** menu, and select **Normal** or choose **Normal View** from the View buttons at the bottom left of your screen).
2. Click the **Tools** menu, and then select **Options.**
3. When the Options dialog box appears, click the **View** tab (see Figure 8.3).

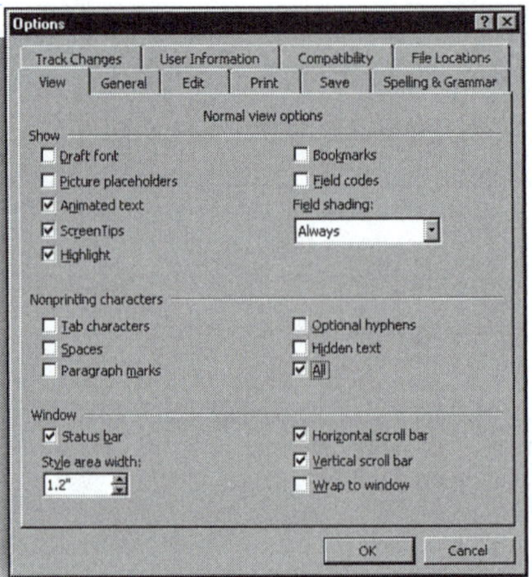

FIGURE 8.3
Increase the **Style area width** to create the style area pane next to your document window.

4. In the **Window** section, change the **Style area width** to a positive number (such as 1 inch).
5. Click **OK**. A style area pane appears on the left side of the document, and the style names of the paragraphs in your document show in that pane (see Figure 8.4).

The style area pane only appears when you are in Normal view.

If you want to resize the style area, drag the border left or right.

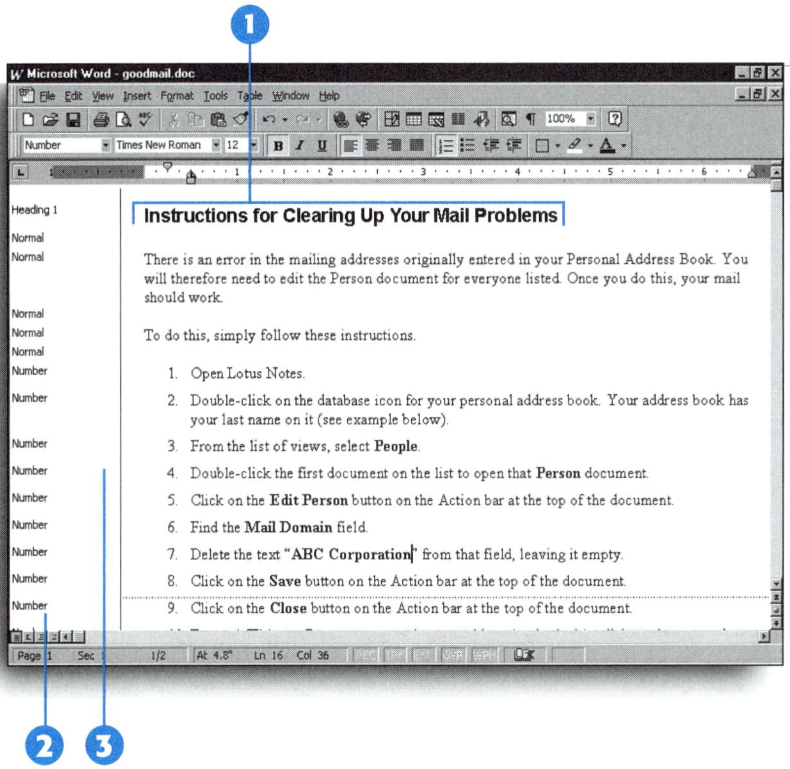

FIGURE 8.4

The style area pane shows the styles of the paragraphs to the right.

1. Paragraph with Heading 1 style
2. Style name
3. Style Area pane

Use Word's Default Styles

Word provides a set of predefined styles, some of which it automatically applies to your text as you write. Other styles you must apply manually. If your document doesn't have any special or unusual formatting, you can use just the predefined styles. If you don't like the way they are formatted, you can either reformat the text directly or redefine the styles to your liking.

The predefined styles include a default paragraph style called *Normal*, a set of heading paragraph styles called Heading 1 through Heading 9, and styles for special types of text, such as headers, footers, and footnotes. When you create a new document using the default *template* (normal.dot), you can see some of these styles in the style list. Others only appear in the style list after you create a paragraph of the type that the style governs.

Word templates

All Word documents are based on templates, which are separate Word document files to which Word assigns the extension .dot. Besides the default template, normal.dot, that Word assigns to all new, blank documents that you create, Word also provides a series of special templates. If you want to create a letter, a memo, or a report, you can use templates that Word provides just for those types of documents. Those templates include additional styles for the special types of paragraphs included in those types of documents.

To see what we mean, try this exercise. Create a new document using the New icon on the Standard toolbar. Unless you have made changes to the program, Word automatically bases the new document on the default template (normal.dot). Now open the style list (click the arrow next to the word *Normal* in the toolbar). You will see five styles listed: Normal, Headline 1, Headline 2, Headline 3, and Default Paragraph Font. The first four are paragraph styles, the last is a character style. If you see additional styles, then changes have been made to your normal.dot template.

Normal is the default paragraph style that Word automatically applies to all paragraphs in the body of your document. Enter some text in your document. As you create a few paragraphs, notice that the word "Normal" always appears in the Style box on the toolbar. Your document might look like the one in Figure 8.5.

FIGURE 8.5
Create this document to test Word's predefined styles.

Now move the insertion point into one of your paragraphs and choose Heading 1 in the style list. You'll see the word *Heading 1* appear in the style box.

Assign the styles *Heading 2* and *Heading 3* to the same paragraph. Notice that each time you assign a new style, the formatting of that paragraph changes to reflect the definition of the new style.

Click the **View** menu, and select **Header and Footer**. (This is what you do to create a header or footer.) Notice that the word Header appears in the style box. Open the style list again.

Notice that now two new styles, Header and Footer, appear in the list. Word added the two new styles and assigned them to the header and footer paragraphs that you haven't even typed yet.

If you add a footnote, a table of contents, or any number of other predefined constructs to your document, you will notice that Word automatically adds one or more predefined styles to the text you added. And each new style is preformatted for you. If you don't like the formatting that Word assigned to your Heading 1 paragraph, you can reformat the paragraph directly or you can redefine the style and Word automatically reformats your paragraph (and all others based on the style) in accordance with your redefinition of the style.

SEE ALSO

➤ *Learn more about Word templates, see page 238*

➤ *Create headers and footers, see page 187*

Create and Apply a New Style

If the predefined formats don't meet your needs, you can create your own styles. The two methods to create styles are by using current formatting as an example or by specifying options in the Style dialog box.

Create a new style from existing formatted text

1. Select a paragraph to which you want to apply the new style.
2. Apply the formatting to the paragraph that you want included in the new style definition. You can include both paragraph and character attributes such as font, bold, italic, and so forth.
3. With the insertion point anywhere in the paragraph, click in the **Style** box on the Formatting toolbar (or press Ctrl+Shift+S) to highlight the current style name.
4. Type the new style name and press Enter.

You can't create character styles using the method outlined previously—only paragraph styles. To create a character style, you have to use the Style dialog box. This is also an alternative method for creating paragraph styles.

The current style overwrote my new formatting!

Don't enter the name of an existing style when you create your new style. If you do, that style's formatting is applied to the paragraph and the formatting changes you made are lost. If this happens, you can recover the formatting by choosing the **Edit** menu, and selecting **Undo**. Then repeat steps 3 and 4 with a new name.

Creating character styles

1. Open the **Format** menu, and select **Style** to open the Style dialog box (see Figure 8.6).

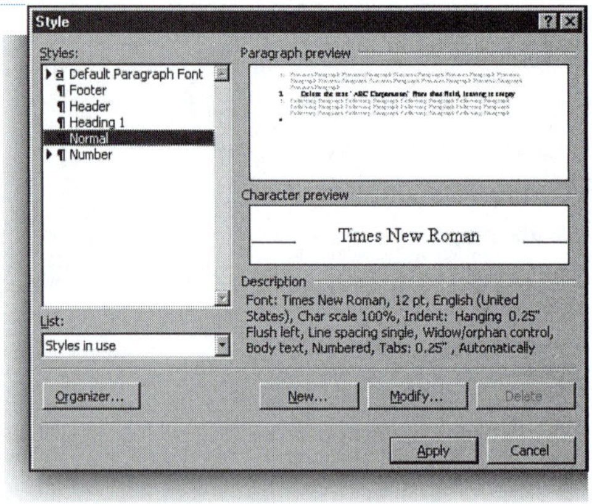

FIGURE 8.6
The Style dialog box previews the style you select from the **Styles** list.

2. Click **New**. The New Style dialog box appears (see Figure 8.7).

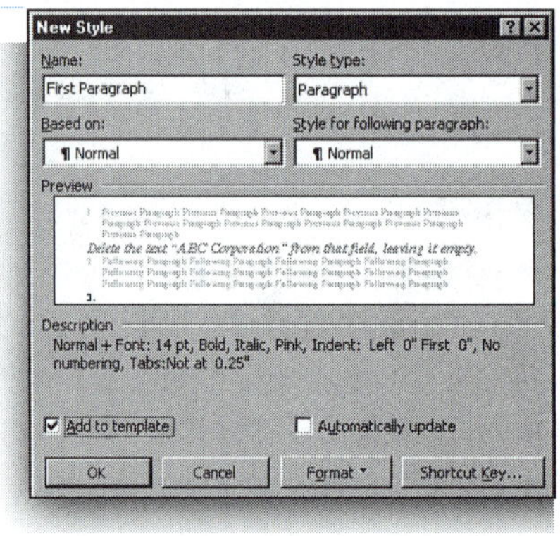

FIGURE 8.7
Specify the name of your new style and select the style type.

3. In the **Name** text box, enter the name for the new style.
4. From the **Style type** drop-down list, select **Character** or **Paragraph**.
5. If you want to base the new style on an existing style, select the base style you want to use from the **Based on** drop-down list. The new style is identical to the base style, except for changes you make in the definition of the new style. Changes you make to the base style also affect the new style,

as long as the change to the base style does not conflict with a defined attribute of the new style.

6. If paragraphs of this style will always be followed by a paragraph of another specific style—for example, a heading paragraph always followed by a body text paragraph—choose the following style in the **Style for following paragraph** drop-down list.

7. If you want the new style to be part of the template on which the current document is based, click **Add to template** to place a check mark there. If you don't check this option, you can use only the new style in the current document.

8. Click **Automatically update** if you want any manual formatting changes you make to any paragraph assigned this style to automatically be added to the style definition. This causes all manual changes to a paragraph's formatting to appear immediately in all paragraphs of the same style. This applies only to paragraph styles and does not apply to the Normal paragraph style. It works with all manual paragraph formatting but only with manual character formatting if you format the paragraph end mark (¶).

9. Choose **Format** and select **Font** or **Border** to specify the font or border and shading of the new style. The appropriate dialog box opens for you to select formatting options. Click **OK** to return to the New Style dialog box. Notice that the **Preview** box shows how the style will look, and the Description area defines the style in words.

   For paragraph styles only: choose **Format** and select **Paragraph** to set the style's alignment, indents, and line and paragraph spacing, **Tabs** to set the new style's tab stops, or **Numbering** to specify a numbering or bullet style.

10. Click **OK** to return to the Style dialog box.

11. Choose **Apply** to assign the new style to the current text or paragraph. Choose **Close** to save the new style definition without assigning it to any text.

SEE ALSO

➤ *Learn more about Word templates, see page 238*

Updating styles automatically

If the idea of having a change in one paragraph automatically appear in other paragraphs makes you nervous, don't choose **Automatically update** in the New Style or Modify Style dialog box. Instead, when you make a manual change to a paragraph's formatting, if you then want to apply that change to all paragraphs having the same style, reapply the style to the paragraph. A dialog box appears giving you the choice of updating the style with the manual change you just made or removing the manual changes by reapplying the style formatting. If you choose to update the style, all paragraphs having that style assigned also update.

Modify Styles

Whether you defined the style or it's one of Word's predefined styles, you can change the styles formatting settings. Be aware, however, that when you modify the style, all text in the document that has that same style also changes.

Modify a style

1. Open the **Format** menu, and select **Style** to open the Style dialog box (see Figure 8.8).

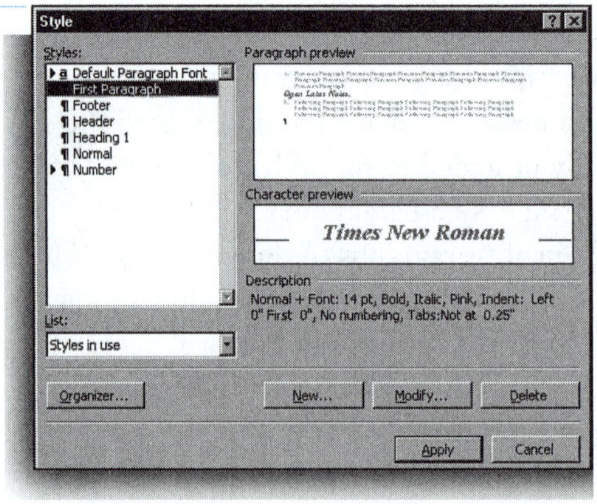

FIGURE 8.8
Choose the style you want to change from the **Styles** list and click **Modify**.

2. Select the style you want to modify from the **Styles** list. If the style you want to change isn't displayed, select which styles you want displayed from the **List** drop-down list:
   - **All Styles** displays all styles available to the current document, whether or not they're currently assigned to text in the document. "Available to" means all styles defined in the document or in a template attached to the document or in a global template.
   - **Styles in Use** shows all styles that have been assigned to text in the current document.
   - **User-Defined Styles** shows any user-defined styles in the current document.

3. Choose **Modify**. The Modify Style dialog box appears, which looks the same as the New Style dialog box (refer to Figure 8.7). Specify the style's new format settings.
4. Click **OK** to return to the Style dialog box.
5. Choose **Close** to exit the dialog box.

A quick way to modify a style is to make your formatting changes to a paragraph assigned that style. Select the paragraph, open the Style list in the toolbar, and reselect the currently assigned style. The Modify Style dialog box appears (see Figure 8.9). Click **Update the style to reflect recent changes**. Click **OK**.

The one thing you can't do in the Modify Style dialog box

You can make any change you want to an existing style, except one. You can't change a character style into a paragraph style or vice versa.

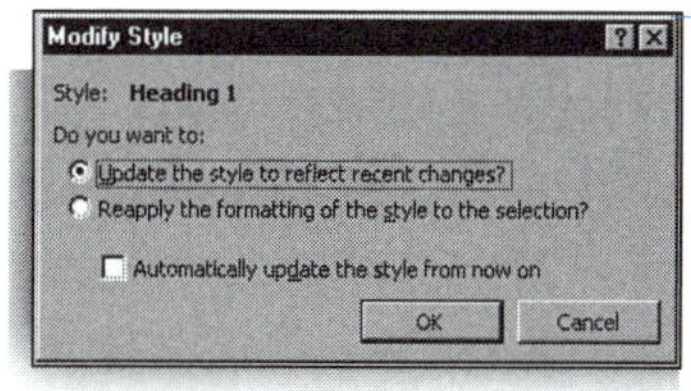

FIGURE 8.9
Choose to update the style so that your formatting changes become part of the style definition.

Apply Automatic Formatting

Microsoft has automated a lot of small, tedious chores that had to be done manually in older word-processing programs. Many of these are formatting chores and Word collects them under the term AutoFormat. You can control what formatting chores Word performs automatically in the AutoFormat tabs of the AutoCorrect dialog box. The benefit of using AutoFormat is that you can concentrate more on the content of your document, and less on the details of formatting.

AutoFormat works two different ways—as you type or on command:

- **AutoFormat As You Type.** Automatically formats headings, bulleted and numbered lists, borders, numbers, symbols, and so on, as you type.
- **AutoFormat on Command.** Automatically formats selected text or the entire document in one pass.

You don't have to do anything to activate AutoFormat. By default, **AutoFormat As You Type** is enabled—you just enter text and Word formats it as you go. You can change the default to **AutoFormat on Command**, which allows you to manually run AutoFormat. This is similar to the way in which you can spell check a document—as you type, or manually, using the menu commands or toolbar icons.

To AutoFormat text

1. To AutoFormat a block of text, select it. To AutoFormat the entire document, make sure that no text is selected.
2. From the **Format** menu, select **AutoFormat** to open the AutoFormat dialog box (see Figure 8.10).

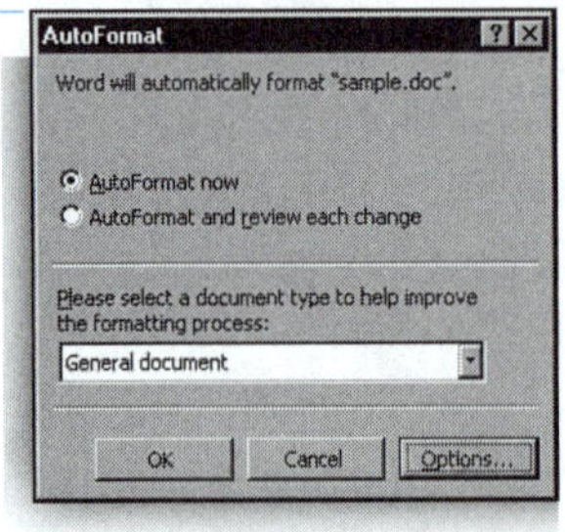

FIGURE 8.10
When you click **OK**, Word AutoFormats your entire document in one pass.

3. Click **AutoFormat now** if you want Word to format the document without prompting you to review the changes.

   Click **AutoFormat and review each change** if you want the opportunity to accept or reject each change proposed by Word.
4. Choose the type of document you have created in the drop-down list labeled **Please select a document type to help improve the formatting process**. This helps Word to AutoFormat the document properly.
5. If you want to limit the types of formatting Word does, choose the **Options** button to display the AutoFormat tab of the AutoCorrect dialog box. Make your selections, then click **OK** to return to the AutoFormat dialog box. The

AutoFormat options are described more fully later in this chapter.

6. Click **OK** to begin the AutoFormat process.

If you choose **AutoFormat now**, Word formats the document, and that's that. If you choose **AutoFormat and review each change**, Word formats the document, then presents a new AutoFormat dialog box (see Figure 8.11). This version of the document looks very different from the first version.

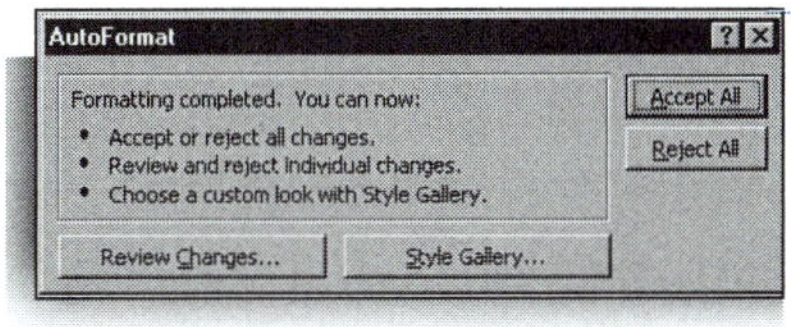

FIGURE 8.11
Accept or reject formatting changes, or use the **Style Gallery** to apply further formatting to the document.

In the new AutoFormat dialog box, you can do the following:

- Accept or reject all Word's formatting changes without further review.
- Review each change that Word made and accept or reject each change individually.
- Use the Style Gallery to apply a new template to the document and, in so doing, completely change the look of the document.

If you choose to review each change, all changes that Word made are displayed in your document as *revision marks* and the Review AutoFormat Changes dialog box appears (see Figure 8.12). You can scroll manually through your document and highlight any changed text, or you can use the two **Find** buttons in the dialog box to have Word search for and highlight changes for you.

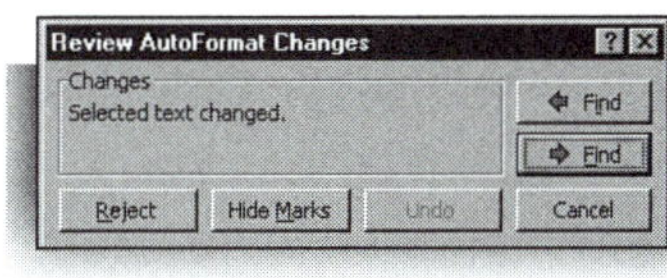

FIGURE 8.12
Because Word has already made changes, you don't have to do anything to accept them. That's why this dialog box has a **Reject** button.

When a change is selected, you can click the **Reject** button. This deletes the change and restores the original formatting. If you then change your mind, you can click the **Undo** button. When you are finished reviewing, click **Cancel**, then, in the AutoFormat dialog box, click **Accept All** to accept the changes that you did not manually reject in the Review AutoFormat Changes dialog box.

SEE ALSO

➤ *Using revision marks, see page 434*

Change Templates with the Style Gallery

AutoFormat assigns styles to every paragraph in your document. This is good because, once a document is completely styled, you can make wholesale formatting changes quickly and easily. You can edit the styles or, better yet, you can switch to other templates that use styles with the same names.

The Style Gallery streamlines the formatting process for you. It enables you to try out different templates on your document, to preview how your document looks in a given template, and then to switch to that template if you like it.

If you choose Style Gallery in the AutoFormat dialog box, the Style Gallery dialog box appears, looking similar to that in Figure 8.13, but with your document displayed, not the one pictured.

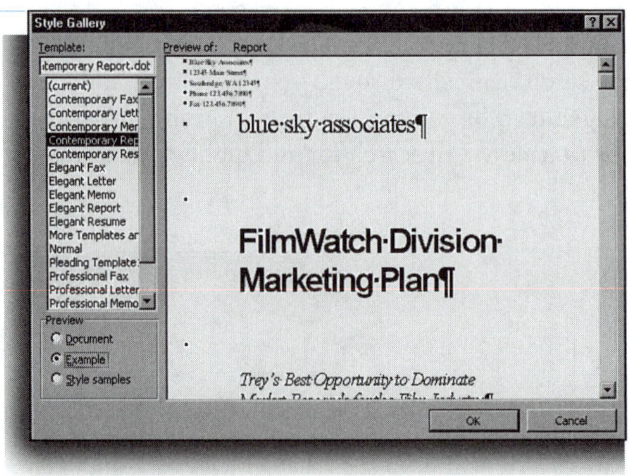

FIGURE 8.13
The Style Gallery lets you see what your document would look like using different templates.

In the list on the left side of the screen, you can choose from the available templates. In the list, **(current)** is the template currently attached to your document. As you choose each template in the list, you can see, in the picture at right, how your document looks as formatted by the chosen template. By clicking the choices in the **Preview** section, you can also see sample documents and examples of the styles in the template to get a further idea of what each template offers.

When you choose another template and click **OK**, Word replaces your current template with the one you chose and applies the new formatting of the template to your document.

How AutoFormat Works and How You Can Help It Work Better

AutoFormat changes the formatting in your document based on a set of rules that it follows. That is, it looks for specific patterns of characters and makes corresponding format changes. For example, it changes some hyphens to em dashes, others to en dashes, and leaves yet others alone, depending on the context of each hyphen.

If you know the character patterns AutoFormat looks for, you can help it along by entering text in those patterns. For example, you can follow a word with two hyphens, then another word (no spaces around the hyphens), knowing that AutoFormat will convert the hyphens to an em dash. Therefore, you may find it useful to review Appendix A, "Changes Made by AutoFormat," which lists the things AutoFormat can do for you.

Controlling AutoFormat Options

All AutoFormat options are turned on by default when you install Microsoft Word. You can, however, disable selected AutoFormat options or turn off AutoFormat entirely by disabling all AutoFormat options. You can set options for **AutoFormat As You Type** separately from options for **AutoFormat on Command**.

Set AutoFormat options

1. From the **Tools** menu, select **AutoCorrect** to open the AutoCorrect dialog box.
2. Choose the **AutoFormat As You Type** tab to display those options.

   Choose the **AutoFormat** tab to display the **AutoFormat on Command** options.
3. Select and deselect the options you want. If you are not sure what effect an option will have, click the **Help** icon, then choose the option.
4. When you have selected all options that you want, click **OK** to set them.

You can also set AutoFormat options during an AutoFormat by choosing the **Options** button in the AutoFormat dialog box.

PART

III

Create Professional-Looking Documents

CHAPTER

9

Lay Out Pages and Sections

- Configure page setup, margins, paper size, and orientation
- Create headers and footers, page borders, and sections
- Add page numbering
- Apply page borders

About Page and Section Formatting

Page formatting in Word refers to the overall look of the printed page. It includes such things as the page margins, the paper size and orientation, column formatting, headers, footers, and page numbering. In a simple document, when you set these parameters, they affect the whole document. For most documents, that is good enough. However, if you need to set up different pages or parts of pages differently from one another, Word permits you to divide a document into *sections* and then set page formats differently for each section.

Create and Remove Sections

If your document needs more than one section, you can create new sections by inserting section breaks. You can insert breaks manually or Word may insert them for you. Section breaks mark the division between two sections, and like the paragraph marker, a section break marker stores the page formats of the preceding section. There are three kinds of section breaks:

- *Continuous.* A continuous section break forces a paragraph break, so that the new section begins immediately following the preceding section, typically on the same page as the previous section, so you can have two types of formatting on the same page. This type of section break is useful in documents such as newsletters, in which the titles of the articles may stretch across the page but the text of the articles is formatted in two columns.
- *Next page.* A next page section break forces a page break, so that the new section begins at the top of the next page. This type of section break is useful for setting major breaks in a document such as the start of a new chapter. If you need to restart the page numbering for each chapter, a next page section is a logical choice.
- *Odd page* or *Even page.* When you use an even page or odd page section break, the section break forces either one or two page breaks so that the new section begins on the next

even- or odd-numbered page. Use this type of section break in a bound document, where a major break in the document, such as a new chapter, should always begin on an even or an odd page.

As you can see in Figure 9.1, Word marks the location of section breaks by displaying a double horizontal line with the label "Section Break" followed by the type of break. You can see section break markers in Normal view but they aren't displayed in Page Layout view (unless you make your hidden characters visible by clicking Show/Hide ¶ [¶] on the Standard toolbar), Print Preview mode, or the printed document.

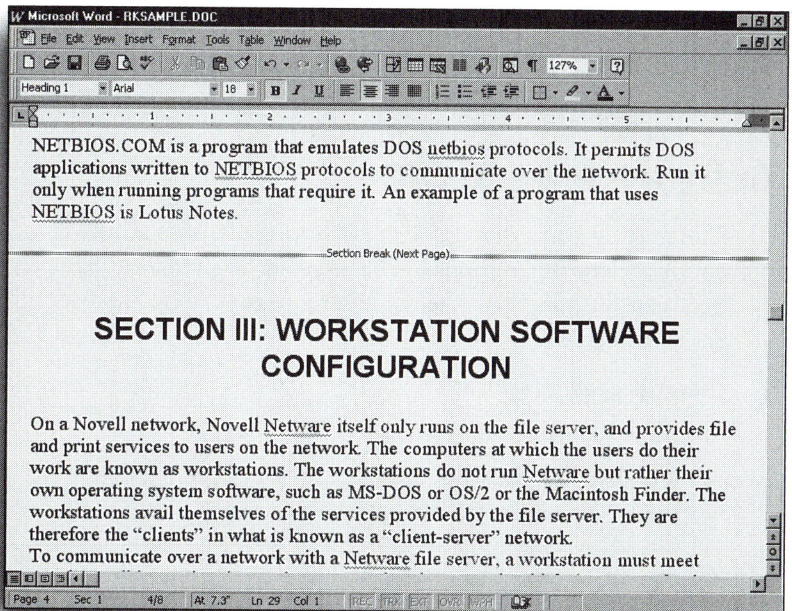

FIGURE 9.1
Section breaks as they appear in Normal view.

Insert a manual section break

1. Position your insertion point where you want the new section to begin.
2. From the **Insert** menu, select **Break** to open the Break dialog box (see Figure 9.2).

FIGURE 9.2

Select the type of section break you want to insert.

Deleting section breaks can delete formatting

When you delete a section break, text in the section before the break assumes the page formatting that was set for the section that follows the break.

3. Under **Section breaks**, click the type of section break you want to insert: **Next page**, **Continuous**, **Even page**, or **Odd page**.
4. Click **OK**.

To remove a section break, position the insertion point right after the break marker and press Backspace. Or position the insertion point on the break marker and press Delete.

Configure Page Setup

The starting point of page layout is setting the page setup options. Use setup options to change your document's orientation, margins, or paper size. Configure page setup in the Page Setup dialog box.

Change page setup options

1. Click the **File** menu, and select **Page Setup**.
2. The Page Setup dialog box appears (see Figure 9.3). Select the tab that contains the options you want to set:

FIGURE 9.3

Select the tab that contains the options you want to set, such as the **Paper Source** tab.

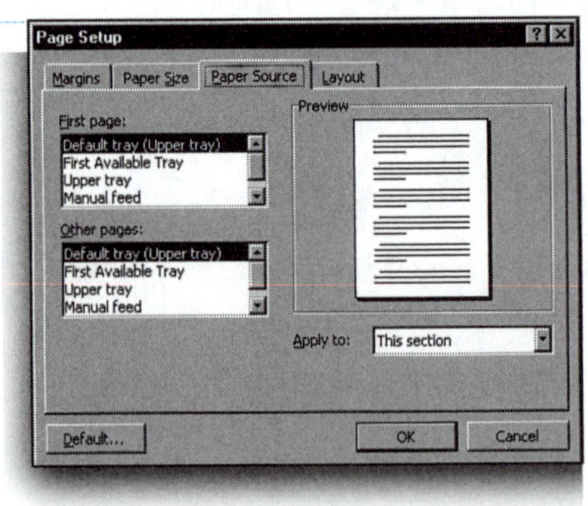

- *Margins*. Set the top, bottom, left, and right margins for your pages. See the "Set Margins" section later in this chapter for more details.
- *Paper Size*. Specify the paper size you're using and whether the page will print in portrait or landscape orientation. See the "Control Paper Size and Orientation" section for more details.
- *Paper Source*. If you have a printer with more than one tray, specify which tray your first page paper is in and which tray contains the paper for your other pages.
- *Layout*. Select the types of headers and footers you need for your document (see "Create Alternating Headers and Footers" later in this chapter), what type of vertical alignment you want to use on your pages, or turn on line numbering (useful where you need to reference different lines in a document).

3. From the **Apply to** drop-down list, select the portion of the document to which you want to apply your settings: **This section**, **This point forward**, **Whole document**, or **Selected sections**. These options appear frequently when you're setting page formats.
   - **Whole document**. Word applies your changes to the whole document.
   - **This point forward**. If you choose this, Word inserts a next page section break at the insertion point when you choose OK and apply your changes to all sections below the new section break.
   - **This section**. This option appears only if the document has more than one section. Word applies your changes only to the current section.
   - **Selected sections**. This appears only if text is selected that straddles more than one section. Word applies your changes to the selected sections.
4. To save the settings as the new default settings for the current document, as well as all new documents based on the

same template, choose **Default**. When a dialog box appears asking if you want the change to become the default for all new documents using this template, choose **Yes**. Choose **No** to make the settings the default for only the current document.

5. Click **OK** to accept your changes and close the dialog box.

SEE ALSO

➤ *For more information on the vertical alignment of text, see page 122*

Set Margins

The distance from the edge of the paper to the beginning of your text area is the *margin*. Each page has four margins: left, right, top, and bottom. Change margin settings when the default settings are not suitable for your document layout or printing preferences. Changing the margin settings affects the entire document, unless you have created sections and you specify that the margins apply only to specific sections.

Our preferences for setting margins

We find the ruler provides the fastest way to set margins. We reserve using the Page Setup dialog box for large documents that have special margin needs, such as a larger inside margin for bound documents.

The two methods for changing margins are the dialog box method and the ruler method. The ruler method is available in two views—Page Layout view and Print Preview—and it works the same way in both places.

The advantage of using the dialog box method is that you can set all four margins at once and you don't have to change to the Page Layout view. However, you do need to enter precise margin values.

Set page margins using the dialog box

1. Click the **File** menu, and select **Page Setup**, or when you're in Page Layout view double-click in the gray area to the left of the ruler.
2. When the Page Setup dialog box appears, select the **Margins** tab (see Figure 9.4).
3. Enter the desired margin size (you don't need to enter the inch mark) in the **Top**, **Bottom**, **Left**, and **Right** text boxes, or click the up and down arrows to set the desired value. The **Preview** area shows you the effect of your margin settings.

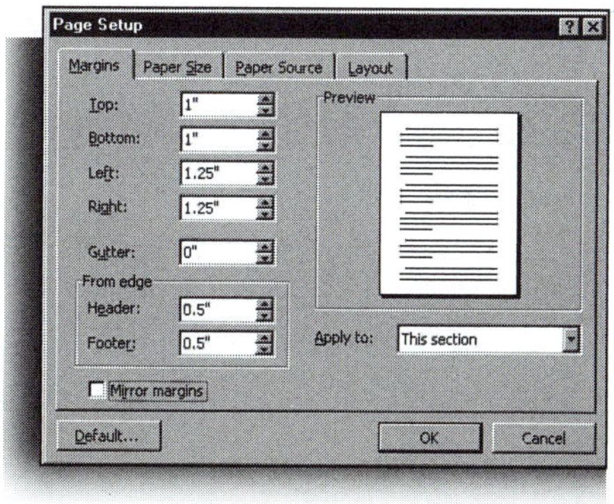

FIGURE 9.4
Specify your margins in the Page Setup dialog box.

4. For documents that will be bound with spiral binding or in a three-ring binder, you may need to leave extra space to allow for the part of the page that will be hidden in the binding, which is called the *gutter*. To do this, enter the desired width of this binding area in the **Gutter** text box. Normally, Word adds this gutter on the left side of the page. However, if you plan to print on both sides of the paper, you should choose **Mirror margins**. With *mirror margins* selected, the gutter space appears on the left side of odd-numbered pages and the right side of even-numbered pages (notice that your left and right margins become inside and outside margins) so the gutter is always on the inside part of the pages.
5. In the **From edge** area, enter the distance the **Header** and **Footer** appear from the top and bottom edge of the paper.
6. From the **Apply to** drop-down list, select where the new margins will apply: **Whole document**, **This point forward**, **This section**, or **Selected sections**.
7. If you want to save the settings as the new default settings for this document or all new documents based on the current template, choose **Default**. When a dialog box appears asking if you want the change to become the default for all new documents using this template, choose **Yes**. Choose **No** to make the settings the default for only the current document.

8. Click **OK** to close the dialog box and apply the margins to your document.

SEE ALSO

➤ *Learn about Print Preview mode, see page 260*

The second method for setting page margins uses the mouse and the ruler. This method enables you to work visually instead of doing arithmetic in your head, because you can immediately see how your changes affect your document.

To display the ruler, choose the **View** menu, and select **Ruler** or position the mouse pointer near the top edge of the work area and hold it there. If you use the second method, the ruler stays visible until you move your mouse pointer away from the top of the document window.

See your entire page

You don't have to switch to Print Preview to see the entire page from Page Layout view. Select **Page Width** from the Zoom drop-down list on the Standard toolbar.

Warning! Be careful not to use indent markers

The indent markers on the rulers do not change the margins of your document, only the indentation for your current or selected paragraphs. To change margins using the ruler, change to Page Layout view first, and use the margin markers as described here.

You must be working in Page Layout view or Print Preview mode if you want to use the ruler to set margins. You'll probably find it easier to work in Page Layout view, because the ruler is usually larger in this view, therefore easier to work with. But in Print Preview, you can see the entire page on the screen, so you can really get a view of the results of any changes you make.

In both of these views, you can see both the horizontal ruler at the top of the page and a vertical ruler on the left edge of the page. To switch to Page Layout view, click the **View** menu, and select **Page Layout** or choose the **Page Layout View** button in the bottom left corner of the screen. To switch to Print Preview mode, choose the **File** menu, and select **Print Preview**, or click the **Print Preview** button.

On each ruler, the white area of the ruler displays the typing area between the margins. The dark gray areas on each side of the typing area display the margins, as shown in Figure 9.5. A light gray line between the white and dark gray areas is the margin marker (don't confuse these with the triangular indent markers).

Quickly display ruler settings

To view ruler settings such as margins, indents, and tabs, point to the ruler element whose setting you want to see, then hold down both the Alt key and the mouse button. The settings appear on the ruler and remain until you release the Alt key.

Change a margin using the ruler

1. Point at the margin marker on the horizontal ruler, at the left or right end of the white bar, or at the top or bottom margin markers on the vertical ruler.

2. When the mouse pointer changes to a two-headed arrow (the help tip displays Left Margin, Right Margin, Top Margin, or Bottom Margin), click and drag the margin to a new position.

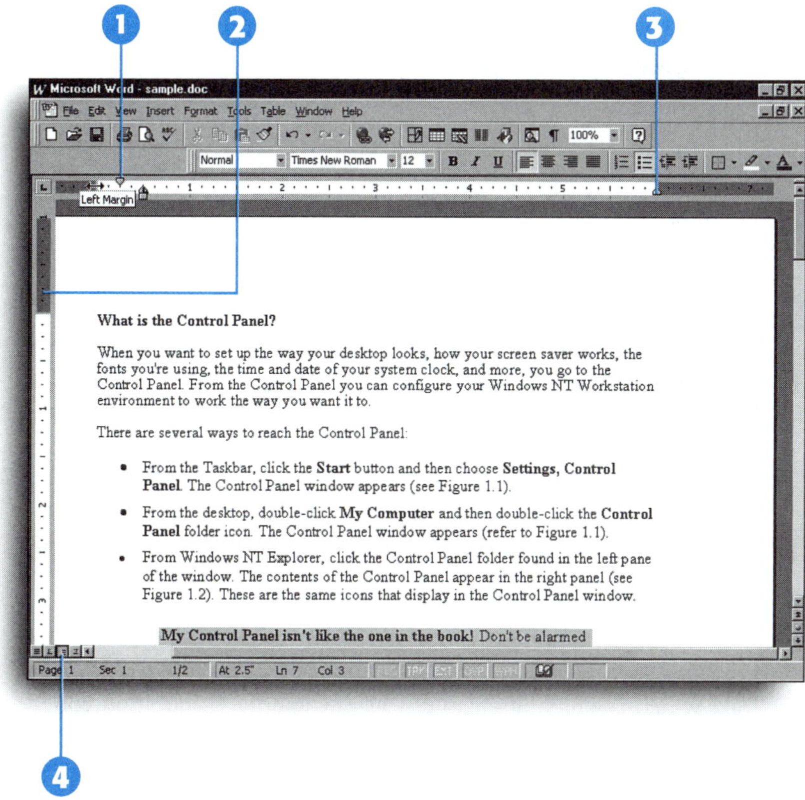

FIGURE 9.5

Drag the margin markers on the horizontal or vertical rulers to change the margins.

1. Left margin marker
2. Top margin marker
3. Right margin marker
4. Page Layout view button

Control Paper Size and Orientation

The default paper size is set at 8 1/2"×11" and in *portrait* orientation (the shorter edge of the paper is the top). To specify a different paper size, select from several standard paper and envelope sizes or define a custom paper size. You can also print in *landscape* orientation so that the long edge of the paper is the top.

Specify paper size and orientation

1. Click the **File** menu, and select **Page Setup** on the menu. The Page Setup dialog box opens.
2. Select the **Paper Size** tab to display the paper size and orientation options (see Figure 9.6).

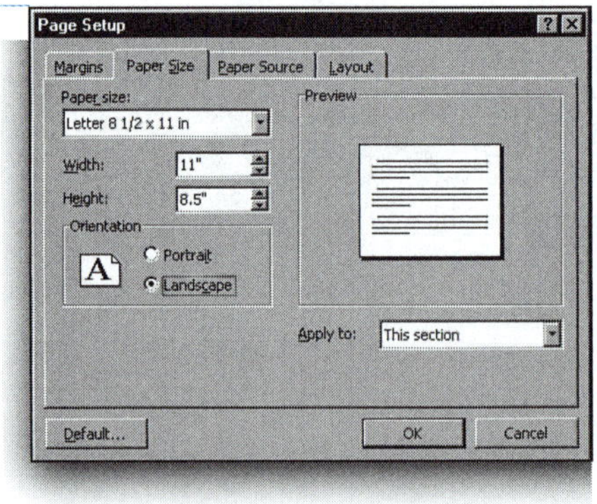

FIGURE 9.6
Choose your paper size and orientation in the Page Setup dialog box.

3. From the **Paper size** drop-down list, select a predefined paper size. If the paper size you need isn't listed, select **Custom Size** and enter the appropriate values in the **Width** and **Height** boxes.
4. Under **Orientation**, select **Portrait** or **Landscape**. See the tiny page sample next to these options if you're not sure which is which; it changes to show you the orientation you selected.
5. From the **Apply to** drop-down list, select the portion of the document to which you want your settings to apply: **Whole document**, **This point forward**, or **This section**.
6. To save the settings as the new default settings for the current document, as well as all new documents based on the same template, choose **Default**. When a dialog box appears asking if you want the change to become the default for all new documents using this template, choose **Yes**. Choose **No** to make the settings the default for only the current document.
7. Click **OK**.

About Headers and Footers

Text that repeats at the top of every page is a *header*; text that repeats at the bottom of every page is a *footer*. Use headers and footers to help readers know which document they've picked up, what page they're on, or what chapter they're currently reading.

Normally, the header and footer text appears 1/2 inch from the edge of the page. You change this in the Page Setup dialog box, as described in the "Set Margins" section of this chapter, in the **From edge** section of the **Margins** tab. The body text starts and ends at the top and bottom margins unless you have several lines in the header, or footer or you change the **From edge** values to be greater than the margin. In those circumstances, the margins adjust so the body text starts after the header and ends just before the header.

Headers and footers can vary within a document. Choices include

- The same header and footer on every page
- A different header and footer for the first page only
- Different headers and footers for odd-numbered pages than those on even-numbered pages
- Different headers and footers for each section of the document

A complex document with multiple sections—for example, a technical manual—might combine all the possible variations. That is, each section might have its own set of headers and footers of all three kinds—first page, odd pages, and even pages.

Add a header or footer to your document

1. Click the **View** menu, and select **Header and Footer**. The document appears in Page Layout view with the header area indicated by a nonprinting dashed-line box (see Figure 9.7). Regular document text is gray, and the Header and Footer toolbar is displayed.

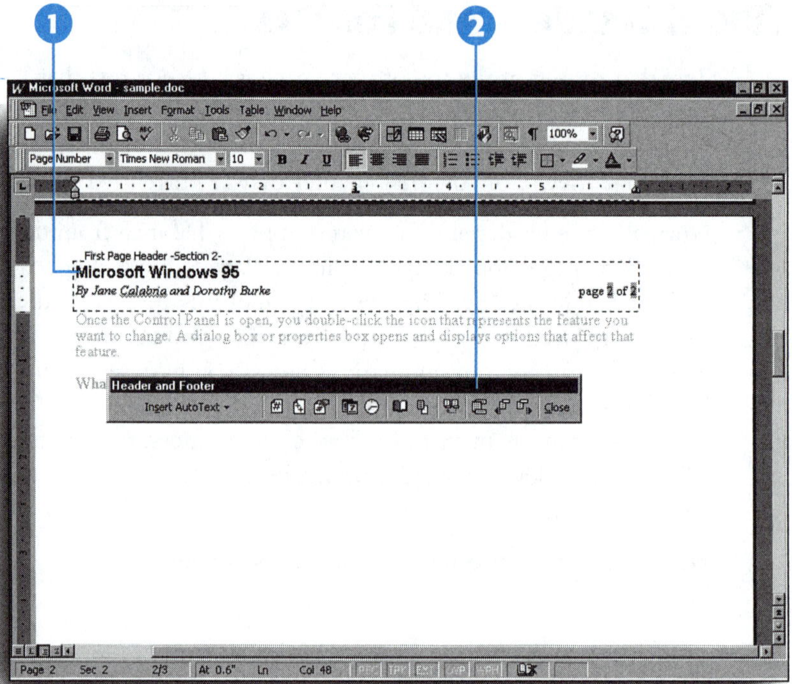

FIGURE 9.7

The header or footer appears in a dashed-line box, and the document text is gray.

1. Header box
2. Header and Footer toolbar

2. Type the header or footer text. Edit and format the text as you would anywhere else in the document. Both the header and the footer have two tabs set to help you align your text: a center tab at the center of the page and a right tab at the right margin.
3. Use the toolbar buttons, described in Table 9.1, to add page numbers, total page numbers, date, time, and so on.
4. Choose **Close** on the Header and Footer toolbar to return to the document.

TABLE 9.1 Header and Footer toolbar buttons

Action:	Button:
Inserts an AutoText entry	Insert
Inserts a page number code	

Action:	**Button:**
Inserts the total number of pages in the document	
Opens the Page Number Format dialog box	
Inserts a date code for the current date	
Inserts a time code for the current time	
Opens the Page Setup dialog box	
Displays or hides the document text	
Makes the header or footer the same type of header or footer (first page, odd pages, or even pages) as the one in the previous section or breaks that link when you deselect it	
Switches between the header and the footer on the same page	
Shows the previous header or footer	
Shows the next header or footer	
Closes the Header and Footer toolbar and returns to document editing	Close

SEE ALSO

➤ *Learn more about AutoText, see page* 77

➤ *Find out more about inserting date and time fields, see page* 444

Create Alternating Headers and Footers

Normally, the same header and footer appear on every page of your document. However, if you plan to print on both sides of the paper and bind the document, you may find it more visually pleasing to have the page numbers on the outside corners of the pages, which means the left side of even-numbered pages and the right side of odd-numbered pages.

Not just for page numbers

Alternating headers and footers give you quite a few page layout opportunities besides changing the placement of your page numbers. For example, you may have the company logo appear in the even page header and the company name in the odd page header. Then, when you open the document, you'll see the logo across from the company name. Or, you might want the author's name on the even pages and the document title on the odd pages.

Set up different odd and even page headers or footers

1. Click the **View** menu, and select **Header and Footer** and then choose **Page Setup** on the Header and Footer toolbar. Or, click the **File** menu, and select **Page Setup**. The Page Setup dialog box opens (see Figure 9.8).

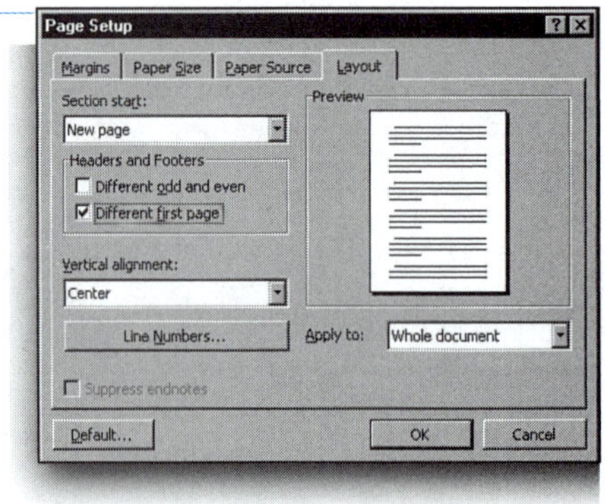

FIGURE 9.8
The Headers and Footers options enable you to have different headers and footers on odd or even pages or a different header and footer for just the first page.

2. Click the **Layout** tab if it's not already selected.
3. Click **Different odd and even** to place a check mark there.
4. Click **OK** to close the Page Setup dialog box.

Using the instructions from the "About Headers and Footers" section earlier in this chapter, you need to create a header and footer on an even page. Then click **Show Next** on the Header and Footer toolbar to see the header or footer for an odd-numbered page. Create the header and footer that you want to appear on all the odd-numbered pages. Choose **Close** to return to your document.

Edit Headers and Footers

Editing headers and footers is similar to making changes in the main body of your document. Adding, removing, and formatting text follows the same procedures.

Edit a header or footer

1. Click the **View** menu, and select **Headers and Footers**. The header on the current page appears in edit mode,

outlined by a dashed box. The Header and Footer toolbar also appears.

If you need to modify the footer, click **Switch Between Header and Footer** from the Header and Footer toolbar.

2. Click in the Header or Footer box and then edit or format the text as you would in any other portion of your document.
3. When your modifications are complete, choose **Close** on the Header and Footer toolbar to return to normal editing of your document.

While you were in Headers and Footers view, the body text of your document was grayed out and uneditable. When you close Headers and Footers view and return to Page Layout view, you can see your headers and footers grayed out and uneditable.

You should keep a couple of cautions in mind when you want to edit different types of headers and footers within the same document:

- *Edit the correct header or footer*. When you have alternating headers and footers, different first page headers and footers, or different headers and footers for different sections of your document, it's very easy to edit the wrong one. Before you start editing, position your insertion point on a page that uses the type of header or footer you want to modify. Then follow the steps for editing. Also check the text at the top of the header or footer box to verify which one you're editing.
- *Make sure* ***Same as Previous*** *is not on*. This is important if your document has multiple sections. If **Same as Previous** is active, the current header or footer inherits its contents from the header or footer of the same type (first page, odd pages, or even pages) in the previous section of the document. You could accidentally change the header or footer in another section without meaning to. To avoid this, look for the words "Same as Previous" in the top border of the header or footer that indicate this feature is active. To turn off

A handy shortcut

When you are in Page Layout view, you can toggle quickly between editing body text and editing headers and footers by double-clicking on the grayed-out text. Double-clicking a header or footer puts you in header/footer edit mode. Double-clicking body text closes header/footer edit mode.

Left-, center-, and right-aligned text on one line

Word automatically assigns the built-in styles Header and Footer to header and footer paragraphs. The special characteristic of both of these styles is that they have a center-aligned tab at the center of the page and a right-aligned tab at the right margin. This lets you enter left-aligned text, then press Tab to enter centered text, then press Tab again to enter right-aligned text, all on one line.

Same as Previous, click the **Same as Previous** icon in the Headers and Footers toolbar.

SEE ALSO

- *Set tabs for different alignments on the same line, see page 127*
- *Use tables as an alternative solution to placing different text alignments on the same line, see page 283*
- *Learn more about styles, see page 157*

Use a Different Header or Footer for the First Page

The first page of a document such as a multipage letter or a report may need a different header or footer than the remainder of the document. For example, the first page of a letter might look much the same as any letter but the subsequent pages might have a header that identifies the recipient, the date of the letter, and the page number.

Make a different header or footer for the first page

1. Click the **File** menu, and select **Page Setup** or choose **Page Setup** from the Header and Footer toolbar. The Page Setup dialog box opens (refer to Figure 9.8).
2. Click the **Layout** tab.
3. Click **Different first page** to place a check mark there.
4. Choose **OK** to close the Page Setup dialog box.

When you create the header and footer for the first page (see the instructions for adding headers and footers in "About Headers and Footers" earlier in this chapter), the header box is marked "First Page Header" and the footer box is "First Page Footer." If you want nothing to appear on the first page, don't enter any text in the box. When you choose **Show Next** on the Header and Footer toolbar, the header and footer boxes on the next page are labeled "Header" and "Footer." Enter the text in these boxes that you want to appear on all later pages.

For information on formatting the page numbers in your headers and footers, or starting the page numbering with a different number (making the page after the title page start at page 1), refer to the "Add Page Numbering" section of this chapter.

Add Page Numbering

Documents longer than one page that you plan to print should have page numbers. You can set up page numbering in two ways. Either insert a page number code while editing headers and footers. Or insert page numbers from the **Insert** menu.

Both methods insert a page number code in your document's header or footer, but there are two differences. If you insert the page number code manually while editing a header or footer, you can embed the number in other text. This enables you, for example, to have your page number look something like this: `Page x of y.`

If you use the **Insert** menu method to have Word insert the page number code for you, the page number will stand alone. However, when you use this method, Word puts the page number code inside a *frame*, then inserts the frame into your header or footer.

A *frame* is a box which you can move anywhere on the page. You can put borders around a frame, put shading inside a frame, insert graphics into a frame, and edit the text inside a frame separately from other text in your document. By inserting your page numbers this way, you can achieve special effects, such as having the page number appear in a shaded, bordered box set outside the normal page margins of your document.

To add a page number code while editing a header or footer, follow the "Add Headers and Footers" instructions earlier in this chapter. When the header or footer box appears in the edit mode, position your insertion point where you want the page number to appear and then click **Insert Page Number** on the Header and Footer toolbar. If you want to note the total number of pages in the document (such as Page 1 of 12), add the appropriate text and then click **Insert Number of Pages** where you want the total to appear.

Add page numbering

1. Click the **Insert** menu, and select **Page Numbers** to open the Page Numbers dialog box (see Figure 9.9).

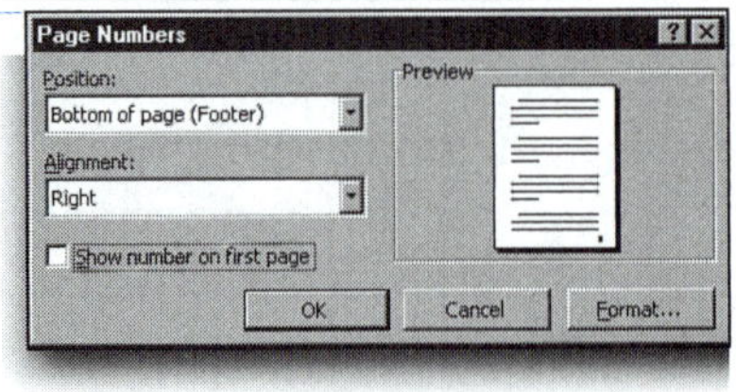

FIGURE 9.9

Deselect **Show number on first page** if you don't want a page number to appear on the first page.

2. From the **Position** drop-down list, select the position on the page where you want your page numbers to appear: **Top of page (Header)** or **Bottom of page (Footer)**.
3. From the **Alignment** drop-down list, select **Left**, **Center**, or **Right** to specify the horizontal position of the page number in relation to the right and left margins. If you're printing on both sides of the paper (and have set up mirror margins) and you want the page numbers positioned near the binding, select **Inside**; to put them away from the binding select **Outside**. This creates the page numbers that alternate position on even or odd pages without creating alternating odd/even headers or footers as described earlier in this chapter.
4. If you want the page number to appear on the first page, click **Show Number on first page** to place a check mark there. Deselecting this option creates a separate header or footer for the first page as discussed earlier in this chapter.
5. Click **OK**. A number appears in the position you specified on the page.

When you insert a page number, Word automatically switches you to Page Layout view so you can scroll to the portion of the page where the page number appears to check its appearance.

Page numbers are grayed out!

The **Page Numbers** option is grayed out on the **Insert** menu when you're in Online or Outline view. Switch to Normal or Page Layout view to add page numbers. You can only see the page numbers in Page Layout view.

Format Page Numbers

You can define the style of page numbering used in your document or in a section of your document, combine the page number with a chapter number, or set the starting number for your page numbering. Word automatically inserts the correct codes and formatting for you.

Format page numbers

1. Click the **Insert** menu, and select **Page Numbers** to open the Page Numbers dialog box (refer to Figure 9.9).
2. Choose **Format** to open the Page Number Format dialog box (see Figure 9.10).

FIGURE 9.10
Enter "1" as the starting page number for the section that starts on the page after the title page.

3. Select the style of numbering you want to use from the **Number format** drop-down list: Arabic (1, 2, 3), lowercase letters (a, b, c), uppercase letters (A, B, C), lowercase Roman numerals (i, ii, iii), or uppercase Roman numerals (I, II, III).
4. (Optional) To have Word insert a combined chapter and page number, so that the page numbers might look like "I-1" or "A:1," there are a couple of steps you must take before you format the page numbering. You must use a consistent paragraph style for your chapter titles (such as Heading 1). Do not apply the chapter title style to any other paragraphs in your document. The chapter titles also have to be numbered (click the **Format** menu, and then select **Bullets and Numbering**. Select the **Outline Numbered** tab, and then choose a multilevel list type that is linked to the Heading styles from the bottom row of options). Then, in the Page Number Format dialog box, click **Include chapter number** to place a check mark there. Select the name of the chapter title style you are using from the **Chapter starts with style** box. From the **Use separator** drop-down list, select a number separator to appear between the chapter number and the page number—hyphen (I-1), period (1.1), colon (A:1), em dash (II—1), en dash (A–1).

5. Click **OK** to return to the Page Numbers dialog box.
6. Click **OK** to accept your formatting changes, or **Close** to close the dialog box without accepting your changes.

SEE ALSO

➤ *Learn more about styles and how to apply them, see page 165*
➤ *For more information on multilevel numbering, see page 147*

Modify Page Numbering for Different Sections of a Document

If you have different sections in your document, you can set up page numbering differently in each section. For example, you might want to number your table of contents in lowercase Roman numerals, but start the first chapter as page 1 using Arabic numerals.

Start new page numbers for another section

1. Set up the page numbering for the first section (your table of contents) using the instructions in the "Format Page Numbers" section earlier in this chapter.
2. Move your insertion point to the next section.
3. Click the **Insert** menu, and select **Page Numbers** and set the position and alignment for your page numbers. Then choose **Format** to open the Page Number Format dialog box (refer to Figure 9.10).
4. Follow the instructions under Format Page Numbers to set the format of page numbering you want to use or to include chapter numbers in the page numbering.
5. Under **Page Numbering**, click **Start at** and type a starting page number in the text box.
6. Choose **OK** to return to the Page Numbers dialog box.
7. Click **OK** to accept your formatting changes.

Repeat these steps for each section in which you want to have different page numbering.

Alternately, you can format page numbers from the Header and Footer view. Just click the **Format Page Numbers** button on the Header and Footer toolbar to reveal the Format Page

Numbers dialog box, then follow the numbered instructions that appeared earlier in this section.

Create an Unnumbered Title Page

One problem you may have when you don't show the page number on the first page is that on the next page the number is "2." After a title page, you want the number to be "1." The solution is to insert a next page section break after the title page and number the pages differently in each section.

Create an unnumbered title page

1. Place your insertion point after the text on your title page and then click the **Insert** menu and select **Break**.
2. From the Break dialog box, click **Next page** under **Section breaks** and then click **OK**.
3. Don't assign page numbers to the title page section, but insert them in the second section. Follow the instructions under the "Modify Page Numbering for Different Sections of a Document" section, entering "1" as your page number in the **Start at** box.

Other formatting differences between the first page and the rest of the document or section, such as margins or vertical centering, can also be accomplished using a section for the first page and another section for the remainder of the document. Refer to "Create and Remove Sections" earlier in this chapter.

Create Page Borders

Use page borders when you want to dress up a document for presentation, such as a title page, an announcement, or an invitation. Borders can be a single line outline, have a shadow, be three-dimensional, be decorative, or combine thick and thin lines.

Word offers several predefined border settings:

- **None** removes all borders from the page.
- **Box** inserts a box border around the page.

- **Shadow** inserts a box border around the page and applies a preset shadow formatting to the border.
- **3-D** inserts a box border around the page and applies preset 3-D border formatting.
- **Custom** lets you create a border using the options you click in the **Preview** window.

Add a border to a page

1. Click the **Format** menu, and select **Borders and Shading**. The Borders and Shading dialog box appears (see Figure 9.11).

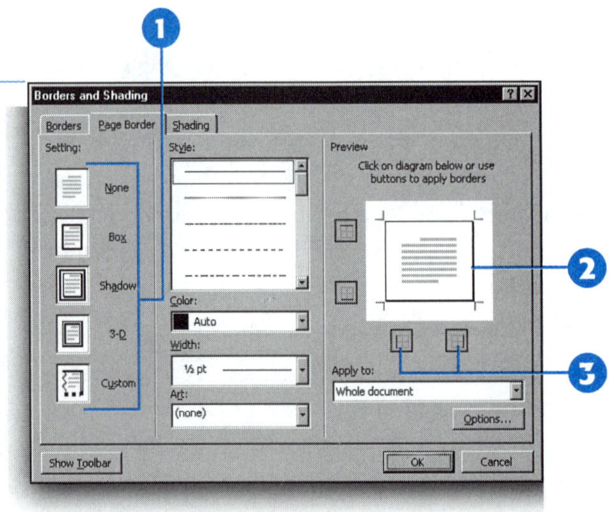

FIGURE 9.11
Select a predefined border under **Setting** or create your own by specifying style, color, width, art, or position.

1. Predefined borders
2. Preview
3. Buttons to apply borders

2. Select the **Page Border** tab.
3. Specify the options you want:
   - Under **Setting**, select one of the preset border options listed earlier in this section. When you choose any of these settings, the current selections in **Style**, **Color**, and **Width** apply to the borders.
   - From the **Style** list, select the type of line you want to use for the border, including dotted, dashed, and wavy lines.

- Click the **Color** drop-down list to select a color to apply to the border.
- From the **Width** drop-down list, choose the thickness of the border line from 1/4-point to 6 points (more for decorative borders).
- From the **Art** drop-down list select a graphical border design.
- From the **Apply to** drop-down list, select the portion of the document on which you want the border to appear (the options are described in the "Configure Page Setup" section). Note that these options also include **This section—First page only** and **This section—All except first page**.

4. Choose **Options** to open the Border and Shading Options dialog box (see Figure 9.12), where you specify the exact position of the border on the page in relation to the edge of the page or the text (the default setting is 24 points, about 1/3 inch from the edge of the paper). Choose **OK** to return to the Borders and Shading dialog box.

Using preview to make custom borders

The Preview box shows you how your borders will look but also lets you define different borders on different sides of the page or have no borders on designated sides of the page. Choose the **Custom** setting and then select the border attributes. In the Preview box, click on the individual border lines or use the border line buttons to apply or remove borders. Change the attributes and then use the Preview box again to apply a different line style on another side (this doesn't work with art borders).

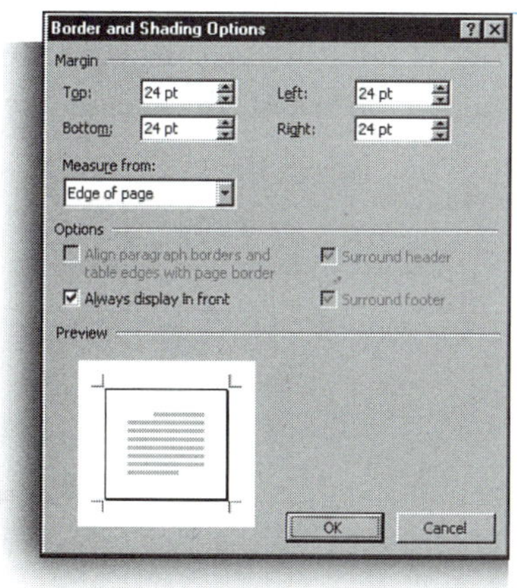

FIGURE 9.12

Specify the location of the border on the page by entering values in the **Margin** boxes and designating where the measurements start in the **Measure From** box.

5. Click **OK** to apply your border to the page or pages you specified (see Figure 9.13).

SEE ALSO

➤ *Learn about text borders, see page 127*

FIGURE 9.13

A page border makes a handsome title page.

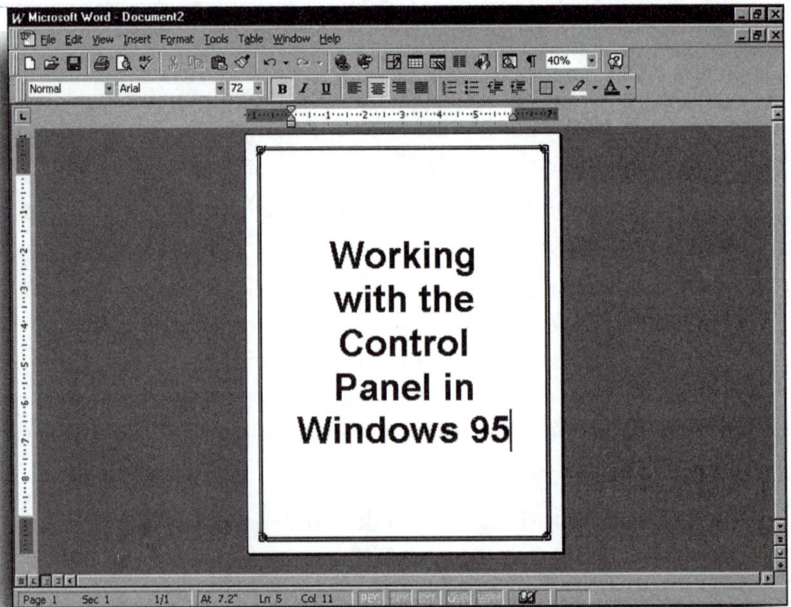

Modify an existing border

1. Click the **Format** menu, and select **Borders and Shading**.
2. In the Borders and Shading dialog box, select the **Page Border** tab (refer to Figure 9.11).
3. Select the options you want using the instructions from the previous section. To change only one side of a border, click **Custom** in the **Setting** area. Specify the new border attributes. Then, under Preview, click the border you want to change.
4. Click **OK** to apply your modifications to the page border.

Page borders add distinction to certificates and awards and make title pages stand out. You want to be conservative, however, in your use of boxes. If you have a page border, you should think twice about also adding lines between columns, boxes around graphics, and borders on paragraphs. Too many lines detract from your page content.

Apply Shading to Online Pages

Although you can apply shading to paragraphs and tables, you can't apply shading to whole pages to be printed. However, if you intend your document to be viewed online—that is, on a computer screen—then you can apply a background color by switching to Online Layout view.

Online Layout view is a new feature of Word 97 that is intended to make online viewing of documents easier. In Online Layout view, Word automatically switches to a larger font and wraps text within the window boundaries rather than the printed page margins (see Figure 9.14). Click the **View** menu, and select **Online Layout** to switch to Online Layout view or click the Online View button at the bottom left corner of the screen.

Easy navigating

The Document Map is automatically a part of the Online Layout view. It appears on the left side of the screen and displays the headings in your document (if you used Word's default styles). Click a heading to quickly move to that location in the document.

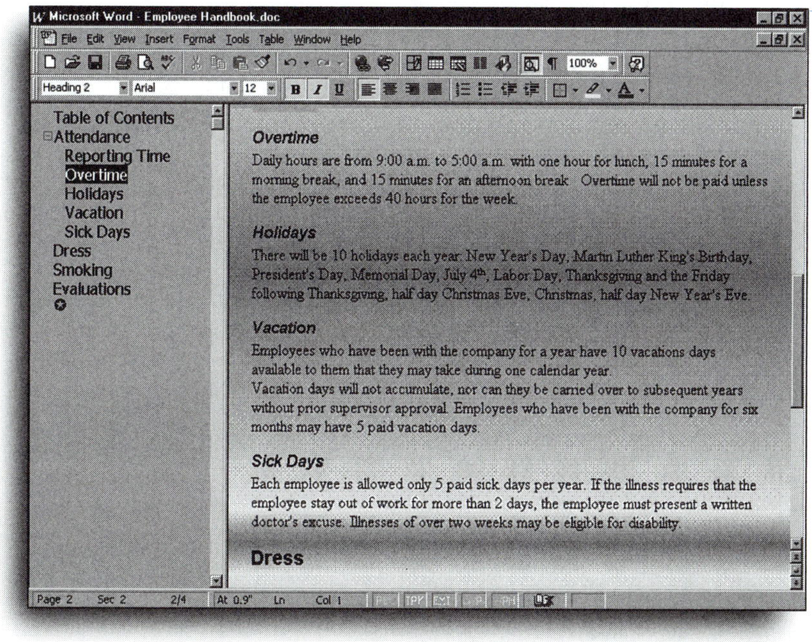

FIGURE 9.14
Backgrounds can be viewed only in Online Layout view.

Add a background to an online page

1. Switch to Online Layout view.
2. Click the **Format** menu and select **Background**.

3. A submenu appears with color choices. Select a color swatch to have that color become the background color. That color is applied uniformly across the entire page.
4. (Optional) If you aren't satisfied with the color choices offered, do one of the following:
   - Click **More Colors** to see a greater selection of colors. Select a color swatch from the **Standard** tab, or mix a color based on color values on the **Custom** tab. Choose **OK**.
   - Click **Fill Effects** to select from various gradients (colored in varying shades, such as light to dark of the same color), textures (such as marble), patterns (such as checks), or pictures (logos or clip art) to fill the background of the page. Click **OK** to apply your selection to the page background.
   - Click **No Fill** to remove the color.

SEE ALSO

➤ *For more information about Online animated text, see page 47*
➤ *For more information on fill effects, see page 369*

CHAPTER 10

Organizing Documents with Outlines, Footnotes, and Endnotes

Generate outlines

Create footnotes and endnotes

Generate Outlines

The purpose of an outline is to organize a document by setting forth its basic parts in a logical order. The outline becomes the framework on which you build your document.

Outline view versus outline numbering

Don't confuse Word's Outline view with paragraph outline numbering (which is discussed in Chapter 7, "Work with Lists"). Paragraph outline numbering refers to the assignment of numbers to paragraphs in a multilevel fashion, and Word also helps you to do that. Outline view works with paragraph heading styles to help you organize an entire document.

Word's Outline view lets you reduce a large document down to its headings for easier viewing and organization of the document. When a document is in Outline view, you can reorganize it quickly and easily by rearranging the order of the headings, demoting headings to lower levels, and promoting headings to higher levels. All text (including lower-level headings) nested beneath a heading goes with it when you move, demote, or promote the heading.

To view a document in Outline view, click the Outline View icon at the bottom of the screen or click the **View** menu and select **Outline**. When you switch to Outline view, the Outlining toolbar appears on your screen and a heading symbol appears in front of each paragraph of your document. If a paragraph has a heading style attached to it, it is a heading paragraph and its heading symbol is a plus or minus sign. It is a plus sign if the heading has subheadings or body text below it. It is a minus sign if the heading has no subheadings or body text below it. If a paragraph does not have a heading style attached, Outline view treats it as a body text paragraph (even though you might intend it to be a heading) and its "heading" symbol is a small square (see Figure 10.1).

To see your document headings in the hierarchical form shown in Figure 10.1, either promote your heading paragraphs to outline headings in Outline view or apply Word's predefined heading styles (Heading 1 through Heading 9) to your headings. Both methods accomplish the same thing, which is the assignment of Word's predefined heading styles to your heading paragraphs. You may change the format of these styles to suit your document, but don't change the names or their hierarchical relationship. Heading 1 is a major heading, Heading 2 is a subheading under Heading 1, Heading 3 is a subheading under Heading 2, and so on.

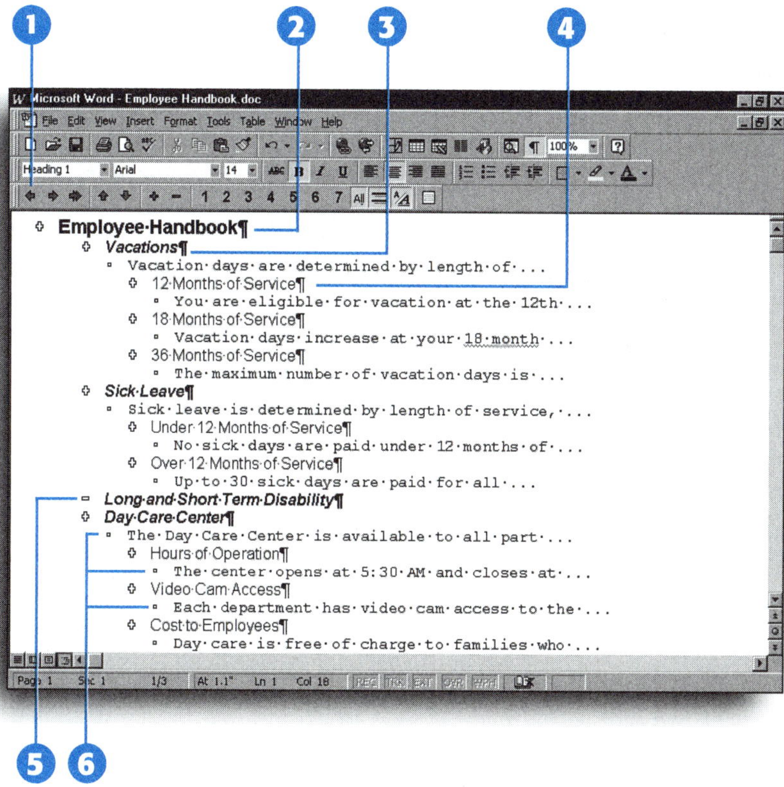

FIGURE 10.1

In Outline view, you can hide nonheading paragraphs to more easily see your document's structure, and you can hide all but the first lines of paragraphs.

1. Outlining toolbar
2. Level 1 heading
3. Level 2 heading (indented)
4. Level 3 heading (indented further)
5. Heading with no subordinate text (shows a minus symbol)
6. Body text paragraphs (showing only the first line)

You can hide the *subordinate text* in Outline view (the body text under the heading) and show only the main headings. You may also show only the first line of every paragraph, as we did in Figure 10.1. When the subordinate text is hidden, the outline is *collapsed*. A line under the heading represents the subordinate text, and a plus sign symbol appears in front of the heading indicating that there is subordinate text. When you show the subordinate text again, the outline is *expanded*. Keep in mind that selecting a heading (by clicking its heading symbol) also selects the subordinate text under it, whether collapsed or not. Therefore, if you move, copy, or delete the heading, you'll also be moving, copying, or deleting its subordinate text.

Table 10.1 describes how to collapse and expand headings.

TABLE 10.1 **Collapsing and expanding headings**

To:	Do this:
Collapse all text below a specific level of heading	Choose the number button on the Outlining toolbar for the lowest heading you want to display. For example, choose Show Heading 4 [1] to show heading levels 1 through 4.
Collapse or display all subheadings and body text under a heading	Double-click the plus sign next to the heading.
Collapse or expand text under a heading, one level at a time	Click the heading text, and then choose Collapse [-] or Expand [+] on the Outlining toolbar.
Collapse or expand all body text in the document	Choose All on the Outlining toolbar.
Display only the first line of body text	Choose Show First Line Only [=] on the Outlining toolbar. An ellipsis (...) after the first line indicates that additional lines of text are collapsed.

SEE ALSO

➤ *For more information on creating, applying, and modifying styles, see page 158*

Creating Outlines from Scratch

The best way to start writing a long document is to organize it with an outline. When you create the outline in Outline view, you're also creating the document by creating its headings.

Create and organize a document with an outline

1. Start a new document.
2. Switch to Outline view by choosing Outline View from the view buttons at the bottom left of the screen or by clicking the **View** menu, and selecting **Outline**.
3. Type each heading you want to include in the document, pressing Enter after each one. Word automatically applies the Heading 1 style to each heading.
4. To change the heading level (and also its style), drag the plus or minus sign that precedes the heading. Drag the sign to the right to demote the heading to a lower level or drag it to

the left to promote the heading to a higher level.
Alternately, place the text cursor anywhere in a heading paragraph and then choose the Demote icon or the Promote icon on the Outlining toolbar.
To demote a heading to body text, click on the Demote to Body Text icon in the Outlining toolbar.

5. To change the order of the headings in the document, drag the plus or minus symbol in front of the heading up or down to the desired location. Or put the text cursor anywhere in the heading paragraph, then choose Move Up or Move Down on the Outlining toolbar.
6. When you have the headings in the desired order and at their proper levels, switch to the Page Layout view or the Normal view (click the appropriate view button at the bottom of the screen) to add the body text, graphics, tables, charts, and so on.

SEE ALSO

➤ *Learn how to create a PowerPoint presentation from a Word outline, see page 352*

Using Outline Views to Rearrange Existing Text

If you created a document without using outlining and later you want to use Word's Outline view to review or reorganize it, you can do so at any time by switching to Outline view. If you assigned any of Word's predefined heading styles (Heading 1 through Heading 9) to any paragraphs, they automatically show up as the corresponding outline levels. If you assigned custom styles to which outline levels had been assigned (in the Paragraph dialog box), or if you assigned outline levels directly to any paragraphs (again in the Paragraph dialog box), those paragraphs will also appear as the corresponding outline levels. All other paragraphs—even your heading paragraphs—appear in Outline view as body text paragraphs. But you can promote any body text paragraph to any level of heading that you want, and you can demote a heading to body text.

Do any of the following:

- *Demote the heading level.* Drag the plus or minus symbol preceding the heading to the right. A vertical line appears as you drag, showing the heading level. When the line is at the level you want, release the mouse button. Or place the insertion point in the heading and then choose Demote on the Outlining toolbar. To demote the heading to body text, choose Demote to Body Text on the Outlining toolbar.

- *Promote the heading level.* Collapse the heading. Drag the plus or minus symbol preceding the heading to the left. A vertical line appears as you drag (see Figure 10.2), showing the heading level. When the line is at the level you want, release the mouse button. Or place the insertion point in the heading and then choose Promote on the Outlining toolbar.

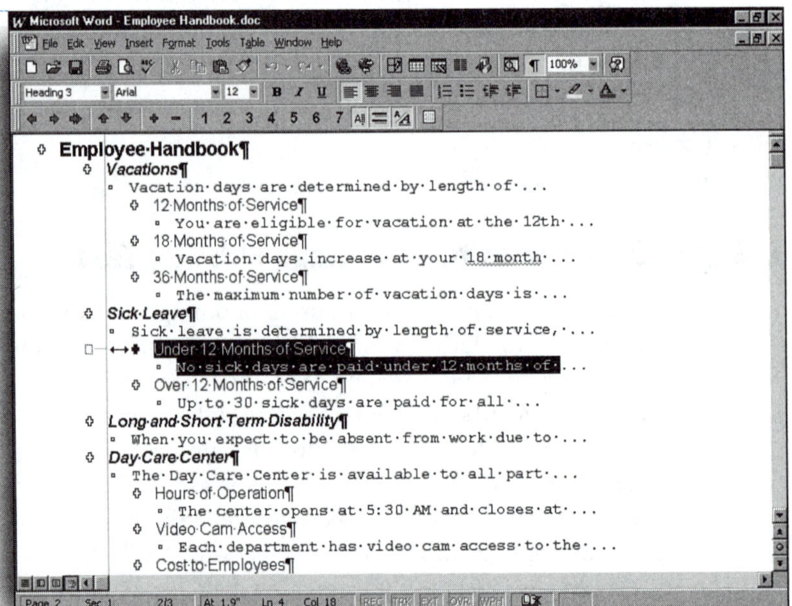

FIGURE 10.2
A vertical line indicates the heading level when you drag a heading to the left or right.

- *Promote body text to a heading.* Drag the small square icon next to a body text paragraph to the left to promote that paragraph to a heading and assign the corresponding heading style to it. Alternately, place a text cursor anywhere in the paragraph, then choose Promote in the Outlining toolbar.

- *Demote a heading to body text.* Select a heading paragraph, then click the Demote to Body Text icon in the Outlining toolbar. The heading paragraph becomes a body text paragraph as Word assigns the Normal style to it. The plus or minus symbol that preceded it becomes a small square symbol.
- *Move text.* Unless you are moving body text paragraphs, you might want to make it easier to see what you are doing by collapsing all headings first (choose 7 on the Outlining toolbar). Then drag the plus or minus symbol in front of the heading up or down in the document. As you drag, you'll see a horizontal line (see Figure 10.3). When that horizontal line stops at the location where you want to put the text, release the mouse button. Or place the insertion point in the heading and then choose Move Up or Move Down on the Outlining toolbar to move the heading up or down one line at a time. Each time you click one of these icons the selected heading moves above the one above it or below the one below it.

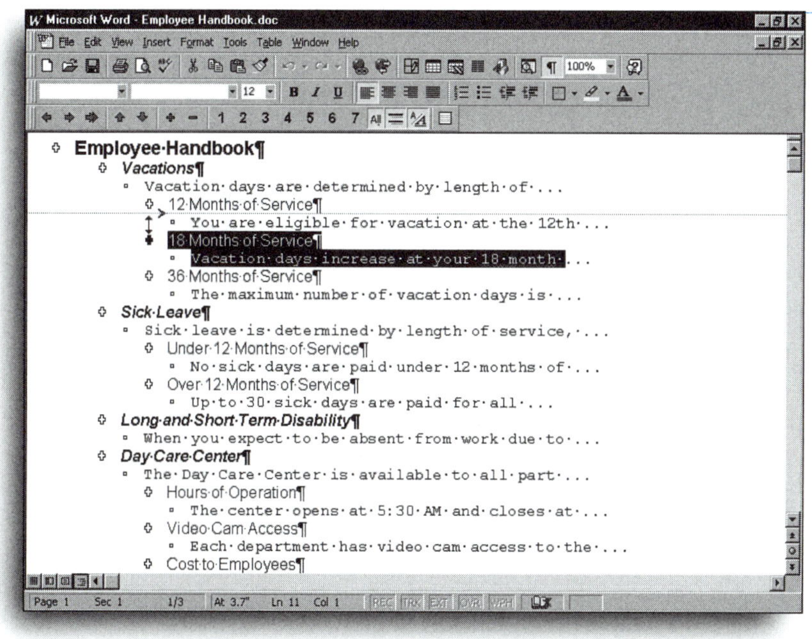

FIGURE 10.3
When you drag headings up or down the document to move them, a horizontal line indicates where the heading will appear after you release the mouse button.

- *Cut, copy, or paste text.* Collapse the heading. Click the plus or minus symbol to select the heading and its subordinate text. Cut or copy the selected heading. The cut or copy also takes the heading's subordinates—all subheadings and body text that are nested beneath it. Move the insertion point to the location where you want the text to appear, then paste. The heading (and all its subordinates) appear at the new insertion point.
- *Delete text.* Collapse the heading. Click the plus or minus symbol to select the heading and its subordinate text. Press the Delete key to delete the heading and its subordinate text.

Whether you're moving or deleting entire sections of a document (in which sections might span multiple pages and include graphics, charts, and the kitchen sink) or just rearranging paragraphs, Outline view provides the easiest way to do it. Outline view lets you do the operations on the heading symbols. When you click a symbol, Word automatically selects the heading and all its subordinate headings and text for you, instead of requiring you to manually select the text, as you would have to do in other views.

Useful Keyboard Shortcuts in Outline View

Use keystrokes instead of the mouse in Outline view to organize a document by moving, promoting, and demoting headings. Using keystrokes, you don't have to waste time moving your hand back and forth between the keyboard and the mouse.

Most outline manipulation keystrokes use the Alt and Shift keys and the arrow keys. So you can use the arrow keys to move the insertion point into a paragraph, then use Alt+Shift+the same arrow keys to move the paragraph in the outline hierarchy. You never have to take your hands off the keyboard, and you can work very fast. Try it! Table 10.2 shows the outline keystrokes.

TABLE 10.2 **Keystrokes to manipulate text in Outline view**

To:	Press these keys:
Promote text to a higher-level heading	Alt+Shift+Left arrow
Demote text to a lower-level heading	Alt+Shift+Right arrow
Demote a heading to body text	Alt+Shift+Keypad 5 (if Num Lock is off) or Ctrl+Shift+N
Move selected headings up	Alt+Shift+Up arrow
Move selected headings down	Alt+Shift+Down arrow
Expand text under selected heading	Alt+Shift+Plus sign
Collapse text under selected heading	Alt+Shift+Minus sign
Expand or collapse all text	Alt+Shift+Alphabetical Keyboard Asterisk or Alt+Shift+A
Hide or display character formatting	Keypad Slash (/)
Show only the first line of body text	Alt+Shift+L
Show only headings down to heading level *n*	Alt+Shift+*n* (where *n* is a number from 1 to 9 on the top row of the alphabetical keyboard)

Notice in the last entry of Table 10.2 that to display only outline headings down to level *n*, you press Alt+Shift+a number key *n* on the top row of the alphabetical keyboard, not on the numeric keypad. Also notice that, for most of the arrow keys and the plus and minus keys, you can use the ones on the numeric keypad only if Num Lock is turned off, but that the Numeric Keypad Asterisk never works and the Numeric Keypad Slash always works. Go figure!

Add Footnotes and Endnotes

Writers use *footnotes* and *endnotes* to provide references to *source documents* for the document text, to provide more detailed explanations or definitions that might otherwise distract the reader if left in the main body of the document, or to make comments on the text. Footnotes appear at the bottom of the page with the text they reference. Endnotes appear at the end of a chapter, section, or document.

Which to use–footnote numbers or footnote symbols?

Should you use footnote numbers or symbols? The general rule is: Use numbers if you have a large number of footnotes or if you intend to use endnotes; use symbols (asterisks, and so on) if you have just an occasional footnote, no more than one every few pages.

The two parts to each footnote or endnote are the reference mark—a number, character, or combination of characters appearing in the body of the document—and the note text. You may automatically number the marks or create your own custom marks. If you use the automatic numbering, Word renumbers the note reference marks if you add, delete, or move notes.

The note text can be any length and format, and you can format the line that separates the notes from the body of the document.

To view the note text, rest the mouse pointer on the note reference mark. The note text appears in a pop-up above the mark (see Figure 10.4). Double-click the note reference mark to display the note text in a note pane at the bottom of the screen. If you are using Page Layout view, footnotes display at the bottom of the page, endnotes at the end of the document.

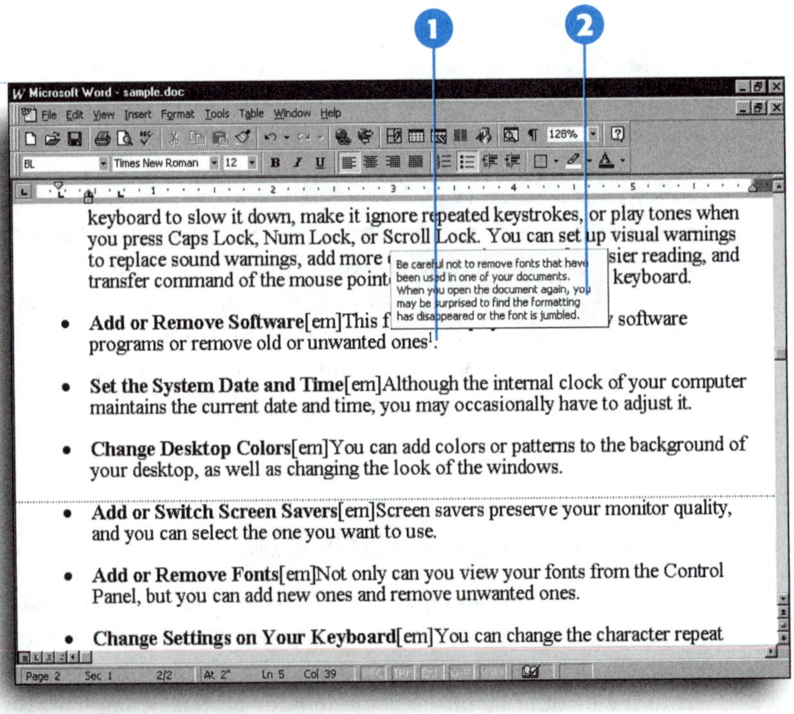

FIGURE 10.4

Point to the reference mark to see the note text appear in a pop-up above the number.

1. Reference number
2. Note text

Add a footnote or endnote

1. Place the insertion point where you want the note reference mark to appear.
2. Choose the **Insert** menu, and select **Footnote** on the menu. The Footnote and Endnote dialog box appears (see Figure 10.5).

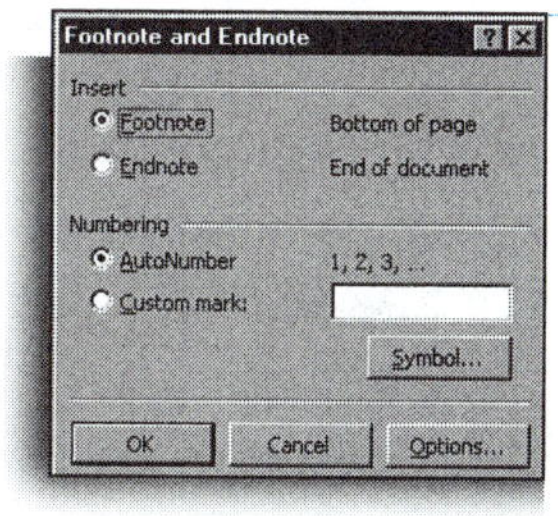

FIGURE 10.5
Choose **Footnote** or **Endnote** and then select a numbering option.

3. Select **Footnote** or **Endnote**.
4. Under **Numbering**, select **AutoNumber** or **Custom Mark**. If you choose **Custom Mark**, insert the symbol or symbols for the reference mark or choose **Symbol** to open the Symbol dialog box (see Figure 10.6), where you can choose one or more symbols. Choose a font, click the symbol you want to use, and then click **OK**.

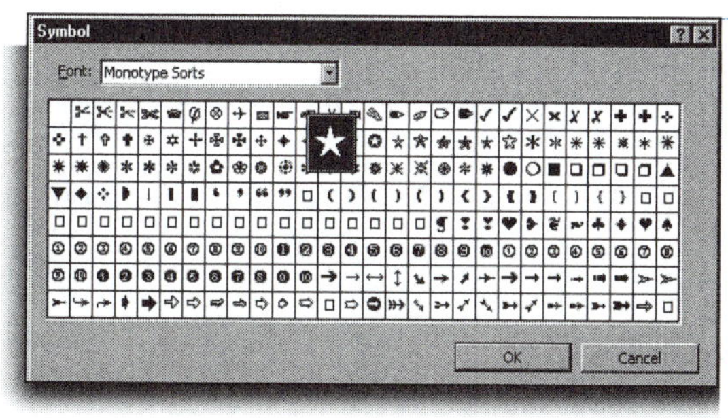

FIGURE 10.6
Select the font that contains the type of symbol you need, click a symbol, and click **OK**.

5. (Optional) Choose **Options** to open the Note Options dialog box (see Figure 10.7). Click the **All Footnotes** or **All Endnotes** tab, depending on the type of notes you're creating. The following options are available:

- From the **Place at** drop-down list, select where you want to place the note on the page or in the document.
- If you chose **AutoNumber** in step 4, select the numbering system you want to use from the **Number Format** drop-down list. In the **Start At** box, enter or select the number you want to start the note numbering with. Click **Continuous**, **Restart Each Section**, or **Restart Each Page** to specify that you want the numbering to be continuous or to have it start over at each section break or page break in your document.

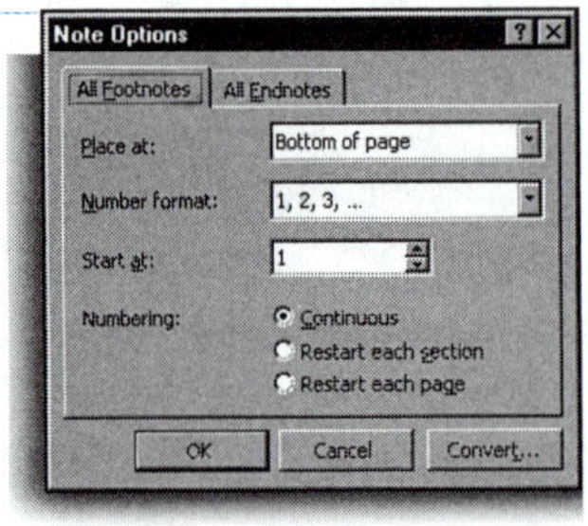

FIGURE 10.7
Set options for where the note will appear and how the numbering will be done.

6. Choose **OK** to close the Note Options dialog box, if you opened it in step 5. Choose **OK** again to close the Footnote and Endnote dialog box.

   Type the note text in the footnote pane (see Figure 10.8). Apply formatting as desired or, better yet, reformat the footnote text style (which automatically appears in the **Style** list when you insert your first footnote).

7. Choose **Close** to close the footnote pane or click in the document to continue typing.

Edit Footnotes and Endnotes

After your footnotes or endnotes are in place, you might need to change the note text, move the reference marks, change the number format, convert the footnotes to endnotes or vice versa, and so on. Follow these instructions to revise your footnotes and endnotes:

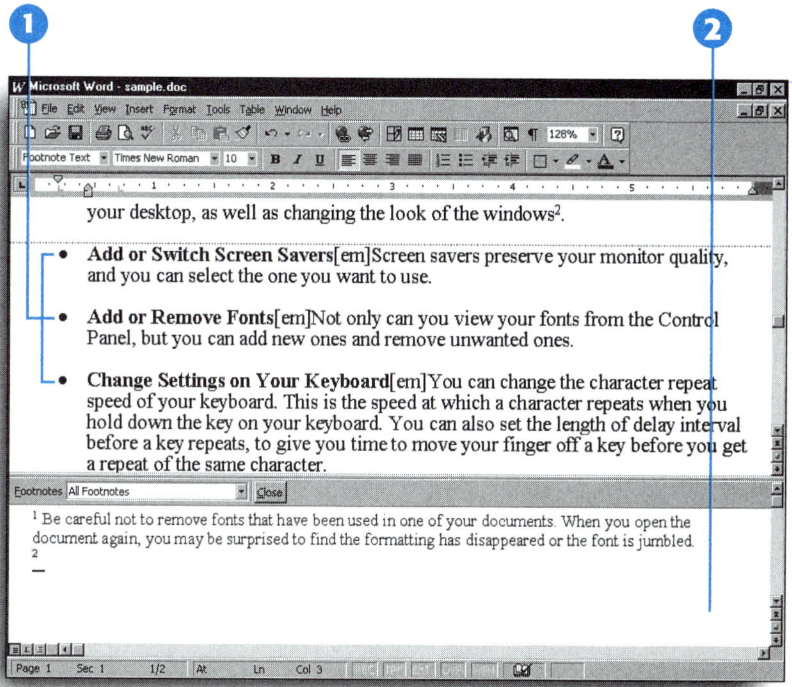

FIGURE 10.8

Enter the footnote or endnote text in the footnote pane.

1. Document text
2. Footnote pane

- To change note text in Normal view, double-click the note reference mark to open the footnote pane. Edit the text in the footnote pane as you would the document text. Choose **Close** to close the footnote pane or click in the document text to continue typing. In Page Layout view you can edit note text directly, because footnote text appears at the bottom of the page and endnote text appears at the end of the section or document.
- To format the note text or reference mark, you can format the note directly or format the styles Word assigns to them. When you create footnotes or endnotes in a document, Word automatically assigns two predefined styles to the note and reference mark. The note text receives the paragraph style called Footnote Text, which inherits the formatting of the Normal style, but is reduced in size. The reference mark receives the character style called Footnote Reference, which includes the superscript font attribute.

- To move the reference mark, select the mark and drag it to its new location. Or cut it and paste it to its new location. If you move text that has a note reference associated with it, make sure you move the note reference mark too. Word renumbers the reference if necessary.
- To change the number format of the notes, choose the **Insert** menu and select **Footnote** to open the Footnote and Endnote dialog box. Choose **Options** and specify the numbering system you want to use (refer to Figure 10.7). Choose **OK** to close the dialog box and then choose **OK** to return to the document.
- To convert footnotes to endnotes, or vice versa, choose the **Insert** menu and select **Footnote** to open the Footnote and Endnote dialog box. Choose **Options** and then choose **Convert**. In the Convert Notes dialog box (see Figure 10.9), click the conversion option you want—**Convert all footnotes to endnotes**, **Convert all endnotes to footnotes**, or **Swap footnotes and endnotes**—and choose **OK**. Choose **OK** to close the Note Options dialog box and then **Close** to return to the document.

FIGURE 10.9
Select the conversion option you want.

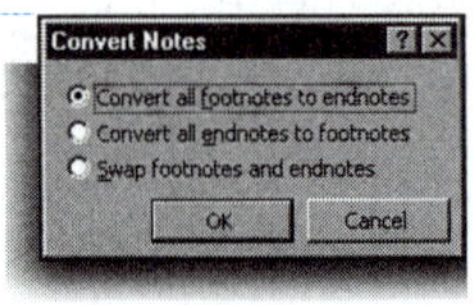

Go To or browse footnotes

You can jump directly to any footnote or endnote reference in your document with Go To (F5, Ctrl+G, or from the **Edit** menu, select **Go To**). You can browse your footnote/endnote references with the Browse buttons below the scrollbar on the right.

To delete an individual footnote or endnote, select the note reference mark and press Delete. Don't merely delete the note text; the reference remains in the body of your document and a blank line appears in your footnotes.

Delete all automatically numbered footnotes or endnotes

1. Click the **Edit** menu and select **Replace**.
2. When the Find and Replace dialog box appears (see Figure 10.10), click the **Replace** tab if it's not already selected.
3. Choose **More** to see more options.

4. Click in the **Find what** box and then choose **Special**. From the pop-up menu, select **Endnote Mark** or **Footnote Mark**.

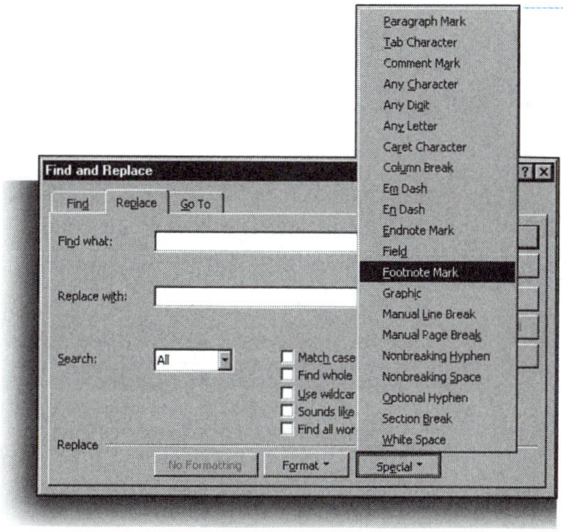

FIGURE 10.10
With the insertion point in the **Find what** box, click **Special** and choose **Endnote Mark** or **Footnote Mark**.

5. Leave the **Replace with** box empty. Choose **Replace All**.
6. Choose **Close** to close the dialog box.

Unfortunately, you can't remove all custom note reference marks at one time. You must delete them one at a time.

Edit Note Separators

Footnotes are separated from the body of the page by a short line called a *footnote separator*. If a footnote continues on the next page, the continued portion of the footnote is separated from the body of the page by a longer line called a *footnote continuation separator*. You can also define a footnote continuation notice—text that appears below the footnote and notifies the reader that the footnote continues on the next page. See the example in Figure 10.11. Endnotes have the same features, only they are called the endnote separator, endnote continuation separator, and endnote continuation notice.

Show one document in two windows

To show one document in two windows in Figure 10.11, we chose the **Window** menu, and then selected **New Window**. Both windows use Page Layout view. To hide the menus, we chose the **View** menu, and then selected **Full Screen**.

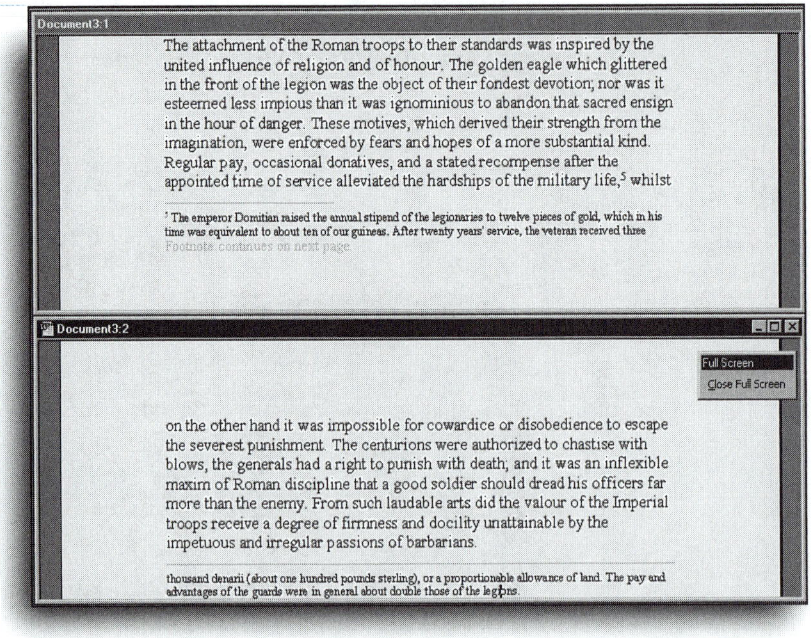

FIGURE 10.11

The footnote in the top window is too long to fit on one page, so it continues on the next page, shown in the bottom window.

Change any footnote separator items

1. Go to Normal view, if you are not already there, by choosing the **View** menu and selecting **Normal**.
2. Open the Footnotes or Endnotes pane by choosing the **View** menu and selecting **Footnotes**.
3. In the **Footnotes** or **Endnotes** drop-down list, choose the item you want to change (see Figure 10.12). If you are in the Footnotes pane, you can choose the **Footnote Separator**, **Footnote Continuation Separator**, and **Footnote Continuation Notice**. If you are in the **Endnotes** pane, you can choose the **Endnote Separator**, **Endnote Continuation Separator**, and **Endnote Continuation Notice**. If you have both footnotes *and* endnotes in your document, switch between the **Footnote** pane and the **Endnote** pane by choosing **All Footnotes** or **All Endnotes** in the **Footnotes** or **Endnotes** drop-down list.

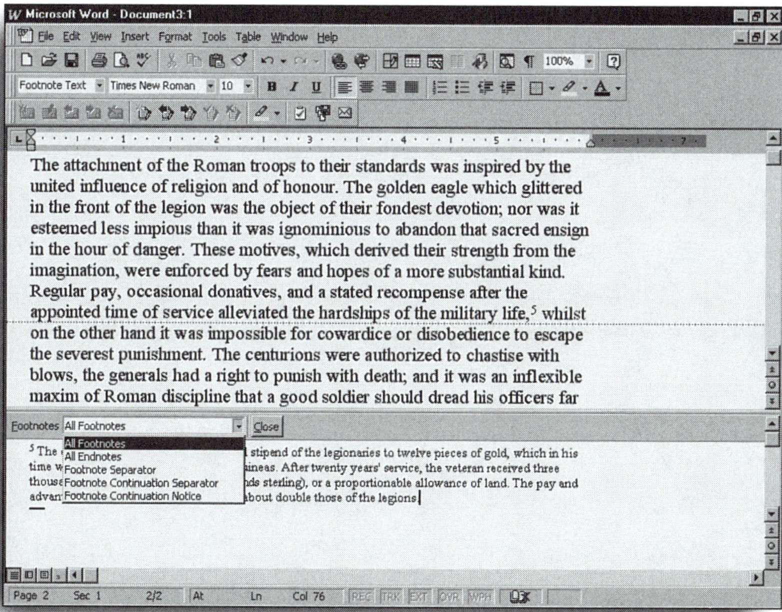

FIGURE 10.12

If your document has both footnotes and endnotes, choosing **All Endnotes** here would switch you to the **Endnotes** pane.

4. Make any changes you want to the item you have chosen. You can edit the separators, remove them, or add text, graphics, or borders to them. It is the same with the continuation notices.
5. Choose **Close** when you are finished. To see the results of your changes, switch to Page Layout view.

If later you want to restore a separator to its original format, you can go back into the **Footnotes** or **Endnotes** pane, choose the item you want to restore, and then choose **Reset**.

CHAPTER

11

Apply Columns

Create columns

Edit columns

Use newspaper columns

Use Newspaper Columns

An attractive way to lay out a large document or a promotional publication is to use *columns*. Columns break the page into two or more vertical segments so that the lines of text are shorter and easier to read. This type of layout is also more flexible for placing graphics, tables, and graphs in combination with text. That's why you see columns used frequently for brochures, pamphlets, and newsletters. In Figure 11.1, you see a document laid out in a three-column format.

FIGURE 11.1

This document, based on Word's Directry.dot template, has heading text, an introductory paragraph, and is formatted into three columns.

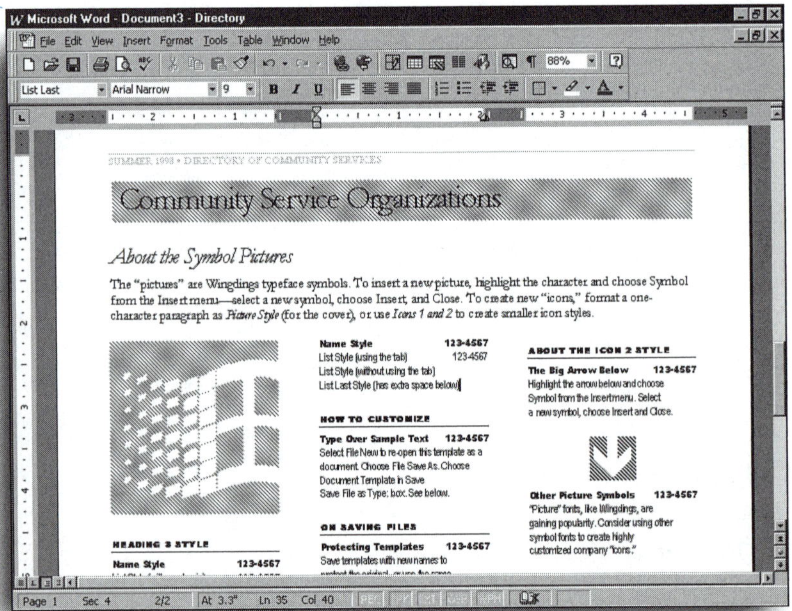

The two types of columns in Word are

- *Side-by-side columns.* These are useful for video scripts, three-fold brochures, résumés, invoices, or phone lists. Set them up using Word's table feature. With the table borders eliminated, the document doesn't resemble an ordinary table.
- *Newspaper columns.* These are used in newsletters, where text flows from one column to the next. When the text reaches

the bottom of the first column, it continues at the top of the column to its right.

SEE ALSO

➤ *Learn more about using tables to create side-by-side columns and grids, see 280*

Create Columns

A column definition applies to the entire document, unless that document has sections. In that case, each section may be formatted with different column settings. If you select text before defining columns, the column definition applies only to the selected text. Word inserts continuous section breaks before and after the selection.

To see the columns on your page, you must be in Page Layout view. Open the **View** menu and select **Page Layout** or click the Page Layout View button at the bottom left corner of your screen. In Normal view you see only one column, even if you have three or four columns defined, and text wraps within the space defined as the width of the column it is in, which usually makes the text crowd over to the left side of the screen.

You have to have at least one

Although we speak of adding columns to a document, there is always at least one column in a document—Word won't let you set zero columns.

Word has five preset column layouts:

- **One**. One column of text stretches from the left to right margin on the page. This is the default column setting.
- **Two**. The page is divided into two columns of equal width.
- **Three**. The page is divided into three columns of equal width.
- **Left**. The page is divided into two unequal width columns with the wider column on the right, and the left column one half the size of the right column.
- **Right**. The page is divided into two unequal width columns with the wider column on the left, and the right column one half the size of the left column.

Define document or section columns with preset column types

1. Unless you specify otherwise, Word formats the entire document in columns. To apply columns to only a portion of

the document, select the paragraphs involved. Word inserts section breaks before and/or after the text, as needed. To apply columns from the position of your insertion point to the end of the document, move the insertion point to the location where you want columns to begin.

2. Open the **Format** menu and select **Columns** to open the Columns dialog box (see Figure 11.2).

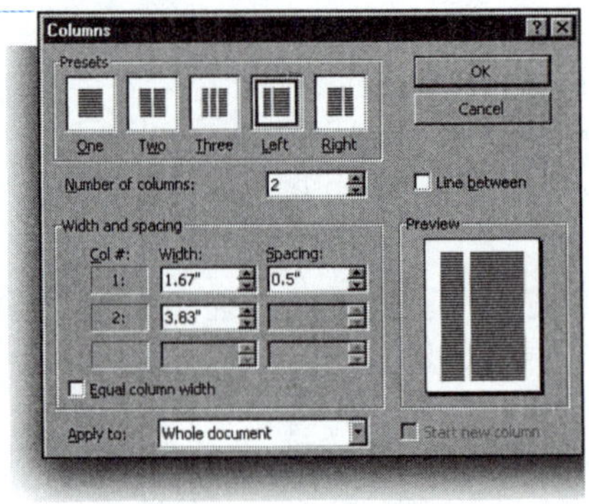

FIGURE 11.2
The Columns dialog box gives you a choice of five preset column definitions.

3. Under **Presets**, click the format you want: **One**, **Two**, **Three**, **Left**, or **Right**.

4. From the **Apply to** drop-down list, select one of the following options:

   - **Whole document**. Applies column definition to entire document. This is available only if the document has not been divided into sections.
   - **This section**. Applies the column definition to the current section (where your cursor is). Available only if you have divided the document into sections.
   - **This point forward**. Word inserts a section break at the current cursor location and applies the new column setting to the section after the break.

5. To display a vertical line between your columns, click **Line between** to place a check mark there.

6. Choose **OK**.

A quick method for applying columns, provided you want columns of equal widths, is to use the Columns button on the Standard toolbar (see Figure 11.3). Choose Columns and then drag over the desired number of columns (only four show initially but keep dragging to the right if you need five or six). When you release the mouse button, your document or section formats in the number of columns you specified.

FIGURE 11.3
Choose the Columns button and then drag to the right until the number of columns you want are highlighted.

Enter and Edit Text in Columns

Although it's usually easier to apply column settings to existing text, there's no reason why you can't first define the columns and then enter the text. Entering, editing, and formatting text in columns is no different than working in a document with only one column, except that your text will wrap at the column margin instead of the page margin. Cutting, copying, pasting, deleting, and inserting text is the same, except that it affects how the text flows from one column to another rather than from one page to another.

Figure 11.4 shows a technical document as it was originally submitted in plain text. Although it's in Courier font, which is easy to read, the document is long. Figure 11.5 shows the same technical document formatted into two columns for easier reading. Note how the same text flows between columns and adjusts after headings are added.

FIGURE 11.4

A document that doesn't have columns can be difficult to read.

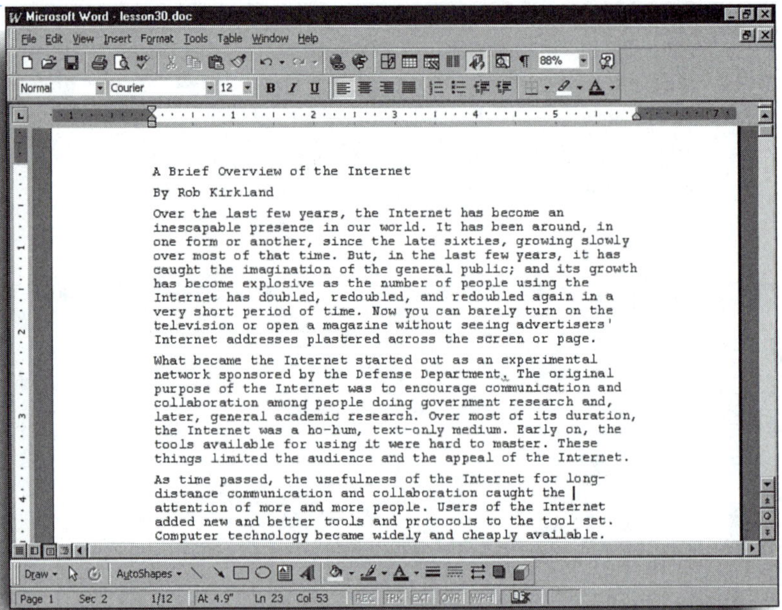

FIGURE 11.5

A document that is formatted into columns is easier to read. When you add the headings, the text adjusts by flowing to the next column.

1. Left margin of left column
2. Right margin of left column
3. Space between columns
4. Left margin and indent markers for right column
5. Right margin of right column

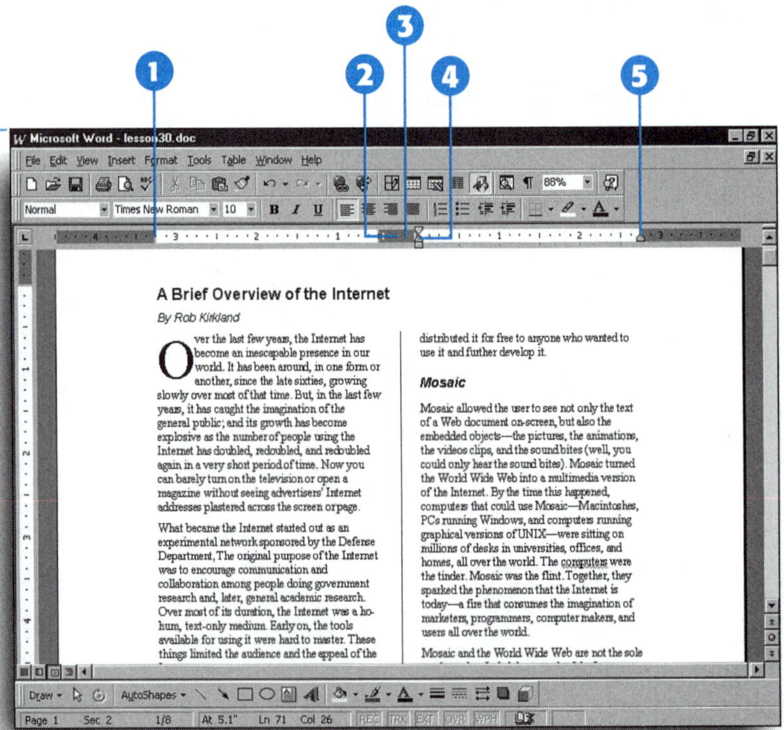

When you enter text and it reaches the bottom margin, the text wraps to the top of the next column (or to the top of the next page, if it's the last column on the page). You can change the text flow, ending the first column and starting in the next column by inserting a break.

Insert a manual column break

1. Position your insertion point where you want the column break to occur.
2. Open the **Insert** menu and select **Break** to open the Break dialog box (see Figure 11.6).
3. Click **Column break** and click **OK**.

Like a manual page break, the column will always break at that point you have placed it in the text. The column break can be deleted by clicking it or by clicking just before it and pressing Delete; or click just after it and press Backspace.

The quickest way to insert a column break

The quickest way to insert a column break is by pressing Ctrl+Shift+Enter.

FIGURE 11.6
Click **Column break** to break the column and continue the remainder of the text in the next column.

To move between columns of text, click in the column where you want to place your cursor.

Revise Column Structure

Even if you selected a preset column definition, you can still change the number of columns, the width of the columns, and the spacing between columns.

Change number, width, or spacing of columns

1. Move the cursor to the columns you want to modify.
2. Open the **Format** menu and select **Columns** to open the Columns dialog box (see Figure 11.7). The options in the dialog box reflect the current settings for the columns where your cursor is located.

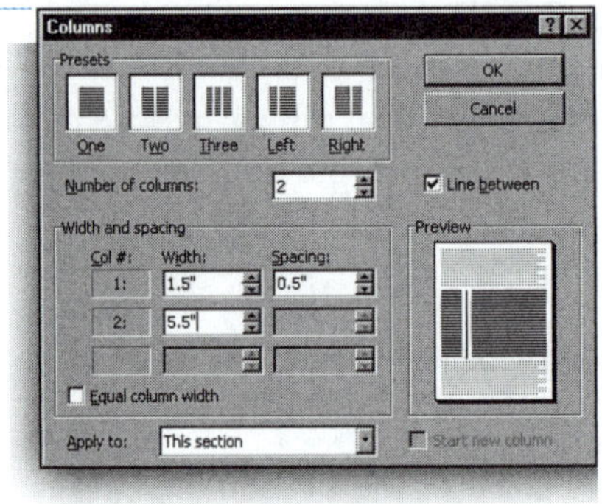

FIGURE 11.7
One way to change the column widths is to modify the settings in the Columns dialog box.

3. To apply a different predefined column format, click the desired format in the **Presets** area of the dialog box.
4. To change the width of or spacing between columns, change the values in the **Width** and **Spacing** boxes for the column you want to change (deselect the **Equal column width** option if you want to make the column widths different sizes). The **Preview** area shows you how the settings affect your document.
5. Choose **OK**.

The column width and spacing can also be changed using the mouse and the ruler. As you can see in Figure 11.8, a column marker appears on the ruler to show the separation between the columns. Point to the middle of the column marker and then drag left or right to change the width of the columns (if you set equal columns, all the columns change). Drag the left or right side of the column marker to change the spacing between the columns.

For complex documents, such as newsletters, sections help you define articles. One article can be formatted in two columns and another in three columns (see Figure 11.9).

Defining different column settings for a new section

1. Position your insertion point at the beginning of the text where you want the new column format to start.
2. Open the **Format** menu and choose **Columns**.
3. When the Columns dialog box appears, choose the options you want for the columns.

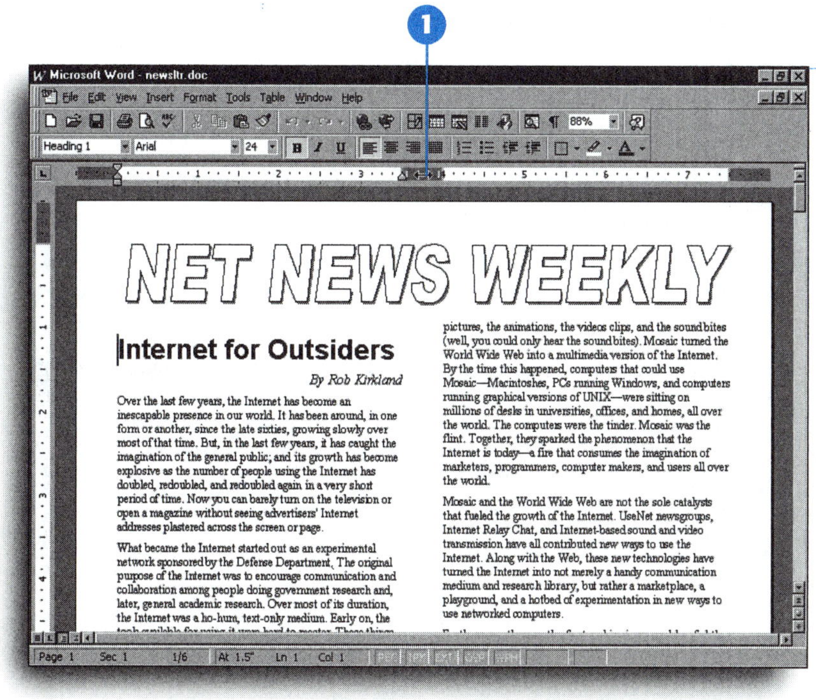

FIGURE 11.8

Drag the column marker to change the column size.

1 The mouse pointer changes to a double-headed arrow to adjust column width.

4. In the **Apply to** box, select **This Point Forward**. If you click the **Start new column** box, a page break is inserted and your new format options appear on a new page. If you leave the box blank, your formatting options change the columns, but keep them on the same page.
5. Click **OK**.

When you get to the end of the article and you want to switch back to the original column settings or an entirely different set, follow the preceding procedure again.

SEE ALSO

➤ *To learn more about section breaks, see page 178*

Delete and Move Columns

When you want to delete (or remove) the column settings from your document or a section of the document, convert the column text back to one column of text.

Converting multiple columns to one column

1. Select the text that you want to change from multiple columns to a single column (place your insertion point in the document or section).
2. Open the **Format** menu and select **Columns** to open the Columns dialog box (refer to Figure 11.7).
3. Under **Presets**, click the **One** option.
4. Click **OK**.

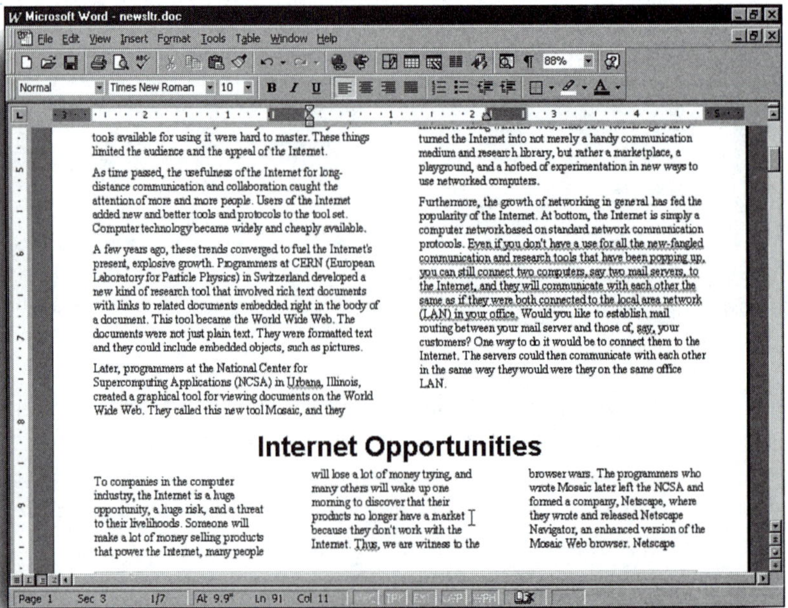

FIGURE 11.9
When you switch column formats, Word adds a section break. In this document, one section has a two-column format and the other has a three-column format.

A quick way to convert text in columns back to single-column text is to select the text (or click in the document or section). Then choose the Columns button on the Standard toolbar and drag to the left to select a single column.

Newspaper columns don't work like columns in tables or worksheets, so you can't select the entire column and then move it elsewhere—cut and paste the text instead. When you remove the text from one column, the text below moves up to fill the gap.

Then when you paste the text in another column, the text moves down to make room for the text you pasted.

Balance Column Length

Balancing column length becomes important when the last page of your document doesn't have a full page of text but your text is formatted into columns. The columns are not of equal length, and one or more columns on the page may be empty. When you balance the column length, Word puts text in each of the columns on the page and makes the columns of equal length.

For example, in Figure 11.10 you see a document where the columns on the final page only partially fill the page.

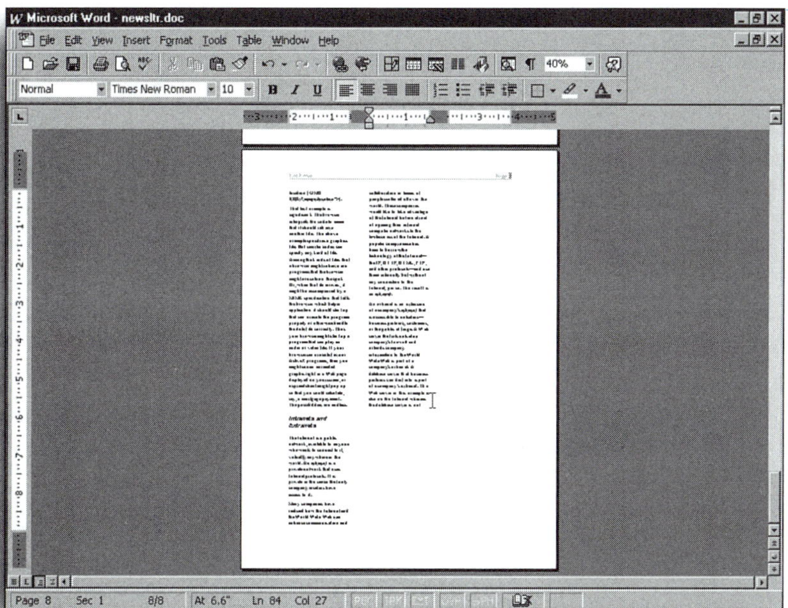

FIGURE 11.10
On the final page of this document, the text doesn't fill the page.

The person who created this document needs to put a mailing label at the bottom of the page and would like to have the text columns distributed across the top of the page and all of equal length. To do this, the columns need to be balanced. Figure 11.11 shows the result of balancing the columns.

FIGURE 11.11

Each of the three columns contains text, and the column lengths are even.

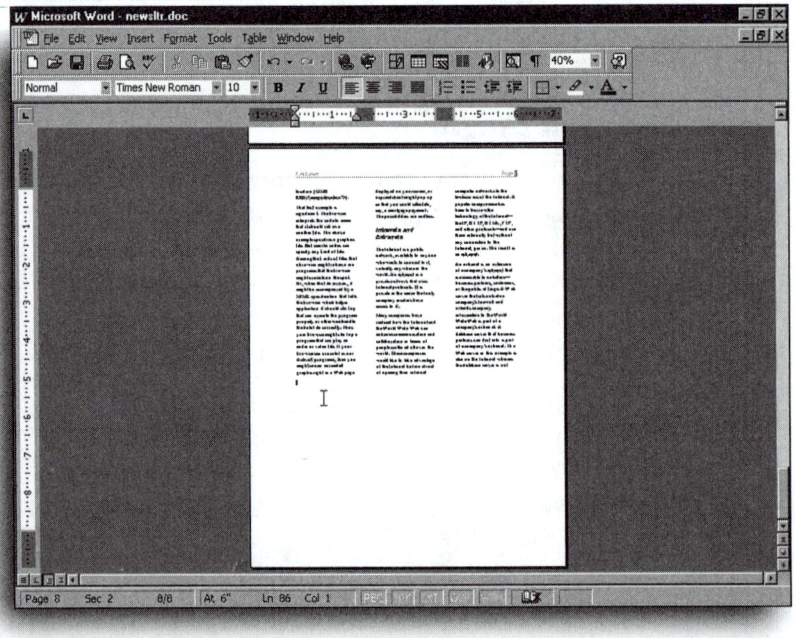

Balance column length

1. Create your columns, if your text is not already set up in columns.
2. Switch to Page Layout view (open the **View** menu, and select **Page Layout** or choose the Page Layout View button).
3. Click at the end of the rightmost column of the columns you want to balance.
4. Open the **Insert** menu and select **Break**. The Break dialog box appears (see Figure 11.12).
5. Select **Continuous** under **Section breaks**.
6. Click **OK**. Word inserts a continuous section break.

FIGURE 11.12

Select a continuous section break to balance your columns.

Keep Text Together in Columns

If you're not worried about balanced columns, but you would like to ensure that specific text does not get split from one column to the next, keep the text together by forcing the start of a new column. Figure 11.13 shows an example of text that has been separated awkwardly by the column break in the document.

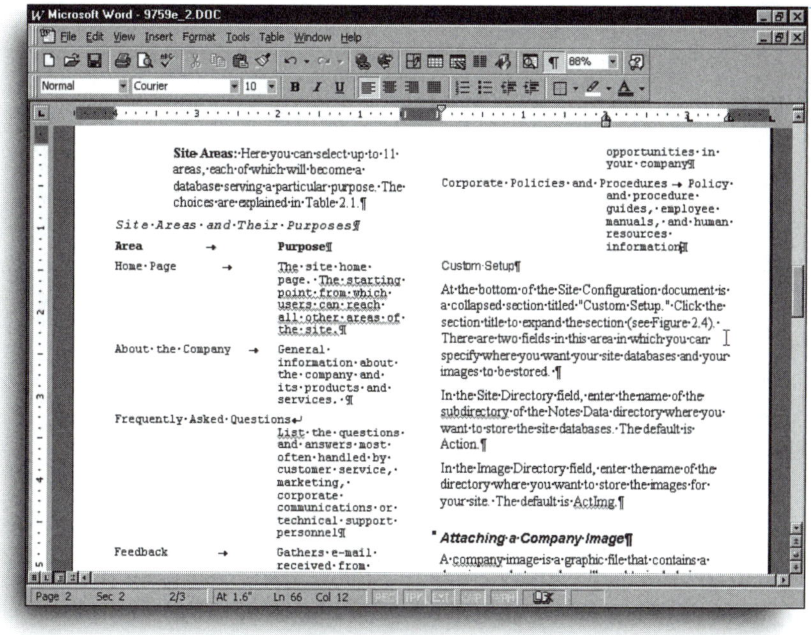

FIGURE 11.13
The automatic column break awkwardly splits the tabbed list between columns.

Forcing text to start at the top of a column

1. Switch to Page Layout view (open the **View** menu and select **Page Layout** or choose Page Layout View in the lower-left corner of your screen).
2. Click where you want the new column to start.
3. Open the **Insert** menu and select **Break** (refer to Figure 11.12).
4. Select **Column break**.
5. Click **OK**. The text after your cursor moves to the top of the next column.

Figure 11.14 shows the result of adding a column break before the tabbed text. It moves the text to the top of the next column.

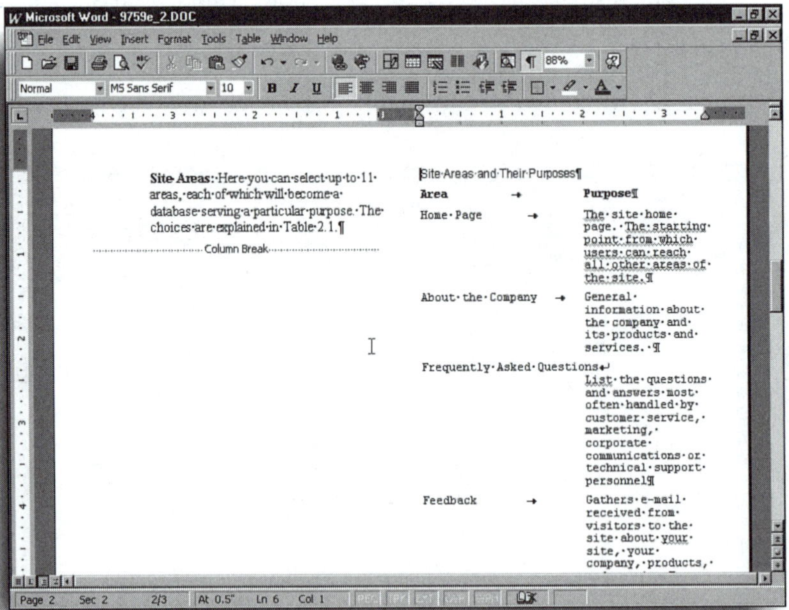

FIGURE 11.14
Inserting a column break forced the tabbed text to the next column.

This technique is also useful for putting headings and headlines at the top of a column. Insert a column break just before the heading or headline text.

Add a Heading that Spans Columns

When you're creating a document such as a newsletter, making a title run across more than one column can effectively define an article (see Figure 11.15).

Create a title or heading spanning more than one column

1. Format your text in columns, if it isn't already.
2. Switch to Page Layout view (open the **View** menu and select **Page Layout** or choose the Page Layout View button).
3. Select the heading text.

4. Choose the Columns button on the Standard toolbar and then drag to the left to select a single column. Word creates a continuous section break before and after the heading, with single-column formatting for that section.

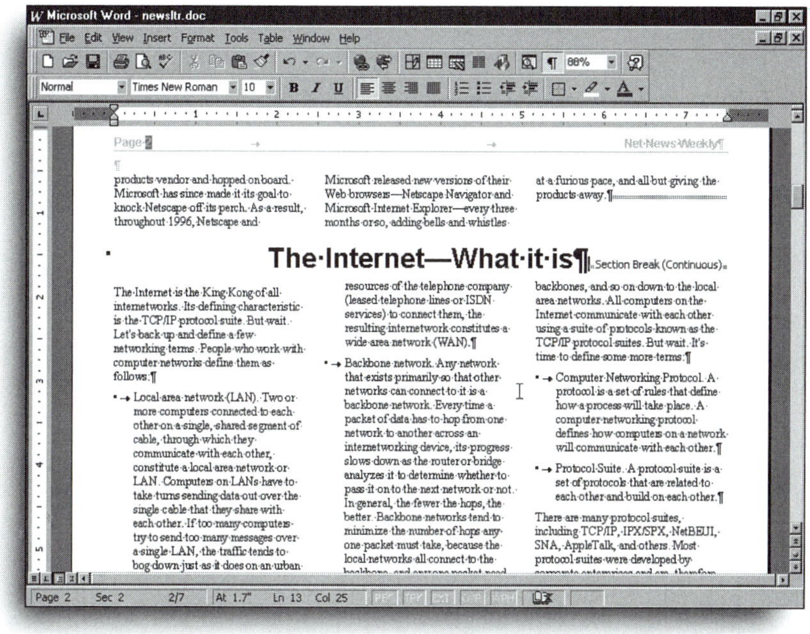

FIGURE 11.15
Use section breaks to make the heading span all the columns.

CHAPTER

12

Create, Modify, and Apply Templates

Select and modify templates

Update documents with template changes

Create new templates

Create a template from a document

About Templates

Templates are one of the fundamental features of Microsoft Word. They are the basis of all Word documents. If you choose the correct template when you create a new document, the template can do much of the work of styles and page layout for you. You definitely want to understand the significance of templates and how to use them to your advantage.

Every time you create a document, you are using a template. Even when you open the **File** menu, choose **New**, and then select **Blank Document**, your new document uses the template called "NORMAL."

Templates are Word files that usually have the extension .dot, as opposed to the .doc extension that Word assigns to regular (nontemplate) documents. (Templates may, however, have any extension—including .doc.) The contents and settings of a template are available to any document based on it, and can include the following:

- Boilerplate text and graphics
- Page layout characteristics
- Paragraph and character styles
- AutoText entries
- Customized toolbars, menus, and shortcut keys
- Programming, including wizards, WordBasic macros, and projects—programs written in Visual Basic for Applications

SEE ALSO

➤ *Learn how to create a custom letterhead template, see page 516*

About the Default Template—normal.dot

Word's default template is called *normal.dot* and all documents are based on it. Optionally, you may attach any other template to a Word document. If you do, the document is based on both that template and normal.dot.

Word creates a new document based on normal.dot if you do any of the following:

- Start up Word in any way that does not open an existing document.
- Create a new document by clicking New on the Standard toolbar.
- Open the **File** menu and choose **New**, then choose **Blank Document** (which is how the normal.dot template is identified in the New dialog box).

You can change the initial settings of new documents by changing the settings of normal.dot. If normal.dot ever becomes corrupted or if you want to quickly return it to its original settings, you can simply delete it or move it out of the folders in which Word looks for templates.

When Word fails to find normal.dot, it creates a new normal.dot file that has the settings of the original, default normal.dot file.

Protect Templates from Viruses

In working with templates that contain macros, you may see warning messages displayed when you first open the template. This is because macro *viruses* can affect a document template. Opening a document with a macro virus infects your Normal template and the virus can be transmitted to other users who open the file, and other documents based on that template. The warning message that appears does not necessarily indicate that the template is infected with a virus, only that it contains macros and, therefore, has the potential for carrying a virus. When the message appears, you have two choices: to use the template with the macros or to use the template without the macros.

You can obtain a virus protection macro at the Microsoft Word Web site that helps to protect your Normal template from virus infection. This macro *MVTOOL* (Macro Virus Protection Tool) locks and password protects your normal.dot file. This macro prevents an infected Word 97 file from infecting your Word environment. The protection is active as long as you do not edit or modify the macros in your normal.dot template. If you want to edit or modify them, you must provide a password (which you assign the first time you run the downloaded macro). After you use your password, the virus protection is no longer active and you must restart Word for the protection to become activated again. Visit the Microsoft site at `www.microsoft.com` and search for "virus" or MVTOOL. Keep in mind that you should read all Word virus information at the Microsoft site when you visit, as new viruses pop up all the time and virus information is updated frequently. The instructions for downloading and installing the MVTOOL are provided by Microsoft at their site.

If you regularly use antivirus software and have scanned files and templates for viruses, you may feel confident enough to disable the macro virus warning. To do this, from the **Tools** menu select **Options** and the Options dialog box appears. Select the **General** tab and clear the **Macro virus protection** box.

If you aren't running antivirus software, it's a good idea to purchase and run this software on a regularly scheduled basis. Virus protection software is a critical tool when you are downloading files from other sources or sharing files at work. You can purchase virus protection software at your local software supplier. This software usually runs around $50.00.

SEE ALSO

➤ *Learn how to run macros, see page 500*

About Other Templates and Where to Find Them

Word comes with numerous templates in addition to normal.dot. You should base your documents on these whenever possible because they generally make the job of creating attractive, functional documents much easier than using just normal.dot, which merely gives you a blank document.

The other templates help you create nicely formatted letters, memos, reports, fax cover sheets, resumes, newsletters, Web pages—almost any kind of standard document. They include features specific to the kind of document you would create with them.

For example, Word comes with four templates for creating interoffice memos. The first three each set up memos for you, with all the boilerplate text ("To:", "From:", "Date:", "Subject:", second page headers and footers, and so on) in place, and labels to show you where to insert your own content. Each template includes page formatting, styles, and graphical elements that lend a special look to your memo—professional, contemporary, or elegant. All you have to do after choosing one of these templates is enter your text (see Figure 12.1).

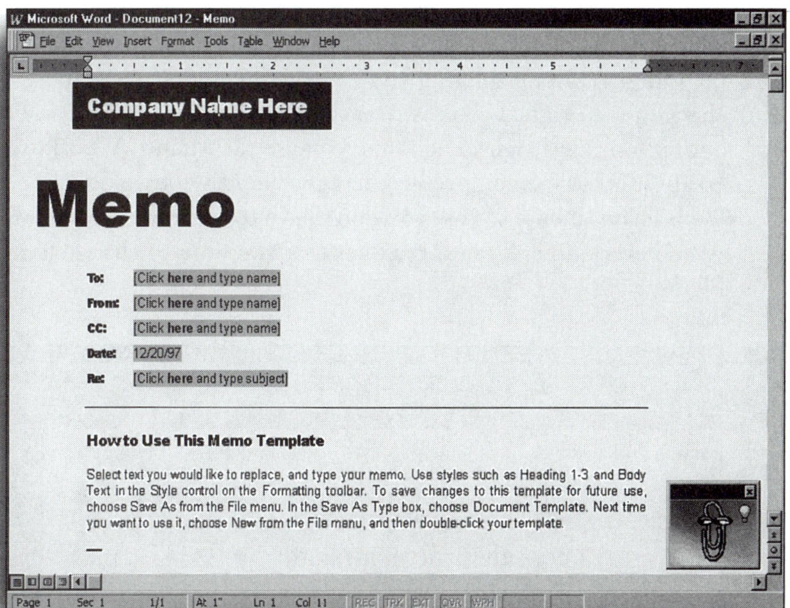

FIGURE 12.1
This document is based on the Professional Memo template and is ready for you to replace the sample text with your own.

The fourth memo template is really a wizard—the Memo Wizard. It prompts you for all sorts of variables, such as which of the three memo templates you want to use, what boilerplate text will be included, who the recipients will be, and what text will appear in the headers and footers (see Figure 12.2).

SEE ALSO

➤ *For more information on wizards, see page 510*

FIGURE 12.2
On the left side, the opening screen of the Memo Wizard displays a map of all the steps the wizard takes you through.

After you have made your choices and the memo appears onscreen, the wizard remains in memory and, in the guise of the Office Assistant offering you a menu of choices, lets you change your original choices. You can keep tweaking the memo until it looks just right. Each time you use the Memo Wizard to create another memo, it remembers the choices you made for the previous memo so that you don't have to rechoose every option every time, but just the ones that you want to change (see Figure 12.3).

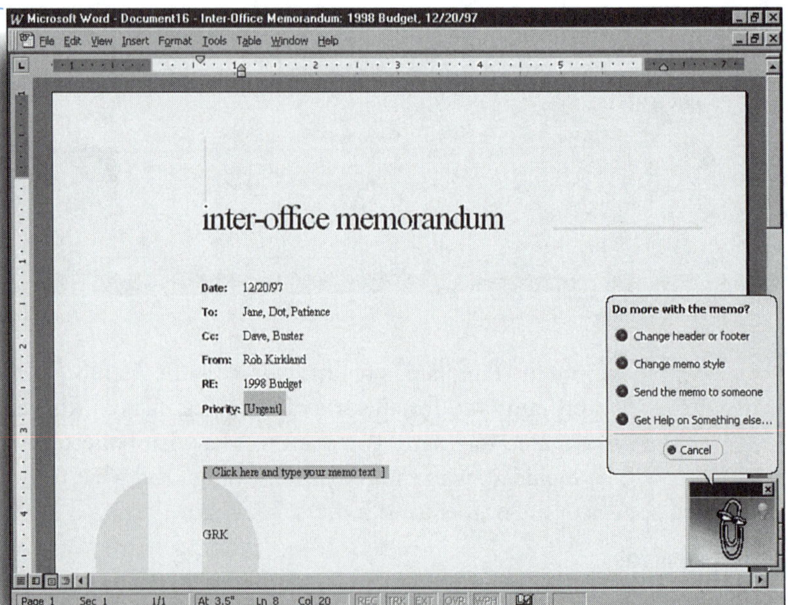

FIGURE 12.3
After the Memo Wizard displays your document, it remains in memory and displays a menu of choices in the Office Assistant balloon. Choose **Cancel** to turn off the Memo Wizard.

You can get lots of templates in addition to those that are installed with Word. If you didn't install all the templates during the initial installation of Word, you can get more from the Word or Office CD by re-running Install. The Microsoft Office CD includes even more templates in the ValuPack\Template\Word folder. If you have access to the World Wide Web, you can download even more templates from Microsoft's Web site. Go to the Microsoft Web site from within Word by opening the **Help** menu and choosing **Microsoft on the Web**, then **Free Stuff**. Figure 12.4 displays the Microsoft Free Stuff Web page, where you can find templates for customer invoices, human resource forms, and sales and marketing forms, as well as additional wizards.

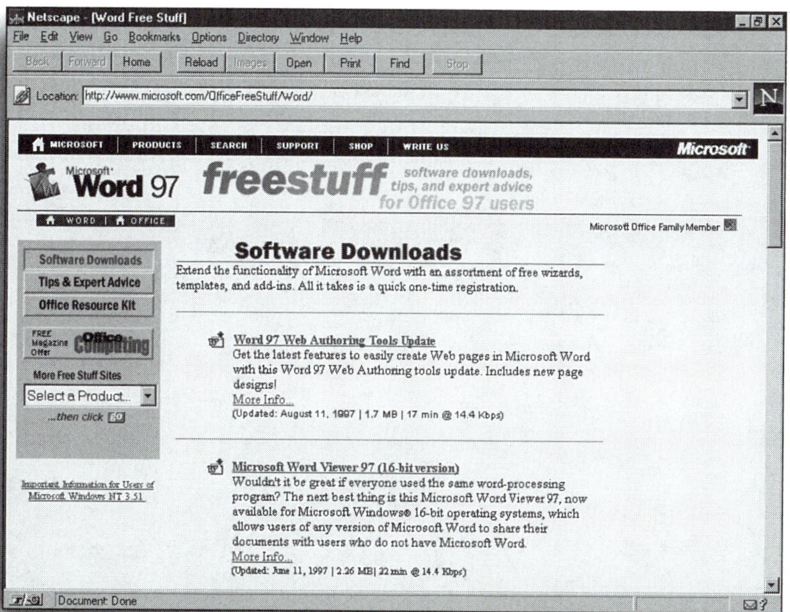

FIGURE 12.4

On the Microsoft Free Stuff Web page you can find additional templates and wizards.

Where Templates Are Stored

You can store a template anywhere you want. However, when you open the **File** menu and choose **New**, Word looks for templates in the following locations:

- The User Templates location, as set in the Options dialog box or the Workgroup Templates path if no template files appear in the User Templates location.
- The Word program folder.

For a standalone machine (one not running on or connected to a network) the default User Templates location is set at Program Files\Microsoft Office\Templates. On a workstation (network-connected PC) templates are located where the Network Administrator determines. If you are running Microsoft Office, all Office applications look to the same locations for their templates so you may see templates in these folders for Excel, Access, and so forth.

The Word or Office setup program places normal.dot in the Templates folder and the specialized templates in subfolders. When you open the New dialog box, the folders appear as tabbed panels. The templates in the Templates folder appear in the panel labeled **General**. The templates in the subfolders appear in panels having the subfolder names (see Figure 12.5).

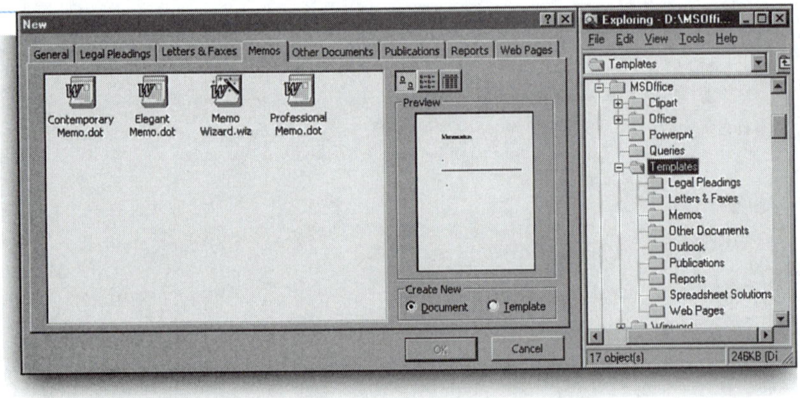

FIGURE 12.5
The titles on the tabs in the New dialog box match the names of the folders under Templates, as shown in Windows Explorer on the right.

Notice in Figure 12.5 that some of the folders under Templates (in the Explorer window on the right side of the figure) do not appear in the New dialog box (left side of the figure). Those folders don't contain any Word templates, only templates for other Office programs—Word doesn't display them. Word's New dialog box only displays a folder if it contains templates

(*.dot), documents (*.doc), or wizards (*.wiz), and only displays files with those extensions when you select a tab—even though other types of files may reside in the folder corresponding to the displayed tab.

SEE ALSO

➤ *For more information on file management and creating subdirectories, see page 108*

Attach a Template to a Document

You can attach a template to a document either when you create a new document or later. You can also make global templates available to a document.

If you attach a template to a document when you are creating a new document, the boilerplate text and graphics stored in the template become part of the document. If you attach a template to an existing document, the boilerplate text and graphics do not become part of the document, but the page formatting, styles, AutoText entries, and special menus and toolbars become available to the document.

SEE ALSO

➤ *Learn how to apply styles, see page 165*
➤ *Learn how to apply automatic formatting, see page 169*
➤ *Use AutoText efficiently, see page 81*
➤ *Customize toolbars and menus, see page 527*

Choose a Template for a New Document

Create a new document using a template other than normal.dot

1. Open the **File** menu and choose **New** to open the New dialog box (see Figure 12.6).
2. Select the tab containing the template you want to use. Then select the icon for the template on which you want to base your document. (If the template you want to use does not appear in any tab, choose **Cancel**; then move the template you want to use into the Templates folder or a subfolder; then start over at step 1.)

Using a wizard

Some of the files in the Template folders are actually wizards. When you choose a wizard instead of a template, the wizard prompts you for information in a series of steps, then uses one of the templates and the information you provide to build your document for you.

3. In the **Create New** section, select the **Document** option. (It may already be selected.)
4. Click **OK**.
5. Replace any sample text on the template with your text and add any additional text necessary to finish the document. Use the provided styles to format your text.

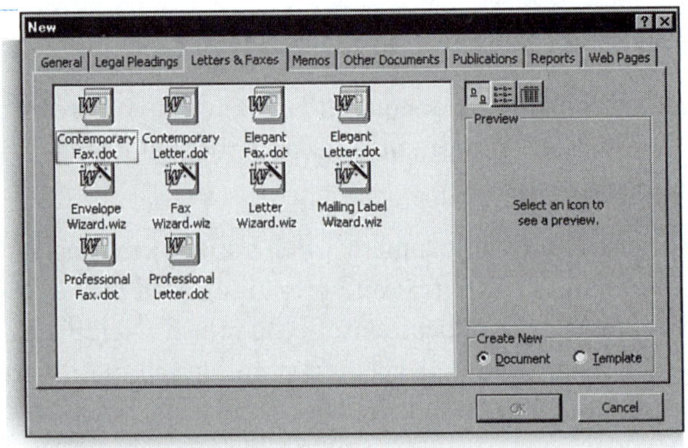

FIGURE 12.6
In the New dialog box, templates are categorized under tabs.

Attach a Template to an Existing Document

Attach a different template to an existing document

1. Open the document to which you want to attach the template.
2. Open the **Tools** menu and choose **Templates and Add-Ins**. This opens the Templates and Add-ins dialog box (see Figure 12.7).

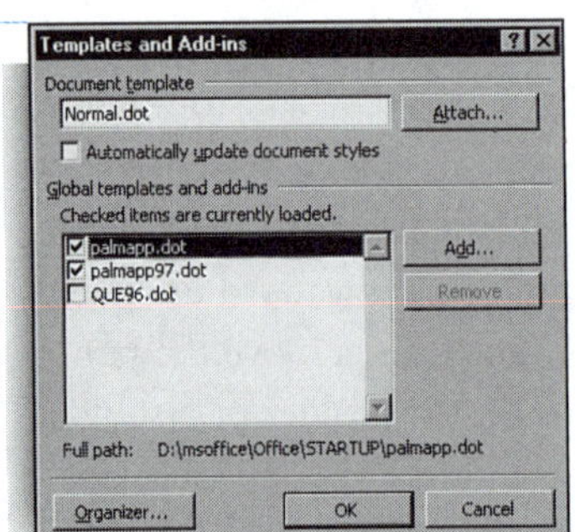

FIGURE 12.7
Attach a different template to your document to use that template's styles.

3. Click the **Attach** button. The Attach Template dialog box opens (see Figure 12.8).

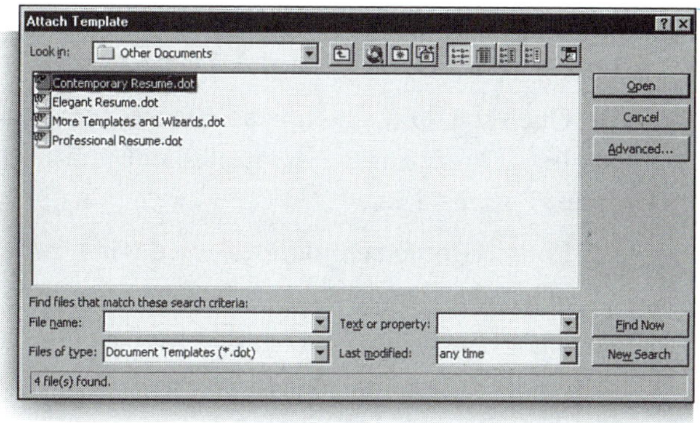

FIGURE 12.8
The Attach Template dialog box is a standard directory-browser dialog box.

4. Select the template you want to attach, then click **Open**. The pathname of the template appears in the **Document template** field.
5. To have style formatting from the new template automatically override style formatting already used in the document, select the **Automatically update document styles** option.
6. Click **OK**. The settings of the new template are now available to your document. If you selected **Automatically update document styles** in step 4, style formatting in your document may automatically change to reflect the formatting of styles in the new template.

Use Global Templates

You can make the settings of one or more templates available to a document without actually attaching the templates to the document. Instead, you can declare them global templates. A global template resides in RAM throughout a Word session and makes its settings available to all documents opened during that session. If you copy a global template into the Startup folder, it then loads into RAM at computer startup and is automatically available to all Word documents during all Word sessions.

To set up a template as global, you have to add it to the list of global templates. To use a global template with a particular document, you have to open the document in Word while the global template is in memory.

Add a template to the list of global templates

1. Open the **Tools** menu and choose **Templates and Add-Ins**. This opens the Templates and Add-ins dialog box (refer to Figure 12.7).
2. In the **Global templates and add-ins** section, choose **Add**. The Add Template dialog box appears. (It is the same dialog box pictured in Figure 12.8, but with a different title.)
3. Choose the template that you want to make global, then click **OK**. The template appears in the list of global templates.

To make a global template available to documents during the current Word session, load it into memory. Open the Templates and Add-ins dialog box, add a check mark to the check box next to the global template, then click **OK**.

To make a global template available to documents during all future Word sessions move the global template to the Windows Startup folder or to the Microsoft Office Startup folder. With the template in the Windows Startup folder, each time you restart the computer, the template loads into memory at system startup. When the global template is stored in the Office Startup folder, it starts when you start Office.

To make a global template temporarily unavailable to documents, remove it from RAM. To do that, open the Templates and Add-ins dialog box, remove the check mark from the check box next to the global template, then choose **OK**.

To make a global template permanently unavailable to documents, remove it from RAM, then remove it from the list of templates by selecting it in the list in the Templates and Add-ins dialog box and choosing the **Remove** button.

About Modifying and Creating Templates

The ready-made templates don't always meet your needs completely. Perhaps you would like to modify one slightly (or radically) to conform it to company standards or to your personal preferences. It's a simple matter either to modify an existing template or to create a new one.

You can create a new template in any number of ways. You can create it from scratch, just as you would create a new, blank document. You could turn a suitable document into a template. You could open another template, make changes in it, then save your changes as a new template.

Having created a new template, you can add features to it from other documents or templates and you can rename those features. Alternately, you can modify an existing template by opening and editing it, by copying features into it from other templates or documents, or by renaming its features.

Create a New Template

You can create a new template based on an existing template, and the new template will contain all the elements of the base template plus any text or formatting you add.

Create a new template

1. Open the **File** menu and choose **New** to open the New dialog box.
2. Select the template on which you want to base your new template. If you want the new template to start out blank, base it on the **Blank Document** template on the **General** tab.
3. Under **Create New**, select the **Template** option.
4. Click **OK**. A new document-editing screen appears based on the template you selected. Its default name (in the title bar) is Template*n*, where *n* is a number.

5. Enter the boilerplate text and other items that you want to be part of the new template. Make changes to any existing text or formatting. Apply new formatting to the text as desired. Create any new styles you might need. Define AutoText. Create custom toolbars, menus, and keystrokes.
6. Open the **File** menu and select **Save As** to open the Save As dialog box or click the Save button on the Standard toolbar.
7. Select the folder in which you want to store the template. If you want the template to be available when you create new documents, be sure to select a folder where Word looks for templates (by default, that's MSOffice\Templates and its subfolders).
8. Enter your filename in the **File name** text box. Be sure to use a different name from the template you selected in step 2, or the new template will replace the original one.
9. Click **Save**. The template is now available for use the next time you start a new document. Be sure to close the new template file before using it.

Create custom letterhead

Create a template to use as your custom letterhead. Include a date and time field (see Chapter 21, "Design Custom Forms") and add graphics, logos, or watermarks. Make the template available for use by all in your company by distributing the template or placing it on a shared network drive.

Create a Template from a Document

Sometimes you will find it useful to create a template based on an existing Word document. If you have applied a considerable amount of formatting and styles in a document, creating a template from the document saves you from having to re-create the formatting by creating a new template. This is especially useful for documents whose formatting you intend to use again and again.

Create a template from a document

1. Open the document on which you want to base the new template.
2. Make desired changes in the document.
3. Save the document as a template by opening the **File** menu and choosing **Save As** to open the Save As dialog box.

4. Select **Document Template** from the **Save as type** drop-down list. The **Save in** box automatically changes to display the Templates folder.
5. Open the folder where you want the template saved. Because Word organizes its templates by category, storing your template in the correct folder makes it easier to find when you want to use it.
6. Type a descriptive name for the template in the **File name** text box.
7. Choose **Save**.

Modify an Existing Template

When you modify a template, changes that you make are not reflected in existing documents that were created based on the template. Only new documents are affected. Rather than modifying a template, it's often better to create a new template based on it. This way the original template is still available should you change your mind.

Modify a template

1. Open the **File** menu and choose **Open** to open the New dialog box.
2. In the **Files of type** drop-down list choose **Document Templates (*.dot)**.

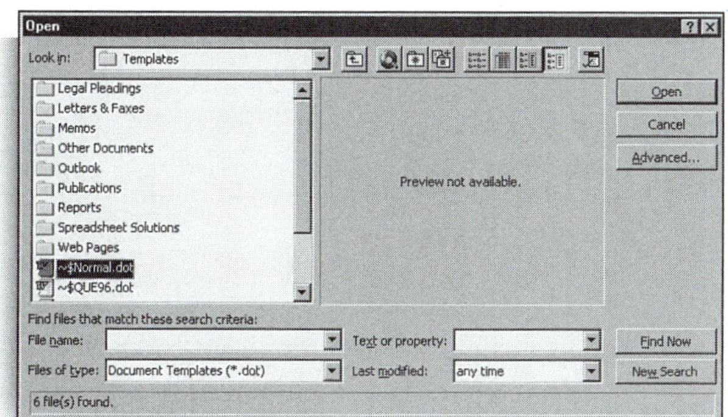

FIGURE 12.9
Only document templates appear in this dialog box.

Recycle old templates

You can use old templates from earlier versions of Word (Word for Windows 95 and Word for Windows 6.0) to create new documents in Word.

3. Navigate to the folder containing the template you want to modify. By default, Word stores templates in the MSOffice\Templates folder, on the drive on which you installed Word or Office. Select the template you want to change. Choose **Open**.
4. Make the desired modifications and additions to the template's text and styles.
5. Save and close the template when you are finished modifying it.

Update Documents with Template Changes

After you modify a template, you can force the style formatting in existing documents to update to the new formatting of the template.

Automatically update template changes to documents

1. Open the **Tools** menu and choose **Templates and Add-ins**.
2. Select the **Automatically update document styles** option. Click **OK**.

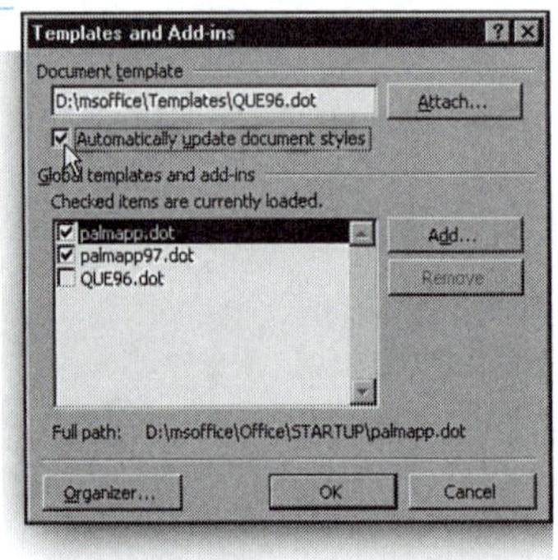

FIGURE 12.10
Be sure to check **Automatically update document styles** when you want template changes reflected in your document.

3. Open the document you want to update. The paragraph and character styles in the document automatically update to reflect the styles in its attached template.

4. If you don't want other documents to be updated automatically the next time you open them, go back into the Templates and Add-ins dialog box and turn off the **Automatically update document styles** option after you have updated your document.

Use the Organizer to Copy, Delete, or Rename Template Settings

When you create or modify a template, you might want to copy settings from other templates, rather than re-create the settings from scratch. After you have copied a setting into a template, you might want to rename it to conform to the naming convention you have adopted in the new template. If you copy a setting by mistake, you will want to delete it from the target.

You can use the Organizer to do all these things. The Organizer lets you easily copy settings to or from templates or documents, rename, or delete settings in templates or documents.

You can copy styles, macros, and custom toolbars to either templates or documents. You can copy AutoText entries only to other templates. You can't copy page layout settings or customized menus or shortcut keys with the Organizer.

Use the template Organizer

1. Open the **Tools** menu and choose **Templates and Add-Ins**.
2. In the Templates and Add-ins dialog box, choose **Organizer**. The Organizer dialog box opens (see Figure 12.11).
3. If the source template does not appear in the left window (labeled **In 15686_12.DOC** in Figure 12.11), choose **Close File**, then **Open File**. If the target template does not appear in the right window (labeled **To Normal.dot** in Figure 12.11), choose **Close File** then **Open File**. (Each of these is really just one button whose label changes when you choose it.)

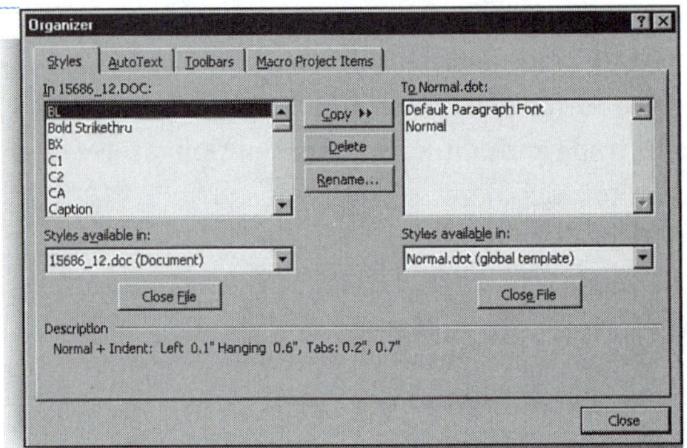

FIGURE 12.11
The Organizer shows the settings of two templates or documents, side by side. You can copy settings from the left to the right.

4. When you choose **Open File** (for the source template) or **Open File** (for the target template) the Open dialog box appears. Select the template or document that you want, then choose **Open**. The settings of the chosen document then appear in the **In [*filename*]** window (for the source template) or the **To [*filename*]** window (for the target template).
5. Choose the tab for the type of setting you want to copy—**Styles**, **AutoText**, **Toolbars**, **Macro Project Items**.
6. In the left window, select one or more features you want to copy. (You can use the Shift and Control keys to select multiple items.) Then choose **Copy**. The selected items appear in the right window. (You also can copy items from the right to the left. When you select an item in the right window, the copy button changes to indicate that it copies from right to left.)
7. If you copy an item by mistake, select it in the right window, then choose **Delete**. If you want to rename an item after you have moved it, select it in the right window, then choose **Rename**. (You can also delete or rename items in the left window.)
8. Repeat steps 5 and 6 for each tab. Choose **Close** when you are finished.

PART

IV

Print with Ease

CHAPTER 13

Use Advanced Printing Options, Print Faxes, and Send Mail

- Edit, print, and change document margins while in Print Preview mode
- Enable/disable background printing and use printing options effectively
- Print multiple copies or pages, portions of text, documents properties, envelopes, and labels
- Print to a fax program or send a document using an email program
- Change print defaults

About Printing in Word

A document printed from Word takes its printing preferences from two areas in the Word program: the Print dialog box and the Page Setup dialog box.

The Print dialog box contains information about the print job, such as which printer to use, what to print (documents, document properties, and so forth), and how many copies to print (see Figure 13.1).

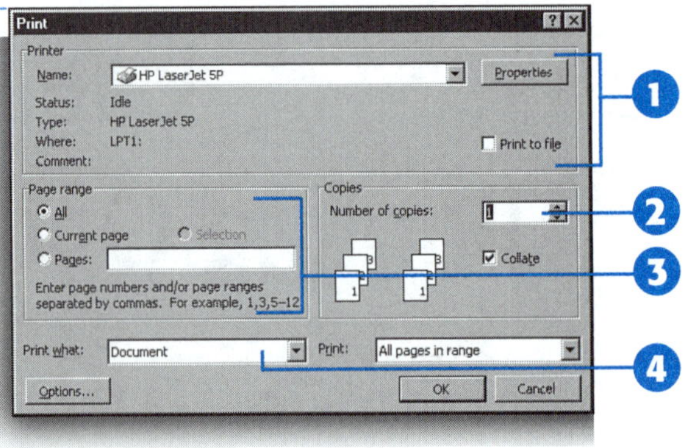

FIGURE 13.1
Choose the **File** menu, and select **Print** or Ctrl+P to view the Print dialog box and change print job settings.

1. Select printer
2. Indicate number of copies
3. Select print range
4. Select what to print

The Page Setup dialog box contains the document paper size as well as the paper source. Here, you indicate if you are going to manually feed a paper source, such as an envelope or special preprinted form (see Figure 13.2).

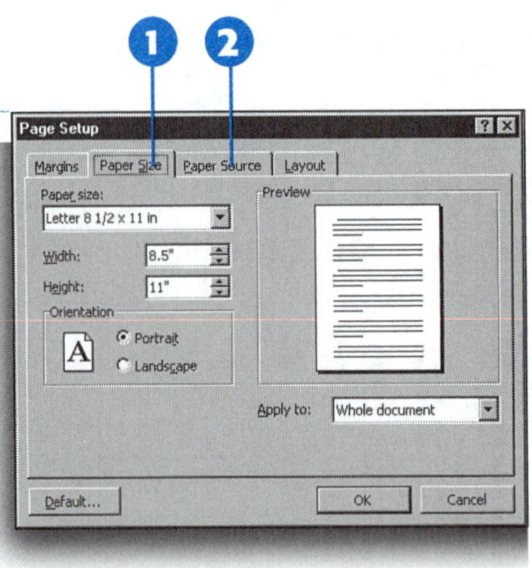

FIGURE 13.2
Choose the **File** menu, and select **Page Setup** to indicate paper source and size.

1. Indicate paper size
2. Indicate paper source

One-page documents sent to a local printer usually require little or no intervention on your part. It's possible that you will not need to access the Print or Page Setup dialog box if your printing needs are small, infrequent, or your documents are simple in layout and small in size.

It's very simple to print a single copy of the entire document on the default Windows printer using the default print options. The default print options, set in the Print dialog box, drive what happens when you click the Print button on the Standard toolbar. Using the Print button, you can quickly print a single copy of the document and bypass the Print dialog box.

Enable Background Printing

Background printing enables you to continue working in Word while your print job is being sent to the printer. If you have not enabled background printing, when you print a document, the Print dialog box appears on your screen and stays on your screen as long as it takes for the print job to be sent to the printer (see Figure 13.3). Background printing comes with a small cost, however. Background printing needs more memory than printing without background capabilities, and print jobs can take longer.

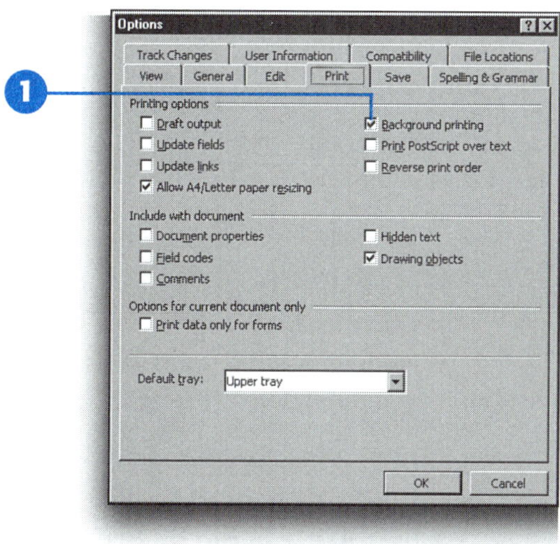

FIGURE 13.3

Enabling Background printing in the Options dialog box **Print** tab prevents the pesky Print dialog box from appearing and allows you to continue to work in Word during the printing process.

1. Disable/enable background printing here

To enable/disable background printing, open the **Tools** menu and choose **Options**. On the **Print** tab of the Options dialog box, click the **Background printing** box to place a check mark and enable it, click again to remove the check mark and disable it. When background printing is enabled, the status bar indicates the page numbers of documents being printed—while they are printing—as you continue to work in Word.

If system memory or printing speed is a concern to you, disable background printing by opening the **Tools** menu, selecting **Options**, and then clicking the **Print** tab. Remove the check mark in the box under **Printing options**.

Modify Documents and Views in Print Preview Mode

Word's Print Preview feature lets you view your document on the screen exactly as it will be printed. While Page Layout view also displays your document in its final form, Print Preview offers some additional features that you may find useful.

For example, you can change margins while in Preview mode, view multiple pages at one time, zoom, and edit text.

To preview an open document, click the Print Preview button on the Standard toolbar. Figure 13.4 displays a document in Preview mode.

To navigate, edit, print, or change margins while in Print Preview mode:

- Press Page Up or Page Down, or use the scrollbar to scroll through pages.
- To view multiple pages, click the Multiple Pages button, then drag over the page icons to preview more than one page at a time (see Figure 13.5).
- To view only one page, click the One Page button.
- To select zoom magnification preferences, use the **Zoom Control** drop-down list (see Figure 13.5).

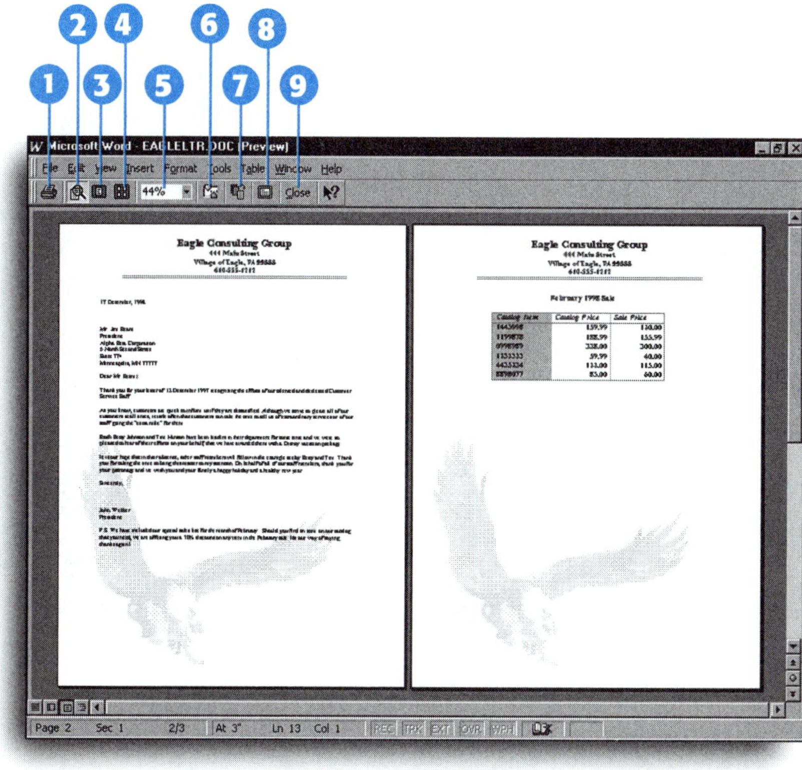

FIGURE 13.4

View multiple pages and vertical and horizontal rulers while in Preview mode.

1. Print
2. Magnifier
3. One Page
4. Multiple Pages
5. Zoom Control
6. View Ruler
7. Shrink to Fit
8. Full Screen View
9. Close

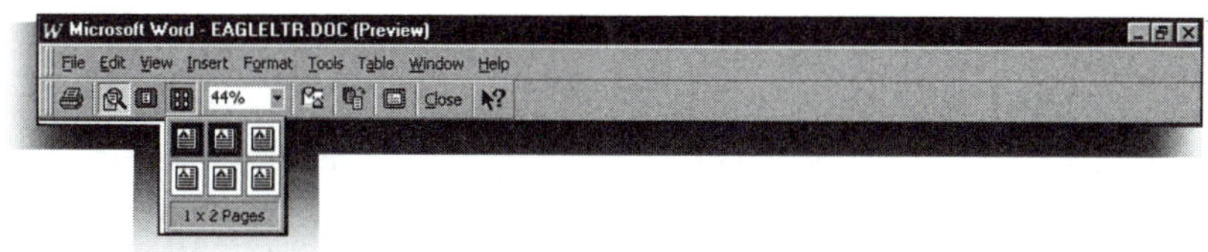

FIGURE 13.5

Select the number of pages and layout for viewing from the **Multiple pages** drop-down menu.

- To change margins, view the ruler and use horizontal and vertical rulers to adjust margin settings and indents.
- To view the document full screen without the Word program framing your document (see Figure 13.6), click the Full Screen View button. To exit Full Screen view, press the Esc key. Alternately, click Close Full Screen on the Full Screen floating toolbar that appears when you enter Full Screen view.

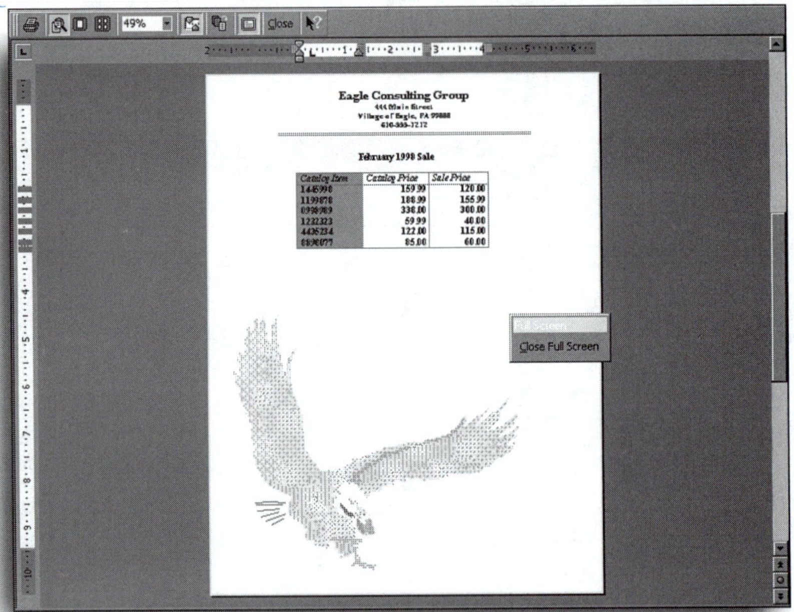

FIGURE 13.6
Navigate through document pages while in Full Screen view using the Page Up and Page Down keys on your keyboard.

- The mouse pointer looks like a magnifying glass in Print Preview. Click with the magnifying glass in the document to enlarge that part of the document. Click again in the document to return to the previous magnification.
- To edit text, click the Magnifier button on the Print Preview toolbar and click in the text to edit it.
- To fit your document on one page, click the Shrink to Fit button. Word adjusts formatting, such as font size, to reduce the page count to one page, when possible. This is useful when you have a small amount of text that spills onto the document's last page. If you save your document after using the **Shrink to Fit** option, the document is saved with new formatting, including the change in font size that was necessary to fit the document on a single page. After you save, there is no quick way to restore the original font size.
- To print the entire document, click the Print button.

- To print with options, open the **File** menu and choose **Print**. The Print dialog box appears. Select your print options in the dialog box.
- Click **Close** or press Esc to close the Print Preview window and return to your document.

SEE ALSO

➤ *To learn how to set indents using the ruler, see page 123*

Select a Printer and Paper Source

To change printers, choose a printer from the drop-down list of the Print dialog box (see Figure 13.7). Printers that are currently installed on your system are listed in the drop-down list.

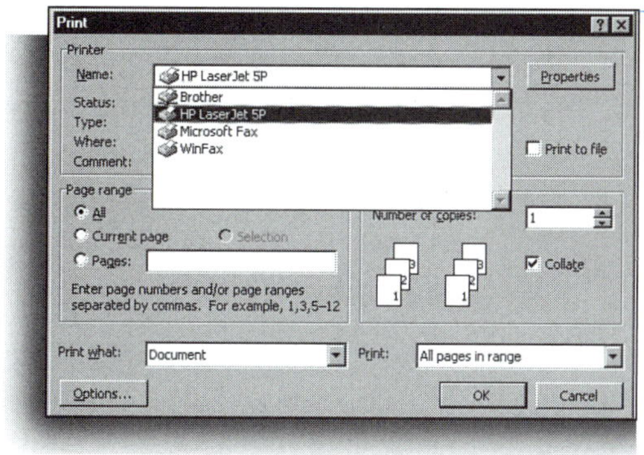

FIGURE 13.7
Printers are selected from the drop-down list in the Print dialog box. Printers may include a fax software program, such as WinFax.

Depending on your printer, printing envelopes can require that you change the paper source on the printer. In most cases, however, when you print envelopes, Word changes the paper source to manual feed. The paper source determines which tray the printer pulls from when printing the document. You might also need to change the paper source when you are printing to preprinted forms. For example, companies with shared printers often load their preprinted company letterhead in one tray, while another tray contains plain, blank paper. One of those two trays is the default tray and it might not always be the paper you need. And, depending on the printer model you are using, you can tell Word to print from one paper tray for the first page of a document and a different tray for the balance of the document.

To change the default paper source

1. Open the **File** menu and choose **Print**.
2. Click the **Options** button in the Print dialog box.
3. Select the default paper source from the **Default tray** drop-down list.

To change the paper source for the current document

1. Open the **File** menu and choose **Page Setup**.
2. Click the **Paper Source** tab and select the paper source from the drop-down list.
3. For a different first page, specify a tray in the **First Page** box and then a tray in the **Other** pages box.

Print Multiple Copies

When you print multiple copies of a document, it is helpful to collate those copies. In this way, sets of your document print in the order that you need them—so that you can staple or bind your copies.

Print multiple copies

1. Open the **File** menu and choose **Print** or press Ctrl+P. The Print dialog box appears.
2. In the **Number of copies** box, enter the desired number of copies or click the up or down arrow to set the number you want.
3. Verify that the **Collate** option is selected to have the copies collated.
4. Click **OK**.

Print Specified Pages or Portions of Text

Most of the time you will want to print the entire document, but you can print just part of a document, ranging from a single sentence to multiple pages.

If you want to print a selection of text, you must first select the text. To print a single page within a multiple page document, position your cursor on that page before you select an option from the Print dialog box.

Open the **File** menu and choose **Print**. Select one of the following options in the **Pages** text box of the **Page range** section in the Print dialog box:

- To print selected text, choose **Selection**.
- To print the current page choose **Current**.
- To print specified pages, choose **Pages** and enter the page numbers in the text box. For example, entering 1–3 prints pages 1 through 3, and entering 2,4 prints pages 2 and 4. You can also enter a combination, such as 1–3,5,7,12.
- To print a section, type `s` followed by the section number (as in `s1`).
- To print a range of sections, type `S` followed by the section number, and separate the section range with a dash (as in S2–S4). To print noncontiguous sections, separate sections with a comma (s1, s5). To print sections that contain pages that span the sections, type `p3s1-p5s4`.

SEE ALSO

➤ *To learn how to create mail merge documents, see page 399*

Print two-sided pages

To print two-sided output to a standard one-sided printer, select odd or even pages in the **Print:** drop-down list of the Print dialog box. Print the odd-numbered pages, flip the printed pages over and place them back in the paper tray, and print the even-numbered pages. Select **All Pages in-Range** to return to printing all pages. Check your printer's manual to ensure that you flip or turn the pages over correctly for printing.

Print Document Properties or Document Information

Document property information is printable and you can print property information for a current document or for several documents at once. In addition, you can print styles, comments, AutoText, and key assignments.

To print document information, select the item to print in the **Print what** drop-down list of the Print dialog box. Figure 13.8 displays a document properties printed page.

SEE ALSO

➤ *To learn how to add revision marks and comments to documents, see page 422*
➤ *To add summary information to documents, see page 106*

You can make document information print by default

To print document information each time you print a document, or to print field codes, hidden text, and other nonprinting characters, open the **Tools** menu and select **Options**. On the **Print** tab indicate which items you want under the **Include with Document** section.

Filename:	EAGLELTR.DOC
Directory:	F:\Q\UWord
Template:	C:\Program Files\Office97\Templates\eagle.dot
Title:	17 December, 1998
Subject:	
Author:	Jane Calabria
Keywords:	
Comments:	
Creation Date:	12/19/97 1:37 PM
Change Number:	2
Last Saved On:	12/25/97 11:27 PM
Last Saved By:	Jane Calabria
Total Editing Time:	23 Minutes
Last Printed On:	12/23/97 9:42 PM
As of Last Complete Printing	
Number of Pages:	2 (approx.)
Number of Words:	223 (approx.)
Number of Characters:	1,272 (approx.)

FIGURE 13.8
When you select an item other than **Document** in the **Print what** box, the print job goes directly to the printer. You cannot Print Preview document information.

Print Envelopes

Word can send envelope information to your printer and depending on your printer, you can select the envelope size you need.

Instant address

Word automatically picks up an address from your letter and inserts the address on your envelope—but not if your address is more than five lines of text. If you have a long address, highlight the entire address, then select the **Tools** menu and choose **Envelopes and Labels**. Word inserts the highlighted address.

Help the post office help you

Postal regulations suggest envelopes and mailing labels be printed in all caps with no punctuation.

Print envelopes

1. Open the **Tools** menu and choose **Envelopes and Labels**.
2. Click the **Envelopes** tab (see Figure 13.9).
3. Enter the mailing address information in the **Delivery address** area (the address appears automatically if you have a letter open that has an inside address). To format the address, select the address text, right-click it, and then click **Font** on the shortcut menu.
4. If the return address is not automatically supplied from your User Information or you need to put a different return address on the envelope, enter the address in the **Return address** area. Select **Omit** if you have pre-printed envelopes and don't need a return address.

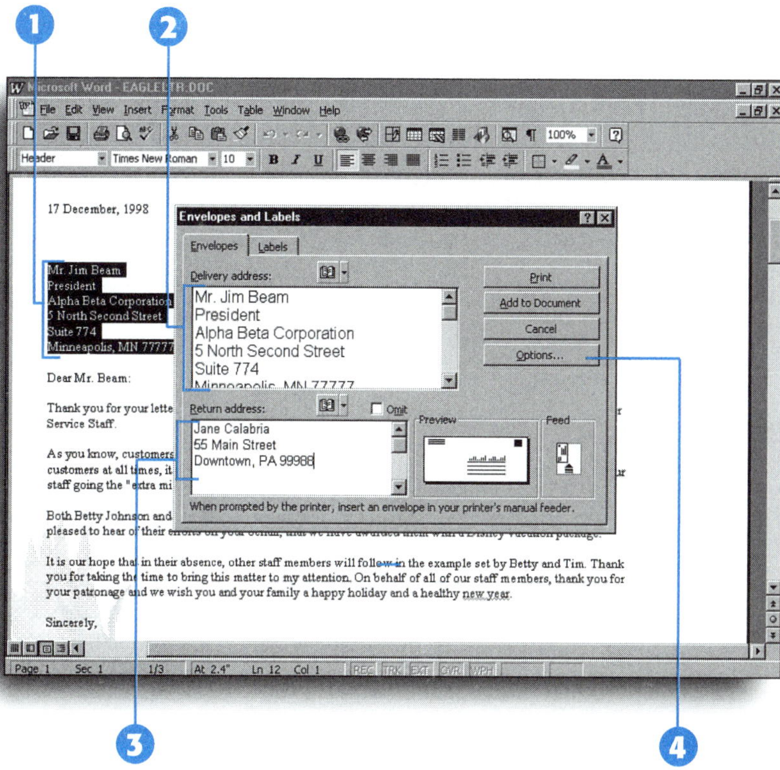

FIGURE 13.9
Select the **Envelopes** tab of the Envelopes and Labels dialog box to create and print envelopes.

1. Mailing address in document
2. Mailing address for envelope
3. Return address
4. Click **Options** to choose a size

5. To select an envelope size, the type of paper feed, whether to add a bar code, and other options, click the **Envelopes Options** tab (see Figure 13.10). After you have selected the options you want, click **OK**.

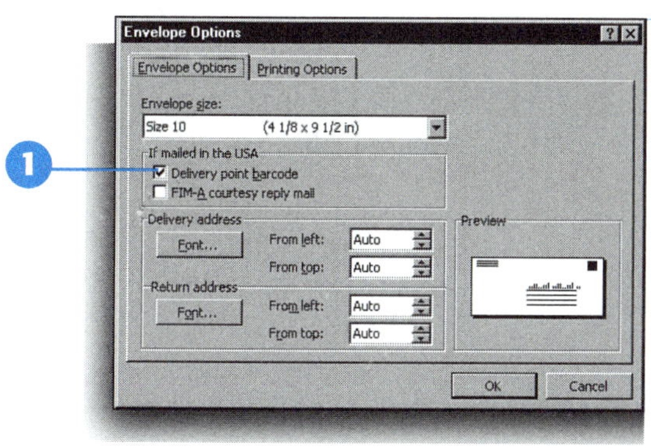

FIGURE 13.10
In the Envelope Options dialog box, select the size envelope you want to print and then click **OK**.

1. Barcode option

Avoid paper jams and sealed envelopes

To avoid gummed-up envelopes as they come out of your laser printer, purchase envelopes designed for laser printers. The glue on laser printer envelopes is designed to "take the heat" as it passes through the printer. And to avoid creased envelopes and paper jams, use your printer's straight paper path—don't let the envelopes curl as they go through the printer. Using the straight paper path helps reduce jams, creases, folds, and even reduces the likelihood of heating up the envelope glue.

Barcodes

Don't forget to add barcodes. One of the options found in the Envelopes dialog box is the printing of a barcode. According to the United States Post Office, using barcodes helps to speed your mail.

6. To print the envelope, insert the envelope in the printer as shown in the **Feed** box, and then click **Print**.

To add the envelope as a separate section at the beginning of the document, click **Add to Document**. This is particularly useful if you print this document often and need to send it to the same address each time. Then, every time you update the file and print it, the envelope is also printed. To change an existing envelope that's already a section in a document, click **Change Document**. You can print the envelope when you print the document.

Print Labels

You can print return address mailing labels or individual shipping labels (if your printer can accommodate them). Use labels when you are mailing to many recipients: it will save you from running to the printer to hand feed or stack envelopes and it is a faster method than printing envelopes individually. If you want to print labels with a different address on each label, you should use a mail merge document.

Print labels

1. From the **Tools** menu, select **Envelopes and Labels**.
2. Select the **Labels** tab (see Figure 13.11).
3. Enter the address information, and then select the options you want. To format the address, select the address text, right-click it, and then click **Font** on the shortcut menu.
4. Under **Print**, select **Full page of same label** if you want a sheet of the same addresses or **Single label** if you only want one label to print.
5. To select the label size you'll be printing, click **Options** (see Figure 13.12).
6. To print the label(s), insert the label or sheet of labels in the printer and then click **Print**.

SEE ALSO

➤ *To print sheets of labels that contain different names and address, see page 411*

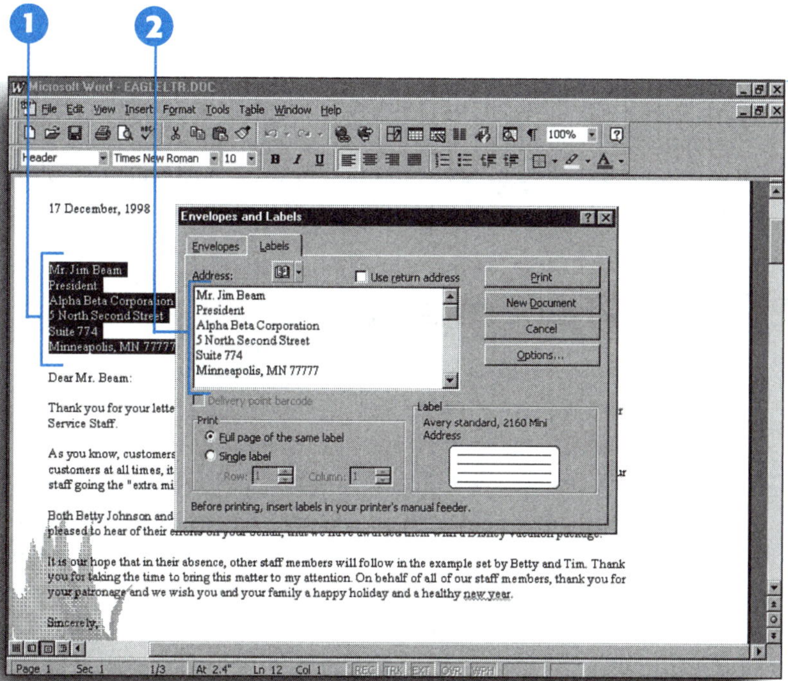

FIGURE 13.11
Print a single shipping label or an entire page of labels to the same address.

1 Mailing address in document

2 Mailing address for label

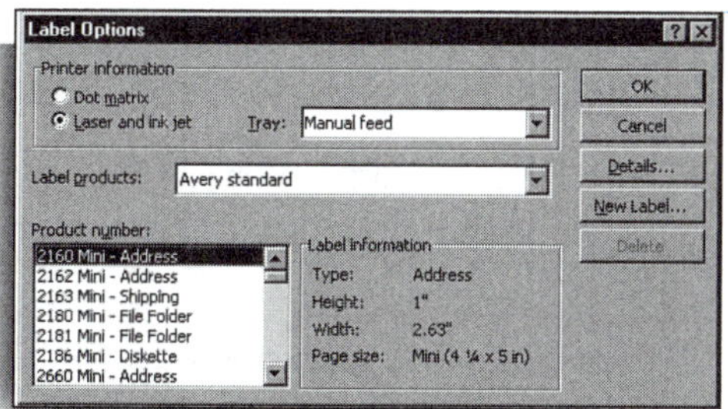

FIGURE 13.12
Choose the type of printer, select from the list of available label sizes, and then click **OK**.

Cancel Print Jobs

After a job has been sent to the printer, you can cancel a print job from Word without having to switch to the Printer control box in Windows.

You may have to act quickly to cancel print jobs

When printing a single page document using background printing, the printer icon may disappear from the status bar before you have a chance to double-click it. In that case, the job is probably already printing and you cannot stop it.

Caution: Do not let Word create a cover sheet for other fax programs

If you are using a program other than Microsoft Fax and choose **Send to Fax Recipient** from the menu, Word prompts you for a cover sheet during the faxing process. At the end of the Fax Wizard, Word starts your fax program. Do not create the cover sheet during the Word Wizard or Word creates a new document consisting of the cover sheet only and that is the document your fax program attempts to send. If you need a cover sheet, wait until Word starts your fax program, at which point you can send a cover sheet from within your fax program.

To cancel a print job with background printing turned off, press Esc or click the **Cancel** button.

To cancel a print job while background printing is enabled, double-click the printer icon located on the status bar. This icon only appears if you have background printing enabled, and during the print job.

Print to a Fax Program

If your system has been set up for faxing (you must have a fax/modem and fax software), you can fax a document directly to one or more recipients using your computer as a fax machine.

Faxing a document can be handled in two ways: depending on how your fax system is installed, you may find the fax program (such as Microsoft Fax or WinFax) listed as a printer in the Print dialog box. If this is the case, the quickest way to send a fax is to print the document with the fax program selected as the printer. As a result, your document does not print to the printer, but starts the fax program, prompts you to fill in the address and phone number and so forth, and faxes the document when you are ready. During this process, most fax software also asks you if you want to send a cover sheet and you can include a cover sheet with the information you specify.

You may have a fax program that does not show in the list of your printers. In that case, you can send a fax using the **Send to** command in Word.

Use the Send To command to send a fax

1. Open the **File** menu and choose **Send To**, and then select **Fax Recipient**.
2. Select Microsoft Fax (or your installed fax program) as the destination printer in the Print dialog box, and click **OK**. The Fax Wizard starts. The wizard is a step-by-step program that takes you through the process of preparing the fax, choosing a cover page, and selecting recipients. After each step, click **Next** to continue the process. Click **Back** to go back to the previous step. After the final step, click **Finish**.

3. If you requested a cover sheet, Word displays it. You can make any additions or changes to the cover sheet at this time.
4. Click the **Send Fax Now** button to send the fax.

Word also provides a fax cover sheet template wizard. To create a cover sheet, open the document you want to fax and do the following steps.

Create a fax cover sheet

1. Open the **File** menu and choose **New**.
2. When the New dialog box appears, select the **Letters & Faxes** tab.
3. Word offers three fax templates: Contemporary Fax, Elegant Fax, and Professional Fax. Although you may choose any of these, using the Fax Wizard may be more helpful for your first fax because it not only creates the fax cover sheet but helps send the fax too. The following steps take you through creating your fax using the Fax Wizard, so select that icon and click **OK**.
4. After the Fax Wizard introductory screen appears, click **Next** to continue (when using a wizard, **Next** continues to the next step, **Back** takes you back to the previous step, **Finish** ends the task, and **Cancel** exits the wizard without completing the task).
5. The Fax Wizard asks you to specify the document you want to send. Select from one of the following choices:
   - Select **The Following Document** if you plan to send a document that's already prepared. Then choose the name of the document from the drop-down list (the document must be open). Then select **With a Cover Sheet** or **Without a Cover Sheet**. Click **Next**.
   - Select **Just a Cover Sheet with a Note** if you only plan to put a note on the cover sheet and don't want to send an accompanying document.
6. The Fax Wizard asks what program you plan to use to send the fax: **Microsoft Fax** or **A Different Program Which Is**

Installed On This System. If you select **A Different Program**, you must then choose the program from the drop-down list in **Which of the Following is your Fax Program?** If you don't have a fax program or a modem installed on your system, you must select **I Want to Print My Document So I Can Send It From a Separate Fax Machine**.

7. Click **Next**. The Fax Wizard asks you to enter the names of the recipients (see Figure 13.13) of your fax. If you are working with Microsoft Outlook 97 or Microsoft Schedule+ 95 and maintain a personal address book in one of those programs, you can click the **Address Book** button and select a recipient's name. If not, enter the recipients' names and fax numbers (including area code) in the **Name** and **Fax Number** boxes (notice that you can address the same fax to different people at different fax numbers). After you've used the Fax Wizard, you'll be able to pick the names of previous recipients from the drop-down list the next time you use the wizard.

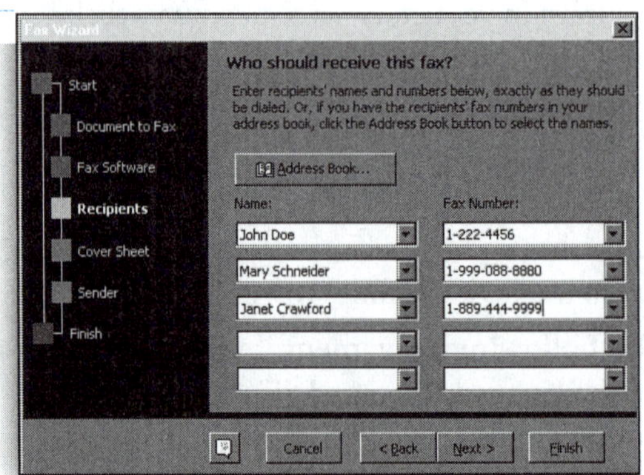

FIGURE 13.13
Enter the names and fax numbers of the people to whom you are sending the fax.

8. Click **Next**. Select the style of fax cover sheet you want to use (if you chose to use a fax cover sheet): Professional, Contemporary, or Elegant. Click **Next**.

9. Enter the information about the sender of the fax on this screen (you) filling in the Name, Company (if there is one),

Mailing Address, Phone, and Fax boxes if Word has not filled these in for you. Click **Next**.

10. Click **Finish**. The fax cover sheet document appears on your screen. Enter any additional information you need on the cover sheet, replacing any of the **Click here and type** fields by clicking them and typing over the field text with your own information. To place a check mark in any of the check boxes, double-click the box. Add any message you want to send on the fax cover sheet in the Comments area.
11. When your fax cover sheet is ready, click **Send Fax Now.**

If you do not have a fax program or modem and choose to print the cover sheet for faxing on a separate machine, the **Send Fax Now** button doesn't appear; just print the cover sheet as you would any other document.

Fax cover sheet templates

If you choose to use the Professional, Elegant, or Contemporary fax templates, your document opens with the boilerplate text and you must replace any sample text or **click here** fields with your own information. Then you print the document so that you can send the fax on a separate fax machine or choose the **File** menu, and select **Send To**. From the submenu choose **Fax Recipient** if you have a fax program and modem installed on your system.

Email a Document from Word

If you have Microsoft Messaging or another email program installed on your system, you can send a document directly to a mail recipient. Here are the steps to take:

1. Open the **File** menu, and choose **Send To**. Then choose **Mail Recipient** from the submenu.
2. Depending on the specifics of your system, Word may ask you to select a profile setting. Generally, the default setting is the one you should select.
3. Next, you see your usual New Message window. The appearance of this window varies depending on the mail system you are using, but it is the same mail form that you use for other email messages.
4. The document is already inserted in the message as an icon. You can add text to the message if desired. You must also fill in the **To** text box of the message with the recipient's address.
5. When the message is complete, click the **Send** button.

When the recipient receives your message, (depending on his mail program) he can double-click the document icon to open the document in Word for printing, editing, and so on.

Change Print Defaults

You can set document print defaults by clicking the **Options** button in the Print dialog box. Figure 13.14 lists these various printing options.

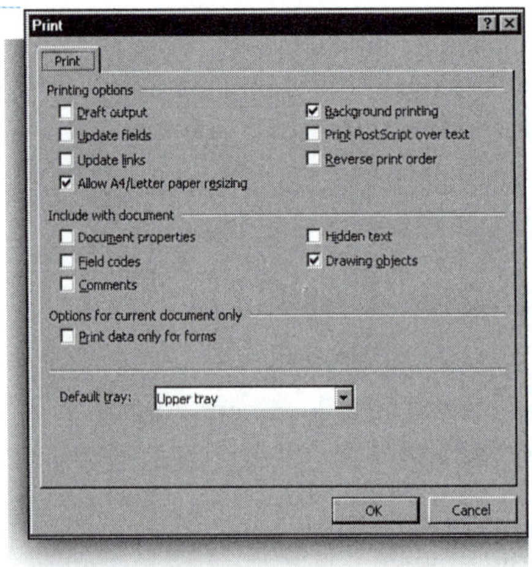

FIGURE 13.14
Click the **Options** button in the Print dialog box to see all the printing options.

These default settings apply for all new documents. Some of the most commonly used options include

- **Draft output.** Produces draft output that prints faster but may lack some graphics and formatting (depending on your specific printer).
- **Reverse print order.** Prints pages in last-to-first order. This setting produces collated output on printers that have face-up output.
- **Background printing.** Permits you to continue working on the document while printing is in progress. This setting uses additional memory and usually results in slower printing.

- **Update fields.** Updates the contents of all document fields before printing.
- **Document properties.** Prints the document's properties in addition to its contents.
- **Comments.** Includes document comments in the printout.

After setting the desired printing option defaults, click **OK** to return to the Print dialog box.

PART V

Add Objects to Documents

CHAPTER 14

Use Tables to Organize Information

- Create, modify, and format tables
- Enter, sort, and rotate text
- Import, link, and embed worksheets
- Perform calculations in tables

Insert Tables

Margins count

Before you create a table, set your page margins. Word automatically draws the table between the margins and then divides that space equally into the number of columns you specified. If you set your margins after you create the table, you will have to adjust the width of your table to match the margins. You may also have to adjust your column widths, especially if you've set them randomly to fit the table contents.

A *table* organizes information in *columns* and *rows*. You enter table information in *cells*, which are the rectangles made by the intersection of the columns and rows. Each cell is independent of all other cells. You can have almost any number of rows and columns in a table. You also have a great deal of control over the size and formatting of each cell. A table cell can contain text, graphics, and just about anything that a Word document can contain. A table cannot, however, contain another table.

Use tables to organize information in your documents, even when you want information to appear in columns, but not as if it is in a table. You can print tables without borders, so the end result is columns of information. The advantage of using tables to enter the data instead of tabbed columns, is that text will wrap within a table cell and formatting table cells is an easy task.

Create a table

1. Place your insertion point where you want to insert the table.
2. Open the **Table** menu and choose **Insert Table**. The Insert Table dialog box appears (see Figure 14.1).

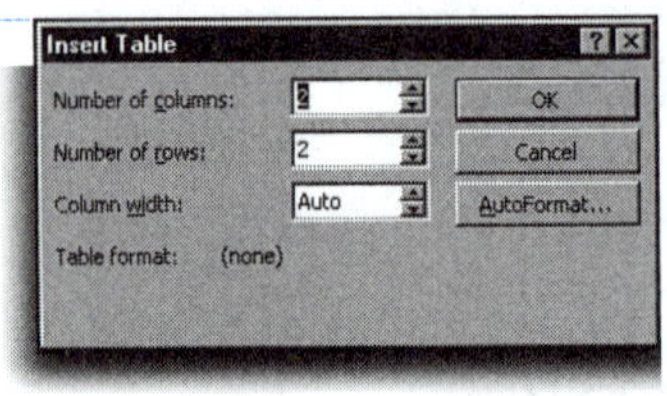

FIGURE 14.1

Enter or select the number of columns and rows you want in your table.

Caution: Leave a blank space before you create a table

It's a good idea to leave a blank space (press Enter) before you create a table on a blank page. If you forget to do this, and at some later point need to type text above and outside of the table, place your cursor in the first cell of the table and press Ctrl+Shift+Enter.

3. In the **Number of columns** and **Number of rows** text boxes, enter the values for the number of columns and rows you want your table to have. Don't worry about knowing the exact number, you can adjust these later.
4. To apply one of Word's automatic table formats to the table, choose **AutoFormat**, select the desired format, and then choose **OK** (see more on AutoFormat in the "Apply Automatic Formatting" section later in this chapter).

5. In the **Column width** text box, select the desired width for each column, in inches. Select **Auto** to have the page width evenly divided among the specified number of columns.
6. Choose **OK**. A blank table appears in your document with your insertion point in the first cell.

A quick way to insert a table is to choose Insert Table on the Standard toolbar and then drag over the desired number of rows and columns (see Figure 14.2). When you release your mouse button the table appears in your document.

Use the Table and Borders toolbar

When working in tables, you'll find the Tables and Borders toolbar helpful. Display the toolbar by opening the **View** menu and selecting **Toolbars**, then select **Tables and Borders** (see Figure 14.3).

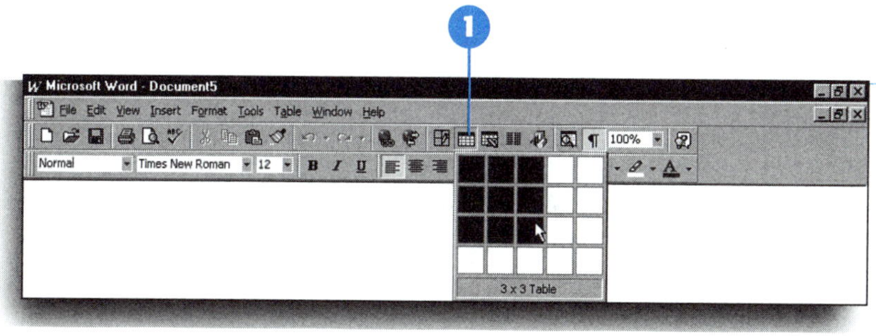

FIGURE 14.2

To create a table with evenly spaced columns, choose the Insert Table button on the Standard toolbar.

1 Insert Table button

Draw Tables

When you insert a table in your document, it stretches from the left to right margin and evenly divides that space into the number of columns you specified (unless you selected a column width in the Insert Table dialog box).

Another option for inserting a table in your document is to draw your table. That way you draw the table to the size and shape you want. You can add columns and rows in a variety of configurations.

Should you insert or draw your table?

Which method you use to create a table is a personal decision. However, 90% of the time, we find ourselves inserting a table. It's faster than drawing and we find that we don't need to be concerned about size and shape. Inserting seems to meet our needs for most tables.

Draw a table

1. Place your insertion point where you want your table to appear in the document.
2. Click the **Table** menu and select **Draw Table**. The Tables and Borders toolbar appears and your mouse pointer becomes a pencil (see Figure 14.3). When you draw a table, Word places you in Page Layout view.

FIGURE 14.3

Use the pencil to draw the outside border of the table by drawing a rectangle where you want the table to appear.

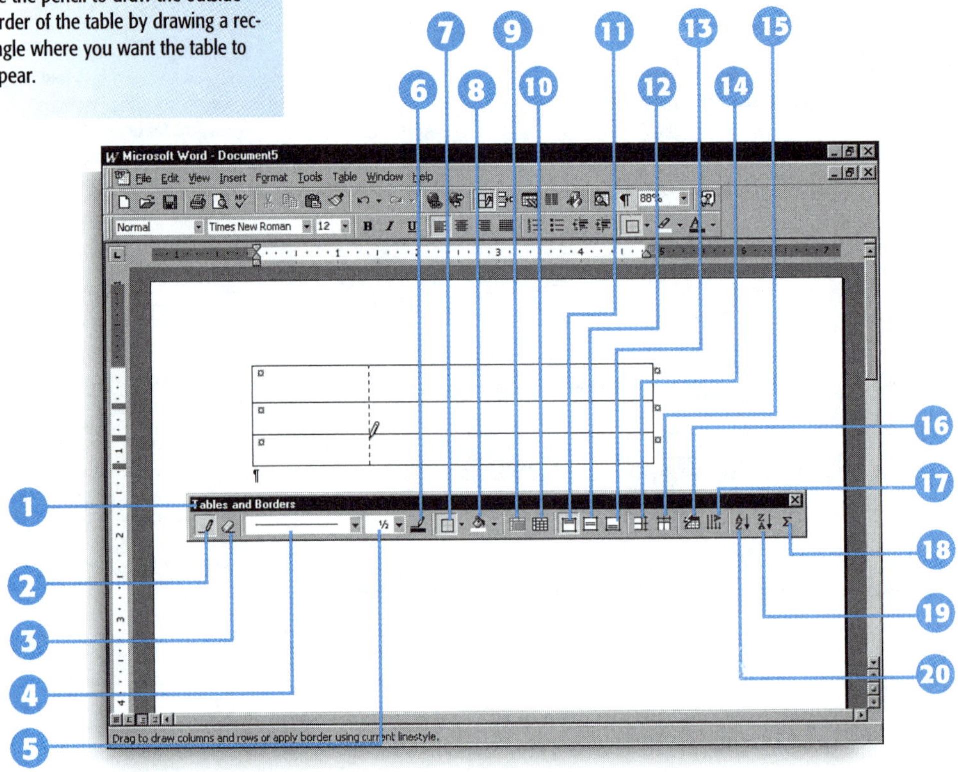

1. Tables and Borders toolbar
2. Draw Table
3. Eraser
4. Line Style
5. Line Weight
6. Border Color
7. Border Option
8. Shading Color
9. Merge Cells
10. Split Cells
11. Align Top
12. Center Vertically
13. Align Bottom
14. Distribute Rows Evenly
15. Distribute Columns Evenly
16. Table AutoFormat
17. Change Text Direction
18. AutoSum
19. Sort Descending
20. Sort Ascending

If the Tables and Borders toolbar is already showing, choose Draw Table on the toolbar to display the pencil cursor.

3. To set the outside dimensions of the table, move your mouse pointer to the spot where you want the upper left corner of the table to be, and then drag diagonally. Release the mouse button when the mouse pointer is at the spot where you want the lower right corner of the table to be.
4. Then use the pencil to draw the lines for the column and row borders, by dragging from one edge of the table to the other, or from one column or row border to the other (Word keeps your lines straight). If you draw a line by mistake, choose Eraser from the Tables and Borders toolbar and click the line you drew to remove it.
5. When you've finished drawing the table, disable the pencil cursor by double-clicking in one of the cells to begin entering text.

SEE ALSO

➤ *To learn how to change margins, see page 182*

Format Tables

Formatting options for tables are extensive. You can apply borders and shading to cells, groups of cells, or the entire table. Text can be rotated and cells can be merged.

Shading and borders give a professional look to tables and assist in the readability of the data contained in the table. Formatting can be applied using Word's automatic formatting options or by manually selecting options.

Learn table skills quickly

A good way to master table creation is to create a table from your newspaper's TV listing. In most cases, you'll find the need to create headers, rotate text, merge cells, and shade. Although the TV listing isn't helpful at the office, it's a great way to spend 20 minutes or so mastering the skills of table creation, preparing you for quick table creation at work.

Apply Automatic Formatting

The quickest and easiest way to format a table is to use one of Word's predefined table formats.

AutoFormat a table

1. Place the insertion point anywhere in the table.

2. Click the **Table** menu and select **Table AutoFormat** to open the Table AutoFormat dialog box, as shown in Figure 14.4. (Another way to open this dialog box is to choose **AutoFormat** in the Insert Table dialog box when you create a table.)

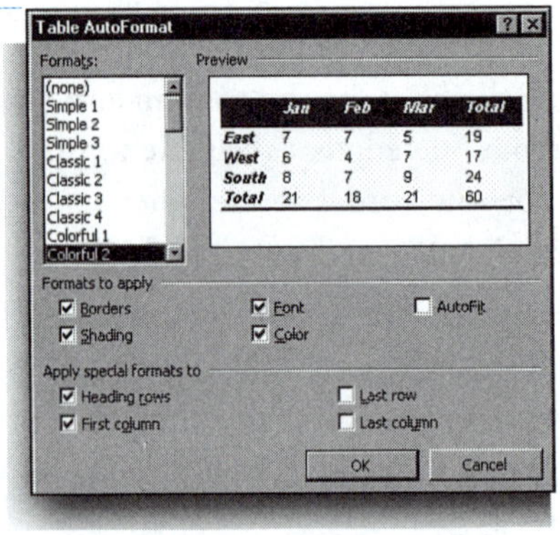

FIGURE 14.4

The Table AutoFormat dialog box offers several preset formats that you may apply to your table.

3. A list of available formats appears in the **Formats** box. When you click one of the formats, the **Preview** box displays a sample of the format.

4. Under **Formats to apply**, click the check boxes to select or deselect the options you want applied to your table (look at the **Preview** to see how the items you check affect the table format):

   - **Borders** turns on or off the border style specified by the format.
   - **Shading** turns the shading for that format on or off.
   - **Font** uses the font specified by the format or returns to the default font for the template on which the document is based.
   - **Color** retains or removes the color that the format adds to a table.
   - **AutoFit** fits the table and column width to the text in the table, and turning it off spaces the columns evenly over the width of the table (between the left and right margins).

5. Under **Apply special formats to**, select the options you want to use for specific rows or columns of your table (look at the **Preview** to see how your selections affect the table format):

   - **Heading rows** adds or removes special formatting (shading, boldface, colored text, and so on) applied to the heading row of your table. A heading row, which is generally the first row of your table, is the row that repeats at the top of each page of your table.
   - **First column** adds or removes special formatting applied to the first column of your table, where you may have row titles entered. The table format may add shading or bold text to that column to make it look different from the rest.
   - **Last row** adds or removes special formatting applied to the last row of a table, such as borders or shading.
   - **Last column** adds or removes special formatting applied to the last column of the table, such as shading, bold text, or borders.

6. Choose **OK**. The selected formatting is applied to the table.

Automatic formatting of a table is convenient when you need to make a table look good fast.

To undo table formatting

You can undo table formatting by clicking the Undo button on the Standard toolbar. You might want to save several versions of your document with different table formatting options to compare them before you make a final decision on table formatting.

Select Table Components

To perform some operations on your table, you must be able to select cells, rows, and columns. Table 14.1 provides you with tips on how to select areas of your table.

TABLE 14.1 **Selecting table components**

To Select:	Do This:
Cell	Click the left edge of the cell between the text and the cell border (when you see a pointer). *or* Triple-click inside the cell.

continues...

TABLE 14.1 **Continued**

To Select:	Do This:
Row	Click to the left of the row (in the margin area) when you see a pointer. *or* Put your insertion point in the row and open the **Table** menu and choose **Select Row**.
Column	With your insertion point in the column, click the column's top gridline or border when you see a down-pointing arrow. Alternately: Hold down the Alt key and click the column. *or* Open the **Table** menu, and choose **Select Column**.
Multiple cells, rows, or columns	Drag across the cell, row, or column; or select a single cell, row, or column, hold down the Shift key, and then click another cell, row, or column where you want the selection to end.
Text in the next cell	Press Tab.
Text in the previous cell	Press Shift+Tab.
Entire table	Click the table and then press Alt+5 on the numeric keypad (Num Lock must be off); or press Alt and double-click the table. *or* Open the **Table** menu, and choose **Select Table** (with your insertion point somewhere in the table).

If you need to reduce a selection to fewer cells or extend a selection to adjacent cells, hold down the Shift key and press an arrow key repeatedly.

After you select cells you can apply table formatting or text formatting to the contents of those cells using the standard techniques for changing fonts and paragraph attributes.

SEE ALSO

➤ *To change fonts and font attributes, see page 36*

Apply Manual Formatting

To customize the appearance of your table, you apply formatting such as borders, shading, or fonts to individual cells, rows, or columns of the table. You need to select the cells, columns, rows, or the entire table to indicate to which cells you want to apply formatting. Then choose the formatting options you want to apply to your selection, including font, font size, bold, underline, italic, centering, left or right alignment, text color, and so on.

Apply Table Borders and Shading

Normally, a new table in Word has a single, thin border around each cell in the table. There is no shading.

Use the Tables and Borders toolbar for formatting

Instead of menus, consider using the icons on the Tables and Borders toolbar as shown in Figure 14.3.

Add table borders and shading

1. Select the table cells that you want to modify.
2. Click the **Format** menu and select **Borders and Shading**. The Borders and Shading dialog box opens.
3. Click the **Borders** tab to work with border options (see Figure 14.5).

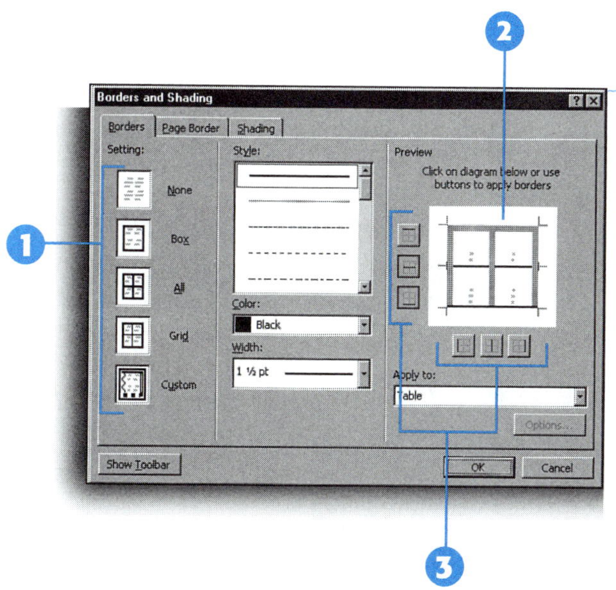

FIGURE 14.5

Select the style of the border line, the color, and the width.

1. Predefined borders
2. Preview
3. Border buttons (to add or remove lines)

Adjacent borders

Border formatting can create conflicts when adjacent cells share a border that is formatted differently for each cell. For example, if you format a thin right border in cell 1 and format a heavy left border in cell 2, what happens? Word accepts formatting options in chronological order, so, the cell 2 border options win. The common border is a heavy border.

- Under **Setting**, click one of the preset border options: **None** to remove all borders from the selected cells, **Box** to insert a box border around the selected cells. Select **All** to insert a box border with shadow formatting around the selection, **Grid** to place a 3-D box border around the selection to make the border look like a window frame, or **Custom** to create a border using the options you click in the **Preview** window. When you choose any of these settings, the current selections in **Style**, **Color**, and **Width** apply to the borders.
- From the **Style** list, select the type of line you want to use for the border, including dotted, dashed, and wavy lines.
- Click the **Color** drop-down list to select a color to apply to the border.
- From the **Width** drop-down list, choose the thickness of the border line, from 1/4-point to 6 points.
- In the **Preview** box, click the individual border lines or use the border line buttons to apply or remove borders or change the attributes for a particular border (select the attributes first and then add the border).
- From the **Apply to** drop-down list, select whether to apply the border to **Cell** or **Table**.

4. Select the **Shading** tab to choose shading options (see Figure 14.6):

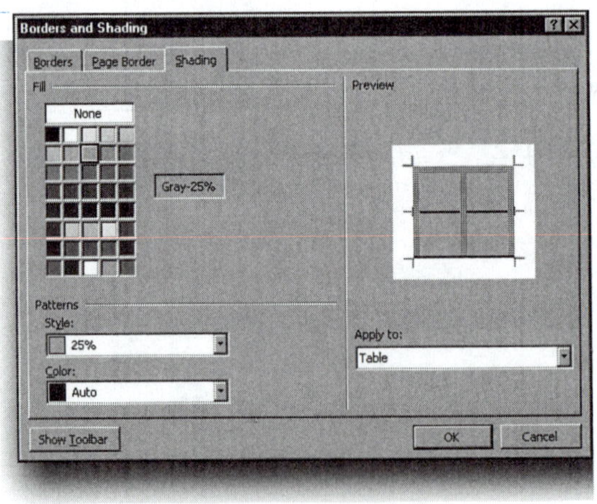

FIGURE 14.6
On the **Shading** tab, select the background fill color for the selected cells.

- Under **Fill**, select the color or shade of gray with which you want to fill the selected cells.
- From the **Patterns Style** drop-down list, choose a shading percentage for the color you selected under **Fill** or a pattern of lines such as **Lt Horizontal** or **Dk Trellis**.
- If you selected a pattern of lines, select the **Color** of the lines from the drop-down list. The Fill color then becomes the background color for the pattern. When using patterns behind text, make the pattern small, the color light, and the text big and bold.
- From the **Apply to** drop-down list select whether to apply the shading options to **Cell** or **Table**.

5. Choose **OK**.

To quickly choose shading colors, border line styles, border line colors, and border line widths, use the Tables and Borders toolbar. Open the **View** menu and select **Toolbars**, then **Tables and Borders** to display the toolbar, or choose Tables and Borders on the Standard toolbar 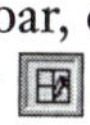. Select the cells to which you want to add borders and shading, and then click the appropriate button on the toolbar. Table 14.2 lists the buttons on the toolbar that you can use for borders and shading. Refer to Figure 14.3 to view the full toolbar.

TABLE 14.2 Tables and Borders toolbar buttons

Button	Description	Icon on Toolbar
Line Style	Sets the style of the border lines (dotted, dashed, wavy, double, and so on)	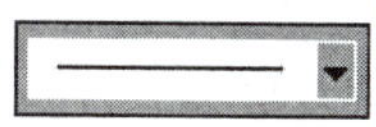
Line Weight	Sets the thickness of the border lines	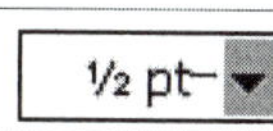
Border Color	Sets the color of the border lines	
Border Options	Specifies where the border appears (top, bottom, left, right, box)	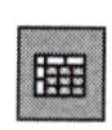
Shading Color	Sets the color of the background shading for the selected cells (you cannot specify the percentage)	

When you have to use a similar table structure and format again and again, don't go through all that work more than once. Select the table and save it as an AutoText entry. Then all you have to do is call for the AutoText entry when you want a similar table.

SEE ALSO

➤ *To learn more about creating AutoText entries, see page* 77

Enter Data in Tables

Entering and editing text in tables is similar to performing these operations in other areas of your document. Click in the table cell where you want to enter text and type. The text wraps within the cell, and pressing Enter starts a new paragraph within that cell. You use the Delete and Backspace keys to remove unwanted text.

To start a new line within a cell, press Enter. To start a new paragraph within a cell, press Shift+Enter. The difference between pressing Enter and Shift+Enter might not be apparent to you at first. The difference lies in the spacing between lines. If you have not changed the default paragraph spacing, you will see no difference. To insert a tab within a cell press Ctrl+Tab.

To move from cell to cell within the table, click in the cell where you want to place your insertion point or use the arrow keys. For some navigation tips, refer to Table 14.3.

Need more rows?

Pressing the Tab key while you are in the last cell of a table automatically adds a new row to your table.

Setting tabs within tables

When you insert a tab (Ctrl+Tab) within a cell of a table, the default tab settings are used. When you set a tab within a cell (click the ruler) the tab setting applies to that cell only, as Word treats each row like a different paragraph. To set a tab setting for an entire column, select the column first, then set the tab using the ruler. All types of tabs can be set within a table, such as decimal, right-aligned, and so forth.

TABLE 14.3 **Keyboard shortcuts to move around in a table**

Press This:	To Move Here:
Tab	The next cell in the row (if you press Tab when you're in the last cell of the table, Word adds another row to the table).
Shift+Tab	The previous cell in a row.
Alt+Home	The first cell in the current row.
Alt+Page Up	The top cell in the current column.
Alt+End	The last cell in the current row.
Alt+Page Down	The last cell in the current column.

Because Tab moves you to the next cell, you must press Ctrl+Tab to insert a tab in a table cell.

SEE ALLO

➤ *To change line and paragraph spacing, see page 118*
➤ *To set tabs using the ruler, see page 123*

Rotate Text

Because horizontal space may be at a premium, you might want some of your table text to appear in a vertical orientation.

Rotate text in a table

1. Select the text you want to rotate.
2. Click the **Format** menu and select **Text Direction** or choose Change Text Direction on the Tables and Borders toolbar.
3. When the Text Direction - Table Cell dialog box appears (see Figure 14.7), click the **Orientation** you want to use. The **Preview** window shows you how the text will look.
4. Choose **OK**.

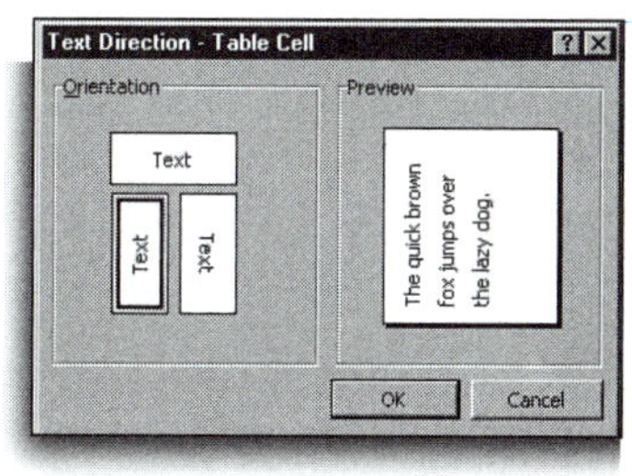

FIGURE 14.7
Select the orientation you want to make your text display vertically.

The selected text changes direction to match the orientation option you chose in the dialog box.

Sort Table Data

When you sort a table, you set the order of the rows in the table based on a value or text in one of the columns. You can indicate that you have headings in your table, to prevent them from being melded into the table data and you can set additional parameters for your sort.

To perform a quick alphabetical sort based on the first word in a cell, place your cursor in the table and click the Ascending Sort or Descending Sort button on the Table toolbar. To sort by a single column, select the column and click the ascending or descending buttons. The following instructions teach you how to perform more complex sorts.

Sort data in a table

1. Select the columns you want to sort. If you are sorting the entire table, click somewhere within the table to place your insertion point there or select the table.
2. Click the **Table** menu and select **Sort**. The Sort dialog box appears (see Figure 14.8).

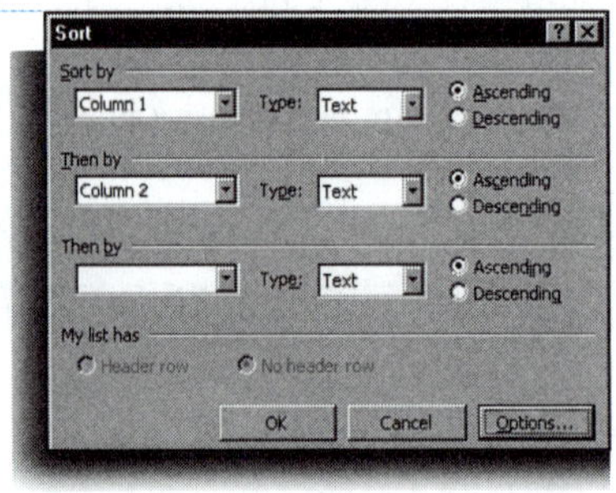

FIGURE 14.8
Specify how you want the table text sorted.

3. From the **Sort by** drop-down list, select the column on which you want to base the sort. If you select **Header row** under **My list has**, the text in the first row replaces the choices **Column 1**, **Column 2**, and so on options in the **Sort by** list.
4. From the **Type** drop-down list select one of the following:
   - Select **Text** to sort the list alphabetically
   - Select **Number** to sort numerically
   - Select **Date** to sort by date or time

5. Click **Ascending** to sort the list in A to Z, 0 to 99 order. Click **Descending** to sort the list in Z to A, 99 to 0 order.
6. When you choose a column for the first (primary) sort, the **Then by** drop-down list is available. This lets you set a secondary sort criteria, so if two items in the first sort are the same, the secondary sort sets the order.
7. If your list has a row of column titles, click **Header row** under **My list has** to avoid including that row in the sorting.
8. Choose **OK**.

Do you need a second sorting order?

Typically, you sort a list of names alphabetically by last name. The second sort order addresses those instances where you have more than one "Smith" or "Jones." For a secondary sort order, select the options for the **Then by** sort the same way you did for the primary sort.

Although you rarely sort one column individually, there are occasions when the information in one column is independent of the columns next to it and may need sorting. It is possible to sort a single column without sorting the entire table.

Sort a single column

1. Select the column you want to sort.
2. Choose the **Table** menu and select **Sort**.
3. Choose **Options** to open the Options dialog box (see Figure 14.9).

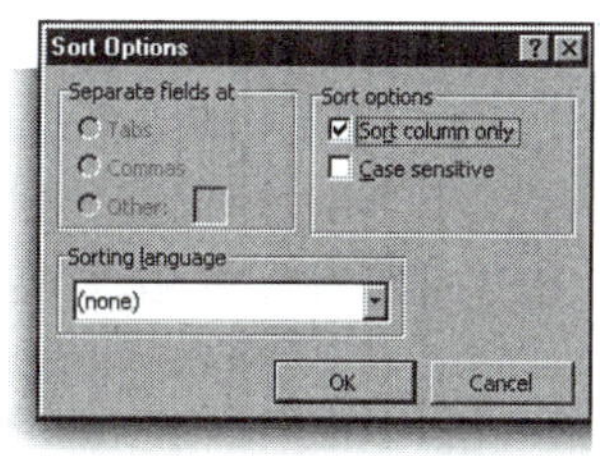

FIGURE 14.9
Select the **Sort column only** option.

4. Click **Sort column only** option.
5. Choose **OK** to close the Options dialog box.
6. Choose **OK** to close the Sort dialog box and apply the sort options to the column.

SEE ALSO

➤ *To learn more about sorting of lists, see page 154*

Convert Text to a Table

Often a list makes a perfect table. This is particularly true when you create a list and later decide to add a column to the list. You'll find adding data is easier in a table than in a column or a list created with tabs. You also can convert columns to a table, using the same procedure. When you convert columns to a table, the number of columns you are converting should match the number of columns in the table (see step 2).

Convert a list to a table

1. Select the text and open the **Table** menu. Choose **Convert Text to Table**.
2. The Convert Text to Table dialog box appears. Indicate the number of columns you want, and how to separate the columns:
   - **Paragraphs**. Choose this if you want to break to a new column when Word encounters paragraph marks.
   - **Tabs**. Choose this to break to a new column when Word encounters a tab mark.
   - **Commas**. Choose this to break to a new column when Word encounters a comma. This is useful when you have a list of names separated by commas, such as Jones, Peter.
   - **Other**. Choose this if you have consistently used a character such as a dash or a colon and type the character in the text box.
3. To have Word AutoFormat the table, click the **AutoFormat** button and choose a layout. Otherwise, skip to step 4.
4. Click **OK**. Word converts your list to a table.

Convert a Table to Text

If you decide that you no longer want a table, convert your table to text in much the same way as "Converting Text to a Table," described previously.

Select the table and open the **Table** menu, choose **Convert Table to Text** and indicate how you want the columns separated—by paragraph marks, tabs, commas, or other marks.

Delete and Insert Rows, Columns, and Tables

Removing the contents of a cell or cells and leaving a blank cell is an easy matter of selecting the cell(s) and pressing Delete (choose **Undo** or press Ctrl+Z if you didn't mean to do that).

Delete a row or column

1. Move the insertion point to any cell in the row or column to be deleted, or select the cells to be deleted.
2. Choose the **Table** menu and select **Delete Cells**. The Delete Cells dialog box appears (see Figure 14.10).

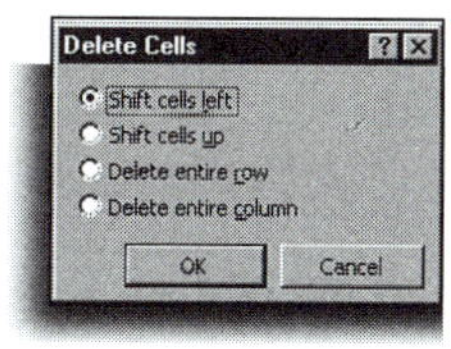

FIGURE 14.10
Choose **Delete entire row** or **Delete entire column**.

3. Click **Delete entire row** or **Delete entire column**.
4. Choose **OK**. The row or column is deleted.

Quickly delete rows or columns

Select the row or column to be deleted and right-click the selection. Choose **Delete Column** or **Delete Row** on the shortcut menu. Or, choose Cut on the Standard toolbar.

When you choose to insert rows or columns, rows are added above the row in which you have positioned your cursor and columns are added to the left of the column in which you have positioned your cursor. When you choose to append a row or column, rows are added to the bottom of the table and columns are added to the far right of the table.

Insert rows or columns

1. Select the column to the right of where you want to insert new columns or select the row below where you want to insert new rows. To insert more than one column or row, select the same number of rows or columns that you want to insert.

Inserting multiple columns or rows

New multiple rows are inserted above the selected multiple rows, new multiple columns are inserted to the left of the selected multiple rows. Remember that if you are simply adding (not inserting) rows, press the Enter key just outside the last row in the table, and a new row appears automatically.

2. Choose the **Table** menu and select **Insert Columns** to insert a new, blank column (or the same number of columns as you selected) to the left of the selected column. Open the **Table** menu and select **Insert Rows** to insert a new, blank row (or the same number of rows as you selected) above the selected row.

You can append rows or columns to your table at any time. To append, or add a row at the bottom of the table, move the insertion point to the last cell in the table and press Tab. To append, or add a column after the last column on the right, click just outside the table's right border, open the **Table** menu and select **Select Column**, and then choose **Table, Insert Columns**.

Here's how to copy or move an entire column or row from one location in a table to another.

Copy or move a table column or row

1. Select the column or row you want to move or copy.
2. To copy the selected row or column, choose Copy on the Standard toolbar or press Ctrl+C. To move the selected row or column, choose Cut on the Standard toolbar or press Ctrl+X.
3. Move your insertion point to the new location for the row or column. Your selected row or column will be inserted above or to the left of the location of the insertion point.
4. Choose Paste on the Standard toolbar or press Ctrl+V.

To delete a table, select the entire table and cut the table or open the **Table** menu and choose **Delete Columns**. If you press the Delete key, you will only delete the contents of the cells, not the table itself.

Modify Tables

The width of columns and the height of rows in Word tables are adjustable. Cells can be split into more cells or merged together in one cell. Tables can be split also, or headers can be added to the top of each column when tables run over one page in length.

Change Column Width

The text you enter in a column of cells may need more or less room than the width of the column. To adjust the spacing, you must change the width of the table column. To quickly change the width of a column using the mouse, use one of these methods:

- Point at the right border of the column whose width you want to change. The mouse pointer changes to a pair of thin vertical lines with arrowheads pointing left and right. Drag the column border to the desired width (see Figure 14.11).

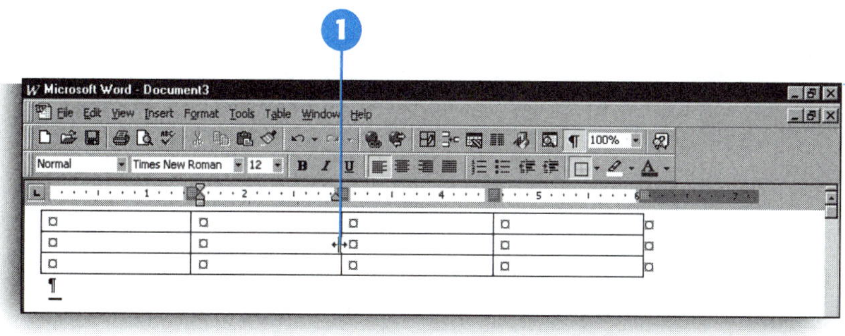

FIGURE 14.11
One way to change the column width is to drag the column border.

1. Double-headed arrow for mouse pointer indicates changing column width

- With your insertion point in the table, the ruler shows the column separators. Point to the column separator over the right border of the column until the mouse pointer becomes a two-headed arrow (the Move Table Column ToolTip appears). Then drag the separator until the column is the desired width (see Figure 14.12).

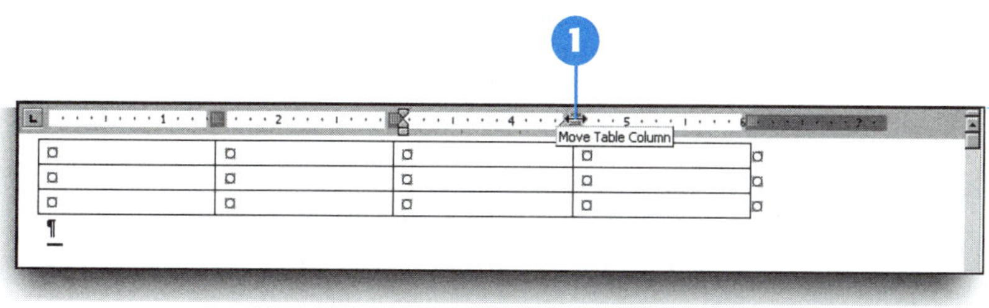

FIGURE 14.12
Another method for changing the column width is to drag the column separator on the ruler.

1. Two-headed arrow mouse pointer and ToolTip

When you need to be exact in setting the column size, use the Cell Height and Width dialog box.

Change cell height or width using the dialog box

1. Move the insertion point to any cell in the column you want to change.
2. Open the **Table** menu and select **Cell Height and Width**. The Cell Height and Width dialog box appears. Click the **Column** tab (see Figure 14.13).

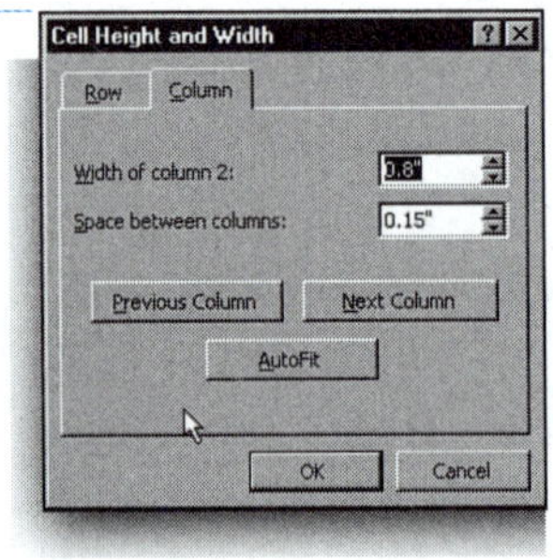

FIGURE 14.13

Enter the column width in inches or click **Autofit** to have Word adjust the column to the length of the widest entry.

3. Enter the desired column width in the **Width of column** text box or click the up and down arrows to change the setting. To automatically adjust the column width to fit the text in the column, choose **Autofit**.
4. To modify the spacing between columns, change the value in the **Space between columns** text box to increase or decrease the amount of space between the text in each cell and the cell's left and right borders.
5. Choose **Next Column** or **Previous Column** to modify the width of other columns in the table.
6. Choose **OK** when you've finished specifying column widths to apply your changes to the table.

To evenly space two or more adjacent columns over their entire width and make the columns the same width, select the columns and then open the **Table** menu and select **Distribute Columns Evenly**.

To automatically fit a column to the widest entry in that column, double-click the right border of the column. To display the column widths for the entire table, hold the Alt key down as you click one of the borders of the table or the column markers in the ruler.

Fast access to the Cell Height and Width dialog box

Double-click in any cell to access the Cell Height and Width dialog box.

Change Row Height

Row height in a table is usually based on the font size or the greatest number of lines in any cell in that row. To adjust the row height using the mouse:

- Select the row you want to change. Point at the top or bottom border of the row whose height you want to change. The mouse pointer changes to a pair of thin horizontal lines with arrowheads pointing up and down (see Figure 14.14). Drag the row border to the desired height.

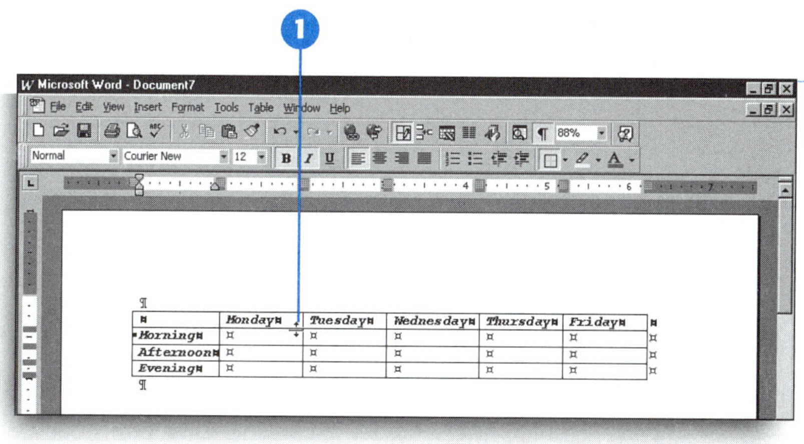

FIGURE 14.14

Drag the border of the row to increase or decrease the height of the row.

1 Double horizontal lines with arrowheads indicate changing row height

- When in Page Layout view, select the row that you want to change. The vertical ruler shows the row separators. Point to the row separator over the border of the row until the mouse pointer becomes a two-headed arrow and the **Adjust Table Row** ToolTip appears (see Figure 14.15). Then drag the separator until the row is the desired height.

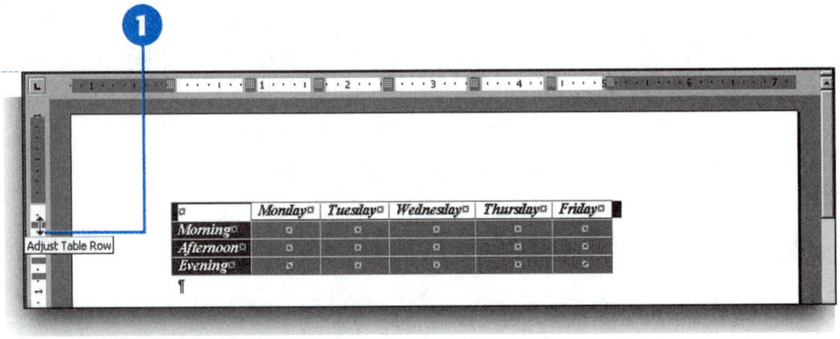

FIGURE 14.15

Drag the row separator on the vertical ruler to change the height of the row.

1 Two-headed arrow and ToolTip

Change row height using a dialog box

1. Select the rows that you want to change.
2. Open the **Table** menu and select **Cell Height and Width** to open the Cell Height and Width dialog box. Select the **Row** tab (see Figure 14.16).

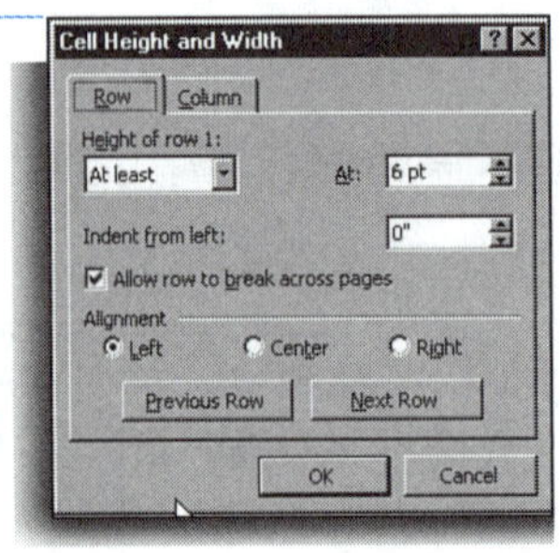

FIGURE 14.16

In addition to row height, you can set the alignment of the table on the page, indent the table from the left margin, or allow a row to break across pages.

3. From the **Height of row** drop-down list, select one of the following options:
   - To automatically adjust to the height of the tallest cell in the row, select **Auto**.
   - To specify a minimum row height (entered in the **At** box, in points) that automatically adjusts to a larger size to fit the row contents, select **At least**.
   - To specify a fixed row height (entered in the **At** box in points), select **Exactly**. When you use **Exactly**, Word prints only the contents that fit in that specified height.

Using tables as forms

If you want to use a table to create a fill-in form that will be printed after it is filled in, be sure to specify fixed row heights for all the rows in the table. Otherwise, the table rows might change size and make the table too big for your page if too much information is entered in a table row. The drawback is that excess text will not be seen or printed. Consider using a fill-in form for this purpose as discussed in Chapter 21, "Design Custom Forms."

4. Choose **Previous Row** or **Next Row** to set the row height for other rows in the table.
5. Choose **OK**.

To evenly space two or more adjacent rows over their entire height and make them the same height, select the rows and then open the **Table** menu and select **Distribute Rows Evenly**.

SEE ALSO

➤ *To change font and font size, see page 38*

Merge and Split Cells

Word tables have the flexibility to enable you to merge several cells into one. The cells must touch each other horizontally or vertically (cells in the same row, cells in the same column, or cells that make a rectangle).

Merge cells

1. Select the cells you want to merge.
2. Click the **Table** menu and select **Merge Cells**.

Split cells

1. Select the cell or cells you want to split (it doesn't have to be a cell that was merged earlier).
2. Click the **Table** menu and select **Split Cells**. The Split Cells dialog box appears (see Figure 14.17).

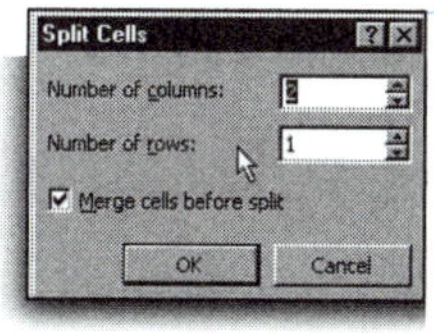

FIGURE 14.17
Enter the number of rows and columns into which you want to split the selected cell(s).

3. Enter the **Number of rows** or **Number of columns** into which you want to split the cell.
4. (Optional) If you want to quickly change your entire table to a new configuration of columns and rows, click **Merge cells before split** to place a check mark there. This option merges all the cells in the table into one cell, and then splits

the table into the number of rows and columns specified in the Split Cells dialog box.

5. Choose **OK**.

Split a Table

Split a table

1. Place your insertion point in the row that you want to be the first row of the second table.
2. Click the **Table** menu and select **Split Table**. Alternately, press Ctrl+Shift+Enter.

To join the tables together again, delete the hard return between the tables (or choose Undo on the Standard toolbar or press Ctrl+Z if you just split the table).

Use Headings

Sometimes your tables are split by a page break. When this happens, the column headings you had on the first page won't appear on the second page unless you instruct word to repeat the headings.

Create table headings

1. Select the rows of your table that you want to use as headings.
2. Choose the **Table** menu and select **Headings**.

Perform Calculations in a Table

Table calculations resemble some worksheet operations. Word is designed to handle simple calculations in a table. If you find you need to perform many or complicated formulas, you should consider using Excel and importing or embedding a worksheet into your document. For simple calculations, use a Word table.

Perform calculations

1. Click in the cell where you want the results of the calculation to appear.

2. Open the **Table** menu and select **Formula**. The Formula dialog box appears (see Figure 14.18).

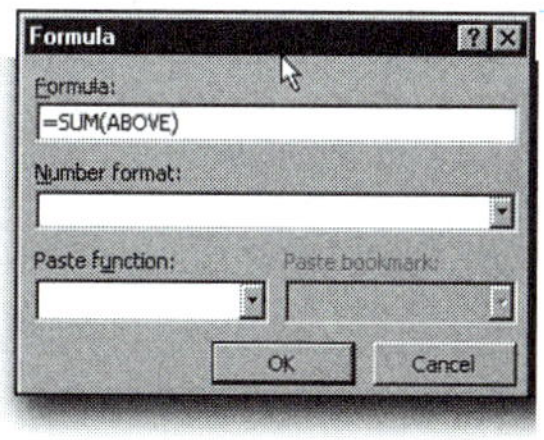

FIGURE 14.18
Enter the formula you want or choose one from the **Paste function** list.

3. Word tries to anticipate your needs by entering a formula for you. If you don't want to use that formula, delete it and enter your own formula or choose a function from the **Paste function** drop-down list (click on this with the Help question mark to see a button that opens a list of function definitions).
4. To reference the contents of a table cell, type the cell addresses in the parentheses in the formula. Each cell has an address, which is a combination of its column name and its row number. The first column on the left is A, the second is B, and so on. The first row is 1, the second is 2, and so on. Therefore, the address (or cell reference) of the cell in the third row down and second column across is B3. A formula might be =B3+B6; a function might be =SUM(B3,B6).
5. From the **Number format** drop-down list, select a format for the numbers (currency, percentage, and so on).
6. Choose **OK** and the result appears in the selected cell.

Keep in mind that the result of the calculation is a field. If you change the data in the referenced cells (changing a number), update the calculation by selecting the field and pressing F9.

SEE ALSO

➤ *To learn how to import or create worksheets, see page 346*

CHAPTER

15

Insert Graphics and Special Characters

- Insert graphics and clip art
- Crop, resize, move, and delete graphics
- Wrap text around graphics
- Use special characters and symbols
- Create a watermark

Add a Graphic Image

A *graphic* is a drawing or picture that is created by a graphics application or scanned and stored on disk. Graphic files created by a variety of applications, including Windows Paint, Microsoft PowerPoint, CorelDRAW!, and AutoCAD, can be incorporated into Word documents (see Figure 15.1). Word also provides its own library of clip art.

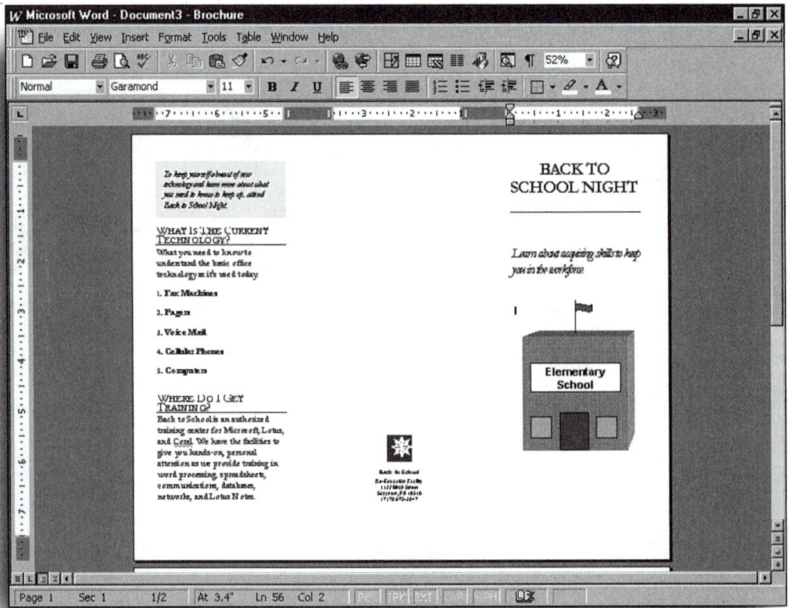

FIGURE 15.1
This document uses a graphic that was drawn in Microsoft PowerPoint.

Whether you create a graphic yourself, using a drawing or graphics program, or you scan an image from a drawing, painting, or photograph, the picture can be inserted into Word provided you saved it in a graphics format that is acceptable to Word. Be careful scanning photographs or pictures from published materials, such as books or magazines, as these items usually are copyrighted. You or your company can be sued for using them without permission.

Add a graphic to a document

1. Place your insertion point where you want the graphic to appear.
2. Open the **Insert** menu and choose **Picture**. From the submenu, select **From File** to open the Insert Picture dialog box (see Figure 15.2).

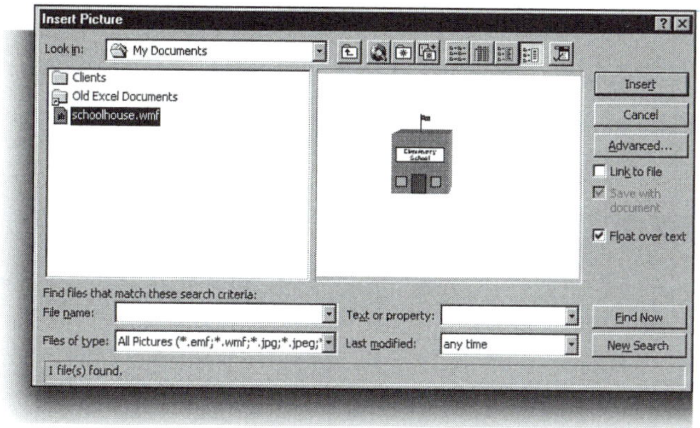

FIGURE 15.2
Select the graphics file and click **Insert**.

3. If necessary, select the folder where the graphic is stored from the **Look in** drop-down list.
4. From the **Files of type** drop-down list, select the type of graphics file you want to appear in the list.
5. Select the name of the file you want to use from the listed files or enter the name in the **File name** text box. Choose **Preview** on the toolbar to see a preview of the selected file.
6. Click any of the following options, if appropriate:
   - **Link to file.** The graphic in the document updates automatically if the original graphic file changes.
   - **Save with document.** Saves a copy of the picture with the document if you selected **Link to file**. This increases the size of the file, but it allows the picture to be displayed even if the original file is no longer available.

Graphic file formats

Graphics formats or file types differ depending on the program used to create the graphic. *TIF* files are usually scanned files, *PCX* files are from paint-style programs, *WMF* are Windows *Metafile* files that have generally been converted to that standardized format for use in other programs, *JPEG* and *GIF* are compressed graphics formats frequently used when putting pictures on Web pages.

Check float over text

Float over text is the default setting, unless you are using the SR1 version of Word 97. In that version, this feature is deselected by default. If you have SR1, your inserted pictures will automatically act as characters in the text and you won't be able to move them to other parts of the page unless you enable **Float over text**.

- **Float over text.** Enables the picture to be displayed behind or over text and other objects. Otherwise, the graphic is displayed inline with text (as if it were another character) and you won't be able to move it.

7. Choose **Insert** to add the graphic image to your document.

The graphic appears near your insertion point, or as near as Word can place it. You may have to move it and size it to fit your layout. The instructions to help you do that are in the sections "Crop and Resize Graphics" and "Delete, Move, and Copy Graphics" later in this chapter.

Insert Clip Art

Word comes with a library of *clip art*, which are drawings and pictures for you to use to add visual appeal and interest to your documents (check your software agreement on the clip art to see if there are any limitations in using the art in items you sell).

Add Word clip art to a document

1. Place your insertion point where you want to put the clip art picture or drawing in your document.
2. Open the **Insert** menu and choose **Picture**, then choose **Clip Art** from the submenu to open the Microsoft Clip Gallery (see Figure 15.3).

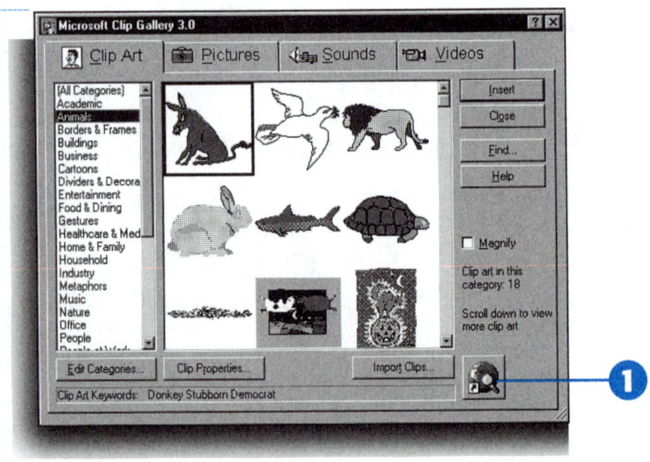

FIGURE 15.3

Choose a clip art category and then select a picture to insert in your document.

1 **Connect to Web** button

3. From the category list on the left of the Microsoft Clip Gallery dialog box, select the category of image you want. Select **(All Categories)** to view all the clip art.
4. Scroll through the picture list until you find the piece of clip art you want and then click it to select it. Click **Magnify** to get a close-up view of the image.
5. Choose **Insert**.

If you want to see even more clip art, insert your Office CD in your CD-ROM drive before you open the Clip Gallery. Then the Gallery displays those images as well as the ones installed on your hard disk.

If you have Internet access and are connected, click the **Connect to Web** button (see Figure 15.1) in the Microsoft Clip Gallery dialog box to connect to Microsoft's Web site. Access additional clip art at this site.

No Clip Art Gallery?

Although the Clip Art Gallery normally installs as part of Office 97, it's possible that the installer opted not to load the clip art to save disk space or time. To load the Gallery files, you must insert the setup disk into your disk drive and run a Custom setup, which allows you to load only those items you need.

Display Graphics

Although it's nice to see your graphics as you work, displaying them can slow down screen scrolling in Page Layout or Online Layout view (images are automatically hidden in Normal and Outline view unless they are inline graphics).

One way to speed up the screen refresh so scrolling is faster is to replace the graphics with empty rectangles called placeholders. These placeholders mark where the graphics will appear in the printed document. The graphics aren't eliminated from the document; they're just temporarily hidden.

To display placeholders instead of the graphics, open the **Tools** menu and select **Options**. Then on the **View** tab, click **Picture placeholders** to place a check mark there before you choose **OK** (see Figure 15.4).

Word inserts *field codes* in the document where linked graphics appear. Linked graphics are created when you select the **Link to file** option when you insert the graphic. The screen shows this field code instead of the picture when field codes are displayed (see Figure 15.5).

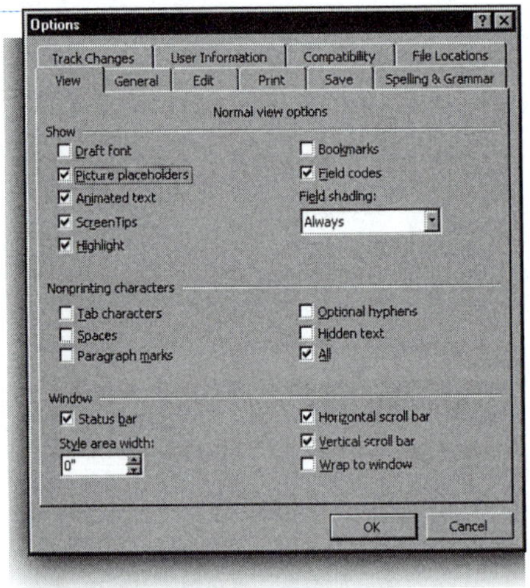

FIGURE 15.4
Display your graphics as placeholders from this dialog box.

FIGURE 15.5
A picture field code tells the filename and location of the picture file.

Although the field code shows in your document onscreen, the picture still prints properly. The picture also appears when you preview the file.

SEE ALSO

➤ *To learn other ways that Word uses fields and field codes, including displaying field codes, see page 444*

Crop and Resize Graphics

Before you can crop and resize a graphic, you must select it using one of these methods:

- To select a single graphic, click it. *Sizing handles* (small hollow boxes) appear around the graphic to indicate that it's selected (see Figure 15.6). A small anchor may also appear next to the closest paragraph if the **Move object with text** box is checked on the **Format Picture Position** tab (this means that the picture will remain close to that paragraph if the text moves in the document).

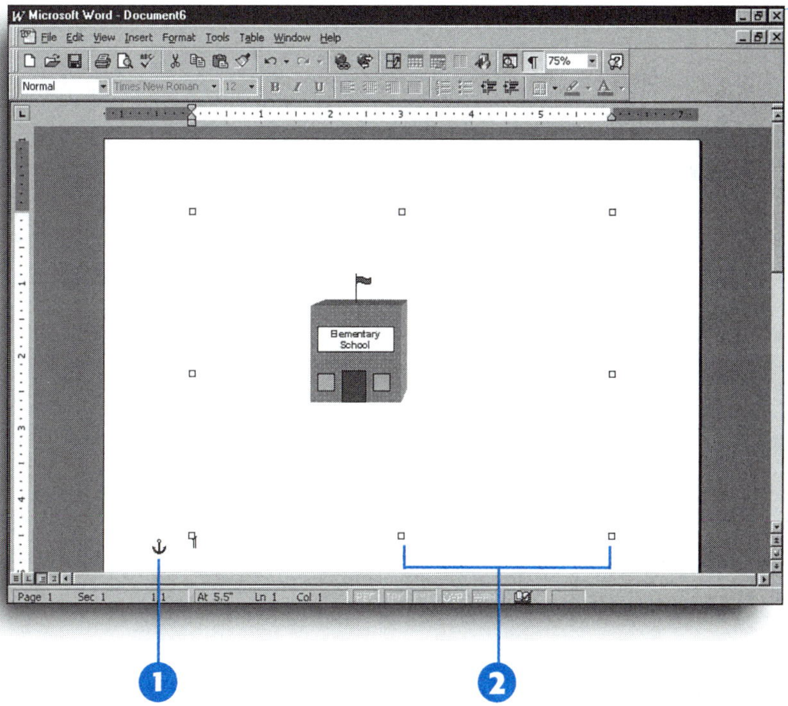

FIGURE 15.6
Eight sizing handles appear around a selected object.

1. Anchor
2. Sizing handles

- To select more than one graphic, click the first item you want to select, hold down the Shift key, and then click each additional item you want to select.
- If you accidentally select an item that you didn't want, hold down Shift and click the item to remove the sizing handles and deselect it.
- To deselect an item, click in a blank area away from the graphic.

Make the selected graphic larger or smaller by dragging one of the sizing handles. When you point at the handle, the mouse pointer becomes a two-headed arrow showing the direction in which you may drag (see Figure 15.7). Drag toward or away from the center of the graphic until the image is the size you need.

Don't distort the graphic

When you size the graphic you can make it too thin or too wide, too short or too tall. To keep the image in proportion (the height-to-width, or aspect, ratio remains the same), use a corner handle when sizing the image and drag toward or away from the center of the graphic. If you do distort the image, use the Undo feature as many times as necessary to get back to the original shape or size.

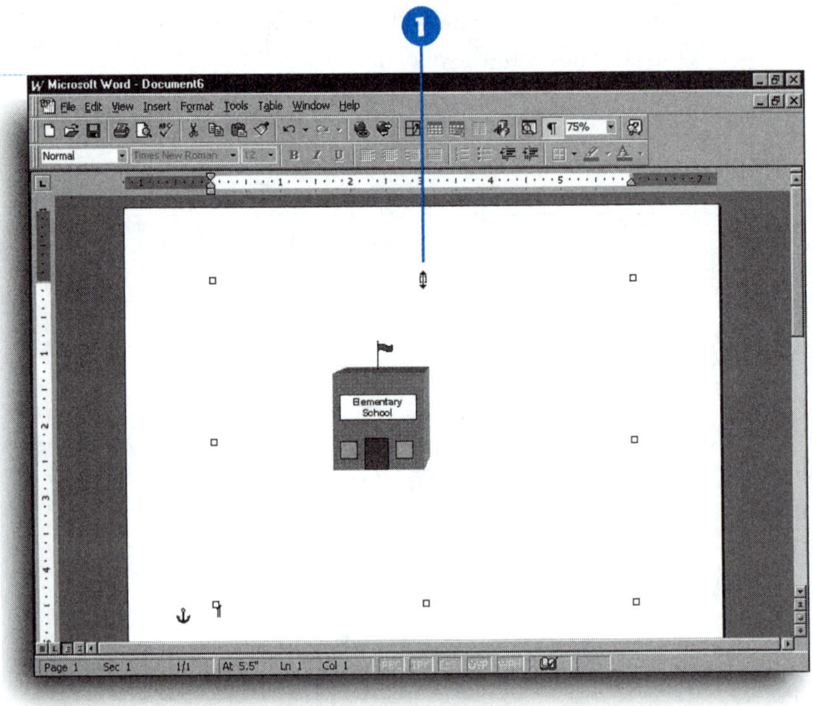

FIGURE 15.7
The mouse pointer becomes a two-headed arrow when you point at a sizing handle.

1 Two-headed arrow for resizing

Your image may have more background than you need. You can trim (crop) the excess from a selected graphic.

Crop a graphic

1. Select the graphic and choose Crop on the Picture toolbar.
2. Position the mouse pointer over the handle on the side you want to crop and drag toward the center of the image until the portion of the picture you wanted to trim disappears.
3. Release the mouse button.

This displays the portion of the graphic that you want to show. Cropping doesn't eliminate the rest of the graphic; it's still stored in your document file. You can drag the cropping handles back out to see part of the original picture. Although using the mouse immediately shows you the result of your cropping and sizing, it isn't precise. When you need to enter exact measurements to get the correct size or trim you should use the options in the Format Picture dialog box.

Size a picture using the Format Picture dialog box

1. Select the graphic and open the **Format** menu and select **Picture**, choose Format Picture on the Picture toolbar, or right-click the graphic and select **Format Picture** from the pop-up menu.
2. When the Format Picture dialog box appears, select the **Size** tab (see Figure 15.8).

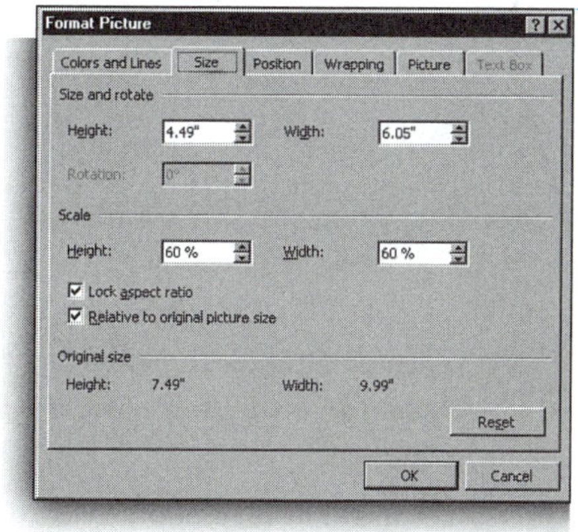

FIGURE 15.8
Enter the dimensions or the scale percentage to size your image.

3. To keep the image in proportion (maintain the ratio between the width and height), click **Lock aspect ratio** to place a check mark there.
4. Under **Size**, change the **Height** or **Width** measurement (the other dimension automatically adjusts when you press Tab to keep the graphic in proportion if you locked the aspect ratio). Or, to use percentages instead of exact dimensions, change the **Height** or **Width** percentage in the Scale area.
5. Choose **OK** to apply your modifications to the image.

Crop a picture using the Format Picture dialog box

1. Select the image and open the **Format** menu and choose **Picture**, choose Format Picture on the Picture toolbar,

or right-click the graphic and select **Format Picture** from the pop-up menu.

2. When the Format Picture dialog box appears, select the **Picture** tab (see Figure 15.9).

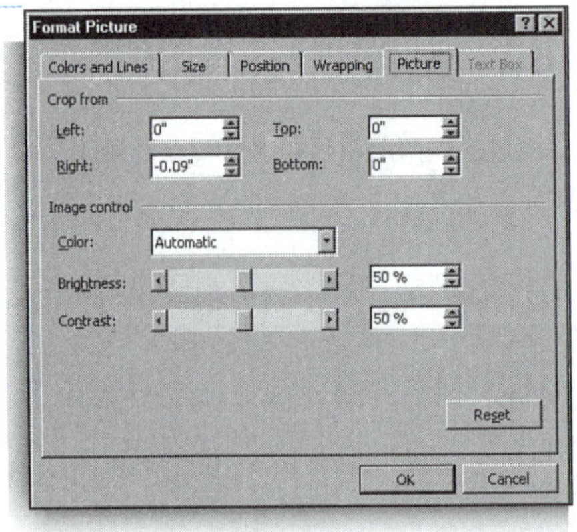

FIGURE 15.9

Enter the amount you want to trim from the left, right, top, or bottom of the picture.

3. Enter the exact measurement (in inches) of the amount you want to crop from the **Left**, **Right**, **Top**, or **Bottom** of the picture.

4. Choose **OK** to apply your modifications to the image.

Although using the dialog box to crop your pictures is a more accurate method, you have to know exactly how much you want to trim to get the desired effect. Using the Cropping tool gives you more immediate visual feedback. Try combining the methods—first cropping with the tool and then refining with the dialog box options—for the best results.

Delete, Move, and Copy Graphics

Deleting a graphic is a simple matter of selecting the graphic and then pressing the Delete key.

To move a graphic, point to the middle of the graphic until your mouse pointer becomes a four-headed arrow (see Figure 15.10), hold down your mouse button, and drag the outline of the graphic to the new location. Then release the mouse button, and the graphic appears at the new location.

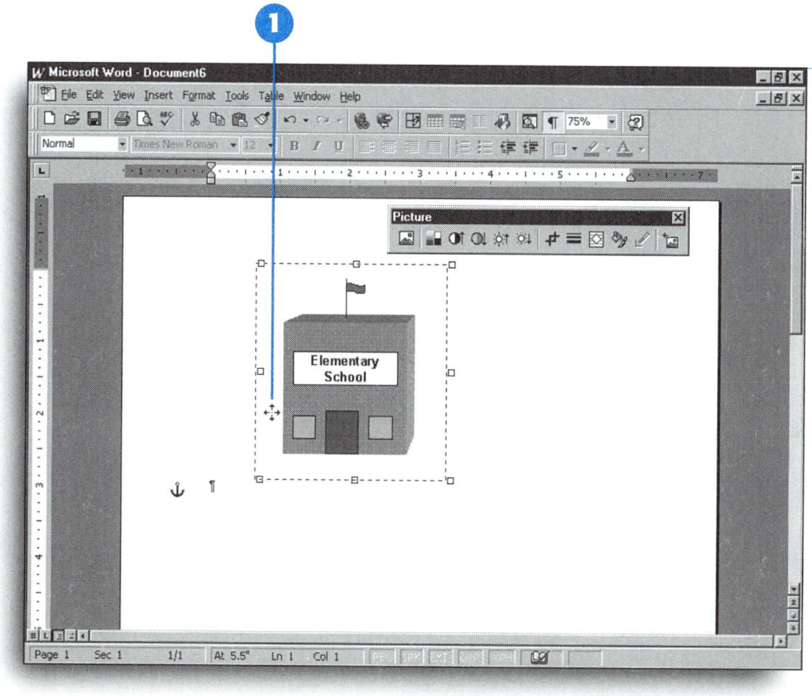

FIGURE 15.10

When your mouse pointer becomes a four-headed arrow you can drag the selected, graphic to its new location.

1 Four-headed mouse pointer for moving graphics

Position a graphic using the Format Picture dialog box

1. Select the image and open the **Format** menu and choose **Picture**, choose Format Picture on the Picture toolbar, or right-click the graphic and select **Format Picture** from the pop-up menu.
2. When the Format Picture dialog box appears, select the **Position** tab (see Figure 15.11).
3. To set the horizontal position of the graphic on the page, specify the distance in the **Horizontal** box and choose **Page**, **Margin**, or **Column** in the **From** drop-down list.
4. To set the vertical position of the graphic on the page, specify the distance in the **Vertical** box and then choose **Margin**, **Page**, or **Paragraph** in the **From** drop-down list.
5. Click the **Move object with text** option to have the graphic move with the text where your insertion point was at the time that you inserted the graphic in your document. As you

add or delete text before the paragraph, the graphic moves up and down the page the same number of lines as the paragraph unless it's close to the bottom or top of the page. Click **Lock anchor** to anchor the graphic to the same page where that text is (even though the paragraph moves, the graphic remains where you placed it on the page until the text moves to another page and it jumps to the same page as the text). Deselecting both these options lets you move the graphic freely around the page.

6. Choose **OK** to have your modifications apply to the graphic.

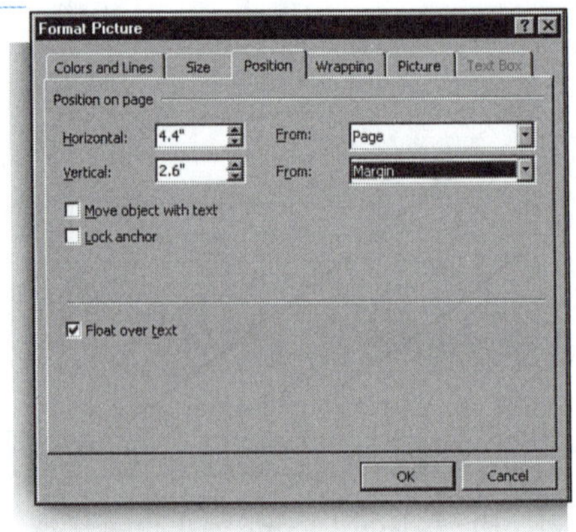

FIGURE 15.11
Enter the measurements for the location of the upper-left corner of the graphic to specify the position.

To move the graphic to another page or another document, select it, choose Cut on the Standard toolbar, position your insertion point where you want the graphic to appear, and then choose Paste on the Standard toolbar. To copy a graphic, select it, choose Copy on the Standard toolbar, position your insertion point where you want the copy to appear, and then choose Paste on the Standard toolbar.

Wrap Text Around Graphics

A graphic causes a break in your text (this doesn't apply to inline graphics). The text immediately after the graphic doesn't start until the next line after the picture, leaving whitespace to the left or right of the graphic. This is called a top-and-bottom text wrap and is Word's default setting for wrapping text around a picture. However, you may want your text to wrap around the image, as shown in Figure 15.12.

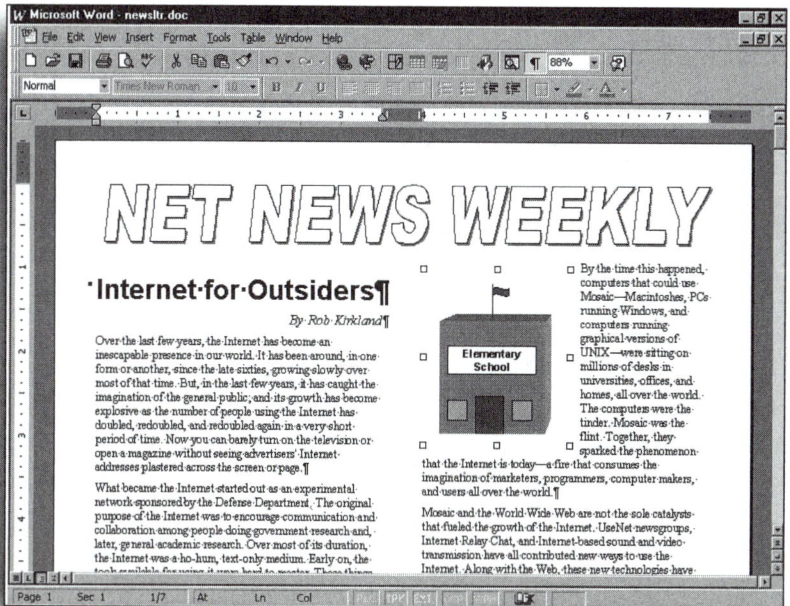

FIGURE 15.12
The text wraps around this graphic.

Set text wrap options

1. Select the image.
2. Open the **Format** menu and select **Picture**, choose Format Picture on the Picture toolbar, or right-click the graphic and select **Format Picture** from the pop-up menu.
3. When the Format Picture dialog box appears, select the **Wrapping** tab (see Figure 15.13).
4. Under **Wrapping style**, select a style of text wrap—**Square**, **Tight**, **Through**, **None**, or **Top & bottom**—depending on how close you want the text to wrap around the picture.
5. Under **Wrap to**, select the sides on which you want the text to wrap—**Both Sides**, **Left**, **Right**, or **Largest Side**.
6. To set the distance between the edge of the picture and the

Adjusting the wrap

The text-wrapping options are available when you click Text Wrapping on the Picture toolbar. There is one more option available that isn't in the dialog box. Choose **Edit Wrap Points** to see a dotted-line outline showing the text wrap boundary (this choice automatically changes the wrap type to **Tight**). Move the points on the boundary line to eliminate awkward breaks in words or lines that make reading difficult. Choose **Edit Wrap Points** again when you finish adjusting the boundary to turn off the display.

beginning of the text wrapping around it, enter the distance in the **Top**, **Bottom**, **Left**, and **Right** boxes under **Distance from text**.

7. Choose **OK**.

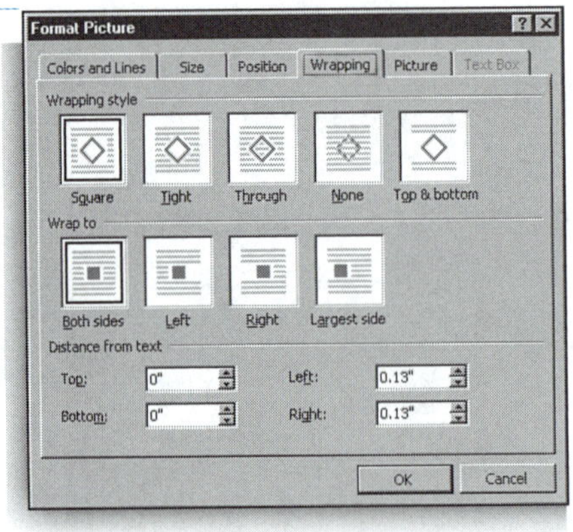

FIGURE 15.13
Select the options for how you want the text to wrap around your picture.

About Special Characters and Symbols

Symbols are characters that do not appear on your computer keyboard, such as letters with accents used in words from languages other than English, stars, bullets, happy faces, the copyright symbol, the registration mark, long (em) dashes, and Greek letters used in mathematical expressions. Even though these characters aren't on your keyboard, Word can still insert them in your documents.

What's the difference between special characters and symbols? Special characters also don't appear on your computer keyboard, and some items appear as both symbols and special characters. Special characters are more the type of characters needed by typesetters, such as the copyright symbol (©), ellipses (…), em spaces (a wider than normal space), and em dashes (—). Table 15.1 gives an example of or describes what the special characters are.

TABLE 15.1 **Special characters**

Name:	Description:
Em dash	— a typographer's long dash (use instead of two hyphens)
En dash	– a typographer's dash (as opposed to a hyphen)
Nonbreaking hyphen	Keeps a hyphenated word from being split between two lines
Optional hyphen	Marks where a word should be hyphenated if it appears at the end of a line (it doesn't appear until the word needs to be broken at the end of a line)
Em space	A larger than normal space
En space	A larger than normal space, but not as large as an em space
Nonbreaking space	A space between words that prevents the words from being split between two lines
Copyright	©
Registered	®
Trademark	™
Section	§
Paragraph	¶
Ellipsis	… (use instead of three periods)
Single opening quote	‘
Single closing quote	’
Double opening quote	“
Double closing quote	”

Insert a Symbol

Insert a symbol

1. Place your insertion point where you want the symbol to appear.
2. Open the **Insert** menu and choose **Symbol** to open the Symbol dialog box (see Figure 15.14). Click the **Symbols** tab if it's not already on top.

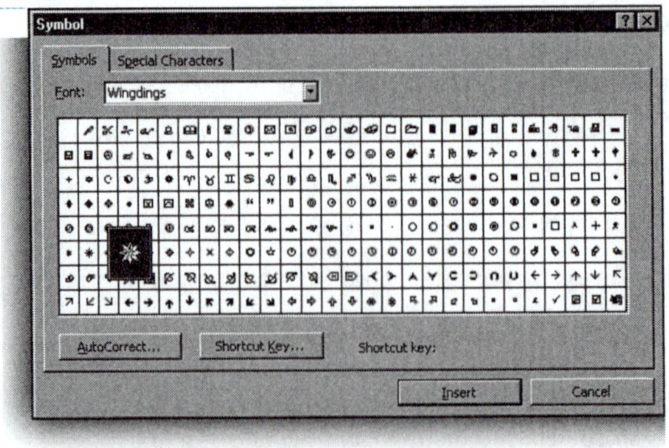

FIGURE 15.14
Select the symbol you want to insert and choose **Insert**.

Not enough fonts and symbols?

You can purchase font software as well as graphics software that includes fonts not found in a standard Windows install. For the most part these software programs install their fonts in Windows, adding the fonts to your lists of available fonts and symbols. Most software packages also enable you to select which fonts to install, and we recommend that you install only the fonts you think you will use. Fonts can take large amounts of disk storage space.

3. From the **Font** drop-down list, select the symbol set you want to use. **Normal Text** is the list for the current font and includes letters with diacritical marks, currency symbols, the paragraph symbol, the registered mark, the trademark symbol, the copyright symbol, and so on. There are a number of symbol fonts, such as Symbol, Wingdings, Zapf Dingbats, or Monotype Sorts, that have Greek letters, mathematical symbols, arrows, pointing hands, snowflakes, bullets, and more.
4. Look through the grid of symbols for the one you want. Click a symbol square to see an enlarged view of the symbol.
5. To insert the selected symbol in your document, choose **Insert** or double-click the symbol.
6. Choose **Close** to close the dialog box after you insert one or more symbols. Choose **Cancel** to close the dialog box without inserting a symbol.

AutoCorrect

Choose **AutoCorrect** to add a symbol or special character to the AutoCorrect list.

Although some symbols are available in Normal Text (such as the copyright, registration mark, em dash), you may also use symbols from the Wingdings font to enhance your documents. Wingdings is shipped with Windows. If you have added other fonts, you may have more symbol fonts to choose from—Bookshelf, Common Bullets, Marlett, Monotype Sorts, Zapf Dingbats, and so on.

SEE ALSO

➤ *To learn how to create AutoCorrect entries, see page 76*

Insert a Special Character

Insert a special character

1. Put your insertion point where you want the special character to appear.
2. Open the **Insert** menu and choose **Symbol**.
3. When the Symbol dialog box appears, click the **Special Characters** tab (see Figure 15.15).

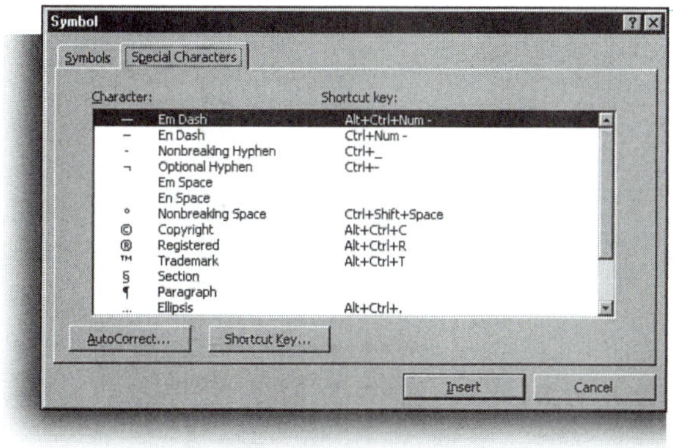

FIGURE 15.15
Insert the special character from the dialog box or use the keyboard shortcut.

4. Select the special character you want from the list and then choose **Insert**, or double-click the character to insert it in your text.
5. Choose **Close** to close the dialog box after you insert a character. Choose **Cancel** to close the dialog box without inserting a character.

Although some items (such as the copyright symbol) appear on both the **Symbols** tab and the **Special Characters** tab, it's easier to access them in **Special Characters** where you don't have to search through the grid to find them. If you have deleted the AutoCorrect entries for the copyright © and registered trademark symbols ®, you can still insert them as special characters or symbols.

Assign Shortcut Keystrokes to Symbols

To quickly insert symbols or special characters that you use frequently, use the keyboard shortcut keys assigned to them (refer to Figure 15.15). For those symbols or special characters that don't already have keyboard shortcuts, you need to assign keys.

Assign shortcut keystrokes to symbols

1. Open the **Insert** menu and choose **Symbol**. Click the symbol to which you want to assign the shortcut keys (refer to Figure 15.15).
2. Choose **Shortcut Key**. The Customize Keyboard dialog box appears (see Figure 15.16).

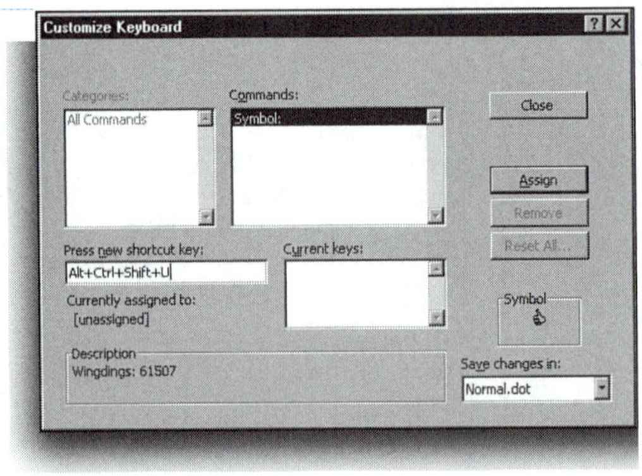

FIGURE 15.16
Displaying assigned shortcut keys.

3. Click in the **Press new shortcut key** text box.
4. Press the shortcut key combination you want to assign (the shortcut keys are a combination of Shift, Ctrl, and/or Alt, and a letter or number key, such as Alt+Ctrl+C that produces the copyright symbol). Its description appears in the **Press new shortcut key** text box. Underneath the text box Word displays **Currently assigned to** and the symbol or operation to which the shortcut key combination is assigned. If it has already been assigned, clear the **Press new shortcut key** text box and try another combination. If Word displays `[unassigned]` then choose **Assign** to assign your combination to the symbol.

5. Choose **Close** to return to the Symbols dialog box, and then choose **Close** to return to your document.

Apply a Watermark

A watermark is text or graphics that appear on the top of or behind document text. Watermarks are often found on preprinted letterhead. With Word, you can create your own watermarks, such as a logo that appears behind the text of your letter, or the word DRAFT to indicate that a document is not in it's final form (see Figure 15.17). Another example of the use of watermarks is for proprietary documents where the word "CONFIDENTIAL" appears behind the text of each page.

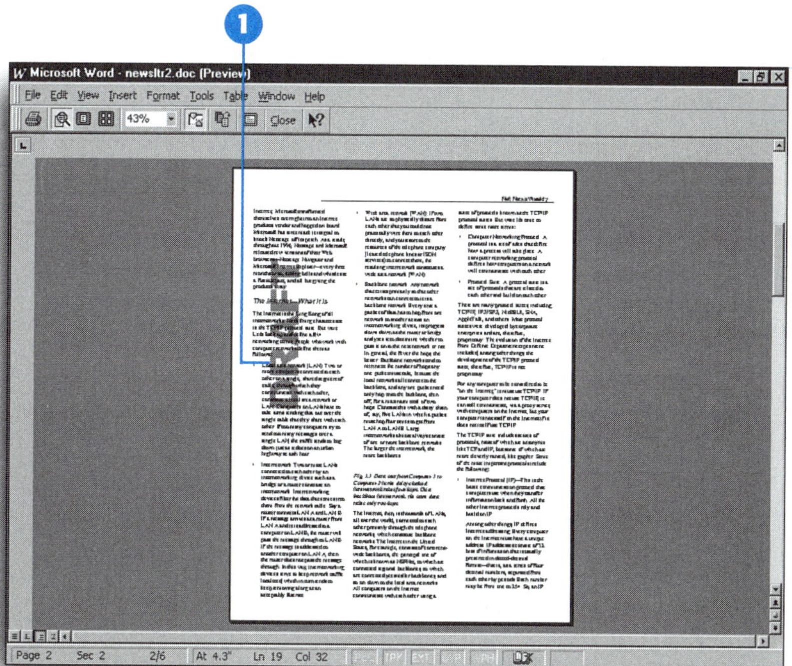

FIGURE 15.17
The watermark "DRAFT" indicates that this newsletter is a work in progress.

1 Watermark

Single-page watermarks

If you only want a watermark to appear on a single page, you don't have to put it in a header or footer. Just insert a picture, text box, or WordArt on the page. After you size and position it, apply the watermark coloring and send it behind the document text.

When you create a watermark for your document, you must start it in a header or footer if you want it to appear on every page. This doesn't confine it to the top or bottom of the page but simply gives it an anchor; then it prints wherever you place it on the page.

Watermark creation is a two-step process:

1. Insert the graphic, object, or text.
2. Format the graphic, object, or text as a watermark, or with light fill colors so that it appears faded like a watermark.

The details of these two steps are explained in the following two sections.

Insert Objects to Be Used as Watermarks

To insert the watermark, complete the following steps.

Create a watermark

1. Click open the **View** menu and choose **Header and Footer**.
2. Choose Show/Hide Document Text on the Header and Footer toolbar to hide the document text.
3. To insert a graphic in your header or footer, go to the **Insert** menu and select **Picture**. From the submenu select **Clip Art**. You also can insert a graphic by selecting the **Insert** menu and then choosing **Picture**. From the submenu choose **From File**. Select the piece of clip art or the graphic file you want to insert, and then choose **Insert**.

   To insert text (such as "DRAFT") click the **Insert** menu and then select **Text Box**. Then drag the rectangle shape in the approximate position where you want the text to appear on your page. Type the watermark text in the box.

   To insert WordArt as a watermark (see Figure 15.18), insert the WordArt while you are in Header/Footer view, then position the WordArt where you want it on the page. Then, change the WordArt fill and line color to a light shade.

FIGURE 15.18

After you insert the graphic into the header or footer, you can size it, position it, and format it for use as a watermark.

1. Graphic as watermark–resized and repositioned
2. WordArt object as a watermark

SEE ALSO

- *To learn how to insert, size, and reposition pictures and graphics, see page 309*
- *To learn how to insert, format, and reposition WordArt, see page 378*

Format Objects as Watermarks

Format an object as a watermark

1. Open the **Format** menu and choose **Picture** or **Object** from the submenu. Alternately, choose the Format Picture icon on the Picture toolbar. The **Format** menu is context-sensitive, it may read Object, Picture, WordArt, and so forth, depending on the item you have inserted and selected.
2. Select the **Picture** tab. Under **Image control**, select **Watermark** from the **Color** drop-down list to format the picture with settings that work well for watermarks (see Figure 15.19).
3. To control how the document text wraps around the picture, select the **Wrapping** tab and then click the **None** option.
4. Choose OK.

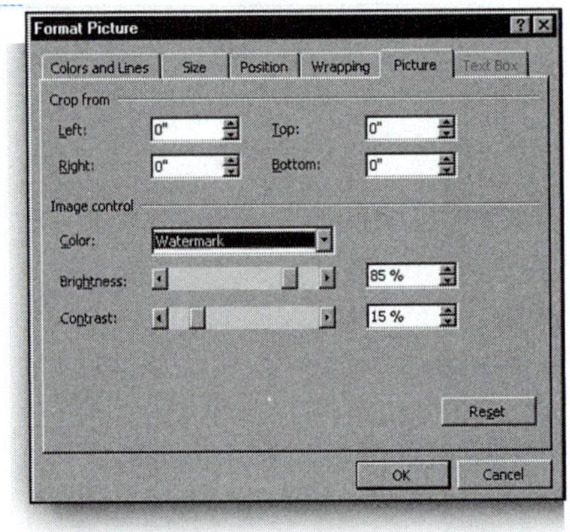

FIGURE 15.19
Use the Watermark color setting to use Word's preset options for your watermark.

Before you print a large document that has a watermark, print a page or two to make sure that the watermark doesn't obscure the text. It may look fine in Print Preview, but some printers may darken the watermark or may not be able to print the watermark and text in the same spot. You can make adjustments after you see the print sample.

Some graphic files just won't translate well to watermarks and appear too dark on a printed page. Should you have this problem try one of the following methods to lighten the graphic:

- Lighten the text in a text box by choosing a text color such as light gray (select the text and choose Font Color on the Formatting toolbar to pick a color).
- Lighten a WordArt object by choosing the **Format** menu and selecting **WordArt.** Then select a lighter fill color on the **Colors and Lines** tab.
- Lighten drawing objects by choosing the **Format** menu and selecting **AutoShape.** Then choose a lighter fill color from the **Colors and Lines** tab.
- Click the **Format** menu and select **Picture** or choose the **Format** menu and select **Object** for imported graphics. Then change the fill color on the **Color and Lines** tab. On the **Picture** tab select **Watermark** from the **Color** drop-down list. For scanned pictures you can adjust the brightness

or contrast, but you may have to edit the picture in an image editing program.

SEE ALSO

➤ *For more information on formatting graphics, see page 378*

Format a text box

1. Select the text box. Open the **Format** menu and choose **Font**. Select the options to format the text as you want it (you should change the **Color** to a lighter shade) and choose **OK**.
2. To rotate the text within the box, choose the **Format** menu and select **Text Direction** and select the rotation option you want (see Figure 15.20).
3. Use options on the Drawing toolbar to format the borders and background color of the text box.
4. Choose **Close** on the Header and Footer toolbar.

SEE ALSO

➤ *To learn more about text boxes, see page 361*

I can't see the watermark!

You must switch to Page Layout view or open Print Preview to see the watermark as it will appear when printed.

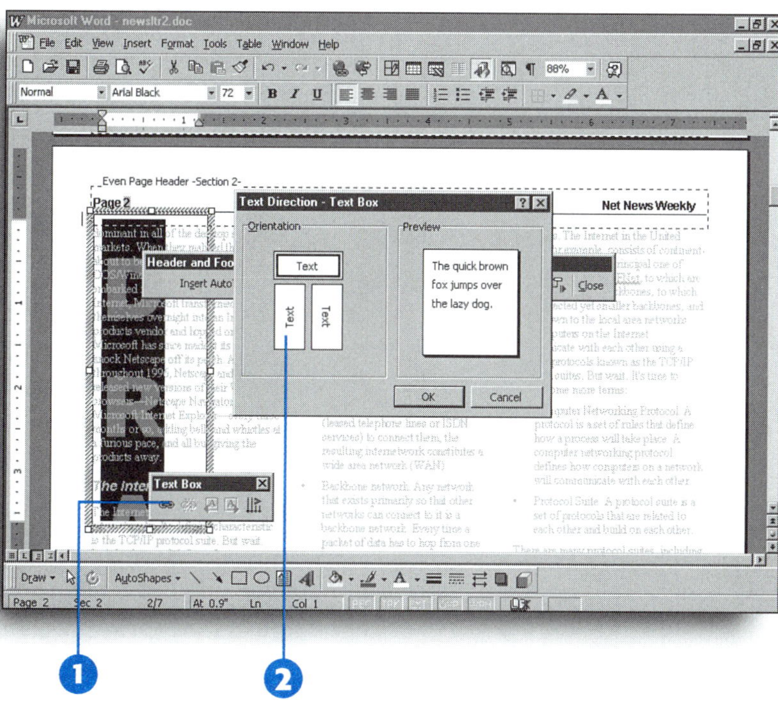

FIGURE 15.20
Select the text direction to rotate your text within the text box.

1. Text Box toolbar
2. Change text direction

Letterhead

Watermarks can be used in templates to make letterhead. To learn how to create templates, see p. 238.

To remove a watermark from your document, you must delete it from the header or footer.

Remove a watermark

1. Open the **View** menu and choose **Header and Footer**.
2. Switch to the header or footer box that contains the watermark.
3. Select the watermark text box or graphic and press the Delete key.
4. Choose **Close** (X) on the Header and Footer toolbar.

CHAPTER

16

Integrate Word Data with Other Applications

- Import files from other applications
- Link files
- Embed objects
- Integrate Excel worksheets
- Create PowerPoint presentations from Word documents

About Data Integration

Word works well with all Microsoft Office applications as well as non-Microsoft applications, such as Lotus 1-2-3. Word is capable of recognizing and converting to and from a wide variety of foreign file formats. In addition, like most Windows-based programs, Word supports *Object Linking and Embedding* (*OLE*), a standard set of tools for integrating data from diverse programs. As a result, you can work with data from other programs in a variety of ways. For example:

- You can use Access data files as data sources in mail merges in Word.
- You can link Excel ranges to reports you create in Word.
- You can open either Access or Excel files directly in Word, which converts them to text and formats them as tables.

Several ways to integrate Word documents with data from other programs are

- Copy and paste
- Insert a file into a Word document
- Link and embed
- Import and export
- Create hyperlinks

This chapter discusses pasting, file insertion, linking, embedding, and importation/exportation of files. We define each method, discuss the differences between them and suggest when to use each to integrate Word data with data created in other applications.

SEE ALSO

➤ *To learn how to create hyperlinks, see page 463*

Copy and Paste

Copy and paste are standard Windows skills. You have undoubtedly been cutting/copying and pasting within Word and between applications for as long as you've been working with Windows.

However, when you paste information from the Clipboard into a Word document, Word may handle the information in different ways, depending on where the information originated.

- If the data came from a Word document, Word simply pastes it in, retaining its original format.
- If the data is textual in nature and came from a program for which Word has a conversion program, Word converts the information to Word text format.
- If the data came from a database program such as Access or a spreadsheet program such as Excel, Word converts the information to Word text, and formats it as a table so as to retain the original column and row format of the data.
- If the data in the Clipboard is in a format that Word cannot convert or is not textual in nature (for example, graphics or sound), but Word can associate the data with an *OLE object application*, Word embeds the data as an object.
- If Word cannot convert the data in the Clipboard and cannot associate the file with an OLE object application, Word pastes the data as is, which may mean the data is unrecognizable and you have to use the **Undo** command (or Ctrl+Z) to remove the pasted data.

Instead of using the **Paste** command and relying on Word to decide what format to use on the pasted data, you can use the **Paste Special** command (on the **Edit** menu) to control the format of the pasted data.

Paste objects using Paste Special

1. Copy your object to the Windows Clipboard.
2. Position your cursor in the receiving document at the position you want to paste the object. Open the **Edit** menu and choose **Paste Special**.
3. The Paste Special dialog box appears (see Figure 16.1).
4. Click **Paste** to embed the Clipboard contents in your document. No link is made to the source file, so the data does not change when the source file is modified.

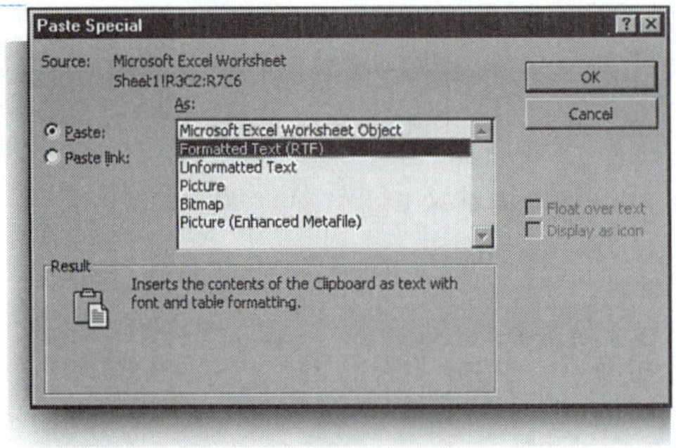

FIGURE 16.1
In the Paste Special dialog box you can choose the format of the pasted data.

Click **Paste link** to insert the Clipboard contents and create a link to the source file (save the source file before you link it in Word). The object in Word updates when the source file is modified.

5. Select the formatting options for your object in the **As** box. The options change depending on the type of object you're inserting. When you select an option, a description appears under **Result**. For example, if you select Formatted Text (RTF) for an Excel worksheet, Word inserts the Clipboard contents as text, but with font and table formatting. Selecting Microsoft Excel Worksheet Object lets you edit the inserted object using Microsoft Excel tools if you are embedding the object, or inserts it as a picture if you linked the file.
6. Enable the **Float over text** option to be able to position the object in front of or behind text or other objects using the drawing commands. If this option is deselected, Word places the object inline where it acts like another character in the text as far as moving the object is concerned.
7. Check **Display as icon** to have the object appear as an icon in your document. You have to double-click the icon to open or edit the object.
8. Choose **OK**.

SEE ALSO

➤ *To learn more about cut, copy, and paste, see page 27*

Insert Files into Word Documents

If you need to paste an entire file into a Word document, you can *insert* the file instead. That way you don't need to open the file to get at its contents. Open the **Insert** menu and choose **File** to open the Insert File dialog box, which is a standard file browser dialog box. Locate and select the file you want to insert and choose **OK**.

If the file you insert is not a Word file and is textual in nature (as opposed to graphics or sound), Word uses its file conversion filters to convert the contents to Word format. If the file is not textual, you should not try to insert it as a file but rather as a picture or an object. (To insert a picture choose the **Insert** menu and select **Picture**. To insert an object, choose the **Insert** menu and select **Object**.)

If Word cannot convert the file, consider re-running the Office or Word Install program to see if you can install a *filter* for the file type in question. Alternately, just open the program and copy the contents to the Clipboard, then paste it into your document.

SEE ALSO

➤ *To insert pictures into Word documents, see page 306*

Importing and Exporting Files

You can easily import files into Word or export files from Word. Importing and exporting converts files to and from Word format. When you import a file Word automatically converts it to Word format if it can. To export a file, you save it in Word by choosing the **File** menu and selecting **Save As**, but choose another file format in the **Save as type** field before you choose **Save**. Word then automatically converts the file to the chosen file format.

When you open a non-Word data file in Word, it detects the file format of the file, converts the file to Word format, then opens it. All you have to do differently from opening a Word file is choose **All files (*.*)** in the **Files of type** field of the Open

For a complete list of Word file conversion formats

Search the Help Index for "file" and open the document called "File Format Converters Supplied with Microsoft Word". If you need a converter not supplied with Word, contact the source application manufacturer and search the Microsoft Web site at `www.microsoft.com`.

dialog box, then choose the foreign file. Alternately, if you know the filename, just type it in and choose **Open**.

Occasionally, Word might not be able to convert the type of file you want to open. If not, consider re-running the Office or Word Install program to see if you can install a *filter* for the file type in question. Alternately, just open the program in which the file was created and try saving it in a file format that Word can recognize. (To save, go to the **File** menu and select **Save As**.) Then, try opening the file again in Word.

The following list displays file formats that Word can open or save to (see Table 16.1). This is not a complete list of file formats, but rather of those that are most popular:

- HTML
- WordPerfect for DOS (versions 5.x and 6.0)
- WordPerfect for Windows (versions 5.x and 6.0)
- Excel (versions 2.x through 97)

TABLE 16.1 File formats recognized by Word

Program or File Format:	Versions:	Open:	Save:
HTML	Up to 2.0	X	X
WordPerfect for DOS	5.x and 6.0	X	
WordPerfect for Windows	5.x and 6.x	X	
Excel	2.x through 97	X	
Word	2.x through 97	X	X
Word for Macintosh	4.x and 5.x	X	X
Works	3.0	X	
Works	4.0	X	X
Lotus 1-2-3	2.x, 3.x, 4.x	X	

SEE ALSO

➤ *To open and save documents, see page 86*
➤ *To save documents as HTML documents, see page 460*

Understanding Object Linking and Embedding

Word supports the OLE2 (Object Linking and Embedding, version 2) standard. To Word users that means that you can either link to data created in another program or embed data created in another program, and that the data linked to or embedded retains its identity with the program in which it was originally created.

Contrast this to pasted or inserted data (described earlier in this chapter). When you insert a file (and if possible when you paste data), the inserted data is converted to Word format, just as if you had entered it manually into your document. But embedded or linked data does not become Word data. Rather, it is a "foreign object" which is "contained" by the Word file. That is why OLE is called object linking and embedding. The source application is called the object application and the destination application is called the container application.

You cannot edit linked or embedded data with Word. Rather, you have to edit it with the program in which it was created. If you try to edit the linked or embedded data, Word will try to open the program in which the data was created. If the program isn't available, you can't edit the data.

If the source program supports OLE2, you can edit the data in-place, that is, within a window that appears around the data object right in your Word document (see Figure 16.2); and Word's menus and toolbars are replaced temporarily by those of the source program. (Clicking in the Word document outside the data object causes Word's menus and toolbars to reappear.) If the source program supports OLE1 or DDE (Dynamic Data Exchange, the predecessor to OLE), the data object appears in its own program's window when you try to edit it.

Understanding Linking

When you link to data created in another program, for example to cells in an Excel spreadsheet, the data appears in your Word document but actually continues to be stored in the Excel data file. All that is stored in your Word file is a pointer to the location of the Excel file.

Linking to data has its benefits. First, if someone updates the data in the spreadsheet file, the update appears automatically in your Word document. If you have access to the program in which the data was created, you can update the original data by simply double-clicking the linked data object in your document. This causes the original file to be opened in the program, and when you save your changes you are saving them to the original file. Second, because your file only contains a pointer to the original object, your file does not get appreciably bigger. The drawback to linking is that you may not be able to update the data in your file if the source file is moved to another location or deleted.

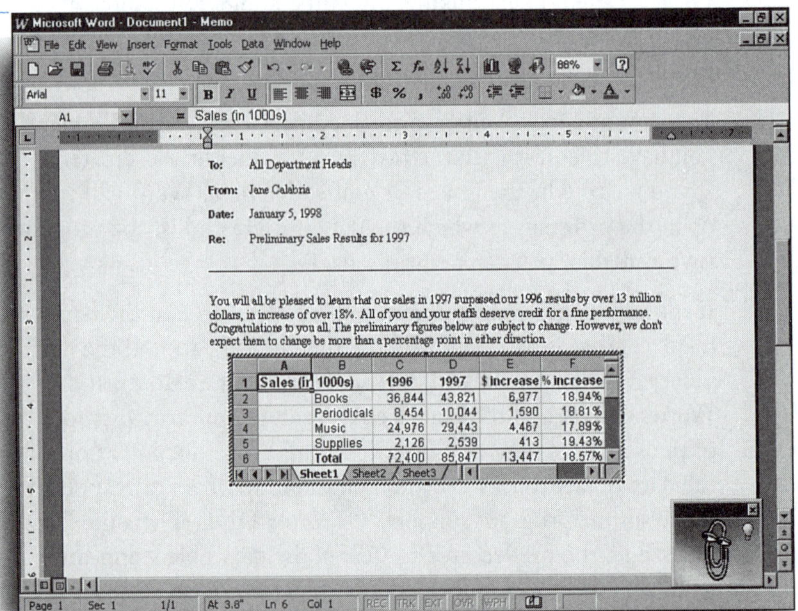

FIGURE 16.2
When you double-click the embedded spreadsheet range, it appears in an Excel window inside of your Word document, and the Excel menu and toolbars replace the Word menu and toolbars.

Understanding Embedding

When you embed data in a Word document, you insert a *copy* of the original data object, and Word does not maintain a link to the original. If someone changes the original copy of the data, that change is not reflected in the copy embedded in your document. If you have the program with which the embedded data object was originally created, you can double-click the data object to open it in that program and edit it. But you are editing your copy only, not the original data.

Embedding data has its benefits. First, you can change the embedded data without affecting the original. Second, you don't have to maintain any link to the original data file.

With either linked or embedded data, you can see the data in your Word file whether or not you have access to the program that created it. But you must have access to the program that created the data if you want to edit it.

When Should You Paste, Insert, Link, or Embed?

You can insert a file if you want to bring an entire file into your Word document. Generally, if you only want to bring part of a file you must paste, link, or embed the data. One exception is spreadsheet files, where a dialog box appears to ask which sheet you want to insert.

Link to external data if any of the following conditions is true:

- When you want updates to the original data object to appear automatically in your document.
- When the data being linked to will be maintained in the original file to which you are linking.
- When you expect that you will be able to maintain the link to the original file.

Embed external data if any of the following conditions is true:

- When you want to be able to manipulate your copy of the embedded data independently of the original object.
- When there is a likelihood that you will not be able to maintain the link between your Word document and the object to which it is linked.

Insert a file or paste data if the other program does not support OLE.

Link to an Object

There are two ways to link to an object—inserting or pasting—as long as you select the linking options. Pasting, however, makes it easier to link to just part of the file.

Link an entire file to your document

1. Position your insertion point in the document where you want the linked object to appear.
2. Open the **Insert** menu and choose **Object**.
3. When the Object dialog box appears, click the **Create from File** tab (see Figure 16.3).

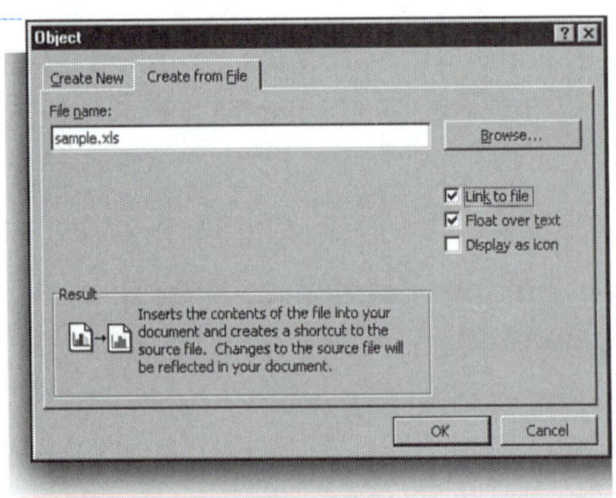

FIGURE 16.3
To link to an existing file, open the Object dialog box and check **Link to file** after you enter the filename.

4. Type the name of the file you want to insert in the **File name** box, or choose **Browse** to select the file from a list.
5. Click **Link to file** to place a check mark there.

6. Click **Float over text** to remove the check mark so that the linked object isn't displayed as a drawing object that you position in front of or behind text.
7. (Optional) If you want to display the linked object as an icon (useful for online documents), click **Display as icon** to place a check mark there. An icon appears in your document text, and you must double-click it to open or edit the object. When you print the document, the icon is printed.
8. Click **OK**. Figure 16.4 shows a linked object, which is a slide from a Microsoft PowerPoint presentation.

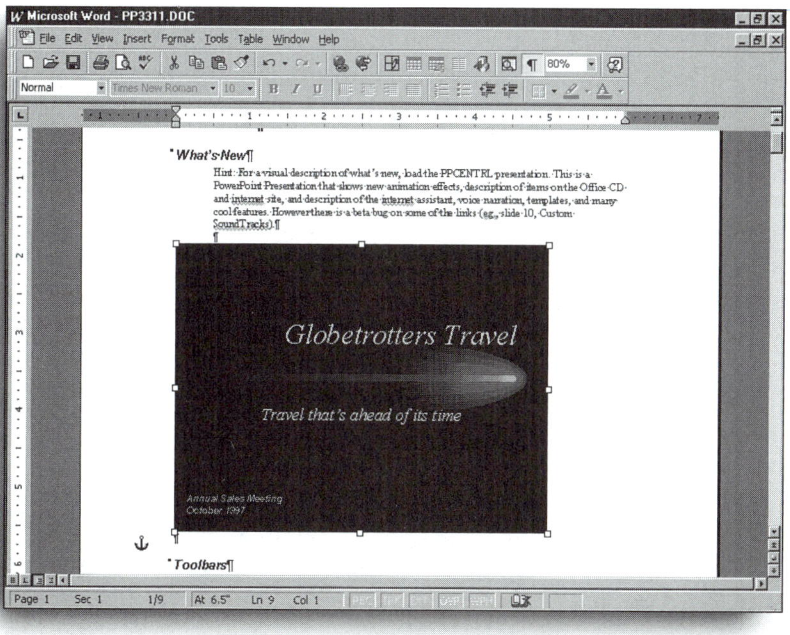

FIGURE 16.4
This illustration is a linked object; the source is a PowerPoint presentation file.

You may not be able to insert some graphics files as linked objects. These must be added by opening the **Insert** menu and selecting **Picture**.

SEE ALSO

➤ *For more information on inserting pictures, see page 306*

Link to part of a file

1. Open the file that contains the data that you will link to in Word. If you have not saved the file yet, save it now. You cannot link to data that has not been saved to disk.
2. Select the data, open the **Edit** menu and choose **Copy** to place a copy in the Clipboard.
3. Position your insertion point in the Word document where you want the linked object to appear. Then open the **Edit** menu and choose **Paste Special** to open the Paste Special dialog box.
4. In the dialog box, choose **Paste link** and a data format.
5. (Optional) Depending on what format you choose, you may also be able to choose **Float over text** if you want to display the object as a drawing object that you position in front of or behind text.
6. (Optional) If you want to display the linked object as an icon (useful for online documents), click **Display as icon** to place a check mark there.
7. Choose **OK**.

Drag-and-drop linking

You can also set up an object link by holding down the Ctrl and Shift keys while dragging the object to be linked from the source file to the target Word file.

To make changes to a linked object, you must open the source file in the application where it was created and modify it there. To do this, you may either open it in the standard way or you may double-click the object in your Word document. If you open the source file by double-clicking the object in Word, the originating application opens in a separate window with the source file in edit mode. Click outside this window to return to Word without closing the source application. The modifications appear in the object in Word, even if you haven't saved the file in the source application. When you do close the source application window, you'll be prompted to save the source file.

If your Word document is open when you make changes to the source file, the object in your document is updated immediately. If not, the next time you open your document, the data will be updated automatically. If you don't want the automatic updating, open the **Tools** menu and choose **Options**, select the **General** tab, and deselect the **Update automatic links at open** option. To update the object manually, select it and press F9.

Word does have an option to automatically update linked files when you print the document. To enable this option, open the **Tools** menu and choose **Options**. Then click the **Print** tab on the Options dialog box (see Figure 16.5). Click **Update links** to put a check mark in the box, and then choose **OK**.

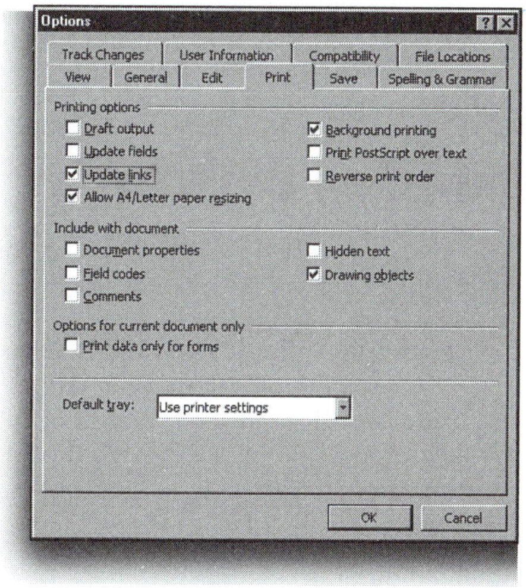

FIGURE 16.5

To have your linked files update automatically when you print, select **Update links**.

If you would rather update the linked object manually, open the **Edit** menu and choose **Links** (see Figure 16.6). Select the object you want to update manually (hold down Ctrl and click on each object to select more than one). Click **Manual** and then choose **OK**.

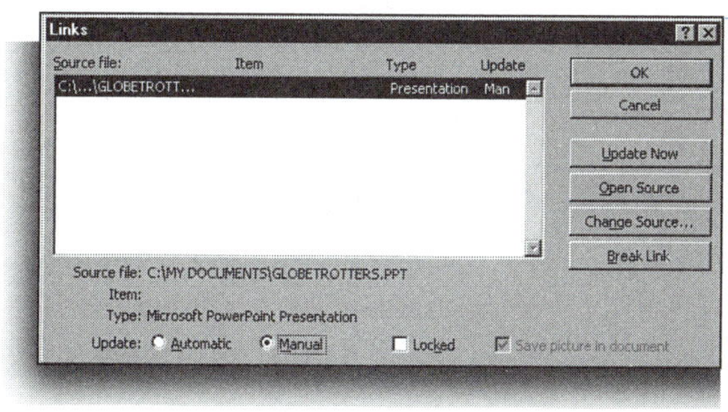

FIGURE 16.6

To switch to manual updating of your links, click **Manual**.

Caution: Don't move linked files

Word cannot update a linked object if the source file is moved or renamed. If you move or rename a linked object's source, open the Links dialog box, select the linked object, and choose **Change Source**. Enter the name of the file to which you want to reconnect to in the **File name** box and choose **Open** to return to the Links dialog box. Then choose **OK**.

To manually update the linked object, open the **Edit** menu and choose **Links**. Select the object you want to update manually and choose **Update Now**. Choose **OK** to close the dialog box. Alternately, select the object in your document and then press F9. You are not prompted by Word to update the link if you turned off automatic linking, so you have to be careful to update the object in Word every time you modify the source file.

To prevent a linked object from being updated, open the Links dialog box and click **Locked** to place a check mark there. Choose **OK**.

Embed an Object

You can embed an entire file or part of a file, such as a spreadsheet range.

Embed an entire file in a Word document

1. Position your insertion point in the document where you want the embedded object to appear.
2. Open the **Insert** menu and choose **Object**.
3. When the Object dialog box appears, click the **Create from File** tab (see Figure 16.7).

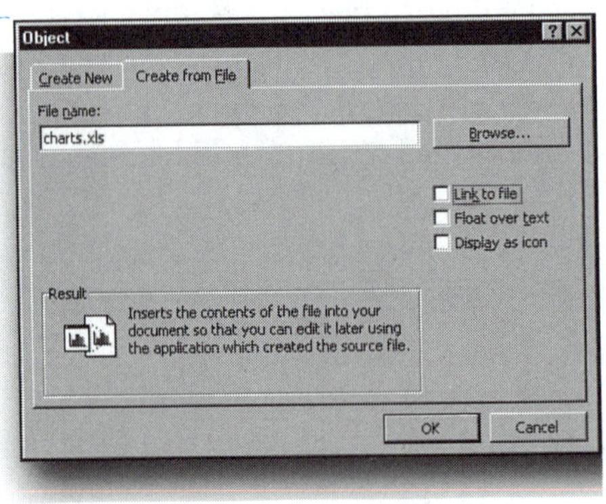

FIGURE 16.7

To embed an existing file, open the Object dialog box and remove the check from **Link to file** after you enter the filename.

4. Type the name of file you want to insert in the **File name** box, or choose **Browse** to select the file from a list.
5. Click **Link to file** to remove the check mark there.

6. Click **Float over text** to remove the check mark, so the object isn't displayed as a drawing object that you position in front of or behind text.
7. (Optional) If you want to display the object as an icon (useful for online documents), click **Display as icon** to place a check mark there.
8. Choose **OK**. Figure 16.8 shows an embedded object, which is a Microsoft Excel workbook. The entire file is contained within the Word document, so when you double-click the object to edit it you can change the worksheet being displayed.

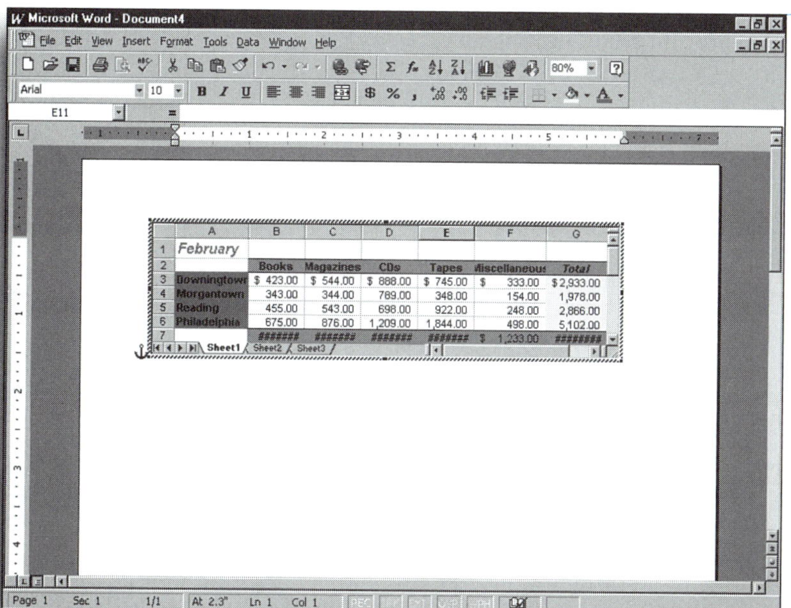

FIGURE 16.8
When you double-click an embedded Excel workbook, you can display different worksheets in that file by clicking the sheet tabs.

Embed part of a file in a Word document

1. Open the file that contains the data that you want to link to in Word. Select the data and paste it into the Clipboard.
2. Position your insertion point in the Word document where you want the linked object to appear. Open the **Edit** menu and choose **Paste Special** to open the Paste Special dialog box.

Drag-and-drop embedding

You can also embed an object by dragging the object to be linked from the source file to the target Word file. Because you must select the object before dragging, you don't have to embed the entire object when you use drag-and-drop. **Float over text** and **Display as icon** options are not applied when using this method.

3. In the dialog box, choose a data format.
4. (Optional) Depending on what format you choose, you may also be able to choose **Float over text** if you want to display the object as a drawing object that you position in front of or behind text.
5. (Optional) If you want to display the linked object as an icon (useful for online documents), click **Display as icon** to place a check mark there.
6. Choose **OK**.

You update the embedded object by double-clicking it and making the changes directly from Word. Many of the toolbar and menu selections from the source program are available when you are editing an embedded object. However, any changes made to the source file aren't reflected in the embedded object and modifications you make to the embedded object from Word do not appear in the source file.

Creating and Embedding a New Object

It's also possible to embed a blank embedded object, such as a blank Excel worksheet, into a Word document. You might want to do this if you intend to create the embedded object on the spot. For example, you may want to embed sales figures that are not yet part of an Excel worksheet. You might prefer to enter the sales figures into a worksheet rather than directly into your Word document, because then you can use Excel's features to calculate the totals and format the numbers.

In another example, you might want to create an expense report form in Word. You might want to embed an Excel expense worksheet in the form where users would enter their numeric expense data so that the form would total up the data automatically. If such an Excel worksheet did not exist yet, you could embed a blank Excel worksheet object in your form and create the expense worksheet on the spot. The interesting aspect of this is that the Excel worksheet object would exist only in your Word document; there would be no copy of it in any Excel file.

Embed a new, blank object into a Word document

1. Place your insertion point in the document where you want the object to appear.
2. Open the **Insert** menu and choose **Object**.
3. When the Insert dialog box appears, click the **Create New** tab (see Figure 16.9).

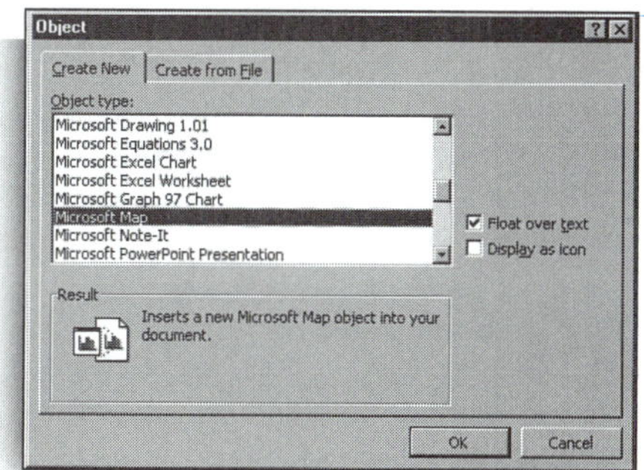

FIGURE 16.9
Select the type of object you want to insert in your document and choose **OK**.

4. From the **Object type** box, select the type of object you want to create.
5. Click **Float over text** to remove the check mark, so the object isn't displayed as a drawing object that you position in front of or behind text.
6. (Optional) If you want to display the object as an icon (useful for online documents), click **Display as icon** to place a check mark there.
7. Choose **OK**. A blank embedded object appears in your document (see Figure 16.10). Double-click the object to enter data.

To enter data into an embedded object, double-click it. When you finish adding data to the embedded object, click outside the border around the object to return to document editing.

Embedding a blank Excel worksheet does not embed the Excel program!

Users who double-click an embedded blank Excel worksheet must have Excel installed on their PC to open the worksheet, even though it is blank. This is true of any source application for any embedded object.

FIGURE 16.10
When editing an embedded object, such as with Microsoft Map, you have access to the tools and menu commands from the source program.

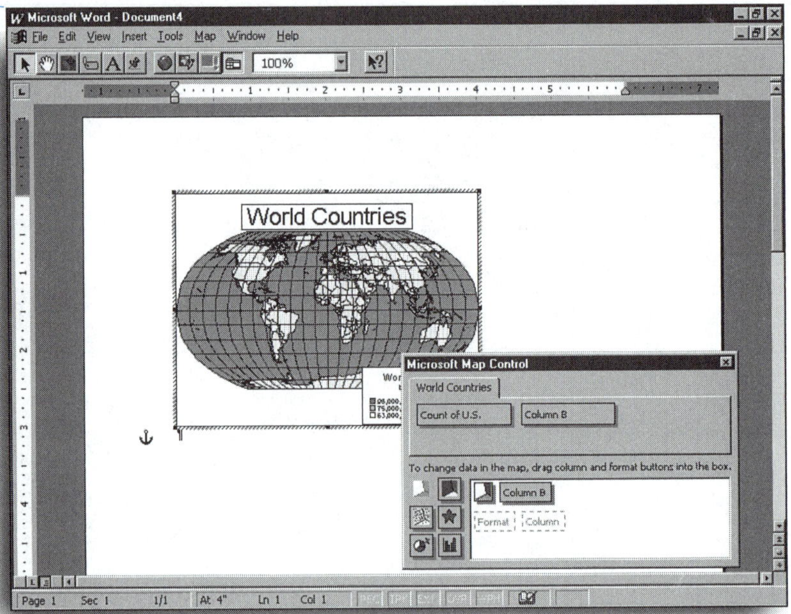

Integrate Excel Data

Word processing and spreadsheet programs are two of the most frequently used PC applications. Microsoft Office includes both Word and Excel and these two programs work closely together to enable you to exchange and import data.

Import Excel Worksheets into a Table

There are several ways to insert Microsoft Excel worksheet data into a document. One way is to insert the worksheet as a linked object or embedded object. Another is to copy and paste a worksheet from Excel into Word.

A *linked* worksheet appears in your document, but its data is stored in the original Microsoft Excel workbook. Word automatically updates the worksheet in your document when changes are made to the Excel worksheet. If you want to edit the worksheet data when you are in Word, select the object, click the **Edit** menu and select **Links**, select the name of the workbook, and choose **Open Source** to open Microsoft Excel with the workbook open.

Insert a linked Excel worksheet

1. Open the Word document into which you want to insert the worksheet and the Microsoft Excel workbook that contains the data you want.
2. Switch to Excel and select the entire worksheet or a range of cells.
3. Open the **Edit** menu and choose **Copy**. Alternately, click the Copy icon on the Standard toolbar.
4. Switch to the Word document and position your insertion point where you want the Excel data to appear.
5. Open the **Edit** menu and choose **Paste Special**. The Paste Special dialog box appears (see Figure 16.11).

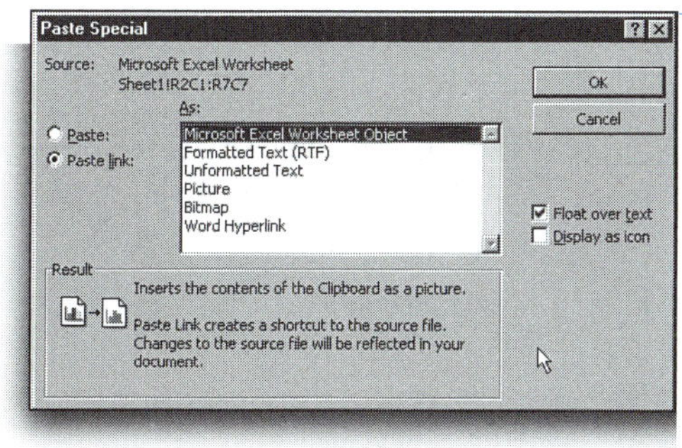

FIGURE 16.11

Choose **Paste link** from the Paste Special dialog box.

6. Select **Paste link**.
7. From the **As** box, select the option you want (a description of the option appears in the **Result** box at the bottom of the dialog box when you select it). Usually you would choose a Microsoft Excel Worksheet Object.
8. Choose **OK**. The worksheet appears in the document and looks like a table.

When the Excel workbook is modified, Word updates your table automatically.

Excel charts and graphs

Embedding isn't limited to worksheet data only. The graphs and charts you create in Excel can also be embedded in your Word documents. Instead of selecting a range of cells, select the chart or graph when following the procedures.

SEE ALSO

➤ *To learn more about Word hyperlinks, see page 463*

Storing and Modifying Excel Data in Word Documents

An *embedded* worksheet stores its data in a Word document. When you want to edit an embedded object, you double-click it. The toolbars and commands from Microsoft Excel temporarily replace the Word toolbars so you can make your changes and return to your Word document. Or, right-click the object and select **Microsoft Worksheet** and then **Open** from the shortcut menu, which opens the source file in Microsoft Excel where you can edit the data.

Where did all my data go?

If the embedded worksheet looks blank after you entered data and saved your file, do one thing before you panic. Double-click the embedded object and check the bottom left of the worksheet area. You'll see some sheet tabs there. Excel allows you to have multiple worksheets, so make sure the correct sheet tab is selected. The other sheets may be blank.

Quickly embed entire worksheet

An entire worksheet object can be quickly embedded. Open the **Insert** menu and select **Object**. Click the **Create from File** tab. In the **File name** box, enter the name of the workbook from which you want to create the embedded object (choose **Browse** to select the filename). Deselect the **Link to file** option. Choose **OK**.

Embed an Excel worksheet in a Word document

1. Open the Word document where you want to embed the Excel worksheet.
2. Open the Microsoft Excel workbook that contains the data that you want to use to create an embedded object.
3. Select the entire Excel worksheet or a range of cells.
4. Still in Excel, open the **Edit** menu and choose **Copy**. Alternately, click the Copy icon on the Standard toolbar.
5. Switch to your Word document and position your insertion point where you want the worksheet to appear.
6. Open the **Edit** menu and choose **Paste** to open the Paste Special dialog box (see Figure 16.12).

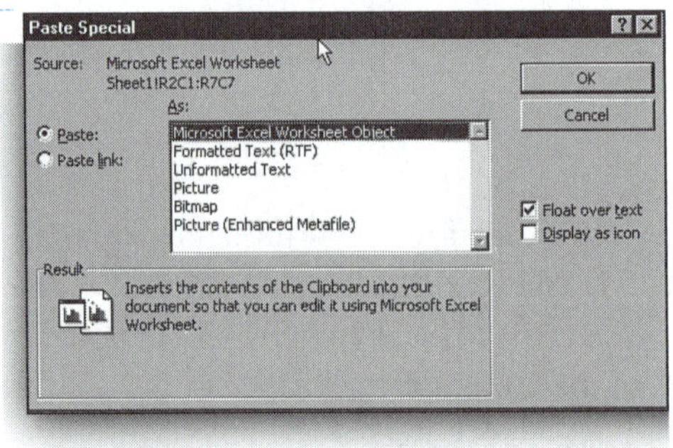

FIGURE 16.12
Select **Paste** when you want to embed the worksheet.

7. Select **Paste**.
8. In the **As** box, select **Microsoft Excel Worksheet Object**.
9. Choose **OK**.

Although the object appears as a table when you click it, you cannot format it as a table. Any formatting and editing must be done using Excel's tools. Double-click the object to edit it. When you double-click it, an Excel window opens and Excel's tools are available for editing and formatting (see Figure 16.13). When you are ready to return to your document, click outside the border around the worksheet.

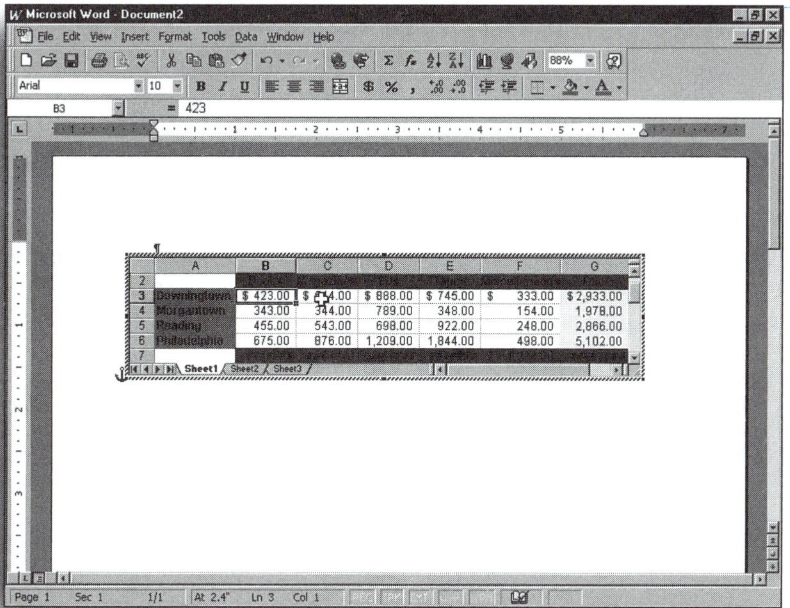

FIGURE 16.13
When you double-click an embedded Excel worksheet, the toolbars from Excel appear on your screen.

You don't have to embed or link files. You can take data that exists in Excel and put it into your document but still be able to format it like a Word table and edit it from Word. You copy the cells in Excel and paste them into Word (don't use the **Paste Special** command). The layout, the data, and style are copied to Word as a table. None of the formulas are active; it's as though the data was simply typed.

SEE ALSO

➤ *To create Word tables, see page 280*
➤ *To master cut, copy, and paste, see page 27*

Update Excel Worksheets

Linked objects are automatically updated to reflect changes in the original worksheet every time you open the document that contains the linked worksheet or whenever changes are made while both the worksheet and the document are open. If you don't want the automatic updating, open the **Tools** menu and choose **Options** then select the **General** tab, and deselect the **Update automatic links at open** option. To update the object manually, select it and press F9. You won't be prompted to update the object, so remember to do it when you modify the source file.

Word does have an option to automatically update linked files when you print the document. To enable this option, click the **Tools** menu and select **Options**. Then click the **Print** tab on the Options dialog box (see Figure 16.14). Click **Update links** to put a check mark in the box, and then choose **OK**.

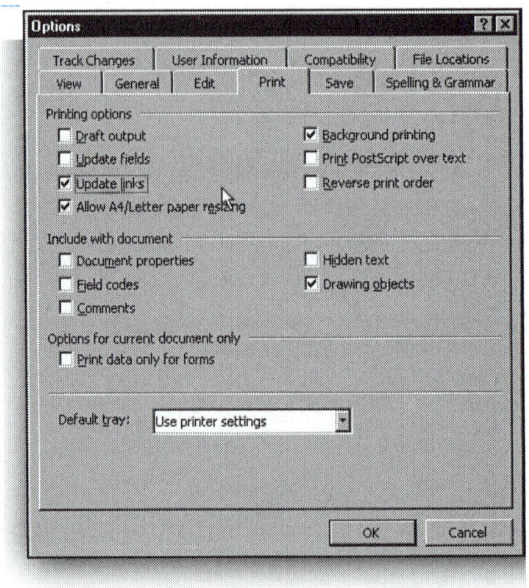

FIGURE 16.14
To have your linked files update automatically when you print, select **Update links**.

If you would rather update the linked worksheet manually, click the **Edit** menu and select **Links**. Choose the object you want to update manually (hold down Ctrl and click each object to select more than one). Click **Manual** and then choose **OK**.

When you want to manually update the linked object, open the **Edit** menu and select **Links**. Choose the object you want to update manually and choose **Update now**. Choose **OK** to close the dialog box. Or, a faster way to update your linked object is to select the object in your document and then press F9.

Embed a Blank Excel Worksheet

Although you can embed an existing *worksheet*, you can also start from scratch by *embedding* a new, blank worksheet in your document.

Starting with a blank embedded worksheet gives the functionality of Microsoft Excel without having to create the worksheet in Excel, then embed it in Word.

Embed a new, blank Excel worksheet into a Word document

1. Position your insertion point in your Word document where you want to insert the object for a worksheet.
2. Open the **Insert** menu and choose **Object**. Select the **Create New** tab (see Figure 16.15).

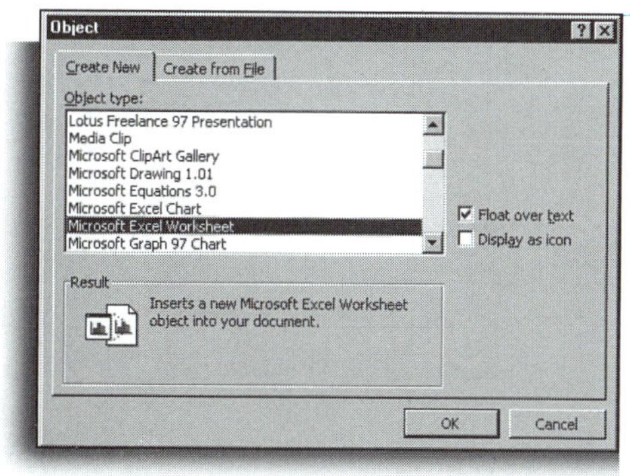

FIGURE 16.15
Select **Microsoft Excel Worksheet** to insert a worksheet object in your document.

3. From the **Object type** list, select **Microsoft Excel Worksheet**.
4. Choose **OK** and begin creating the worksheet (choose **Microsoft Excel Help** from the **Help** menu for assistance if you're not familiar with Excel).

Another method for embedding a blank worksheet is to choose Insert Microsoft Excel Worksheet on the Standard toolbar. As with the Insert Table button, a drop-down area appears where you drag across the boxes to select the number of rows and columns you want in the worksheet. After you release the mouse button, the object is inserted at your insertion point. From that point it behaves as any other embedded worksheet.

Integrate PowerPoint Data

PowerPoint and Word information is interchangeable in many ways. You can, of course, copy and paste text and graphics between the two programs. You can also:

- Create a PowerPoint presentation from a Word outline
- Link a PowerPoint slide(s) or presentation into a Word document
- Embed a PowerPoint slide(s) or presentation into a Word document

Create a Presentation from a Word Outline

With Microsoft PowerPoint installed on your computer, you can create a PowerPoint presentation from a Word document if you use heading styles in your Word document. When PowerPoint reads the Word document, it converts heading styles to outline levels in your presentation. For example, a Word Heading 1 style becomes the title of a new slide in PowerPoint. Heading 2 styles become the first level of text and so forth. A good way to be sure that you have the appropriate heading styles where needed is to view the document in Outline view.

Figure 16.16 shows a Word document in Outline view that contains heading styles. Figure 16.17 shows the resulting PowerPoint slides created from the Word document.

Create a PowerPoint presentation from a Word document

1. Open the document in Word. Check to ensure your heading styles are correctly formatted.

2. Open the **File** menu and choose **Send To**, then select **Microsoft PowerPoint**.

3. The Microsoft PowerPoint program opens, displaying your Word document in outline form.

SEE ALSO

➤ *To learn how to work with heading styles, see page 158*

➤ *To create Word outlines, see page 204*

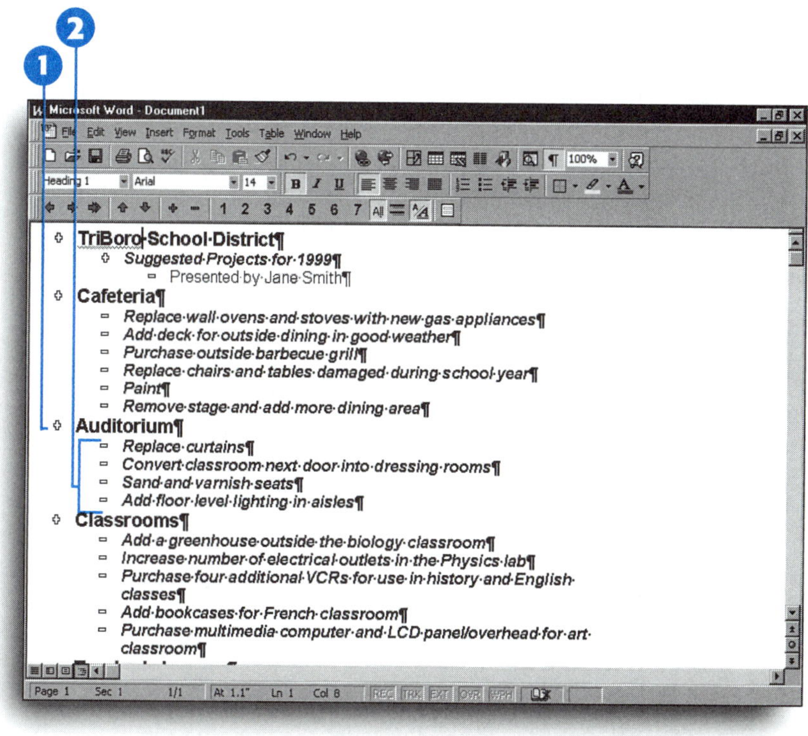

FIGURE 16.16

PowerPoint slides can be created from Word documents using heading styles.

1. Heading 1 paragraph will become a slide title

2. Heading 2 text becomes the slide bullet text

Embed PowerPoint Slides

A single slide, several slides, or an entire PowerPoint presentation can be embedded into a Word document. When you embed multiple slides or an entire presentation, the first slide is displayed in the document. To view the other slides, double-click the first slide and the PowerPoint slideshow begins. Embedding part or all of a presentation file is useful when you're preparing an online document that others may share and use even if they don't have PowerPoint. It's also helpful if you have slides such as organization charts or graphs that you'd like to change from your Word document without changing the original presentation.

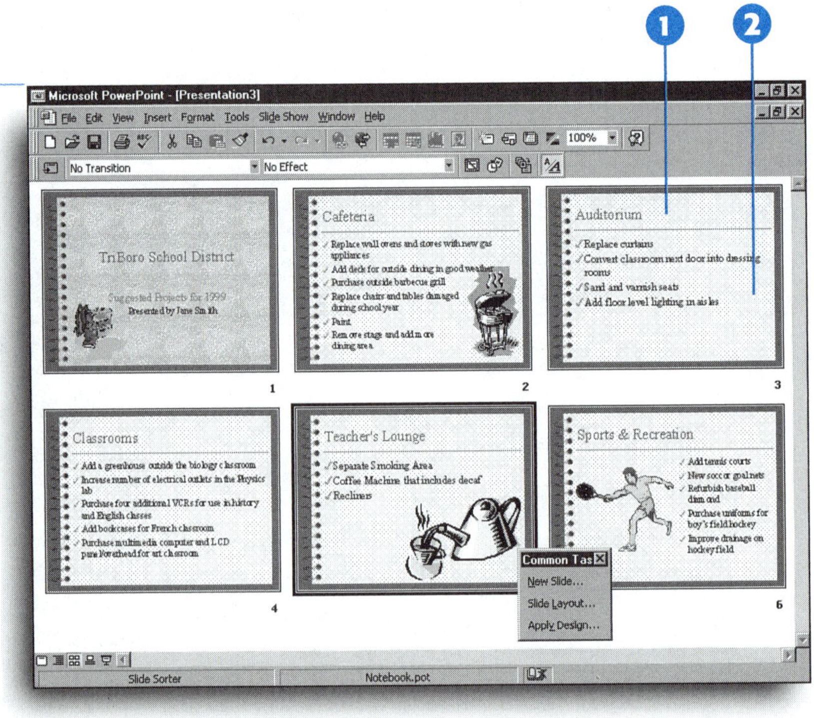

FIGURE 16.17

In the PowerPoint slide sorter you see the resulting slides, where the titles are the Heading 1 paragraphs from the Word document.

1. Slide title is same as Heading 1 paragraph
2. Bullet text is the same as Heading 2 text

Embed a PowerPoint object into a Word document

1. Open the document in Word and the presentation in PowerPoint that you want to embed into the Word document.
2. Switch to PowerPoint Slide Sorter view.
3. Select and copy the slide or slides, or the entire presentation.
4. Switch to the Word document. Position your cursor where you want to insert the objects.

5. Open the **Edit** menu and choose **Paste Special**. If you are embedding a single slide, choose **Microsoft PowerPoint Slide Object** in the **As** box. If you are embedding multiple slides or the entire presentation, click **Microsoft PowerPoint Presentation Object** in the **As** box.

Others must have PowerPoint to run the slideshow

When you embed a PowerPoint presentation, others will be able to view a single slide; but if they don't have PowerPoint installed, they cannot see the slideshow when they double-click. You should consider packing the PowerPoint viewer with the presentation and emailing them to non-PowerPoint users so that they can view the slideshow even if they can't edit the file.

Link PowerPoint Slides

To link PowerPoint slides to your Word document, save the PowerPoint presentation. Open both the Word document and the Power Point presentation you want to link.

Link a PowerPoint slide to a Word document

1. With both programs and files open, switch to PowerPoint Slide Sorter view.
2. Select and copy the slide(s) you want to link.
3. Switch to Word and open the **Edit** menu and select **Paste Special**.
4. Choose **Paste link**.
5. In the **As** box, click **Microsoft PowerPoint Slide Object**.

Link a PowerPoint presentation to a Word document

1. Open Word and the document in which you want to place the link.
2. Open the **Insert** menu and choose **Object**.
3. Click the **Create from File** tab. In the **File name** box, type the name of the PowerPoint file.
4. Click the **Link to file** check box.
5. Click **OK**.

Like an embedded object, Word displays the first slide in the document. Double-click the slide to view the entire slideshow.

CHAPTER

17

Add Drawings and WordArt

- Create drawings in Word documents
- Edit and modify drawings
- Add 3-D and other special effects to drawing objects
- Insert a WordArt object

Create a Drawing

Although you can insert graphics and clip art to your Word document, Word provides tools to create your own drawings. Use these tools when you want to draw lines, boxes, or create flowcharts and organization charts. By using Word tools, you don't need to switch to a graphics or drawing program unless you need a powerful program for your artwork and you can draw exactly the item you need.

With Word drawing tools you can create simple shapes, lines, boxes, text boxes, ovals, and circles. To these shapes you can add text, shadows, and 3-D effects. You can also rotate, flip, and resize objects (see Figure 17.1).

When you choose Drawing on the Standard toolbar to display the Drawing toolbar, Word automatically switches to the Page Layout view. Page Layout view is necessary to work with drawn objects.

To create drawing objects—lines, arrows, rectangles, ovals, text boxes, 3-D shapes—select the object or tool on the Drawing toolbar. Table 17.1 lists and briefly describes the buttons on the Drawing toolbar.

TABLE 17.1 Drawing tools

Button:	Name:	Description:
	Draw	Displays a menu of drawing commands
	Select Objects	Selects drawing objects
	Free Rotate	Rotates objects to any angle
	AutoShapes	Displays a pop-up menu of different shapes
	Line	Draws straight lines
	Arrow	Draws arrows

Button:	Name:	Description:
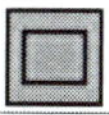	Rectangles	Draws rectangles and squares
	Oval	Draws ovals and circles
	Text Box	Creates a box to place text anywhere on the page without putting it inside another shape
	Insert WordArt	Lets you create a WordArt object in your document
	Fill Color	Applies fill colors or attributes to selected objects
	Line Color	Applies color or patterns to selected lines or outlines
	Font Color	Applies color to selected text
	Line Style	Applies a line thickness or style to a selected line or outline
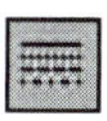	Dash Style	Applies a dashed line style to a selected line or outline
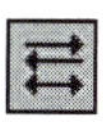	Arrow Style	Applies an arrow style or direction to a selected line or arrow
	Shadow	Applies a shadow to a selected object
	3-D	Applies a three-dimensional (3-D) setting to a selected object

Each Word drawing object has attributes, many of which can be changed. For example, you can change the thickness or position of a line, or the color of a box. The procedures for changing object attributes are found throughout this chapter.

SEE ALSO

➤ *To learn to insert graphics and clip art, see page 308*

FIGURE 17.1

All the objects shown here can be created in Word with the tools available on the Drawing toolbar.

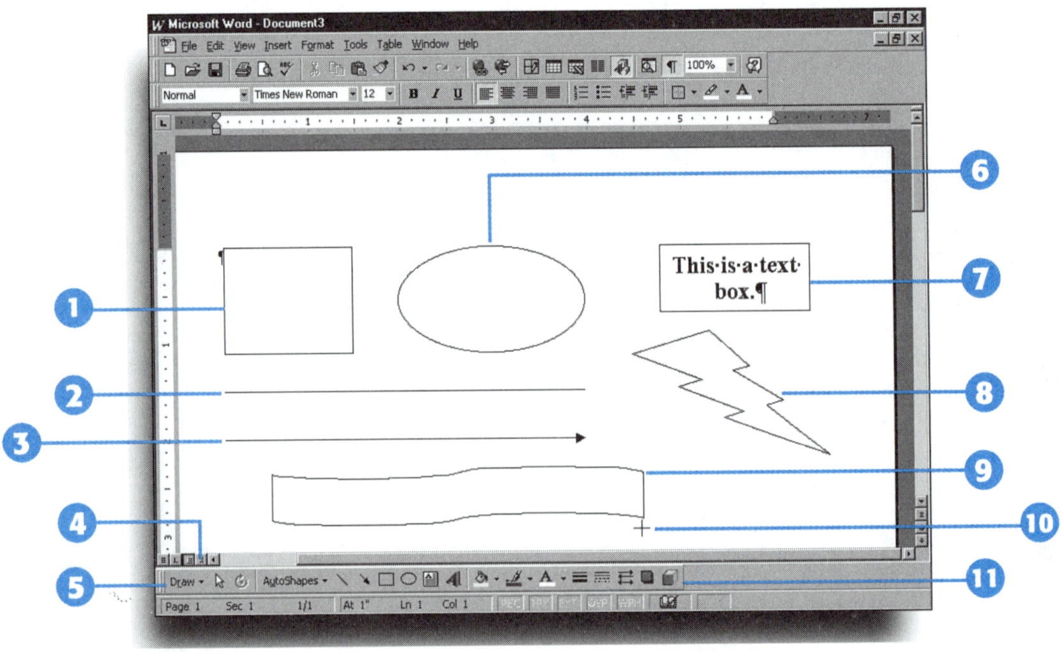

1. Rectangle
2. Line
3. Arrow
4. Page Layout View button
5. Draw button
6. Oval
7. Text box
8. AutoShape (lightning bolt)
9. AutoShape (banner) being drawn
10. Crosshair
11. Drawing toolbar

Draw Lines and Boxes

To draw a line or arrow, choose Line or Arrow on the Drawing toolbar, position the mouse pointer (crosshair) where you want the line or arrow to start. Then hold down the mouse button and drag to the end of the line or arrow, and then release the mouse button. Hold down the Shift key as you drag to make a straight horizontal or vertical line or arrow.

To draw a rectangle, choose Rectangle on the Drawing toolbar, position the mouse pointer (crosshair) where you want one corner of the rectangle to be, hold down the mouse button and drag diagonally to the opposite corner, and then release the mouse button.

To draw an oval, choose Oval on the Drawing toolbar, position the mouse pointer (crosshair) where you would imagine one corner of a rectangle surrounding the oval to be, hold down the mouse button and drag diagonally to the opposite corner, and then release the mouse button.

Draw the perfect circle or square

Hold down the Shift key as you draw an oval or rectangle, and when you release the mouse button you will have the perfect circle or square.

Add a text box

1. Choose **Text Box** on the Drawing toolbar.
2. Position the mouse pointer (crosshair) where you want one corner of the box to be, hold down the mouse button and drag diagonally to the opposite corner, and then release the mouse button.
3. After the box is drawn, enter your text by clicking inside of the text box and typing. Your text wraps within the margins of the box.
4. (Optional) Format the text using the formatting tools or menu commands.

Figure 17.1 displays some of these different objects drawn on a page.

SEE ALSO

➤ *To format text, see page 36*

Select Shapes from a Menu

Word contains too many objects you can draw to display them on the Drawing toolbar. Additional shapes not displayed on the Drawing toolbar such as block arrows, *flowchart items*, stars and banners, hearts, smiley faces, and *callouts* can be found when you choose **AutoShapes** on the Drawing toolbar.

Insert AutoShapes

1. Open the **AutoShape** drop-down menu on the Drawing toolbar. Select the category of shape you want on the Drawing toolbar and click the shape. The following list describes the techniques for drawing items found on the Lines category.
   - For lines, arrows, and double arrows (arrowheads at both ends), click at the beginning of where you want the line to begin and drag to the point you want the line to end. Release the mouse button.
   - For curves, click in your document to begin the curve and click at each point you want the curve to bend. End the curve by double-clicking.
   - For freeforms, click in your document to begin the freeform, and click at each corner to create a series of straight lines joined at sharp angles. Alternately, click to begin the freeform and drag to draw in any direction. Double-click to end the freeform.
   - For scribbles, click in your document and drag in any direction you want to draw. Double-click to end the scribble.
2. Position the mouse pointer (crosshair) where you want one corner of the box to be, hold down the mouse button and drag diagonally to the opposite corner, and then release the mouse button.
3. (Optional) To keep the autoshape proportional, hold down the Shift key as you drag your mouse.

Use the tear out menu

To make AutoShape selections quickly, float the **AutoShapes** menu by "tearing it out" of the Drawing toolbar. To do this, click the AutoShapes drop-down menu on the toolbar, grab the gray bar at the top of the **AutoShapes** drop-down menu and drag it to your work area.

Modify Lines and Objects

Before you modify, move, or size lines and objects, you must be able to select the lines or objects. A selected line or object displays *sizing handles* (small hollow boxes) at the line endpoints or on each side and corner of an object (see Figure 17.2).

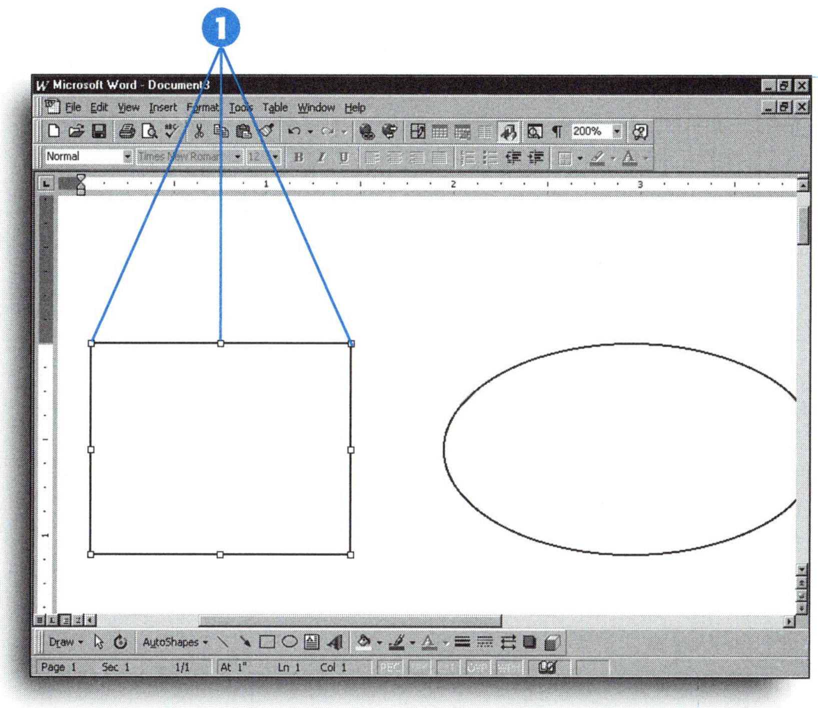

FIGURE 17.2
The small hollow boxes on this rectangle show that it is currently selected.

1 Sizing handles

To select a drawn object, do the following:

- To select a single line or object, click it.
- To select more than one line or object, click the first item you want to select, hold down the Shift key, and then click each additional item you want to select.
- To select a group of adjacent objects, choose Select Objects [icon] on the Drawing toolbar and drag a rectangle (selection box) around the items you want to select. When you release the mouse button, all items totally within the rectangle will have sizing handles and the selection box will disappear.

Don't overlook the power of grouping objects

Grouping objects can save you from formatting or moving objects individually. To group objects, select the objects and choose **Draw** and then **Group** from the Drawing toolbar. Once grouped, selected objects appear "as one" when you select them again. For more information on grouping items, see section "Order, Align, Group, and Layer Objects" later in this chapter.

- If you want the selected objects to always act together as if they were one object, choose **Draw** on the Drawing toolbar and click **Group** from the pop-up menu.
- If you accidentally select an item that you didn't want, hold down Shift and click the item to remove the sizing handles and deselect it.

SEE ALSO

➤ *To resize clip art and imported graphics, see page 308*

Change the Size of Lines and Objects

It's not easy to draw an item the exact size you want it, but changing the size after you draw it isn't difficult.

Change line and object size

1. Select the item.
2. Point to one of the sizing handles and drag it in the appropriate direction (see Figure 17.3).

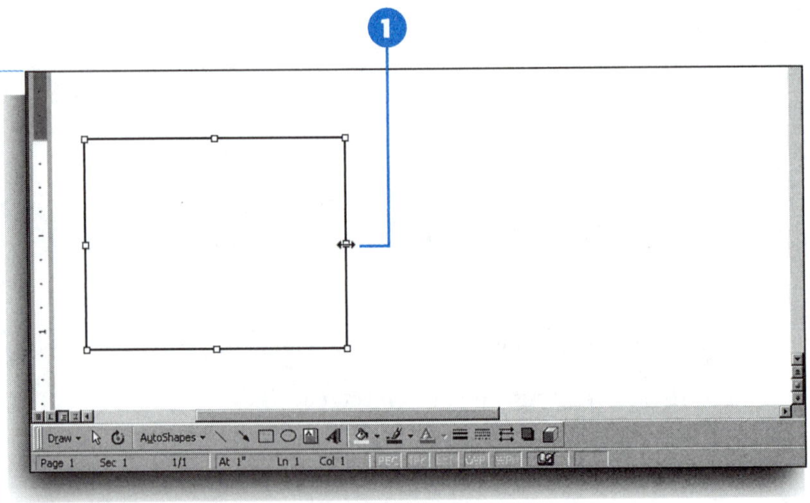

FIGURE 17.3

When you point to a sizing handle, the mouse pointer changes to a two-headed arrow showing in which direction you can drag the handle.

1 Two-headed arrow mouse pointer

- Drag the handles at either end of a line or arrow in any direction to shorten or lengthen the line or change the position of the endpoint. To keep the line straight as you drag, hold down the Shift key.

- Drag the center top and bottom handles of an object toward or away from the center of the object to make it shorter or taller.
- Drag the center left and right handles of an object toward or away from the center of the object to make it narrower or wider.
- Drag the corner handles diagonally away or toward the center of the object to make it bigger or smaller. Dragging the corner handles in other directions changes the overall dimensions of the object. To keep the dimensions in the same proportions as the original, hold down the Shift key as you drag.
- AutoShapes have an additional handle (a small yellow diamond, as seen in Figure 17.4). When you drag this handle, it adjusts the shape.

3. As you drag, you'll see a dotted line outline of the shape or line showing you how the item will look when you release the mouse button.
4. When the item is the size you want, release the mouse button.

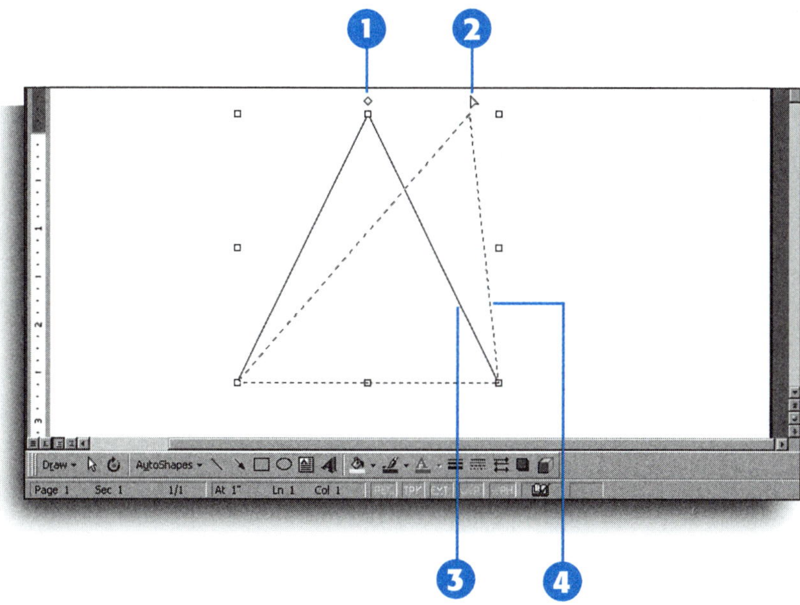

FIGURE 17.4
When you drag the yellow diamond on the triangle, it changes the angle of the triangle. The dotted outline shows how the shape will appear when you release the mouse button.

1. Yellow diamond
2. Mouse pointer
3. Original shape
4. New shape

If you add text to a shape, as explained in the section "Add Text to Shapes" later in this chapter, you may have to size the object again to accommodate the text.

To set the exact size of an item (height, width, length) in inches, double-click the item to open the Format AutoShape dialog box. Alternately, right-click the object and click **Format AutoShapes** on the pop-up menu. Then select the **Size** tab, enter the dimensions you want in the **Height** and **Width** boxes, and then choose **OK** (see Figure 17.5). To keep the height and width in the same proportions when you size the item, check **Lock aspect ratio** before you change the dimensions.

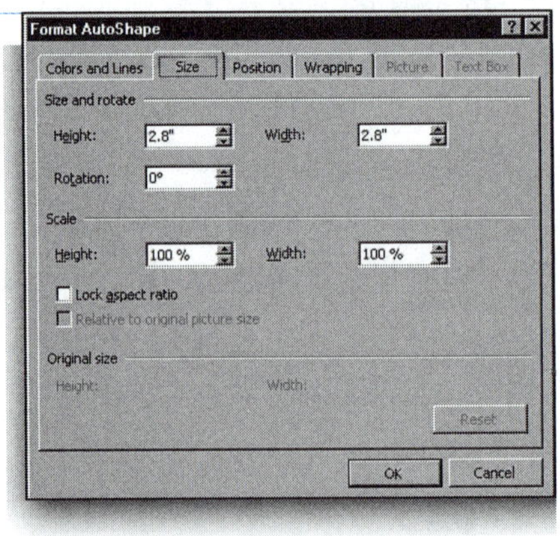

FIGURE 17.5
Enter the exact dimensions you want to apply to the object.

Move Lines and Objects

Move lines and objects within a page

1. Select the line, arrow, or object.
2. Point in the middle of the line, arrow, or object (or on the outline of the object if it has no fill). Be sure to avoid the sizing handles. The mouse pointer becomes a four-headed arrow (see Figure 17.6).
3. Hold down the mouse button and drag the dotted-line duplicate of the item to its new location.
4. Release the mouse button when you have the dotted-line duplicate in the position where you want the item to go. The item appears in that spot.

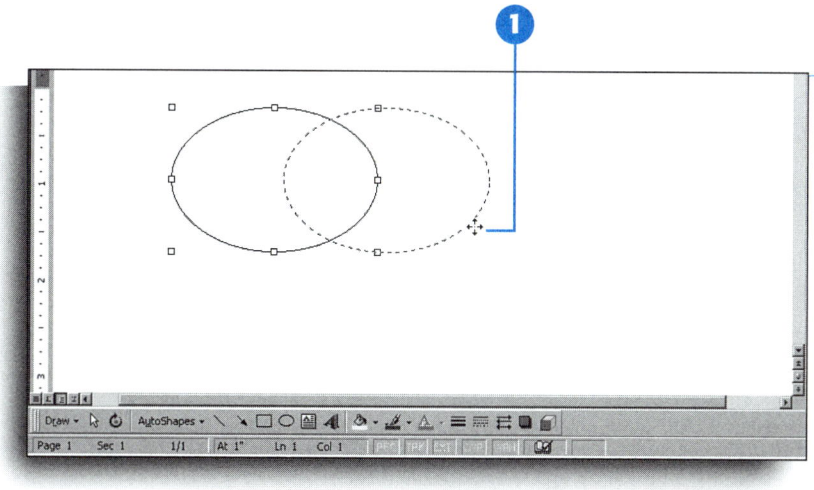

FIGURE 17.6

The mouse pointer becomes a four-headed arrow, which indicates you're ready to move the item.

1 Four-headed arrow mouse pointer

To set the exact position of an item on a page, double-click the item to open the Format AutoShape dialog box (see Figure 17.7), select the **Position** tab, enter the **Horizontal** distance **From** the **Margin**, **Page**, or **Column** and the **Vertical** distance **From** the **Margin**, **Page**, or **Paragraph**. Choose **OK**.

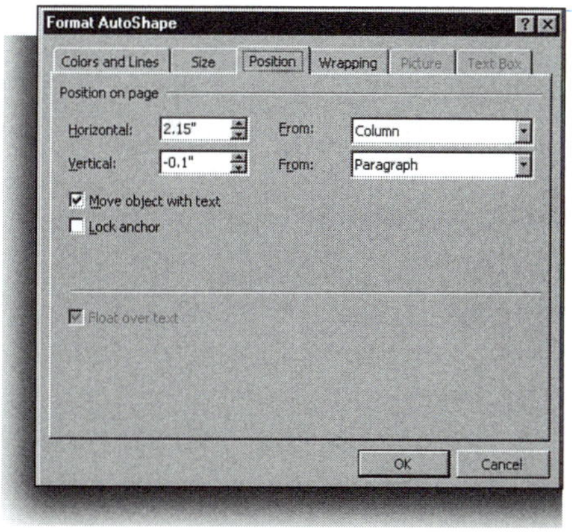

FIGURE 17.7

Enter the vertical and horizontal distances to precisely position the object on the page.

Dragging a line, arrow, or object to another page is not practical, so if you must move an item to another page, use the **Cut** and **Paste** commands. Right-mouse click the object and choose **Cut** on the pop-up menu. Right-click to position your insertion point on the page where you want to put the item, and then choose **Paste** from the pop-up menu.

Modify Line Attributes

Lines have characteristics such as thickness, style, dash, arrowheads, and color. Some of these attributes may also be applied to the outlines of rectangles, ovals, and shapes.

To apply a line attribute to a selected line, arrow, or shape outline, do one of the following:

- Choose Line Style on the Drawing toolbar to select line thickness or style (double, thin-thick, thick-thin, and so on). Click **More Lines** on the **Line Style** palette to open the Format AutoShape dialog box (see Figure 17.8) to the **Colors and Lines** tab, which offers a greater selection of line style options.

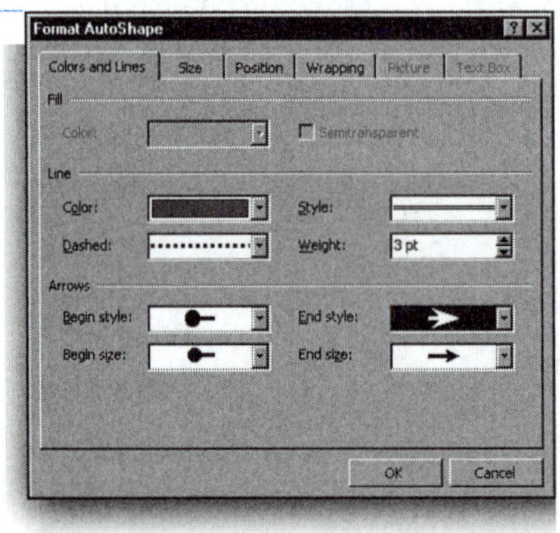

FIGURE 17.8
Double-click the object or right-click it and choose **Format AutoShape** to open the Format AutoShape dialog box.

- Choose Dash Style on the Drawing toolbar to select a dashed or dotted line style.
- Choose Arrow Style on the Drawing toolbar (not applicable to object outlines) to set the style and direction of arrowheads. Click **More Arrows** on the **Arrow Style** palette to open the Format AutoShape dialog box, which offers a greater selection of arrowhead options (refer to Figure 17.8).

- Choose Line Color on the Drawing toolbar to apply the current color to the line, arrow, or outline. Click the down arrow next to the button to see a greater selection of colors. Click No Line to remove a shape's outline (if you choose this option with a line or arrow, the item becomes invisible but it is still there). Click **Patterned Lines** to add dot, crosshatch, diagonal line, and other patterns to the line. Choose **More Line Colors** to see a greater selection of colors.
- Double-click the line, arrow, or outline to open the Format AutoShape dialog box (refer to Figure 17.8) that offers all the line attribute options and allows you to set the line thickness in 1/4-point increments. You can also open the Format AutoShape dialog box by right-clicking the line, arrow, or outline and then selecting **Format AutoShape** from the shortcut menu, or by opening the **Format** menu and selecting **AutoShape**.

Modify Fill Attributes

Ovals, rectangles, and shapes have fill attributes. The available types of fills include

- **No fill**. Leaves the item empty so that you can see any text or objects behind it.
- **Solid color**. Fills the item with one color.
- **Pattern**. Fills the item with a pattern (dots, crosshatch, diagonal lines, horizontal lines, vertical lines, and so on) in two colors—one for the pattern (Foreground) and one for the Background behind the pattern.
- **Gradient**. The fill varies from light to dark shades of the same color (One-Color), from one color to another color (Two-Color), or in a preset pattern of many colors (Preset). You then pick the Shading Style to specify in what direction the gradient should display.
- **Texture**. Fills the item with texture graphics such as green marble or granite.

Removing a line or outline

Removing the line around an object, which is really the outline, is different from removing a line. When you remove the outline, you leave only the fill color of the item (a nice way to get a shaded shape). You select the item and choose **No Line** from the **Line Color** options. Applying **No Line** as the color of a line, however, does not remove the item from your page—only the color from the line. If you accidentally click the part of the page where the line is, you'll see the handles that show it's still there. To remove a line, you must delete it. Select the line and press the Delete key.

- **Pictures**. Fills the item with repeated copies of a picture you have on file (such as a logo or the Windows wallpaper graphics).

To apply fill attributes to a selected object:

- Choose Fill Color on the Drawing toolbar to apply the current fill color.
- Click the down arrow next to the Fill Color to choose from a palette of colors. Click **No Fill** if you don't want the item to have a fill. Choose **More Fill Colors** if you want to see a larger selection of colors or you want the color to be semi-transparent so that you can see items or text behind it but still have a fill color in your item.
- To choose a fill other than solid color, click the arrow next to the Fill Color, and then select **Fill Effects**. This opens the Fill Effects dialog box (see Figure 17.9).

When you open the Fill Effects dialog box, you have the advantage of seeing how your choices will look before you click OK. In the lower-right corner of the dialog box is a **Sample** box that previews the fill you've chosen.

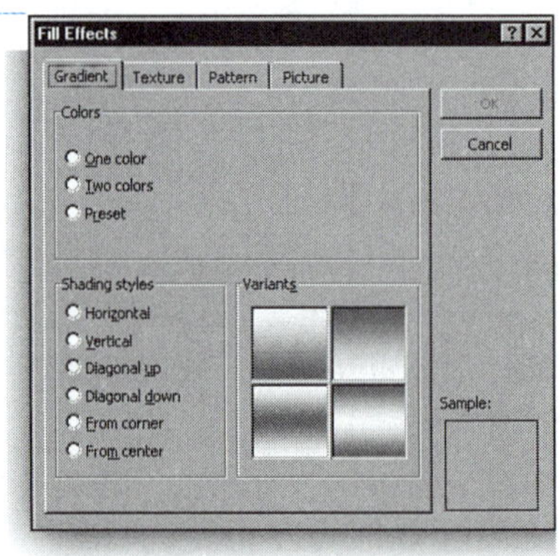

FIGURE 17.9
Select the tab for the type of fill you want to use and then select a fill or specify how you want the fill to appear.

Rotate, Flip, Add Shadows, and Order Objects

Many drawing objects can be rotated, flipped, or enhanced with shadows. Select the item you want to enhance and apply any of these effects:

- **Free Rotate.** To rotate a selected object, choose Free Rotate on the Drawing toolbar, position the mouse pointer over one of the four rotating handles at the corners of the object, and drag in a circular motion until the object is at the desired angle.
- **Rotate 90°.** To rotate a selected object 90° clockwise or counterclockwise, choose **Draw** on the Drawing toolbar, click **Rotate or Flip** on the pop-up menu, and then select **Rotate Right** or **Rotate Left**.
- **Flip.** To flip an object horizontally (so it looks like its mirror image) or vertically (so it's upside down), choose **Draw** on the Drawing toolbar, click **Rotate or Flip** on the pop-up menu, and then select **Flip Horizontal** or **Flip Vertical**.
- **Shadow.** Apply a shadow to a selected object by choosing Shadow on the Drawing toolbar and selecting the style of shadow you want from the pop-up palette. To adjust the position of the shadow, choose **Shadow Settings** from the pop-up palette to make the Shadow Settings toolbar appear (refer to Figure 17.9) and use the nudge buttons on the toolbar to move the shadow. Click the down arrow next to the Shadow Color button on that toolbar to pick a color for the shadow.

  Shadow On/Off adds or removes the shadow from the item.

  Nudge Shadow Up moves the shadow up (in relation to the item) by small increments.

  Nudge Shadow Down moves the shadow down by small increments.

  Nudge Shadow Left moves the shadow to the left by small increments.

  Nudge Shadow Right moves the shadow to the right by small increments.

  Shadow Color lets you change the color of the shadow by picking one from the selection provided (choose More Colors to see a larger selection), or allows you to make the shadow color semitransparent.

Order, Align, Group, and Layer Objects

As you add objects to your drawing, they appear on top of the ones you drew first and sometimes they cover up the objects you want to appear on top. For example, you may draw a circle and then draw a bigger circle around it, but you won't be able to see the small circle because it's covered up—send the bigger circle to the back. To address this problem, change the order of an object in the stack.

Change object order

1. Select the object you want to reposition.
2. Choose **Draw** on the Drawing toolbar.
3. From the pop-up that appears, click **Order**.
4. Then pick an ordering command from the submenu:
   - **Bring to Front** puts the item on top of the stack.
   - **Send to Back** puts the item at the bottom of the stack.
   - **Bring Forward** brings the item up one layer in the stack.
   - **Send Backward** sends the item down one layer in the stack.
   - **Bring in Front of Text** puts the item in front of the document text.
   - **Send Behind Text** puts the item behind the document text.

To line up two or more selected objects or space them evenly apart, choose **Draw** on the Drawing toolbar, click **Align or Distribute** on the pop-up menu, and then select one of the alignment or distribution options such as **Align Center**, **Align Top**, **Distribute Horizontally**, and so on.

Items can be grouped, or viewed by Word, as a single item. This is particularly useful if your drawing is made up of many components and you want to move those components. By grouping them first, you can then select and move one item, instead of many. You can have as many groups in your drawing as you like and you can ungroup items at any time. To create a group, hold down the Shift key while you select the items to be grouped and from the **Draw** menu, select **Group**. To break the grouping back into individual components, select the item and choose **Ungroup**. To create a group from the same items again without having to select each item, select one of the items and choose **Regroup** from the **Draw** menu.

Ungrouping clip art

Some of the pictures in the Clip Art Gallery can be ungrouped, which allows you to remove unwanted parts of the picture or select and change colors of specific items (like the hair or clothing colors). After you insert the picture, select it and then click **Draw**. If the **Ungroup** command is available, then you can do it. Be careful–you may delete too much or have difficulty regrouping the pieces back into one picture (you'll find out quickly if you move the pieces and find one left behind).

Add Text to Shapes

Instead of creating text boxes for diagrams, you can add text in any of the Word drawing shapes (except arrows, lines, and freeforms). To add text, right-click the object and then click **Add Text** on the pop-up menu. An insertion point appears in the shape; enter your text.

If the object already has text and you want to change it, right-click the object and choose **Edit Text** from the pop-up menu.

Edit Curves, Freeforms, and Scribbles

Creating the exact curve, freeform or scribble you want, at the time you draw it, is difficult. It's likely you will have to edit these shapes to refine them.

Edit curves, freeforms, or scribbles

1. Select the curve, freeform, or scribble you want to modify.
2. On the Drawing toolbar, choose **Draw**.
3. From the menu that pops up, click **Edit Points**. A small black dot appears at each point the line bends or changes angles (see Figure 17.10). These black dots are *points*.
4. To move the point, place your mouse pointer over it, hold down the left mouse button, and drag the point to another location.

   To delete a point, place your mouse pointer over it, hold down Ctrl, and click.

   To add a point, place your mouse over the curve, freeform, or scribble where you want the new point to appear, hold down Ctrl, and then click.
5. When you are finished editing points, click somewhere off the curve, freeform, or scribble.

FIGURE 17.10
As you drag a point to move it, you see a dotted outline of how the shape will change.

1. Points
2. New shape
3. New position of point
4. Original position of point

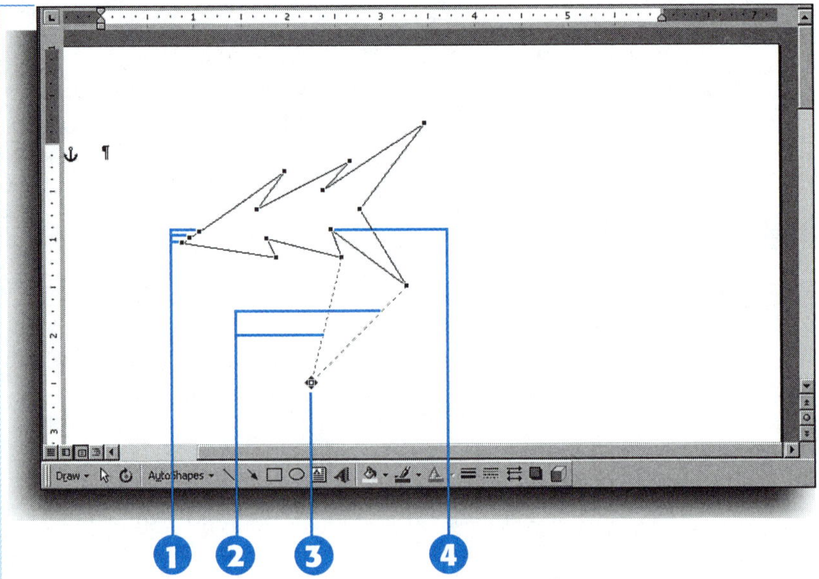

Use 3-D Shapes and Effects

To give your lines and shapes a three-dimensional look, add 3-D effects to them.

Create a 3-D object

1. Draw or select the item you want to make three-dimensional.
2. Choose the 3-D button on the Drawing toolbar.
3. Select the 3-D style you want from the pop-up palette (see Figure 17.11).

FIGURE 17.11
Select the 3-D look you want to apply to the selected object.

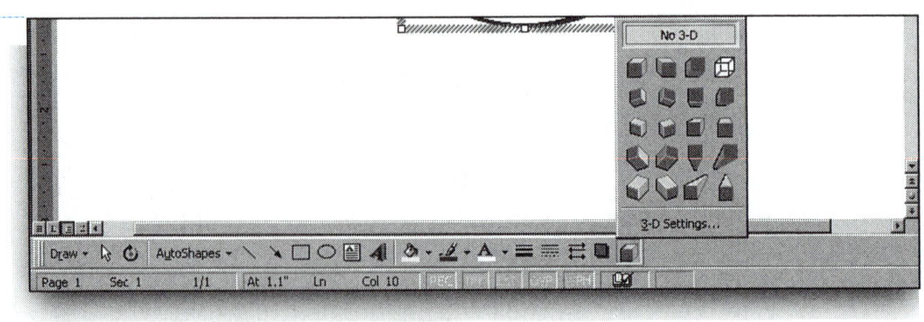

When you want to adjust the 3-D effect, choose 3-D  on the Drawing toolbar and select **3-D Settings** to display the 3-D Settings toolbar (see Figure 17.11). Use the buttons on this toolbar to tilt the object, change the depth of the 3-D effect, change the direction of the 3-D effect, change the location of the light source, select a material finish, and choose a color for the 3-D portion of the object. Table 17.2 describes the 3-D Settings toolbar buttons.

TABLE 17.2 **3-D Settings toolbar buttons**

Icon:	Button:	Function:
	3-D On/Off	Turns the 3-D effect on or off.
	Tilt Down	Makes the top of the object look like it's tilting toward the viewer.
	Tilt Up	Makes the top of the object look like it's tilting away from the viewer.
	Tilt Left	Makes the left side of the object look like it's going away from the viewer as the right side comes closer.
	Tilt Right	Makes the right side of the object look like it's going away from the viewer as the left side comes closer.
	Depth	Makes the object look thicker. You select the depth (in number of points) from a list or enter a custom depth.
	Direction	Lets you select the direction you want the 3-D effect to extend from the samples. Perspective makes the 3-D effect extend toward a single point, while Parallel extends all sides of the 3-D effect parallel to one another.
	Lighting	Sets which direction the light is coming from and where the shadows fall. Select **Bright**, **Normal**, or **Dim** for the brightness of the light.

continues...

Apply 3-D to several objects at one time

To add the same 3-D effects to several objects at one time, select the objects by holding down the **Shift** key while you click them, then click the 3-D effect.

TABLE 17.2 **Continued**

Icon:	Button:	Function:
	3-D Color	Lets you apply a color to the 3-D effect (use **Fill Color** to color the object itself). Select from the colors displayed or click **More 3-D** colors to see a greater selection.
	Surface	Lets you choose one of four surface options: **Wireframe** to see only the outlines of the object and the 3-D effect without the surfaces being filled in, **Matte** to make the surfaces look unreflective or dull, **Plastic** to make the surfaces look like plastic, or **Metal** to make the surfaces look like polished metal.

Insert a WordArt Object

WordArt is a program packaged with Microsoft Office. WordArt allows you to add interest to your text with preset shapes. With WordArt objects, your text can be curved, twisted, and rotated. If WordArt is not available on your computer, it may not have been installed during the setup of Office 97. By doing a custom setup, you may add this program without reinstalling the entire suite.

Access WordArt while in Word by choosing **Insert WordArt** on the Drawing toolbar or by opening the **Insert** menu and selecting **Picture**, and then **WordArt**. The WordArt window appears at your insertion point.

Insert a WordArt object

1. Select the WordArt effect you want from the WordArt Gallery dialog box (see Figure 17.12). Choose **OK**.
2. When the Edit WordArt Text dialog box appears (see Figure 17.13), replace the "Your Text Here" in the **Text** box with your own text.

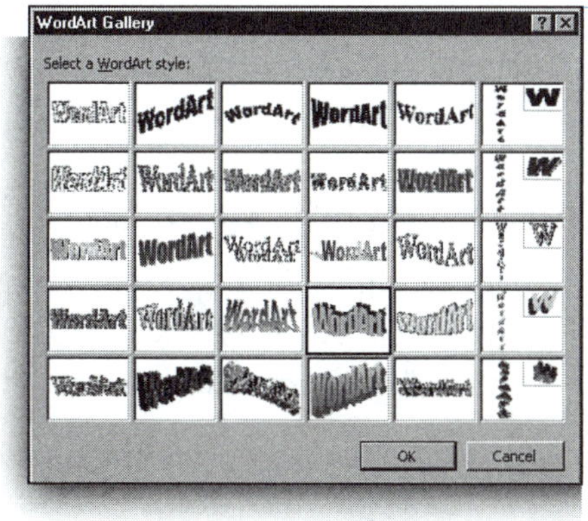

FIGURE 17.12

Select the WordArt effect you want to use.

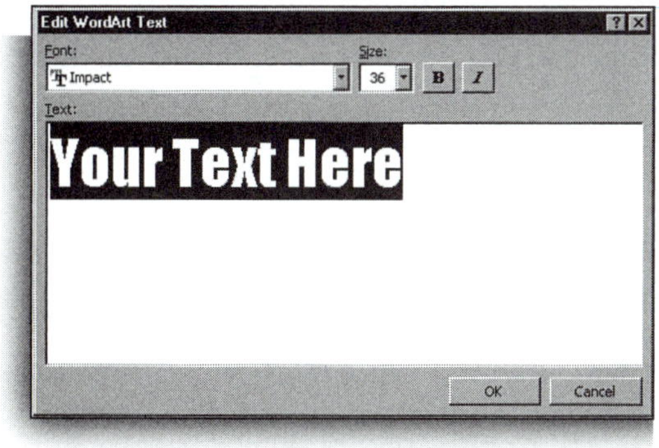

FIGURE 17.13

Enter your text in the Edit WordArt Text dialog box.

3. Choose a **Font** from the drop-down list and choose a **Size**. If you want bold or italic type, click the appropriate buttons.
4. The WordArt object appears in your document, with sizing handles around it to show it's still selected. Word also displays the WordArt toolbar (see Figure 17.14).

FIGURE 17.14

The WordArt toolbar has the tools you need to modify the WordArt object.

Deselect the WordArt by clicking somewhere else in your document. The WordArt object can then be moved and sized like other graphics objects.

Format and Edit WordArt Objects

To edit the text of the WordArt object, double-click in the middle of the WordArt and change the entry. To modify the WordArt object, click it once to display the WordArt toolbar.

- Use the sizing handles to change the height and width of the graphic.
- Use the yellow diamond handles to adjust the shape of the WordArt.
- Use the buttons on the WordArt toolbar to modify the WordArt. See Table 17.3 for a list of the buttons and what they do.

TABLE 17.3 WordArt toolbar buttons

Button:	Name:	Description:
	Insert WordArt	Inserts a new WordArt object in your document at the cursor position
	Edit Text	Opens the Edit WordArt Text dialog box so that you can change the text of your WordArt
	WordArt Gallery	Opens the WordArt Gallery of predefined effects
	Format WordArt	Opens the Format WordArt dialog box where you select fill colors, position, size, and text wrapping options
	WordArt Shape	Displays a palette of preset shapes to apply to the WordArt object
	Free Rotate	Enables the Free Rotate tool (drag a corner of the object to set it at a new angle)
	WordArt Same Letter Heights	Changes the height of the lowercase letters to match that of the uppercase letters

Button:	Name:	Description:
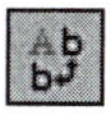	WordArt Vertical Text	Gives the text a vertical orientation
	WordArt Alignment	Offers a set of alignment options to align the WordArt text within the boundaries of the object
	WordArt Character Spacing	Changes the spacing between the letters of the WordArt text (selections range from Very Tight to Very Loose)

CHAPTER 18

Add Interest with Charts

Create, embed, import, and link charts

Modify and edit charts

Create a Chart

Charts and graphs, such as pie charts or column graphs, are valuable tools in illustrating data. Often, reports such as a business annual report contain charts illustrating data such as sales and profits. Word doesn't create charts, but uses a program called Microsoft Graph 97, which is packaged with Word. There are several ways to include charts in a Word document:

- Create a chart while working in Word, using Microsoft Graph 97.
- Paste a chart from another application into a Word document.
- Import data or a chart from other programs (such as Excel or Lotus 1-2-3) into a Microsoft Graph 97 chart.
- Paste a chart or insert a chart file from another application into your Word document but link it back to the original file and application so that the chart in your document updates when changes are made to the original.
- Embed a chart object from another application (such as a Microsoft Excel chart) into your document.

SEE ALSO

➤ *To learn more about importing files, see page 333*
➤ *To understand pasting and linking files, see page 338*
➤ *To embed objects, see page 342*

Create a Chart with Microsoft Graph 97

To insert a chart using Microsoft Graph 97 into your Word document, follow these steps:

Create a chart with Microsoft Graph 97

1. Place your insertion point where you want the chart to appear.
2. Open the **Insert** menu and select **Object**.
3. When the Object dialog box appears, click the **Create New** tab (see Figure 18.1).

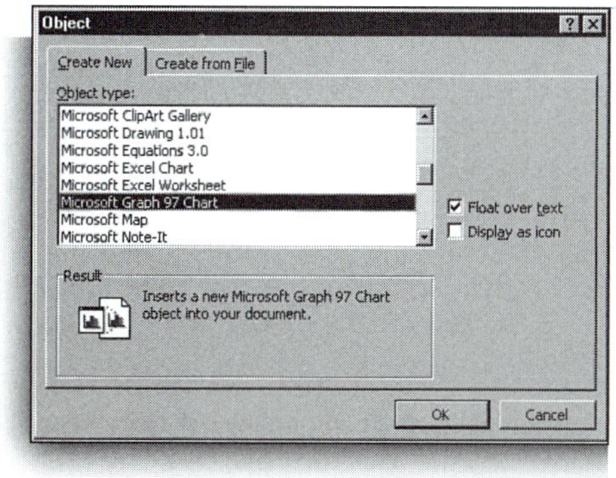

FIGURE 18.1

Select **Microsoft Graph 97 Chart** from the Object dialog box and click **OK**.

4. From the **Object type** box, select **Microsoft Graph 97 Chart**.
5. To position the chart using the commands on the Drawing toolbar, enable the **Float over text** option by clicking the box to place a check mark there. If you want the chart to flow with the text in the current paragraph, deselect that option.
6. Choose **OK**.
7. A column chart and a Datasheet window appear (see Figure 18.2). The Datasheet contains sample data that you replace to create your own graph. The chart is transformed automatically as you add your data and select formatting options, until it becomes the chart you want. To replace the sample data, click in the cell in the Datasheet where you want to put new data and then type your own data there. Press Enter to accept the data and move down one row; press Tab to move one cell to the right and Shift+Tab to move one cell to the left (the arrow keys also help you navigate in the Datasheet). Choose View Datasheet on the Standard toolbar to close the Datasheet.

   Each number or value in the Datasheet is plotted as a data point on the chart, represented as points on a line: the top of columns, the end of bars, dots in a scatter chart, points in an area, or pie slice percentages. The data that appears in the rows of the Datasheet is called series or *series data*. Each row represents a line, a set of bars or columns of the same color,

Editing embedded objects

When you edit embedded objects, such as a Microsoft Graph 97 chart, the object appears in a box. Outside the box, you can still see your document. As long as you work in the box, the toolbars and menu commands change to those used in the application in which the object is created. When you click outside the box, the document becomes active and the tools and menus return to the Word toolbars and menu commands.

or area on a chart. The words at the beginning of each row are the Legend labels. The *Legend* is the area on a chart that has a small symbol or color next to a label so that you can tell what series the lines or bars on the chart represent. The titles at the top of each column (the first row of the Datasheet) are the categories. They appear on the chart as the labels for the *category axis*, which is also called the X-axis.

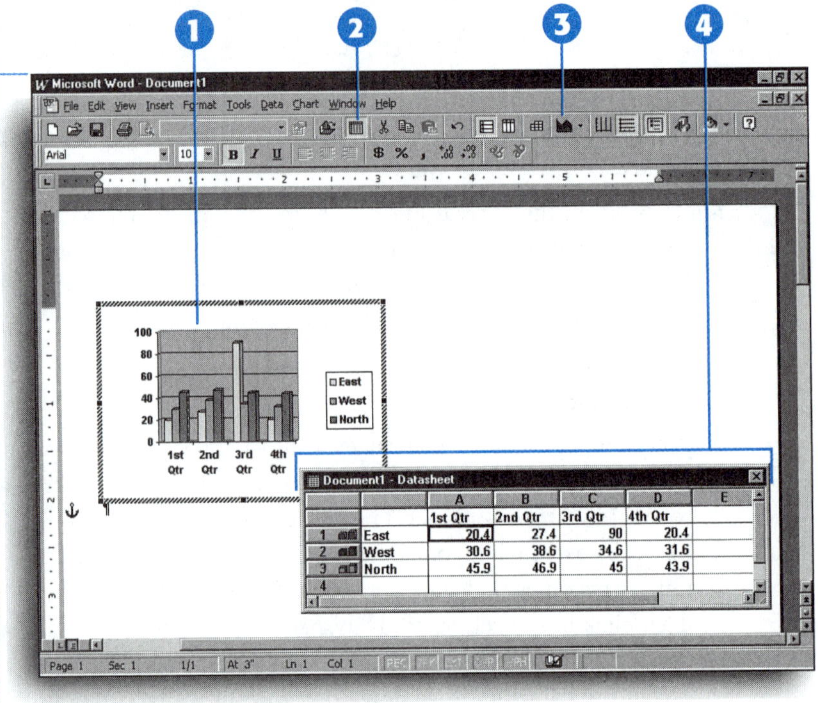

FIGURE 18.2

The Datasheet contains the data that generates the graph. Note that the toolbars and menus change to include buttons and commands you'll need to work with charts.

1. Chart
2. View Datasheet button
3. Chart Type button
4. Datasheet

8. Click the down arrow next to the Chart Type button on the Standard toolbar to select a chart from the types shown. Then click the picture of the type of chart you want to create.

9. Click outside the border around the graph to return to the Word document (double-click the chart to return to the Microsoft Graph 97 program).

The sample data that appears in the Datasheet when you start a new chart is always the same. It serves as an aid that helps you enter the data in the right places. Be sure to delete any of the sample data that remains after you've entered your own information.

SEE ALSO

➤ *To learn how to work "in-place" on embedded objects, see page 342*

Create a Chart from a Table

Data that exists in a table (such as sales and profit data) can act as the data for your chart. If you have the data you need for a chart in a Word table, there's no need to enter the data again in the Datasheet. Instead, start the chart by following these steps:

Create a chart from a table

1. Create the table in Word. Put text labels in the cells in the top row and in the left column. Put numbers in the other cells.
2. Select all the cells in the table (click in the table to put your insertion point there and then open the **Table** menu and choose **Select Table**), unless your table includes a row or column of totals. In that case, select all the cells except those total rows or columns.
3. Open the **Insert** menu and select **Object**, and then select the **Create New** tab in the Object dialog box.
4. Select **Microsoft Graph 97 Chart** from the **Object type** box.
5. Choose **OK**.
6. The data from your table appears in the Datasheet.
7. Choose Chart Type on the Standard toolbar and then select a chart type.
8. Click outside the graph area to return to your Word document.

SEE ALSO

➤ *To learn how to create tables, see 280*

This is a quick method of entering data without having to type it in the Datasheet. It eliminates the step of replacing or deleting the sample text and your readers will see the original data in the document in the form of a table.

Modify a Chart

After a Microsoft Graph 97 chart is embedded in your document, double-click the middle of the chart to activate Microsoft Graph 97 and modify the chart.

To help you in modifying the chart, tips pop up when you point to the various components of the chart. This helps you in identifying the item you want to change (see Figure 18.3).

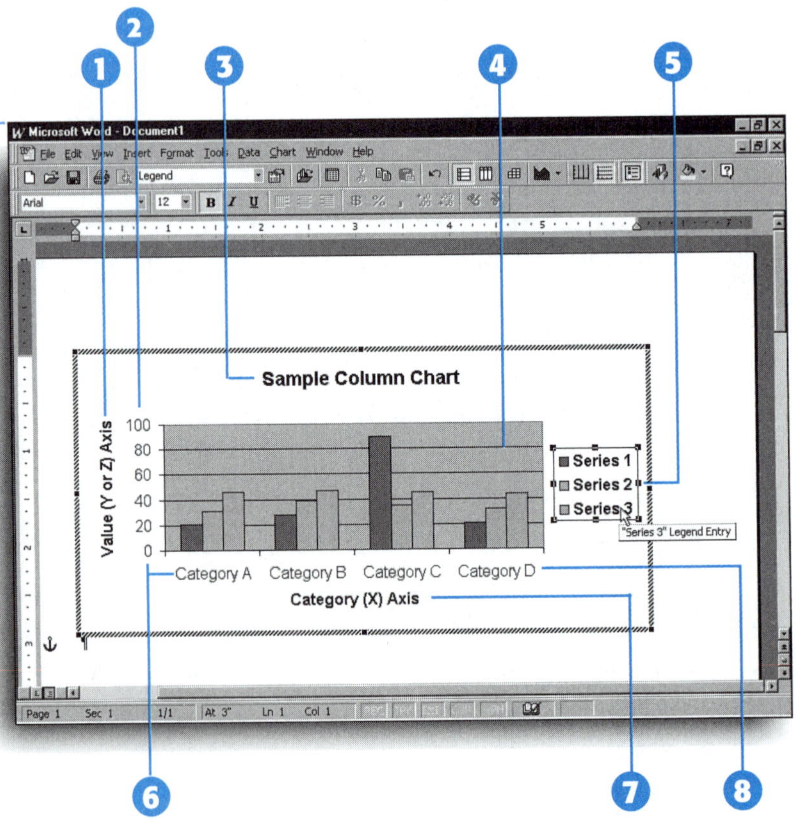

FIGURE 18.3

Point to a component of the chart to see a identifying label pop up.

1. Value Axis title
2. Value Axis
3. Chart title
4. Gridline
5. Legend
6. Axis labels
7. Category Axis title
8. Category Axis

You can modify the chart when you're in Microsoft Graph 97 in a number of ways, from changing the data to altering its appearance. The following list gives you some suggestions on how you can modify your chart:

- To edit the data, open the Datasheet by choosing View Datasheet on the Standard toolbar. Replace data by clicking in the cell and typing the new value or label. Press Enter or move the insertion point to the next cell to accept the change.
- To change the chart type, open the **Chart** menu and select **Chart Type** to open the Chart Type dialog box (see Figure 18.4). From the **Chart type** list, select the type of chart you want. Then make a selection from the **Chart sub-type** options and choose **OK**.

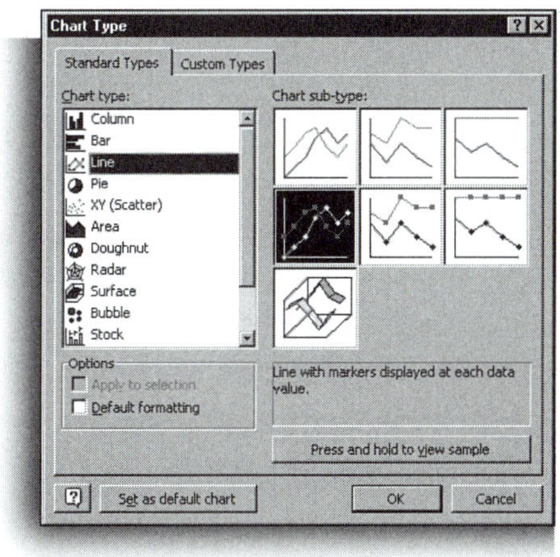

FIGURE 18.4
When you select a chart type, a set of chart sub-types appears.

Be careful how you click

When you are trying to double-click an item, be careful not to pause too long between clicks, and definitely don't click to select the item and then double-click it to change its attributes. A single click on an item selects all the items in a series (click a red bar and all the red bars are selected). If you pause and then click that item again, only that item is selected. Therefore, if your double-click pauses, only one of the series items gets selected and the options you choose apply only to that one item. Watch the selection handles around the items that indicate if they're selected; if the series is already selected click somewhere off the items first and then double-click one of the items in the series to open the dialog box.

- To change the color of bars, lines, or areas, double-click on the item to open the Format Data Series dialog box, as shown in Figure 18.5. For pie chart slices, click once on the pie and then double-click the slice you want to change to open the Format Data Point dialog box. Set the line style and color or the area color or pattern (click **Fill Effects**) by clicking the appropriate options. If you are working on a bar or column chart, click the **Shape** tab and select a shape for the bars or columns (cylinders, cones, pyramids, and so forth). Then choose **OK** to apply them to the chart.

FIGURE 18.5

Select the line color, style, or thickness for line charts or the area color for other charts.

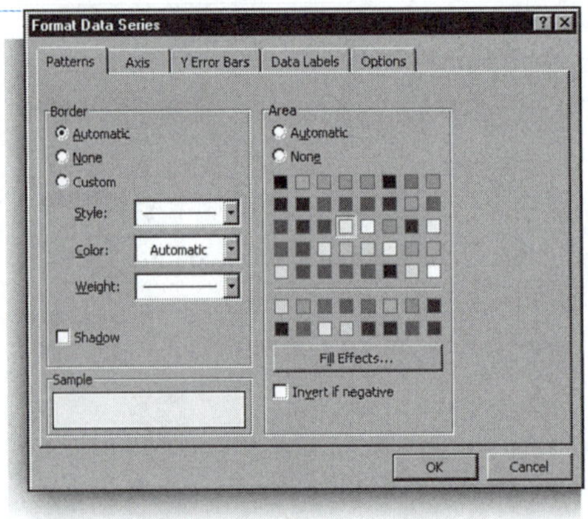

- To change the number format (how the numbers appear) of the chart values, double-click the numbers on the value axis (Y-axis) to open the Format Axis dialog box and then select the **Number** tab (see Figure 18.6). Choose a number format (such as currency or percentage) from the **Category** box. The options vary with each category, so you may have to specify number of decimal places, symbols, appearance of negative numbers, use of a thousand separator, date and time formats, and so on. Choose **OK**.

FIGURE 18.6

Select the format category and then enter the specific options. The sample shows the result.

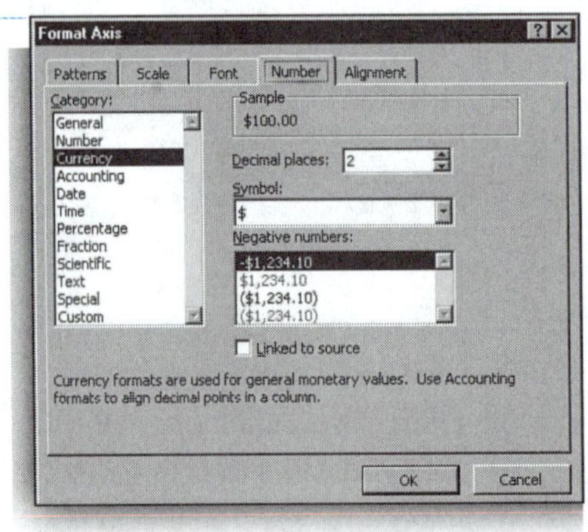

- To set the interval between the numbers or specify the minimum or maximum values, double-click the numbers on the value axis (Y-axis) to open the Format Axis dialog box and then select the **Scale** tab (see Figure 18.7). Change the **Major unit** number to specify the interval between numbers, which also sets the spacing between the *gridlines* (lines that act as a reference to help you evaluate data in relation to the axes). Enter values in the **Minimum** and **Maximum** boxes to change those values. Choose **OK**.

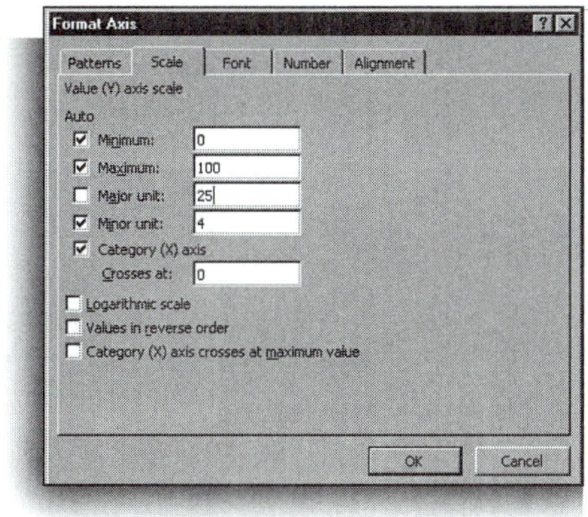

FIGURE 18.7
Specify the interval between numbers on the value axis by changing the **Major unit** value.

- To change the appearance or position of the legend, double-click the legend to open the Format Legend dialog box. On the **Patterns** tab, set the border style around the legend and the background color. On the **Font** tab, set the font of the legend text. On the **Placement** tab (see Figure 18.8), select the position for the legend in relation to the graph. Choose **OK**.

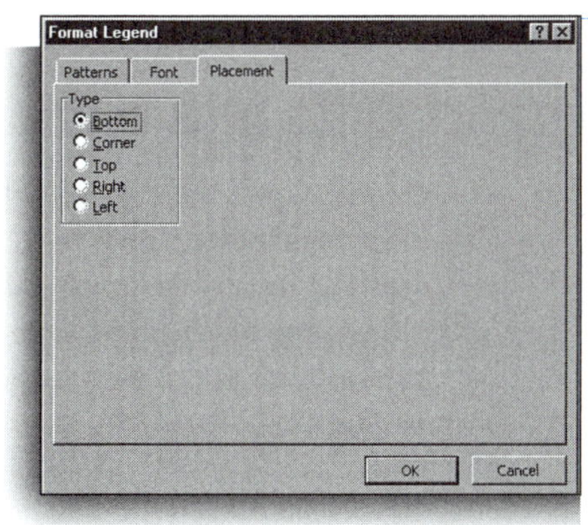

FIGURE 18.8
Select the position where the legend appears in relation to the graph.

- To add titles to the value and category axes, click open the **Chart** menu and select **Chart Options** to open the Chart Options dialog box (see Figure 18.9). Select the **Titles** tab and enter the title text in the **Category (X) axis** or **Value (Z) axis** box. Click **OK**.

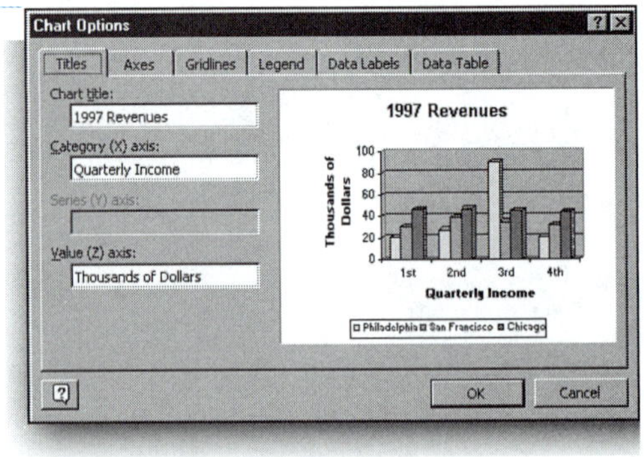

FIGURE 18.9
Enter the titles you want to appear next to the axes or for the chart as a whole.

When you complete your modifications, click outside the graph border to return to your Word document. Move the graph by pointing in the middle of it and dragging it to a new position on the page. Change the size of the chart by selecting it and then dragging one of the handles (small hollow boxes surrounding the chart) toward or away from the center of the graph. After you click outside the graph, it acts like any graphic inserted into a Word document.

SEE ALSO

➤ *To learn more about sizing and moving graphics, see page 363*

Import Data into a Chart

Although you have the capability to enter data directly in the Datasheet to generate your chart, you don't want to enter figures that you already have stored in a file in another application. Microsoft Graph can import that data for you and then generate the chart, as long as the originating file is a delimited text file (separated by tab characters, commas, or spaces) or a spreadsheet file.

Microsoft Graph can import files that have the following file extensions: TXT or CSV (delimited text files), WKS or WK1 (Lotus 1-2-3 files), XLS (Microsoft Excel worksheet or workbook), XLW (Microsoft Excel 4.0 workbook), XLC (Microsoft Excel 4.0 or earlier chart), or SLK (SYLK, or symbolic link, files). If you have data in another type of file, check your application and see if it can save the file in one of the listed formats.

The imported data cannot have more than 4,000 rows or 4,000 columns. Microsoft Graph won't display more than 255 data series.

Import a file

1. Create a new graph.
2. When the Datasheet appears, click in the cell where you want the upper-left corner cell of your imported data to appear.
3. Open the **Edit** menu and select **Import File**. The Import File dialog box appears (see Figure 18.10).

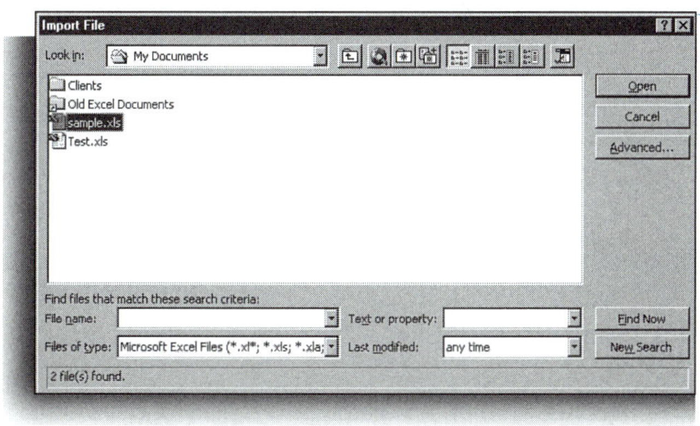

FIGURE 18.10
Select the file you want to import.

4. From the **Look in** drop-down list, select the drive and folder where the file you're importing is stored.
5. From the **Files of type** drop-down list, select the file format of that file.
6. Select the file you want and choose **Open** or double-click the filename (if the file isn't listed, enter the name in the **File name** box).

7. If the file you selected is a text file, the Text Import Wizard opens. Following the steps in the wizard, you specify how the imported data is currently organized and how you want it arranged in the Datasheet.

   If the file you're importing is a spreadsheet, a dialog box appears (see Figure 18.11). Specify which sheet you want to use in the dialog box (if it's a Microsoft Excel worksheet). Specify whether you want to import the entire worksheet or a range (enter the range reference or the range name), and if you want to **Overwrite existing cells** to replace all the current data in the Datasheet. Choose **OK**.

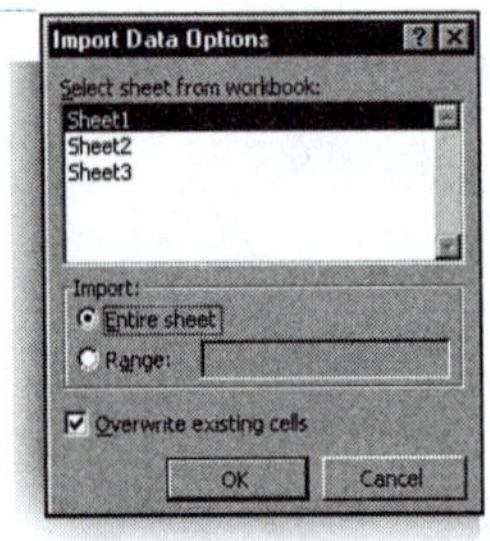

FIGURE 18.11

When you import spreadsheet data, it's useful to name the range in the worksheet first.

Bring only the data you need

When you're selecting the data to import, don't include blank rows, columns, or any columns or rows that have totals in them. If you do accidentally import a file with rows or columns you don't want included in the chart data, double-click the column or row header. The data turns gray. If necessary, delete rows or columns.

Instead of using the **Import** command, it may be easier for you to copy the data and then paste it into the Datasheet. This gives you more control over which cells you copy.

Copy data into a datasheet

1. Open the program, document, or worksheet where the data is stored.
2. Select the data.
3. Open the **Edit** menu and select **Copy**.
4. Switch to your Word document and double-click the Microsoft Graph chart.
5. Open the Datasheet, if it's not already on the screen (choose View Datasheet on the Standard toolbar).
6. Click in the cell where you want the upper-left corner of the copied data to appear.
7. Open the **Edit** menu and select **Paste**.

To have the chart update automatically when the original data is modified, open the **Edit** menu and select **Paste Link** when you paste it into the Datasheet.

SEE ALSO

➤ *For more information on linking, see page 335*

Paste a Chart

Charts created in other applications can be pasted into Word. By pasting charts, you can use the features many chart and graphing programs contain that are not a part of Microsoft Graph 97.

Paste a chart into a Word document

1. Open the program, document, or worksheet where the chart is stored.
2. Select the chart.
3. Open the **Edit** menu and select **Copy**.
4. Switch to your Word document and position your insertion point where you want the chart to appear.
5. Open the **Edit** menu and select **Paste**. The chart is inserted and can be moved or sized using the same method as you use for graphics.

If you want the chart to update automatically when the original data is modified, open the **Edit** menu and select **Paste Special**. When the Paste Special dialog box appears, click **Paste Link** and then choose **OK**.

Embed a Chart

Another alternative for placing an existing chart in your document is to embed it.

Embed a chart

1. Place your insertion point where you want the chart to appear in your document.
2. Open the **Insert** menu and select **Object**.

3. When the Object dialog box appears, select the **Create from File** tab.
4. Enter the name of the file in the **File name** box or choose **Browse** to select the file.
5. If you want the changes in the source file (the file where the original chart is stored) to be automatically reflected in the chart in your document, click **Link to file** to place a check mark there.

   If you don't want to have the chart automatically updated each time the original file changes but you do want to edit the chart using the application that created the original file, remove the check mark from **Link to file**. When you do this, Word embeds the file in the document.
6. Choose **OK**.

After the chart appears in your document, you can size and move it as you would any graphic. If you embedded the file, double-click in the middle of the chart to see the toolbars and menu commands of the source application so that you can modify the chart.

PART

VI

Create Special Purpose and Custom Documents

CHAPTER

19

Create Mail Merges, Catalogs, and Lists

Create mailing lists and generate personalized form letters

Create databases and product catalogs or lists from those databases

---

Import or merge data from other database programs

Print envelopes or mailing labels from a database

About Mail Merges and Databases

A mail merge is an operation that takes the information from a *database* (such as a mailing list) and merges it with a document to create a set of form letters, envelopes, or labels.

A database is a collection of information that can be sorted, extracted, and queried. An example of a database is an address book which stores a persons first name, last name, street address, city, state, and zip code. Each unique piece of information, such as the last name is a *field* and the complete set of information for each person is a *record*. These terms are standard database terms and their use and description apply to Word as well as other programs in which you can create databases. Many databases are created and stored in table format. In a table, columns represent the database fields and rows represent the database records.

Word provides several methods of working with database information. You can:

- Create and maintain a database in Word and use it to generate letters, documents, envelopes, faxes, or labels.
- Retrieve data from existing databases created in other programs.
- Update or add new data to databases created in other programs.

In Word, documents used for mail merge purposes are called *main documents* and databases are referred to as the *data source*.

As is the case with spreadsheets, Word has somewhat limited capabilities when it comes to databases, although those capabilities will probably serve you well for most of your mail merge needs. However, when databases are extremely large (thousands of records), database information changes frequently (needs daily updating) or needs to be accessible to many people for the purposes of entering, sorting or retrieving data, use a bona fide database program, such as Microsoft Access for your data source.

Word can provide direct access to other database programs that support *Open Database Connectivity* (*ODBC*). An industry standard, ODBC enables database and other programs to share information. For example, Word can create envelopes based on data stored in Microsoft Access or Lotus Approach. In this chapter, we discuss the most commonly used, basic communications with external databases; through importing and merging.

Merge Documents Using Variable Data

A Word mail merge involves three pieces:

- *Data source*. The data source (database) contains the individualized information that "personalizes" each version of the final merged document. Frequently this is a list of names and addresses, but it doesn't have to be limited to mailing information. It can also contain information such as an employee date of hire.
- *Main document*. This document holds the static text that remains the same in each merge. It also contains a set of field codes that tell Word where to put the information from the data source.
- *Merged document*. The result of the merge operation, this document can be a set of labels, envelopes, or form letters. Each, label, envelope, or page is a combination of the data from one record in the data source and the common text in the main document.

Word organizes the process of merging the main document with the data source and helps you through the merge in a step-by-step manner using the Mail Merge Helper (see Figure 19.1).

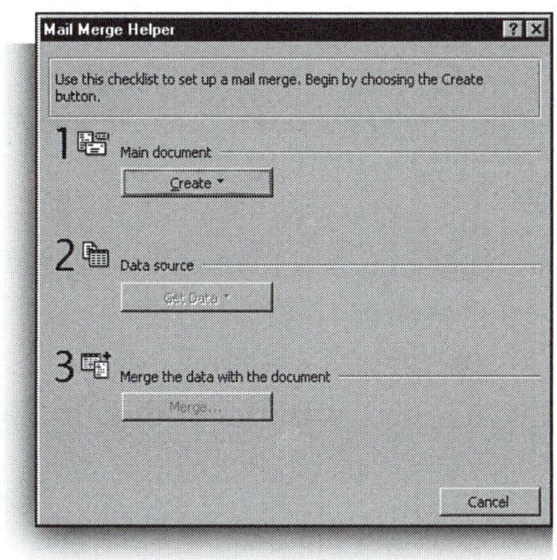

FIGURE 19.1

Follow the three steps of the Mail Merge Helper to perform your mail merge.

Begin a mail merge

1. Click the **Tools** menu and select **Mail Merge** to open the Mail Merge Helper dialog box.
2. Under step 1, **Main document**, choose **Create**.
3. On the menu that appears, click the type of main document you want to create—**Form Letters**, **Mailing Labels**, **Envelopes**, or **Catalog**.
4. After you make the selection a dialog box appears. Choose **Active Window** to turn the document you currently have open into your main document for the mail merge. Choose **New Main Document** to open a new document to create the main document.
5. Under step 2, **Data source**, choose **Get Data**.
6. A new menu appears. You need to identify your data source through this menu. Choose from the following:
   - Select **Create Data Source** to start a completely new data source document. If you make this selection, skip to page 403 "Create a Database" for instructions on creating a new database.
   - Select **Open Data Source** to use an existing data source document (you then specify the filename and location).
   - Select **Use Address Book** to use an electronic mail address book or contact list from Microsoft Outlook or Schedule+. (You specify which program your address book is in and the Exchange profile.)
7. Under **Main document**, choose **Edit**. Select the main document you want to edit (such as "Form Letter: Document1"). Insert the text, graphics, and merge fields you need for the main document (see the sections later in this chapter on creating form letters, labels, and envelopes). Save and name the file.
8. Return to the Mail Merge Helper. Under step 3, **Merge the data with the document,** choose **Merge**. The Merge

dialog box appears (see Figure 19.2). From the **Merge to** drop-down list, specify how you want to output the merge:

- **New Document**. Creates a document that has each of the merged form letters, labels, or envelopes in it. If you don't have a large number of records, this selection gives you the opportunity to view the result of your merge or edit each merge before you print it.
- **Printer**. Sends the merged document directly to the printer.
- **Electronic Mail**. Sends each document to the recipient via electronic mail. Your system must include a MAPI-compatible (Messaging Application Programming Interface) electronic mail program such as Microsoft Schedule+ or Microsoft Exchange. There must be a field in the data source containing the email address. Choose **Setup** to specify that field, enter a subject line for the email memo, and select whether to send the merged document as an attachment. Choose **OK** to return to the Merge dialog box.
- **Electronic Fax**. Sends each document to the recipient via electronic fax (your system must include a MAPI-compatible electronic fax program). There must be a field in the data source containing the fax address. Choose **Setup** to specify that field and enter a subject line for the fax memo. Choose **OK** to return to the Merge dialog box.

9. Under **Records to be merged**, click **All** or **From**. If you select **From**, enter the record numbers in the **From** and **To** boxes that specify the range of records you want to merge. If you only want to merge specific records or records of a certain type, choose **Query Options** and set conditions on the merge.
10. Under **When merging records**, click **Don't print blank lines when data fields are empty**. This prevents blank lines from appearing in your letters, labels, and envelopes as

Returning to the Mail Merge Helper

At any stage in the mail merge process, you return to the Mail Merge Helper dialog box by opening the **Tools** menu and selecting **Mail Merge** or by choosing Mail Merge Helper on the Mail Merge toolbar, if it is displayed.

To create a data source without starting mail merge

If you want to create a data source, such as a mailing list, before you begin a mail merge, it's still easiest to go through the mail merge process. Follow the steps described here, but leave the main document blank and delete it when you are finished. Alternately, create a data source in a table, merging it later.

a result of blank fields (which is the default for merging). For example, a Suite or Address2 field might be blank if there is no suite number or building name for an addressee.

11. Choose **Merge**.

SEE ALSO

➤ *To learn how to query, see page 415*

Depending on the **Merge to** option you select, Word will begin printing the merged documents, sending email messages or faxes, or displaying the merged documents on your screen.

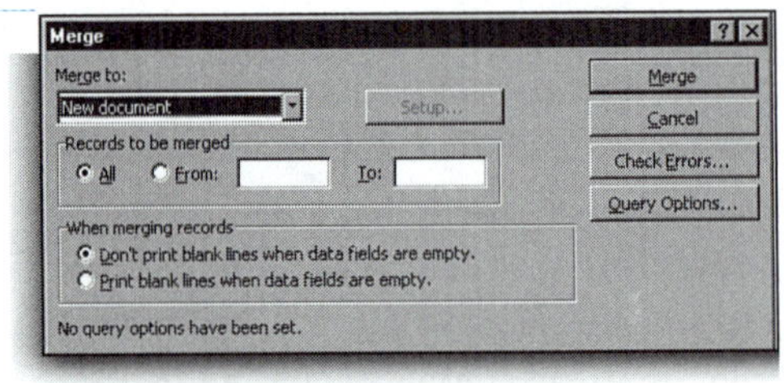

FIGURE 19.2
Set the options for your merge output.

After you create the main document, the Mail Merge toolbar appears. Table 19.1 describes the tools on this toolbar.

TABLE 19.1 Tools on the Mail Merge toolbar

Button:	Name:	Click To:
	Insert Merge Field drop-down list	Select from a list of database fields that you want to add to your main document.
	Insert Word Field drop-down list	Select from a list of nondatabase fields that you can add to your document (such as Fill-In which prompts the the user for text to insert in the document, or Merge Record #, which inserts the number of the current merge record).
	View Merged Data	See how the database information will look in the final merged document.

Button:	Name:	Click To:
	First Record	Go to the first record in the data source file.
	Previous Record	Display information from previous data record.
	Go to Record	Enter the number of the record you want to see, and then press Enter to go to that record.
	Next Record	Display information from the next data record.
	Last Record	Go to the last record in the data source file.
	Mail Merge Helper	Open the Mail Merge Helper dialog box.
	Check for Errors	Report errors in the main document or data source that may cause merging problems.
	Merge to New Document	Start the mail merge and create a new document that contains the results of the merge.
	Merge to Printer	Start the mail merge and automatically print the resulting document.
	Mail Merge	Open the Mail Merge dialog box so you can set options for the mail merge.
	Find Record	Search for specified data records.
	Edit Data Source	Open the Data Form dialog box so that you can view, modify, add, or delete records.

Create a Database

Word keeps Data Source files in table form. Each column of the table represents a field; each row represents a record (see Figure 19.3). The first row of the table (called the header row) shows the field names used in the data source.

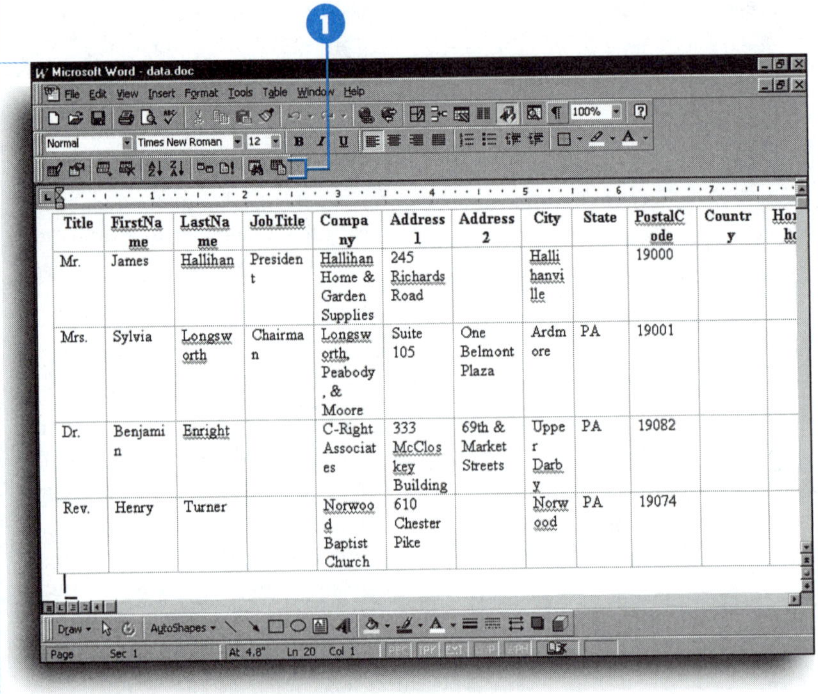

FIGURE 19.3

Word data source files are stored in tables. The table columns represent fields and rows represent records.

1 Database toolbar

Creating a useful data source

The key to creating a useful data source is to create a separate field for each piece of data on which you may need to sort or use alone. For example, a data source that contains a single field name in which you enter a first and last name would make it impossible to create a letter that starts "Dear Tom." A single name field would result in "Dear Tom Jones."

Create a data source file

1. Select **Create Data Source** from the Mail Merge Helper. The Create Data Source dialog box opens (see Figure 19.4). Word provides a list of suggested field names for your data source, and they are listed in the **Field names in header row** box. Do one of the following to customize the list:

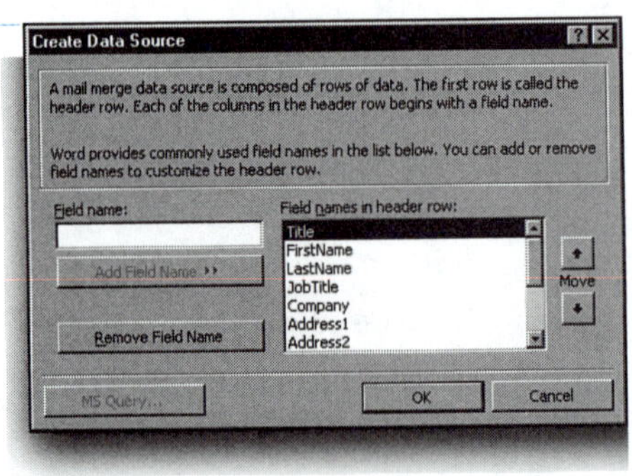

FIGURE 19.4

Customize the field names for your data source file in the Create Data Source dialog box.

- To remove a field name from the list, select the name and choose **Remove Field Name**.
- To add a new field name, enter the field name in the **Field name** box and then choose **Add Field Name**. If the **Add Field Name** button is grayed out, the field name you entered isn't legal. The field name must start with a letter, followed by letters, numbers, or underscore (_) characters. Spaces aren't allowed, and the name can't be more than 40 characters long.
- To change the order of the field names, select a field name and click the up or down **Move** button next to the **Field names in header row** box to move the field up or down in the list. Although the order doesn't matter to the merging process, it does help to have a logical order for data entry.

2. Choose **OK**. The Save As dialog box appears. Type a name for the data source file in the **File name** box, and specify where you want the file stored from the **Save in** drop-down list. Choose **Save**.
3. A dialog box appears telling you that you have not added any records to the data source file. To begin adding records, choose **Edit Data Source**.
4. The Data Form dialog box opens (see Figure 19.5). The field names are listed on the left side of the dialog box in the order you set. A text box follows each field name. Enter the information for the first record in the data source by filling out the text boxes. Press Enter or Tab to move to the next box down; press Shift+Tab to move to the previous box. The up and down arrow keys also help you move from box to box.
5. When you finish entering the data for one record and press Enter after completing the last field, a new record automatically opens. Use the record navigation buttons at the bottom of the dialog box to move from record to record ◄ ► or to the beginning |◄ or end ►| of all the records.

Required fields

You choose the field names and order in which your data sources should appear. Word doesn't require you to use a certain number of fields. However, field names must be unique (such as **fname** for first name and **lname** for last name) and if you plan to distribute the merged output via electronic mail or fax you must include a field that has the email address or fax address.

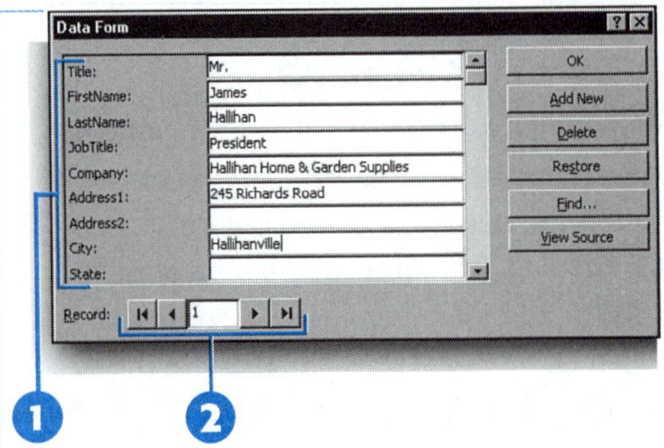

FIGURE 19.5

Enter the field information for each record in the Data Form dialog box.

1. Field names
2. Record navigation buttons

Merging an Access database

When selecting the data source for the merge, specify the filename and location of the Access database and click **Open**. If the data you want to use is in a table in the database, click the **Tables** tab of the Microsoft Access dialog box, select the table, and choose OK. If it's in a query, click the **Queries** tab, select the Query, and choose **OK**. The remainder of the merge process is the same as creating a data source in Word.

6. If you don't complete all the fields in a record and you want to start a new record, choose **Add New** to add a new, blank record to the end of the data source. Then type the field information into that record.

   To delete an entire record, display the record you want to remove from the file and then choose **Delete**.

   To undo any changes you made to the displayed record, choose **Restore**.

7. When you've finished adding records, choose **OK** to return to the main document.

Add and Delete Records

Forgot a field or record? Need to add or remove a record? Editing the data source can be done from the data form or from the table in the data source file.

Modify the database from the data form

1. Click the **Tools** menu and select **Mail Merge** to open the Mail Merge Helper.

2. Then under **Data source,** choose **Edit** and select the name of your data source file. Or, choose Edit Data Source on the Mail Merge toolbar. The Data Form dialog box appears (see Figure 19.6).

3. Do one of the following:
   - To start a new record, choose **Add New** to add a new, blank record to the end of the data source. Then type the field information into that record.
   - To delete an entire record, display the record you want to remove from the file and then choose **Delete**.
   - To undo any changes you made to the displayed record, choose **Restore**.
4. Click **OK**.

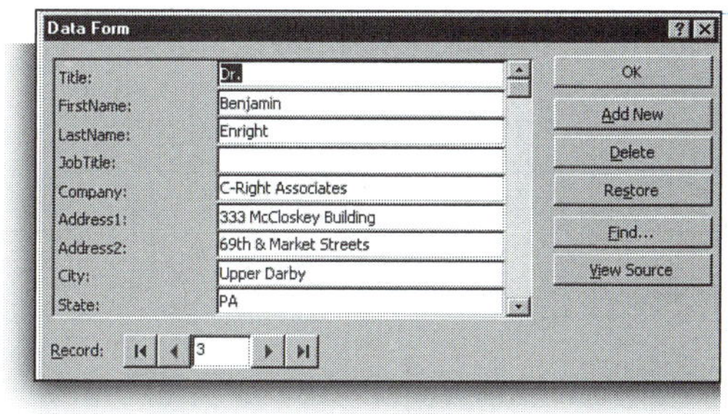

FIGURE 19.6
Add or delete records from the Data Form dialog box.

Modify the database from the data source

1. Click the **Tools** menu and select **Mail Merge** to open the Mail Merge Helper.
2. Under **Data Source** choose **Edit** and select the name of your data source file. Or, choose Edit Data Source on the Mail Merge toolbar. When the Data Form dialog box appears, choose **View Source** from the data form.
3. Do one of the following:
   - To add a new record, choose Add New Record on the Database toolbar. Word appends a new row at the bottom of the table. Enter the information for each field for that record. Save the file to save the information you added.
   - To delete a record, click in the row where the record appears and then choose Delete Record on the Database toolbar.

- To add, remove, or rename the fields in the data source, choose Manage Fields on the Database toolbar to open the Manage Fields dialog box (see Figure 19.7). To add a field, type the name of the new field in the **Field name** box and choose **Add**. To remove a field, select the name from the **Field names in header row** list and choose **Remove**. To rename a field, select the name from the **Field names in header row** list and choose **Rename**. Choose **OK**.

4. Save and close the file.

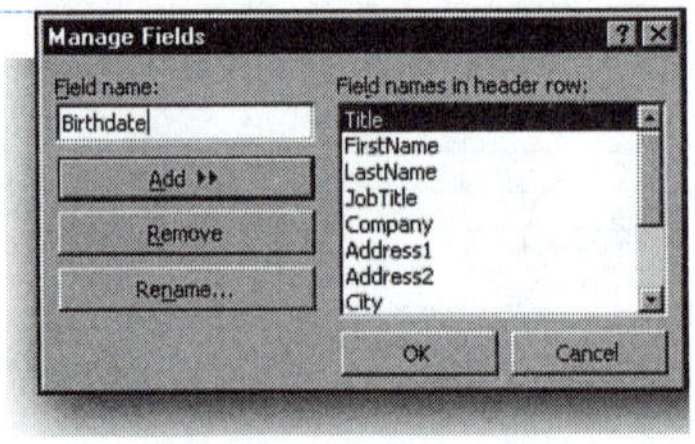

FIGURE 19.7
Add, remove, or rename fields in the Manage Fields dialog box.

If you're no longer in the main document where you can easily access the file through the Mail Merge Helper, open the file by clicking the **File** menu and selecting **Open**, or choose Open on the Standard toolbar. Edit the data as you would any table in a Word document (add a column to add a field; add a row to add a record) and then save the file.

SEE ALSO

➤ *To learn more about navigating through tables, see page 290*

Sort Records

In a mail merge, the main documents are generated in the order in which you entered your records. You may want to sort records so your output is generated in a certain order, such as zip code order or alphabetical order.

Sort mail merge records

1. Click the **Tools** menu and select **Mail Merge** to open the Mail Merge Helper, or choose Mail Merge Helper on the Mail Merge toolbar.

2. Under step 3, **Merge the data with the document**, choose **Query Options**.
3. Select the **Sort Records** tab (see Figure 19.8).

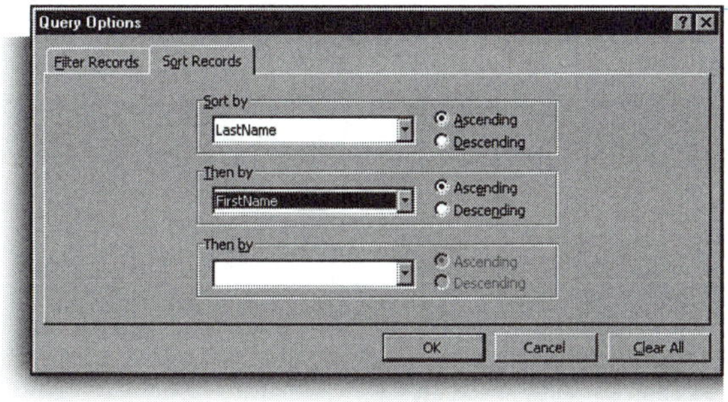

FIGURE 19.8
Select the field in the data source that you want to sort by and then choose the order.

4. From the **Sort by** drop-down list, choose the field you want to use to sort the records.
5. Click **Ascending** if you want the records sorted by that field in an A–Z, 1–99 order. Choose **Descending** to sort the files in Z–A, 99–1 order.
6. Steps 4 and 5 set up the primary sort. If you want to set up a secondary sort, select a field from the **Then by** drop-down list and click **Ascending** or **Descending**. A secondary sort is useful when you have a mailing list sorted by the last name. If there is more than one person with the same last name, the secondary sort by first name will list those people in order of their first names.
7. If necessary, the sort can be refined further. Select a field from the **Then by** drop-down list, and then click **Ascending** or **Descending**.
8. Choose **OK** to close the Query Options dialog box and continue with the merge.

This method assumes that you have already initiated the mail merge process, specified a main document, and created or opened a data source file. If you're not in the middle of a mail merge and you want to sort a data source file, open that file and sort the data table in the document using table sorting methods.

Finding records

To locate specific records in a large table, use the Find Record button on the Database toolbar. In the **Find what** box, type the text you want to locate and indicate the name of the field to search in the **In field** box.

SEE ALSO

➤ *To learn more about sorting tables, see page 291*
➤ *To find and replace text, see page 68*

Prepare the Main Document

Main documents in a mail merge can be form letters, mailing labels, envelopes, or catalogs. Several different types of main documents can use the same data source, so you can make form letters, envelopes, and mailing labels from the same mailing list file.

Write a Form Letter

A form letter consists of text and graphics that you want to appear on each recipient's letter, plus a series of merge fields in which the information relating to that recipient appears. The information in the merge fields is what "personalizes" the form letter.

After you've created your data source file, you're ready to prepare your form letter. When you close the data form, Word returns you to the main document; or click the **File** menu and select **Open**, and then select the main document file to open it.

The Mail Merge toolbar appears on your screen, but the document is blank. Enter any text or graphics you want to appear on each recipient's letter. When you want to insert a piece of information from your data source, choose Insert Merge Field on the Mail Merge toolbar and select the field name you want. A field code appears in the document (see Figure 19.9). It acts as a placeholder for the data from each record in the data source.

Remember to add any required punctuation so that the information flows with the rest of the document text. To be sure that the data displays properly, choose View Merged Data on the Mail Merge toolbar to see the information from your first record displayed.

Formatting fields

To apply character formatting to fields, select the field(s) and use the formatting toolbar or the **Font** or **Format** menu to choose formatting options.

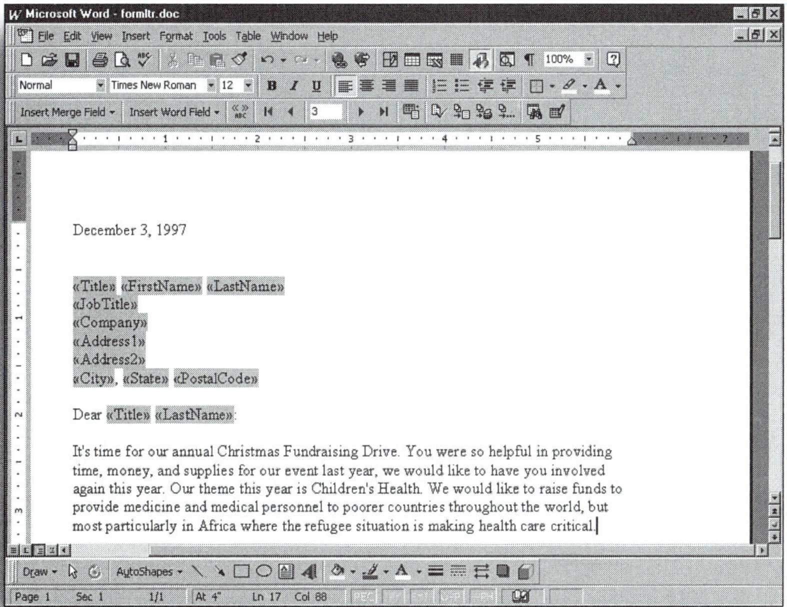

FIGURE 19.9

The field codes appear in the form letter with double-angle brackets around them.

When you've completed the document, save it. Then, choose Mail Merge Helper on the Mail Merge toolbar to continue with the mail merging process. Alternately, choose Mail Merge to specify mail merging options, choose Merge to New Document to activate the merge and create a new document that combines the main document text with the records in the data source, or choose Merge to Printer to print the mail merge documents.

Create Mail Merge Labels

To create mailing labels from the data source, begin following the mail merge process steps from "Merge Documents Using Variable Data," making sure to select **Mailing Labels** as the type of main document you want to create. Then complete the following steps.

Create mail merge labels

1. Click the **Tools** menu and select **Mail Merge** to open the Mail Merge Helper dialog box.
2. Under step 1, **Main document**, choose **Create**.

3. On the menu that appears, click **Mailing Labels**.
4. After you make the selection a dialog box appears. Choose **Active Window** to turn the document you currently have open into your main document for the mail merge. Choose **New Main Document** to open a new document to create the main document.
5. Under step 2, **Data source**, choose **Get Data**.
6. On the menu that appears, select **Create Data Source** to start a completely new data source document, select **Open Data Source** to use an existing data source document, or select **Use Address Book** to use an electronic mail address book or contact list from Microsoft Outlook or Schedule+.
7. If you are using an existing data source file, the Label Options dialog box appears (see Figure 19.10).

   If you created a new data source file, Word returns you to the blank main document. Open the **Tools** menu and select **Mail Merge** or choose Mail Merge Helper on the Mail Merge toolbar to open the Mail Merge Helper dialog box. Click **Setup** to open the Label Options dialog box.

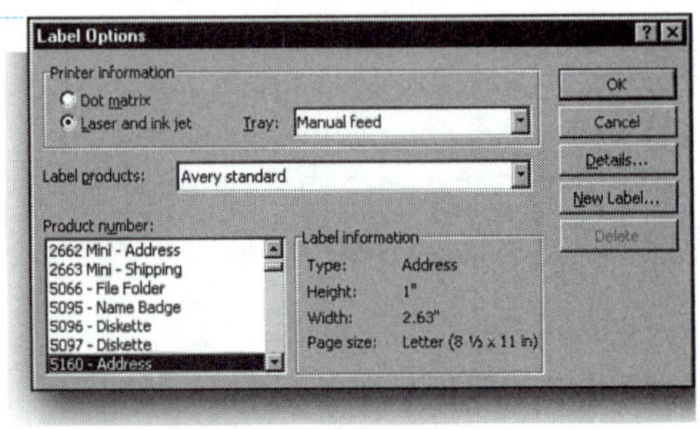

FIGURE 19.10
Select the manufacturer and product number of the labels you plan to use.

8. Under **Printer information**, select the type of printer you'll be using—**Dot matrix** or **Laser and ink jet**. From the **Tray** drop-down list, select the tray or bin where you put the labels for printing.
9. From the **Label products** drop-down list, select the brand or type of labels you use. The **Product number** listings differ depending on your selection. Choose the **Product**

number you use, or the nearest in size. If the size label you want to use isn't listed, choose **New Label** and fill in the dimensions.

10. Choose **OK**. The Create Labels dialog box opens (see Figure 19.11).

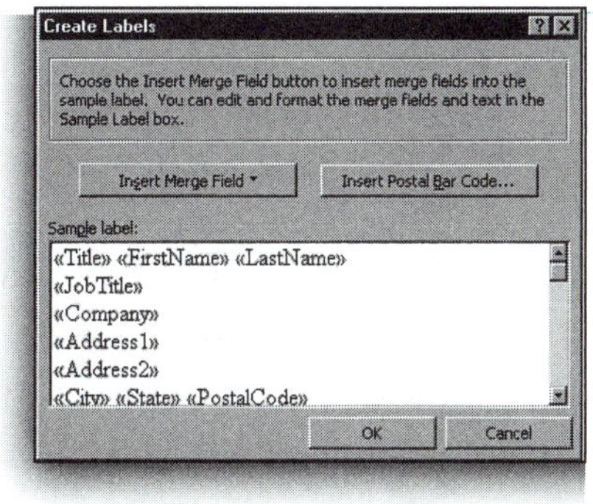

FIGURE 19.11
Add the merge fields to organize the data on the labels.

11. Choose **Insert Merge Field** and select the merge field code you want to insert in the label. Repeat this for each merge field you want to use. Remember to add the correct spacing and punctuation so that the label prints correctly.
12. If your label has room and you want to speed your mail through the United States postal system, choose the **Insert Postal Bar Code** button to print the delivery bar code on the label.
13. Choose **OK** to return to the Mail Merge Helper.
14. Choose **Merge** and select the appropriate output options to print the labels or to create a new document.

U.S. Post Office bulk mail requirements

For bulk mailing, refer to the requirements of the U.S. Post Office regarding proper addressing (all uppercase, no punctuation). Create your envelope form with those requirements in mind.

SEE ALSO

➤ *For additional information on printing labels, see page 268*

Create Mail Merge Envelopes

Create mail merge envelopes

1. Click the **Tools** menu and select **Mail Merge** to open the Mail Merge Helper dialog box.
2. Under step 1, **Main document**, choose **Create**.

3. On the menu that appears, click **Envelopes**.
4. A dialog box appears. Choose **Active Window** to turn the document you currently have open into your main document for the mail merge. Choose **New Main Document** to open a new document to create the main document.
5. Under step 2, **Data source**, choose **Get Data**.
6. On the menu that appears, select **Create Data Source** to start a completely new data source document, select **Open Data Source** to use an existing data source document, or select **Use Address Book** to use an electronic mail address book or contact list from Microsoft Outlook or Schedule+.
7. Depending on your choice in the previous step, you need to do one of the following:

   If you created a new data source, click Mail Merge Helper  on the Mail Merge toolbar to return to the Mail Merge Helper dialog box. Then choose **Setup** under **Main document**.

   If you opened an existing data source file from the Mail Merge Helper, a dialog box appears saying that you need to set up the main document. Choose **Set Up Main Document**.
8. The Envelope Options dialog box appears (see Figure 19.12). Select the **Envelope size** you want to print from the drop-down list.

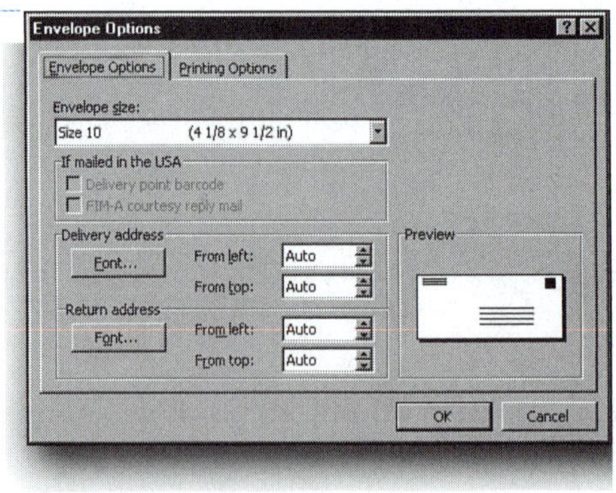

FIGURE 19.12
Select the size of envelope you want to print and how you want the return and delivery address to look.

9. To set the appearance of your envelope, choose **Font** under **Delivery address** or **Font** under **Return address** and make your font choices for the address. To position the addresses on the envelope, set the distance **From left** and **From top** of the envelope for the delivery address and **From left** and **From top** for the return address.
10. Choose **OK** and the Envelope address dialog box appears (see Figure 19.13). Choose **Insert Merge Field** and select the merge field code you want to insert in the envelope. Repeat for each merge field you need to insert. Remember to add the correct spacing and punctuation so the address prints correctly.

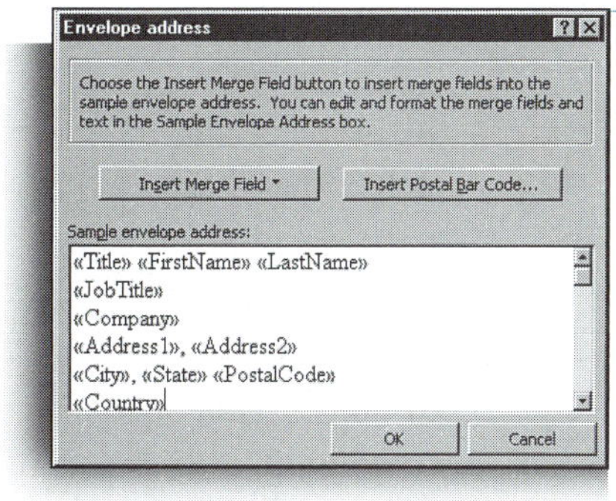

FIGURE 19.13
Add the field codes you need for your envelope.

11. To speed your mail through the U.S. postal system, choose **Insert Postal Bar Code** to print the delivery bar code on the label.
12. Choose **OK** to return to the Mail Merge Helper.
13. Choose **Merge** and select the appropriate output options to print the envelopes or to create a new document.

SEE ALSO

➤ *To learn additional information on printing envelopes, see page 266*

To change label or envelope size

If you change printers or need to change the size or modify envelopes, open the envelope main document and open the **Tools** menu and select **Envelopes and Labels**. In the Envelopes and Labels dialog box, make your changes. To change labels, open the **Tools** menu, choose **Mail Merge** and create a new mailing labels main document.

Select Data

Your data source file may be a generalized file, such as a large mailing list, but you only want to send a particular form letter to a select group of members of the list. In the case of a mailing list, you may need to select addresses in one city or state.

To set up the conditions of a selective merge, you need to use the Query Options feature of the mail merge process.

Filter records prior to a merge

1. Access Query Options from the Mail Merge Helper prior to doing the merge by choosing the **Query Options**, or if you have clicked **Merge** and opened the Merge dialog box, choose **Query Options** there. The Query Options dialog box opens (see Figure 19.14).

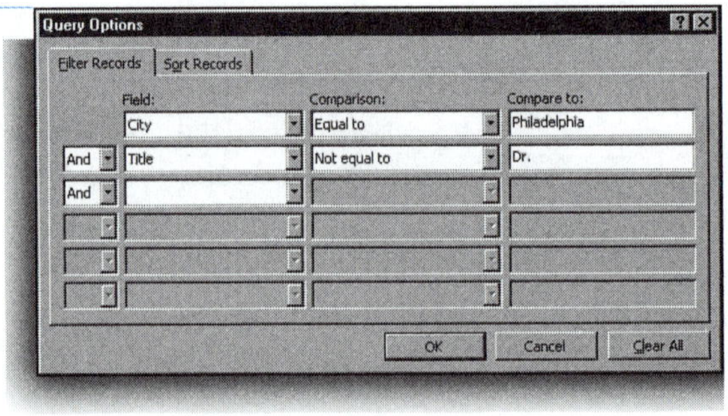

FIGURE 19.14
Use the Query Options dialog box to set conditions for selecting particular records for your merge or to sort the records in a certain order.

2. Select the **Filter Records** tab if you plan to set conditions to select only certain records for your merge.
3. In the **Field** box, select the field you want to use to set the conditions of your merge. For example, if you only want to send your form letter to people in a particular city, choose the **City** field.
4. From the **Comparison** box, select the type of comparison you want to make (**Equal to**, **Not equal to**, **Greater than**, **Less than**, **Is blank**, and so on).
5. In the **Compare to** box, enter the exact value to which you want to compare the field information. In the **City** example, you would enter the name of the city.
6. If you want to evaluate more than one condition, fill out the boxes in the second row. In the first box of the line, select **And** to select records that match all the filter criteria or

Filter criteria

The information entered in the **Field**, **Comparison**, and **Compare to** boxes is called the *filter criteria* because they filter out any records that don't meet that criteria.

select **Or** to select records that match any of the filter criteria.

7. If you want to sort the records, click the **Sort Records** tab and follow the instructions under the "Sort Records" section earlier in this chapter.
8. Choose **OK** to close the Query Options dialog box and continue with the merge.

The merged documents include only those records that meet the conditions of your query.

Create Catalogs and Lists

Using the Word's mail merge feature and its capability to pull unique pieces of information from a data source (database) file, it's possible to create a catalog, membership directory, parts list, or similar document. The method is similar to merging a form letter with a mailing list. The resulting document however, is quite different. With catalogs, directories, and lists, data is stored in a source document, but the merged information is combined into a single document.

Create a catalog or list

1. Start a new document.
2. Click the **Tools** menu and select **Mail Merge** to open the Mail Merge Helper dialog box.
3. Under step 1, **Main document**, choose **Create**.
4. On the menu that appears, click **Catalog**. With a catalog main document, all the merged data is placed in one resulting merged document and the text you add to the main document is repeated for each set of data.
5. After you make the selection, a dialog box appears asking whether you want to use the active document window when you create the document or a new document window. Choose **Active Window** to turn the document you currently have open into your main document for the merge.
6. Under step 2, **Data source**, choose **Get Data**.

7. On the menu that appears, click **Create Data Source**. Set up the fields you want to use. Choose **OK**.
8. The Save As dialog box appears. From the **Save in** drop-down list, select the drive and folder where you want to store the data source file. Enter the name of the data source in the **File name** box. Choose **Save**.
9. When the dialog box appears asking if you want to add data records or edit the main document, choose **Edit Data Source** to enter the data to create the data source.
10. In the **Data Form**, enter the specific information for each record that you want to add to the database (see Figure 19.15). Choose **Add New** to add a new record. When you've added all the records, choose **OK**.

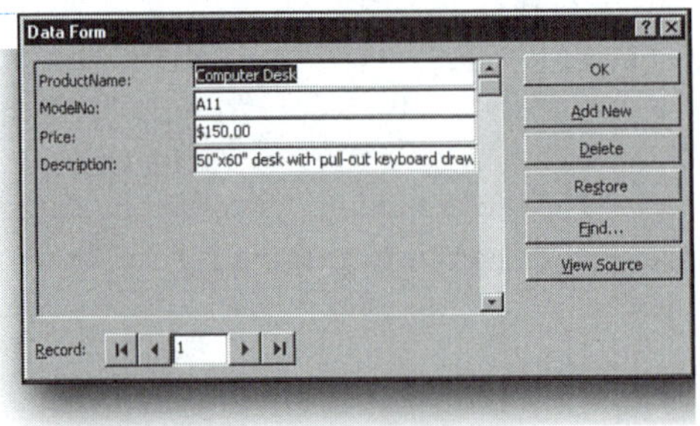

FIGURE 19.15
This database for a price list uses only four fields.

11. In the main document, insert the text and graphics you want repeated with each data record. With your insertion point where you want the data from the data source to appear, choose Insert Merge Field on the Mail Merge toolbar and click the field name that you want to insert from the menu that appears. Repeat this for each field you want to display for all the records in your data source (see Figure 19.16).
12. Return to the Mail Merge Helper by choosing Mail Merge Helper on the Mail Merge toolbar. Under step 3, **Merge the data with the document**, choose **Merge**. In the Merge dialog box, select **New Document** from the **Merge to** drop-down list.

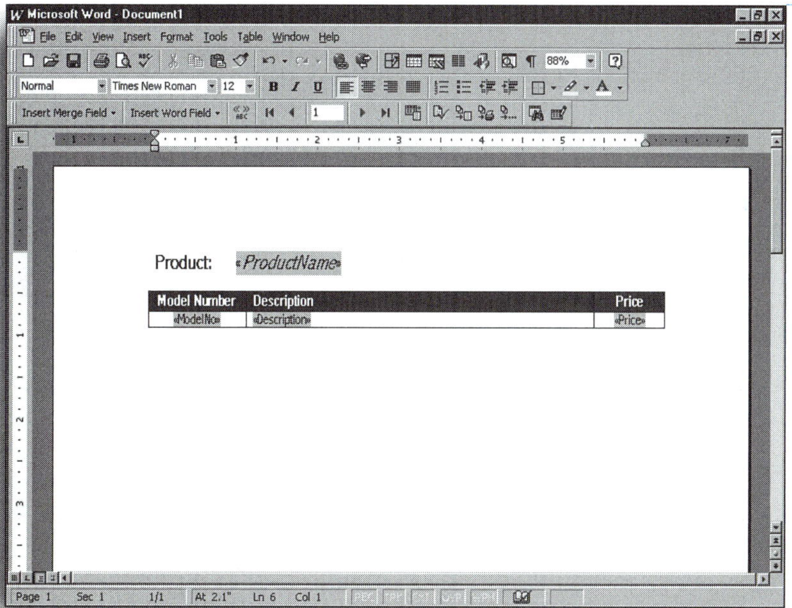

FIGURE 19.16

The main document contains the boilerplate text, formatting, and fields needed to create the final document.

13. Under **Records to be merged**, select **All** or **From**. If you chose **From**, enter the range of record numbers in the **From** and **To** boxes that you want to merge. If you only want to merge specific records or records of a certain type, choose **Query Options** and set conditions on the merge.
14. Under **When Merging Records**, click **Don't print blank lines when data fields are empty** if you don't want any blank lines in your catalog, directory, or list because there was no entry in a particular field.
15. Choose **Merge**.
16. After the catalog or list document appears (as shown in Figure 19.17), add headers, footers, or any additional text you need for the overall document. Then print the document as you would any other Word document.

FIGURE 19.17
The resulting price list has an entry for each record in the database.

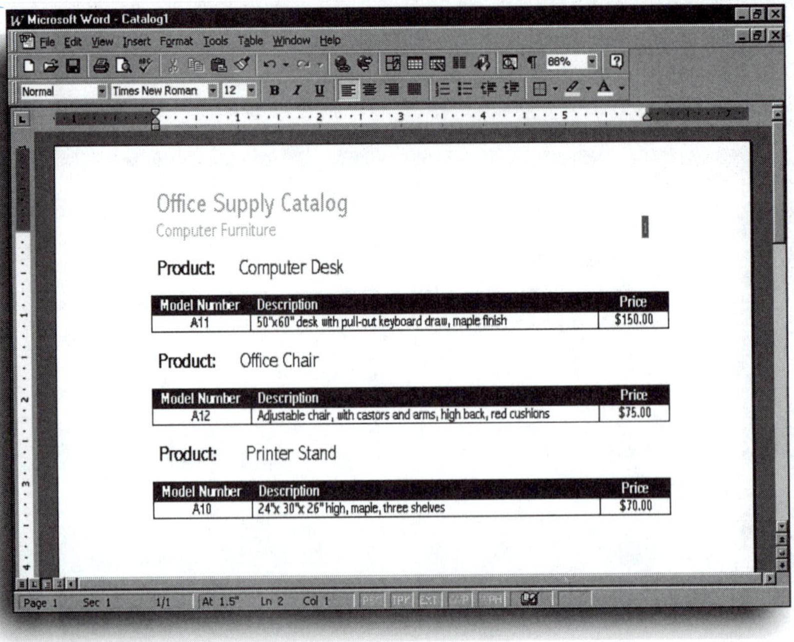

CHAPTER

20

Manage Workgroup Documents

- Track document changes through revision marks
- Insert comments into documents that are not part of the document printed text
- Route documents (through email) to various recipients
- Create multiple versions of a document

About Workgroups

A *workgroup* is a number of people whose combined talents are utilized on a specific project or event. The members of a workgroup might belong to a single department, represent technical talents from many departments, or they might be a group of administrators whose only shared workgroup interests are the use of standard forms or letters.

But most often, workgroup focuses are project-oriented. Word provides workgroup support through document routing, versioning, and comments and revisions. Consider using these tools when you are sharing documents, working as part of a group, or want to keep several versions of a document as you prepare for the final version.

Track Document Changes

Not all changes are marked as revisions to a document

Some formatting changes (including font styles and paragraph formatting) are not tracked and marked as revisions when tracking is turned on. For example, if tracking is activated, and you bold some text, the text appears as bold in the document, with no tracking references. We know of no reliable method for tracking formatting changes in Word.

When several people are working on the same document, it may be important to know who made which changes. Word does this through the use of *revision marks*. Each person's modifications to a document appear in a different color, provided revision marks are enabled during the editing process. Revision marks can track colors for as many as eight authors.

To assign different color text to each reviser of a document, Word pulls information from the **User Information** tab of the Options dialog box. If someone revises a document while working on your computer, Word extracts your user information.

SEE ALSO

➤ *To set user information, see page 546*

Turn on revision marks

1. Open the document that you want to edit.
2. Open the **Tools** menu and select **Track Changes, Highlight Changes** to open the Highlight Changes dialog box (see Figure 20.1). Click **Track changes while editing** to enable that feature. If you want to see the revisions when you view the document, click **Highlight changes on screen**

to place a check mark in the box. To see the revisions in the printed document, click **Highlight changes in printed document** to place a check mark in the box. Choose **OK**.

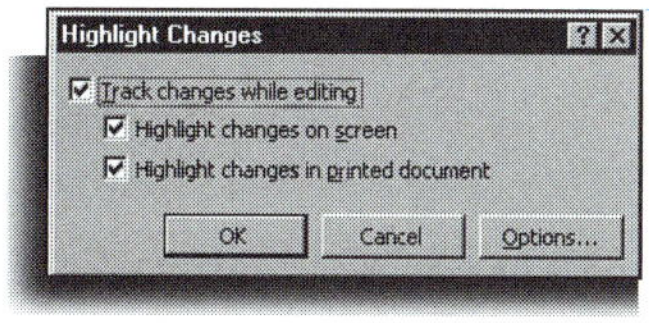

FIGURE 20.1

In the Highlight Changes dialog box, indicate if you want the text highlighted on the screen or in the printed document.

Or, choose Track Changes on the Reviewing toolbar (see Figure 20.2). To display the Reviewing toolbar, open the **View** menu and select **Toolbars**, and then **Reviewing** or right-click a toolbar and click **Reviewing** on the pop-up menu. When changes are being tracked, TRK appears on the status bar, as shown in Figure 20.2. When changes are not being tracked, TRK is dimmed. Table 20.1 lists the tools available on the Reviewing toolbar.

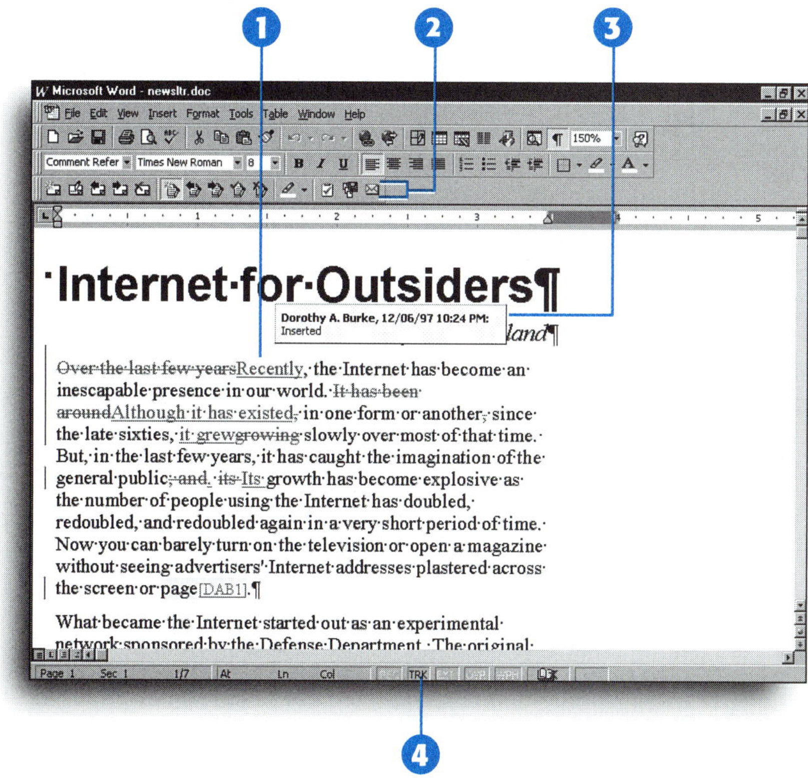

FIGURE 20.2

Use the Reviewing toolbar to quickly insert or review comments; highlight text; and track, accept, or reject changes.

1. Revision
2. Reviewing toolbar
3. Reviewer pop-up
4. TRK

3. Make modifications as you would in any Word document. Any additions you make appear in color and are underlined. Deletions are in color, underlined, and have strikethrough applied. A vertical line appears in the left margin wherever a change appears in the document. Note that you won't be able to change the revision formatting (for example, you won't be able to remove the underlining).
4. Save the document.

TABLE 20.1 **Reviewing toolbar**

Button:	Tool:	Description:
	Insert Comment	Inserts a comment into the document at the insertion point.
	Edit Comment	Displays all comments in the Comments pane for editing or viewing.
	Previous Comment	Goes to previous comment in document and displays comment text in pop-up.
	Next Comment	Goes to next comment in document and displays comment text in pop-up.
	Delete Comment	Deletes the selected comment from the document.
	Track Changes	Marks revisions in the document and tracks them by the name of the modifier.
	Previous Change	Locates and selects the previous tracked revision.
	Next Change	Locates and selects the next tracked revision.
	Accept Change	Accepts the selected revision and removes the highlighting.
	Reject Change	Rejects the selected revision and removes the highlighting.
	Highlight	Highlights text when you choose this button and then select the text.
	Create Microsoft Outlook Task	Opens Microsoft Outlook (if you have the program) and allows you to enter a task there.

Button:	Tool:	Description:
	Save Version	Saves a version of the document.
	Send to Mail Recipient	Sends the current file as an attachment to a mail message.

To change the color or formatting that Word uses to mark your revisions, open the **Tools** menu, select **Options**, and then click the **Track Changes** tab (see Figure 20.3). For any of the following categories, choose a different type of formatting with **Mark** or **Color**:

- **Inserted text**
- **Deleted text**
- **Changed formatting**
- **Changed lines** (lines that appear by the margin to indicate changed text or formatting within the paragraph)

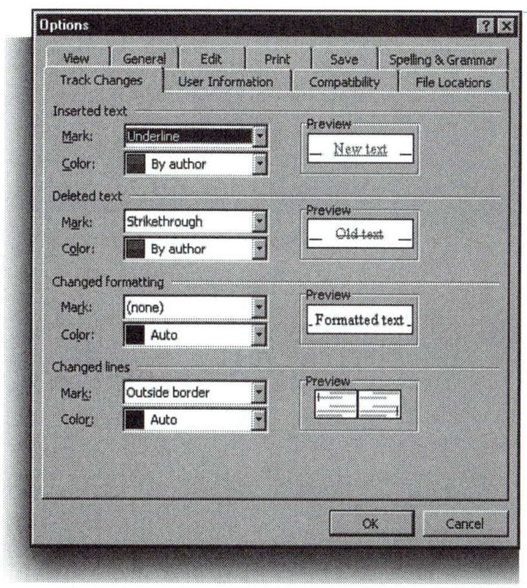

FIGURE 20.3
Make changes to the formatting settings in the **Mark** boxes or select different colors for different events.

When the document author or the final editor receives the document with the changes from all the editors, that person determines whether to accept or reject the changes by doing one of the following:

- Select the revised text. Open the **Tools** menu and select **Track Changes**, and then **Accept or Reject Changes** to open the Accept or Reject Changes dialog box (see Figure 20.4). This dialog box stays on the screen while you edit the document or scroll to find changes, until you choose **Close**.

  Under **View**, click the option that displays the revisions in the manner easiest for you to use: **Changes with highlighting** shows both changes and revision marks, **Changes without highlighting** shows the changes but doesn't display the revision marks, **Original** doesn't display changes or revision marks. Choose **Accept** to accept the selected change, **Accept All** to accept all the changes in the document, **Reject** to reject the selected change, or **Reject All** to reject all the changes in the document. Choose ← **Find** or → **Find** to move to the previous or next revision.

- Select the modification and then choose Accept Change or Reject Change on the Reviewing toolbar.

- Choose Previous Change or Next Change on the Reviewing toolbar to move from one revision to another. Then choose Accept Change or Reject Change.

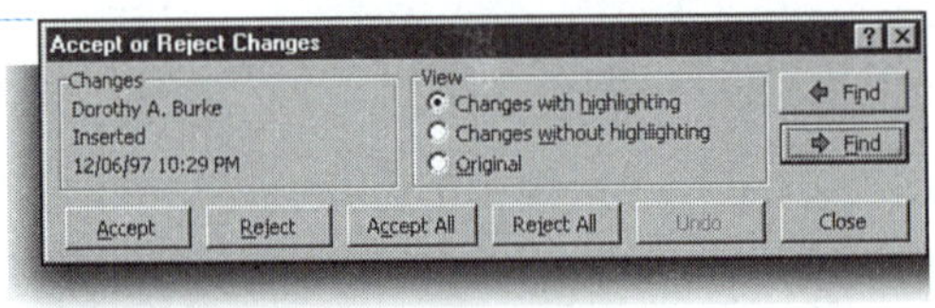

FIGURE 20.4
The Accept or Reject Changes dialog box also tells you who made the revision and when.

When you accept changes, any inserted revisions become part of the document, deletions are removed from the document, formatting changes are applied permanently to the appropriate text, and the revision marks disappear. When you reject changes, inserted modifications are removed, deletions are restored to the document, formatting changes are removed, and revision marks disappear.

The only way to prevent unauthorized persons from changing the document or from removing marked revisions is to protect the document and give it a password. Open the **Tools** menu and select **Protect Document**. Select **Tracked** changes and then type a password in the **Password** box. Click **OK**. Only those users who possess the password can unprotect the document and remove the tracking changes.

SEE ALSO

➤ *Protecting documents, see page 448*

Insert Comments

As you're making revisions to a document, you may want to add a comment to the author or pose a question without changing the document text. To add a comment, choose Insert Comment on the Reviewing toolbar or open the **Insert** menu and select **Comment**. Type your comment in the comment window at the bottom of the screen (see Figure 20.5).

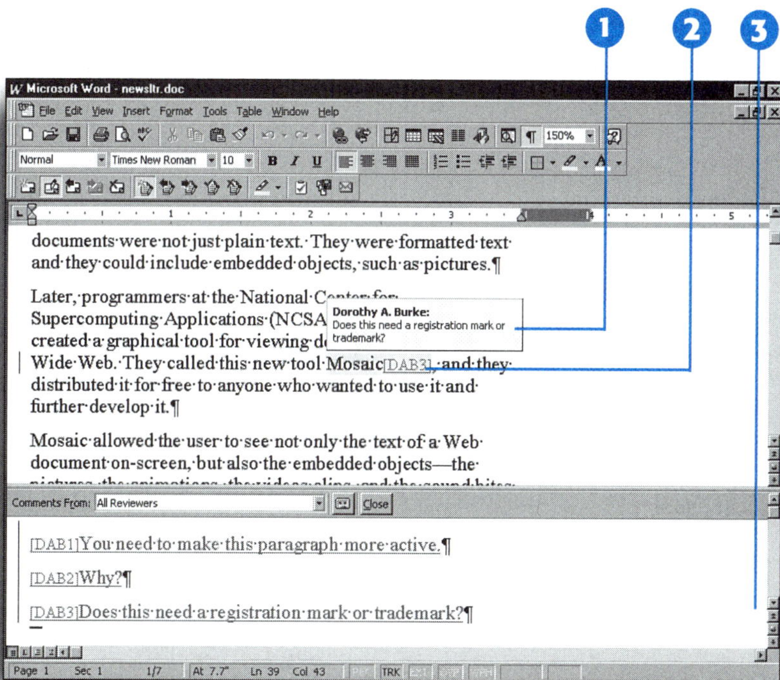

FIGURE 20.5
Point to a comment reference to see the comment text in a pop-up.

1. Comment pop-up
2. Comment reference
3. Comment window

Adding a comment to the text

To make a comment part of the document text, choose Edit Comment on the Reviewing toolbar. Select the comment text in the **Comment** pane, choose Copy on the Standard toolbar or press Ctrl+C, click in the document where you want the comment text to appear, and then choose Paste on the Standard toolbar or press Ctrl+V.

A comment reference mark appears next to the text on which you're commenting. When reading a document with comment marks, point to the comment reference mark. The comment pops up above the text.

After entering the comment in the comment window, choose **Close** to close the window. Choose Edit Comment on the Reviewing toolbar to open the comment window again or double-click the comment reference mark. Or, leave the comment window open as you work through the document. Edit and review comments in the comment window.

Route Documents

If you're using your email program to mail documents to members of your workgroup, consider routing them instead. When you *route documents*, use the same distribution list as you would when you email—the difference here is how Word handles the mail. With routing, you list the mail recipients at the time you mail the document, but the document arrives in the first recipient's mailbox only. After that person is done with his revisions, the document is routed to the next person on the list and so forth, ultimately being returned to the original sender.

This, of course, only works when you are email enabled and Word is configured properly with your email program. You must have an email system using Microsoft Exchange, Lotus cc:Mail, a MAPI (Messaging Application Programming Interface), or VIM (Vendor Independent Messaging) compatible system.

Be sure to include a message when routing

Although Word includes a text message in your routed document that instructs the recipient to continue, the message does not contain a list of all recipients. The first person in the routing list sees that the message is from the sender. However, the second person sees that the message is from the first person, not the original sender. Consider putting a message or list of recipients in the routing slip as a courtesy.

Create a Routing Slip

To route a document, you must first prepare a routing slip.

Create a routing slip

1. Open the document you plan to route.
2. Open the **File** menu and select **Send To**, and then select **Routing Recipient** to open the Routing Slip dialog box (see Figure 20.6).

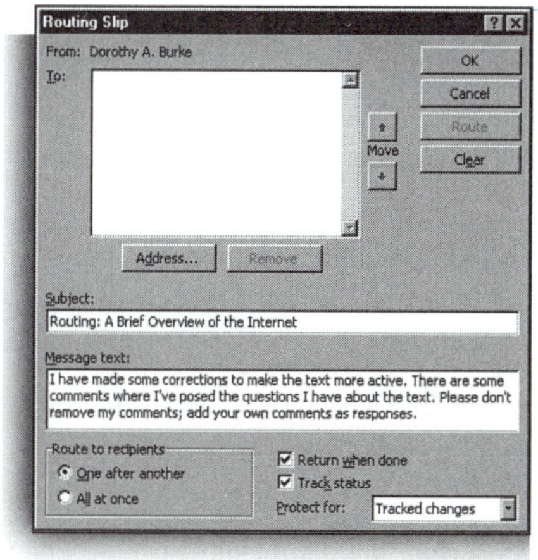

FIGURE 20.6
Set up your routing options from the Routing Slip dialog box.

If you haven't set up Microsoft Exchange on your system, a wizard appears to help you specify your Exchange Server, the mail software you'll be using, the name and location of your mailbox file, any passwords you need to open your mail software, and the location of your address book. After you finish the wizard, the Routing Slip dialog box appears.

3. Choose **Address** to select the recipients of the document (see Figure 20.7).

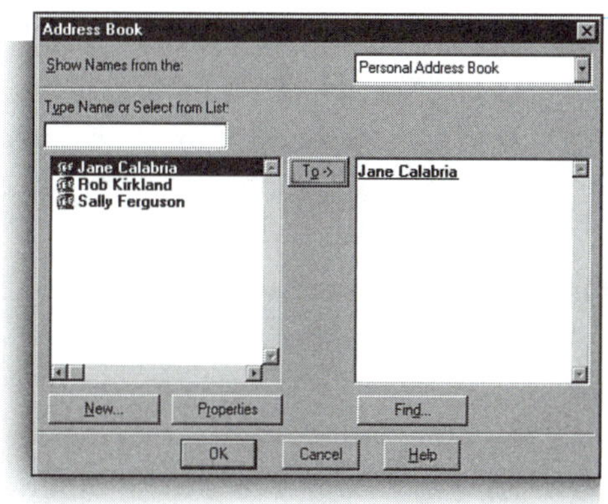

FIGURE 20.7
Enter the names of the recipients or select them from the list of names in your Address Book.

4. Select the database, distribution list, or address book that contains the names you want to use for routing in the **Show names from the** drop-down list.

Avoid selecting distribution groups

Word treats a group as if it were one person and sends the document to everyone in the group at once, instead of routing it to each one in turn. Instead of selecting a group, specify the names of the individuals in the group to preserve the sequential ordering necessary to routing.

5. In the **Type Name or Select from List** box, enter the recipient's name or select the recipients from the list of people in your address book (hold down Ctrl while clicking names to select more than one name).
6. Choose **To** and then choose **OK**. The names you selected or entered appear in the **To** box. After you have entered names, the **OK** button (see Figure 20.6) changes to **Add Slip**.
7. To set the order of names in the routing list, click a person's name and then click the up or down **Move** arrow to move the name up or down the list.
8. Word automatically enters a subject for the message in the **Subject** box, based on the opening lines of the document. Edit or replace the subject text.
9. In the **Message text** box, enter the message you want to accompany the document.
10. Under **Route to recipients**, click **One after another** to have the document routing to the first person on the list, and then to the second, and then to the third, and so on. If you click the **All at once** option, everyone on the routing list will receive the message at the same time. The recipients won't have the opportunity to read the comments and revisions of others before passing the document on to the next person, which may result in duplication of effort.
11. Click **Return when done** to enable that option. This makes sure that the document is routed back to you after everyone on the list is finished with it.
12. Click **Track status** to place a check mark there. When you enable this option you will receive a message whenever someone forwards the document on to the next person on the routing list.
13. From the **Protect for** drop-down list, select one of the following options:
    - **Comments** lets reviewers insert comments but not change the contents of the document.

- **Tracked Changes** turns on revision marking to track all changes the reviewer makes in the document.
- **Forms** routes a form that you want recipients to complete without modifying the form itself.
- **(None)** doesn't track the reviewers' changes, so you can't highlight or merge them.

14. Choose **Route** to route the document.

Choose **Add Slip** to close the dialog box without routing the document. When you're ready to route the document, open the document, choose the **File** menu and select **Send To**, and then select **Next Routing Recipient**.

Caution! Protecting for tracked changes protects the original file

When you protect the routed document for tracked changes, any changes you make to the original after the file has been sent are entered into the document as revisions. You cannot turn off revisions or accept your own changes until the original document is routed back to you. Even if you save the document with a different name, changes you make are treated as revisions.

SEE ALSO

➤ *To email word documents, see page 273*

Edit the Routed Document

When you receive an email message with a routed document attached, open the attachment per the instructions in your email software (in most cases, you double-click the attachment icon). Figure 20.8 shows a Word-routed document received by a Lotus Notes Mail User. When the user double-clicks the attachment, Word starts.

After you double-click an attachment and make your revisions or comments, you're ready to send the document along to the next person on the routing list. Remembering that you are now working in Word (regardless of the email program you used when you received this attachment), open the **File** menu and then select **Send To**. From the submenu select **Next Routing Recipient**.

If you want to route the document to someone who isn't on the original routing list, open the **File** menu and select **Send To**. From the submenu select **Other Routing Recipient**.

When document routing is completed and returned to the originator, Word creates a message indicating that the routing process is complete. Figure 20.9 shows the routed document returned to the originator in Microsoft Outlook.

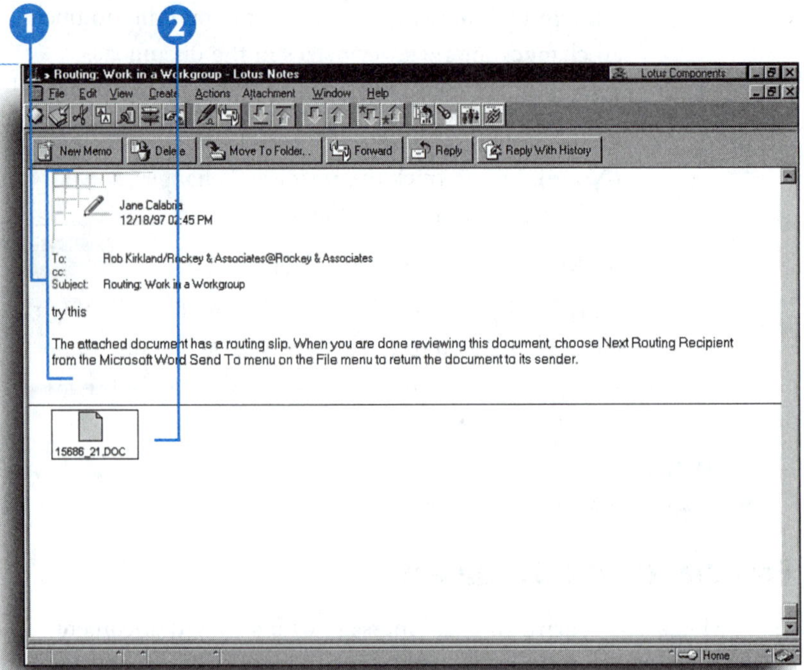

FIGURE 20.8
Word generates this accompanying message when you route a document.

1. Word-generated message
2. Routed document is mailed as attachment

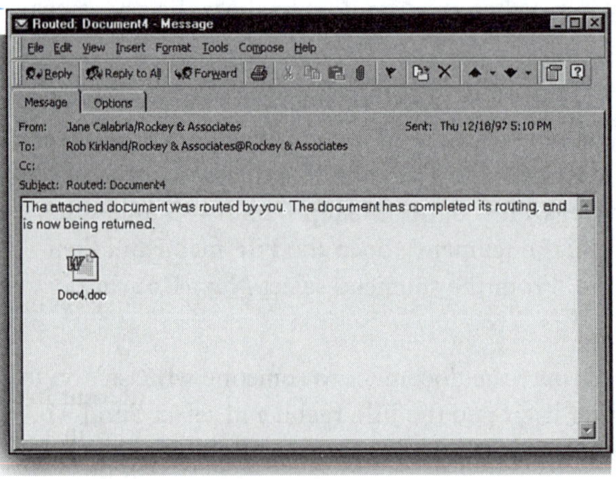

FIGURE 20.9
Word indicates that the routing process is complete, and presents an opportunity to merge the routed document with the original.

Double-clicking the document icon starts Word and opens the file. A message appears (see Figure 20.10) asking if you want to merge the document changes with the original file. Your choices are

- **OK**. Word merges the routed document with the original document (you must indicate the filename during this process). The original document now contains revisions and you can accept or reject the changes.
- **Cancel**. Ends merging and routing processes.

FIGURE 20.10
When you open a routed document at the end of its travels, the Office Assistant prompts you to merge the document with the original file.

Indicate how you want to treat the returned message, and the routing process is complete.

Highlight Text

Just as you use a highlighter pen on printed text, Word has a highlighter for you to use to emphasize text in your printed document as well as onscreen. When you share the document with others, they can easily spot the important points in the document.

To highlight text in your document, click the Highlight button on the Reviewing or Formatting toolbar and then select the text you want to emphasize. Or, select the text first, then choose Highlight.

If you want to change the color of the highlighting, click the down arrow next to the Highlight button and then click on one of the colors.

This type of highlighting is done manually and is different from the automatic highlighting Word uses to track revisions in a document (see "Track Document Changes" earlier in this chapter).

Create Multiple Versions of a Document

Another option for working with documents that you want reviewed by several people is to have Word save the current version of the document automatically each time you or another person closes the document after modifying it. All the versions are stored in a single document, but only the most current version displays. The date and time the version was saved is automatically recorded, as is the name of the person making the revisions.

You can view any one of the previous versions in a separate window by opening that version from the Versions dialog box.

Prepare a document for versioning

1. Open the document to be reviewed. Make sure you set it up to track changes if you want to see the revisions made by the reviewers (refer to "Track Document Changes" earlier in this chapter).
2. Open the **File** menu and select **Versions** to open the Versions dialog box (see Figure 20.11).

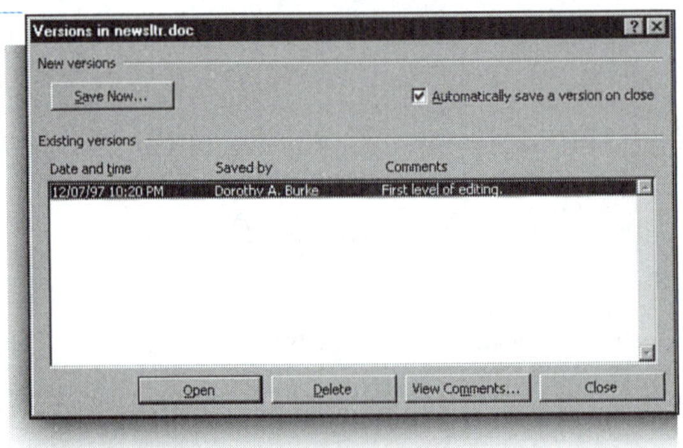

FIGURE 20.11
Any existing versions of the document appear in the Versions dialog box.

3. Choose **Save Now** to store the current state of the document as a separate version and open the Save Version dialog box (see Figure 20.12). In the **Comments on version** box, enter any information that will help identify the purpose or special characteristics of that version. Then click **OK.** To read the full text comments for each version of a document,

open the **File** menu and choose **Versions**. Select the version, and choose **View Comments**.

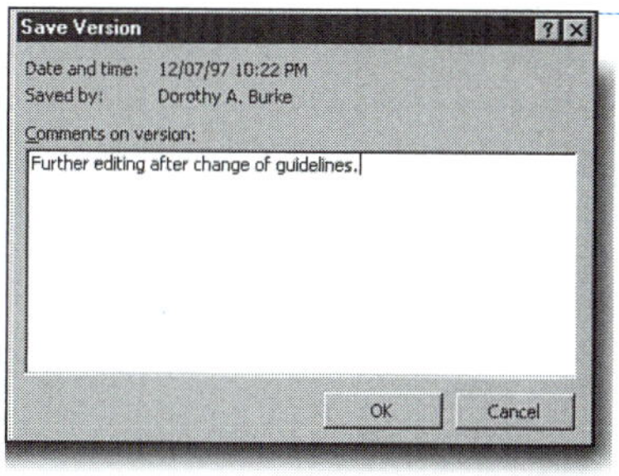

FIGURE 20.12
Enter comments that provide information on the types of revisions made in that version.

4. Click **Automatically save a version on close** to save a new version whenever the file is closed.
5. Choose **Close** to close the dialog box.
6. Send the document to the reviewers.

If you want to view a specific version of the document, open the **File** menu and select **Versions** to open the Versions dialog box. Click the version you want to see from the list of **Existing versions** and then choose **Open**. Word opens the version as a second document window (see Figure 20.13).

Word can compare two versions of the document to see how they differ, but they must be separate files.

Quickly save a version

When you want to quickly save a version of the document, choose the Save Versions icon on the Reviewing toolbar. It opens the Save Version dialog box where you enter a comment and click **OK**.

Save a version of a document

1. Open the **File** menu and select **Versions** to open the Versions dialog box.
2. In the **Existing versions** box, select the version you want to save as a separate file.
3. Choose **Open** to open the version in its own document window.
4. Open the **File** menu and select **Save As** .
5. Enter a name for the file in the **File name** box.
6. Choose **Save**.

FIGURE 20.13
Word shows the two versions of the same document in separate windows.

Compare file versions

1. With one version open, open the **Tools** menu and select **Track Changes**, then choose **Compare Documents**.
2. The Select File to Compare With Current Document dialog box opens (see Figure 20.14).

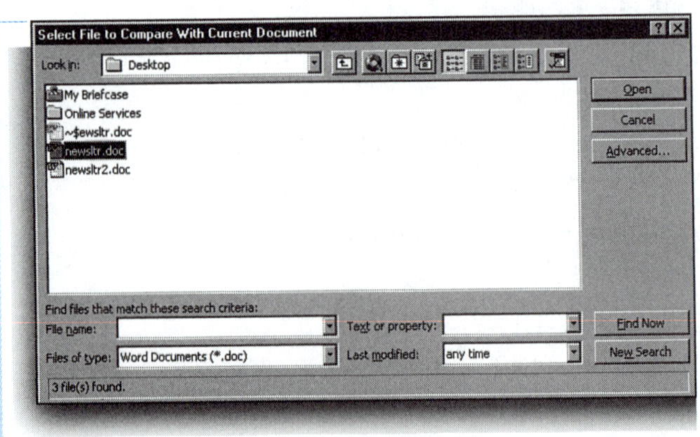

FIGURE 20.14
Select the name of the file you want to compare with the current document.

3. Click the name of the file to which you want to compare the current document or enter its name in the **File name** box.
4. Choose **Open**.

Any modifications in the other file appear as revisions in the current document.

One problem with using different versions or allowing several reviewers to each work on a copy of the same document is gathering all the comments and modifications into one document. You can merge all versions into one document.

Merge file versions

1. Open the document (usually the original) in which you want all the changes and comments to appear.
2. Open the **Tools** menu and select **Merge Documents**. The Select File to Merge Into Current Document dialog box opens (see Figure 20.15).
3. Select the document that has changes that you want to merge with the current file.
4. Choose **Open**.
5. Repeat steps 2 to 4 for each document you want to merge with the current document.
6. Review all the comments and accept or reject the changes.
7. Save the document.

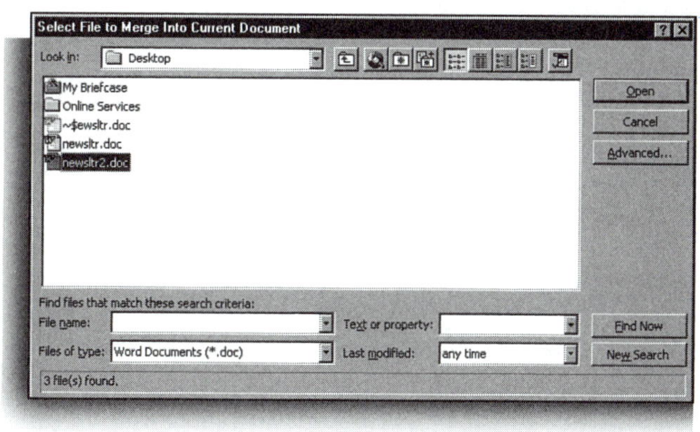

FIGURE 20.15
Select the name of the file that has the changes you want to merge with the current document.

CHAPTER 21

Design Custom Forms

Create online and printed forms

Edit, modify, and fill in forms

Control layout with tables, frames

When preparing forms, it's important to control text placement on the form. Tables do that easily, but to keep the table cells a certain size, you need to choose **Exactly** when specifying row height (in the Cell Height and Width dialog box). You also need to deselect **Allow row to break across pages** in the same dialog box. Putting text in frames or text boxes are also good ways to control the placement of text on your form.

Good form design begins on paper

One sheet of paper and a few minutes of time are all you need to plan a form. Unless design is not a consideration, save time later by taking a moment to plan and lay out your form elements on paper before you create the form in Word.

Design Forms

Forms are useful documents for gathering and displaying information. Create forms for fill-in by others to capture information such as employee information, client information, and so forth.

A form consists of *boilerplate* information (information that cannot be changed by users) and fields where users fill in information. You can create two types of forms in Word:

- *Printed forms* designed to print first and then fill in on the printed copy.
- *Online forms* designed to fill in while working in Word.

SEE ALSO

➤ *To learn more about tables, see page 296*

Create a Printed Form

Some forms need to be printed before they can be filled in by others. These types of forms include fax cover sheets. Even with fax modems on every PC in the company, there is often a need to fax information from hard copy (such as a magazine article). Most companies maintain fax machines for this purpose and keeping a stack of fax cover sheets in the fax room saves others from having to run back to their PC to create a cover sheet in Word. Other printed forms used in the office include phone message pads and supply requisitions.

Create a printed form

1. Create a new document.
2. Add any text or graphics you want on the form.
3. To insert a text box where users enter their responses, click where you want to place the text box and then choose Text Form Field on the Forms toolbar (see Figure 21.1). If the Forms toolbar is not showing, open the **View** menu and select **Toolbars**. From the submenu, select **Forms**.
4. To insert check boxes, click in the document where you want to place the check box. Then choose Check Box Form Field on the Forms toolbar.

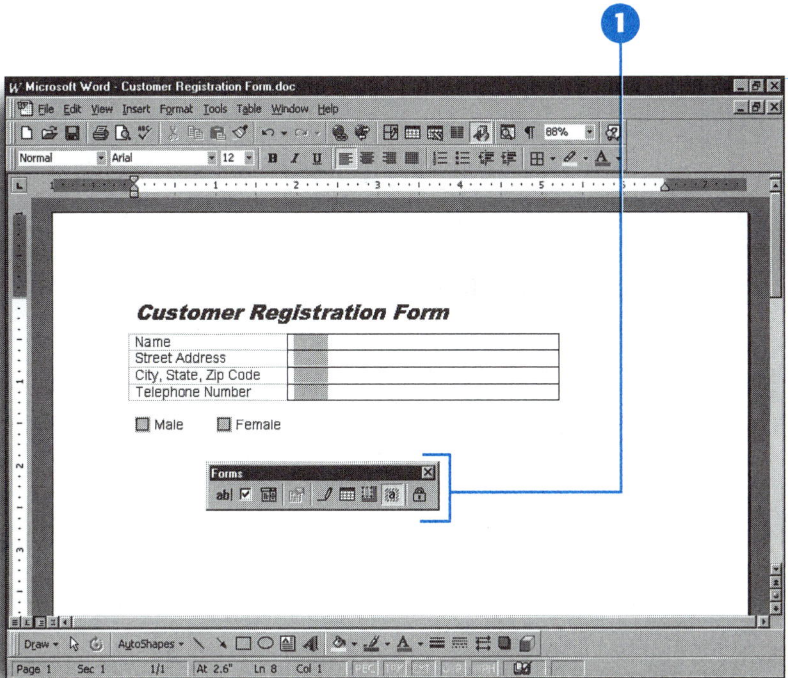

FIGURE 21.1

Tables help you organize the text on a form.

1 Forms toolbar

5. Save and print the form.

You now have a form you can duplicate so others can fill it in.

Create Online Forms

An *online form* is one filled out on the computer screen in Word or on the Web. Use online forms for registrations, customer orders, surveys, and evaluations, for example.

The online form is based on a template. After created, users fill in the form by opening a new document based on that template. The resulting form is saved as a document and the unaltered template can be used again to create new documents.

Consider using tables to create the form, as they help you organize the layout of form elements. The Forms toolbar has both the Draw Table and Insert Table buttons to help you create tables where you need them.

Create an online form

1. Open the **File** menu and select **New**. When the New dialog box appears, select the **General** tab if it's not already selected. Click the Blank Document icon.
2. Under **Create New**, select **Template** and choose **OK**.
3. Add the boilerplate text or graphics you want in your form (refer to the "Insert Text" section of this chapter for more information on adding boilerplate text).
4. Turn on the Forms toolbar by opening the **View** menu and selecting **Toolbars**, and then select **Forms**.
5. To add the fields you want the user to fill in, click in the document where you want the field to appear, and then insert the appropriate form field from the Forms toolbar (see the "Insert Fields" section later in this chapter for instructions on adding fields to your form).
6. After the form is complete, choose Protect Form on the Forms toolbar. When you protect the form, the users can enter information only in the form fields. They can't change any other part of the form. This also helps the user move from field to field quickly in the form (for more information, see "Protect Forms" later in this chapter).
7. Save and close the template.

SEE ALSO

➤ *To learn more about templates, see page 238*
➤ *To create tables, see page 280*

Warning! Boilerplate text can be changed

Unless you protect your form (see "Protect Forms" later in this chapter), users can change the boilerplate text and alter your template.

Insert Text

When you're building a form, it's generally easier to enter the boilerplate, or static information first. This includes the form title, instructional or explanatory text, labels for fields, and so on.

The Forms toolbar (refer to Figure 21.1) contains tools to help you create tables or isolate text from other text in the form:

- Draw Table lets you draw a table wherever you want it on the page.

- Insert Table inserts a table at your insertion point.
- Insert Rows appears on the Forms toolbar if your insertion point is in a table and replaces the Insert Table button. Choose Insert Rows to insert a row before the row where your insertion point is.
- Insert Frame creates a box (called a *frame*). Choose Insert Frame on the Forms toolbar and then drag a rectangle to specify the position, size, and shape of the frame (see Figure 21.2). Enter text or insert graphics inside the frame, add a border to the outside of the frame, or shade the interior of the frame. The frame can be moved to any location on the page by dragging it, and document text automatically wraps around the frame. When you click the frame to select it, tiny black boxes appear (called handles). Drag any of these handles to change the size or shape of the frame. Click the **Format** menu and select **Frame** to open the Frame dialog box and specify text wrapping, position, and size options for the frame.

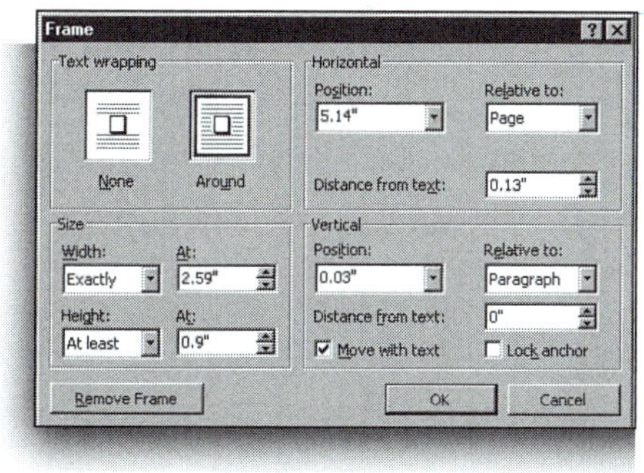

FIGURE 21.2
Specify options for the selected frame in the Frame dialog box.

SEE ALSO

➤ *To learn more about inserting, drawing, and formatting tables, see page 280*
➤ *For more information about wrapping text around a frame is available, see page 316*
➤ *To learn how to customize your toolbars and add an Insert Frame button, see page 527*

Insert Fields

Fields are placeholders for *variables* (information that may change in a document). Word has many different types of fields for different purposes. For example, when you insert page numbers, Word inserts a page number field in the document. Word adds a date field to your document when you click the **Insert** menu and select **Date and Time**. You learn more about date and time fields later in this chapter and more about page numbers later in this section.

You can't see the field codes in a document unless you click the **Tools** menu and select **Options**, then select the **View** tab, and click **Field Codes** under **Show** to enable the option. The field codes in a document appear between braces (curly brackets {}), as shown in Figure 21.3.

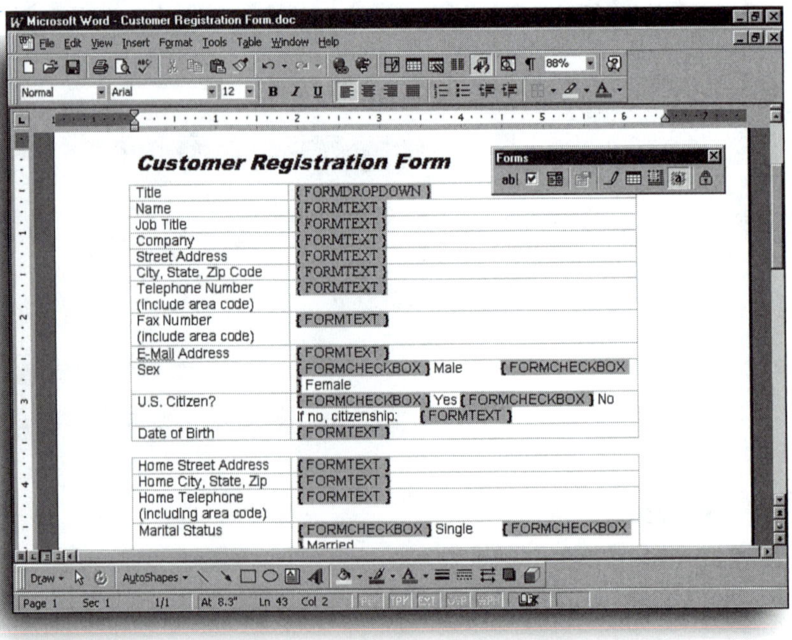

FIGURE 21.3
The field codes in this form appear with gray shaded backgrounds.

Forms have three special types of fields:

- *Text Form Field.* A fill-in field in which users insert text.
- *Check Box Form Field.* Puts a check box next to an option.
- *Drop-Down Form Field.* A drop-down list box from which users may select from one of several options.

To insert a field in your form, click where you want the field to appear and then click the appropriate button on the Forms toolbar.

You need to define the field options to determine how the field will work in your form. Each type of field has its own options. To set the options, double-click the field or choose Form Field Options on the Forms toolbar to open the Field Options dialog box for that particular type of field. Specify the options and then choose **OK**. You won't be able to see the full functionality of the form fields until you protect the document (see "Protect Documents").

For a Text Form field, you specify the type of text the user can enter in the field—regular text, numbers, date, time, calculation, and so on. You can enter the default text that appears in the field, set the maximum length of the field, or specify the format for the text, date, time, or numbers. Figure 21.4 shows the Text Form Field Options dialog box. Choose **OK** to accept your settings and close the dialog box.

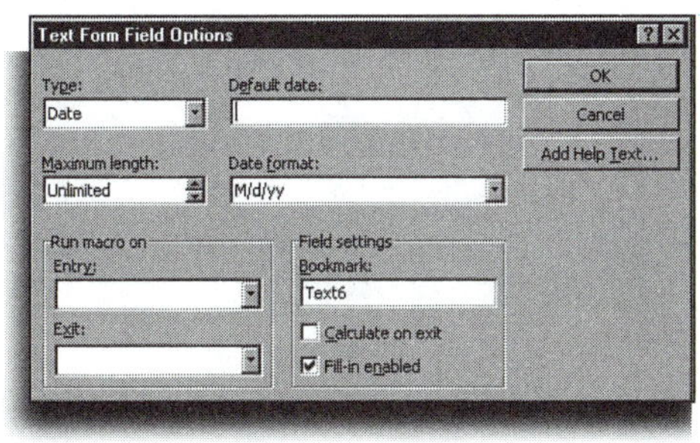

FIGURE 21.4
The options in the Text Form Field Options box are set for the Birthdate field on the form.

The options in the Text Form Field Options dialog box are set for the Birthdate field on the form. For a Check Box Form field, you specify the size of the check box and decide whether the box should be checked automatically when the user opens the document (the user can change that) by clicking **Not checked** or **Checked** under Default Value. Choose **OK** to accept your settings and close the dialog box. Figure 21.5 shows the Check Box Form Field Options dialog box.

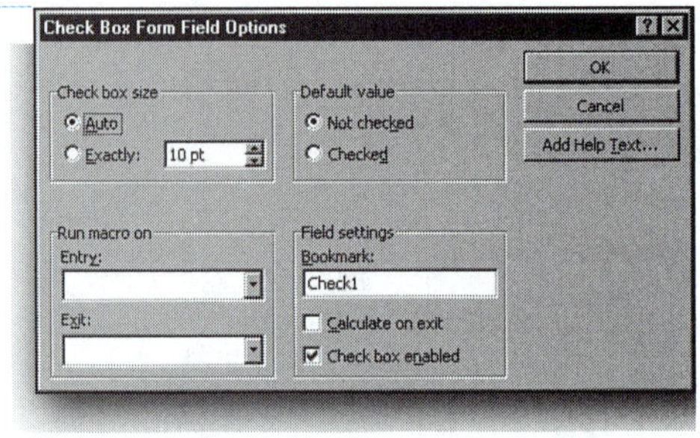

FIGURE 21.5
Set the size of the box and choose whether or not it should be checked by default.

The Drop-Down Form Field options let you add the list of options from which the user chooses, as shown in Figure 21.6. Enter an item for the list in the **Drop-down item** box and then click **Add** to add it to the list. Use the **Move** arrows to set the order of the items in the list. The first item in the list will be the default option in the drop-down box. Choose **OK** to accept your settings and close the dialog box.

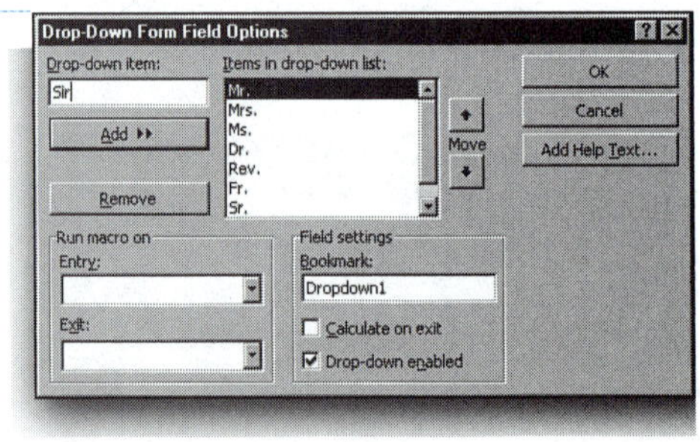

FIGURE 21.6
Create the list of items that appear when the user clicks on the field in the form.

When you select the options for the field, choose **Add Help Text** to enter information that guides the user in filling out the form (see Figure 21.7). On the **Status Bar** tab, click in the **Type your own** box and enter the text to appear on the status bar when the user clicks on the field. Alternately, click **AutoText**

entry and select the AutoText entry that acts as the help message (you must create the appropriate AutoText entry before opening this dialog box). On the **Help Key (F1)** tab, enter the text that appears when the user presses F1 for help on a field or select the appropriate AutoText entry. Choose **OK** to return to the Field Options dialog box.

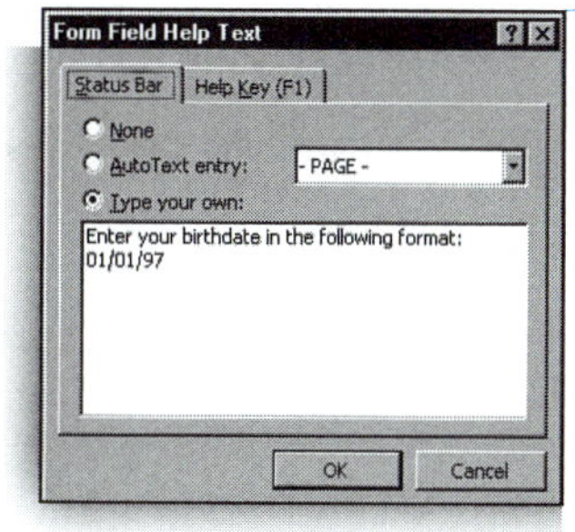

FIGURE 21.7
Enter instructions that you want the users to see on the status bar when they click the field.

To trigger a macro when users enter text in a field, or exit from a field, specify the macro name in the **Run macro on** area of the Field Options dialog box, in either the **Entry** or **Exit** box (depending on when you want to activate the macro).

To help the users of the form locate fields, turn the field shading on by choosing Form Field Shading on the Forms toolbar. Normally, the form field shading is on, in which case choosing Form Field Shading would turn the shading off.

SEE ALSO

➤ *For more information on fields and formatting fields, see page 410*
➤ *To learn how to create macros, see page 494*
➤ *To learn more about AutoText, see page 77*

Edit and Modify a Form

Modifying printed forms is easy—open the document, edit it, and save your changes.

Modifying online forms is a little more complicated. You must open and modify the template, removing any protection assigned to the template.

Modify an online form

1. Click the **File** menu and select **Open**, choose Open on the Standard toolbar, or press Ctrl+O. The Open dialog box appears. From the **Files of type** box, select **Document Templates (*.dot).**
2. In the **Look in** box, specify the drive and folder where the form template is stored (such as \Program Files\Microsoft Office\Templates\Other Documents). Select the template from the list of files and click **Open**.
3. If you protected the form when you created it (see "Protect Documents" later in this chapter), click the **Tools** menu and select **Unprotect Document.**
4. Make your changes to the form template.
5. Protect the form again before you save it by choosing Protect Form on the Forms toolbar or by clicking the **Tools** menu and selecting **Protect Document**, clicking **Forms**, and choosing **OK**.
6. Save and close the template.

You must close the form template before you can use it to fill out a form online.

SEE ALSO

➤ *To learn more about AutoText, see page* 77

Protect Documents

When you create a document that may be used by other people, you can restrict access to that document. Word enables you to create the following document and field protection:

- Require users to enter a password to open or edit a document
- Allow users to open the file in read-only mode
- Control data entry to fields by adding restrictions

Assign Passwords

Use password protection when documents contain sensitive material or you want to limit the number of people who are authorized to edit the document. Only those who know the password may open or edit the document.

Assign a password to a document

1. With the document open, click the **File** menu and select **Save As**. The Save As dialog box appears.
2. Choose **Options**. The Save dialog box appears (see Figure 21.8).

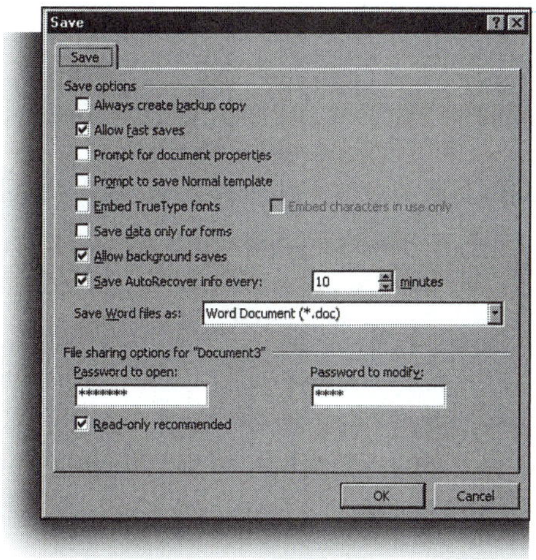

FIGURE 21.8
You enter passwords in the **File sharing** section of the Save dialog box.

3. To restrict who may open the document, enter the password you want to assign the document in the **Password to open** box. Passwords can be as many as 15 characters long and can include letters, numbers, symbols, and spaces. As you enter a password, only asterisks appear in the box. This keeps anyone from reading the password over your shoulder, but it also means you must type carefully to avoid misspellings.
4. People who know the "Open" password can open the document and read it. They can't necessarily make modifications to the document. To restrict who may edit the document, enter the password in the **Password to modify** box (you

may enter both passwords for any document). Only those people possessing this password may modify the document.

5. To prevent errors or changes in the original file, click **Read-only recommended** to enable that option. When a user opens the file, a recommendation displays a suggestion that they open the file as a read-only document. If that user makes changes, the user must save the file with a different name. The original is thus preserved. You can enable this option even if you don't set passwords for the document.
6. If you entered a password in the **Password to open** box, the Confirm Password dialog box appears when you choose **OK** (see Figure 21.9). Confirm the password by entering it again exactly as before (passwords are case-sensitive, so be sure to capitalize the password the same way as the original). The password appears as asterisks in the text box. Then choose **OK**.

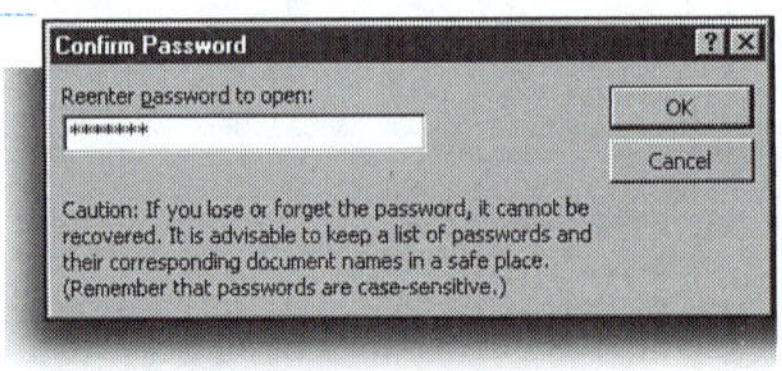

FIGURE 21.9
You must confirm the password you entered.

7. If you entered a password in the **Password to modify** box, the Confirm Password dialog box appears when you choose **OK**. Confirm the password by entering it again exactly as before and then choose **OK**.
8. Click **Save** to save the file with its password.

When anyone attempts to open the document, a dialog box appears requesting the password (see Figure 21.10). The user must enter the password exactly as you did when you created it. After a user enters the password correctly and chooses OK, the document opens.

Users are prompted to enter a password when they try to open the document if you enter a password to modify the document (see Figure 21.11).

FIGURE 21.10

You must enter a password to open a password-protected document.

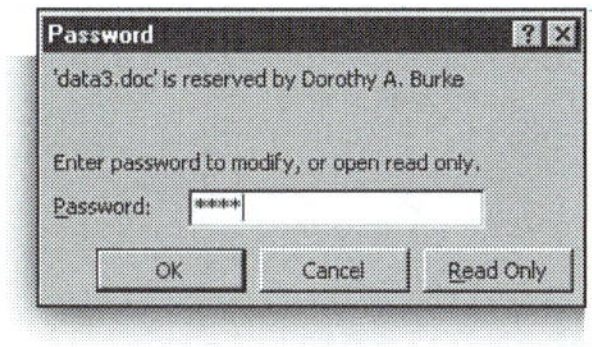

FIGURE 21.11

You must enter a password before you can edit a protected document.

Users who don't know the password can click **OK** and the document opens in read-only mode. Users who enter the correct password can make changes and save the modifications in the original file.

If you selected the **Read-only recommended** option when you saved the file, a dialog box appears (see Figure 21.12) when a user opens the document, recommending that the document be opened as read-only unless changes to it need to be saved. The user clicks **Yes** to open the file as read-only. After the document has been opened in read-only mode, the user must save it with a new filename to edit it.

SEE ALSO

➤ *To password protect files, see page 109*

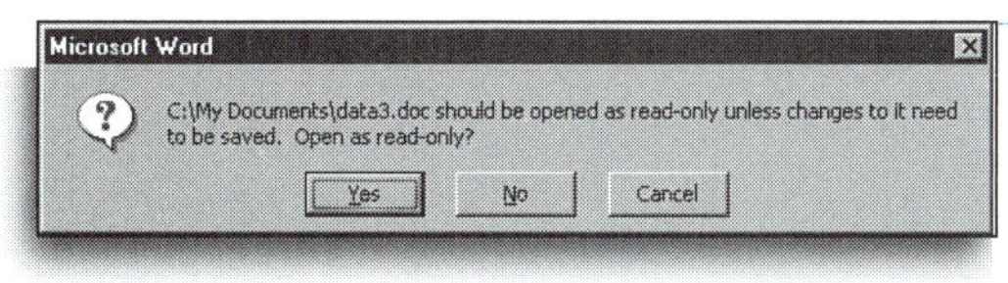

FIGURE 21.12

Click **Yes** to accept the recommendation that the file be opened as read-only.

Protect Forms

It's a good idea to restrict users to designated areas (sections) of a form so that they can't change your boilerplate text, graphics, headers or footers, page numbering, fields, and so on.

Protect a form

1. With your form document open, open the **Tools** menu and select **Protect Document**. The Protect Document dialog box appears (see Figure 21.13).

FIGURE 21.13
Choose **Forms** to restrict users to entering data in fields on the form.

2. Click **Forms**. This prevents changes to the form, except in form fields where the user is expected to enter data or in unprotected sections. If the document is divided into sections, specify which sections are to be protected by choosing **Sections** and selecting the sections you want to protect, as shown in Figure 21.14.

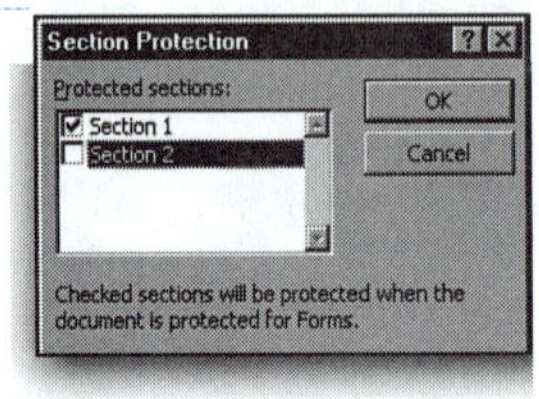

FIGURE 21.14
Designate the sections of your document to be protected.

3. Enter a password in the **Password** (Optional) box so only authorized users can remove the protection and change the form; otherwise any knowledgeable user can unprotect the document.
4. Choose **OK**.

SEE ALSO

➤ *To learn how to create sections, see page 178*

When users open a protected form, they may enter information only in unprotected fields and sections. For online forms, this simplifies data entry in addition to keeping unauthorized people from changing your form.

Fill In a Form

After the form template has been created, the form is ready for users to populate.

Fill in an online form:

1. Open the **File** menu and select **New**. In the New dialog box, select the appropriate tab and then click the icon for the form template you want to use. Select **Document** under **Create New** and choose **OK**.
2. Enter information in the form fields (see Figure 21.15). For check boxes, click to check the box or press X when the box is highlighted. For drop-down fields, click the down arrow next to the field to see the list of available items and then click the item you want. If you're unsure what to enter, check the Status bar or press F1 to see any help text on how to fill in the field.

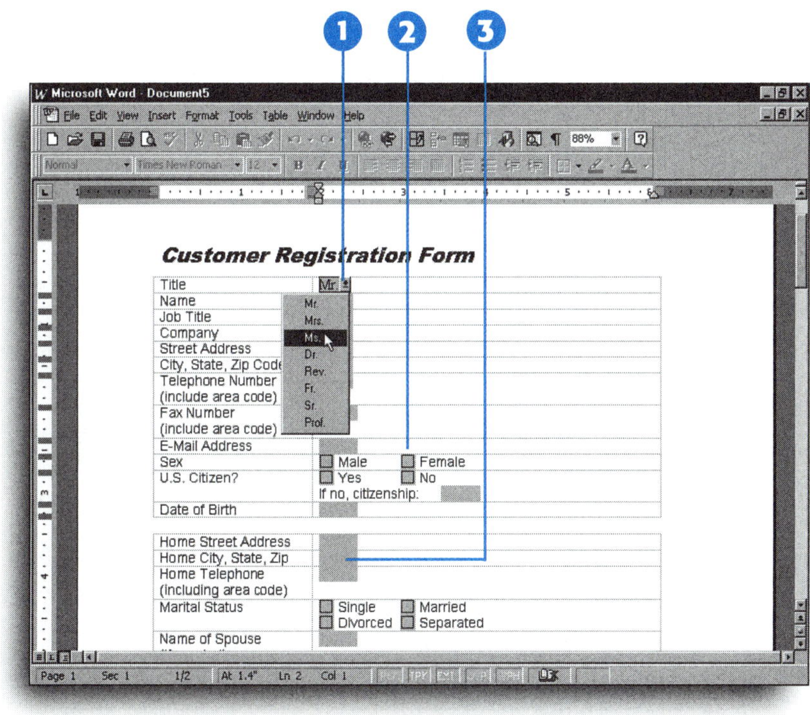

FIGURE 21.15

Use Tab, Shift+Tab, the arrow keys, or the mouse to move from field to field.

1. Drop-down form field
2. Check box form field
3. Text form field

Press Tab and Shift+Tab to move forward or backward through the fields. The arrow keys also help you navigate through the form.

3. When you have completed the form, save it.

After the file is saved, you can print it, fax it, or email it. If you're on a network with shared access to files, others can open the file and view it.

CHAPTER

22

Generate Internet and Intranet Documents

- Understand basic Internet and intranet terms
- Use Word to browse HTML or Word documents or Web pages
- Create your own HTML documents from Word
- Add links from your document to other locations, pages, or Web sites

Web and Internet Basics

The *Internet* is a worldwide conglomeration of computer networks. The Internet isn't owned and operated by any one company. It is one network of computers that can talk to another, and then in turn talk to another network of computers, and so on.

The *World Wide Web* (or just *Web*) is a component of the Internet. It's a collection of documents accessible through the Internet. These documents contain a special technology called *hypertext*. When you click your mouse on hypertext, you'll be taken to a new document or *Web page*, maybe even to a Web page on a different computer (or *Web site*). Web pages are read through programs called *Web browsers*, such as Internet Explorer or Netscape Navigator. The Web uses a type of address called a *uniform resource locator (URL)* (such as `www.microsoft.com`) to identify specific documents and locations.

Hypertext Markup Language (HTML) dictates how Web pages look and work. HTML is a collection of instructions, or tags, that tell a browser program how to display a document—when the text is bold, italic, and so on. A Web page has a series of tag entries such as <B> to turn on bold and </B> to turn off bold. Unfortunately, using these tags is complicated. Fortunately, Word saves you the pain of learning HTML by converting your documents to Web pages for you.

Intranet Basics

An *intranet* is your company's computer network working with software that serves HTML documents to Web browsers. Your company's network server handles all the data traffic of sending and receiving files. A Web server program on that computer tells the computer how to deal with requests and transmissions so any computer can communicate on an intranet, no matter what type of computer it is or what operating system it's using.

The individual workstations in the company have browser programs that receive the output from the Web server and translate the HTML code in the Web documents into a visible layout.

Browse HTML Files

Word can open documents on your company's intranet or at Internet sites, if you have a connection to the Internet. You must have a Web browser program, such as Internet Explorer or Netscape Navigator, installed on your computer. Word can open Web documents stored in HTML on your computer or network, as well as regular Word documents.

To preview your HTML pages in a Web browser program that you have installed on your computer, click the **File** menu and select **Web Page Preview** to open your browser program offline and view your page.

Use Word to browse when you want to preview the Web documents you are creating, view related documents, or test links. Having browser capabilities in Word saves you time.

Open a Web page or Word document and work with browser-like tools

1. Display the Web toolbar by choosing Web Toolbar on the Standard toolbar or by clicking the **View** menu and selecting **Toolbars**, and then selecting **Web** from the submenu.
2. Type the URL for the Web page or the filename and path in the Address box on the Web toolbar, such as `http://microsoft.com` or `http://www.dba.com/homepage.html` or `\\Server1\files\document.doc`.
3. Press Enter.

To open files or documents you've opened before, try one of these methods:

- The Address box maintains a list of recently visited Web sites and documents you opened. To revisit a site or open a document you recently visited, click the down arrow next to the Address box and select the site or document you want.
- If you opened the file or visited the Web page in this Word session, Word maintains a history of where you have been. This list also contains the names of Web pages and files you

viewed by following *hyperlinks*. Hyperlinks are the graphics or colored or underlined text you point to that jumps you to another location on the page, another page, or another Web site. To view a previously opened document, choose Back on the Web toolbar. To go to the next document in the history list, choose Forward on the Web toolbar.

- Make it easy to return to files or Web pages you visit frequently by adding them to your Favorites folder. Choose Favorites on the Web toolbar and click **Add to Favorites** to add the currently open document or Web page to the Favorites folder. To view one of the items you added to the Favorites folder, choose Favorites and choose **Open Favorites**. Then select the file and choose **Open**.

Being able to browse through files from Word gives you the opportunity to see how your own HTML documents look, as well as search out other documents to which you want to link.

Web pages versus Web site

Word does not create a Web site for you. It creates HTML documents, which may be home pages or Web pages after you turn them over to the Web site or network administrator. That person adds the pages to your Web site or includes them in the site on your company's intranet.

Create a Web Document

Word can convert any document to HTML format for use on the Web. You create the document, edit and format the text, and add graphics as you would with a document you intended to print (see Figure 22.1). When you save the file, Word adds the HTML codes required to produce the same or a similar appearance. However, HTML is somewhat limited in dealing with some layout and formatting commands, so your Web page may not look exactly like your document when you created it. You need to view the page on a browser to see the final output, as shown in Figure 22.2.

Formatting Differences

Here are some of the things you need to know about how your formatting will change:

- Whitespace automatically appears before and after paragraphs. Press Shift+Enter to create paragraphs without whitespace between them.

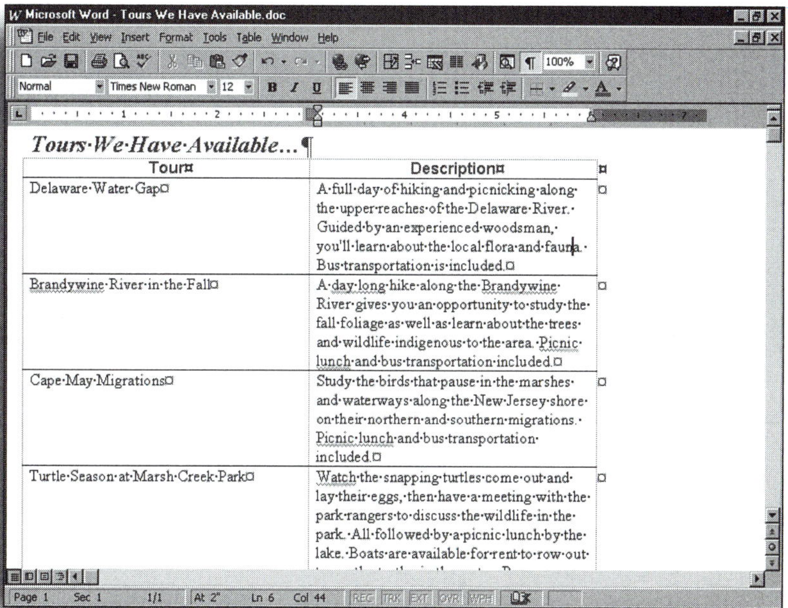

FIGURE 22.1

A word document prior to saving it as HTML.

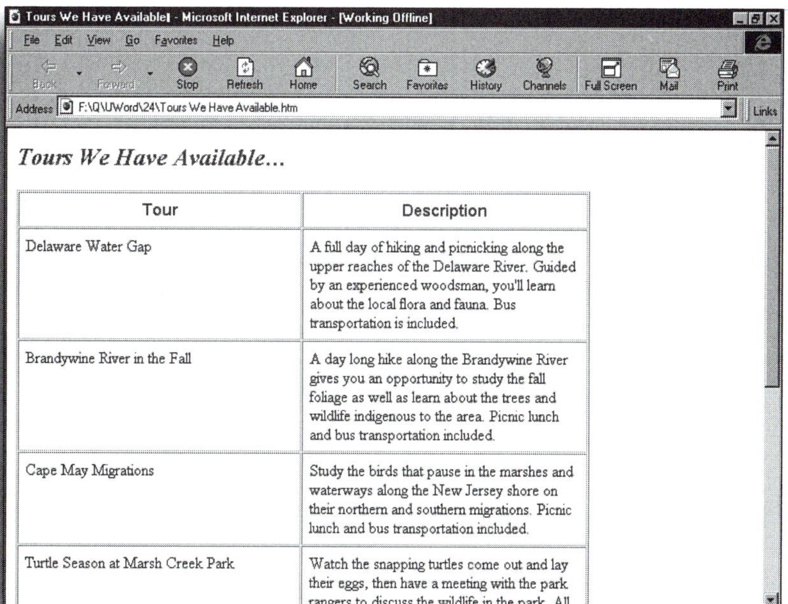

FIGURE 22.2

The HTML version of the document displayed in a browser.

- Text columns aren't supported. Use table columns instead.
- Tab settings aren't maintained. Use table columns instead of tabs. To shift the first line of text to the right, use an indent.
- Indents are supported by HTML.
- Text alignment is in relation to the width of the screen or the cell in a table. HTML doesn't support full justification.
- Bold, italic, underline, strikethrough, superscript, and subscript formats appear on Web pages, but emboss, text animation, all caps, small caps, outline, double strikethrough, shadow, and engrave do not.
- Settings for line spacing, margins, character spacing, kerning, text flow, and spacing before and after paragraphs are lost when the document is converted to HTML.
- Font sizes are limited to major sizes in HTML, so your setting may convert to the closest size. Also, you should keep in mind that people who view your Web pages might not have the same set of fonts you do. The browser converts an unknown font to its default font.
- Use font colors to liven up your page. They are supported in HTML.

Use the Web Page Wizard

A great way to start creating a Web page is to use the Web Page Wizard (see Figure 22.3) or the Blank Web Page template, both of which are available when you click the **File** menu and select **New**, and select the **Web Pages** tab in the New dialog box.

However, you can convert any Word document to an HTML document.

Save as HTML menu change

After you save a document as HTML, the **File** menu changes. **Save as HTML** is replaced by **Save as Word Document**.

Save a Word document as an HTML document

1. Open the **File** menu and choose **Save As HTML** to open the Save As HTML dialog box. HTML document is automatically selected as the **Save as type**.
2. Select the drive and folder where you want to store the file. Enter a filename (Word automatically adds the extension

"html" or "htm" to the filename) and choose **Save**. After you save the document, you will see that Word has inserted a field called {PRIVATE} at the top of the HTML document (see Figure 22.4). This field holds the data Word needs to convert the HTML document back to a Word document.

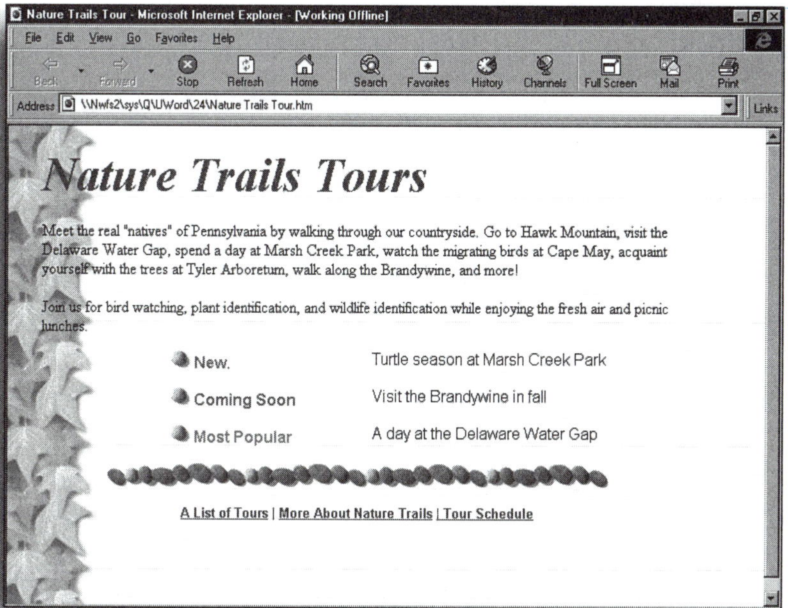

FIGURE 22.3
This home page was designed using the Web Page Wizard.

If you included graphics in your document, they will be saved as separate ***.gif** files in the same folder as your document. The files do not always have the same name as the original picture file, but might be called Image1.gif or Photo1.gif. Be sure to include these files when you copy your HTML to a disk or another network disk.

You might be prompted to access the Internet to check for a new version of Web authoring tools after you save the file as HTML. If you have an Internet connection from your computer, click **Yes** to get a newer set of tools. Click **No** if you don't want to go to the Internet at this time. To never be bothered by this dialog box again, check **Don't ask me again**.

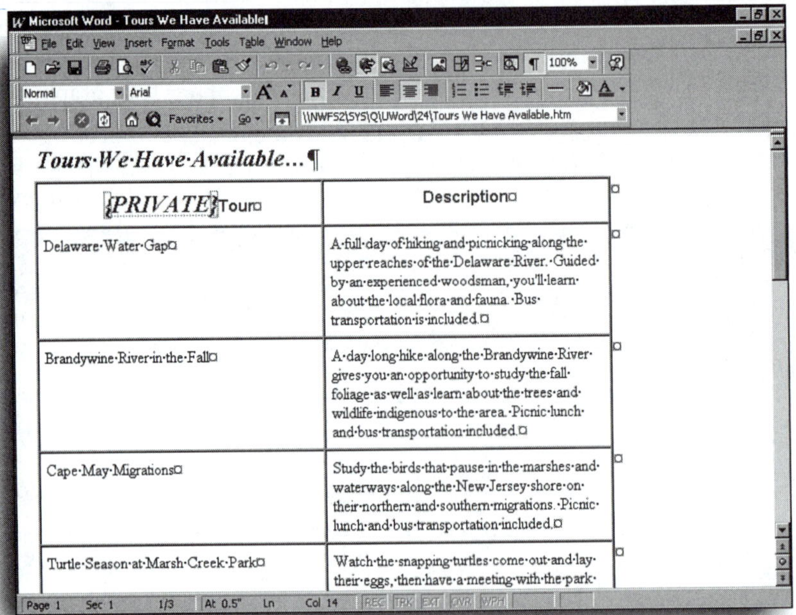

FIGURE 22.4

A {PRIVATE} field code appears after you save the file as an HTML document.

Previewing your Web page

If you have a Web browser such as Netscape Navigator or Internet Explorer, it's easy to preview your Web page as you're working on it. Choose Web Page Preview on the Standard toolbar (it won't be available if you haven't already saved your document as HTML). To switch back to Word, choose the Word icon on the Windows taskbar or close the browser.

If your company has a Web site, the manager of that Web site can add your document to the Web server and link it to other documents from your company. If not, store the file on your file server and others in the company can access it by entering its name and location in the address field of their Web browsers or in Address box on the Web toolbar.

When you have an HTML document open, there are three buttons on the Standard toolbar that directly relate to the creation of Web pages.

- Insert Hyperlink adds a hyperlink to your document (you must specify the destination file or URL for the link). See "Create Links" later in this chapter for more information.
- Web Toolbar displays or hides the Web toolbar.
- Web Page Preview, which only appears when the current document is in HTML format, opens your default Web browser and displays the current page.

Create Links

On Web pages, you see colored and underlined text or graphics that you click to go to another location on the current page, another Web page, an HTML page on the World Wide Web, or an HTML page on an intranet. The colored and underlined text or the graphic is called a *hyperlink*.

When the hyperlink consists of text, it's called a *hypertext link*. Hypertext links identify Web documents by their URL (uniform resource locator), such as `http://www.microsoft.com`.

On a Web page (see Figure 22.5), you identify a hypertext link by the following:

- The link text is a different color than the regular text and/or is underlined.
- When you point at the text with your mouse, the mouse pointer changes to a pointing hand.
- When you click a hypertext link, your Web browser automatically searches for and then displays the Web page to which the link points.

One way to have the text in your document marked as a hypertext link is to have Word automatically detect the text as you type and create the hypertext link in your document for you.

Set AutoFormat to create hyperlinks

1. Open the **Tools** menu and choose **AutoCorrect** on the menu.
2. When the AutoCorrect dialog box appears, select the **AutoFormat As You Type** tab (see Figure 22.6).
3. Under **Replace as you type**, click **Internet and network paths with hyperlinks** to enable that option.
4. Choose **OK**.

After activating this feature URLs (such as `http://www.microsoft.com`) automatically convert to hypertext links as you enter them in your document. This can be disconcerting, however, if you are writing about URLs in a document (such as providing a reference list of useful Web sites) and Word automatically changes them to hypertext links.

SEE ALSO

➤ *For more information on AutoCorrect, see page 77*

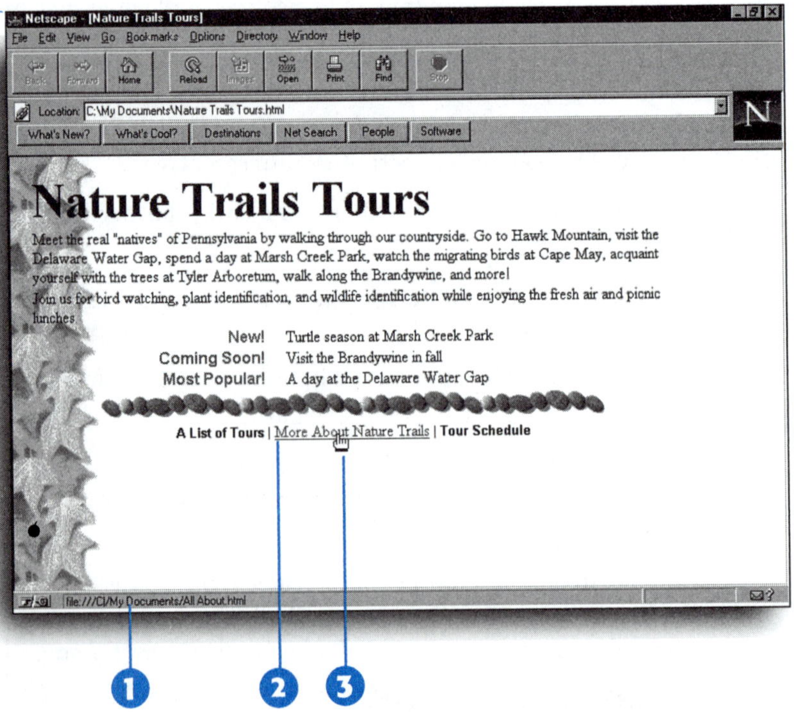

FIGURE 22.5
The mouse pointer changes to a pointing hand when it encounters a hypertext link.

1. The file referenced by the hypertext link.
2. Hypertext link
3. Mouse pointer

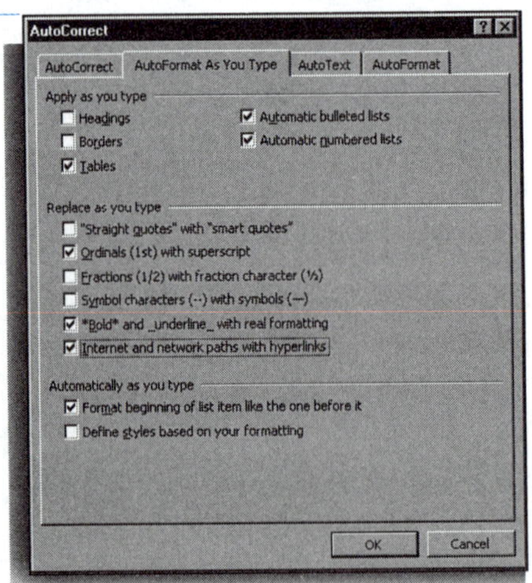

FIGURE 22.6
To have Word identify and automatically create hypertext links for you, check **Internet and network paths with hyperlinks**.

If you've elected not to have Word automatically create hyperlinks for you, you need to insert your links manually as you enter text.

Manually insert a hyperlink

1. Save your document.
2. Position your insertion point where you want to place the hyperlink if you want the URL address or path to appear in the document. If you want to turn existing text into a hyperlink, select the text.
3. Open the **Insert** menu and select **Hyperlink on** or choose Insert Hyperlink on the Standard toolbar. The Insert Hyperlink dialog box appears (see Figure 22.7).

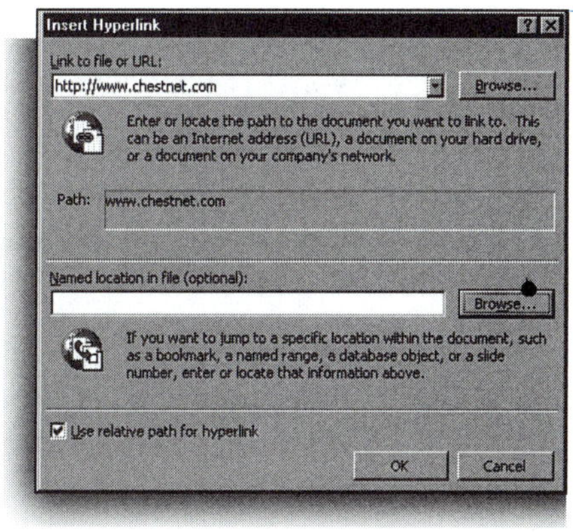

FIGURE 22.7
Enter the name and path (or URL) of the document or Web page you want to open.

4. In the **Link to file or URL** text box, enter the filename and path or the URL for the document or Web page to which you want to link. If you're not sure of the location or filename of a file on your computer or on your network, choose **Browse** and use the Link to File dialog box to locate the file.
5. To link to a specific location in the file (such as a bookmark, named range, database object, or slide number), enter the name in the **Named location in file (optional)** text box. Or, choose **Browse** to select from a list of locations that are available in the file you designated in step 4.
6. Choose **OK**.

This manual method of inserting hyperlinks gives you more control over where you place your hyperlinks and how they appear.

Edit a Web Document

Word can edit existing Web documents in HTML format. When you open an HTML document, it's converted into Word format. Then, when you save it after making any modifications, Word converts the document back into HTML.

The place to create Web pages

Although you can create Web pages in Word, it has some limitations. You may want to consider an alternative to Web page design in Word, such as using FrontPage. Programs like FrontPage have more flexibility in design, plus they include features meant exclusively for Web page design.

Edit an HTML document

1. Open the **File** menu and choose **Open** or click Open on the Standard toolbar. Select **HTML document from files of type**. Choose the location and then the file you want, and click **Open**.
2. Use Word's regular editing commands to make changes to the document.
3. Click the **File** menu and select **Save** or choose Save on the Standard toolbar. The document is automatically saved in HTML format.

You can now store the file on your company's file server for browsing by your coworkers as part of an intranet, or give the file to your Web site manager for loading on the Web server.

CHAPTER

23

Build Reference Documents

- Create and modify a master document to manage and bind several files into one
- Generate a table of contents
- Create an index
- Insert, display, and delete bookmarks

Navigating a long document

When working with long documents, you'll find Word's **Go To** command very useful. Open the **Edit** menu and select **Go To** (alternately, press F5). The Find and Replace dialog box appears. Click the **Go To** tab and indicate the page, section, bookmark, and so forth, that you want to go to. For more information on using the Find and Replace dialog box, see Chapter 4, "Use Proofing Tools."

About Master Documents

Working with long documents is cumbersome, particularly when several files created by several users need to be combined into one seamless report. For example, documents and reports such as annual reports, corporate policies, or employee handbooks are often the combined efforts of a team of people representing several departments. Each of these people creates a separate file for their contribution to the report from which a final product is generated. When the files are bound into one large report, the need for page numbers, headers and footers, a table of contents, an index, and consistent formatting becomes apparent (and often a headache) to the individual responsible for the final, printed version.

Word's solution to this problem is the *master document*, which acts as a binder for a set of separate files called *subdocuments*. The master document helps manage all the subdocuments that are its components. A master document can be managed by one person, or managed as a cooperative effort of many.

A master document contains links to separate files, which can be opened and edited while working in the master document, or individually outside of the master document. The master document manages the "big picture," keeping a total of page count, viewing all files as the sum of the whole, enabling you to create and work in a single file.

SEE ALSO

➤ *To learn how linking works, see page 335*

Create a New Master Document

Create a new master document

1. Start a new document.
2. Click the **View** menu and select **Master Document** to switch to the Master Document view. In Figure 23.1 you see the headings that are the beginning of an employee handbook. The Master Document view closely resembles an Outline view.

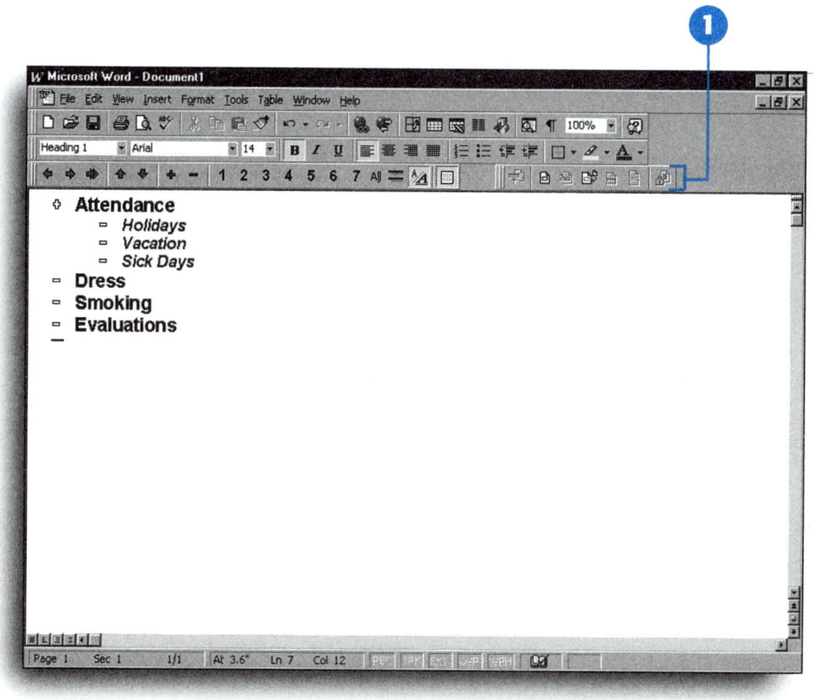

FIGURE 23.1

The seven headings in this document will become the titles of seven subdocuments in the master document.

1. Master Document toolbar

3. Create an outline for the master document to serve as the skeleton of the master document. Use Word's built-in heading styles (Heading 1, Heading 2, and so on) or use Promote and Demote on the Outlining toolbar to set the outline levels (Demote indents the heading to the right, Promote moves the heading to the left, while in Outline view).
4. Select the headings and text you want to divide into subdocuments. The first heading in the selection must be formatted with the heading style or outline level that you want to use to designate the beginning of each subdocument, such as Heading 1.
5. Choose Create Subdocument on the Master Document toolbar (see Figure 23.2).

FIGURE 23.2
Section breaks appear between the subdocuments in the master document.

❶ Subdocument icon

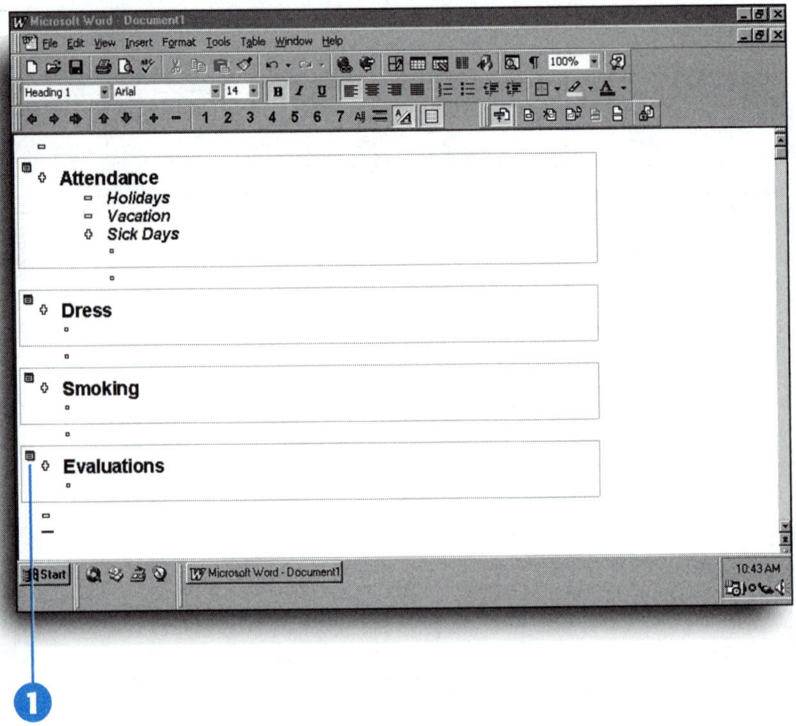

6. Save the master document by clicking the **File** menu and selecting **Save As** on the menu. When the Save As dialog box appears, select a location for the master document from the **Save in** drop-down list. Enter a name for the document in the **File name** box. Choose **Save**. Word assigns a filename for each subdocument based on the first characters in the heading for the subdocument. For example, in the employee handbook example illustrated in Figure 23.2, Word also saved four documents (Attendance.doc, Dress.doc, Smoking.doc, and Evaluations.doc) when the master document was saved as Employee Handbook.doc.

SEE ALSO

➤ *To learn more about creating outlines and using the Outlining toolbar, see page 206*

➤ *For more information on using styles, see page 158*

By default, subdocuments are collapsed (you only see the document names, as in Figure 23.3) when you open a master document. Choose Expand Subdocuments on the Master Document toolbar to see all the text in a subdocument. The same button becomes the Collapse Subdocuments button when the subdocuments are expanded.

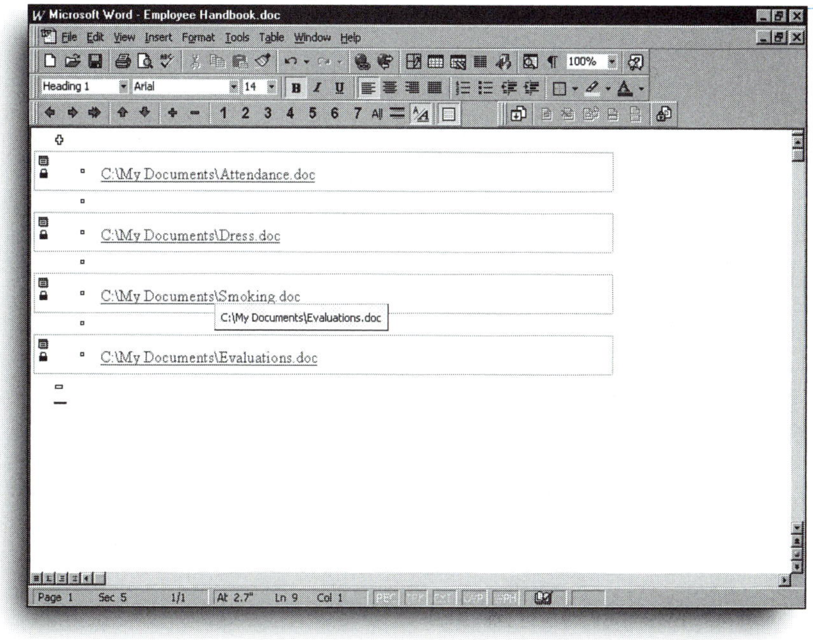

FIGURE 23.3
When the subdocuments are collapsed you see only the document names. The names are links–click the name to jump to that document.

To edit text or print a subdocument from within the master document, you need to expand the subdocument first.

After all the subdocument text in the master document is complete, add your headers and footers, a table of contents, and an index from the master document.

Create a Master Document from an Existing Document

What do you do when you've already started the document and realized that you should have created it as a master document? You convert the document into a master document.

Convert a document to a master document

1. Open the document you want to convert to a master document.
2. Click the **View** menu and select **Master Document** to open the Master Document view.
3. Apply Word's built-in heading styles or specify outline levels to set up the outline of the master document.
4. Select the headings and text you want to divide into subdocuments. Remember to format the first heading you select with the heading style or outline level that you want to use to designate the beginning of each subdocument.
5. Choose Create Subdocument on the Master Document toolbar.
6. Save the master document by clicking the **File** menu and selecting **Save As**. Enter a filename and location for the master document. Choose **Save**. Word assigns a filename for each subdocument based on the first characters in the heading for the subdocument.

After you've converted your document into a master document, you can insert or create subdocuments to add to it.

Edit and Modify Master Documents

Editing the text of a master document can be handled two ways: directly in the master document or from the subdocument files.

When you want to modify the text contained in a subdocument, you can open that file directly. For example, to change the employee handbook, you open Attendance.doc and make your changes there. Because the subdocument in the master document is only a pointer to this file, any modifications to Attendance.doc automatically appear in the master document after Attendance.doc is saved.

This capability to open the subdocuments as separate files is what makes it possible for several authors to work on the same master document simultaneously.

If you have the master document open and you would like to work directly in the subdocument file, double-click the subdocument icon at the top of that subdocument and the subdocument file opens. If the subdocuments are collapsed, the names of the subdocuments become hyperlinks to the subdocument files—click the name of the file, and the file opens. When you save the subdocument file, the modifications appear in the master document.

SEE ALSO

➤ *To learn more about hyperlinks, see page 457*

Add an Existing Document to the Master Document

To insert an existing document into the master document, see the steps that follow.

Insert a subdocument

1. Open the master document in the Master Document view.
2. Place your insertion point where you want to insert the existing document. This should be in a blank line between existing subdocuments.
3. Choose Insert Subdocument on the Master Document toolbar.
4. In the Insert Subdocument dialog box, select or enter the filename of the document you want to add. Choose **Open**.

Remove a Subdocument from the Master Document

At some point you may decide that one of the subdocuments in your master document does not need to be set up as a separate document. Its text can be incorporated into the master document. You usually do this when there is not sufficient text in the subdocument to warrant a separate file.

Remove a subdocument

1. Open the master document.
2. Select the subdocument you want to remove (click the subdocument icon).

Hyperlinks

Hyperlinks are specially marked text that jumps you to a specific address on the Web, to a specific file on your hard disk or network drive, or to a specific location in a document (such as a bookmark). In long documents, combining hyperlinks with bookmarks can help anyone reading the document online in navigating the document. You can create your own hyperlinks from text in your document by highlighting the text and then clicking Insert Hyperlink on the Standard toolbar.

3. Choose Remove Subdocument on the Master Document toolbar. Any text from that subdocument is incorporated into the master document.

If, instead of removing the separate subdocument and making its text part of the master document, you meant to totally remove the subdocument and its contents, you must *delete* the document and its text.

Create a Table of Contents

A *table of contents* lists all the main topics in your document and notes on which page number each topic starts.

Word helps you generate a table of contents for your document automatically. The easiest method for doing this is to assign one of Word's built-in heading styles (Heading 1 through Heading 9) to the headings you want to include in the table of contents. If you don't want to use Word's heading styles, you must assign a table of contents level to the styles you're using or mark text for inclusion in the table of contents.

Create a table of contents using Word's built-in heading styles

1. Apply the built-in heading styles Heading 1 through Heading 9 to the headings in your document that you want to include in the table of contents.
2. Place the insertion point in the document where you want the table of contents to appear. You may want to add a section or page break before your document text so the table of contents is on a separate page.
3. Click the **Insert** menu and select **Index and Tables**. The Index and Tables dialog box appears (see Figure 23.4).
4. Select the **Table of Contents** tab if it's not already selected.
5. From the **Formats** list, select the format that you want to apply to the table of contents. As you click a format, a sample appears in the **Preview** window.

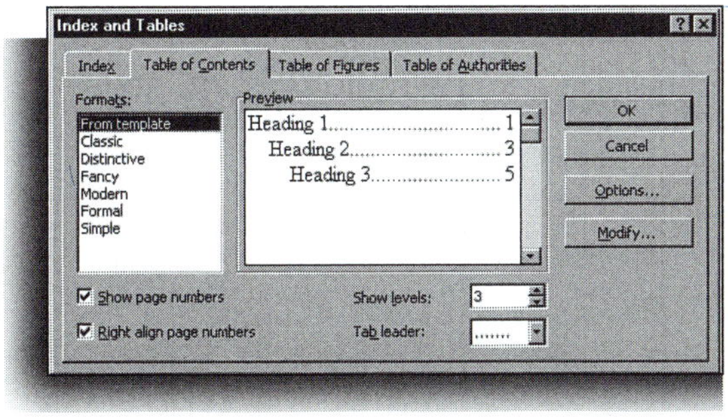

FIGURE 23.4

Select the format you want to use for your table of contents.

6. If you want the page numbers to appear for each topic, click **Show page numbers** to enable that option. Click **Right align page numbers** if you want the page numbers lined up on the right margin.
7. In the **Show levels** box, enter the number of heading levels you want to appear in the table of contents, or use the up and down arrows to select the number.
8. From the **Tab Leader** drop-down list, select the repeat character (leader) you want to appear between the heading and the page number (dots, dashes, or underscores). Select **None** if you don't want any leaders.
9. (Optional) If you want to change the format, choose **Modify** (only available if you selected **From Template** as the format) to open the Style dialog box (see Figure 23.5). From the **Styles** box, select the heading level you want to change in the table of contents and then choose **Modify** to open the Modify Style dialog box. Choose **Format** to select the type of format you want to specify and then select the formatting options you desire. Choose **OK** to return to the Style dialog box, and then choose **Apply**.
10. Choose **OK**. Word generates the table of contents for your document.

Don't include table of contents

When you're assigning styles to your headings, be careful not to assign a style to the heading of your table of contents. Otherwise, when you generate your table of contents, "Table of Contents" will be one of the entries.

SEE ALSO

➤ *To learn more about applying styles to document text, see page 159*

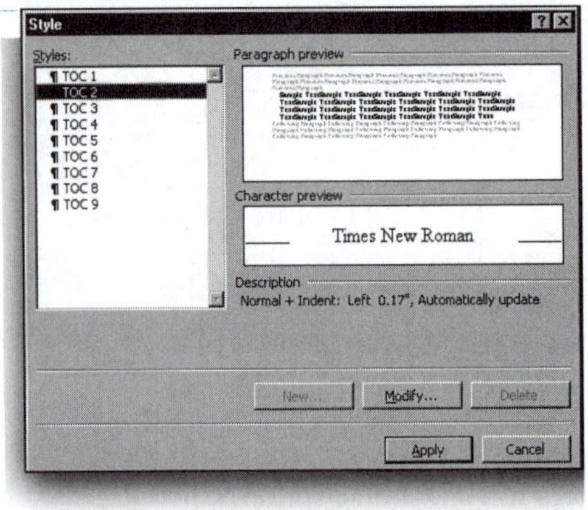

FIGURE 23.5

Select the table of contents style and level you want to change and then choose **Modify**.

Generate a Table Using Styles

If you don't want to use Word's built-in heading styles and would prefer to assign table of contents levels to the styles currently in the document, complete the following steps.

Create a table of contents using styles

1. Place the insertion point where you want the table of contents to appear.
2. Click the **Insert** menu and select **Index and Tables**. The Index and Tables dialog box appears (refer to Figure 23.5).
3. Select the **Table of Contents** tab if it's not already selected.
4. Choose **Options** to open the Table of Contents Options dialog box (see Figure 23.6). Click **Styles** to enable that option. Enter a number from 1 to 9 in the **TOC level** boxes across from the styles you want to assign to the table of contents. Choose **OK**.

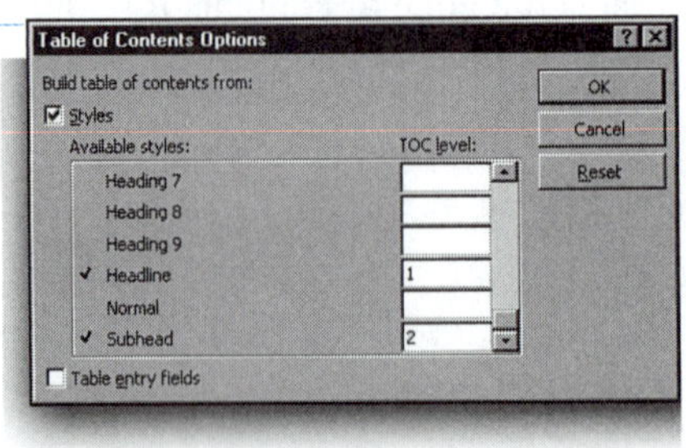

FIGURE 23.6

Put a table of contents level number next to each heading style you want to use to generate the table of contents.

5. Follow steps 5 through 10 of the "Create a table of contents using Word's built-in heading styles" section.

Mark Text for Table of Contents

Using styles is not the only method to indicate which text should appear in the table of contents. Table of contents entries can be marked by field codes, marking each entry as you type. Use this method if you have items you want to include in the table of contents, but those items do not have styles associated with them. You can use this method in combination with creating tables of contents using styles.

If a table already exists

When you insert a table of contents, Word will ask you if you want to replace the current table of contents (if one already exists). Click **Yes** to replace the current one; **No** to add a second one.

Mark entries for a table of contents

1. Place your insertion point immediately before the text you want to include in the contents.
2. Click the **Insert** menu and select **Field**. The Field dialog box appears (see Figure 23.7).

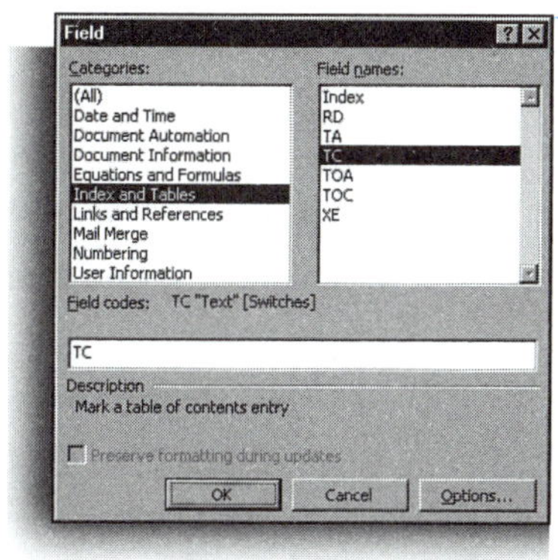

FIGURE 23.7

Select the **Index and Tables** category and then the **TC** field name. Then enter the remainder of the code in the **Field codes** box.

3. From the **Categories** list, select **Index and Tables**.
4. From the **Field names** list, select **TC**.
5. Following the "TC" in the **Field codes** box, enter the text that you want to appear in the table of contents. The text should be enclosed in double quotes.
6. Choose **OK**. A field code is inserted in the document text but is hidden. Choose Show/Hide ¶ [¶] on the Standard toolbar to see the code (see Figure 23.8).

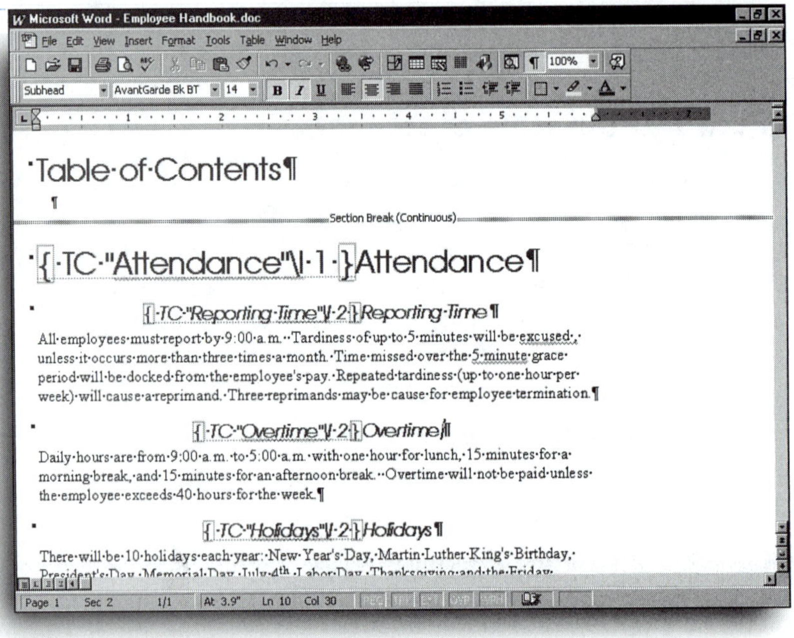

FIGURE 23.8

A code is inserted that marks the text for the table of contents.

Perform the following steps to generate a table of contents from your marked entries.

Generate a table of contents from marked entries

1. Place the insertion point where you want the table of contents to appear.
2. Click the **Insert** menu and select **Index and Tables**. The Index and Tables dialog box appears.
3. Select the **Table of Contents** tab if it's not already selected.
4. Choose **Options** to open the Table of Contents Options dialog box (see Figure 23.9). Click **Table entry fields**. Choose **OK** to return to the Index and Tables dialog box.
5. Choose **OK** to generate the table of contents.

Update and Delete a Table of Contents

The table of contents does not automatically change when you make changes to the heading text in your document or you add or delete text. Although it's possible to edit the text within the table of contents, any changes won't match your document text. You need to refresh the table of contents.

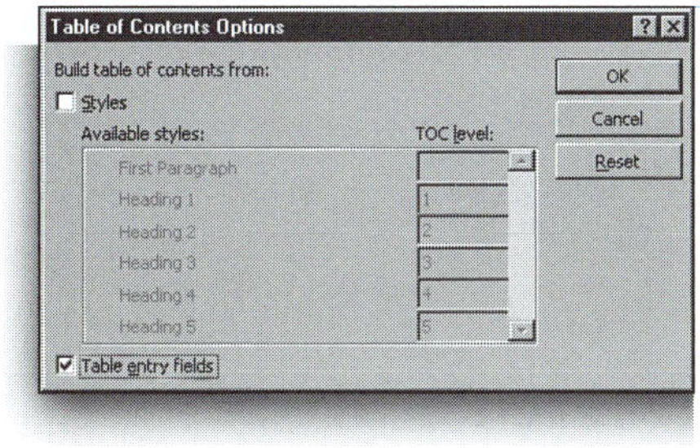

FIGURE 23.9
Enable the **Table entry fields** option to generate a table of contents based on fields.

Update a table of contents

1. Click in the table of contents.
2. Press F9, or right-click the table of contents and click **Update Field** from the shortcut menu. The Update Table of Contents dialog box appears (see Figure 23.10).

FIGURE 23.10
Choose to update only the page numbers or the entire text.

3. Click **Update page numbers only** if you've only moved text around or added or deleted body text. Click **Update entire table** if you've added or deleted headings or if you changed the style of some of the headings.
4. Choose **OK**.

Perform the following steps to remove a table of contents.

Remove a table of contents

1. Click in the table of contents.
2. Press Shift+F9 if you don't see a field code (or click the right-mouse button and select **Toggle Field Codes**). The code would look something like:

```
{ TOC \o "1-3" }
```

3. Select the field code, including the brackets {}, and press the Delete key.

If you're not familiar with field codes and your table of contents isn't lengthy, try this instead: select the text of the entire table of contents (the text appears white in a gray field) and then press the Delete key.

SEE ALSO

➤ *To learn more about field codes, see page 444*

Create an Index

An *index* is a listing that usually appears at the end of the book. The listing is a set of topics covered in the document along with the pages on which the topics are mentioned. The topics are generally listed in alphabetical order.

You start by indicating which words, phrases, or symbols you want to include in the index for your document by "marking" them. Then you choose an index design and generate the finished index. To make the index, Word collects all the index entries, sorts them alphabetically, references their page numbers, finds and removes duplicate entries from the same page, and displays the index.

Mark Text for Index

To create a topic and page reference in your index, you must mark the words or phrases you want to appear in the index so Word will know what and where they are in your document.

Perform the following steps to mark an index entry.

Quick index marking

A quick way to open the Mark Index Entry dialog box is to select the text you want to mark for the index and press Alt+Shift+X.

Mark index entries

1. Select the text that you want for the index entry.
2. Click the **Insert** menu and select **Index and Tables** to open the Index and Tables dialog box.
3. Select the **Index** tab (see Figure 23.11).
4. Choose **Mark Entry**. The Mark Index Entry dialog box appears (see Figure 23.12).

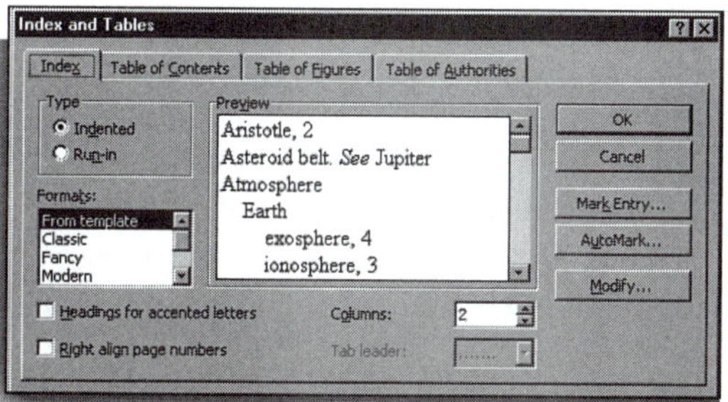

FIGURE 23.11

Select the style of index you want for your document.

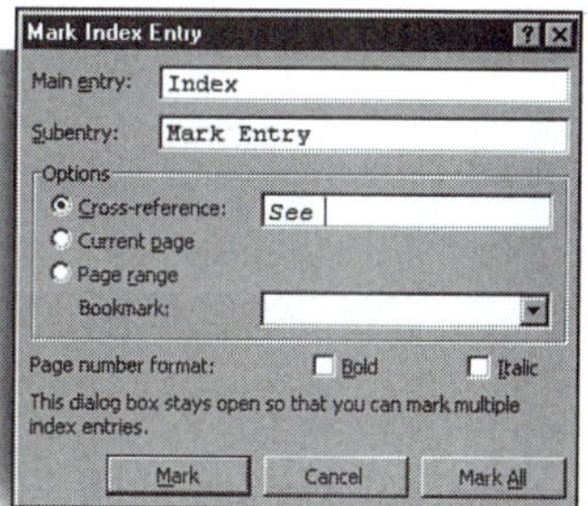

FIGURE 23.12

Specify the text for the index entry.

5. The selected text appears in the **Main entry** box. Edit that text or enter new text if the selected text is not exactly what you want to display in the index.
6. Under Options, click **Current page** as the page number you want cited in the index. If you want to add formatting to the page numbers as they appear in the index, click **Bold** or **Italic** under **Page number format**.
7. Choose **Mark** to mark the entry. Choose **Mark All** to mark the first occurrence in each paragraph of your document that exactly matches the text and case of the entry.
8. The dialog box remains open so you may make additional index entries. To make another entry, click in the document to make it active, then select the text in the document or click immediately after it, click back in the Mark Index Entry dialog box to make it active, and repeat steps 5 through 7.

9. Repeat step 7 for each index entry you want to make in this session. Choose **Close** to close the Mark Index Entry dialog box.

Word marks each index entry by inserting a field immediately after the entry text in your document (see Figure 23.13). If the field isn't visible, choose Show/Hide ¶ [¶] on the Standard toolbar.

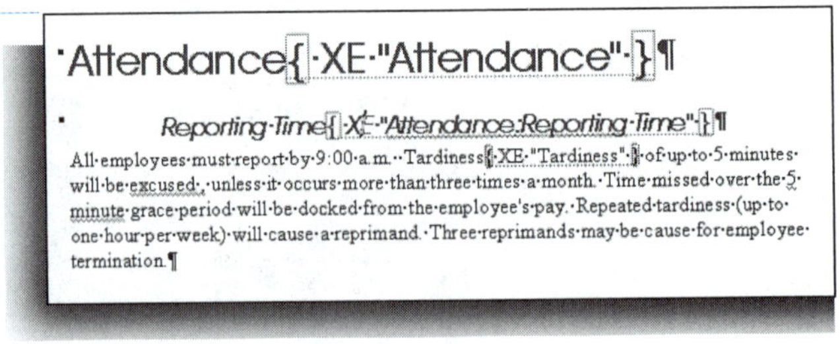
·Attendance{·XE·"Attendance"·}¶

Reporting·Time{·XE·"Attendance:Reporting·Time"·}¶

All·employees·must·report·by·9:00·a.m.··Tardiness{·XE·"Tardiness"·}·of·up·to·5·minutes·will·be·excused·,·unless·it·occurs·more·than·three·times·a·month.·Time·missed·over·the·5·minute·grace·period·will·be·docked·from·the·employee's·pay.·Repeated·tardiness·(up·to·one·hour·per·week)·will·cause·a·reprimand.·Three·reprimands·may·be·cause·for·employee·termination.¶

FIGURE 23.13
A field appears after the text you marked for the index.

Use a Concordance File

An alternative to marking each index entry in your document is to use a concordance file. A *concordance file* is an index file with two columns—the first column lists the text in the document that you want to index, and the second column lists the index entries to generate from the text in the first column. You use the concordance file to automatically search your document and mark all the matching entries for the index. With a large document, this can save you considerable time in building an index.

Create a concordance file

1. Start a new file.
2. Create a two-column table.
3. Enter the words or phrases that you want to mark as index entries in the first column of the table. Because Word will search your document for all the occurrences of this text, you must enter it exactly as it appears in the document. To be sure, make a separate row for all forms of the text you want to search (such as search, searching, searched, searches). Press Tab to move to the second column.

4. Type the text for the main index entry as it will appear in the index. To create a subentry, follow the main entry text with a colon (:) and then the subentry text. Press Tab to go to the next row.

5. Repeat steps 3 and 4 until you've entered all the reference information (see Figure 23.14).

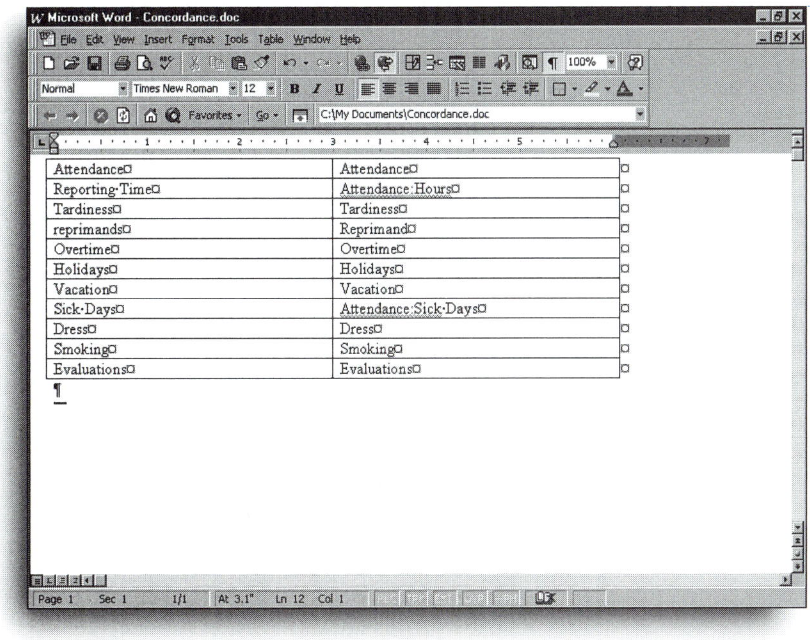

FIGURE 23.14
A concordance file consists of a two-column table with text to be indexed in the left column and index entries in the right column.

6. Save the concordance file.

To be sure you get the correct entries and to avoid typing each one, use the copy and paste commands. Open both the concordance file and the document you're indexing at the same time. Click the **Window** menu and select **Arrange All** to see both documents. Copy the text from the document and paste it into the first column of the concordance file.

After you have a concordance file, perform the following steps to use it to automatically mark your index entries.

Mark index entries using a concordance file

1. With the document you want to index open, click the **Insert** menu and select **Index and Tables**.
2. Select the **Index** tab.
3. Choose **AutoMark**. The Open Index AutoMark File dialog box appears.
4. Select the file you want to use as the concordance file or enter the name in the **File name** box.
5. Choose **Open**. Word searches the document text for each text entry you made in the first column of the concordance file. For each exact match found, Word inserts an index entry field with the text from the second column of the concordance file as the index entry text.

Add Index Cross-References

Terms that are synonyms or that may be fully referenced under another topic generally have a "See topic" or "See also topic" reference in an index. These are index cross-references.

Create a cross-reference for an index entry

1. Select the text for which you want to create an index entry.
2. Press Alt+Shift+X to open the Mark Index Entry dialog box (see Figure 23.15).

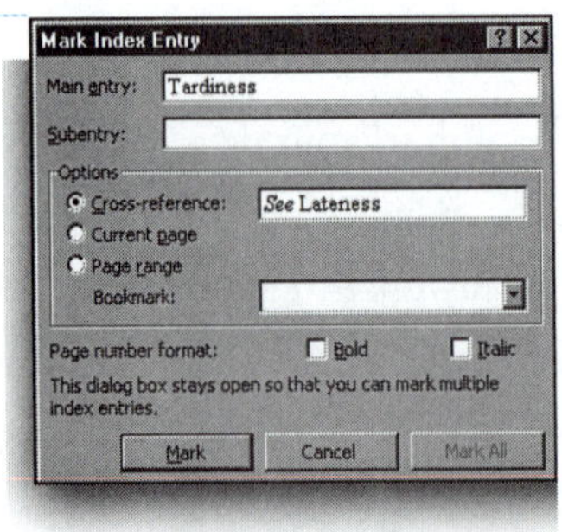

FIGURE 23.15
Enter the cross-reference text and then choose **Mark**.

3. Under **Options**, click **Cross-reference**.
4. Enter the text you want to use as a cross-reference after the word "See."

5. Choose **Mark**.
6. Choose **Close** to close the dialog box.

Modify or Delete Index Entries

Word marks each index entry by inserting a field immediately after the entry text in your document. If the field isn't visible, choose Show/Hide ¶ [¶] on the Standard toolbar. The field is similar to the entry for the phrase "Attendance" you see in Figure 23.19 as:

{ XE "Attendance" }

If you want to delete an index entry, select the field that follows the index text in your document (including the {} brackets), and then press the Delete key.

To change the text or formatting of an index entry, you must also work with the index entry field. Click inside the quotation marks and edit the text, or select the text inside the quotes and then make your formatting choices.

Generate an Index

After you have all the index entries marked in your document, you're ready to generate the index. You may want to insert a section or page break at the end of the document where you want the index to start so it begins on a new page.

Generate an index

1. Put your insertion point at the location in your document where you want the index to appear.
2. Click the **Insert** menu and select **Index and Tables**. When the Index and Tables dialog box appears, select the **Index** tab (see Figure 23.16).
3. Under **Type**, click **Indented** or **Run-in**. An indented index lists the subentries as indented paragraphs under the main topic. A run-in index lists all the subentries in a single paragraph, separated by semi-colons. When you choose a type, a sample appears in the **Preview** window.

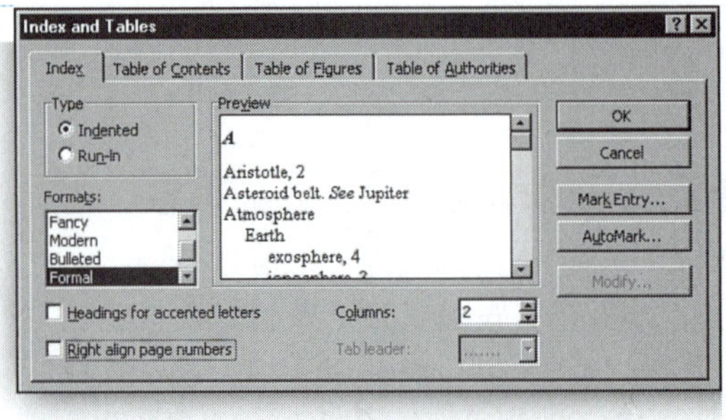

FIGURE 23.16

Select the type and format of the index and then click **OK**.

4. To choose from the predefined index formats available in Word, select one from the **Formats** list. When you do, the **Preview** changes to show you an example of that format.
5. If the format you selected has letter of the alphabet headings, click **Headings for accented letters** to encompass any non-English words that may begin with accented letters.
6. Because the index can be lengthy but the lines are short, you may want to set it up to run in columns. Enter the number of columns you want in the **Columns** box.
7. Page numbers in an index generally follow immediately after the topics. If you would rather have your numbers appear on the right side of the line, click **Right align page numbers**. Choose a character from the **Tab Leader** drop-down list if you want to join the entry text with the page number by a tab leader.
8. Choose **OK** to generate the index.

Update and Delete an Index

After your index is in place, you might need to update it to reflect additions or deletions in your text or new index entries. To update the index, click in the index and then press F9.

To remove the entire index from your document, perform the steps that follow.

Remove an index

1. Click in the index.

2. Select the index field code including the {} brackets (press Shift+F9 if you can't see the code).
3. Press the Delete key.

If you're not familiar with field codes and your index isn't lengthy, try this instead: select the text of the entire index (the text is white in a gray field) and then press the Delete key.

Incorporate Cross-References

A *cross-reference* refers you to another part of the document or to another document where there is more information on the topic being discussed. Word enables you to create different types of cross-references—numbered items, headings, bookmarks, footnotes and endnotes, equations, figures, listings, and tables.

Create a cross-reference

1. Enter the beginning text for the cross-reference, such as "For more information on this topic, see."
2. Click the **Insert** menu and select **Cross-reference**. The Cross-reference dialog box appears (see Figure 23.17).

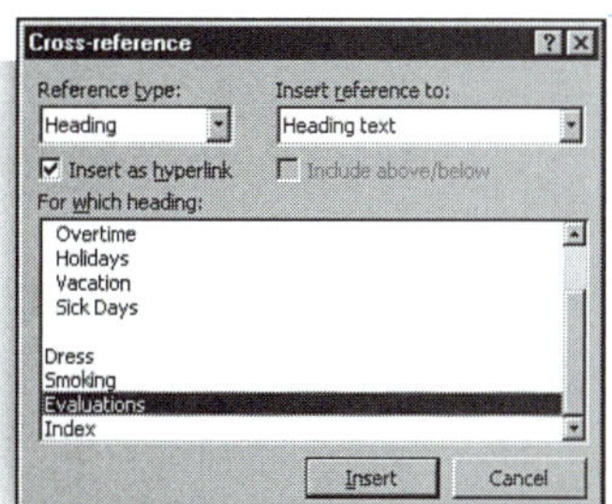

FIGURE 23.17
Select the type of cross-reference you want.

3. From the **Reference type** drop-down list, select the type of item to which you want to refer—numbered items, headings (must be Word styles Heading 1, Heading 2, and so on), bookmarks, footnotes and endnotes, equations, figures, listings, or tables.
4. From the **Insert reference to** drop-down list, select the type of reference you want inserted in the document.

5. In the **For which heading** box, click the item to which you want to refer. If no items appear, you may need to select a different type of reference.
6. If you're preparing a document that will be used online, click **Insert as hyperlink**. The reader will then be able to click the cross-reference and then jump to the place to which you referred.
7. Choose **Insert**.
8. The reference is inserted but the dialog box remains open to allow you to create additional cross-references. To close the dialog box, choose **Close**.

SEE ALSO

➤ *To learn more about hyperlinks, see page 463*

Modify or Delete a Cross-Reference

Modify a cross-reference

1. Select the cross-reference in the document. Do not include the introductory text, such as "For more information, see."
2. Click the **Insert** menu and select **Cross-reference**.
3. From the **Insert Reference to** box, select the new item to which you want to refer.
4. In the **For which heading** box click the item to which you want to refer.
5. Choose **Insert** and then choose **Close**.

To delete a cross-reference, select the entire cross-reference in the document including the introductory text. Then press the Delete key.

Use Bookmarks

A *bookmark* is a location in your document or a selection of text that you name for reference purposes. After you place a bookmark, you can return to the same location again and again by selecting the bookmark when you use Word's **Go To** feature (press Ctrl+G or F5). Bookmarks are especially useful when you're modifying or editing a large document. Create a bookmark when you close the document so on opening it again, you can find where you left off. Bookmarks are also useful as reference points for cross-references, index entries, and macros.

To add a bookmark

1. Place your insertion point where you want to insert the bookmark.
2. Click the **Insert** menu and select **Bookmark** to open the Bookmark dialog box (see Figure 23.18).

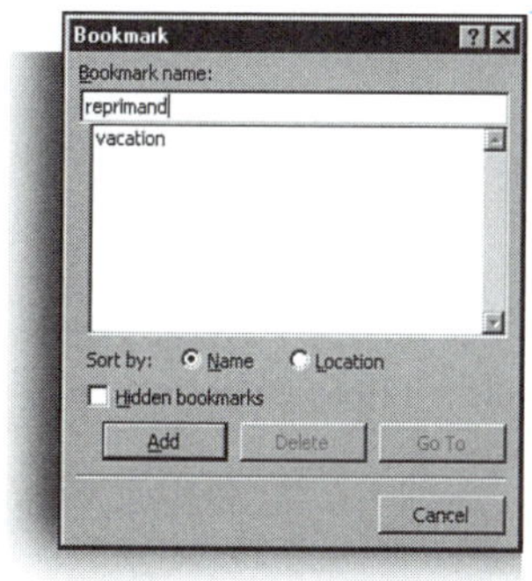

FIGURE 23.18
Type the name of the bookmark and click **Add**.

3. Type a name for the bookmark in the **Bookmark name** box (don't enter any spaces in the name) or select one from the list. If you select the name of an existing bookmark, it will move the bookmark location to the current position of your insertion point.
4. Choose **Add**.

Displaying Bookmarks

Bookmarks are not normally visible in your document. They appear in square brackets ([ ]). To see the bookmarks in your document, complete the following steps.

Display bookmarks

1. Click the **Tools** menu and select **Options**.
2. Select the **View** tab.

3. Under **Show**, click **Bookmarks**.
4. Choose **OK**.

Deleting a Bookmark

Delete a bookmark

1. Click the **Insert** menu and select **Bookmark**.
2. Select the name of the bookmark you want to remove.
3. Choose **Delete**.
4. Choose **Close**.

PART

VII

Automate and Customize

CHAPTER

24

Write Simple Macros

Record, test, and run macros

Edit macros

Write a macro to create templates

Understand Macros

Repetitive tasks involving several steps are prime candidates for macros. A *macro* is a set of commands and instructions that is recorded and played back when you command it to run. By creating a macro to perform the steps of a repetitive task, you save yourself time and avoid possible errors.

What could you do with a macro? You could make a macro to perform routine editing or formatting, to combine several commands so you can access them with one keyboard shortcut, to use an option without having to go through one or more dialog boxes, or to automate a complicated set of tasks.

Macro viruses

Macros can be carriers for computer viruses. When you open a document that has a macro virus your computer becomes infected. The macro virus is stored in your Normal template and infects every document you create based on that template. Other users who open those documents become infected also. Word can't protect you from macro viruses, although it issues a warning every time you open a document with macros, and gives you the opportunity to open it without macros. To avoid spreading viruses through your own macros and documents, use up-to-date antivirus software to keep your system clean.

Word has two methods for creating macros—the *macro recorder* or the *Visual Basic Editor*. The recorder acts almost like a tape recorder, noting each command and set of instructions you use in doing a task so it can play back those commands and instructions the next time you ask for them. Word records these commands and instructions for a macro in Visual Basic for Applications programming language. Using the Visual Basic Editor, you modify the instructions or create more flexible and powerful macros.

Because you have to be able to access the macro after you create it, Word allows you to assign the macro to a toolbar, a menu command, or shortcut keys.

The macro is stored, by default, in the Normal template for use in every Word document. However, you may want to store specific macros in the templates where they would be most useful.

SEE ALSO

➤ *To learn about macro viruses and templates, see page 239*

Record a Macro

Recording macros is similar to making a tape recording of all the steps you perform to do a particular task. However, the macro recorder has some limitations. You can't use the mouse to move the insertion point because the macro recorder doesn't record mouse movements. Instead of using the mouse to select, copy, or move items by clicking or dragging, you must use the keyboard. However, any mouse movements that activate menus, buttons, and commands are recorded.

Here are some tips to keep in mind when working with macros:

- Always plan the steps you want to include in the macro before you start recording. You might even want to run through the task once to be sure what commands you use; write them down if it's a complicated task. Although you can correct a mistake as you're recording, the error and the correction will become part of the macro. You'll have to go back later and edit the macro to remove any unnecessary steps.
- Think ahead to avoid unnecessary steps in the macro. A different order or different method might be cleaner and faster, or prevent having to set up conditions or open an additional dialog box. For example, using the **Find** command is a great way to position your insertion point at a particular phrase, but the Find dialog box retains its last entries. If the last setting was to search up or down, the macro may stop when it reaches the beginning or end of the document. Instead, you should include in the macro a step to change the Search setting to **All**.
- If the macro will be used in many types of documents, don't include anything that is specific to the document you have open when you create the macro.
- Whenever you create a macro it's a good idea to assign it to a toolbar button, a menu, or a shortcut key so you don't have to open the Macro dialog box every time you want to use the macro.

Record a macro

1. Open the **Tools** menu and choose **Macro**, then select **Record New Macro** from the submenu. The Record Macro dialog box appears (see Figure 24.1).

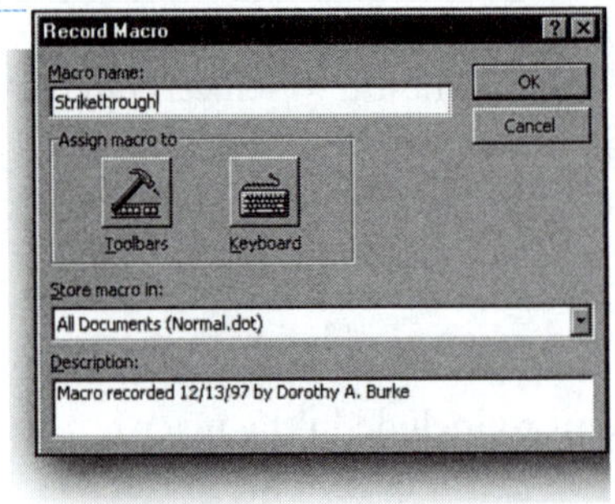

FIGURE 24.1
Enter a name for the new macro and then choose whether you'll assign it to a toolbar or keyboard shortcut.

Built-in macros

The templates Macros8.dot and Support8.dot contain macros you can copy into your documents or global template for your own use, such as TableCellHelper, that display the column and row of a table cell in the status bar.

2. In the **Macro name** box, type a name for the macro you're about to record. The name must begin with a letter and can contain as many as 80 letters and numbers, but it can't include spaces or symbols. If the **OK** button is grayed out (unavailable), the macro name isn't valid. Be careful not to give the macro the same name as an existing, built-in macro in Word because the new macro actions will replace the existing actions for the built-in macro.
3. From the **Store macro in** drop-down list, select the template or document in which you want to store the macro. **All Documents (Normal.dot)** is the default setting.
4. Type a description for the macro in the **Description** box. Word automatically enters the date the macro was recorded and who recorded it.
5. To assign the macro to a toolbar or menu, choose **Toolbars** (see the "Assigning a macro to a toolbar" steps for full instructions). To create a keyboard shortcut to activate the macro, click **Keyboard** (see the "Assigning a keyboard shortcut to a macro" steps for instructions).

   After you've assigned a macro to a toolbar or menu and you want to create a keyboard shortcut, choose **Keyboard** in the Customize dialog box to open the Customize Keyboard dialog box. Then choose **Close** to return to the Customize dialog box.
6. If you aren't assigning the macro to a toolbar, menu, or keyboard shortcut—or after you have assigned the macro to a toolbar or keyboard shortcut—choose **OK** to begin recording the macro.

7. The Stop Recording toolbar appears, and your mouse pointer changes to resemble a tape cassette with a pointer. Do the steps, choose the commands, and enter the instructions to perform the task for which you're creating the macro. The macro recorder records them as you do them (see Figure 24.2).

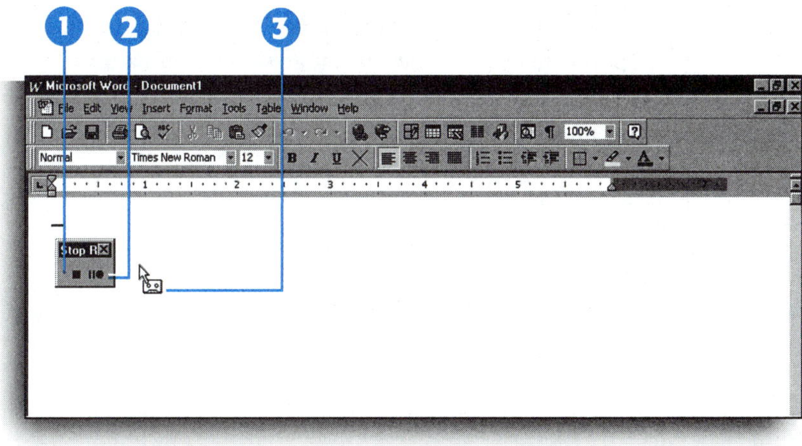

FIGURE 24.2
The Stop Recording toolbar appears on your screen, and your mouse pointer has a little cassette tape attached to let you know that everything you do is being recorded.

1. Stop Recording
2. Pause Recording
3. Mouse pointer when recording macro

8. You can pause the macro recorder and then resume recording where you stopped. To pause the recorder, choose Pause Recording on the Stop Recording toolbar. Choose that same button again to resume recording. The pause is not recorded as part of the macro.
9. When the task is finished and you want to stop recording, choose Stop Recording on the Stop Recording toolbar.

Assigning a macro to a toolbar

1. When you click the **Toolbar** button while creating a macro (see the preceding procedure), the Customize dialog box appears (see Figure 24.3).
2. Select the name of the macro you're recording from the **Commands** box.

3. Drag the macro name to the toolbar or menu to which you want to assign it. As you drag it onto the toolbar, a thick black vertical line appears indicating where the button will appear when you release the mouse button; when you drag it to a menu, a black horizontal line indicates where the command will appear when you release the mouse button.
4. If you assigned the macro to a toolbar, choose **Modify Selection** in the Customize dialog box to display a menu with options that allow you to change the button name (click **Name**, edit the name, and then press **Enter**). To pick a button image (click **Change Button Image** to pick a picture from the submenu or click **Edit Button Image** and draw a symbol).
5. Choose **Close** to close the Customize dialog box and begin recording the macro.

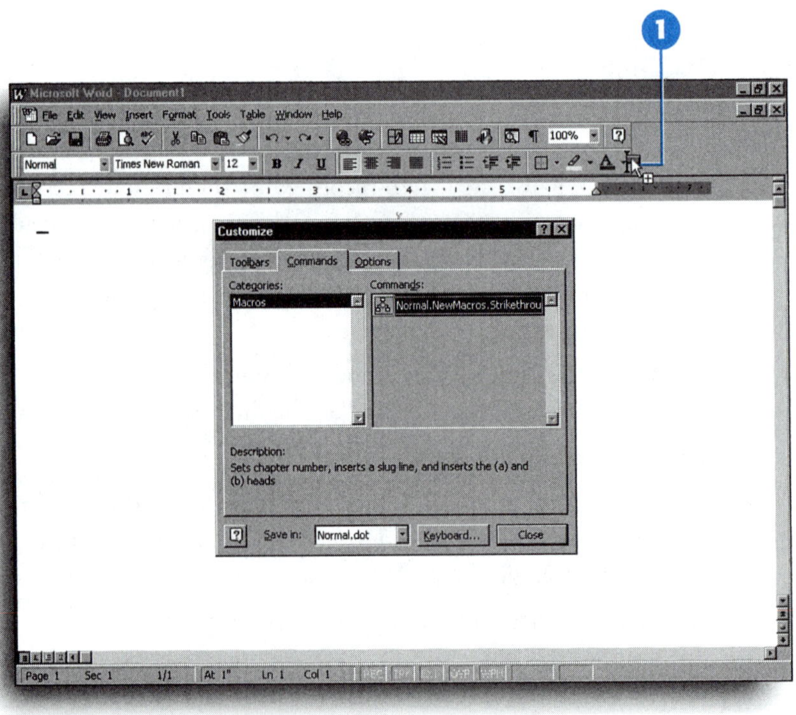

FIGURE 24.3
When you drag the macro name to a toolbar, a thick vertical line appears showing where the button will be displayed when you release the mouse button.

1 Vertical line

Assigning a keyboard shortcut to a macro

1. When you click the **Keyboard** button while creating a macro (see step 5 of the recording macros procedure), the Customize Keyboard dialog box appears (see Figure 24.4).
2. Select the name of the macro you're recording from the **Commands** box.
3. Type the key sequence you want to use as the keyboard shortcut in the **Press new shortcut key** box. If the text below the box says the key combination is `[unassigned]`, choose **Assign**; if the key combination is assigned to another task, delete it and try another combination.
4. Choose **Close** to begin recording the macro.

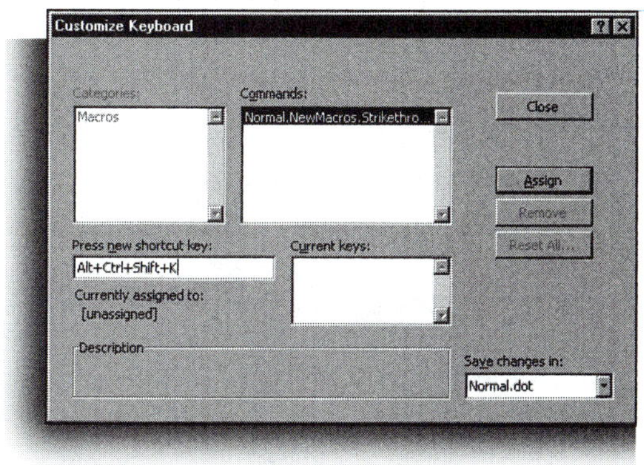

FIGURE 24.4
Enter the key combination you want to use as the keyboard shortcut.

SEE ALSO

➤ *To customize toolbars, see page 527*
➤ *To create keyboard shortcuts, see page 535*

Test a Macro

After you finish creating your macro, test it out a few times. Vary the circumstances to make sure it works in all conditions. If you have problems, edit the macro to fix it.

Here are some tips when testing your macro:

- Work with files or text that will not be permanently injured if your macro doesn't work correctly. Or, make a copy of the file you want the macro to work with and give the file another name so the original file is protected.
- If you assigned the macro to more than one method—keyboard shortcut, toolbar, or menu—test all the methods to make sure it works equally well in all situations.
- Open a new file (one that uses the same template where you stored the macro) and test the macro there.
- Make sure your macro works when you change the situation. For example, if your macro applies a font attribute, make sure it works when you are using another font. It may always change your font to the one you were using when you recorded the macro.
- If your macro doesn't work properly, note what it isn't doing the way you want it to.

Run a Macro

To run a macro after you've created it, do one of the following:

- Click the button you added to the toolbar.
- Choose the menu and command you added to the menu.
- Press the key combination you created as the keyboard shortcut.
- Click the **Tools** menu and select **Macro**, then select **Macros** from the submenu. The Macros dialog box appears (see Figure 24.5). Select the name of the macro you want to use and then choose **Run**.
- Press Alt+F8, and the Macros dialog box appears. Select the name of the macro you want to use and then choose **Run**.

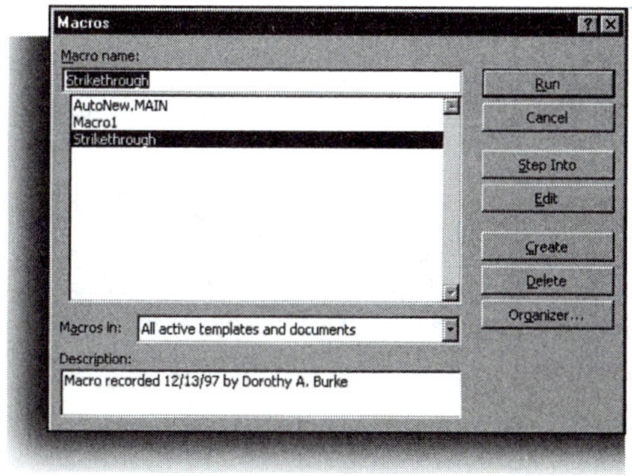

FIGURE 24.5
Select the name of the macro and choose **Run**.

Edit a Macro

If you need to change or remove a step in your macro, you have two choices: either record the macro again from the start or open the Visual Basic Editor and modify the macro.

Edit a macro

1. Open the **Tools** menu and select **Macro,** then select **Macros** from the submenu. The Macros dialog box appears (refer to Figure 24.5).
2. From the **Macro name** box, select the name of the macro you want to edit.
3. Choose **Edit**. The Microsoft Visual Basic window opens (see Figure 24.6).
4. Make the necessary changes in the **Code** window (some suggestions follow these steps). You can scroll through all your macros in this window, so be sure you are in the correct macro before making changes.
5. Click the **File** menu and select **Close** and **Return to Microsoft Word** after you complete your modifications.
6. Test your macro to see that your changes worked.

After the Microsoft Visual Basic window is open, the individual lines of code involved in the macro appear in the **Code** window on the right of the screen. Although it's helpful to have a knowledge of the Visual Basic programming language and how it works (especially if you want to add steps and conditional statements), there are some simple things you can do to the macro code to correct or adjust the steps you recorded.

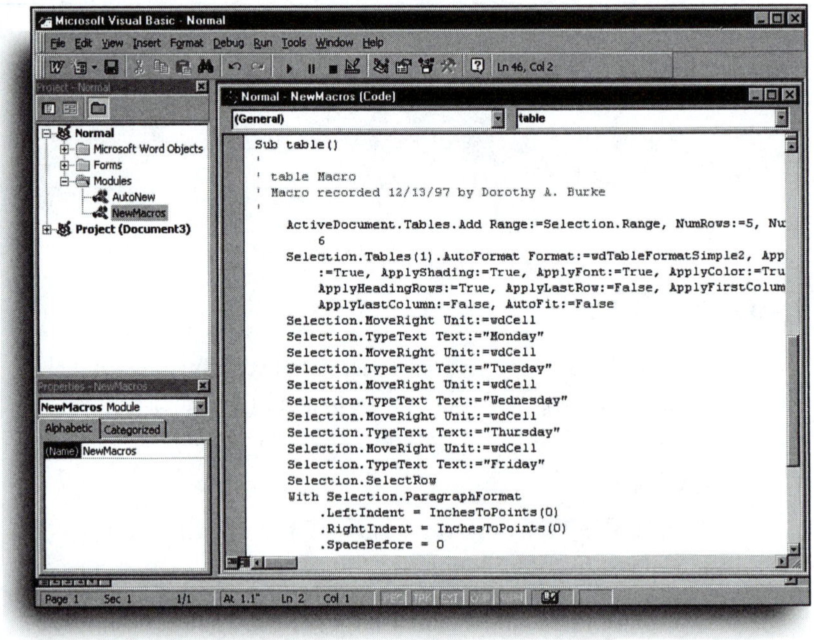

FIGURE 24.6
The macro being edited is designed to create a table with the days of the week as the headings.

One adjustment you can make to increase the speed and efficiency of your macro is to remove unnecessary lines of code. For example, when you record a macro that selects an option from a dialog box, the macro recorder records all the settings in the dialog box. You should remove the unnecessary ones from the recorded macro by deleting those lines of code.

The following lines of code are for a recorded macro that changes the selected text to the color blue:

```
Sub BlueText()
'
' BlueText Macro
' Macro recorded July 30, 1997 by Dorothy Burke
'
With Selection.Font
.Name = "Courier"
.Size = 12
```

```
.Bold = False
.Italic = False
.Underline = wdUnderlineNone
.StrikeThrough = False
.DoubleStrikeThrough = False
.Outline = False
.Emboss = False
.Shadow = False
.Hidden = False
.SmallCaps = False
.AllCaps = False
.ColorIndex = wdBlue
.Engrave = False
.Superscript = False
.Subscript = False
.Spacing = 0
.Scaling = 100
.Position = 0
.Kerning = 0
.Animation = wdAnimationNone
End With
End Sub
```

Several lines of code that are unnecessary to the macro can be deleted. The macro could be as simple as:

```
Sub BlueText()
'
' BlueText Macro
' Macro recorded July 30, 1997 by Dorothy Burke
'
    With Selection.Font
         .ColorIndex = wdBlue
End With
End Sub
```

You could even change wdBlue to wdGreen to change blue text to green text.

For more information on using Visual Basic with Word macros, open the **Help** menu and choose **Contents** and **Index**. Select the **Contents** tab and then select the **Microsoft Word Visual Basic Reference** topic. (This reference may not have been installed when you installed Word, so you may not have a copy on your computer. You will have to install it from the Word setup CD or disks.)

Copy, Rename, and Delete a Macro

Deleting a macro can be done from the Macros dialog box; however, you will still have to remove the menu commands and toolbar buttons you assigned to the macro—they remain but they won't work without the macro.

Delete a macro

1. Open the **Tools** menu and choose **Macro**, then select **Macros** from the submenu to open the Macros dialog box (refer to Figure 24.5).
2. From the **Macro name** box, select the name of the macro you want to delete.
3. Choose **Delete**.
4. When Word asks for a confirmation that you want to delete that macro, choose **Yes**.
5. Choose **Close** to close the Macros dialog box.
6. To remove the toolbar buttons and menu commands you assigned to the macro, open the **View** menu and choose **Toolbars**, and then select **Customize** from the submenu. When the Customize dialog box appears, drag the button for the macro from the toolbar on the screen or the macro menu command from the menu.

SEE ALSO

➤ *To learn more about customizing toolbars and menus, see page 527*

Copying a macro to another document or template, renaming a macro, or deleting a macro can all be done from the Organizer. You reach the Organizer through the Macros dialog box, by completing the steps that follow.

Copy, rename, or delete a macro

1. Open the **Tools** menu and choose **Macro**, and then select **Macros** to open the Macros dialog box.

2. Choose **Organizer**.
3. The Organizer dialog box appears with the **Macro Project Items** tab selected (see Figure 24.7).

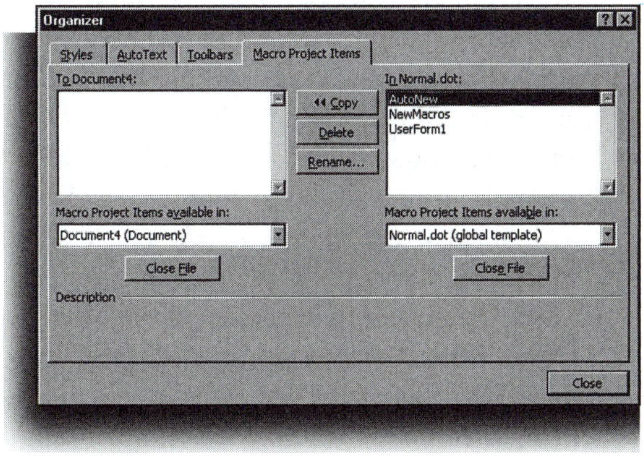

FIGURE 24.7
Use the Organizer to copy, delete, or rename macros.

4. The two boxes in the dialog box are the **In Normal.dot** box on the right that displays the macros in the Normal document template and the **To Document** ***x*** box on the left that displays the macros used in the document you have open. From either list, select the macro you want to copy, rename, or delete.

   If the macro is in another template that's attached to the current document, select that template from the **Macro Project Items available in** drop-down list on the right.

   If the document you want isn't listed, choose **Close File** and then choose **Open File**. Select the file you want to use and then click **Open**. The file's macros will appear in that box.
5. Click the appropriate button for the action you want to perform:
   - **Copy** copies the macro from one box to the other, thus copying it from the Normal template to the current document or vice versa, depending on where the macro was stored.
   - **Delete** deletes the selected macro (to delete more than one macro, hold down the Ctrl key and click each one you want to delete before choosing **Delete**).

- **Rename** opens the Rename dialog box. Enter the **New name** for the macro and choose **OK**.

6. Choose **Close**.

Word supplies a set of useful macros for you. The Macros8.dot template contains macros that you may find useful in your daily work or as samples to review and modify. The macros include one to find the ANSI value for a selected character, another to add the Symbol dialog box to the find and replace function. There is also one to insert footnotes in the Chicago Manual of Style format, and another to add a header and footer view pane to the Normal view. To use the macros, click the **File** menu and select **Open**, and then change to the Microsoft Office\Office\Macros folder. From the **Files of type** drop-down list, select **All Files**. Then double-click the Macros8.dot filename. Run the macros you want and then copy any you need to other documents using the Organizer.

Create a Template Containing Macros

Although macros can be attached to a document, they are a powerful tool when combined with templates. They can automate the task of completing documents created with a template and are particularly useful when working with online forms.

When you create a template for an online form, you insert fields on that form. Any macro in the form template can run automatically when the insertion point enters or exits a form field.

Create a template containing macros

1. Create the macros that you want to include in your new template. Create or open the form template that you want to automate.
2. If protection has been applied to the form, choose Protect Form on the Forms toolbar or click the **Tools** menu and select **Unprotect Document**.
3. Create the macros you want to use in the template and store them in the template.

4. Add the form fields you need in the template.
5. For each form field to which you want to attach a macro, double-click the form field to see the Field Options dialog box (this box differs slightly depending on the type of field you're working on).
6. Under **Run macro on** (see Figure 24.8), select the macro you want to use with that field from the **Entry** drop-down list (if you want the macro to run when the insertion point enters the field) or from the **Exit** drop-down list (if you want the macro to run when the insertion point exits the field).

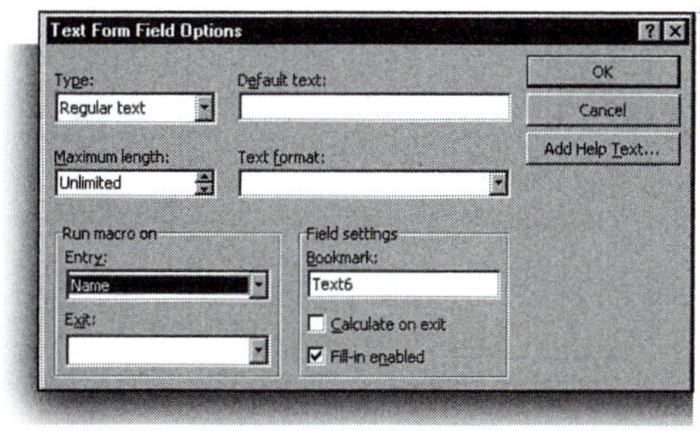

FIGURE 24.8
The Name macro automatically enters the user name when the user clicks in that field.

7. Choose **OK**.

Test the template to see that your macros work properly when you use the template to create new documents.

SEE ALSO

➤ *To learn more about creating templates, see page 249*
➤ *To learn more about designing forms, see page 440*

CHAPTER

25

Real-World Solutions

- Create and send a fax using the Fax Wizard
- Design a newsletter with the Newsletter Wizard
- Create a résumé with the Résumé Wizard
- Create custom letterhead
- Create business cards
- Create a memo
- Perform a mail merge

How to use this chapter

This chapter is designed as a refresher and provides the step-by-step instructions for creating some popular specialized and customized documents in Word. Use this chapter when you need to create these documents quickly, and you don't need the background and supporting information, the steps to create the types of documents covered here.

Missing wizards?

If you don't see the wizards mentioned here, more templates and wizards are available on the CD you used to install Word. They are stored in the ValuPack folder. Copy the files you want to c:\program files\microsoft office\templates. You can also download additional templates and wizards from the Microsoft Web site by opening the **Help** menu and choosing **Microsoft on the Web,** and then selecting **Free Stuff**.

Create and Send a Fax with the Fax Wizard

The Fax *Wizard* helps you send an electronic fax, merge several names to a fax, or print a cover sheet to send using a fax machine.

Run the Fax Wizard

1. Open the document you want to fax (unless you're sending only a cover sheet with a note). Click the **File** menu and select **New**.
2. When the New dialog box opens, select the **Letters & Faxes** tab.
3. Click the **Fax Wizard** icon to select it and then choose **OK**.
4. The Fax Wizard dialog box appears. The left side of the dialog box has a progress chart.
5. Choose **Next**; the Fax Wizard asks `"Which Document Do You Want to Send?"` The name of the document that is currently open automatically appears in the drop-down list box under **The following document**.
6. To send the current document, click **The following document** and leave the name of the current document in the box.

   To send a short message, you can include the message on the cover sheet and send it alone. To do this, click **Just a cover sheet with a note**.
7. If you are sending a document with your cover sheet, click **With a cover sheet** to send a cover sheet with the document you chose or **Click without a cover sheet** to send the document by itself.
8. Choose **Next**. The Fax Wizard asks you to identify the fax software you are going to use to send the fax. **Microsoft Fax** is one of the choices. If you have another fax program, click **A different fax program which is installed on this system**. Then select the name of your fax program from the drop-down list below **Which of the following is your fax**

program? If you don't see your fax program listed, choose **Other** and select the name of your fax software.

If you don't have fax software loaded on your system, click **I want to print my document so I can send it from a separate fax machine**.

9. Choose **Next**. The Fax Wizard asks you for the names of the recipients of your fax. If you have used the Fax Wizard before, the names of recent recipients appear in the drop-down boxes and you can click a name to select it as a recipient. Or, you can click in a box and enter a name and then the corresponding fax telephone number (exactly as they should be dialed, including numbers your system requires to reach an outside line). If you use Microsoft Outlook, choose **Address Book** and select a name from your address book.
10. Choose **Next**. If you chose to create a cover sheet, the Fax Wizard lets you select one of the three styles of cover sheets it has available—**Professional**, **Contemporary**, or **Elegant**. Click the style you want to use.
11. Choose **Next**. This screen asks whom the fax is from. The Fax Wizard automatically pulls information from Word's User Information (click the **Tools** menu, select **Options**, and select the **User Information** tab to see what data is stored about you and make any necessary changes). Enter or replace the information in the **Name**, **Company**, **Mailing Address**, **Phone**, and **Fax** fields. Or, click **Address Book** and select information from your Outlook Address Book.

    If you elected not to use a cover sheet, you won't see this screen.
12. Choose **Next**. The final screen of the wizard reminds you to add any prefixes to the phone numbers that you need to access an outside line.
13. Choose **Finish**. The fax cover sheet document opens. Enter or modify information on the cover sheet, but don't delete any of the fields with the double-angle brackets (<< >>) because the recipient information you specified will be merged into those fields.

14. Choose **Send Fax Now** on the Fax Wizard toolbar to send the fax.

    If you chose to send only a cover sheet with a note, click the field where it says "Click here and type any comments" and type your note. Then choose **Send Fax Now**.

    If you are printing the fax so you can send it on a separate fax machine, you won't see the Fax Wizard toolbar. For a fax addressed to a single recipient, just print the document. For a fax addressed to multiple recipients, choose Merge to Printer on the Mail Merge toolbar.

SEE ALSO

➤ *Use the Print command to fax a document, see page 270*

Create a Résumé with the Résumé Wizard

Whether you're job hunting or you need a professional-looking employment biography to accompany business documents, the Résumé Wizard helps you prepare a neat, professional, and organized document.

Create a résumé using the Résumé Wizard

1. Click the **File** menu and select **New**.
2. When the New dialog box appears, select the **Other Documents** tab.
3. Click the **Résumé Wizard** icon to select it and then choose **OK**.
4. The Résumé Wizard dialog box appears.

   Choose **Next**. The wizard offers you three styles of résumés—**Professional**, **Contemporary**, or **Elegant**. A preview of each style appears beneath the option. Click the style you want to use.
5. Choose **Next**. The Résumé Wizard lets you select the type of résumé you're preparing. Use **Entry-level résumé** if you're entering the job market or have limited experience, **Chronological résumé** to list your experiences in chronological order, **Functional résumé** to show your

administrative-level experience in several areas, or **Professional résumé** to highlight your education and accreditation.

6. Choose **Next**. On this screen, enter your contact information in the **Name**, **Address**, **Phone**, **Fax**, and **Email** fields. Be sure to include area codes with the phone numbers.
7. Choose **Next**. The Résumé Wizard lists a series of headings that can appear on the résumé style you chose. Click the ones you want included on your résumé to check those boxes and remove the check marks from the headings you don't want to use.
8. Choose **Next**. Another set of heading choices appears. These can be included, but you probably won't use them unless they're relevant to the objective of the résumé. Click to check the headings you want to use.
9. Choose **Next**. The résumé headings you selected are listed on this screen. If you want to add another heading, type the heading in the text box and then choose **Add**. To set the order of appearance in your résumé, select a heading by clicking it and then choose **Move Up** or **Move Down** to move the heading up or down in the list. To remove a heading from the list, select it and then choose **Remove**.
10. Choose **Next**. You've filled in all the information needed for the résumé, so choose **Finish**.

When the résumé document opens, it displays a series of fields (marked in gray and enclosed by [ ] brackets). Click those fields and enter the necessary information to complete the résumé document. Then you save and print the résumé as you would any document.

The Office Assistant may appear, offering help options, you might need in finishing your résumé:

- **Add a cover letter**. When you select this option, a sample letter appears that you can modify and save.
- **Change visual style of the résumé**. This option returns you to the screen where you may choose a professional, contemporary, or elegant style to set the appearance of the résumé.

- **Shrink to fit**. Choose this option if you need to squeeze your résumé on one page. Be aware that sometimes this option doesn't work because you have too much text to fit on one page.
- **Send résumé to someone**. When you select this option, Word asks if you want to **E-mail** or **Fax** the résumé. Click the appropriate choice and then choose OK. If you selected **E-mail**, Word sets up a mail message and attaches the résumé to it. If you chose to send the résumé by fax, the Fax Wizard opens (see the instructions on using the Fax Wizard earlier in this chapter).

Click one of those topics to get more help, or click **Cancel** to close the Office Assistant.

SEE ALSO

➤ *To email a document, see page 273*

Create a Newsletter with the Newsletter Wizard

Newsletter layout can be a daunting task. Word's Newsletter Wizard provides easy and attractive layout of your document. Run the wizard first, and write the articles (or paste the text) into the newsletter after you have finished with the wizard.

Create a newsletter with the Newsletter Wizard

1. Open the **File** menu and choose **New**.
2. When the New dialog box appears, select the **Publications** tab.
3. Click the **Newsletter Wizard** icon to select it and then choose **OK**.
4. The Newsletter Wizard dialog box appears. Choose **Next**. The Newsletter Wizard offers three general layout styles: **Professional**, **Contemporary**, or **Elegant**. Click one of the options to select it. Then click **Black and white** or **Color** to choose how the newsletter will appear.

5. Choose **Next**. Type the name of your newsletter in the text box. Click **Date** if you want to include the date by the title, and then enter the date in the text box. If you want volume and issue numbers, click **Volume and Issue** and enter the text in the box.
6. Choose **Next**. If you want to leave room on the back of the newsletter for a mailing label, click **Yes**; otherwise, click **No**.
7. Choose **Next**. The wizard is done collecting information. Choose **Finish**.

The newsletter appears, but the articles are instructions for using the newsletter template. One of your first steps should be to print the sample newsletter so that you can read and refer to the articles. The articles include information on the styles used in the newsletter and to what paragraphs you should apply them, about column formatting, text boxes and linking text boxes to continue articles on another page, and inserting and editing pictures. There are also suggestions for customizing the template by adding footers, symbols to mark the end of articles, and page borders.

Next you need to replace the sample articles with your own text. The pictures in the newsletter are from Word's Clip Art gallery, and you'll probably have to replace those, too.

The Office Assistant appears with some help options to guide you through completing your newsletter:

- **Add or remove a picture.** When you click this option, the Office Assistant provides simple instructions for replacing a picture. To delete a picture, click it to select it and then press Delete. To add a picture, click the **Insert** menu and select **Picture**, and then select **From File**.
- **Regenerate the Table of Contents**. Click this option and Word regenerates the table of contents for you.
- **Cancel**. Choose **Cancel** to close the Office Assistant.

You don't have to go through this entire process to create your next issue of your newsletter if you save your document as a template. Open the **File** menu and select **Save As**. From the

Linked text boxes

Linked text boxes are a way to begin an article on one page and then finish it on another page, which is not necessarily the next page. Create the text boxes you want to use for the article, select the first box and then click it using the right mouse button. On the pop-up menu, click **Create Text Box Link**. Then click the text box where you want the remainder of the text to flow.

Save as type drop-down list, and select **Document Template**. Then click **Save**.

SEE ALSO

- *For information on inserting pictures, see page 372*
- *To learn how to create text boxes, see page 361*
- *For information on working with styles, see page 158*
- *To learn how to regenerate a table of contents, see page 468*
- *For information on creating templates from documents, see page 250*

Create a Letterhead Template

Two ways that you can create custom letterhead in Word are

- Edit a Word letterhead template, adding your own headers and footers, logo, graphics, and so forth.
- Custom design a letterhead template from scratch.

Here, we discuss the custom design of a letterhead template from scratch, using some advanced features. The benefit to the design-from-scratch approach is that you will spend most of your time building and creating. If you redesign an existing Word letterhead template, you may find yourself spending more time undoing and deleting design elements before you build. After you create a custom letterhead, you can share the letterhead template by distributing it to others or by placing it on a shared network drive.

The following steps outline the method for quickly creating a template file. Many types of Word skills are used in creating letterhead templates and you will need to draw upon such skills as adding headers and footers, working with graphics, and creating fields, to build your template.

Create a new letterhead template

1. Click the **File** menu and choose **New** to open the New dialog box.
2. Click the **General** tab, if it's not already selected.
3. Select the **Blank Document** icon.

4. Under **Create New**, click **Template**.
5. Choose **OK**.
6. Enter any text or fields that you want to be part of the new template, create headers and footers, add page numbering, insert graphics or watermarks, create any styles that you want to use, and apply formatting to the text.
7. Click the **File** menu and choose **Save,** or choose Save on the Standard toolbar. When the Save As dialog box appears, select the folder to store your template and name and save the template.

The template is now available for use the next time you start a new document. Be sure to close the new template file before using it.

SEE ALSO

➤ *To modify existing Word templates, see page 251*

➤ *To create online forms using templates, see page 441*

➤ *For more information on creating headers or footers, see page 187*

➤ *For more information on adding page numbers to a document, see page 189*

➤ *To learn how to create fields, see page 444*

Insert Graphics

Typically, a letterhead contains a company logo, a graphic, or even a picture of a person (such as a real estate agent, insurance agent, or consultant).

Inserting a logo or other graphic on the first page of your template

1. Position your insertion point on the first page of the template. Don't worry if you don't want the graphic at exactly that position on the page, because you can move it later.
2. Open the **Insert** menu and choose **Picture** then choose **From File**. The Insert Picture dialog box opens.
3. From the **Look In** drop-down list, select the drive and folder where the graphic is stored.
4. From the **Files of Type** drop-down list, select the graphic format of the file (choose **All Pictures** if you aren't certain of the format).

Custom templates: page 2

Custom templates typically consist of one page. What happens when your business letter is two pages long? You don't want to use your first-page letterhead for the second page of your letter. Anticipate that users will have second pages and select **Different First Page headers and footers** on the **Layout** tab of the Page Setup dialog box when you first begin your template design. This will result in blank second pages when users insert a page break. To format your second page with header, footer, or logos, enter a page break at the end of your Template page 1 and then set up the headers, footers, and logos on page 2.

Template folder structure

Word comes with several template folders such as General, Letters & Faxes, and Web pages. When you open the **File** menu and choose **New**, folders are represented by tabbed pages in the dialog box. If you save templates in the Templates folder, you will see them on the **General** tab. If you save templates in a subfolder of Templates, you will see them in the corresponding tab and a new tab will appear when you create a subfolder.

5. Select the file from the list or type the name of the graphic file in the **File Name** box.
6. Choose **Insert**.
7. Size and move the graphic as needed.

SEE ALSO

➤ *To learn more about inserting graphics into documents, see page 306*
➤ *For more information on sizing and cropping graphics, see page 310*
➤ *For more information on moving graphics, see page 314*
➤ *To apply a watermark, see page 323*

Insert Time and Date Field

Saving time is one purpose behind using a template. You want to add any elements to your letterhead template that would be repeated in all the letters written by you or your company.

One element that is common to all letters is the date. To save the user of the template time, you should add a Date and Time field to your template that automatically inserts the current date in the letter being created.

Inserting a Date and Time field in your template

1. Place your insertion point where you want the Date and Time field to appear.
2. Open the **Insert** menu and choose **Field**. The Field dialog box opens.
3. Select **Date and Time** from the **Categories** list.
4. From the **Field Names** list, select the field that produces the date that you want added to your template.
   - **CreateDate** inserts the date the document was created.
   - **Date** enters today's date, so the date changes whenever you open the document.
   - **EditTime** inserts the total amount of document editing time.
   - **PrintDate** inserts the date the document was last printed.

- **SaveDate** inserts the date the document was last saved.
- **Time** inserts the current time.

5. Choose **Options** to set the date and time format you want to use From the **Date-Time** formats, select the date and time formatting you want applied to the date. Choose **Add to Field** and then choose **OK** to return to the Field dialog box.
6. To keep the character formatting you apply to the resulting date whenever Word updates the field, click **Preserve Formatting During Updates** to enable that option.
7. Choose **OK**.

The current date appears in your document, but the gray shading behind it indicates that the date is a field and not plain text.

Create a Letter Using the Custom Template

After you create your template follow these steps to create a letter.

Creating a letter

1. Click the **File** menu and choose **New**. When the New dialog box opens, select the template you have created.
2. Be sure **Document** is selected under **Create New**.
3. Choose **OK**. The template opens with the fixed elements you created in place, such as the headers and footers, page numbers, graphics, watermarks, and boilerplate text.
4. Enter the text for the letter and save the file.

Create a Memo with Memo Wizard

Memorandums, or memos, are basic business documents. Memos should be easy to read, concise, and meaningful. Word's Memo Wizard helps you set up and format your memo document.

Run the Memo Wizard

1. Open the **File** menu and choose **New**.
2. Click the **Memos** tab of the New dialog box.
3. Select the Memo Wizard icon and choose **OK**.
4. When the Memo Wizard dialog box opens, click **Next** to continue.
5. Select the style of memo you want to create—**Professional**, **Contemporary**, or **Elegant**—and then click **Next**.
6. If you want to include a title at the top of your memo document, click **Yes** and then enter the title text in the text box. If not, click **No**. Then click **Next**.
7. Indicate which items you want to include in the header of your memo document: **Date**, **From**, **Subject**, or **Priority**. In the text boxes next to these options, enter the **Date**, **From**, and **Subject** text you want to appear in the header. Click **Next**.
8. Specify who should receive your memo by checking **To** or **Cc** and then entering the names of the recipients in the appropriate boxes. Or, click in the appropriate text box and then choose **Address Book** to select people listed in your Address Book.
9. If you have a large distribution list, you may want to have the list of recipients appear on a separate cover page. In that case, click **Yes**. Otherwise, click **No**. Click **Next**.
10. Select the closing items you want at the end of the memo—**Writer's initials**, **Typist's initials**, **Enclosures**, or **Attachments**. In the appropriate text boxes, enter the initials or the number of enclosures. Click **Next**.
11. For memos that have more than one page, select the items you want to appear in the header and footer for subsequent pages: **Date**, **Topic**, **Page Number** for the header or **Date**, **Confidential**, **Page Number** for the footer. If you chose to include a topic, enter the text for the topic. Click **Next**.
12. Click **Finish**. The Office Assistant appears and offers you the opportunity to change the header or footer, change the

memo style, or send the memo to someone else via email or fax (starts the Fax Wizard). Close the Office Assistant if you don't need help, or click the item with which you need assistance.

13. Click the **Click here and type your memo text** field and begin typing the body of your memo. The field is indicated by gray background shading and the square brackets surrounding the click here text. Click any other editable fields in your memo, such as **Priority**, and make the appropriate adjustments.
14. Save your memo and print it.

SEE ALSO

➤ *For information on creating templates from documents, see page 250*

Save time by reusing this memo

Do you like the way your memo looks? Rather than going through this entire process the next time you do a memo, you should save your document as a template. Open the **File** menu and select **Save As**. From the **Save as type** drop-down list, select **Document Template**. Then click **Save**.

Create Business Cards

Business cards can be expensive to a small or upstart business. Often you can print business cards inexpensively by purchasing business card stock and creating the cards in Word. Some stationery manufacturers supply business card templates for use in Word. We recommend that you use these templates if available.

Otherwise, you can create your own template and print it on perforated business card stock available from your office supply store or paper product catalog. All you have to do is get your card text and artwork to fit properly in the business card spaces.

Create business cards

1. Open the **Tools** menu and choose **Envelopes and Labels**.
2. Click the **Labels** tab on the Envelopes and Labels dialog box.
3. Choose **Options**.
4. Under Printer Information, select **Laser and ink jet** as the type of printer you have (dot matrix printers aren't recommended for creating business cards).
5. From the **Label products** drop-down list, select **Avery standard** or **Avery A4 and A5 sizes**.

6. From the **Product number** list, select one of the business card options. If the business card stock you chose is an Avery product, look for the same number that appears on the box. Otherwise, click each of the business card options and then check the Label information area until you see dimensions that match the size of one card (such as 3.5 inches wide by 2 inches high).
7. Choose **OK**.
8. In the **Address** area, enter the text you want to appear on a single business card. Or, leave this area blank if you want to format the text after you create the business card document (it's often easier to add the text in the document to make one business card that suits you, and then copy the text to each of the other cards on the page).
9. Select **Full page of the same label** under Print.
10. Choose **New Document**.
11. From the **Table** menu, select **Show Gridlines** to see the outline of each business card.
12. Format and align the text.
13. To add graphics to the business cards, insert the picture or object and then remove the **Float over text** attribute. Size the graphic to fit on the business card. Copy the graphic to each card on the page.
14. Print a test page and see if your cards fit on the business card template. Adjust any spacing if needed.
15. Save and print your document.

SEE ALSO

➤ *To learn more about inserting, sizing, and formatting graphics, see page 310*
➤ *For more information on tables, see page 280*
➤ *For more information on creating labels, see page 268*

Perform a Mail Merge

Mail merges are covered extensively in Chapter 19, "Create Mail Merges, Catalogs, and Lists," but here we provide a quick refresher for those who have created existing data sources and main documents.

To perform a Mail Merge

1. Click the **Tools** menu and choose **Mail Merge** to open the Mail Merge Helper dialog box.
2. Under Main Document, choose **Create**. Select the type of document you want to create: **Form Letters**, **Mailing Labels**, **Envelopes**, or **Catalog**.
3. A dialog box appears. Choose **Active Window** to use the document you currently have open as your main document, or **New Main Document** to open a new document.
4. Under Data source, click **Get Data**. Choose **Create Data Source** if you need to create the data you want to use in your mail merge or **Open Data Source** to select an existing data file.
5. If you specified an existing data file, click **Edit Main Document** in the dialog box that appears.

   If you created a new data file, you return to the main document after you finish adding records.
6. Type the contents of the form letter. Whenever you need to add data from the data source, click Insert Merge Field on the Mail Merge toolbar and select the field name from the menu.
7. When the main document is complete and saved, click Merge to New Document or Merge to Printer on the Mail Merge toolbar.

SEE ALSO

➤ *For more information on mail merge, see page 398*

CHAPTER

26

Customize Word

- Arrange your toolbars on your screen and customize the buttons to suit the way you work
- Add or delete commands on the menu and the shortcut menus
- Create additional keyboard shortcuts to speed repetitive tasks
- Set up your program and document defaults to tailor Word to your work habits and needs
- Make the Office Assistant work and look the way you want

Position Toolbars

Microsoft Word has a variety of toolbars available for your use. Some you display by clicking the **View** menu, choosing **Toolbars** and then selecting the toolbar from a submenu (see Figure 26.1). Alternately, right-click any toolbar to select from the same list.

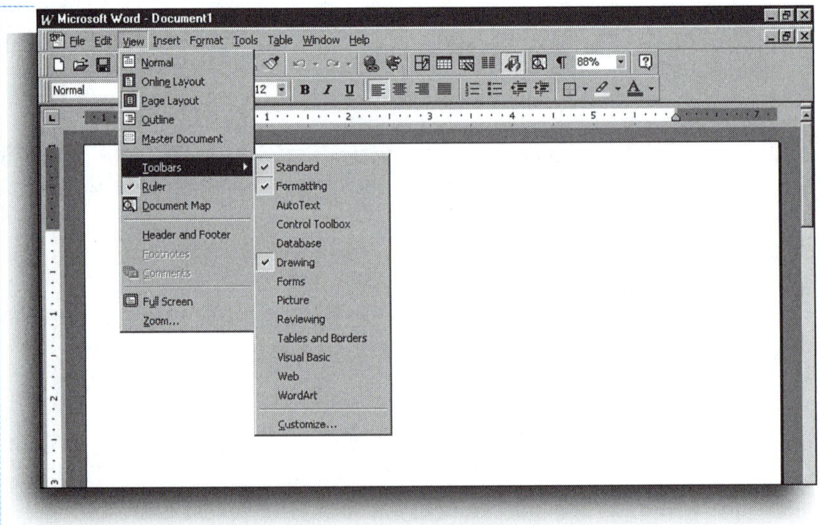

FIGURE 26.1

When you click the **View** menu and select **Toolbars**, a submenu of toolbars you can display appears.

Other toolbars, such as the Mail Merge toolbar or the Stop Recording toolbar, appear automatically when you begin specific tasks.

The Standard toolbar has three buttons that display other toolbars: Web Toolbar, Tables and Borders, and Drawing. If any of these toolbars is already on the screen, choosing that same tool will close the toolbar.

Toolbars in Word can be docked or floating. A *docked* toolbar is one that's attached to one side of the program window. A *floating* toolbar is not attached and can be moved to any part of the document window.

Docked toolbars have a *move handle* at the top or left side (see Figure 26.2). To change the position of a docked toolbar, drag the toolbar by its move handle. When you drag it to any edge of the program window, the toolbar attaches itself to that side and becomes a docked toolbar once again.

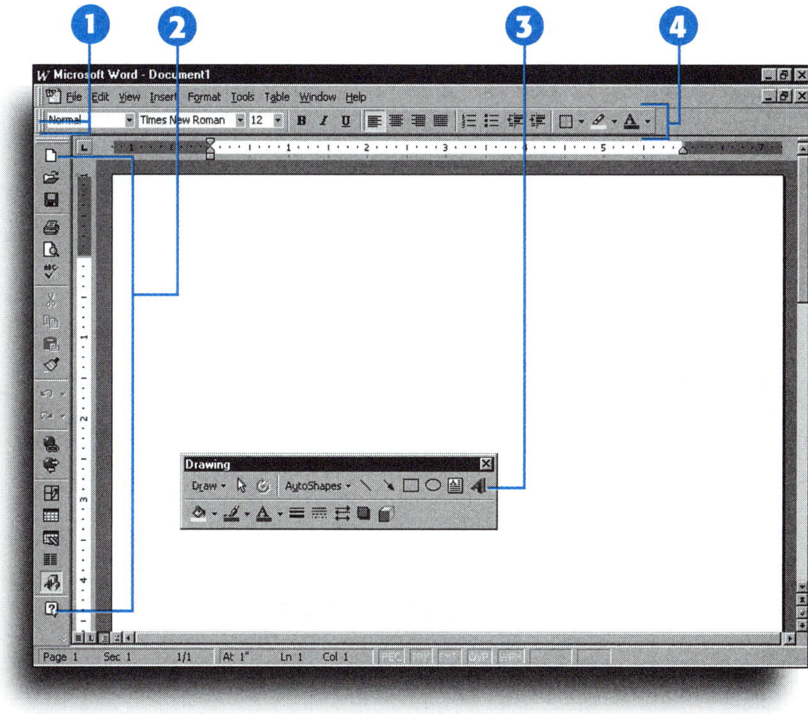

FIGURE 26.2
Toolbars can be floating or docked.

1. Move handles
2. Toolbar docked at left
3. Toolbar docked at top
4. Floating toolbar

If you drag a toolbar out into the document window, the toolbar becomes a floating toolbar. You move a floating toolbar by dragging the title bar. Click the Close (X) button to close the toolbar. Drag any edge of a floating toolbar to change the size and shape of the toolbar. To dock a floating toolbar, drag it against the side of the program window to which you want to attach it.

Customize Toolbars

Word's toolbars provide shortcuts to commands and dialog boxes, and there are many tools available to you with these toolbars. You still have the capability, however, to add more tools, remove unnecessary tools, or create your own tools or toolbars.

Add or Remove Buttons

Add or remove toolbar buttons

1. Display the toolbar to which you will add or remove buttons, if it's not already showing on your screen.
2. Click the **View** menu and select **Toolbars**, then choose **Customize** from the submenu, or right-click a toolbar and click **Customize** on the shortcut menu.
3. When the Customize dialog box appears, click the **Commands** tab (see Figure 26.3).

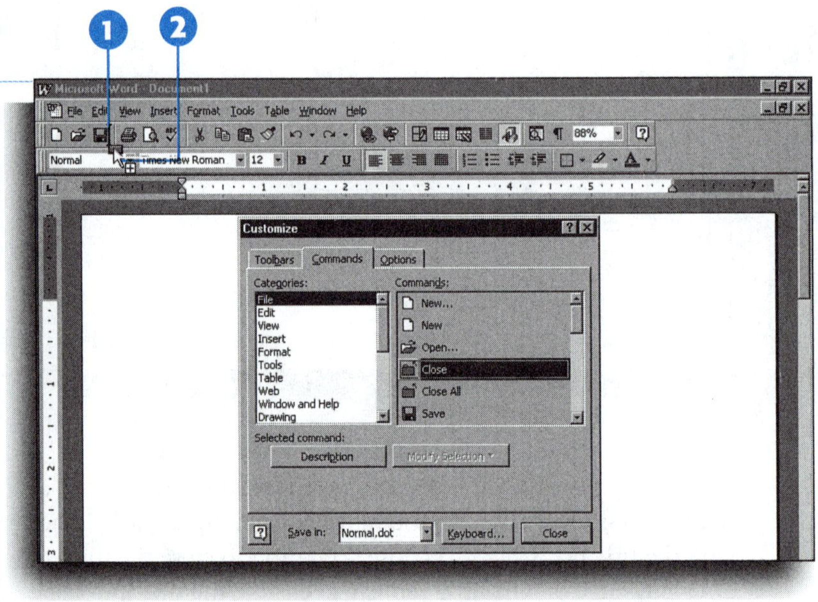

FIGURE 26.3
Select the category and then drag the command to the toolbar.

1 Black line

2 Mouse pointer

4. From the **Categories** list, select the menu title for the command you're adding as a tool or choose **All Commands**, **Macros**, or **Fonts** for additional commands. If you're creating a new tool, you must create a macro first that will perform the commands you want to occur when you choose that tool.
5. From the **Commands** list, click the command you want to use. Drag the command from the **Commands** list to the

toolbar. As you bring the mouse pointer over the toolbar a thick vertical or horizontal line appears on the toolbar. That line moves to follow your mouse pointer as you continue to drag along the toolbar. When you release the mouse button, the new button appears at the position of that line. If you accidentally drop the button in the wrong position, drag it to the correct location (you can do this as long as the Customize dialog box is open). If you want to group buttons, click **Modify Selection** and choose **Begin a Group** to add a gray vertical line before the button.

6. Choose **Close** to close the dialog box.

To remove a button from a toolbar, open the Customize dialog box as described in steps 1 and 2. Click the button you want to remove and then drag it off the toolbar. Make sure you don't release the mouse button while your mouse pointer is over another toolbar.

SEE ALSO

➤ *To learn more about creating tools based on macros, see page 493*

Add built-in menus

Want to add a menu to a toolbar? Display the toolbar to which you want to add the menu. When the Customize dialog box is open, select the **Commands** tab. Click **Built-In Menus** in the **Categories** box. Drag the menu you want from the **Commands** box to the toolbar.

Create a New Toolbar

If you have a set of favorite tools you'd like to see together, create a toolbar that contains them all. That will save you steps in opening and closing several different toolbars.

Create a new toolbar

1. Display the toolbar to which you will add or remove buttons, if it's not already showing on your screen.
2. Click the **View** menu and select **Toolbars**, and then choose **Customize** from the submenu, or right-click a toolbar and click **Customize** on the shortcut menu.
3. When the Customize dialog box appears, click the **Toolbars** tab (see Figure 26.4).
4. Choose **New** to open the New Toolbar dialog box (see Figure 26.5).
5. In the **Toolbar name** text box, type the name of your new toolbar.

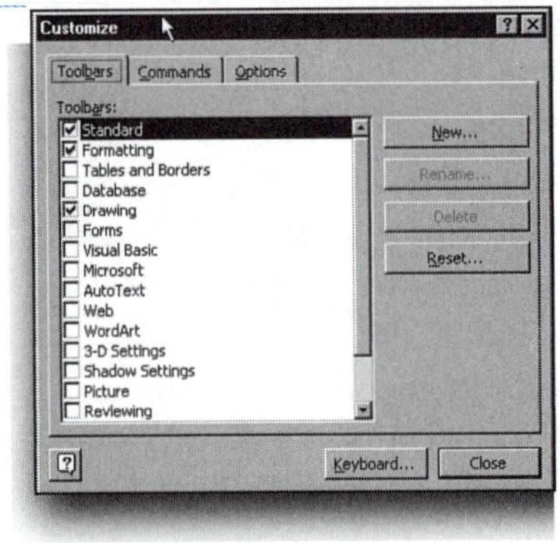

FIGURE 26.4

Choose **New** to create a new toolbar; choose **Reset** to return a selected toolbar to its original setting.

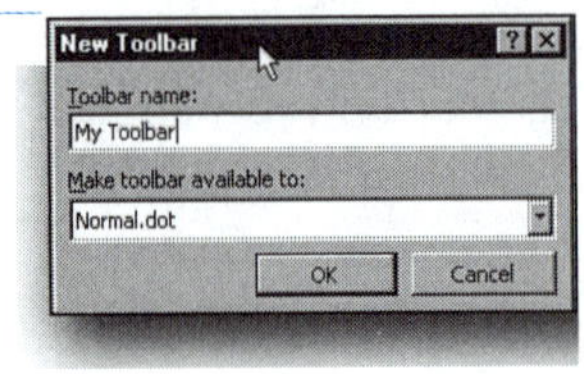

FIGURE 26.5

Enter the name of your new toolbar and select the template or document where you want to store it.

6. From the **Make toolbar available to** drop-down list, select the template or file in which you want to store the toolbar. Storing it in Normal.dot will make it available to most of your documents.
7. Choose **OK** to return to the Customize dialog box.
8. A small floating toolbar appears on the title bar with the name you selected. Following the instructions under "Add or Remove Buttons" earlier in this chapter, add the tools you want to appear on that toolbar.
9. When the toolbar is complete, choose **Close** to close the dialog box. Move your toolbar to position or dock it.

To delete a toolbar from Word, open the Customize dialog box, select the **Toolbars** tab, click the toolbar name in the **Toolbars** list, and then choose **Delete**. When Word asks if you're sure you want to delete it, choose **OK**.

Set Toolbar Options

Word enables you to choose larger icons for your toolbars, turn the ScreenTips on or off, or add the keyboard shortcut keys to the ScreenTips. ScreenTips are the little yellow tags that appear when you point at a toolbar button that tells you what the button is.

Set toolbar options

1. Open the **View** menu and choose **Toolbars**, then select **Customize** from the submenu, or right-click a toolbar and click **Customize** on the shortcut menu.
2. When the Customize dialog box appears, click the **Options** tab (see Figure 26.6).

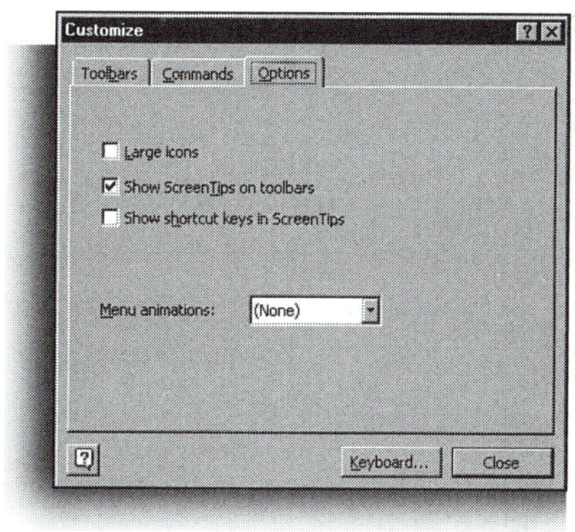

FIGURE 26.6
Check the toolbar options you want to use.

3. Click the appropriate option to enable it:
   - **Large icons** enlarges the toolbar buttons to make them easier to see.
   - **Show ScreenTips on toolbars** turns the ScreenTips on (click to remove the check mark if you want to turn the ScreenTips off). You can also turn on ScreenTips by clicking the **Tools** menu and selecting **Options**, choosing the **View** tab, and then enabling **ScreenTips under Show**.
   - **Show shortcut keys in ScreenTips** adds the keyboard shortcut combinations to the ScreenTips. For example,

when you point to Italic on the Formatting toolbar, "Ctrl+I" displays after "Italic" in the ScreenTip.

4. Choose **Close** to close the dialog box.

Add Menu Commands

Ever wish you could just click a command in the menu, instead of having to open dialog boxes and choose options to get the result you want? The answer to your wish is to add the command to the menu.

Add a menu command

1. Open the **Tools** menu and choose **Customize** on the Customize dialog box (see Figure 26.7).

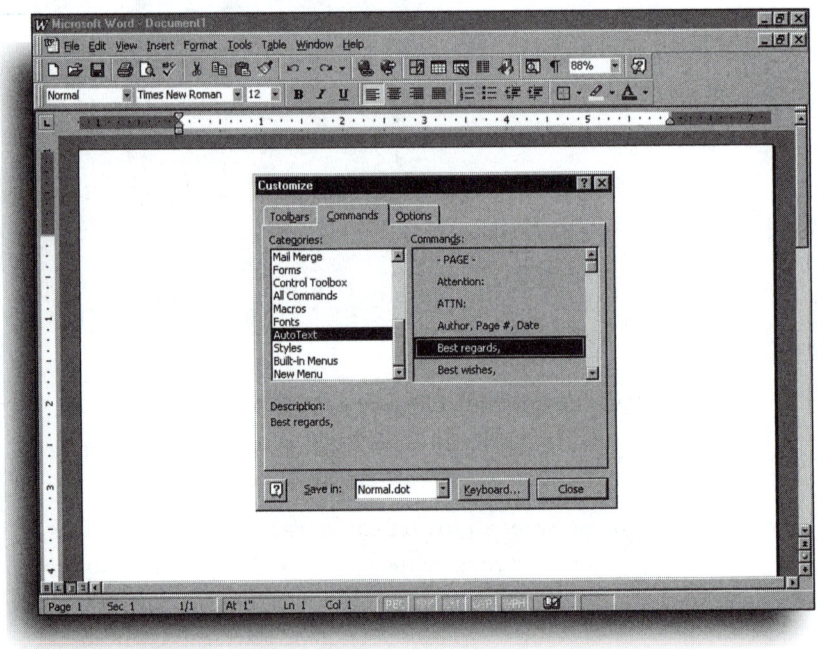

FIGURE 26.7
Select the **All Commands**, **Macros**, **Fonts**, **AutoText**, or **Styles** category when adding menu commands.

2. Select the **Commands** tab.
3. From the **Categories** box, select a command category:
   - **All Commands** to select from all available commands.

- **Macros** to add a menu command that runs a macro (you must create the macro first).
- **Fonts** to add a command that applies a particular font.
- **AutoText** to add a command that inserts an AutoText entry (create the AutoText entry first).
- **Styles** to add a menu command to apply a style.

4. Select the command you want to add from the **Commands** list. Then drag it to the appropriate menu. As you move your mouse pointer over the menu, a thick horizontal line appears. When you release the mouse button, the new command appears at the location of the horizontal line (see Figure 26.8).

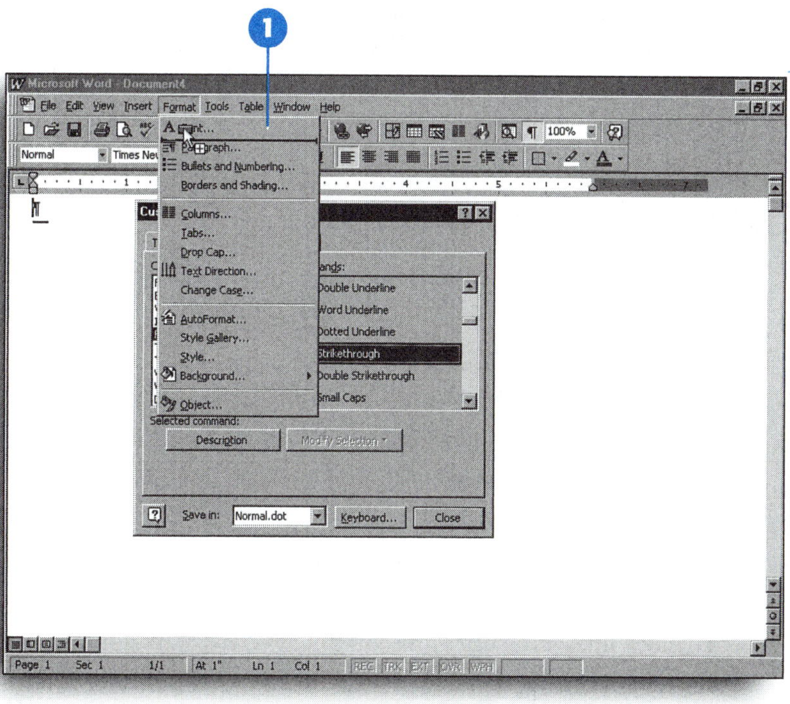

FIGURE 26.8
Drag the command to the menu and release the mouse button when the dark line is where you want the command to appear.

1 Line indicates where new command will be added to menu.

5. (Optional) If you want to change the name of the command, choose **Modify Selection**. In the **Name** box on the pop-up menu, click the name to edit it. Press Enter when your modifications are complete.

6. (Optional) The commands on the menus are grouped to keep similar commands together. Thin horizontal lines separate these groups on the menu. To create a group that includes your new command, choose **Modify Selection** and then click **Begin a Group** on the pop-up menu. To move other commands into that same group, click and drag them below the thin horizontal line.
7. Choose **Close** to close the dialog box.

If you need to delete a menu command, open the Customize dialog box. Click the menu command you want to delete and then drag it off the menu.

To create a new menu on the menu bar, open the Customize dialog box and select the **Commands** tab. Select **New Menu** from the **Categories** list. Drag **New Menu** from the **Commands** list to the menu bar. Choose **Modify Selection** and click in the **Name** box to modify the menu name. Press Enter to accept the new menu name. Then add commands to the new menu.

Change Shortcut Menus

In addition to adding commands to the menu on the menu bar, Word allows you to modify the shortcut menus that appear when you right-click an item.

Modify shortcut menus

1. Open the **Tools** menu and select **Customize** on the menu.
2. When the Customize dialog box appears, click the **Toolbars** tab.
3. Click **Shortcut Menus** on the **Toolbars** list to check the box. The Shortcut Menus toolbar appears (see Figure 26.9).
4. Click one of the categories on the Shortcut Menus toolbar. Then click the shortcut menu you want to modify.
5. To add a command, select the **Commands** tab and then select a category for the command from the **Categories** list. Drag the command from the **Commands** box to the appropriate location on the shortcut menu. Using the position of

the horizontal line as a guide, release the mouse button when the mouse pointer is in the correct location.

To delete a command, click the shortcut menu that contains the command you want to delete. Drag that command off the menu.

6. Choose **Close** to close the Customize dialog box.

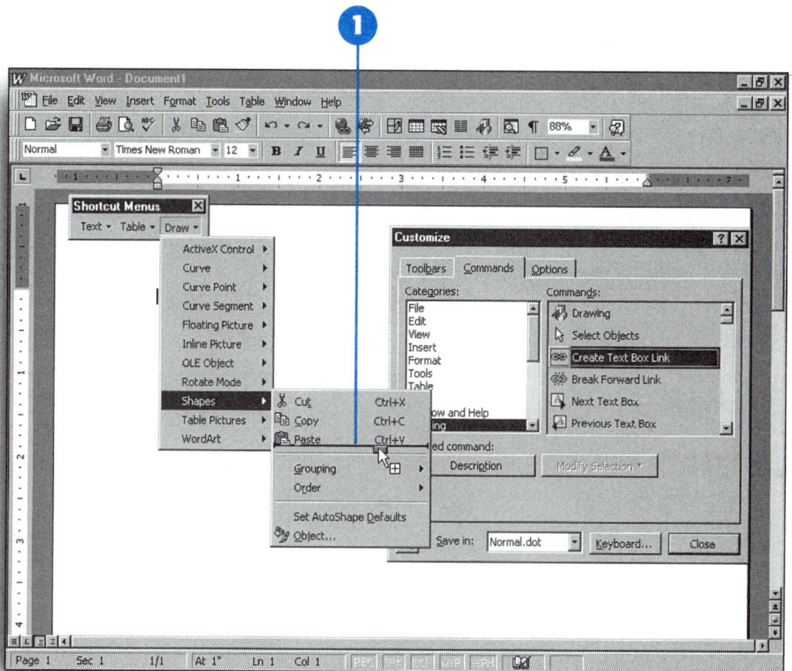

FIGURE 26.9

Check the Shortcut Menus toolbar to make it visible.

1 Line indicates where command will be added to menu

The Shortcut Menus toolbar only remains visible while you are modifying the shortcut menus.

Make Your Own Keyboard Shortcuts

Word has keyboard shortcuts for many of the menu commands. By using these key combinations, you save time (if you're a touch typist) by not having to move your hands from the keyboard while you're typing. Learning the key combinations requires memorization—you either sit down and memorize the key combinations or you learn them by repetition. These shortcut keys appear next to the command on the menu, so you see them each time you use the command on the menu. For a full list of keyboard shortcuts, check the **Help** index for **Keys, Shortcut**, and then select the type of shortcuts you need. For commands that you use frequently but don't have keyboard shortcuts, you may want to create your own.

Create keyboard shortcuts

1. Open the **Tools** menu and choose **Customize**.
2. When the Customize dialog box opens, choose **Keyboard**.
3. The Customize Keyboard dialog box appears (see Figure 26.10).

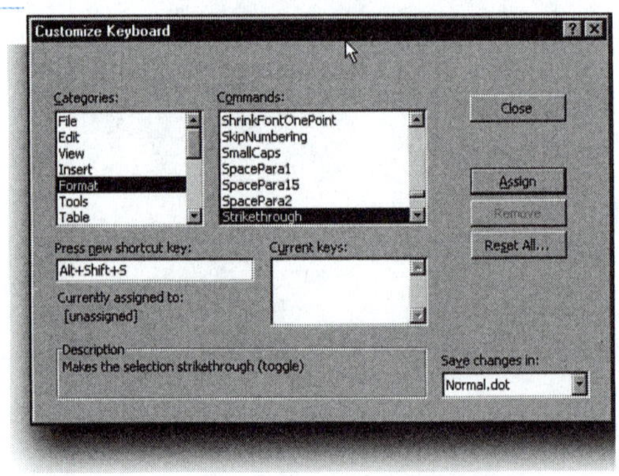

FIGURE 26.10
Enter your new keyboard combination in the **Press new shortcut key** box.

4. Click the **Save changes in** drop-down list and select the template or document in which you want to save the keyboard shortcut.
5. From the **Categories** box, select the category that contains the command for which you are creating the shortcut.
6. From the **Commands** box, select the item for which you are creating the shortcut. If there is a shortcut already assigned to that command, it will appear in the **Current Keys** box.
7. Click in the **Press new shortcut key** box and type the keyboard shortcut key combination you want to assign to the selected command. For example, press Ctrl+Shift+S.

If the combination you enter is already assigned to a command, that command will appear below **Currently assigned to** (for example, Ctrl+Shift+S is currently assigned to Style). In that case you need to delete the key combination and try another one, unless you want to replace the old assignment with your new command.

When the combination you enter is not already assigned to a command, "[unassigned]" appears below **Currently assigned to.** Choose **Assign** to assign that combination to the selected command. The key combination moves to the **Current keys** box.

8. Choose **Close** to close the Customize Keyboard dialog box.
9. Choose **Close** to close the Customize dialog box. In the future you can use your newly created shortcut instead of the menu commands to do the task you selected.

Shortcut keys are also assigned to macros, styles, or symbols.

SEE ALSO

➤ *To learn more about assigning keyboard shortcuts to macros, see page 494*
➤ *To learn more about styles, see page 157*
➤ *For more information about symbols, see page 318*

Set Program Options and Defaults

Default settings specify which options are in effect when you start a document or set up how a particular operation works *unless* you change the settings. In other words, default settings are how things work normally. If you don't like the default settings used by Word for fonts, margins, file locations, styles, and so on, Word lets you change the defaults. After you make the modifications, your new settings become the default for documents created from that moment on.

Set View Preferences

To control what normally appears on your screen, and how your program window looks, you need to set the View options. Some of the View options displayed in the dialog box depend on the current view (Normal, Page Layout, Outline, or Online), so you should switch to the view for which you want to set the defaults. Then click **Tools** on the menu and select **Options** to open the Options dialog box. Click the **View** tab. Table 26.1 describes the view options.

TABLE 26.1 View options

To:	Enable:
Display drawings created with drawing tools. Deselect this option to hide the drawings and speed up the screen refresh (drawings will still print normally).	**Drawings**
Display object anchors (show that an object is attached to the paragraph next to the anchor symbol) if Show/Hide ¶ button on the Standard toolbar is clicked or **All** is checked under **Non-printing Characters** in the Options dialog box.	**Object Anchors**
Display dotted lines around page margins, text columns, and objects that are helpful when working with the document layout.	**Text Boundaries**
Speed up screen display in documents with a great amount of formatting by displaying all character formatting as bold and underlined and graphics as empty boxes.	**Draft Font**
Increase the refresh speed on your screen so you can scroll faster through a document that has lots of graphics; displays boxes in the place of each graphic in the document.	**Picture Placeholders**
Display animated text onscreen; deselect this to see how the printed text will look.	**Animated Text**
Display ScreenTips when you point to a button on a toolbar. See "Set Toolbar Options," earlier in this chapter, for more information.	**ScreenTips**
Display highlight shading applied by the Highlight tool on the Formatting toolbar.	**Highlight**
Make any bookmarks in your document appear with square brackets ([]) around them.	**Bookmarks**

To:	Enable:
Display field codes in curly brackets ({}) instead of displaying the results of fields (for example, {USERNAME* Caps\ *MERGEFORMAT} appears in place of your name as the Word user).	**Field Codes**
Easily identify fields by shading them. Choose **Always** or **When Selected** from the drop-down list.	**Field Shading**
Display symbols or characters to indicate where you inserted **Tab Characters**, **Spaces**, **Paragraph Marks**, **Optional Hyphens**, or **Hidden Text** in your documents. Click **All** to display all these marks.	**Nonprinting Characters options**
Display the status bar at the bottom of your program window.	**Status Bar**
Display the vertical ruler at the left of the document window.	**Vertical Ruler**
Display a horizontal scrollbar at the bottom of your document window.	**Horizontal Scroll Bar**
Display a vertical scrollbar on the right side of the document window.	**Vertical Scroll Bar**
Wrap text to the width of the document window. Deselect to wrap text as it will print.	**Wrap to Window**
Display the style area, where the style names appear across from the paragraphs. Enter a measurement to display the style area; enter 0 to remove the style area from the screen.	**Style Area Width**
Makes any font smaller than the specified size at least as large as the specified size so it's easily readable online. Enter a font size. "Appears only in Online view."	**Enlarge Fonts Less Than**

Set General Options

For generalized defaults that control the operation of Word and help WordPerfect users adjust to Word, you need to set general options. Click the **Tools** menu and select **Options** to open the Options dialog box. Then click the **General** tab. Table 26.2 describes the general options.

TABLE 26.2 **General options**

To:	Enable:
Automatically adjust the page numbering and automatic page breaks in your document as you work. Deselect this option to speed up document editing and scrolling (you can't disable this option when in Page Layout view), but select it again before your final save.	**Background Repagination**
Display or demonstrate the Word equivalent of WordPerfect for DOS keystrokes. You'll see WPH on the status bar after you select this option.	**Help for WordPerfect Users**
Switch the functions of Page Up, Page Down, Home, End, and Esc to the WordPerfect for DOS equivalent.	**Navigation Keys for WordPerfect Users**
Change the background color of the document window to blue and the text to white, as it appears on the WordPerfect for DOS screen.	**Blue Background, White Text**
Be alerted by a sound when certain events or actions occur in Word.	**Provide Feedback with Sound**
See special animated cursors and mouse pointers during some Word operations (saving, printing, repagination, AutoFormatting, or find and replace) to help identify the operations.	**Provide Feedback with Animation**
Allow you to select or verify the file format converter to convert a file to a Word document when it's opened (otherwise, Word does it for you automatically).	**Confirm Conversion at Open**
Automatically update any linked objects, pictures, or data in a document when it is opened.	**Update Automatic Links at Open**
Send the current document as an attachment when you choose the **File** menu, select **Send to** and then choose **Mail Recipient** from the submenu. Deselect this option to include the text of the document in the mail message.	**Mail as Attachment**
Display your most recently used files at the bottom of the **File** menu.	**Recently Used File List**
Specify the number of files displayed in the **Most Recently Used File** list. Enter or select a number to change this.	**Entries**

To:	Enable:
Cause a warning message to appear any time you open a document that might contain a macro virus. You then decide whether to open the document with or without the macros enabled.	**Macro Virus Protection**
Select the unit of measurement for the horizontal ruler and for measurements you enter in dialog boxes.	**Measurement Units**

Change Editing Options

The default settings for text selection, copying and cutting, pasting, and moving text are part of the Edit options. To change these options, click the **Tools** menu and select **Options** to open the Options dialog box. Then click the **Edit** tab. Table 26.3 describes the edit options.

TABLE 26.3 **Edit options**

To:	Enable:
Delete and replace selected text as soon as you start typing new text. When this option is deselected, Word inserts the new text immediately before the selected text.	**Typing Replaces Selection**
Move selected text when you drag it (hold down Ctrl to copy it) and insert it at the cursor position when you release the mouse button.	**Drag-and-Drop Text Editing**
Select the entire word and the space after it when you select part of the word.	**When Selecting, Automatically Select Entire Word**
Insert the contents of the Clipboard at the insertion point when you press the Insert key.	**Use the INS key for Paste**
Replace existing text as you type, one character at a time (double-click OVR on the status bar to turn it off and on after you enable this option).	**Overtype Mode**
Add or delete spaces before or after text you paste from the Clipboard or delete (either by cutting it or by using the Delete key).	**Use Smart Cut and Paste**
Increase or decrease left indent when you press Tab or Backspace.	**Tabs and Backspace Set Left Indent**

continues...

TABLE 26.3 Continued

To:	Enable:
Be able to capitalize French words that begin with accented letters, such as Étude.	**Allow Accented Uppercase in French**
Specify which application to use when editing photos. You select from applications that are installed on your computer.	**Picture Editor**

SEE ALSO

➤ *To learn more about how to select and edit text, see page 23*

Set Print Options

Printing options such as reverse order, draft output, background printing, and items to include with the document when printing, can be reached in two ways. The first is by clicking the **Options** button in the Print dialog box. The second is by opening the Options dialog box and selecting the **Print** tab.

SEE ALSO

➤ *To learn more about printing options, see page 274*

Choose How and Where to Save Files

You want to save files quickly and frequently and avoid losing data. The Save options set up how your files are saved, and the File Location options determine where they are saved. Click the **Tools** menu and select **Options** to open the Options dialog box. Then click the **Save** tab. Table 26.4 describes the Save options.

TABLE 26.4 Save Options

To:	Enable:
Save the previous version of a document with a .bak extension each time you save a document. When you save the file again, the new backup copy replaces the previous one. The backup file is stored in the same folder as the current version.	**Always Create Backup Copy**

To:	Enable:
Save only the changes and append them to the document file, which cuts down the time it takes to save files. However, the size of the saved file may increase significantly if you made several modifications because the file keeps all the changes. Deselect this option before your final save to decrease the size of the final file. This option is grayed out when you choose **Always Create Backup Copy**.	**Allow Fast Saves**
Open the Document Properties box when you initially save the file to allow you to enter information such as title, subject, author, keywords, and comments.	**Prompt for Document Properties**
Prompt you each time you save a document to save any changes to the default settings in the Normal template. If you deselect this option, Word automatically saves the Normal template without asking.	**Prompt to Save Normal Template**
Store any TrueType fonts you used as part of the document, so others who open the document can view the formatting even though they don't have the same font set as you do. This increases the size of the document file.	**Embed TrueType Fonts**
Embed only the font used in the document instead of all those available in the font set. This minimizes the the increase in size caused when you selected **Embed TrueType Fonts**.	**Embed Characters in Use Only**
Save only the data entered in an online form, instead of the entire document, and store it as a single, tab-delimited record for use in a database. The file is saved in text-only format.	**Save Data Only for Forms**
Continue working while Word saves files.	**Allow Background Saves**
Create a document recovery file in case you lose power or your system hangs. When you start Word up afterward, Word displays the AutoRecover file, which may contain information that you entered since your last save. Don't think AutoRecover is the same as Save—you must still save your file when you've finished.	**Save AutoRecover Info Every**
Set the time interval at which AutoRecover runs (enter a number between 1 and 120).	**Minutes**
Set the file format Word uses by default each time it saves a file.	**Save Word Files As**

continues...

TABLE 26.4 Continued

To:	Enable:
Specify the password needed for a person to open the file.	**Password to Open**
Specify the password needed for a person to be able to edit the document and save the file with the modifications.	**Password to Modify**
Display a recommendation when someone tries to open the file. The recommendation is that the file be opened in read-only mode, so the document has to be saved with a different name before modifications can be saved. This preserves the original copy.	**Read-Only Recommended**

The default location for storing Word document files is the **My Documents** folder. Of course, at any time you can save to any of your folders, but you can also change the default file locations.

The File Locations options also set the default locations for your clip art files, templates, workgroup templates, user options, AutoRecover files (you should specify a location for these files), tools, and startup files. If some of these files are kept on network drives, you should designate the proper path.

Change the default file locations

1. Open the **Tools** menu and choose **Options** to open the Options dialog box.
2. Click the **File Locations** tab (see Figure 26.11).
3. Select **Documents** from the **File types** box.
4. Choose **Modify**.
5. In the Modify Location dialog box, select the drive and folder where you normally want your documents stored from the **Look in** drop-down list or enter the path in the **Folder name** box.
6. Choose **OK** to return to the Options dialog box.
7. Choose **OK** to close the Options dialog box.

SEE ALSO

➤ *To learn more about saving files, see page 86*

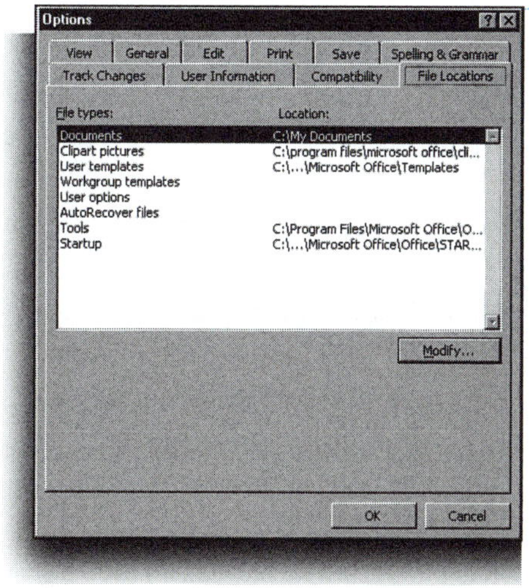

FIGURE 26.11

Select the current file location default and then click **Modify** to change it.

Specify Spelling and Grammar Preferences

Do those green, wavy lines that mark a grammar error annoy you? Turning this option off is only one of the spelling and grammar preferences. To set the options to make spelling and grammar checking work the way you want them to, click the **Tools** menu and select **Options** to open the Options dialog box. Then click the **Spelling & Grammar** tab. Table 26.5 describes the spelling and grammar options.

TABLE 26.5 **Spelling and grammar options**

To:	Enable:
Mark spelling errors with a red wavy underline as you type.	**Check Spelling as You Type**
Hide the red wavy line under potential spelling errors.	**Hide Spelling Errors in This Document**
Display a list of suggested spellings for possible errors whenever you spell check the document.	**Always Suggest Corrections**
Check spelling against the Main Dictionary but ignore any custom spelling dictionaries.	**Suggest from Main Dictionary Only**
Skip words in uppercase during a spell check.	**Ignore Words in UPPERCASE**

continues...

TABLE 26.5 Continued

To:	Enable:
Skip words that contain numbers during a spelling check.	**Ignore Words with Numbers**
Skip any Internet or file addresses during a spell check.	**Ignore Internet and File Addresses**
Specify the spelling dictionaries in use, other than the Main Dictionary.	**Custom Dictionary**
Select, edit, add, or delete custom dictionaries.	**Dictionaries**
Automatically check for and mark possible grammatical errors as you type, marking them with a green wavy underline.	**Check Grammar as You Type**
Hide the green wavy line under possible grammatical errors.	**Hide Grammatical Errors in This Document**
Check spelling as you check the grammar. Deselect this option to check the spelling only.	**Check Grammar with Spelling**
Display the Readability Statistics dialog box after checking the grammar. For most standard documents, you want a Flesch Reading Ease score of 60 to 70 or a Flesch-Kincaid Grade Level score of 7.0 to 8.0.	**Show Readability Statistics**
Set the level which you want the grammar checker to use in finding grammatical errors—**Casual**, **Standard**, **Formal**, **Technical**, or **Custom**. To set your own style, choose **Custom** and then click **Settings** to select the items the checker should look for.	**Writing Style**
Run the spelling and grammar checker on the current document.	**Recheck Document**

SEE ALSO

- *For more information about using the spelling checker, see page 54*
- *To learn more about running the grammar checker, see page 63*

Adding User Information

User Information identifies you for tracking changes, making comments, return addresses on envelopes, and so on. The original entries result from the data you enter when you install Word. If you didn't install Word yourself the data may be incorrect, and in any case it may be incomplete. You want the information to be entered as it would for letters and other formal documents.

To add your complete information, click the **Tools** menu and select **Options** to open the Options dialog box. Then click the **User Information** tab.

Choose **OK** when your information is complete.

Modify Page Setup Defaults

Each template controls the default formatting for the documents created based on that particular template. As you learn to change the defaults for page setup, styles, and fonts, you should note that you are given the opportunity to modify not only the document, but also to add the change to the template on which the document is based. Adding that change to the template makes it the default for all future documents based on that template.

You don't have to open a template to make default formatting changes. For example, to change the default margins, paper size, and alternating headers and footers, you open the Page Setup dialog box while in your current document and set the changes there.

Change default Page Setup options

1. On the **File** menu, select **Page Setup**.
2. When the Page Setup dialog box opens, change the settings that you want to use as your defaults.
3. Choose **Default**.
4. As shown in Figure 26.12, Word asks for confirmation that you want to change the default settings for page setup and tells you that the change will affect all new documents based on the current template. Choose **Yes**.

As you're saving your document be sure to update the template when prompted, so your changes are incorporated into the template.

SEE ALSO

➤ *To learn how to set margins, see page 182*
➤ *For information on setting paper size and orientation, see page 185*
➤ *To learn more about modifying templates, see page 237*

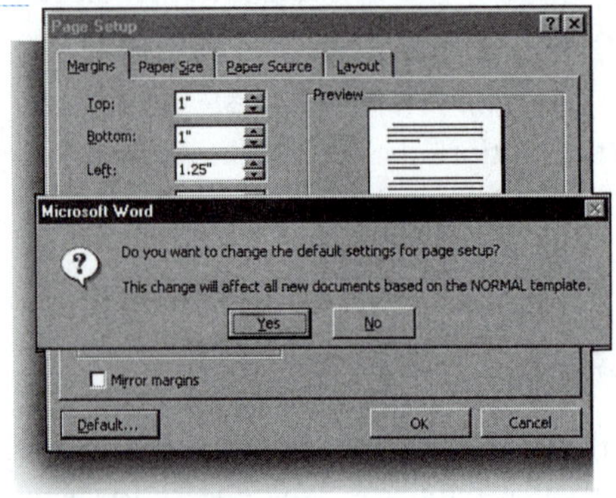

FIGURE 26.12
Click **Yes** to add your formatting changes to the template.

Set Default Fonts

Are you getting tired of Times New Roman? That's the default font in Word, and the default font size is 10 points. Times New Roman is one of the fonts that ships with Windows 95, so in choosing that font Microsoft could be sure that most people would have it. However, if you have more fonts installed on your computer and would prefer to use something other than Times New Roman, you should change your default font.

Change the default font

1. Open the **Format** menu and choose **Font** to open the Font dialog box (see Figure 26.13).
2. Select the font, font style, size, and so forth that you want for your default font.
3. Choose **Default**.
4. Word asks for a confirmation that you want to save the settings as your default font and add them to the template. Click **Yes**.

SEE ALSO

➤ *To learn more about setting font options, see page 35*

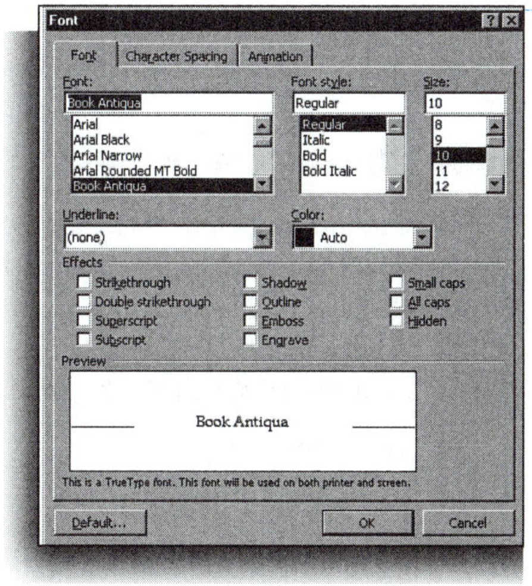

FIGURE 26.13

Click **Default** to make the current font settings into your default font.

Set Default Styles

Styles are stored in the document where you create them or in the template on which the document is based. As you are modifying the Heading 1 through Heading 9 styles or the Normal styles, which are usually generated by the template, you have the option to add your alterations to the template so they are available for new documents.

Set default styles

1. Open the **Format** menu and choose **Style** to open the Style dialog box.
2. Select the style you want to modify from the **Styles** list.
3. Choose **Modify**.
4. In the Modify Style dialog box click **Add to template**.
5. Choose **Format** and then select the formatting options you want to apply to the style.
6. When you return to the Modify Style dialog box, choose **OK** to return to the Style dialog box.
7. Choose **Apply** to apply and save your changes and then close the dialog box. Choose **Close** to save your changes and close the dialog box.

As you save the document, Word may prompt you to save changes to the template. Click **Yes** to save the style changes.

Modify the Normal Template

Because most documents and templates are based on the Normal.dot template, modifying that template changes many of the defaults in effect when you start new documents. For example, to change the Heading 1 through Heading 9 and Normal styles or the tabs, edit the Normal template.

Modify Normal.dot

1. Open the **File** menu and choose **Open**.
2. When the Open dialog box appears, select **Document Templates (*.dot)** from the **Files of type** drop-down list.
3. Locate the template folders (usually in the \Program Files\Microsoft Office\Templates folder).
4. Select **Normal.dot** from the list of files.
5. Click **Open**.
6. Make your formatting changes and then save the template.

Any changes you make to the page setup, styles, tabs, and so forth, will change any new documents you create based on the Normal template.

SEE ALSO

➤ *For more information on modifying templates, see page 237*

Customize Office Assistant

The Office Assistant can use system resources. Depending on your system configuration, you may find that it slows down your computer. If you don't experience problems with the Office Assistant, set options for exactly how much help you require from the Office Assistant in the Office Assistant dialog box.

To customize the Office Assistant, click the Assistant and click the **Options** button. The Office Assistant dialog box appears. Click the **Options** tab to set options. Table 26.6 highlights some important Office Assistant Options.

TABLE 26.6 Office Assistant options

Option:	Description:
Respond to F1 key	Activates the Office Assistant when you press the F1 key. Clear this option and press F1 to bring up the Word Help Topics window.
Move when in the way	Moves the Assistant when dialog boxes are present on your screen. Minimizes the Assistant if it is not used for a five minute period.
Guess help topics	Shows Help topics before you ask for them, based upon the task you are performing.
Make sounds	Turns on Office Assistant sounds.
Using features more effectively	Shows tips on features as you work with them.
Using the mouse more effectively	Shows tips on using the mouse more effectively.
Keyboard shortcuts	Displays shortcut keys you can use while you work.
Show the Tip of the Day at startup	Shows a Tip each time an Office program starts.

Options that you set for the Office Assistant affect how the Assistant works and appears in all Office programs (such as Excel, PowerPoint and so forth).

To choose a different Office Assistant character, click the **Gallery** tab of the Office Assistant dialog box. Click the **Back** or **Next** button until you find the Assistant you want. Figure 26.14 shows the Genius Assistant.

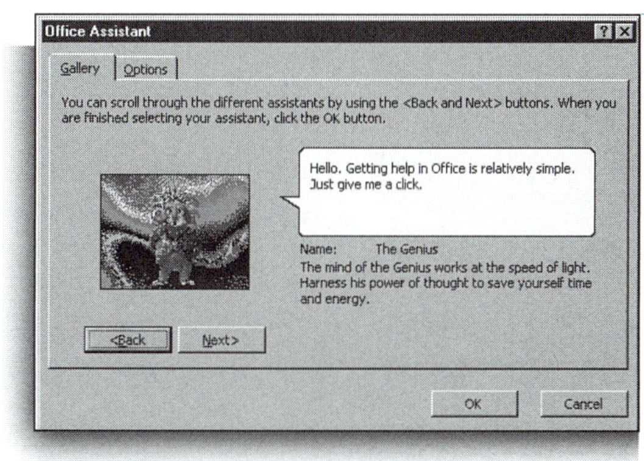

FIGURE 26.14

If you have Internet access, you can visit the Microsoft home page to download additional Office Assistants to add to your Gallery.

APPENDIX

A

Changes Made by AutoFormat

When You Type:	AutoFormat Does This:
A number followed by a period, hyphen, closing parenthesis, or greater than sign and then a space or tab, followed by text.	Turns it into a numbered list.
An asterisk, one or two hyphens, a greater than sign, or an arrow created with a greater than sign and a hyphen or equal sign, followed by a space or tab, and then text.	Turns it into a bulleted list.
A symbol (inserted by using the **Insert** menu's **Symbol** command) followed by two or more spaces and then text.	Turns it into a bulleted list where the symbol is the bullet.
An inline graphic (within 1.5 times the height of the text) followed by two or more spaces and then text.	Turns it into a bulleted list where the inline graphic is the bullet.
Three or more hyphens or underscores. Available only on the **AutoFormat as You Type** tab.	Creates a single, thin-line border above the paragraph.
Three or more equal signs. Available only on the **AutoFormat as You Type** tab.	Creates a double-line border above the paragraph.
Three or more number signs. Available only on the **AutoFormat as You Type** tab.	Creates a decorative-line border above the paragraph.
Three or more tildes. Available only on the **AutoFormat as You Type** tab.	Creates a single, wavy-line border above the paragraph.
Three or more asterisks. Available only on the **AutoFormat as You Type** tab.	Creates a dotted-line border above the paragraph.
A salutation, such as "Dear Mr. Smith:"	Offers to start the Letter Wizard.
Straight quotation marks (" and ').	Turns them into typesetter quotes (curly) such as "" and '.
Fractions, such as 1/2 or 1/4.	Changes them to ½ or ¼.
Ordinal numbers such as 1st or 2nd.	Changes them to 1st or 2nd.
Text, a space, hyphen, another space, and then text.	Changes spaces and hyphen to an en dash (–).
Text, two hyphens, and more text.	Changes the hyphens to an em dash (—).
An asterisk followed by text and then another asterisk.	Turns the text between the asterisks to boldface (by applying the built-in character style named Strong).
An underline followed by text and then another underline.	Turns the text between the underlines to italic (by applying the built-in character style named Emphasis).

When You Type:	AutoFormat Does This:
An Internet, email, or network address.	Formats it as a hyperlink.
A plus sign, a series of hyphens, another plus sign, a series of hyphens, and so on, then press Enter (looks like: +——+——————+————+)	Inserts a table, putting the column borders where the plus signs were. The number of hyphens determines the width of the columns.
A list item that starts with a bullet or asterisk, followed by bold, italic, or underlined text, followed by a period, colon, hyphen, em dash, question mark or exclamation point, and then followed by a space or tab and then plain text. For example: **John*: Marry me, Mary, and make me merry!	Applies the same formatting to the lead text of the next list item. Available only on the **AutoFormat as You Type** tab.
An outline while in Outline view.	Applies styles Heading 1 through Heading 9 to your outline headings.
Text formatted like a heading (for example, Bold, Centered, no punctuation), or text formatted like body text (for example, **based** left-aligned or justified, multiple word-wrapped lines, punctuated).	Creates a new paragraph style based on the formatting you apply, and applies the style to that paragraph. Works only if **Define styles on your formatting** is checked.

Glossary

.BAK The file extension that Word assigns to backup copies of files that it creates during saves when **Always create backup** copy is activated in the Options dialog box.

.DOC The default file extension for Word files (documents).

.DOT The default file extension for a Word template.

.GIF A file extension for graphics saved in the Graphics Interchange Format.

.HTML (also **.HTM**) A file extension for documents saved in HTML format, needed to publish documents on the Web. *See also: Hypertext Markup Language*

.JPEG (also **.JPG**) A file extension for graphics saved in the Joint Photographic Experts Group format.

.PCX A file extension for graphics saved in PC Paintbrush format

.RTF A file extension for rich text files, which are text files that retain their formatting.

.TIF A file extension for graphics saved in the Tagged Image File Format.

.TXT A file extension for text-only files, such as those created in Notepad.

.WMF A file extension for graphics saved in the Windows Metafile Format.

.XLS The default file extension for Excel files.

Alignment The arrangement of items on a document, or on the screen in relation to the margins. *See also: Horizontal alignment, Vertical alignment, Indentation, Center-aligned, Right-aligned and Justified.*

Antonym A word whose meaning is the opposite of another word. Hot and cold are antonyms.

Ascenders In a typeface, the portion of a letter that extends above the "x" height, which is the average height of most lowercase letters. This includes the top of most uppercase letters, but also lowercase b, d, f, h, k, l, and t.

AutoComplete A word feature that automatically inserts items such as AutoText entries when you type the AutoText entry shortcut.

AutoCorrect A Word feature that automatically corrects typos—spelling errors and grammar errors—as you type.

AutoFormat A Word feature that automatically applies styles (such as headings, bullets, and so forth) as you type a document.

AutoRecover A Word feature that periodically saves a temporary copy of a document while you are working.

AutoShapes Drawing objects provided by Word and accessed on the Drawing toolbar.

AutoText A text (name and address) or graphic (logo) entry stored for frequent use. AutoText entries are assigned shortcuts—when you type the shortcut the entire AutoText entry is inserted in your document. In previous versions of Word, AutoText was called *Glossary items*.

Background printing A Word feature that enables you to continue to work in Word while a Word document is being printed.

Boilerplate Static text or graphics that does not change and is used over and over again in many documents, or the same document. Examples of boilerplate text include contracts, logos, and so forth.

Bookmark A placeholder that references a selection of text or a location in a document.

Border The frame of a Microsoft window, table, cell in a table, document, or drawing. Window borders cannot change, but object borders (such as tables, cells and so forth) can have formatting applied that includes colors.

Browser *See: Web browser*

Callout A text label identifying an object. Often applied to identify sections of a drawing, picture, or graph.

Caption A label applied to a table, figure, equation, listing, or graphic to identify it or describe its contents.

Category axis An axis in a graph. In a graph such as a line, bar, area, or column chart, data is generally plotted in reference to two axes. One contains the values and is called the y-axis or Value axis. The x-axis, or Category axis, shows the different categories into which the data falls, such as months, dates, cities, brand names, and so forth.

Cell The intersection of a row and a column in a worksheet or spreadsheet.

Center-aligned Paragraph formatting in which all lines of text appear to the left and the right of a center point. The center point is user-defined and may be the center of a document, table, paper, cell, column, and so forth.

Character styles Attributes assigned to a font. Character styles include such attributes as bold, italic, and underline.

Chart A graphic representation of data or relationships between data.

Client In a network, a computer that uses programs or data files located on the server.

Client/Server The relationship between the server computer, which controls the network and stores files and programs, and the workstation computers that are part of the network and access files and programs on the server.

Clip art A collection of already-prepared drawings, diagrams, and graphic images that are available to the general public or that can be purchased as a software package for your personal use.

Clipboard *See: Windows Clipboard*

Collapsed An outline view of text, usually displaying header information. Clicking the headers expands the view and displays additional content.

Column break Word symbol that instructs the program to begin a new column.

Column A layout arrangement that displays information in vertical alignment. Table columns consist of cells; newspaper columns consist of text wrapped within a vertical area defined by margins.

Concordance file A list of words from a document and the context in which they appear in the document, generally used in creating indexes.

Condensed A font format in which the characters are more narrowly spaced. *See also: Expanded*

Copy To duplicate.

Copyright symbol ©

Cross-reference Text that refers to (points to) a different location in a document or to a different document where additional information on the topic at hand can be found.

Cut To delete or remove.

CV Curriculum Vitae—a resume.

Data source In Word, the original file containing data to be used for merging.

Database A collection of information stored in fields and records that can be sorted and manipulated or merged with forms, letters, envelopes, reports, and so forth.

Datasheet A spreadsheet-like window in Microsoft Graph used to enter the data and labels needed to generate the chart or graph.

Descenders In a typeface, the portion of a letter that hangs below the "x" height, which is the average height of most lowercase letters, as in the letters g, j, p, q, and y.

Default The direction or choice made by a program unless intervention is made by the user. Many program features require values, such as a font size, and defaults are set by the program but can be changed by the user.

Delete To cut or erase.

Delimited text file A text file whose contents are set apart by a symbol that separates the values of fields. The symbol used to separate fields is called a delimiter.

Destination file The receiving file when information is sent to a file from a source file.

Directories A container (also called folder) which lists filenames and is used to organize files on a computer hard drive. Directories created within directories are called subdirectories. *See also: Folders*

Document Map A view in Word that displays an outline view of a document in a separate pane. Documents can be navigated using the Document Map.

Document properties A listing of an object's characteristic. Document properties include size, author, number of pages, and so forth.

Document summary Part of document properties that stores information concerning the document contents. Document summary information is indexed and can be searched.

Dot leader A special tab setting in which the whitespace that precedes the tab stop is filled with dots. This type of tab setting is frequently used in a table of contents.

Drawing An object or graphic inserted into a document. Typically used to define user-created objects such as boxes and lines.

Ellipsis Three dots (...). Commonly found in menus of programs designed to run in Windows and used to indicate that a submenu or dialog box will appear when the user selects the menu choice followed by the ellipsis. Also used in quotations to note that the full text isn't shown.

Em dash A long dash (—) that is as wide as the uppercase M in the specific font being used. It's often used to express a parenthetical thought.

Embedded object Data from one document that is placed or *embedded* into another document. After it is embedded, it becomes a part of the other document, but still retains a separate identity for editing.

En dash A regular dash (–) that is as wide as the uppercase N in the specific font being used. It is often used to separate numbers or dates, to indicate that the numbers or dates between are also included (such as "pages 10–25").

Endnotes Numbered notes appearing at the end of a document that provide information on the source of certain text in a document, or that explain or comment on that text. *See also: Footnotes*

Expanded A font format in which the characters are more widely spaced. Also, in the Outline view, displaying heading information and the body text accompanying it. *See also: Collapsed*

Export Save a file in a different file format for use by another application.

Facsimile *See: Fax*

Fast Save A method of saving a document that only saves any changes made to the document (as opposed to saving the complete revised document) by appending them to the previously saved file. It's usually used with large documents to save time.

Fax (*Also facsimile*) Transmission of a document or picture over a telephone line that is received as a copy of the document or picture.

Field A container, or location that stores a particular type of data, such as number fields or text fields. Fields can be a part of a record in a database, or act individually to store or display information on a document, such as a Date field. Field information may be filled in by the user, or calculated by the program, depending on the form or database design.

Field code A placeholder for field information. Field codes are surrounded by brackets{}.

Field label Text that identifies the purpose or content of a field and that appears as static text on a document or screen, even when the field has not been populated.

File server The computer in a network where the files are stored for access by other computers in the network.

Filter A set of criteria that determines which of the database information to display. For example, a filter can cause a database to display only records that contain a certain area code or zip code.

Filter criteria Parameters used to determine which records a filter will display.

Flowchart A diagram of a process or procedure using specific symbols to indicate decision points and alternate paths.

Folders A container (also called directory) which lists filenames and is used to organize files on a computer's hard drive. Folders created within folders are called subfolders.

Font A character set that has a typeface, size, and style (bold, italic) in common.

Footer Information printed at the bottom of a page. Footer information is determined by the document creator and can contain page numbers, document names, logos, and graphics.

Footnote separator A line that separates the body of a document from the footnotes.

Footnote Numbered notes appearing at the bottom of a page that provide information on the source of certain text on that page, or that explain or comment on that text. *See also: Endnote*

Form *See: Online form or Printed form*

Form letter A standardized letter that differs only in a few pieces of data, such as the name or address of the person to whom it is addressed.

Format Painter A Word feature that enables the copying of formatting options from one selected object to another, or to many throughout the document.

Frame A rectangular object that can be moved anywhere on a Word page. It can contain text or graphics. Text on the page wraps around it. In Word 97 it has been largely replaced by the Text Box object.

Gradient In the Fill Effects dialog box, gradient is the section in which you can define the background shading of an object in which the background color gradually changes from light to dark or from one color to another color.

Graph A picture of the relationship between two or more variables.

Graphic A drawing or picture created by a graphics application or scanned and stored in a file.

Gridlines Optional lines that extend from the tick marks on an axis across the plot area of a chart. Gridlines make it easier to evaluate data values when reading the graph. Also, the nonprinting lines used to define cells in a table.

Group objects Create a single set of objects from two or more individual objects.

Gutter The area of a page that is lost in the binding of a book.

Hanging indent Paragraph alignment in all lines of a paragraph are indented except for the first line.

Hard Page Break *See: Page break*

Header Information printed at the top of a page. Header information is determined by the document creator and can contain page numbers, document names, logos, and graphics.

Heading A main topic in a document that is followed by body text, for example, outline headings, column headings, headlines, and subheads.

Horizontal alignment Controls the location of text between the right and left margins of a page.

HTML *See: Hypertext Markup Language*

Hyperlink A block of text (usually colored and underlined) or a graphic that represents a connection to another place in the document or a separate document. You usually can open the other document or jump to the other place in the currently open document simply by clicking the text or graphic.

Hypertext Markup Language (HTML) A collection of instructions or tags that tell a browser program how to display a document—as in when to bold or italicize. HTML tags typically appear embedded within a document, set apart from the document text by angle brackets. For example, <B> means display the text that follows as boldface; </B> means turn off boldface for the text that follows.

Hypertext *See: Hyperlink*

Hyphen A dash that marks where a word at the end of a line of text has been broken and then continued on the next line. *See also: Nonbreaking hyphen and Optional hyphen*

Import To insert or copy information from one program into another.

Indent Paragraph alignment in which additional whitespace is inserted between the margin and the paragraph text.

Index entry A topic or word marked and identified as belonging to the index.

Index A listing or set of topics derived from document or book text. An index includes the page number of the document or book on which the topic is discussed. An index usually appears at the end of the document or book.

Internet A worldwide conglomeration of computer networks that can communicate with each other.

Intranet A company's computer network, which stores HTML documents and serves HTML documents to clients running Web browsers.

Justification Aligning the ends of lines of text so that each end is flush with the left or right margin, or both. *See also: Alignment*

Justified A paragraph alignment in which the text in the paragraph is even with the right and left margins, except for the last line of the paragraph. The amount of space between words varies to facilitate this balance of text.

Landscape Page orientation in which text runs parallel to the long edge of the paper.

Layer objects To place objects in a document on top of other objects.

Left-aligned Paragraph formatting in which the left ends of lines of text are an even distance from the left margins and the right ends are uneven.

Legend An area on a chart that displays a set of symbols or color boxes that represent each set of series data displayed in the graph. It helps the reader understand what the elements of the chart mean.

Line spacing The vertical distance between lines of text, usually measured as the number of lines (such as single, one and a half, or double).

Link A pointer to a block of data located in an external file. A linked object appears to be in one file but really exists in a second file. The first file only has a pointer or link that tells the first program where to locate the object pointed to.

Linked object Data that is created in one file and then connected to another file. Although the data appears to be part of the second file, it really remains part of the first file.

Local Area Network (LAN) A network that connects a group of computers that are within an immediate area, such as the same building, and are connected to each other by network cable.

Macro recorder Records the steps involved in a task so they can be played back when you run the macro.

Macro A set of program commands and instructions that are recorded and played back on request. Macros can contain lengthy strings of commands but macros can be played using a single menu command or set of shortcut keystrokes.

Macro virus A program that is hidden within a macro. It is designed to destroy files or programs or at least disrupt computer operations. Using a template or document containing such a macro may cause damage to your document files. *See: Virus*

Mail merge An operation that extracts data from a data source and inserts it into fields on a main document to create form letters, envelopes, and labels.

Mail server In an email system, the server that stores email messages for pickup and sorts incoming messages into the mailboxes for delivery to the correct individuals.

Main Document The document that contains the information in mail merge that does not change, for example, the return address on an envelope.

Margin(s) The distances between the text on a document and the edge of the paper.

Master Document A document that acts as a binder for other documents, facilitating the creation of a table of contents, index, headers and footers and uniform formatting for all documents it binds.

Merged Document The third document that results from a merge of a main document and a data source. *See: Mail merge*

Metafile A file that contains information from which a program can create a desired result. A graphics metafile contains a set of vectors from which a graphics program can draw a picture. In Windows printing, an enhanced metafile (EMF) is an intermediate file that the Windows Graphical Device Interface (GDI) creates when you use the **Print** command in Word. It allows you to more quickly return to working in Word after sending a graphics print job.

Microsoft Graph 97 A Microsoft program used for creating simple charts and graphs.

Mirror margins In a document that has facing pages, the right margin on the even page is equal to the left margin on the odd page, and the left margin on the even page is equal to the right margin on the odd page.

Multilevel list An outline.

Newspaper column A page format in which more than one column appears on a page and text flows down one column, then wraps to the next column and flows down it, and so on, down each column on the page, similar to the way text flows in a newspaper or magazine.

Nonbreaking hyphen A type of hyphen that you should use when you want to keep hyphenated words from splitting apart at the end of a line. Word does not insert a line break at a nonbreaking hyphen. Use Ctrl+Shift+Hyphen to insert a nonbreaking hyphen.

Nonbreaking space A type of space that you should use when you want to keep two words from splitting apart at the end of a line. Word does not insert a line break at a nonbreaking space. Use Ctrl+Shift+Space to insert a nonbreaking space.

Normal.dot The default template that Word bases a document on if you don't tell Word to use a different template. Normal.dot is a global template in the sense that its features are always available to all documents, even documents that are primarily based on another template.

Numeric keypad A block of keys to the right of the keyboard set up like a calculator and used to enter numbers, which has keys for performing mathematical functions.

Object Linking and Embedding (OLE) Allows different applications to share and copy information by either linking two files, or by taking selected data from one file and copying or embedding it in another file. Also known as OLE, Microsoft has released two versions of it. Word 97 supports version 2 of OLE.

ODBC *See: Open Database Connectivity*

OLE *See: Object Linking and Embedding*

Online form A form that you can fill in onscreen, as opposed to on paper. You just fill in the blanks. The form designer decides whether, when you save the form, only the variable data or the whole document gets saved or printed.

Open Database Connectivity (ODBC) An industry standard that defines how databases and other programs can share information even though they store the information in different formats.

Optional hyphen A hyphen that is used between syllables when a word is broken at the end of a line.

Orientation The direction the lines print on a piece of paper. *See also: Portrait and Landscape*

Orphan When the first line of a paragraph is at the bottom of one page or column and the rest of the paragraph is continued on the next page or column, that single first line is called an *orphan.*

Outline view A view that shows the various levels of a document by using indentations for headings and text.

Page break A break in the text of a document where a new page is started. Automatic or oft page breaks automatically occur when the amount of text reaches a specified maximum. To change the spot where the text breaks, a *hard* page break can be manually inserted.

Paper source The source where paper is taken from when a document is printed, such as lower tray, upper tray, or manual feed.

Paragraph spacing The distance between the end of one paragraph and the beginning of another, generally measured in points.

Paragraph style A predefined set of formats that are stored together under a name. By applying the style to a paragraph, you apply all the formats at once. You apply a style by picking its name from a list of styles.

Password A word or phrase that must be entered to open or edit a protected document. A password is used to give a document greater security.

Paste A function that takes data that has been cut or copied from one document and places it into another location.

Pattern In the Fill Effects dialog box, a panel in which you can choose from a set of background designs for an object.

Plot area The area in which Microsoft Graph plots your data. This area includes the axes and all markers that represent data points.

Plug and Play A feature of Windows 95 that automatically detects new hardware devices and configures the system to work with them.

Point A unit of measure used in specifying type size. One inch is equal to 72 points.

Populate Use already existing information from another file to supply data for a database.

Portrait The orientation in which the text runs parallel to the short edge of the paper.

Print device A device for making paper copies of documents, or a printer.

Print Preview A view that shows all the pages of a document in the form in which they will be printed.

Printed form A form intended to be filled out on paper. *See also: Online form*

Printer driver A program that provides the operating system with the language and information necessary to run the printer.

Printer font A font that resides in a printer but not in the computer. When you use a printer font in your document, Windows must display the document onscreen using some other font, because the printer font is not available in the computer for display purposes. Windows would normally substitute a *screen font*.

Properties The attributes belonging to an item—file, object, picture, text, document, and so forth. *See also: Document properties*

Ragged-right The lines in a paragraph do not end evenly at the right margin.

Record A collection of related fields in a database (a row of information on a client, person, and so forth).

Registered trademark symbol ® The uppercase letter R enclosed in a circle. Used to inform the reader that a trademark is registered with the U.S. Office of Patents, Copyrights, and Trademarks.

Revision mark An editing mark that shows where changes, such as deletions or substitutions, have been made.

Right-aligned Paragraph formatting in which the right ends of lines of text are an even distance from the right margins and the left ends are uneven.

Route documents A function in email that enables a document to be sent to several people, one after the other, instead of to all of them at once.

Row Items arranged horizontally in a table or spreadsheet.

Ruler Bars at the top and side of the document that display measurements, such as inches, and indicate the location of margins, indentation, column width and row height, paper size, and tab settings.

Scaleable font A font that can be changed to allow different character sizes instead of being restricted to a few specific sizes.

Screen fonts A font that is used for display on a computer monitor to represent the font as it will be printed.

Section break An editing mark used to delineate the end of a section in a document.

Section Division of a document that allows different formatting to appear in the same document.

Series data A row of data in a datasheet that produces a line on a line chart, a set of columns or bars that share a color on column or bar charts, or an area in an area chart.

Server (include Web, Network, file and mail) A computer that stores information or programs for access by other computers.

Service provider An organization that offers a service (such as Internet connection) that users may subscribe to and then access. Internet service providers are often called ISPs.

Shading A background color or shade of gray that you can apply to a block of text, a cell, row, or column in a table, or an object (such as a frame or text box) inserted in a document.

Share Allowing computer resources (files, printers, folders, and so forth) to be used by other computers in the network.

Shareware Software that you are allowed to use for free for a trial period. If you decide to continue to use it, you are supposed to send a payment to the author of the program.

Shortcut keystroke A keystroke or combination of keystrokes that allow a task to be performed more quickly and simply, without using a mouse.

Side-by-side columns Columns that are parallel to each other on the same page, but whose text flows to the same column on the next page instead of going to the top of the next column on the same page (usually accomplished in Word by using tables).

Sizing handles Small hollow boxes that appear at the endpoints of lines or arrows, or on the sides and corners of objects. The appearance of these handles means that a line or object is selected. Dragging the handles changes the size of the selected item.

Source document The document that contains the information that is either linked or embedded into another document.

Source file The file that contains the information that is either linked or embedded into another file or a document.

Spike Stores text so that it can be moved without using the Clipboard. Items can be appended to the Spike so that the Spike grows until you empty it.

Static text The nonvariable parts of a form. The labels that identify what should be filled into the blanks.

Styles Collections of formatting specifications that have been assigned names and saved. These can then be applied to other paragraphs to give them the same formatting.

Subdirectories Directories that are contained in a directory. Beginning with Windows 95, Windows refers to directories and subdirectories as folders and subfolders.

Subdocument A document that is contained within a Master Document.

Subfolders Folders that are contained in another folder.

Subordinate text Text that is nested beneath a heading in an outline.

Summary Information *See: Document summary*

Synonyms Words that have nearly the same meaning as each other.

Tab A keystroke that moves the cursor to a set position on the ruler, where the next text entered will align, or to the next cell in a table. Also, the name of the set position on the ruler.

Table heading A column or row title.

Table of contents Lists all the main topics in your document, and the page on which the topic starts. It appears at the beginning of the document. The topics are generally listed in page order.

Table Organizes information in a row and column format.

Template A Word document, usually having the extension .dot, which includes features such as boilerplate text, styles, AutoText entries, macros, and custom toolbars and menus that are available to any document based on that template.

Texture In the Fill Effects dialog box, a tab in which you can choose background patterns that simulate real-world textures such as marble, granite, wood, or cloth.

Thesaurus A book or file that provides a list of synonyms and antonyms for the selected word in a document.

Trademark symbol™ The letters TM, capitalized and superscripted, appearing next to a trademark to identify it as a trademark.

TrueType A type of scaleable font developed jointly by Apple and Microsoft, in which the characters are described mathematically within the font, and a rendering engine interprets the description to draw the characters on your computer screen, on paper, or wherever the text is to be displayed.

Uniform Resource Locator (URL) A pointer to the location of an object. URLs conform to a standard syntax that generally looks as follows:

[protocol]://[host].[domain].[superdomain]/[directory]/[file] such as `http://www.microsoft.com`.

Universal Naming Convention (UNC) A standard syntax for naming paths to servers, directories, and files.

Value axis The axis in a graph such as a line, bar, area, or column chart that contains the values (also referred to as the y-Axis).

Variable A placeholder that will be replaced by information to be supplied at a later time. For example, a template might include a field code as a variable that will be replaced by the creation date of a document based on the template.

Versioning A feature of Word that permits you to save succeeding versions of a document all within the same file on disk, and to review and revert to earlier versions.

Vertical alignment Controls the location of text between the top and bottom margins of a page.

VIM (Vendor Independent Messaging) An industry standard that allows different applications to interact with different mail messaging systems.

Virus A program designed to destroy files or programs or at least disrupt computer operations. It can be included or attached to an innocent program, file, or disk and so carried from one computer to another. *See also: Macro virus*

Visual Basic Editor An optionally installed component of Word (or Office) that enables you to do basic programming in Visual Basic, an object-oriented programming language used to create and change programs that use a graphical user interface (GUI). You use the Visual Basic Editor when editing Word macros.

Watermark Text or a graphic that is layered either on top of or behind text in a document. For example, a lightly shaded logo may appear in the background on each page of a document.

Web browser A program that enables users to read and download documents on the Web, use hyperlinks, receive email, and access newsgroups.

Web page One of the HTML documents that makes up the World Wide Web.

Web server A server that makes Web pages accessible to users of the Web and maintains Web sites.

Web site A group of related Web pages.

Web The World Wide Web (or just Web) is a component of the Internet. It is a collection of HTML documents accessible through the Internet.

What's This? A type of Windows help that identifies objects that you click with the mouse.

Wide Area Network (WAN) A network that connects computers over a large geographical area, such as a city, state, or country.

Widow When all the lines of a paragraph except the last one are on one page or column, the last line of the paragraph that appears at the top of the next page is called a *widow*.

Windows Clipboard A Windows function that allows data to be cut or copied from one file, stored on the Clipboard, and then transferred to another file.

Wizard An interactive "mini-program" designed to assist users in a particular feature or function of the software program, such as Word's Letter Wizard.

Word wrap The automatic break of lines of text by a word-processing program to fit text within the boundaries set by the user, such as the margins.

WordArt A program that creates special effects for text, such as creating shadows, skewing, and stretching.

Workgroup People who are working together and sharing computer data and resources, often over a company intranet or network.

Worksheet One page, or sheet of an Excel workbook. A worksheet can contain one or more spreadsheets as well as charts. If the worksheet contains a single spreadsheet, it is often simply referred to as a spreadsheet.

Workstation A computer in a network from which the user can access other computers.

World Wide Web *See: Web*

WYSIWYG An acronym for What You See Is What You Get, which means that the appearance of your document on your screen is the same as the printed document.

Index

C

J-K

L

O

Q-R

S

T

U

V

W-X-Y-Z